US-China Relations

US-China Relations

Perilous Past, Uncertain Future

Fourth Edition

Robert G. Sutter

ROWMAN & LITTLEFIELD
Lanham • Boulder • New York • London

Published by Rowman & Littlefield
An imprint of The Rowman & Littlefield Publishing Group, Inc.
4501 Forbes Boulevard, Suite 200, Lanham, Maryland 20706
www.rowman.com

86-90 Paul Street, London EC2A 4NE

British Library Cataloguing in Publication Information Available

Library of Congress Cataloging-in-Publication Data

Names: Sutter, Robert G., author.
Title: US-China relations: perilous past, uncertain future / Robert G. Sutter.
Other titles: United States-China relations
Description: Fourth edition. | Lanham: Rowman & Littlefield, [2022] | Includes bibliographical references and index. | Summary: "This comprehensive and balanced assessment of the historical and contemporary determinants of Sino-American relations explains the conflicted engagement between the two countries. Offering a rich discussion and analysis, Robert G. Sutter explores the twists and turns of the relationship over the past two hundred years"— Provided by publisher.
Identifiers: LCCN 2021040385 (print) | LCCN 2021040386 (ebook) | ISBN 9781538157169 (hardback) | ISBN 9781538157176 (paperback) | ISBN 9781538157183 (epub)
Subjects: LCSH: United States—Foreign relations—China. | China—Foreign relations—United States.
Classification: LCC E183.8.C5 S884 2022 (print) | LCC E183.8.C5 (ebook) | DDC 327.73051—dc23
LC record available at https://lccn.loc.gov/2021040385
LC ebook record available at https://lccn.loc.gov/2021040386

Contents

Chapter One: Introduction   1

Chapter Two: Patterns of US-China Relations Prior to World War II   15

Chapter Three: Relations during World War II, Civil War, Cold War   41

Chapter Four: Rapprochement and Normalization   67

Chapter Five: Tiananmen, Taiwan, and Post–Cold War Realities,
    1989–2000   99

Chapter Six: Early Twenty-First Century Relations: Pragmatism
    and Rising Differences   129

Chapter 7: America's Negative Turn Against China: Determinants,
    Evolution, and Implications   161

Chapter Eight: Security Issues in Contemporary US-China
    Relations   185

Chapter Nine: Economic and Environmental Issues in
    Contemporary US-China Relations   211

Chapter Ten: Taiwan and East Asian Maritime Disputes in
    Contemporary US-China Relations   245

Chapter Eleven: Issues of Human Rights and Governance in
    Contemporary US-China Relations   273

Chapter Twelve: Outlook   305

Notes   327

Selected Bibliography   389

Index   399

Chapter One

Introduction

Relations between the United States and China constitute the most important bilateral relationship in world affairs in the twenty-first century. China's global economic importance and rising political and military power came about in a world order where the United States faced many challenges but still exerted broad leadership reflecting its superpower capacities and status. Whether the two powers will support international peace and development and pursue more cooperative ties, become antagonistic as their interests compete, or pursue some other path in world affairs remains a subject of ongoing debate among specialists and policy makers in both countries and concerned observers throughout the world.[1]

The fourth edition of this volume was written in the fourth year of a remarkably negative turn in American policy toward China begun at the end of the first year of the Donald Trump administration and continuing into the Biden administration. This edition gives special focus to the origins, evolution, and implications of the hardening of US policy that demonstrates its importance as the most substantial change in US-China relations since President Nixon and Mao Zedong opened the way to improved relations over fifty years ago.

The reasons for the American change in policy centered on China's power, policies, and practices. As China rose in power and international prominence, Chinese leaders remained careful to avoid confronting America in ways that would lead to military conflict with strongly negative implications for China's priorities and interests. But the past decade witnessed ever more assertive and expansive Chinese foreign behavior directed by China's quest for wealth and power at the expense of the United States, which was seen as in decline. Gone were the days of the first decade of the twenty-first century and earlier when China followed the dictums of senior leader Deng Xiaoping (d. 1997) to avoid the international spotlight and leadership. Strongman leader Xi Jinping, in power since 2012, promoted a much more prominent role for China in world affairs and backed it up with substantive programs and initiatives that benefited China at the expense of others, notably the United States and its leading allies and partners.[2]

US policy was slow to perceive this change and respond to China's challenges. The Trump administration's first articulation of the new American approach came in its National Security Strategy released in December 2017, which used harsh language unseen in executive branch discourse since before the Nixon administration to emphasize that China posed a greater international danger to the United States than any other country. It took time for observers in the United States and China to appreciate the significance of the shift. The latter became clearer as the Trump administration followed up with punitive tariffs, investment restrictions, and export controls targeted at China and as bipartisan majorities in Congress joined administration leaders in landmark legislation in 2018 making "whole of government" US hardening against wide-ranging challenges posed by China's practices a matter of law.[3]

US countermeasures to Chinese challenges targeted long-standing American differences with China over such issues as Taiwan, human rights, trade imbalances, and the respective Chinese and US arms buildups aimed at each other in Asia, but they also highlighted new issues reflecting heightened urgency, with some viewing China as an existential threat to the United States.[4] Most important was the judgment that China's headlong economic advance, employing widespread espionage, cybertheft, domestic protectionism, and international mercantilism, now led China to seek dominance in the high-tech industries that were key to American economic and military power. This judgment held that if the United States did not sustain leadership in these industries, its economy and national defense would become second to and increasingly dominated by China.[5]

These developments settled one of the points of debate about Chinese foreign policy and US policy toward China discussed in previous editions of this book. That debate centered on whether the accommodation, moderation, and reassurance of the United States seen in Chinese foreign relations since the Cold War, and especially prominent in the first decade of this century, was likely to continue. For many years and until very recently, there was a prevailing expectation that close and cooperative US engagement with China would see Chinese accommodation, moderation, and reassurance of the United States continue into the future, with some foreseeing China gradually conforming to norms of the liberal international order fostered by the United States. However, a pattern of authoritarian initiatives to suppress dissent and strengthen domestic controls as well as dramatic purges of government corruption saw Xi Jinping stoke Chinese nationalistic ambitions with widely publicized and assertive foreign policy initiatives. Chinese international behavior challenged China's neighbors, the United States, and a variety of established international institutions and norms.[6]

Prior to Xi's ascendance, some analysts in China and abroad foresaw a clear road ahead for China. They viewed Chinese leaders as following a moderate strategy that dealt pragmatically with world conditions and conformed to international norms, pursuing Chinese interests focused on development, which required international stability.[7] In contrast, others, including this writer, judged that China's approach to foreign affairs depended on many variables inside China and abroad, and these could change. Many of these variables were beyond the control of Chinese leadership. The leadership also had sometimes contradictory approaches in dealing with these issues. As a result, this author's assessment was that continued moderation in Chinese foreign relations would be contingent on circumstances that could change. Meanwhile, a number of foreign critics portrayed Chinese leaders as authoritarians determined to hold on to power by following an approach of hiding their intentions of dominance as China built greater power through ongoing foreign interactions.[8] In the event, those forecasting continued moderation and pragmatic accommodation by China have been proven wrong. The engagement policies of the past have been attacked by the Trump government and disavowed by the Biden government.[9] Debate continues between those forecasting Chinese foreign policy contingent on circumstances and those seeing a well-crafted Chinese strategy seeking regional dominance and world leadership. For now, what is clear is that Beijing appears determined to continue its ongoing wide array of challenges to the United States and that the US government appears equally determined to counter those Chinese challenges in an acute rivalry that has wide-ranging impacts on international affairs.

BALANCING CONVERGING AND CONFLICTING INTERESTS

The first edition of this book was written in 2010 following the latter years of the administration of President George W. Bush (2001–9) and the first year of the administration of President Barack Obama (2009–17). Officials in China and the United States emphasized positive aspects of their relationship. As explained in detail in chapter 6, these included ever closer trade and investment ties leading to deepening economic interdependence of the United States and China. Converging security interests involved dealing with international terrorism, North Korea's nuclear weapons program, UN peacekeeping, and other issues involving sensitive situations in Asia and the world. China had come far in the post–Mao Zedong (d. 1976) period in adopting norms of free-market economic behavior supported by the United States and essential to China's success in dealing with the conditions of economic globalization of the current era. China also substantially changed policies on proliferation of weapons of mass destruction to conform more to US-backed international rules. US-China collaboration on climate change and environmental issues was prominently featured, and bilateral discussion on human rights continued amid mixed reviews on progress in China toward accepting US-backed international norms. US-China differences over Taiwan subsided with the coming to power of Taiwan president Ma Ying-jeou (2008–16), who sharply shifted Taiwan toward a more cooperative stance in relations with China. In broad terms and with some reservations, the US government accepted and supported the Chinese Communist government as a leading actor in world affairs; the Chinese government seemed to tacitly accept, at least for a time, the existing international order in which the United States exerted leading power in Asian and world affairs.[10]

The Chinese and American governments had strong reasons to emphasize the positive aspects of their relationship and to minimize public discussion of negative aspects. Sino-American differences were dealt with through private conversations among senior leaders and channels of diplomacy called dialogues. The number of these dialogues grew to more than ninety by the end of the Barack Obama administration. The most important was the US-China strategic and economic dialogue, which held its first meeting in July 2009.[11]

During this seemingly positive period, students, media commentators, and other readers inexperienced with the complicated background and context of the Sino-American relationship had a tendency to be misled by the benign image of US-China relations that flowed from the public discourse of US and Chinese officials in the previous decade. Adding to the mix was the point of view of some commentators, particularly in the United States, that emphasized the convergence of interests between the United States and China. At the outset of the Obama administration, some argued for an international order determined chiefly by cooperation between the two governments, what is called a G-2 world order, for the twenty-first century.[12] The first edition of this book took issue with what it saw as an overly benign image of Sino-American cooperation; it concurred more with scholarly and other assessments in the United States, China, and elsewhere that viewed Sino-American relations as more complicated and conflicted than official discourse and arguments by commentators who favored a Sino-American international condominium led many to expect.

The second edition came in 2013 amid the increasing competition and public acrimony evident in Sino-American relations since 2010. It depicted a fragile balance between converging and diverging interests in the relationship, notably with China's newly appointed party leader and president, Xi Jinping (2012–), pursuing assertive and often bold initiatives at home and abroad that seriously challenged key American security, economic, and political interests. Though registering sometimes strong public opposition to China's advances at the expense of its neighbors and the United States and taking some military, economic, and diplomatic moves in response, the Obama government on the whole continued to rely on private summit talks and other dialogues to manage tensions. The Xi Jinping government also avowed support for such diplomatic managing of key differences, but China's actions on sensitive territorial disputes, trade and investment matters, international governance issues, and restrictive treatment in China of Chinese citizens and of US and other foreign businesses and nongovernment organizations undermined the previous benign image of cooperation with the United States.[13]

The Obama government remained positive about the status of US-China relations to the end of its tenure in January 2017. However, sharply critical treatment of China in the 2016 US election campaign came from the leading Democratic Party candidate, Hillary Clinton, the secretary of state in the first term of the Obama government (2009–13). Clinton's negative assessment of Chinese policies and practices complemented criticisms by Republican frontrunner and later president Donald Trump.[14] Together, the two candidates reinforced a broad trend seen among American experts, specialists, members of Congress, and the media that the previous moderate and forthcoming US engagement of China was failing; a new, tougher approach would be required to deal with the rising challenges posed by Xi Jinping's government.[15] For their part, Chinese specialists and media were on guard in the face of these negative trends. They claimed that China would seek to work constructively with the president-elect. Hillary Clinton was viewed negatively as an official who was familiar with Sino-American differences and determined to push Beijing on these matters. Trump was depicted as a newcomer and much less committed to key differences with China; a prevailing view in China saw him as a pragmatic businessman turned political leader who could be "shaped" to accord to Chinese interests through bargaining and negotiations.[16]

The third edition of this book was written against this background after five months of the Trump presidency in 2017, notably prior to the publication in December of the Trump administration's hard-line national security strategy targeting China and its following widely publicized "trade war" involving punitive tariffs and other economic measures targeting Chinese practices. US-China relations were tense when President-Elect Trump in December 2016 took a controversial step in accepting a congratulatory phone call from Taiwan's president. When China complained, President-Elect Trump replied by criticizing Chinese economic policies and military advances in disputed islands in the South China Sea, and he later went on to repeatedly question why the United States needed to support a position calling for one China and avoiding improved contacts with Taiwan.[17]

These rapid-fire actions upended Chinese forecasts of smoother sailing with Trump than with Hillary Clinton. In a few gestures and blunt messages to the media and on Twitter, the president-elect showed President Xi and his lieutenants that the new US leader would be capable of a wide range of actions that could be carried out easily and would surprise Chinese counterparts with serious negative consequences. During the long US election campaign, President Trump made clear that he preferred unpredictability and did not place the high value President Obama did on policy transparency, carefully measured responses, and avoidance of dramatic actions. He was much less constrained than the previous US administration by a perceived need to sustain and advance US-China relations. Like President Xi and unlike President Obama, President Trump was characterized as (1) not averse to conflict, (2) presumably willing to seek advantage in tensions between the two countries, and (3) prepared to seek leverage through linking his policy preference in one area of the relationship with policies in other areas of the relationship.[18]

In sum, the first year of the Trump government saw US-China relations heavily influenced by one bold leader interacting with another bold leader. President Trump eventually was persuaded to publicly reaffirm support for the American one-China policy during his first phone conversation with President Xi on February 9. Xi reportedly refused to speak with President Trump until he did so. The informal summit meeting with President Xi at the Trump resort Mar-a-Lago in early April 2017 went well, though it sandwiched President Trump's surprise announcement of fifty-nine US cruise missiles striking a Syrian airfield that was being used to carry out a widely condemned chemical weapons attack. After the summit, the Trump government kept strong political pressure on China to use its economic leverage to halt North Korea's nuclear weapons development. While stoking widespread fears of conflict on the peninsula, President Trump stressed his personal respect for President Xi. He promised Beijing easier treatment in negotiations on the two countries' massive trade imbalance and other economic issues.[19]

Overall, the US leader put his Chinese counterpart on the defensive, compelling Beijing to prepare for a wide range of contingencies from the American president. Gone was the Obama government's commitment to positive ties with China. It became clear that Beijing could no longer rely on the policy transparency, measured responses, and avoidance of dramatic action or spillovers among competing interests that characterized the previous administration. As discussed in chapter 6, in the view of American critics, "no-drama" Obama enabled Xi to expand in the South China Sea and carry out other bold moves at American expense without the danger that the resulting tensions would lead to serious US retaliation. China's new uncertainty over the American president added to reasons for Beijing to avoid confrontation and conflict with the Trump administration. But China's determined march toward greater wealth and power at the expense of others, including notably the United States, continued, setting the stage for the recent period of unremitting rivalry.[20]

ENDURING DIFFERENCES: DIVERGING INTERESTS AND VALUES

The lessons of history over US relations with China and especially relations with the People's Republic of China (PRC) provide the basis for findings of lasting importance in determining the course of Sino-American relations. The following chapters show that on balance the historical trajectory has not been positive, with tensions reaching a high point of conflict and confrontation during the first two decades of the Cold War and sustained acute rivalry characterizing 2017–21. A major breakthrough took place under the leadership of President Richard Nixon (1969–74) and Chairman Mao Zedong. After that historic thaw, major turning points over the next fifty years showed that without powerful, practical reasons for pragmatic accommodation and cooperation, strong and often deeply rooted and enduring differences between the two governments and their broader societies were likely to emerge. Even in the best of times, those differences tended to obstruct improvement in Sino-American relations.

The differences between the United States and China in the first two decades of the twenty-first century are summarized in the sections that follow.

China

China's many disagreements with the United States can be grouped into four general categories of disputes that have complicated US-China relations for years. Based on Chinese statements and commentary in official Chinese media, the four categories are (1) opposition to US support for Taiwan and to US diplomatic and other involvement with other sensitive sovereignty issues, including Tibet, Xinjiang, Hong Kong, and Chinese territorial disputes with neighbors along China's eastern and southern maritime borders; (2) opposition to actual or perceived US efforts to change China's political system; (3) opposition to the United States playing the dominant strategic role along China's periphery in Asia, including US military involvement in Taiwan and military activities in disputed and other territory along China's rim; and (4) opposition to many aspects of US leadership in world affairs. Some specific issues in the latter two categories include US policy in Iraq, Iran, Syria, and the broader Middle East; aspects of the US-backed security presence in the Asia-Pacific, seen notably in the Obama government's so-called pivot or rebalance policy in the region; US and allied ballistic missile defenses;

periodic US pressure on such governments as Myanmar (Burma), North Korea, Sudan, Zimbabwe, Cuba, and Venezuela; US pressure tactics in the United Nations and other international forums; and at times the US position on global climate change.[21]

United States

US differences with China continue to involve clusters of often contentious economic, security, political, sovereignty, and foreign policy issues. Economic issues center on inequities in the US economic relationship with China that include a massive trade deficit, Chinese mercantilist industrial policies, Chinese currency policies and practices, US dependence on Chinese financing of American budget deficits, and China's lax enforcement of intellectual property rights and wide use of industrial espionage targeting US firms. Security issues focus on the buildup of Chinese military forces and the threat they pose to US interests in Taiwan and the broader Asia-Pacific. Political issues include China's controversial record on human rights, democracy, religious freedom, and family planning practices. Sovereignty questions involve disputes over the status of Taiwan, Tibet, Xinjiang, and Hong Kong and the often intense disputes in contested territory along China's eastern and southern rim that involve maritime transit and security issues of importance to the United States. Foreign policy disputes focus on China's support for states deviating from US-backed norms, notably including at various times North Korea, Sudan, Myanmar (Burma), Iran, Syria, Cuba, Zimbabwe, and Venezuela, and Chinese trade, investment, and aid involving resource-rich and poorly governed states in Africa and other parts of the developing world, which undermine Western sanctions and other measures designed to pressure these governments to reform.[22]

The following chapters show that these differences reflect conflicting interests and values that often bedeviled US-China relations before the establishment of the PRC in 1949 as well as since that time.

On the US side:

- US policy and practice demonstrates the strong rationale to seek change in China in directions favored by the United States. This values-based American approach often clashes with the realities in US-China relations, arguing for greater US policy pragmatism.
- US government and nongovernment opinion shows wariness and is disinclined to accept China until and unless it accommodates satisfactorily to US values and norms.
- US exceptionalism prompts US policy makers backed by broader American opinion to often see their actions in morally correct terms, so

they have a tendency to play down or ignore the negative implications of their actions for China and Chinese interests.

- Nongovernment actors play a strong role in influencing policy, reinforcing the need for US government policy to deal with domestic US determinants in relations with China as well as the international aspects of those relations. These nongovernment actors tend to reinforce the three above-noted elements of a US values-based approach to China seen as less accommodating to Chinese policies and practices at odds with US norms.
- The long-standing US strategic interest in China saw a prolonged reluctance to undertake the risks, costs, and commitments of leadership in relations with China until forced to do so by the Japanese attack on Pearl Harbor at the start of World War II. This period disappointed those in China seeking help from the United States. Since then, US leadership and resolve generally has continued amid often great sacrifice and trauma, caused in particular by repeated, sometimes very costly, and often unpredicted shifts in China. The resulting distrust in Sino-American relations seems strong.

On the China side:

- China's "victim mentality," a long-standing dark view of foreign affairs strongly propagated by the Chinese government, compels China to sustain and advance national power and independence in order to protect its interests in the face of perceived acquisitive and often duplicitous world powers, notably the United States.
- Chinese exceptionalism places the PRC clearly in the lead in the small group of countries that view their foreign behavior in more self-righteous ways than the United States does. Concurrent with the state-fostered "victim mentality," Beijing fosters a view that effectively sways opinion among the Chinese elite and populace that China is always morally correct in its foreign decisions. Information on China's many episodes of aggression and coercive practices for self-interest is suppressed or controlled. In this view, disputes between China and other countries are not China's fault; they arise because of erroneous policies of other countries or sinister manipulation by larger powers, notably the United States. Since China is never at fault, the PRC has never recognized making a mistake in foreign affairs.
- China shows particular worry about the leading world power (usually the United States) and how it will use its presence and influence along China's periphery, its broader international influence, and its

involvement in Chinese internal affairs to enhance its own power and
influence at the expense of Chinese interests and influence.

- As China rises in international power and influence, the leading power
  (the United States) is seen to be inclined to constrain and thwart China's
  rise in order to preserve its own dominant position.
- Chinese suspicions and wariness toward the United States and toward
  foreign affairs in general are reinforced by strong currents of nationalism
  and Chinese domestic politics sensitive to perceived foreign pressures or
  impositions.

Adding to these determinants and values is the fact that the United States
and China are big countries—the world's most powerful. Their approaches
to each other will not be easily changed by smaller powers or other outside forces.

Meanwhile, the checkered record of the United States and China in managing their differences in the interest of pragmatic cooperation since the Nixon-
Mao breakthrough fifty years ago has given rise to experiences on each side
that add to bilateral wariness and friction. They include:

- Taiwan: Private and long held secret Nixon administration interaction
  with China shows US leaders at the outset giving assurances to China
  about Taiwan that appeared to open the way to unification on terms
  agreeable to China. Subsequently, Chinese leaders were repeatedly confronted with US actions that were at odds with earlier US promises and
  impeded Chinese ambitions regarding Taiwan. Chinese distrust of US
  policy, especially regarding Taiwan, became deep and long lasting and
  continues today.
- Secrecy: Beginning with Nixon, various US administrations determined
  to hide US concessions on Taiwan and other sensitive issues through
  secret diplomacy with China in order to keep Congress as well as US
  media and other interested Americans in the dark on these sensitive
  questions. One result was repeated backlash from these forces against
  US administration China policy. Such backlash was seen in congressional action drafting the Taiwan Relations Act of 1979 and congressional
  and media reaction to the George H. W. Bush handling of China policy
  after the Tiananmen incident of 1989. The perceived duplicity of the US
  administration on sensitive issues of China policy led to continued suspicion among congressional officials, the media, and other US opinion
  leaders regarding the purpose and implications of sensitive US policies
  toward China. The US domestic backlash and suspicion imposed a significant drag on US administration efforts to move forward on sensitive
  issues in US-China relations.

- Respective costs and benefits: Debate in the United States and China repeatedly centers on whether one side or the other is gaining disproportionately in the relationship while the other side defers and makes concessions. The Chinese government, given its authoritarian system, has done a better job than the United States in keeping such debate from spilling over publicly to affect policy in negative ways. Nonetheless, the tendency of both sides to be wary of being taken advantage of by the other remains strong.
- Nongovernment actors: Elites in the Chinese and US governments have been the key decision makers in Sino-American relations. However, in the United States, and particularly in US policy toward China, there has been a long history of American nongovernment forces influencing foreign policy. These groups and individuals have been especially important when broader international and domestic circumstances do not support a particular elite-led policy toward China. Thus, they were very important in the years after the Tiananmen incident and the end of the Cold War. Chinese leaders for their part say they are constrained by patriotic public opinion in China, which they aver runs counter to Chinese compromises on Taiwan or other sensitive issues in the interests of fostering better US-China relations.

PURPOSE AND SCOPE OF THIS BOOK

The review offered in this volume synthesizes and analyzes the views of various assessments regarding the background, issues, and trends in Sino-American relations. It shows enormous changes over time, with patterns of confrontation, conflict, and suspicion much more prevalent than patterns of accommodation and cooperation. The past four decades have featured sometimes remarkable improvements in relations as leaders on both sides have pursued practical benefits through pragmatic means. That the base of cooperation was often incomplete, thin, and dependent on changeable circumstances at home and abroad was evident as the societies and governments more often than not showed salient differences over a variety of critical issues involving security, values, and economics. Even during periods of public cooperation, probing below the surface showed officials, elites, and public opinion on both sides demonstrating persistent suspicion and wariness of the other country and its possible negative intentions or implications affecting Sino-American relations.

The purpose of the book is not to argue against continuing efforts in both the United States and China to seek possible ways to promote a positive trajectory in Sino-American relations. Such efforts are viewed as reasonable and are based on common interests of both countries in seeking greater cooperation. Nor does it argue against US and Chinese public disagreements and competition in peaceful pursuit of their respective interests. Instead, this volume conveys the perspective of experienced policy makers and specialists on both sides who understand that perceived advances or setbacks in Sino-American relations involve only part of a complicated relationship. It seeks to assess more fully the complexity of the relationship, so improvements and frictions in official relations between the two nations are placed in balanced context.

Partly because of the salience of US-China relations for international politics, political scientists and other experts devote impressive effort to understanding the relationship and charting its future trajectory, notably using international relations (IR) theories. Nevertheless, experience with many past failed predictions and often unexpected twists and turns in the relationship argues against adherence to only one IR theory in addressing Sino-American relations. Prominent IR scholar Aaron Friedberg early in this century usefully showed how different American and other IR specialists viewed China's rising power and influence through the lens of realism, liberalism, or constructivism—the leading theories in the IR field.[23]

Indeed, as shown in this volume, the complex American relationship with China has many features that may best be assessed using different perspectives from IR theory. Deepening strategic competition and a massive security dilemma between China and the United States in the Asia-Pacific region underline forces and phenomena that seem best understood through a realist lens. At the same time, American stress on open trade and investment, related social and political liberalism, and deepening Chinese engagement with the existing world order seem best assessed through a liberal perspective in IR theory. In addition, a fundamental reason US efforts to engage and change China's policies and practices have occurred on the US side and have been resisted on the Chinese side has to do with a profound gap between the national identity in China and that in the United States, a topic well explained by constructivist IR theory.

While written by a specialist who sees US-China dynamics as best viewed through a realist lens, this study sees the wisdom of using an eclectic approach in applying IR theory to explain varied developments in US-China relations. Meanwhile, the complexities and perceived shortcomings in assessing Sino-American dynamics discussed above lead this author to employ throughout the book the type of contextual analysis used by US government and other policy and intelligence analysts. The author's intention is to offer a comprehensive assessment of the various determinants seen in the context of Chinese and US decision-making in order to provide (1) a realistic view of why and how government officials and others influential in decisions relevant to the US-China relationship have made their choices and (2) a realistic view of the implications of those decisions. Those determinants take into account the changing interplay of power, interests, development, identity, norms, and values present in different countries and regions.

OUTLINE

This book assesses determinants—historical and contemporary—that explain the situation prevailing today between areas of convergence and areas of divergence in contemporary US-China relations. It also thoroughly examines those issues (i.e., areas of convergence and divergence) and offers a likely forecast for US-China relations.

Proceeding from this introductory chapter, which provides a summary of some findings and explains the purpose and scope of the book, chapters 2 through 7 treat the historical development and status of US-China relations with an eye toward discerning determinants relevant to contemporary US-China relations. Chapters 8 through 11 examine four major issue-areas in contemporary US-China relations, endeavoring to discern determinants relevant to the status and outlook of the relationship. Chapter 12 concludes the study by articulating an outlook for Sino-American relations.

Given the importance of the recent hardening of US policy toward China since 2017, this volume devotes more attention to the United States side of the relationship than to the Chinese side in these four years. And viewing the avowed failure of the US policy of engagement with China to reach its objectives over the past fifty years, the assessment here takes a closer look at US policy decision points in the period of engagement since Nixon and Mao. It finds repeated episodes where the administration strongly pushed for advances in American engagement with China, even at the expense of US interests and values, while Congress more often than not reflected greater wariness and opposition to sacrificing existing interests and values for the sake of forward movement in engagement with the Chinese government. Over the years, media discourse and other commentary tended to highlight favorably the actions of the administration in pushing forward the relationship with China and often depicted those resisting in Congress as parochial, myopic, and partisan in their concerns for US interests and values. The brief observations in this volume question those prevailing views in American discourse. These observations will be included in a future study judging with clearer hindsight which part of government, the executive or Congress, were better stewards of American interests in the decades of US engagement with China.

STUDY QUESTIONS

1. What are the main causes of the recent negative turn in US policy toward China?
2. Why did Chinese leaders put aside the advice of senior leader Deng Xiaoping to avoid international prominence and choose to engage in recent assertive and expansionist foreign policies challenging US leadership?
3. Why were US administrations until recently slow to recognize and deal with challenges posed by a rising China?
4. What are the major areas of dispute between the United States and China today? Which ones seem most important and why?
5. Most of these disputes reflect differences in interests and values that have divided the United States and China throughout their recent history. What are those interests and values?
6. What caused US and Chinese leaders until recently to emphasize positive cooperation and to manage differences through private dialogue? What have been the enduring reasons for the United States and China to cooperate and seek closer relations?
7. Why does this volume commonly employ the international relations theory of realism to explain the many turning points in the tortuous development of US-China relations, though it recognizes the need to use the theories of liberalism and constructivism to explain many important developments? Is such an eclectic approach appropriate?

RELEVANT VIDEOS

"China: Power and Prosperity" (documentary, PBS, 2019, 144 minutes) available at https://www.youtube.com/watch?v=JovtmKFxi3c

"What China Will Be Like as a Great Power" Martin Jacques (keynote address at 32nd Annual Camden Conference, more than one hour) available at https://www.youtube.com/watch?v=uBjvklYLShM

"Has China Won?" Kishore Mahbubani, John Mearsheimer, and Tom Switzer (May 11, 2020, one hour) available at https://www.youtube.com/watch?v=ZnkC7GXmLdo

Chapter Two

Patterns of US-China Relations Prior to World War II

Throughout much of the nineteenth century, the United States played a limited role in Chinese affairs. Initial American traders and missionaries had no choice but to accommodate the restrictive and sometimes capricious practices of Chinese regulation of trade and other foreign interaction at Canton in southeastern China, part of the Chinese government's broad tribute system restricting and regulating Chinese interaction with foreigners.[1]

The US government followed the lead of Great Britain, France, and other powers that used wars to compel the declining Qing dynasty (1644–1912) to meet foreign demands and grant privileges to foreigners, including Americans who did not take part in the fighting. Americans in China supported and benefited from the resulting treaty system. The emerging new order gave foreigners extraterritoriality, the right to reside in China under foreign laws and jurisdiction. The series of foreign treaties imposed on China in the nineteenth and early twentieth centuries opened Chinese ports to foreign commerce and residence; established equal diplomatic relations between the foreign powers and China, with foreign diplomats stationed in the Chinese capital, Peking; allowed foreign missionaries and others to live and work throughout China; provided for concessions of land and development rights that made parts of China, like Shanghai, into foreign-ruled enclaves; and allowed foreign military forces to patrol Chinese coastal and inland waterways and eventually to deploy ground forces in China to secure their interests. The treaties also marked the loss of substantial pieces of Chinese territory to foreign ownership.[2]

A few American companies made significant profits in China trade, but the scope of US trade and investment there remained small. Christian missionaries comprised the largest and most influential group of Americans in China until the start of World War II, but for much of the period they numbered only in the hundreds.[3]

American diplomats, merchants, and missionaries reacted with concern as European powers and later Japan began at the end of the nineteenth century to carve up Chinese territory into exclusive spheres of influence. However, US government actions in response were mainly symbolic, using nonbinding measures such as diplomatic notes and agreements to support the principles of free access to China and Chinese territorial integrity. US importance in China also grew by default as previously active European powers withdrew forces and resources during World War I. Imperial Japan used military and other coercion to solidify Japanese control in parts of China, notably Manchuria.[4]

Though there often was strenuous US debate, the prevailing US official position was that limited US capabilities and interests in China argued against the United States confronting increasingly dominant Japanese power in East Asia. US officials endeavored to use international agreements and political measures to persuade Japanese officials to preserve Chinese integrity and free international access to China. The US efforts were seriously complicated by political disorder in China and by US leaders' later preoccupation with the consequences of the Great Depression. In the 1930s, Japan created a puppet state in Manchuria and continued encroachments in northern China. The United States did little apart from symbolic political posturing in response to the Japanese aggression and expansion.[5]

US-China relations in this more than century-long period saw the emergence of patterns of behavior that influenced US and Chinese attitudes and policies toward one another. American officials and elite and popular opinion tended to emphasize what they saw as the uniquely positive role the United States played as a supporter of Chinese national interests and the well-being of the Chinese people, with some commentators seeing the emergence of a US special relationship with China. Chinese officials and elites, including a rising group of Chinese patriots in the late nineteenth and early twentieth centuries, tended to see American policies and practices as less aggressive than those of other powers but of little substantive help in China's struggle for national preservation and development. Chinese officials often endeavored to manipulate American diplomacy to serve Chinese interests, but they usually were disappointed with the results. American government policies and practices were seen at bottom to serve narrow US interests, with little meaningful concern for China. Gross American discrimination against and persecution of Chinese residents and Chinese immigrants in the United States underlined a perceived hypocrisy in American declarations of special concern for China.[6]

US INTERESTS, ACTIONS, AND PERCEPTIONS

Beginning in the late eighteenth century, new American freedom from British rule brought American loss of access to previously British-controlled trade partners. This prompted an American search for new trading opportunities in China. Though actual US trade with China remained relatively small, the China market often loomed large in the American political and business imagination. Meanwhile, US officials sometimes sought to channel US investment in ways that would preserve American commercial opportunities in China in the face of foreign powers seeking exclusive privileges and spheres of influence.[7]

Americans also were in the vanguard of Protestant missionaries sent to China in the nineteenth century. US missionaries came in groups and as individuals to work in the treaty ports and eventually grew to many hundreds working throughout China to spread the gospel and to carry out relief, education, medical, and other activities of benefit to Chinese people. Part of a well-organized network of church groups that reached deep into the United States for prayers and material support, American missionaries explained Chinese conditions to interested Americans, fostering a sense of special bond between the United States and China. They also served as advisers to US officials dealing with China and sometimes became official US representatives in China. Their core interest remained unobstructed access to Chinese people for purposes of evangelization and good works carried out by the American missionaries and their foreign and Chinese colleagues.[8]

Though commercial and missionary interests remained at the center of US priorities in China well into the twentieth century, a related strategic interest also had deep roots. In 1835, several years before the first US treaty with China in 1844, the United States organized the Asiatic Squadron. This US Navy group began in 1842 to maintain a regular presence along the China coast. It later was called the Asiatic Fleet. Initially two or three vessels, it grew to thirty-one vessels by 1860 before forces were recalled on account of the American Civil War. It varied in size after the Civil War but was sufficiently strong to easily destroy the Spanish forces in Manila harbor during the Spanish-American War in 1898. It protected American lives and commerce in China and throughout maritime East and South Asia and reinforced American diplomacy in the region.[9]

Strong American interest in commercial, missionary, and strategic access to China seemed to contrast with only episodic American diplomatic interest in China. The US government occasionally gave high-level attention to the appointment of envoys or the reception of Chinese delegations. Caleb Cushing, Anson Burlingame, and some other nineteenth-century US envoys to China were well connected politically. Some US envoys endeavored to use their actions in China to influence broader US policy or to advance their own political or other ambitions. US envoys sometimes came from the missionary community in China. On the other hand, the post of US minister in China often was vacant, with an interim official placed in charge in an acting capacity. Generally speaking, whenever nineteenth-century US envoys pushed for more assertive US policies that involved the chance of significant expenditure of US resources or political risk, Washington decision makers reflected the realities of limited US government interests in the situation in China and responded unenthusiastically. This broad pattern continued into the twentieth century, though US officials from time to time took the lead in low-risk political and diplomatic efforts in support of US interests in unimpeded commercial and other access to China.[10]

Not surprisingly, the Americans with an interest in China tended to emphasize the positive features of US policy and behavior. Thus, the United States was seen to have behaved benignly toward China, especially when compared with Japan and the European powers that repeatedly coerced and attacked China militarily. The US government repeatedly voiced support of China's territorial and national integrity. Through missionary and other activities, including education activities that brought tens of thousands of Chinese students to the United States for higher education by the 1940s, Americans also showed strong sympathy and support for the broader welfare of the Chinese people.[11]

US officials, opinion leaders, and commentators tended to ignore or soft-pedal negative features of US relations with China. Most notable was the so-called exclusion movement that grossly discriminated against and often violently persecuted Chinese immigrants to the United States. The movement took hold in US politics beginning in the 1870s and lasted for almost a hundred years. At first centered in western states with some significant concentrations of Chinese workers, the exclusion movement reflected widespread American prejudice and fear of Chinese workers amid sometimes difficult economic times in the United States. American elites and common people took legal and illegal actions, including riots and the murder of hundreds of Chinese in the United States, to stop Chinese immigration to the United States and drive away those Chinese already in the United States. Various state governments and the national government passed an array of laws, and the US courts made a variety of decisions that singled out Chinese immigrants for negative treatment and curbed the legal rights of Chinese residents and Chinese citizens of the United States. The movement eventually broadened to include all Asians. The National Origins Act of 1924 barred all new Asian immigration. US mistreatment of Chinese people in the United States became a major issue for the Chinese government, which complained repeatedly against unjust US actions but with little effect. The US mistreatment was the target of a Chinese anti-American boycott in 1905.[12]

CHINESE INTERESTS, ACTIONS, AND PERCEPTIONS

The Chinese side of the US-China relationship during the more than a century long experience prior to World War II saw Chinese officials and elite opinion in the nineteenth and early twentieth centuries remain preoccupied with massive internal rebellions and disruptions. In this context, the United States figured secondarily in Chinese government and elite concerns. The opinion of the Chinese populace was less important in China-US relations until the occurrence of anti-Christian and antimissionary riots later in the nineteenth century and grassroots nationalistic actions like the 1905 anti-American boycott reacting to the US mistreatment of Chinese immigrants.[13]

Qing dynasty officials often were too weak to confront foreign aggression and military pressure in the nineteenth and early twentieth centuries. Their diplomacy frequently amounted to versions of appeasement. Forced to give ground to foreign demands, the Qing officials gave special emphasis to capitalizing on real or perceived differences among the foreign powers, hoping to use some foreign powers to fend off others. Chinese officials repeatedly tried to elicit US actions that would assist Chinese interests against other generally more aggressive and demanding powers. Although US envoys in China often would be caught up in these Chinese schemes and argue for US positions at odds with other powers in China, Washington decision makers tended to adhere to a low-risk approach that offered little of substance to support the Chinese efforts.[14]

Qing dynasty initiatives endeavoring to use possible US support against other foreign powers did not blind Chinese government officials to US interests in China that worked against Chinese government concerns. The spread of foreign missionaries throughout China as a result of treaties reached in 1860 meant that these foreign elites soon ran up against strong resistance from local Chinese elites. The local Chinese leaders, the so-called gentry class, often fomented popular outbursts and riots against the foreigners and their Chinese Christian adherents. The American missionaries sought the support of their official representatives in China who backed their demands to the Chinese government for protection, punishment of Chinese malefactors, and compensation with strong diplomacy and frequent use of gunboats. This posed a very difficult dilemma for Qing officials, who needed to deal with the threats from the Americans and other foreign officials pressing for protection of missionaries and punishment of offending Chinese elites while also sustaining the support of local Chinese elites who provided key elements of Chinese governance at the local levels.[15]

Meanwhile, American government officials were seen by Chinese officials and other elites as transparently hypocritical in demanding protection of special rights for American missionaries and other US citizens in China, while US officials and people were carrying out repeated and often violent infringements on the rights and basic safety of Chinese workers in the United States. In this context, Chinese officials tended to be sympathetic with the merchant-led and student-encouraged anti-American boycott that took hold in Chinese coastal cities in 1905 and that focused on Chinese anger over US discrimination against Chinese immigration to the United States and poor treatment of Chinese in the United States.[16]

With the withdrawal of the European powers to fight World War I, the United States loomed larger in the strategies of the weak Chinese governments following the end of the Qing dynasty in 1912. However, the United States remained unwilling to take significant risks of confrontation with the now-dominant power in China: imperial Japan. The US reaction to the gross Japanese infringements on Chinese sovereignty in the so-called Twenty-One Demands of 1915 elicited statements on nonrecognition and not much else from the United States. President Woodrow Wilson gravely disappointed Chinese patriots by accepting Japan's continued control of the former German leasehold in China's Shantung province at the Versailles Peace Treaty ending World War I.[17]

The Nine Power Treaty at the US-convened Washington Conference of 1921–22 pledged to respect Chinese territorial integrity, but when Japan took over Manchuria, creating a puppet state in the early 1930s, the US government offered little more than words of disapproval. Given this experience, Chinese patriots were not persuaded by the protestations of some American commentators that the United States had developed a special relationship with China based on concern for the well-being of the Chinese people and preservation of China's sovereignty and integrity. When Japan, after occupying Manchuria, moved in 1937 to launch an all-out war against China and the United States did little in response, Chinese patriots became even more cynical about American intentions and policies.[18]

NINETEENTH-CENTURY ENCOUNTERS

American traders and seamen were the first from the United States to interact with China. When American traders went to China prior to the Opium War of 1839–42, Chinese regulations under the tribute system in foreign affairs confined them, along with most other foreign maritime traders, to Canton, in southeastern China. There, local officials supervised and taxed foreign trade, foreigners were required to live and work in a designated area of Canton during the trading season, and foreign interaction with Chinese was kept to a minimum; certain Chinese merchants were designated to deal with foreign merchants.[19]

Chinese foreign relations under the tribute system were unequal; they emphasized the superiority of China, its system of governance, and the emperor. The foreigners were expected to abide by Chinese laws and regulations and to accord with Chinese instructions. As a result, although American and other foreign merchants and their foreign employees benefited from the trading opportunities at Canton, they were subject to interventions from Chinese authority that appeared unjust from a Western perspective and dangerous to those concerned.

A graphic illustration of the vulnerability of foreigners in China was the case of Francesco Terranova. A Sicilian-born sailor on an American ship trading at Canton in 1821, Terranova was accused of the murder of a boatwoman selling fruit to the ship. He and his shipmates denied the charge. A standoff resulted, with Chinese authorities cutting off American trade until Terranova was handed over. The American merchants and shipowners gave in; Terranova was handed over, tried in secret under Chinese procedures with no American present, convicted, and executed. Trade between the United States and China resumed.[20]

Like their British colleagues, American merchants brought opium into China, balancing their purchases of tea and other Chinese commodities. The burgeoning trade in illegal opium entering China in the period before the Opium War was carried out mainly by British merchants, though American merchants carried Turkish opium to China and held about 10 percent of the Chinese opium market. American opium along with British opium was confiscated and destroyed by Chinese authorities in Canton in 1839, leading to Great Britain going to war. The US government took no part in the fighting.[21]

After the British in 1842 negotiated the Treaty of Nanjing, ending the Opium War and opening five Chinese treaty ports for foreign residency and trade, the United States appointed Caleb Cushing as commissioner to China to negotiate a US treaty with China. He negotiated the Treaty of Wang-hsia in 1844, obtaining the rights and privileges Britain had gained by force of arms. Chinese negotiator Ch'i-ying followed a general policy of trying to appease foreign demands, and the US treaty included language to the effect that Chinese concessions made to other foreign nations would apply to the United States as well. American merchants, missionaries, and others were free to settle in the five treaty ports, and Americans, like other foreigners in China, had the right of extraterritoriality. This legal system meant that foreigners and their activities in China remained governed by their own law and not Chinese law.[22]

Emblematic of the wide-ranging influence some American missionaries exerted over the course of US policy toward China during that period was the role of Peter Parker (1804–88). Parker was a medical missionary in Canton in the 1830s. He assisted Caleb Cushing in negotiating the Treaty of Wang-hsia. He was an interpreter and also helped facilitate the talks by being on good terms with the chief Chinese government negotiator and his aides. Parker eventually became US commissioner in China in 1856. Faced with a harder Chinese line at that time toward foreign demands for broader commercial and missionary privileges, Parker favored Britain's approach, emphasizing firmness and appropriate use of force to advance foreign interests. When, in 1856, Chinese forts in Canton fired on US warships under the command of Commodore James Armstrong, Parker backed Armstrong's destruction of the forts. Parker later had ambitions for the United States to gain a foothold in Taiwan and to have a more active naval presence in China, but these initiatives were not supported by the US government.[23]

The upsurge of the massive Taiping Rebellion beginning in 1850 caught Chinese authorities and American and foreign observers by surprise as the rebel movement came to dominate southeastern China and most of the Yangtze River valley. Some Americans at first were attracted by Taiping leader Hung Hsiu-ch'uan's avowed Christian beliefs. Hung came to his own unique views of Christianity, though he had three months of study in 1837 with an American missionary in Canton, Issachar Roberts. As the Taiping leader's warped views of Christianity became clearer to Americans, they added to reasons Americans and other foreigners shied away from the radical rebel leader and his destructive activities.[24]

Though seeing US interests resting with continued Qing dynasty rule, American officials nonetheless were ready to join with Great Britain, France, and others in pressing for treaty revisions that would open more treaty ports, allow for missionary activities outside the treaty ports, and establish foreign legations in the Chinese capital. Britain and France used military force to back up their demands, and in 1858 the Chinese government signed treaties with them as well as with the Americans, who did no fighting. When British and French envoys returned in 1859 to exchange ratification, they refused Chinese ratification instructions, and a battle resulted in which the Chinese drove off the foreigners. During the battle, the US commodore accompanying Minister John Ward, the American envoy, had his forces, with Ward's approval, join with the British in fighting the Chinese. Ward nonetheless followed the Chinese instructions for treaty ratification and managed to exchange ratification. The British and French returned in force in 1860 and marched to Peking before setting forth new conditions in the treaties of 1860 that also benefited the United States.[25]

US policy in China supported stronger Chinese government efforts after 1860 that worked within the confines of the treaty system and accepted Western norms while strengthening the Chinese government, economy, and military. American Frederick Townsend Ward had led a foreign mercenary force paid by Chinese merchants to protect Shanghai during the Taiping Rebellion, and he later worked with Chinese authorities in leading a Chinese force that helped crush the rebellion. Americans supported the newly established Chinese Imperial Maritime Customs Service. This foreign-managed customs service had its roots in Shanghai in the 1850s during the years of threat posed by the Taiping Rebellion; it emerged as a unique Chinese-foreign enterprise (with more than four hundred foreign employees in 1875) that preserved the Chinese government's access to an important and reliable source of revenue. The US government saw its interests well served by cooperating amicably with Britain and France as they worked collaboratively with a newly reformist Chinese government seeking to strengthen China along Western lines. The American Civil War weakened American military presence in China and prompted US policy to place a premium on avoiding disputes with Britain and France that might lead the European powers to be more inclined to support the secessionist South.[26]

Anson Burlingame, US minister to China (1861–67), symbolized American collaboration with other foreign powers and with China in promoting Chinese reforms and greater outreach to advanced Western countries. After leaving his position as minister, Burlingame accepted a Chinese offer to lead a Chinese delegation to observe and have talks with leaders of the West. The trip was moderately successful, meeting acceptance notably in America and England. The so-called Burlingame Treaty was signed during the delegation's visit to the United States in 1868. Among other provisions in the treaty, the United States said it would not interfere in the internal development of China, China recognized the right of its people to emigrate, and the United States gave Chinese immigrants the right to enter the United States. At the time, there were more than one hundred thousand Chinese in the United States. Many had come with the support of American business interests and their national and local US government backers seeking reliable labor for the rapid development of the American West.[27]

Unfortunately, American society showed deep prejudice against Chinese that eventually spread to other immigrants from Asia. Ironically, this came at a time when a wide range of elements in the United States generally welcomed the hundreds of thousands of immigrants coming annually to the United States from Europe. There emerged in the 1870s a broad-based exclusion movement in the United States that was a dominant feature in US relations with China for decades to come. This widespread US movement was grounded in prejudice and fear of Chinese workers amid sometimes difficult economic times in the United States. Showing blatant racism against Chinese, Americans took legal and illegal actions, including riots and the murder of hundreds of Chinese in the United States, to stop Chinese immigration to the United States. In September 1885, mobs of white workers attacked Chinese in Rock Springs, Wyoming, killing twenty-eight in an outburst of burning, looting, and mayhem. State governments and the national government passed an array of laws, and US courts made a variety of decisions that singled out Chinese immigrants for negative treatment and curbed the legal rights of Chinese residents and Chinese citizens in the United States. In 1888, the Scott Act restricted Chinese laborers' entry and denied them reentry into the United States. In 1892, the Geary Act stripped Chinese in the United States, whether citizens or not, of substantial legal rights, requiring them to obtain and carry at all times a certificate showing their right to reside in the United States. Without such proof, the punishment was hard labor and deportation. The movement broadened to include all Asians. The National Origins Act of 1924 barred new Asian immigration.[28]

Chinese officials in the Chinese legation in Washington protested US discrimination and persecution of Chinese and endeavored to reach agreements with the US government that would assure basic protection of Chinese rights. They repeatedly found US actions in violation of treaty obligations and other agreements. US violations seriously undermined diplomatic relations between the two countries in the 1890s. US mistreatment of Chinese people in the United States also prompted patriotic merchants, students, and others to organize anti-American movements. The 1905 boycott closed several coastal Chinese cities to US goods for several months. Nevertheless, the US exclusion movement persisted and grew.

Adding to the friction in Sino-American official relations were the tensions caused by expanding US and other foreign missionary activities in China and the resulting antiforeign backlash in China. Attacks against Chinese Christians and their missionary leaders became common occurrences in the latter part of the nineteenth century, prompting American and other Western governments to press the Chinese government for strong remedial actions and prompting foreign officials to take actions on their own, including the use of foreign gunboats, in order to protect their interests and citizens. The Chinese authorities repeatedly found themselves caught between competing pressures. On the one hand were the strong American and other foreign pressures to protect missionaries and Chinese Christians. On the other hand was the strong need to preserve the support of the local Chinese gentry class, whose cooperation was essential for the maintenance of local governance in the minimally staffed Chinese administration at the grassroots level. The gentry often tended to see the foreign missionaries as posing social, political, and ideological challenges to the Chinese elite, and they frequently took steps to foster antiforeign sentiment against them by the broader Chinese society.[29]

Illustrating the marked shift toward the negative in official US attitudes toward China from the comparatively benign and somewhat paternalistic views of Anson Burlingame was the change in approach of Charles Denby, who served as American minister in China (1885–98). A loyal Democrat appointed by the first Grover Cleveland administration, Denby stayed as US minister through the end of the second Cleveland administration. Initially favoring a temperate position in seeking cooperation with Chinese officials seen as moving toward reform, Denby came later to the view that Chinese government incompetence and weakness endangered American and other missionaries and opened China to unchecked ambitions by outside powers. He saw little alternative to the United States' joining coercive foreign powers in order to protect US interests.[30]

Chinese official disappointment and frustration with the United States were reflected in the experience of Li Hung-chang (Li Hongzhang) (1823–1901). Dominating Chinese foreign policy in the last third of the nineteenth century, this senior regional and national leader and commissioner of trade in northern China repeatedly employed the past practice of Chinese leaders in using initiatives toward the United States in an effort to offset pressures on China from other powers. And, as in those earlier episodes, he found the US response wanting and became increasingly cynical about the utility of appealing to the United States for support.[31]

As in the case of earlier episodes of Chinese efforts to use the United States against more aggressive foreign powers, Li's view was based on the judgment that the United States posed little threat to Chinese territories or tributary states, while its commitment to commerce provided common ground in US-China relations that could be used by Chinese officials to win American support against more grasping and aggressive foreign powers. Li was forced to deal with the growing source of friction between the United States and China posed by US immigration policy discriminating against Chinese. Initially, he endeavored to deal with this issue through negotiation.

Li sought US assistance in dealing with Chinese difficulties with Japan over the Liu-ch'iu (Ryukyu) Islands in the 1870s. President Ulysses S. Grant favored a cooperative US policy toward China and was a personal friend of Anson Burlingame, the prominent proponent of cooperative China-US relations. After leaving office, Grant traveled to Asia in 1879 and was encouraged by Li to intercede with Japan on China's behalf regarding a dispute over the Liu-ch'iu (Ryukyu) Islands. Grant also received a promise from the Chinese government to negotiate treaty restrictions on Chinese immigration into the United States. Li later sought US endorsement of Chinese claims in

Korea in the face of Japanese pressure there in the 1880s. He also sought US mediation in a growing dispute with France over Vietnam in the 1880s. All these initiatives achieved little of benefit to China. By July 1894, Li sought US good offices to avoid a war with Japan over Korea only after exhausting other options. Li then endeavored to rely on Russia and other European powers to deal with Japanese demands after the Japanese defeated China in 1895. Unlike other Chinese officials, including his senior colleague Chang Chih-tung (Zhang Zhidong), Li did not emphasize the option of turning to the United States for meaningful assistance in the period of demands by Russia, Japan, and other imperial powers for major territorial and other concessions from China at the turn of the nineteenth century.[32]

US-CHINA RELATIONS AMID FOREIGN DOMINATION, INTERNAL DECLINE, AND REVOLUTION IN CHINA, 1895–1941

China's unexpected defeat by Japan in the Sino-Japanese War of 1894–95 led European powers to join Japan in seeking exclusive spheres of influence and commercial and territorial rights in China. Alarmed that US interests in free commercial access to China would be jeopardized, US officials formulated a response that led to the so-called Open Door Notes of 1899 and 1900. The notes sought the powers' agreement that even if they established special spheres in China, they would not discriminate against foreign trade or interfere with customs collection. They underlined US interests in preserving equal commercial access to China and the preservation of the integrity of the Chinese Customs Service, a crucial source of revenue for the struggling Chinese government.[33]

Though generally unenthusiastic about the US initiatives, most concerned powers offered evasive and qualified responses, but all in effect endorsed the principles in the Open Door Notes. As the United States and other foreign powers dispatched troops to crush the Boxer Uprising and lift the siege of foreign legations in Peking, the United States in July 1900 sent a second round of Open Door Notes that expressed concern for preserving Chinese sovereignty. The foreign powers went along with the notes.

US policy makers repeatedly referred to the US Open Door policy following the issuing of the Open Door Notes. The William H. Taft administration in 1910 interpreted the policy to extend beyond equal trade opportunity to include equal opportunity for investment in China. The Wilson administration in 1915 reacted to the Japanese Twenty-One Demands against China by refusing to recognize such infringements of the Open Door policy. The related principles concerning US support for the territorial integrity of China were featured prominently in the Nine Power Treaty of the Washington Conference in the Warren G. Harding administration in 1922 and in the nonrecognition of Japanese aggression in Manchuria during the Herbert Hoover administration in 1932. The Harry Truman administration sought Soviet Union leader Joseph Stalin's promise that the Open Door policy would be observed in the Soviet-influenced areas of Manchuria following the Soviet military defeat of Japanese forces there in 1945. In general, American political leaders dealing with China throughout the twentieth century tended to refer to the Open Door policy in positive terms, as a US attempt to prevent China from being carved up into commercially impenetrable foreign colonies. Chinese interpretations often emphasized that Americans were more concerned about maintaining their own commercial access and were prepared to do little in practice to support Chinese sovereignty. The historical record tends to support the Chinese interpretations.[34]

Most prominent in US policy toward China in the tumultuous period of the Open Door Notes was John Hay. Secretary of state under President William McKinley and, after McKinley's assassination in 1901, President Theodore Roosevelt, Hay strove to preserve US commercial access to China and other interests amid widespread foreign encroachment on the weakened Qing dynasty. Responding to the unexpected Japanese defeat of China in 1895 and European powers' extortion of leaseholds and concessions in the following three years, Hay used the work of State Department China expert William Rockhill and his British colleague from the Chinese Imperial Maritime Customs Service, Alfred Hippisley, as the basis for official US messages sent to all foreign powers concerned with China in September 1899.[35]

The first Open Door Notes were followed by the crisis associated with the Boxer Uprising. A grassroots antiforeign insurrection in northern China, known as the Boxers, came to receive support from some Chinese officials, and by 1899 and 1900 it was carrying out widespread attacks against foreign missionaries and Chinese Christians. As the movement grew, it received the support of the Qing court, though regional leaders in most of China did not support the Boxers. The insurgents occupied Peking and Tientsin, besieging foreign legations and settlements. About twenty thousand foreign troops were mustered, including thousands of Americans, to end the siege and put down the insurgents. They ended the siege of Tientsin in July and of Peking in August 1900. Many troops stayed, carrying out punitive expeditions.[36]

As the United States and other foreign powers dispatched troops to crush the Boxer Uprising and lift the siege of foreign legations in Peking, Hay in July 1900 sent a second round of Open Door Notes in which he expressed concern for preserving Chinese sovereignty. He depicted local Chinese authorities as responsible for law and order and the safety of foreigners in China. This helped the United States and other powers continue to work constructively with regional Chinese leaders in central and southern China who were maintaining law and order and to focus their anti-Boxer suppression more narrowly, in northern China.

Though Hay tried to reduce the large size of the foreign indemnity demanded of China, the United States took its $25 million share of the $333 million indemnity China was required to pay the foreign powers under terms of the Boxer Protocol signed in September 1901, and the United States stationed troops along with other powers in northern China under the terms of the protocol. While continuing to work in support of China's territorial integrity and equal commercial access to China, Hay responded to US pressures to obtain a coaling station in China by making a perfunctory and ultimately vain effort in December 1900 to acquire such a station on the China coast.[37]

Meanwhile, as Russia endeavored to consolidate its hold in Manchuria, and Japan and Great Britain worked together against it, ultimately forming an alliance in 1902, Hay attempted to secure US interests with a new Sino-American trade treaty and a request to open two new treaty ports in Russian-dominated areas of Manchuria. Russia at first resisted Chinese acceptance of the US request but decided to withdraw its opposition when it was clear to them that Americans or other foreigners, notably Japanese, would not settle in the ports.[38]

Though Li Hung-chang and his increasingly skeptical view of the utility of overtures to the United States for Chinese interests remained salient in Chinese foreign-policy decision making until his death in 1901, simultaneously, an important force often arguing for closer Chinese coordination with the United States came from Chang Chih-tung (1837–1909). A powerful Chinese official, well entrenched as governor-general in the provinces, Chang endeavored in the period after Japan's defeat of China in 1895 and subsequent European powers' extortion of concessions to cooperate with the United States as a power opposing seizure of Chinese territory. Though he supported China's reliance on Russia after the defeat by Japan in 1895, he came by 1898 to seek the support of Britain and the United States, viewing them as commercial powers with substantial interests in blocking seizures of Chinese territory by Japan, Russia, and others.[39]

That year, he entrusted an American consortium to build the Hankow-Canton railway. The US business group was known as the American-China Development Company. Organized in 1895 and representing US railway, banking, and investment interests, the company received from the Chinese government in 1898 a concession to build and operate a railway between the two Chinese cities. The company demanded and received better terms from the Chinese government in a supplementary agreement in 1900.[40]

Chang made overtures to the United States during and after the Boxer Uprising, seeking US mediation with the foreign powers and US assistance in moderating the foreign reaction to the crisis. Chang sought, without much success, US help in limiting the size of the foreign indemnity and in dealing with Russian military occupation of Manchuria after the Boxer Uprising. He subsequently became disillusioned with the American consortium for the Hankow-Canton railroad. Some of the American shareholders sold interest in the company to a Belgian syndicate, which by 1904 controlled five of seven seats on the company's board of directors. Chang and the Chinese government then sought to buy back the concession, and the US government encouraged efforts by American investors to restore American control to the company. In the end, American shareholders, having restored American ownership of the company, gained considerable profit by selling their interests in the railway concession back to the Chinese government in 1905.

Chang's frustration with the United States also was seen as he intervened at several points with the Chinese central government and the US government, emphasizing strong antipathy among Chinese patriots over the US exclusion of Chinese in the late nineteenth and early twentieth centuries. During the anti-American boycott of 1905, prompted heavily by Chinese resentment over US restrictions on Chinese immigration, Chang privately advised President Theodore Roosevelt to ease the US restrictions.[41]

American officials also were active in the late nineteenth and early twentieth centuries, pressing the Chinese government to protect American and other missionaries and their converts, who were subjected to frequent attacks often fomented by Chinese local elites. The Boxer Uprising added greatly to the anti-Christian attacks and implicated the Qing government in the violence. Hundreds of foreign missionaries and thousands of Chinese Christians were killed. The violence against missionaries subsided but did not end. The Lien-Chou massacre of 1905 represented the most serious incident in US-China relations in the decade. The murder of five US missionaries in this southern Chinese city prompted President Theodore Roosevelt to consider the use of force in Canton, and American forces began gathering in Canton harbor. Roosevelt already was strongly critical of the prolonged anti-American boycott underway in China. Chinese officials ultimately took steps to punish those responsible for the massacre and to pay an indemnity.[42]

The Sino-American maneuvering over the Hankow-Canton railway was emblematic of an erratic pattern of American business and government interest in investment in China in railway and other development plans in the last fifteen years of Qing rule. Also reflected then was erratic Chinese interest in using such US involvement in efforts to offset foreign encroachment. The focus of interest for the United States and China came to rest in Manchuria, where Russia and especially Japan were consolidating spheres of influence. Prominent figures on the Chinese side in this issue were Tang Shao-yi, a governor in Manchuria, and the regional and emerging national leader of China, Yuan Shih-kai, both of whom sought such US support.[43]

A protégé of Li Hung-chang, Yuan emerged as the most important military and political leader in China in the early twentieth century until his death in 1916. His base of power was in northern China, and he was closely involved with efforts to stem the decline of Chinese influence and control in Manchuria in the face of Russian and Japanese advances. He supported the ways Tang Shao-yi and others approached the Theodore Roosevelt administration as they sought US support in order to counter Japanese expansion in Manchuria. Seeking good relations with the United States, he argued for the suppression of the anti-American boycott.[44]

Tang had studied in the United States and worked with Yuan and others in encouraging US government and business to become more involved with railway building in Manchuria as a means to counter Japanese expansion there. Tang sought support from US financial backers and officials in China. As US consul general in Mukden, Manchuria, during the Theodore Roosevelt administration, Willard Straight attempted to work with Tang and other Chinese officials to use US investments to counter Japanese domination in Manchuria. In 1908, Tang traveled to Washington, where he met with Secretary of State Elihu Root, who underlined the Theodore Roosevelt administration's lack of interest in confronting Japan in Manchuria by sharing with Tang the yet-unpublished Root-Takahira Agreement. This was an exchange of notes between Root and Japanese ambassador Takahira Kogoro that underlined US commitment to the status quo in the Pacific region, including China; US desire to maintain friendly relations with Japan; and lack of US interest in considering any Chinese-inspired plan to challenge Japanese interests in Manchuria.[45]

US government policy on supporting railway building as a means to challenge other powers' encroachment and support Chinese influence in Manchuria shifted markedly for a time during the Taft administration (1909–13). The president and Secretary of State Philander Knox tried to use schemes involving US investment in railways to prevent Russia and Japan from dominating Manchuria. A leading example of these plans was a proposed railway in Manchuria between the cities of Chinchow and Aigun. Willard Straight had left US government service and was working with Chinese officials and US and foreign backers to promote plans to build the railroad. Straight signed an agreement with Chinese authorities in Manchuria in October 1909 to have an American banking group finance the Chinchow-Aigun route. Before moving forward with the deal, the Chinese authorities in Peking awaited US efforts to deal with expected Japanese and Russian anger over this challenge to their spheres of influence in Manchuria. In this regard, Secretary of State Knox proposed a bold plan to neutralize or internationalize all railway projects in

Manchuria. Japan and Russia rejected Knox's plan and warned against the Chinchow-Aigun railway. Chinese central government authorities temporized, and US investors showed little enthusiasm. The Taft administration's "dollar diplomacy" failed. The US administration subsequently adopted a more moderate stance emphasizing US cooperation with European powers, and ultimately Russia and Japan, in an international consortium dealing with loans to China. Ironically, Hsi-liang, the Chinese governor-general in Manchuria in the last years of the Qing dynasty, and his Qing dynasty colleagues chose this time to try to consolidate ties with the United States and to seek greater US support against Russia and Japan in Manchuria. However, Chinese government emissaries found the Taft administration now maintained a low profile regarding Manchuria.[46]

The pattern of US government policy on the one hand supporting an open door of international commercial access to China and Chinese territorial integrity, and on the other hand avoiding actions that would complicate US relations with salient foreign powers expanding in China, continued with the fall of the Chinese empire. In the thirty years from the end of the Qing dynasty in early 1912 to the attack on Pearl Harbor in late 1941, US policy and practice endeavored to stake out positions and formulate political measures designed to support Chinese sovereignty and integrity. But they did so while generally avoiding the risk of confrontation with imperial Japan, which emerged as the dominant power in East Asia after the pullback and weakening of European powers in the region with the start of World War I. US policy makers also were challenged by revolutionary movements and violent antiforeign sentiment sweeping China in the 1920s. They tended to adjust to these trends pragmatically, giving way to some of the Chinese demands and eventually establishing good working relations with the Nationalist Chinese government of Chiang Kai-shek, the dominant leader of China by the late 1920s.

Japan moved quickly to consolidate its position in China with the start of World War I. Allied with Great Britain and siding with the Allies in World War I, Japan occupied German concessions in China's Shantung province in 1914. In January 1915, Japan presented the Chinese government with five sets of secret demands that became known as the Twenty-One Demands. The demands were leaked, which compelled Japan to defer the more outrageous ones, but they resulted in May 1915 in Sino-Japanese treaties and notes confirming Japan's dominant position in Shantung, southern Manchuria, and eastern Inner Mongolia, and Japan's special interests in an industrial area in central China. US officials debated how to respond. Secretary of State William Jennings Bryan at first reaffirmed US support for China's territorial integrity and equal commercial access to China but also acknowledged Japan's "special relations" with China. President Wilson subsequently warned that the United States would not accept infringements on its rights, and Bryan said the United States would not recognize infringements on US rights, Chinese sovereignty, or the Open Door policy. In a bid to expand US leverage, Wilson then reversed an earlier decision and supported American banks' lending money to China through an international consortium as a means to balance Japanese expansion in China.

Not seriously deterred, Japan maneuvered to see that its position in Shantung province was secured by the Versailles Peace Treaty ending World War I. Like Japan, the Chinese government had aligned with the victorious allied powers. US and Chinese delegations worked closely at the peace conference to free China from restrictions on its sovereignty, and Chinese negotiators were particularly interested in regaining control of the former German concession in China's Shantung province. Nevertheless, Japan earlier had signed secret agreements with European powers that bound them to support Japan's claims to the Shantung leasehold, and the Chinese government's position was weakened by having agreed as part of the Twenty-One Demands in 1915 to accept German-Japanese agreement on the concessions. Robert Lansing, a counselor at the State Department during the early years of the Wilson administration, argued against confrontation with Japan in defense of China's integrity at the time of Japan's Twenty-One Demands in 1915. As secretary of state in 1917, he negotiated and exchanged notes with Japanese envoy Ishii Kikujiro that acknowledged Japan's "special interests" in China, even though Japan privately agreed not to seek privileges at the expense of other friendly powers in China. The notes were used by Japan as evidence of tacit US support for Japanese expansion in China. Though Lansing opposed President Wilson's decision at the Versailles Peace Conference in 1919 to accept the Japanese claim to the German concessions in China's Shantung province, Wilson felt compelled to accept Japan's claim to the former German concessions. The president's action gravely disappointed Chinese patriots. The provision in the treaty was a catalyst for a demonstration in Peking on May 4, 1919, that led to both intellectual reform campaigns and radical, anti-imperialist movements that spread throughout China in the following years and became known collectively as the May Fourth Movement.[47]

The United States after World War I took the lead in calling a major conference involving powers with interests in the western Pacific, including China but not the Soviet Union, to deal with relevant security issues. The result was the Washington Conference of 1921–22 that saw passage of a Nine Power Treaty supporting noninterference in Chinese internal affairs. US delegates working with others also succeeded in getting Japan to agree to withdraw from Shantung under terms of agreements at the conference. Nonetheless, the treaty and the conference results disappointed Chinese patriots heavily influenced by the strong nationalistic fervor that was growing in China, as they had no enforcement mechanisms and did nothing to retrieve the rights of sovereignty China had been forced to give up to foreign powers over the previous eighty years.[48]

Meanwhile, US policy makers were compelled to react to repeated acts of violence against Americans and other foreigners and their interests, as revolutionary political and military movements swept through China during the 1920s. By 1925, the foreign treaty port rulers and collaborating Chinese provincial rulers seemed to an increasing share of the Chinese public to constitute an evil partnership of "imperialism" and warlords. The rising Chinese Nationalist Party under Sun Yat-sen (d. 1925) and his successor Chiang Kai-shek was receiving substantial military and financial support and training from the Soviet Union and the international Communist organization known as the Communist International or Comintern. Soviet-backed Communist agents were instrumental in assisting the establishment of the Chinese Communist Party, which was instructed to align with Sun and Chiang's much larger Chinese Nationalist Party. These movements were compatible in seeing the evils of imperialism and warlords as enemies of Chinese nationalism. Chinese industrialists had prospered with the withdrawal of competition from Western enterprises and the rise in foreign demand during World War I. They were readier to take a stance against the foreigners in this period of revived foreign economic competition in China.[49]

In Shanghai early in 1925, union organizers were active and strikes increased, and at the same time merchants in the Chinese Chamber of Commerce protested against regulation and "taxation without representation" under the foreign-ruled Shanghai Municipal Council. An incident in Shanghai arising out of a strike against Japanese-owned textile mills led to an outburst of anti-imperialist and antiforeign demonstrations and sentiment. British-officered police under the authority of the foreign-ruled Shanghai Municipal Council killed thirteen demonstrators on May 30, 1925. There ensued a nationwide multiclass movement of protests, demonstrations, strikes, boycotts, and militant anti-imperialism. This May Thirtieth movement dwarfed all previous antiforeign demonstrations. In June, a demonstration in Canton led to shooting between Nationalist Party cadets and Anglo-French troops, killing fifty-two Chinese. The resulting fifteen-month strike and boycott of Hong Kong crippled British trade with South China.[50]

In this revolutionary atmosphere, Chinese Communist Party organizations expanded membership rapidly. Consistent with guidance from the Joseph Stalin–dominated Comintern, the party remained in a wary united front with the larger Chinese Nationalists as Chiang Kai-shek consolidated his leadership and prepared to launch the Northern Expedition from the Nationalist base in Canton in 1926. The military campaign and attendant political agitation were designed to smash the power of the warlords, assert China's rights against imperialism, and reunify China. By 1927, the campaign had gained control of much of southern and central China.[51]

Advancing in Nanking in March 1927, some Nationalist forces attacked foreigners and foreign property in this city, including the American, British, and Japanese consulates. Several foreigners, including Americans, were killed. Looting and threats against foreigners did not stop until British and US gunboats began to bombard the attackers. The Americans joined the other powers in demanding punishment, apology, and compensation from the Nationalist authorities. The Nationalist authorities at the time were in turmoil with a power struggle for leadership that saw Chiang Kai-shek's forces kill several hundred Communist Party and labor leaders in Shanghai the day after the Nanking incident, foreshadowing the start of a broader and violent Nationalist campaign against Communists and other perceived enemies. Maneuvering within the Nationalist leadership resulted in Chiang Kai-shek's emergence as dominant leader in January 1928. US Secretary of State Frank Kellogg reacted with moderation and restraint to the violence and challenges to US and foreign rights in China. This helped facilitate US rapprochement with the Nationalist regime of Chiang Kai-shek once it consolidated power in 1928. In March 1928, Chiang's regime accepted American terms about the Nanking incident while the US government expressed regret about the gunboat bombardment.[52]

Imperial Japan felt threatened by rising Chinese nationalism and endeavored to consolidate its hold in Manchuria. Japanese agents assassinated the Chinese warlord in Manchuria and eventually took control of the territory under the guise of an independent state, Manchukuo, created in 1932 and recognized among the major powers only by Japan. US policy makers did not change their low-risk policy toward Japan despite Tokyo's blatant grab of Manchuria. Dealing with the disastrous consequences of the Great Depression, US president Hoover was reluctant to respond forcefully to Japan's aggression in Manchuria and its breach of US-backed security arrangements in the Nine Power Treaty of 1922 and the Kellogg-Briand Pact of 1928. With his secretary of state, Henry Stimson, in the lead, Hoover favored a moral stance of nonrecognition of the changes brought by Japan's aggression. This so-called Hoover-Stimson doctrine failed in 1932 as Japanese forces expanded their military aggression in China to include attacks on Chinese forces in Shanghai. The Hoover administration formally protested, sent additional forces to China, and appealed to the world not to recognize the Japanese aggression. The Japanese halted the assault on Shanghai, and the League of Nations adopted a resolution of nonrecognition, but Japan created a puppet state of Manchukuo and withdrew from the League of Nations when it approved a report critical of Japan's actions.[53]

The Franklin D. Roosevelt administration continued a cautious stance in the face of Japanese aggression in China, though some administration officials showed sympathy and support for China. Harry Hopkins, a close adviser to President Roosevelt, was sympathetic to China's cause and provided a channel of communication between Chiang Kai-shek's administration and the US president. Secretary of the Treasury Henry Morgenthau endeavored to support the struggling Chinese Nationalist Party government against Japanese aggression. In 1934, the United States inaugurated, primarily for domestic reasons, a silver purchase program, which caused great turmoil in the Chinese economy as massive amounts of silver left China by 1935. In response, Morgenthau initiated a silver purchase program for Nationalist China, paying it hundreds of millions of dollars in gold and US dollars for five hundred million ounces of silver.[54]

Even when Japan engaged in all-out brutal war against China in 1937, Washington showed sympathy to China but offered little in the way of concrete support. Responding to Japanese aggression against China and other military expansion, President Franklin D. Roosevelt in a speech on October 5, 1937, called for a quarantine of an "epidemic of world lawlessness." No specific US actions in Asia followed because the US government was not prepared to stand against Japan as it ruthlessly advanced in China. Indeed, Japanese aircraft in December 1937 sank the US gunboat *Panay* and machine-gunned its survivors in the Yangtze River. US officials accepted Japan's apology and compensation, not choosing to make this an issue of confrontation with Japanese aggression in China.[55]

Stanley Hornbeck, a senior State Department specialist on China, played important roles in advising and implementing US policy toward China during this period. A strong supporter of China, he also was realistic about Chinese weaknesses and capabilities in the face of Japanese power. He was involved in various efforts to provide US support for the Chinese Nationalist Party government and to resist Japanese aggression without directly confronting Japan. Those US efforts were slow in coming.[56]

As secretary of state in the Franklin D. Roosevelt administration in the years prior to World War II, Hornbeck's boss, Cordell Hull, shied away from support of China, then at war with Japan. He sought to avoid US involvement in an Asian war at a time of heightened tensions and war in Europe. Hull disapproved a plan supported by Treasury Secretary Henry Morgenthau to provide China $25 million in credits to purchase supplies in the United States, but President Roosevelt approved the plan while Hull was out of the country in December 1938. Hull resisted efforts to impose sanctions on Japan, but eventually the State Department in January 1940 announced that the United States would not renew a 1911 commercial treaty with Japan. This step allowed the United States subsequently to impose selective embargoes on the sale of strategic materials to Japan, leading to a US oil embargo in 1941.[57]

By this time, with the support of Treasury Secretary Morgenthau and others, President Roosevelt approved the formation of the American Volunteer Group, also known as the "Flying Tigers," to support the beleaguered Chinese Nationalist administration in the face of Japanese aggression. The group arose from plans by retired US general Claire Chennault and others that resulted in a secret presidential order allowing US pilots to resign their commissions and sign contracts with a firm whose operating funds came from the lend-lease air program, for the purpose of flying fighter planes transferred to the Chinese government under lend-lease. The lend-lease program was proposed by the president and approved by Congress in early 1941, and China became eligible to receive lend-lease aid on May 6, 1941. The Flying Tigers helped protect airspace over the Chinese Nationalist capital in China's interior city of Chungking and other Chinese Nationalist holdings against attacks by Japanese warplanes.[58]

Nongovernmental American interaction with China continued to focus on economic exchange and missionary-related activities, although educational exchange separate from missionary activities grew in importance. US trade with China increased to $290 million in 1929, worth almost half of the $692 million value of US-Japanese trade that year. As world trade contracted sharply with the Great Depression, the importance of US exports to Japan relative to US exports to China increased. In 1936, the year prior to the start of the Sino-Japanese War, US exports to China were valued at $47 million, while US exports to Japan were valued at $204 million. The balance of US economic interests appeared to reinforce continued strong isolationist tendencies in the United States to avoid involvement on the side of China in opposition to increasingly apparent aggression by imperial Japan.[59]

Japanese atrocities in the war against China beginning in 1937 and imperial Japan's subsequent alignment with Nazi Germany in 1940 hardened American public attitudes as well as those of US officials against Japan. Individual Americans with close ties to both the Chiang Kai-shek and Roosevelt administrations and a number of organizations such as the Committee for Non-Participation in Japanese Aggression advocated giving US aid to China. Thomas Corcoran, formerly a White House lawyer close to President Roosevelt, was among the group of several former federal officials paid by Chiang Kai-shek's agents to ensure stronger US support for the Nationalist government. Henry Luce, the child of Christian missionaries in China, created a powerful media enterprise in the United States centered on *Time* and *Life* magazines. Luce used these widely read publications to strongly support Chiang Kai-shek and his American-educated wife, Soong Mayling, hailing the nation-building struggles of the Nationalist Party government and its protracted resistance to Japanese aggression. The Committee to Defend America by Aiding the Allies and other groups and individuals worked against those in American politics who continued to adhere to a noninterventionist stance. The latter included the Women's International League for Peace and Freedom and the National Council for Prevention of War. The noninterventionist stance was buttressed by widespread feeling in the United States in the 1930s that the United States had mistakenly intervened in World War I on behalf of the privileges of a few, prompting peace activists to work to prevent repetition of such errors.[60]

The missionary response to China's problems in the early twentieth century went well beyond evangelical matters. Expanding from about a thousand American missionaries representing twenty-eight societies in China in 1900, the respective numbers increased by 1930 to more than three thousand missionaries representing sixty societies. Adjusting to the rise of nationalism in China, the emphasis now focused on making the Christian church in China indigenous, led by Chinese and at least partially self-supporting, with Americans assisting and advising. The YMCA emphasized programs for literacy and social work and proved to be attractive to younger Chinese leaders. The North China famine of 1920–21 saw the creation of the China International Famine Relief Commission that by 1936 used more than $50 million in foreign donations to promote basics in rural development. An interdenominational Protestant conference in 1922 organized the National Christian Council that set to work on social issues in urban and rural China. James Yen, educated at Yale University and with the YMCA, used support from the Rockefeller Foundation to begin to spread literacy and practical education to rural China.[61]

American reformist ideas and influence were notable among the more moderate elements of the Chinese intelligentsia at the time. The latter tended to be foreign trained and to work in academic and scientific institutions. The dozen Christian colleges were coming under more Chinese control and relied on Chinese sources for more than half of their income, though a majority of their faculties were foreign trained. The big national universities also had staffs largely trained abroad, mostly in the United States. Such American influence also was evident in the various research institutes of the central government and the big Rockefeller-supported Peking Union Medical College. Supporting these trends, 2,400 Chinese students entered American universities between 1900 and 1920, and 5,500 did so between 1920 and 1940. They studied in 370 institutions and tended to major in such practical subjects as engineering and business. They returned to China as a new elite in Chinese business, academic, and government circles.[62]

STUDY QUESTIONS

1. US foreign behavior prior to World War II is often labeled "sentimental imperialism." How important were factors of "sentiment" versus factors of "imperialist" control of wealth and power manifest in the following elements of US interaction with China during this period?
- US role in opium trade with China
- US refusal to join foreign powers using military force to coerce concessions from China
- US actively joining foreign powers in expanding power and influence in China under terms of the unequal treaties forced on China
- The expansive role of US missionaries in Chinese society
- Harsh US treatment of Chinese in the United States leading to the so-called exclusion movement blocking immigration from China to America
- US support for the Burlingame mission, the Open Door policy, and China's territorial integrity in the Nine Power Treaty of the Washington Conference of 1921–1922
- US use of the Boxer indemnity to fund education of Chinese students in the United States
2. Chinese patriots call the hundred-year period prior to the 1949 establishment of the People's Republic of China "the century of humiliation."
- What were the main sources of humiliation in the treaty system imposed on China by foreign powers? How important were elements such as loss of territory, concessions allowing foreign rule in areas of major Chinese cities, extraterritoriality, patrols of foreign gunboats in Chinese rivers and coastal waters, and deployment of foreign troops in China to protect foreign interests?
- Is the humiliation in the treaty system seen as stark when compared to the previous tribute system guiding Chinese foreign relations? That system was characterized by explicit and repeated recognition of the superiority of China's state, society, and civilization; overt deference to the Chinese emperor; and acceptance of formal subservience as a means to trade and benefit from interaction with China's rich economy and advanced technology.
3. Were foreign interventions or domestic weaknesses (massive rebellions, loss of central control, myopic leaders, corruption, overpopulation, and declining living standards) the main causes of the century of humiliation?

4. Did the United States, as some have claimed, establish a "special relationship" with China in this hundred-year period? What were the main reasons why or why not?

5. Given the Open Door and related policies, why was the United States reluctant to counter, or ineffective in countering, moves by other powers, especially Japan, challenging China's sovereignty and territorial integrity in the twentieth century? Episodes included "dollar diplomacy"; the Twenty-One Demands; maneuvers to hold the line against Japanese expansion in Manchuria versus the Root-Takahira agreement 1917; United States siding with Japan and not China on the German concession in Shandong in the Versailles Peace Treaty 1919; US efforts to curb Japan's expansion at China's expense seen in the Nine Power Treaty of the Washington Conference 1921–1922; and low-key US reactions to Japan's takeover of Manchuria and the initial years of the Sino-Japanese War.

6. Often radically anti-imperialist movements leading to the consolidation of the Republic of China under Chiang Kai-shek severely challenged US and other foreign holdings in China. Why did the United States accommodate and establish positive relations with Chiang's government?

RELEVANT VIDEOS

"The Story of China" (History, BBC, June 4, 2017, one hour) available at https://www.youtube.com/watch?v=dT6TwsMtTRY

"The Chinese Exclusion Act" (PBS, May 29, 2018, more than one hour) available at https://www.pbs.org/wgbh/americanexperience/films/chinese-exclusion-act/

"The Long History of America-China Relations" (Stanford Professor Gordon Chang lecture, October 24, 2016, forty-eight minutes) available at https://www.youtube.com/watch?v=vW747IAz154

Chapter Three

Relations during World War II, Civil War, Cold War

US-CHINA RELATIONS DURING WORLD WAR II AND CHINA'S CIVIL WAR

US Interests, Actions, and Perceptions

The Japanese attack on Pearl Harbor thrust the United States into a leadership position in China and in global affairs. American debates over international involvement and the long-standing US reluctance to assume the costs and risks of leadership were put aside. President Franklin D. Roosevelt and his war cabinet enjoyed broad domestic support as they mobilized millions of American combatants and enormous contributions of equipment and treasure in working with and leading Allied powers in the largest war the world has ever seen. The coalition eventually defeated the Axis powers. US leaders and interests focused on effectively fighting the massive worldwide conflict and dealing with issues that would determine the postwar international order.

The United States emerged as the most important foreign power in China. However, waging war in China and dealing with complications there, notably the bitter rivalry between Chiang Kai-shek's Nationalist forces and the Communist forces under the direction of Mao Zedong, received secondary attention. Circumstances in China contrary to American plans and expectations also repeatedly forced US leaders to adjust strategies.[1]

Early American assessments that China would provide strong forces and reliable bases for the defeat of Japan proved unrealistic given the many weaknesses of Chiang Kai-shek's Nationalist armies, the inability of the United States to supply and train large numbers of Chinese forces on account of Japan's control of the main surface routes of supply, and the primacy Chiang's Nationalists (KMT) and Mao's Communists (CCP) gave to their struggle with one another. The United States shifted focus to defeating Japan by advancing through the Pacific Islands; it strove to keep China in the war as a means to tie down the one million Japanese soldiers deployed to the country.[2]

The turning tide of the war with Japan caused US planners to look beyond generalities about China's leading role as a partner of the United States in postwar Asia to the realities of preparations for civil war in China possibly involving the United States and Soviet Union on opposite sides. Debate among US officials about how to deal with the Chinese Nationalists and the Chinese Communists and the postwar order in China eventually led to direct US arrangements with the Soviet Union, notably those negotiated at the Yalta conference of February 1945, and continued American support for Chiang's Nationalist government. In this context, US leaders encouraged negotiations and mediated between the Chinese Nationalists and Chinese Communists in order to avoid civil war and shore up China's position as a power in Asia friendly to the United States.[3]

Though they were repeatedly and deeply disappointed with the weaknesses and corruption of the Nationalist Chinese government, American officials tended to follow paths of least resistance when dealing with the dispute between the Chinese Nationalists and the Chinese Communists. US actions and policy choices reinforced existing American proclivities to back Chiang Kai-shek's Nationalists, who continued to enjoy broad political support in the United States. They avoided the difficult US policy reevaluation that would have been required for US leaders to position the United States in a more balanced posture in order to deal constructively with the Chinese Communists as well as the Chinese Nationalists. Though some American officials pushed for a more balanced US approach, others were suspicious of the Communists on ideological grounds and because of their ties to the USSR. There also was skepticism about the strength and prospects of the Communist forces. In the end, it appeared that moving American policy from support for Chiang Kai-shek's Nationalists would be too costly for American interest in shoring up a postwar Chinese government friendly to the United States. The drift and bias in US policy, strengthened by interventions of important US officials such as US presidential envoy and ambassador to China Patrick Hurley, foreshadowed the US failure in China once the Communists defeated the Chinese Nationalists on mainland China in 1949 and moved in early 1950 to align with the Soviet Union against the United States in the Cold War.[4]

Chinese Interests, Actions, and Perceptions

Having survived with enormous cost and deprivation four years of war with Japan, Chiang Kai-shek and his Nationalist government were relieved as the United States entered the war with Japan in 1941. The eventual defeat and collapse of the Japanese empire seemed likely. The Nationalist government was prepared to cooperate with its new US ally in the war effort against Japan, but repeatedly it showed greater interest in using US supplies and support in order to prepare to deal with the opposing Communist forces and secure Nationalist leadership in postwar China. Chiang Kai-shek and his lieutenants sought to maximize the material, training, financial, and political support from the United States while fending off repeated US requests for greater contributions by Nationalist armies in the war effort against Japan. When US officials in China repeatedly became frustrated with the lackluster support of the war effort from what was often seen as a corrupt, repressive, and narrowly self-serving Nationalist Chinese government, Chiang and his allies tried to outmaneuver them through such means as appeals to top US leaders and special US envoys sent to China, lobbying in Washington, and thinly veiled warnings that the Nationalists might seek accommodation with Japan.[5]

The Nationalists also resisted efforts by US officials in China to open direct American communication with and possible support for the Chinese Communist forces. Furthermore, Chiang and his government fended off repeated US calls for greater reform and accountability in the Chinese Nationalist government. They accommodated US mediation efforts to bridge the divide between the Nationalists and Communists. They found strong common ground with US mediator Patrick Hurley. US mediator George Marshall was much more critical of Chiang Kai-shek and Nationalist policies and actions. The Nationalists appeared to have little choice but to grudgingly go along with the humiliating arrangements imposed on them as a result of US-USSR negotiations at Yalta. Their future depended on preserving US support. They strove to continue this support without conditions that would compromise the goal of a Nationalist-ruled China in postwar Asia.[6]

The Chinese Communists under the leadership of Mao Zedong had strong and well-developed ideological and foreign policy leanings opposed to US policy in China and US leadership in world affairs. Their connections with the Soviet Union and the influence of the USSR on their approach to the United States also were significant. They endorsed the twists and turns of Soviet maneuvers in the early years of the war, and they followed Moscow's lead in an overall positive approach to the United States as it entered the war in 1941.[7]

Probably more important in Chinese Communist calculations were the realities of power in China. Like Chiang Kai-shek's Nationalists, the Communists under Mao foresaw the eventual defeat of Japan at the hands of the United States. The United States rapidly became the predominant power in East Asia, and in China it brought its power, influence, and aid to bear solely on the side of Chiang Kai-shek's Nationalists, who were determined to subordinate and suppress the Communists. For CCP leaders, there was a serious likelihood that the United States, because of growing association with Chiang Kai-shek, might use its enormous power against the CCP during the anticipated Chinese civil war following Japan's defeat.[8]

To counter this prospect, the Communists had the option of looking to their Soviet ally for support. But Moscow at that time was showing little interest in defending CCP interests against a challenge by US-backed Nationalist forces. The Communists saw that only at great risk could they ignore the change that had taken place in the balance of forces in China. Seeking to keep the United States from becoming closely aligned with Chiang Kai-shek against CCP interests, the Communists decided to take steps on their own to ensure that Washington would adopt a more evenhanded position. They strove to put aside historical difficulties with the United States and soft-pedaled ideological positions that might alienate Washington as they sought talks with US officials in order to arrive at a power arrangement that would better serve CCP interests in China.[9]

The United States chose to rebuff the Communist initiatives, leaving the CCP facing the likelihood of confrontation with a strong US-backed KMT army at the end of the Pacific war. Fortunately for the CCP, Moscow built its strength in East Asia during the final months of the war and the period following Japan's defeat, and the United States rapidly withdrew its forces from East Asia at the war's end. Later in the 1940s, the Communists obtained more support from the USSR, leading eventually to the Sino-Soviet alliance of 1950. Meanwhile, the Communist forces grew in strength while the larger Nationalist forces suffered from significant weaknesses including poor leadership and morale, paving the way to Communist victory against the US-supported Nationalists in 1949.[10]

Encounters and Interaction in the 1940s

It is hard to imagine a decade of more consequence for modern China and its relations with the United States than the 1940s. The US entry into World War II marked the beginning of the end of Japanese aggression in China and the Asia-Pacific. The stalemate between Japanese forces occupying the more well-developed eastern regions of China and the Chinese Nationalists and Chinese Communist forces holding out in China's interior eventually broke and ended under the pressure of the US-led war effort against imperial Japan. The end of the Japanese occupation of China opened the way to Chinese civil war and resolution of the decades-long conflict between Chinese Nationalist and Chinese Communist forces. As the leading foreign power in China, the United States wielded its influence in ways seen to accord with US interests and goals. At bottom, the US actions and policies did not mesh well with realities in China. The result by the end of the decade was a massive failure of US efforts to establish a strong China, friendly to the United States, in postwar Asia.[11]

The China theater was a secondary concern in the overall war effort, as the United States first focused on defeating Adolf Hitler and the Nazi-led forces in Europe. Initial expectations that China could be built up and play an active strategic role in the war effort, with Chinese armies under Chiang Kai-shek's leadership pushing back the Japanese and allowing China to become a staging area for attack on Japan, proved unrealistic. Chiang's Nationalist armies were weak, and the Americans were unable to provide large amounts of military equipment because Japan cut off surface routes to Nationalist-held areas of China. US strategists turned to an approach of island-hopping in the Pacific, with US-led forces coming from the south and east of Japan, taking island positions in step-by-step progress toward the Japanese home islands. The role for the Chinese armies in this strategy mainly was to stay in the war and keep the many hundreds of thousands of Japanese forces in China tied down and unable to reinforce Japanese positions elsewhere.[12]

The United States recognized Chiang Kai-shek and the Chinese Nationalist government as China's representative in war deliberations and insisted that Chiang's China would be one of the great powers that would lead world affairs in the postwar era. President Roosevelt strongly supported China's leading role and met with Chiang Kai-shek and British prime minister Winston Churchill at an Allied conference in Cairo in 1943 that determined, among other things, that territories Japan had taken from China would be restored to China. US aid in China flowed exclusively to Chiang and his officials. The commanding American general in the China theater, Joseph Stilwell, was appointed as Chiang Kai-shek's chief of staff. American contact with and understanding of the rival Chinese Communists were minimal. Mao Zedong's forces were cut off from American and other contact by a blockade maintained by Nationalist Chinese forces. There were American contacts with the Chinese Communist liaison office allowed in the Chinese wartime capital of Chungking.[13]

Chiang Kai-shek welcomed American support but constantly complained that it was insufficient. General Stilwell and many other US officials in China were appalled by what they saw in the poor governance of the Chinese Nationalist leadership and the unwillingness of Chiang and his lieutenants to use US assistance against Japan as they focused on building capabilities to deal with the Chinese Communists. Stilwell and his American staff were interested in establishing relations with the Chinese Communist forces, who seemed more willing to fight Japan. Chiang resisted these American leanings.[14]

Despite widespread dissatisfaction with Chiang Kai-shek and the Chinese Nationalist government on the part of many American officials as well as media and other nongovernment American observers in China, Chiang Kai-shek maintained a positive public image in the United States. Publicists such as Henry Luce, who used *Time* and *Life* magazines, continued to laud the leadership of the courageous leader of China in the face of Japanese aggression. President Roosevelt's personal emissary to China, Lauchlin Currie, traveled to China in 1941 and again in 1942. He advised the US president to follow policies of strong support for Chiang Kai-shek and the Chinese Nationalists: the Chungking government should be treated as a "great power"; Chiang should be given greater economic and military support and should be encouraged to reform. In Currie's view and the views of other US officials in Washington, close US cooperation with Chiang would promote cooperation within China and ensure a more effective struggle against Japan. While President Roosevelt's private calculations regarding Chiang Kai-shek and the situation in China remain subject to interpretation, his actions and statements generally adhered to this kind of positive American orientation toward Nationalist China.[15]

Emblematic of broader support for the Chiang administration in the United States was the positive reception given to Madame Chiang Kai-shek when she toured the United States from November 1942 to May 1943. In February 1943, she delivered a stirring speech to the US Congress. She appealed for more American aid and higher US priority to the war effort in China. Roosevelt and his war planners were unwilling to change their focus on defeating Germany first, but the US Congress took steps to redress the grossly discriminatory US immigration policies against China. In 1943, it acknowledged China as an ally and amended exclusion provisions to permit 105 Chinese to immigrate annually. Initial steps also were taken to amend the various treaty provisions between the United States and China that supported unequal relations that were offensive to Chinese nationalism. In 1943, the administration signed a treaty surrendering American extraterritorial rights in China, and the Senate readily agreed.[16]

Some influential US military leaders, notably General Claire Chennault of the American Volunteer Group ("Flying Tigers") and the Army Air Force, were much more sympathetic to Chiang Kai-shek than Stilwell and his supporters. Chennault pressed for US military efforts that were supported by Chiang but opposed by Stilwell and his staff. He collaborated with and won Chiang's support for plans involving US use of Chinese Nationalist–defended air bases in China to attack Japanese positions and shipping with US bombers. Stilwell opposed the plans that diverted US supplies from his efforts to build Chinese armies in order to open ground supply routes to occupied China and for other use against Japan. Stilwell warned that once the US bombing attacks from Chinese air bases rose in Japan's war calculus as a result of Chennault's plan, the bases would be subject to Japanese ground attack and might be overrun because of weak Chinese Nationalist defenses for the bases.

Indeed, presumably prompted at least in part by the US air attacks, Japanese forces in 1944 overran the weakly defended air bases and expanded more deeply into Nationalist-held areas, provoking a major crisis between Chiang and Stilwell and between the United States and its Nationalist allies.[17]

The Chinese Communists, for their part, took advantage of limited interaction with US officials, media, and nongovernment representatives in Chungking in order to build on the image they had already established through their brief encounters with American and other Western news personnel at the Communist base in Yenan in north China in the 1930s. Consistent with their approach to Edgar Snow and other American visitors in that period, the Communists emphasized the image of a relatively democratic and honest political administration, positive public support received by the Yenan leadership, and the CCP's reasonably benign attitude at that time toward free enterprise. In this way, they attempted to appeal to American ideals. At the same time, the Communist spokespersons tried to drive a wedge between Americans and Chinese Nationalists by criticizing what they viewed as the corrupt, oppressive, and totalitarian rule of the nationalist government. In line with their approach toward Snow and other visitors in the 1930s, the Communist officials did not disavow the CCP's ultimate Marxist-Leninist goals regarding the future of China but indicated that such objectives were to be achieved at the end of a long "democratic" period. They thus revealed to American officials and other representatives the image of a Chinese party worthy of US support, willing to compromise with Washington, and deserving of a share of power in China. In this context, heavy stress was placed on the Nationalists' unwillingness to share power as the prime cause for continuing Communist-Nationalist confrontation in China.[18] The central role in CCP policy toward and interaction with the United States was played by senior Communist leader Zhou Enlai, the chief Communist representative in Chungking during World War II. In his frequent contacts with American officials and other US representatives, Zhou demonstrated repeatedly a preference for realistic exchange, unencumbered by ideological constraints or bitterness over past Chinese affronts at the hands of US "imperialism." He initiated a CCP proposal for the establishment of an American liaison mission to Yenan, cast doubt on Nationalist willingness to pursue the war against Japan, and attacked Chungking's legitimacy as the regime best serving the interests of the Chinese people. Zhou, along with visiting senior Communist military leader Lin Biao, in Chungking for negotiations with the Chinese Nationalists, appealed for US supplies so that the Communists could go on the offensive against Japan. They also promised close intelligence sharing with the United States regarding enemy activities near the Communist base areas. They condemned the Nationalists' passivity in the war effort while the Chiang Kai-shek forces reinforced their military blockade against the Communists.

Zhou Enlai's initiatives and subsequent interaction with American officials visiting Yenan on the part of Mao Zedong and other senior CCP leaders reflected pragmatic actions to deal with potentially adverse circumstances. The American entry into the war against Japan strengthened the position of the Communists' adversary, Chiang Kai-shek, and raised the strong possibility that the United States would continue to side firmly with Chiang following the defeat of Japan and the establishment of a new Chinese administration. The relatively weak strategic position of the Chinese Communist forces in China at the time and the low probability that the Soviet Union would take decisive actions to protect the Chinese Communists from US-backed pressure from Chiang Kai-shek's Nationalists added to incentives for the CCP to appeal to the United States for closer relations and support.[19]

The depth of the American–Chinese Nationalist alignment meant that the Communists could have little hope of undermining the American-Nationalist relationship. But by opening formal contacts with Americans through a US liaison mission in Yenan or other means, the Communists would at least have the opportunity to encourage the Americans to move away from Chungking over the critical issue of the Chinese civil dispute. In particular, a formal American mission in the Communist base area would allow CCP leaders to present their case to the highest levels in Washington; it would enable Mao and his group to scotch many ill-founded Nationalist allegations concerning the Communist leaders and policies, which had heretofore enjoyed credibility with US policy makers. Further, formal ties with Washington would enhance the Communists' ability to solicit US military supplies. The Communist leaders also seemed confident and proud of the economic, political, and military situation in their base area; if their administrative achievements could be shown to American officials, they would compare favorably with the deteriorating situation in Nationalist-held areas.[20]

In early 1944, there was a formal US presidential request to Chiang Kai-shek for the establishment of an American military observer mission in the Communist-held areas of China. The proposal was grudgingly approved by Chiang Kai-shek during the visit to China of American vice president Henry Wallace in June 1944. Amid the crisis caused by Japanese forces overrunning US air bases in China and penetrating deep into previously Nationalist-controlled territory, Chiang was in a weak position to resist the US request.[21] American officials were not only interested in shoring up Chinese resistance to Japanese aggression and improving military coordination against Japan with the Chinese Communists. By this time US officials were deeply involved in plans for dealing with previously unanticipated divisions that weakened China and posed the danger of Chinese civil war once Japan was defeated. There was concern that the Chinese Nationalists might draw in the United States on their side of the conflict and that the Chinese Communists might draw in the Soviet Union on their side. To deal with this potentially dire situation warranted closer American interaction with, and understanding of, the policies and intentions of the Chinese Communist forces through the establishment of the US military observer mission to Yenan.[22]

Responding to Vice President Wallace's expressions of concern over the Chinese war effort and the Nationalist government's loss of public support, Chiang focused on American and especially Stilwell's responsibility. Chiang impressed the American visitor with his determination to remove Stilwell or to have the United States send a personal representative from Roosevelt to control Stilwell and give Chiang regular access to the president free from the interference of the Departments of War and State, which were seen as influenced by Stilwell and his supporters in the US embassy.[23]

Patrick Hurley, a prominent Republican who served as President Herbert Hoover's secretary of war, was a key figure in US policy toward the KMT and the CCP in 1944–45. His strong support for the Chinese Nationalists and accusations against opponents within the US government had lasting impacts on US relations with China. Hurley was sent to China as a special envoy by President Roosevelt in September 1944. Dealing with the major disputes then causing a crisis between Chiang Kai-shek and General Joseph Stilwell, Hurley sided with Chiang. Roosevelt recalled Stilwell in October 1944, appointing General Albert Wedemeyer as his replacement. Hurley was appointed as ambassador to replace Clarence Gauss, who shared Stilwell's negative opinions about Chiang and the Nationalists.[24]

In November 1944, Hurley traveled to Yenan and negotiated a five-point agreement with Mao Zedong and his senior colleagues. Among other things, the agreement summarized Hurley's promises of equal treatment and US aid to the Communists in a coalition with the Nationalists. Returning to Chungking, he switched and sided strongly with Chiang Kai-shek in his demand that Communist forces be disbanded before the Communists could be brought into a Nationalist-led Chinese coalition government. Much of the US embassy staff in Chungking rebelled against Hurley by sending a collective message to Washington in early 1945 warning of the negative consequences of Hurley's alienation of the Communists and bias toward Chiang's Nationalists. The ambassador disputed the charges in a meeting with President Roosevelt, who supported Hurley, leading to transfers of dissident US staff from Chungking.[25]

As US ambassador, Hurley supported the Nationalist-Communist peace talks in Chungking in September 1945. Chiang Kai-shek, backed by Hurley and the Harry Truman administration, demanded the Communists surrender their forces and territory as a precondition for joining a coalition. Fighting spread in China, and the talks collapsed. Hurley, unsuccessful in urging a full US commitment to Chiang's cause, abruptly resigned as ambassador in November 1945, blaming pro–Chinese Communists in the State Department for thwarting US policy. After the Communist victory in China and the Chinese intervention in the Korean War, Hurley's charges provided a leading wedge for congressional investigators seeking to purge alleged pro-Communists and other security risks from among the ranks of the Chinese affairs specialists in the State Department and other agencies.[26]

US leaders worried about conditions in China and how they would affect the final stages of the war against Japan. They foresaw the inability of weak Chinese Nationalist forces to defeat the hundreds of thousands of Japanese forces in China as the war in the Pacific moved toward an end and the danger of a Nationalist-Communist civil war in China that would drag in the United States and the Soviet Union on opposite sides. As a result of the so-called Far Eastern Agreement of the Allied powers at Yalta in February 1945, Soviet forces, not Chinese forces, would take on the main task of defeating Japanese armies concentrated in Manchuria and northern China. In compensation, Russian territory taken by Japan would be restored; Russian interests in Manchuria, including a naval base, would be restored; and Outer Mongolia would remain independent. The United States promised to obtain the concurrence of China's Nationalist government to provisions regarding Manchuria and Mongolia, which were claimed by China. The Soviet Union also expressed willingness to negotiate a friendship and alliance treaty with China's Nationalist government. The Far Eastern Agreement had negative implications for the Chinese Nationalist government, which was not consulted on the territorial concessions to the Soviet Union, and for the Chinese Communists, who appeared to be isolated from the Soviet Union.[27]

The broad outlines of US policy toward China prevalent in early 1945 persisted as Harry Truman became president upon the death of Franklin Roosevelt in April 1945 and as the war in the Pacific came to an unexpectedly quick end with Japan's surrender after the US atomic bomb attacks in August 1945. US policy strongly supported Chiang Kai-shek's Nationalist forces. US airplanes and other means were used to transport Nationalist forces to various parts of China to take the surrender of Japanese forces. The US government provided hundreds of millions of dollars of military equipment and other assistance. The rival Communists were urged to participate in peace talks and come to terms in a united Chinese government under Chiang's overall leadership. President Truman commanded that Japanese-controlled forces in China surrender their positions and arms to Chiang Kai-shek's representatives, not to Communist forces.[28]

The Soviet army entered the war in China and defeated Japanese armies. The Soviet Union signed a friendship treaty with Chiang Kai-shek's

Nationalist government, as noted in the Far Eastern Agreement at Yalta. Seemingly isolated, the Chinese Communists agreed to join peace talks in Chungking in September where Chiang, backed by US ambassador Hurley and the Truman administration, demanded the Communists surrender their armed forces and territory as a precondition for joining a coalition government under Chiang's leadership.

There was little consideration at high levels of US policy makers for a more evenhanded US approach to the Nationalist-Communist rivalry in China, though some American officials warned of the danger of civil war and were uncertain how the Chinese Nationalists, weakened by years of warfare and led by often corrupt and inept officials, would fare. As the peace talks deadlocked and Communist-Nationalist armed conflict spread in northern China in late 1945, it became clear to US planners that Chiang's forces would not defeat the Chinese Communists without a substantial commitment of US military forces. It was against this background that Ambassador Hurley pushed for an open-ended US commitment to Chiang Kai-shek, but Washington decision makers demurred and Hurley resigned.[29]

President Truman appointed General George Marshall as his personal representative to salvage the deteriorating situation in China. Marshall managed a few months of shaky peace, but they were followed by frequent fighting in Manchuria as Nationalist and Communist forces vied to take control as Soviet occupiers retreated. US aid continued to go exclusively to Nationalist-held areas and increased markedly in mid-1946. On July 1, 1946, Chiang Kai-shek ordered a nationwide offensive against the Communists. Marshall intervened, got Truman to stop US arms aid to Chiang, and Chiang agreed to US-Nationalist-Communist truce teams to prevent fighting in northern China. The fighting still spread, however, and soon became a full-scale war.[30]

The failure to avoid civil war in China did not lead to fundamental change in the broad framework of US policy in China. Even though the Nationalists appeared increasingly weak and inept, and seemed headed for defeat on the mainland by 1948, the Truman administration continued support for them and took no significant steps to reach out to the Chinese Communists. In 1948, the administration supported the China Aid Act providing $125 million for the failing Nationalist government in China. This was done in large measure to avoid resistance from many pro–Chiang Kai-shek congressional members regarding the administration's requests for funding the Marshall Plan for Europe and Japan. Prospects for positive US relations with the Chinese Communists were soured by years of one-sided US support for the Chinese Nationalists.[31]

Given what were seen by Truman administration officials as continued strong US congressional and other domestic constraints against abandoning Chiang Kai-shek and opening US contacts with Chiang's enemy, the Chinese

Communists, the Truman administration officials allowed developments in China to settle the civil war in favor of the Chinese Communists. Over time, they hoped to find constructive ways for the United States to deal with the new Chinese Communist regime. There was strong debate in the administration as to whether the United States should allow Taiwan, the island off the Chinese coast where Chiang and his Nationalist forces retreated after their defeat on the mainland in 1949, to fall to the Communists. The policy decided on was one of no intervention to protect Taiwan.[32]

Secretary of State Dean Acheson was known for his efforts to end US support for Chiang Kai-shek and his KMT regime. He sought publication of the famed "China White Paper." This lengthy (more than a thousand pages) document was issued by the US State Department in August 1949. It was critical of Chiang Kai-shek and his government for corruption and other failings as they lost the Chinese Civil War against the Chinese Communist forces. The report served to support the Truman administration's efforts to cut support for Chiang's Nationalists. It also deflected attention from US policy oversights and mistakes. The report was attacked by Chiang's Nationalists, Mao's Communists, and many US supporters of Chiang Kai-shek.[33]

Also during the last months of the Chinese Civil War on the Chinese mainland, Acheson instructed the US ambassador to Nanking, Leighton Stuart, to seek contacts with the Communist forces advancing on the Nationalist capital. Stuart stayed in the city after Nationalist forces retreated. He made contact with Huang Hua, a former student of his who was sent by the Communist leaders to investigate US intentions. Stuart was invited to meet Communist leaders setting up their new capital in Beijing, but President Truman was unwilling to support a plan to have the ambassador travel to Beijing for talks with the Communist rulers.[34]

The Chinese Communists, meanwhile, reinforced their victory in the civil war with the announcement that they would side with the Soviet Union in the emerging Cold War struggle with the United States and its non-Communist allies. Amid these grim developments for US interests in China, the administration endeavored to adopt a lower profile regarding China. US leaders anticipated Communist victory over Chiang's forces holding out in Taiwan and a subsequent long process of the United States working to build some semblance of workable ties with the new regime in China. The US military position in the region was weak as a result of the rapid US demobilization and withdrawal of forces following World War II. While the United States had shown strong military and political resolve following Pearl Harbor in defeating Japanese aggression and that of the Axis coalition, US leaders were only gradually coming to the realization of a need for continued strong military preparations and presence in Asia in order to deter new sources of expansion and aggression.[35]

CONFLICT AND CONTAINMENT

Chinese Interests, Actions, and Perceptions

Mao Zedong and his CCP-led fighters faced large challenges as they endeavored to consolidate their rule after defeating Chiang Kai-shek's Nationalist forces in the Chinese Civil War and establishing the People's Republic of China (PRC) on the Chinese mainland in 1949. China had been war-ravaged for decades and arguably had been without effective governance for more than a century. The Communists were a rural-based movement with decades of experience in guerrilla war. They also had decades of experience supporting administrative efforts in the Chinese countryside but little experience in managing the complicated affairs of China's cities, its urban economy, or its national administration. Seeking needed technical and economic backing as well as guarantees and support for China's national security, the Maoist leadership endeavored to consolidate relations with the Soviet Union in an international environment heavily influenced by the United States, the main international supporter of its Chinese Nationalist adversary, and American-associated states influential in Asian and world politics.[36]

Taken together, these circumstances and determinants led to a strong current in analyses of Chinese relations with the United States that emphasized Chinese imperatives of consolidation and development domestically and reactions internationally to perceived threats and occasional opportunities posed by circumstances involving the United States. In particular, as the Cold War spread from Europe and came to dominate international dynamics in Asia for several decades beginning in the late 1940s, Chinese relations with the United States were seen as dominated in the 1950s and 1960s by Chinese efforts to deal with what emerged as a massive US-led military, economic, and political containment of China. Chinese interactions with the United States in this period often were assessed in terms of Chinese reactions to perceived threats posed by the strength and actions of the United States and associated powers.[37]

Heading the list of strengths that the Maoist leaders brought to bear as they began national leadership in China were the CCP's broad experience in political organization and related social and economic mobilization and a strong revolutionary ideology. Mao Zedong and supporting leaders were committed to seeking revolutionary changes in China and in international affairs affecting China, and they had the determination and ability to move Chinese people along these paths. This set of determinants and circumstances led to another strong current in analyses of Chinese relations with the United States, one that emphasized the importance of the Chinese leadership's determination to challenge and confront the United States and its allies and associates in Asia as the Chinese Communist leadership sought to promote revolutionary change in Asian and world affairs. The analyses also showed a related tendency of the Chinese leadership to exploit episodes of confrontation with America as means to mobilize greater support within China for the often revolutionary changes sought there by the Maoist leadership.[38]

Assessments of the record of the Maoist period show a complicated mix of imperatives both revolutionary and more conventional—of security and nation building—that drove Chinese decision making. Adding to the mix was the emergence of the dominant role of Mao Zedong and his strong-man rule, which came to determine Chinese decision making with particular regard to Chinese foreign relations—notably, relations with the United States and the Soviet Union. One consequence was the ability and the actual tendency of China to shift direction dramatically in foreign affairs. China's strong alignment with the Soviet Union in 1950 and break with Moscow ten years later exemplified the kinds of major shifts in China's foreign policy on issues important to the United States during this period.[39]

For their part, Chiang Kai-shek and the Chinese Nationalists appeared at the end of their struggle when they retreated to Taiwan after defeat on the Chinese mainland in 1949. Given the Truman administration's decisions to cut ties with the Nationalists and await opportunities to build relations with the triumphant Chinese Communists, it appeared to be only a matter of time before Communist forces would overwhelm the Nationalists on Taiwan. Those Nationalist leaders and officials who were less than fully committed to Chiang Kai-shek and the Nationalist cause and had options other than joining Chiang on Taiwan tended to follow those alternative paths and settled in Hong Kong, the United States, or other safer locations. The two million Chinese who fled the mainland to Taiwan included leaders and officials who were loyal to Chiang and strongly anti-Communist and large numbers of officials, soldiers, and dependents who had few other options.[40]

The outbreak of the Korean War and the subsequent US policy of containment against expansion of Chinese Communist power and influence dramatically reversed the fortunes of Chiang and his associates on Taiwan. They sought to use the new circumstances to strengthen support from the United States and to consolidate their power in Taiwan. On this basis, they endeavored to go beyond US efforts to contain Communist China by striving to lead efforts to roll back Communist rule on the mainland.[41]

US Interests, Actions, and Perceptions

At the start of the Cold War, Asia seemed secondary in US strategy. The United States demobilized rapidly after World War II. US forces occupied Japan and US naval and air forces patrolled the western Pacific, but overall,

US military capabilities appeared unprepared for significant action in Asia. When the Korean War broke out unexpectedly, the United States abruptly reversed practice and began what became massive commitments of military power and related assistance to stop the spread of perceived Communist expansion in Asia. Long-standing US interest in sustaining a balance of power in East Asia favorable to the United States, as well as ongoing US interests in fostering free economic access to the region and the spread of American values there, now were seen to require the United States to undertake the leading role in bearing the major costs, risks, and commitments associated with a system of containment that came to dominate US policy in Asia in the 1950s and the 1960s and to determine the course of American policy toward China during this period.[42]

Dominating the US foreign policy calculus toward China and other East Asian countries were strategic concerns with shoring up the regional balance of influence against Communist expansion in Asia. Strong efforts by the US government to mobilize domestic American support for the costs and risks associated with US leadership of the containment effort overshadowed private calculations of American leaders and strategists. The latter appeared to favor a more nuanced and flexible American approach that would have allowed for possible efforts to seek contacts and accommodation with Communist-ruled China. Eventually, US elites and supporting groups began to chafe publicly in the 1960s at what they saw as a counterproductive US tendency to try to isolate China as part of the Cold War containment strategy in Asia. Their efforts to encourage greater US flexibility in dealing with the Chinese Communists failed in the face of strident Chinese opposition to the United States, a wide range of other adverse foreign influences at the start of China's Cultural Revolution in 1966, and the concurrent large increases in US combat forces fighting Chinese-backed Communist forces in Vietnam.[43]

Encounters and Interaction in the 1950s and 1960s

Neither the government of Mao Zedong nor the Truman administration sought or foresaw US-China war in early 1950. The Americans were surprised when North Korean forces, with the support of Soviet and Chinese leaders, launched an all-out military attack against South Korean forces in June 1950. The Chinese Communist leaders and their Korean and Soviet Communist allies apparently calculated that the better-armed North Koreans would attain victory quickly without provoking major or effective US military response. Thus, it was their turn to be surprised when the United States quickly intervened militarily in the Korean War and sent the Seventh Fleet to prevent Chinese Communist attack on Taiwan. US forces and their South Korean allies halted the North Korean advance and carried out an amphibious landing at Inchon in September 1950 that effectively cut off North Korean armies in the South, leading to their destruction.[44]

The string of miscalculations continued. With UN support, US and South Korean forces proceeded into North Korea. The Chinese Communists warned and prepared to resist them, but US leaders thought the warnings were a bluff. By November hundreds of thousands of Chinese Communist forces were driving the US and South Korean forces south in full retreat. Eventually, the Americans and their allies were able to sustain a line of combat roughly in the middle of the peninsula as the two armies faced off for more than two more years of combat, casualties, and destruction.[45]

Chinese Communist leaders also launched domestic mass campaigns to root out pro-American influence and seize control of US cultural, religious, and business organizations that remained in China. The United States began wide-ranging strategic efforts to contain the expansion of Chinese power and Chinese-backed Communist expansion in Asia. A strict US economic and political embargo against China; large US force deployments, eventually numbering between five hundred thousand and one million troops; massive foreign aid allocations to US Asian allies and supporters; and a ring of US defense alliances around China were used to block Chinese expansion and to drive a wedge between China and its Soviet ally. Meanwhile, led by often irresponsible congressional advocates, notably Senator Joseph McCarthy, congressional investigators in the early 1950s took aim at US specialists on China and Asia, discrediting those with moderate and pragmatic views about the Chinese Communists and endeavoring to silence those in or out of government who were less than uniform in opposing the Chinese Communists and supporting Chiang Kai-shek and the Chinese Nationalists.[46]

The Dwight D. Eisenhower administration used threats and negotiations in reaching an armistice agreement that stopped the fighting in Korea in 1953. American efforts to strengthen military alliances and deployments to contain Chinese Communist–backed expansion continued unabated. They faced off against enhanced Chinese efforts in the wake of the Korean armistice to strengthen support for Communist insurgents working against American-backed forces in French Indochina and direct Chinese military probes and challenges against the United States and their Chinese Nationalist allies in the Taiwan Strait.[47]

Mao Zedong and his CCP-led government continued their consolidation of control inside China, notably through mass campaigns led by Communist activists targeting landlords, the leading urban political and economic elites, and others deemed abusive or uncooperative with Communist goals. They prepared for major nation-building efforts with the support of their Soviet and Warsaw Pact allies to establish a governing structure, often along the lines of that of the Soviet Union, to rule Chinese civil administration, economic planning, military modernization, intelligence collection, and other endeavors. They sought means to tap into the surplus wealth being created in China's rural sector for investment in their planned expansion of China's industrial economy. After a brief period where peasants held land as a result of the mass campaign for land reform in rural China in the early 1950s, Chinese leaders saw the need to emulate the Soviet model and began to collectivize the land under government administration so as to better control the surplus rural wealth and to maximize its utility to the state's interests in promoting industrial development. The Soviet Union was providing more than a hundred major projects in assistance to Chinese industrialization and modernization, but they had to be paid for it. Collectivization of the land and concurrently greater state control of the urban economy along Soviet lines were chosen as the appropriate ways to deal with conditions in China while seeking economic modernization and development of the sinews of national and state power.[48]

These dramatic and massive shifts in domestic policy and direction occurred frequently in conjunction with crises and confrontations with the United States and its allies and associates around China's periphery in Asia. At one level, the Chinese determination to work against and confront the US-backed forces in Indochina and the Taiwan Strait reflected a deeply held determination to confound and wear down the American-fostered containment system. The Chinese Communist leadership held a strong revolutionary commitment to change the international order dominated by the United States and its allies and to support Communist-led forces struggling against this foreign imperialism.[49]

The US effort also directly threatened China's national security and sovereignty, often in graphic and severe ways. The Eisenhower administration threatened China with nuclear attack in order to push it toward an armistice in Korea, and the US government used the threat of nuclear attack at other times in the face of perceived Chinese provocations in the 1950s. Mao Zedong's China had no viable defense against US nuclear weapons and put top priority on developing Chinese nuclear weapons to deal with such repeated US intimidation. At the same time, the Chinese Communist leaders also were seen to continue to use the crisis atmosphere caused by confrontations with outside threats posed by the United States and its allies as a means to strengthen their domestic control and their mobilization of resources for advancement of nation building and administrative competence.[50]

Defeat of US-backed French forces in Indochina led to the 1954 Geneva Conference and accords that formalized French withdrawal from Indochina. After the conference, US policy worked to support a non-Communist government in South Vietnam, backing the regime when it resisted steps toward reunification set forth in the Geneva accords. The United States also deepened and broadened defense and other links with powers in Southeast Asia in order to check Chinese-backed Communist expansion in the region.[51] President Eisenhower and Secretary of State John Foster Dulles were wary of Chiang Kai-shek and Chinese Nationalist maneuvers that might drag the United States into a war with the Chinese Communists over Taiwan. Chiang Kai-shek's Nationalists used the fortuitous turn of fate caused by the Korean War to consolidate their rule in Taiwan, and with American support they rapidly built Taiwan's military forces with the objective of eventually taking the battle to mainland China. The political atmosphere inside the United States was very supportive of Chiang and his harsh anti-Communist stance. The so-called China lobby supporting Chiang and his Nationalist government included liberals as well as conservatives in such respected organizations as the Committee of One Million, which opposed Communist China taking China's seat in the United Nations. US military and economic assistance to Chiang Kai-shek and the Nationalist forces on Taiwan expanded dramatically, and there was little public objection by the American government to Chiang's repressive authoritarian rule.[52]

Though Dulles and other leaders of the US government were privately unsure of the wisdom of such a close and formal US commitment to Chiang's Nationalists, Washington eventually brought Taiwan into the web of formal military alliances that provided the foundation of the US containment system against Chinese-backed Communist expansion in Asia. The United States and Nationalist China signed a bilateral defense treaty in December 1954.[53]

The People's Republic of China reacted with harsh rhetoric and military assaults against Nationalist Chinese–controlled islands off the coast of the Chinese mainland. The new and potentially very dangerous military crisis involving the United States and China so soon after the bloody conflict in Korea was not welcomed by Great Britain and other US allies, nor by some US congressional leaders and other elites. The US administration firmly backed the Chinese Nationalists and their Republic of China. US forces helped Nationalist forces on some exposed islands to withdraw as the Taiwan Strait crisis of 1955 continued, raising renewed fears of US-China war.[54]

Against this background, the Chinese Communist government's stance against the United States moderated. The reasoning appeared related to a shift in Soviet policy toward the West following Stalin's death in 1953. The incoming Soviet leaders were more interested than the now-dead Soviet dictator in arranging advantageous modus vivendi with Western powers in Europe. While they continued to give some public support to their Chinese ally in its dispute with the Chinese Nationalists and the United States, they also signaled Soviet wariness about getting involved in Asian conflicts by playing down the applicability of the Sino-Soviet alliance to Asia, where Soviet commentary implied China was to bear the major responsibility for dealing with the United States and its allies and associates. At the same time, the Chinese government also began to try to broaden productive economic and diplo-matic ties with countries in nearby Asia and in Europe, and Chinese leaders found that their hard-line, confrontational behavior in the Taiwan Strait was counterproductive for this effort. Washington, for its part, had not sought to escalate military tensions with China, which complicated US efforts to work with European and Asian allies in exploring Soviet moderation and building lasting alliance relationships to contain Communist expansion in Asia.[55]

Thus, Beijing by early 1955 was faced with an increasingly counterproduc-tive campaign over Taiwan, a potentially dangerous military confrontation with Washington, lukewarm support from its primary international ally, and increased alienation from world powers now being wooed by the Chinese government. In this context, Chinese leaders understandably chose to shift to a more moderate stance when presented with the opportunity afforded by the American offer in mid-January 1955 of a cease-fire regarding the armed con-flict in the Taiwan Strait. Beijing responded to the US proposal with criticism but indirectly signaled interest in the offer by gradually reducing Chinese demands concerning Taiwan.[56]

Chinese premier Zhou Enlai used the venue of the Afro-Asian Conference in Bandung, Indonesia, in 1955 to ease tensions and call for talks with the United States. Chinese leaders at the time attempted to engage in high-level dialogue with the United States. How serious the Chinese were in pursuing their avowed interest in such engagement with the United States was never shown, as the Chinese overtures met with a nuanced but firm rebuff from the United States. Secretary of State Dulles was wary that direct talks with the PRC would undermine Chiang Kai-shek's Nationalist government on Taiwan. Dulles privately showed an interest in splitting China from align-ment with the Soviet Union; the strategy called for maintaining a tougher US stance against China than the comparatively accommodating US stance toward the USSR. On the other hand, Dulles faced congressional and Allied pressures to meet with the Chinese, so he agreed to low-level ambassadorial talks that began in Geneva in 1955.[57]

The two sides fairly expeditiously reached an agreement on repatriating detained personnel. The Chinese intended the agreement to lay the ground for higher-level talks with the United States. American officials from Dulles on down responded by using the wording in the agreement to make demands on the Chinese for release of detained US personnel, notably captured US spies, which they knew, through private conversations with Chinese officials at the ambassadorial talks leading up to the agreements, that China would not do. Washington soon charged Beijing with perfidy and disregard for agree-ments, souring the atmosphere in the talks. The US side also pressed hard for a Chinese renunciation of force regarding Taiwan. Chinese negotiators came up with various formulas to bridge differences between the United States and

China over this issue; at least one was positively received by the US negotiators but was rejected by Washington. This issue came to stop progress in the talks, which were suspended for a time before resuming in Warsaw in 1958, when the two sides met periodically without much result. The talks did at least provide a useful line of US-PRC communication during times of crisis, as both sides strove to avoid serious military conflict.[58]

Dulles's private strategy of vigorously pursuing a containment policy against China favored a tougher US policy toward China than toward the Soviet Union. He endeavored thereby to force Beijing to rely on Moscow for economic and other needs the Soviet Union could not meet. In this and other ways, he hoped to drive a wedge between China and the USSR.[59]

In 1958, Mao Zedong's Communists used artillery barrages in an effort to challenge and halt the resupply of the Nationalist hold over the fortress island of Quemoy and other Nationalist-controlled islands located only a few miles off the coast of the Chinese mainland. The military attacks predictably created another major crisis and war scare, with the United States firmly supporting Chiang Kai-shek's forces and threatening nuclear attack. Chiang Kai-shek refused to consider withdrawal from the Quemoy fortress, where a large portion of his best troops were deployed as part of his broader military preparations to attack mainland China and reverse Communist rule.

The absence of landing craft and other preparations for an invasion suggested that Mao was testing Nationalist and US resolve regarding the offshore island and did not intend to invade Taiwan itself. The crisis atmosphere played into Mao's efforts at the time to use the charged atmosphere of the mass campaign to mobilize national resources for a massive "Great Leap Forward" in Chinese development. Later, foreign analysts argued persuasively that the domestic mobilization was a major Chinese objective in launching the military aggression on the offshore islands held by the Chinese Nationalists. Another line of analysis argued that the Chinese leader also used the confrontation with the United States to test Soviet resolve in supporting China in what was seen in China as a weakening Sino-Soviet alliance.[60]

The Chinese-Soviet alliance indeed began to unravel by the late 1950s, and 1960 saw a clear public break with the withdrawal of Soviet economic aid and advisers. US policy makers had long sought such a split. Nonetheless, they were slow to capitalize on the situation as China remained more hostile than the Soviet Union to the United States, and deepening US involvement in Vietnam exacerbated Sino-American frictions.

During the 1960 presidential election campaign, Senator John Kennedy criticized the "tired thinking" of the outgoing administration on issues regarding China; however, he said little about China once he assumed office in 1961. US domestic opposition, Chinese nuclear weapons development, Chinese aggression against India, and Chinese expansion into Southeast Asia were among factors that seemed to block meaningful US initiatives toward China. The administration took firm action in 1962 to thwart plans by Chiang Kai-shek to attack the Chinese mainland at a time of acute economic crisis in China caused by the collapse and abject failure of the Great Leap Forward campaign. The staggering damage to China from the three-year effort saw the premature deaths of thirty million people due to starvation and nutrition deficits.[61]

Though publicly reserved about China policy, the Kennedy administration seemed to appeal to emerging American elite opinions seeking some moderation in the stern US isolation and containment of China. However, scholarship has shown there was strong private antipathy on the part of Kennedy administration leaders to China's development of nuclear weapons and support for Communist-led insurgencies in Southeast Asia. The administration's backing of Chiang Kai-shek in the United Nations also went beyond pledges under Eisenhower, with officials privately reassuring Chiang that the United States would veto efforts to remove Nationalist China from the United Nations. Kennedy was actively considering a visit to Chiang in Taiwan.[62]

The administration of Lyndon Johnson, 1963–69, saw US-Asian policy dominated by escalating US military commitment and related difficulties in Vietnam. There was some movement within the US government for a more flexible approach to China, consistent with growing signs of congressional and US interest-group advocacy of a US policy of containment without isolation toward China. But they came to little as China entered the throes of the violent and often xenophobic practices of the Cultural Revolution, and the American forces in Vietnam faced hundreds of thousands of Chinese anti-aircraft, railway, construction, and support troops sent there. Johnson was anxious to avoid prompting full-scale military involvement of China in the Vietnam conflict. US diplomats signaled these US intentions in the otherwise moribund US-China ambassadorial talks in Warsaw, and Chinese officials made clear that China would restrain its intervention accordingly.[63]

By early 1968, the bitter impasse in Sino-American relations had lasted two decades and seemed unlikely to change soon. The net result of the twists and turns in Chinese domestic and foreign policy since the widespread starvation and other disasters caused by the collapse of the Great Leap Forward were years of violence and life-and-death political struggle among elites and other groups mainly in Chinese cities during the Cultural Revolution, which began in 1966 and did not end until Mao's death in 1976. At first, the sharply deteriorating domestic situation in the early 1960s caused Mao to retreat from regular involvement in administrative matters. His subordinates pursued more moderate and pragmatic policies designed to revive agricultural and industrial production on a sustainable basis without reliance on the highly disruptive and wasteful mass campaigns and excessive collectivization of preceding years. The economy began to revive, but the progress was marred in Mao's eyes by a reliance on the kinds of incentives prevalent in the "revisionist" practices of the Soviet Union and its allied states and the controlling bureaucratic elites in those states seen as restoring the kind of unequal and exploitative practices of capitalism.[64]

Mao found that two of the three main pillars of power and control in China, the CCP and the Chinese government, continued to move in the wrong direction. The third pillar of power and control, the Chinese military, was under the leadership of Lin Biao following the purge of Defense Minister Peng Dehuai, who dared to resist Mao's Great Leap policies during a leadership meeting in 1959. Lin positioned his leadership in support of Maoist ideals of revolution, equality, and service to the people. Indoctrination and involvement in civil society and affairs often took precedence over professional military training. The distillation of Mao's wisdom from volumes of selected works was distributed throughout the Chinese military and the broader masses of China in the form of a plastic-covered "little red book," *Quotations from Chairman Mao Tse-Tung*, published with a preface by Lin Biao.[65]

Mao was not prepared to break with his party and government colleagues until 1966. By that time he had become sufficiently opposed to prevailing administrative practices and tendencies. Also, he had built up enough support outside normal administrative structures to challenge and reverse what were later portrayed as a drift toward revisionism and the restoration of capitalism. Relying on his personal charisma, organizational support from military leaders like Lin Biao, security forces controlled by radical leaders like Kang Sheng, and various political radicals and opportunists, Mao launched his unorthodox efforts that saw the creation of legions of young Red Guards leading the attack against established authority in urban China. The result was confusion, some resistance from political and government leaders often unaware of Mao's commitment to the radical Red Guards and their allies, and ultimately mass purges and persecution of senior and lesser authorities amid widespread violence and destruction carried out by Red Guard groups. By 1968, numerous sections in cities in China had burned during clashes of rival Red Guard groups, and the party and government structure had collapsed. The military was called into the cities to restore order. With Mao's support, they proceeded to transport the millions of Red Guards from the cities and to disperse them into various areas in the Chinese countryside, where they were compelled to stay and work for the indefinite future.[66]

The disaster and disruption seen in domestic affairs was duplicated in the shift toward radicalism in Chinese foreign relations. The Chinese public split with the Soviet Union deepened and broadened in the 1960s. Beijing not only opposed the Soviet Union on ideological grounds but also strongly attacked Moscow's willingness to cooperate with the United States in international affairs. Chinese leaders saw the newly independent Asian and African states providing an important arena for struggle with Moscow as well as the United States. Though weak economically and having little to spare following the deprivations of the Great Leap Forward, China provided economic and military aid to left-leaning governments and provided training, military assistance, and financial support to armed insurgents struggling against colonial powers or right-leaning governments of developing countries.[67]

Chinese premier Zhou Enlai visited Africa in 1964 and said it was "ripe for revolution." China endeavored to compete with the Soviet Union in support of various anticolonial insurgencies and to supply significant aid to African governments prepared to align closer to China than the Soviet Union or the West. In Asia, China strongly supported the Vietnamese Communist forces directed by the North Vietnamese government in Hanoi in the face of increased American military involvement in South Vietnam and other parts of Indochina. The Chinese government also organized and/or strengthened support for Communist-led insurgencies against governments in Southeast Asia that were seen by China as pro-American or insufficiently accommodating to Chinese influence and interests. The left-leaning Sukarno government of Indonesia, the largest country in Southeast Asia, was a focus of Chinese support until the military coup in 1965 smashed Communist and Chinese influence in the country through mass killings and arrests.[68]

Maoist China sacrificed conventional diplomacy in pursuing revolutionary fervor during the early years of the Cultural Revolution. The foreign minister and much of the senior foreign policy elite were purged. Ambassadors were recalled and forced to undergo extensive ideological retraining. Lower-level embassy officials often endeavored to show their loyalty to Mao and his revolutionary teaching by unauthorized demonstrations and proselytizing to often unreceptive and hostile foreign audiences. They and the staff of foreign policy organs in Beijing followed a radical line that alienated China from most foreign governments.

The nadir of Chinese diplomacy seemed evident in several developments in 1967. Huge Red Guard demonstrations were mobilized against the Soviet embassy in Beijing, which was kept under siege in January and February. Later in 1967, Red Guards invaded the Soviet Embassy's consular section and burned its files. When Moscow withdrew its diplomats' dependents in February 1967, some were beaten or forced to crawl under pictures of Mao Zedong on their way to planes to take them home. When Red Guard demonstrators in Hong Kong were arrested by British authorities for public disruption and disorder, a major crisis in Chinese-British relations ensued. A mob of thousands of Chinese surrounded British diplomatic offices in Beijing and set fires in the building. Escaping British diplomats came into the hands of the Chinese mob.[69]

The life-or-death struggles for power and attendant violent mass campaigns inside China, combined with militant Chinese policies in support of
the Vietnamese and other Communist insurgencies in Southeast Asia and a
rigid Chinese stance on Taiwan, Korea, and other issues, continued to divide
China and the United States. US leaders saw little prospect for any significant
movement in relations with the PRC as they grappled with consuming preoccupations associated with the failing US effort against Communist insurgents
in Vietnam.[70]

Chiang Kai-shek endeavored to deepen the alliance relationship with the
United States but found the Johnson administration reluctant to take actions
that might embroil China more deeply in the Vietnam War. Despite China's
radical and xenophobic posture, the newly independent developing nations
tended to be supportive of China being diplomatically recognized by them
and by international bodies, notably the United Nations. Sentiment in the
West also shifted somewhat in support of recognition of China, even if it
came at the expense of past ties with Taiwan. France set the precedent by
establishing ties with Beijing in 1964. The successful Chinese nuclear weapons test that year was followed by many more, underlining the rationale for
formal relations with the Asian power.

As Chiang aged, he incrementally passed administrative authority to his
son Chiang Ching-kuo, who focused less on plans for attacking the mainland
and more on strengthening the economy and the KMT's support on Taiwan.
The elder Chiang precluded compromise in the zero-sum competition with
China for diplomatic recognition and representation in the United Nations.
At one level, Taiwan seemed sure to lose this competition, but in 1968, with
China in the midst of the Cultural Revolution and all its radical excesses, such
losses seemed far off.[71]

STUDY QUESTIONS

1. How did the attack on Pearl Harbor fundamentally change America's
   overall international outlook and policy and role in China in particular?
2. Why was the United States ineffective in achieving its wartime goals in
   dealing with Chiang Kai-shek's government?
3. Why did the US government, despite frustration with Chiang Kai-shek's
   government policies, nonetheless maintain overall strong support for
   the Chiang government? What was the role of US domestic politics and
   public opinion in this support for the Chiang government?
4. Why did the often stridently anti-imperialist Chinese Communist Party
   leadership of Mao Zedong seek improved relations with the United
   States, 1943–45?

5. Why did the US government remain wary of the CCP? Could the United States have achieved a breakthrough in relations with Mao's CCP in the 1940s and thereby avoided the damaging failure in the so-called loss of China in 1949?

6. Why did the United States rely on the USSR and not Chiang Kai-shek's forces or Mao Zedong's forces in defeating and disarming the hundreds of thousands of Japanese troops in Northeastern China at the end of World War II?

7. Why did Mao "lean to one side" and align with the USSR in 1949–50?

8. How did North Korea, the USSR, and China miscalculate in starting the Korean War? How did the US government miscalculate in invading North Korea after defeating North Korea forces in the south?

9. What were the purpose and scope of the US containment of China in Asia? How and why is the US containment relevant today?

10. What was Dulles's "wedge" strategy? How did it drive Moscow and Beijing apart? Why didn't US policy take advantage of this outcome until many years later?

11. What drove Chinese actions in support of anti-French forces in Indochina in countering Chiang Kai-shek forces in 1954–55 and 1958 and in splitting from the alliance with the Soviet Union?

12. What made China move toward ideologically driven international isolation in the Cultural Revolution?

RELEVANT VIDEOS

"United States and China: World War and Civil War, 1937–1949" (Arthur Schlesinger Jr., video cassette, 1970, thirty minutes) available at https://www.worldcat.org/title/united-states-and-china-world-war-and-civil-war-1937-1949/oclc/122662194&referer=brief_results

"The Long History of America-China Relations" (Gordon Chang lecture, October 24, 2016, forty-eight minutes) available at https://www.youtube.com/watch?v=vW747IAz154

"China the Roots of Madness" (Theodore White, film, 1967, seventy minutes) available at https://www.amazon.com/China-Roots-Madness-1967/dp/B001BXTPUG

"General 'Vinegar Joe' Stillwell" (film, 1963, forty minutes) available at https://www.youtube.com/watch?v=luRi8qY8hiI

"The Dixie Mission" (CGTN, June 23, 2021, four minutes) available at https://www.youtube.com/watch?v=ycF8G9suXGs

"Meet the Press" (interview with Ambassador J. F. Dulles, June 24, 1951, thirty minutes) available at https://www.worldcat.org/title/meet-the-press-june-24-1951/oclc/8085741789&referer=brief_results

"Meet the Press" (Senator Joseph McCarthy opposes Dean Acheson, June 3, 1951, thirty minutes) available at https://www.worldcat.org/title/meet-the-press-june-3-1951/oclc/8085749533&referer=brief_results

"Behind the Bamboo Curtain" (filmstrip, 1969, fifteen minutes) available at https://www.worldcat.org/title/behind-the-bamboo-curtain/oclc/397281&referer=brief_results

Chapter Four

Rapprochement and Normalization

STRATEGIC IMPERATIVES OPENING US-CHINA RELATIONS

The roots of the contemporary, closely intertwined Sino-American relationship began in what appeared to be very adverse circumstances. Maoist China had descended through phases of ideologically driven excess in foreign and domestic affairs, reaching a point of unprecedented international isolation, ideological rigidity, and wariness in foreign relations bordering on xenophobia. The United States had more than five hundred thousand troops in Vietnam fighting a Communist-led adversary supported by China with supplies, financing, and provision of many thousands of Chinese troops. US leaders were particularly fearful of an escalation of the prolonged and increasingly unpopular conflict that would somehow bring China more directly into a war that they were unsure how to win under existing conditions. The US containment effort along China's periphery continued, as did US political isolation and economic embargo against the Beijing regime. Nascent US efforts to consider greater flexibility in relations with China ran up against Maoist hostility, disinterest, and contempt and were overshadowed by the broad implications of the Vietnam quagmire.[1]

The dramatic turnabout leading to the opening in US-China relations at the end of the 1960s and early 1970s has been subject to some different scholarly interpretations. One view sees a flagging of Mao's revolutionary drive and vigor, opening the way for the Chinese leader to consider and ultimately pursue pragmatic understanding with the United States.[2] Another sees a reconfiguring in the US calculus of China's position in world politics and its implications for the United States. This view highlights the importance of an apparent trend whereby US leaders privately came to see China in the late 1960s as less threatening than in the past; eventually they came to view the Maoist regime as a potential asset in American strategy focused increasingly on dealing with a rising and threatening Soviet Union.[3]

Despite these and other divergent views, assessments of this period and the opening in Sino-American relations find it hard not to give primacy to interpretations, broadly in line with the realist school of thought in international relations (IR) theory, that focused on the acute strategic necessities of both the United States and China amid circumstances of regional and international order featuring a rising and powerful Soviet Union challenging their core national interests. Only the threat of nuclear war with a domineering Soviet Union at a time of acute Chinese internal disruption and weakness appears sufficient to explain the remarkable turnabout in China's foreign policy calculus and approach to the United States. Given China's size and the long-standing preoccupation of Chinese rulers with the tasks of managing the complicated internal affairs of this vast country, China historians and specialists of contemporary affairs often have given pride of place to Chinese domestic determinants in Chinese foreign policy. There was no better example during Maoist rule of the way domestic Chinese policies and practices determined Chinese foreign policy than during the violent and disruptive early years of China's Cultural Revolution. Moving Chinese leaders out of their self-initiated isolation probably would have taken many years under more normal circumstances. But circumstances in the late 1960s were far from normal, giving rise to the real danger of the Soviet Union militarily invading China, destroying its nuclear and other strategic installations, and forcing China to conform to Soviet interests.[4]

For their part, US leaders faced an unprecedented situation of Soviet military power seeming to reach parity with and in some critical areas surpassing that of the United States. The concurrent Vietnam quagmire drained American resources, and Moscow pumped up support for the Vietnamese Communist resistance, seeking to further weaken the United States and strengthen the changing balance of power in Asian and world affairs. Finding a way to break this trend and deal more effectively with the Vietnam situation became critically important issues in American politics.[5]

It was fortuitous that strong strategic imperatives, which drove Chinese and US leaders toward one another, developed at the same time. Otherwise, Maoist China in particular seemed positioned to continue resistance to the United States, while US interest in greater flexibility toward China appeared likely to be overwhelmed by opposing US interests and political inclinations. There had been earlier occasions when one side or the other saw their interests served by a possible improvement in Sino-American relations. But it turned out that when one side showed some interest in improved contacts, the other rebuffed or ignored it. Thus, despite deeply rooted differences between the US government and Chinese Communist leaders on ideological, economic, and international issues, United States–Chinese Communist interchange since the start of World War II witnessed a few instances where one side or the other saw their interests served by reaching out and seeking reconciliation and better ties with the other party. The Chinese Communists in particular tried a moderate and accommodating approach to the United States in greeting the American Military Observer Group to Yenan in 1944 and in the initial ambassadorial talks following Zhou Enlai's moderate overture at Bandung in 1955. The Americans tried more tentative overtures to Beijing in 1949 and showed interest in more flexibility toward China by the 1960s. Unfortunately, these initiatives and overtures failed, as there were never occasions when both sides sought improved relations at the same time, until internal and international weaknesses in 1968 and 1969 drove the United States and China closer together in a pragmatic search for means to deal with difficult circumstances, which appears best understood through the realist lens of IR theory.[6]

ENCOUNTERS AND INTERACTION, 1968–89

Opening Contacts

Difficulties in the United States in 1968 were profound. It is hard to recall a one-year period since the start of the Cold War with so many shocking and adverse developments for American leaders and their constituents. The string of calamities and reversals began in January with the Communist Tet Offensive throughout South Vietnamese cities. The assault often was carried out by Vietnamese who were thought to be supporting the American war effort. The US and Allied forces counterattacked against the guerrillas in their own ranks and elsewhere in the supposedly pacified cities of South Vietnam, killing many thousands, but the uprising and mass killings shattered the Lyndon Johnson administration's predictions of progress in the increasingly unpopular Vietnam War.[7]

US commanders called for two hundred thousand more US troops in addition to the more than half million US forces in the country. The vast majority of these American forces were draftees. They and their families and friends tended in growing numbers to question the purpose of the US commitment to Vietnam and the massive costs in terms of American casualties and economic and military support. Antiwar demonstrations in the United States grew in size and frequency. Protest marches of two hundred thousand or more along the Mall in Washington, DC, became more regular occurrences. Providing security for the White House compound adjoining the Mall became an increasing concern given the size of the demonstrations and the uncertainty over whether they would stay on the Mall or turn against the nearby White House.

The rising antiwar sentiment in the United States changed the course of the 1968 presidential election campaign. President Johnson's mandate appeared to collapse when he did poorly in the New Hampshire primary in February. He ran against Senator Eugene McCarthy, an otherwise unexceptional opponent who emphasized an antiwar platform. Johnson pulled out of the race and redoubled peace efforts in talks with the Vietnamese Communists in Paris.

Civil rights leader and antiwar proponent Martin Luther King Jr. traveled to Memphis in March in support of a strike by city trash handlers. While standing outside his motel, King was killed by a rifleman. The assassination set off a rampage of urban looting and burning that afflicted several American cities. Washington, DC, was closed for days as major parts of the city burned out of control. The fire service was prevented from interceding by snipers and mob violence. Order was restored only after the imposition of martial law by US Army combat troops.

Amid this turmoil over the Vietnam War and race relations in the United States, the contentious Democratic primaries reached a conclusion in California in June, where Senator Robert Kennedy won. Kennedy was critical of the conduct of the war and drew vast crowds of African Americans and others hopeful for government policies to heal fractured race relations in the United States. Like King three months earlier, Kennedy was assassinated, just after the California victory was secured.

With Kennedy dead, antiwar advocates gathered in Chicago in August to protest the likely selection of Johnson's vice president, Hubert Humphrey, as the Democratic standard-bearer. Chicago's mayor Richard Daley and his police officers promised tough measures to deal with unauthorized demonstrations. They delivered on their promise: as American television audiences watched in shock, police officers clubbed and beat demonstrators, reporters, and others they deemed to be obstructing the smooth flow of the convention and nearby hotel receptions.

The Republicans at their convention that summer nominated Richard Nixon. In a political comeback after retreating from public life in the early 1960s, Nixon said he had a plan to deal with the Vietnam morass. He did not speak very much about an opening to China. Nixon won the election and took office amid unprecedented tight security for fear of violence from antiwar protesters and others. Upon entering office, Nixon moved quickly to begin what would turn out to be the withdrawal of more than six hundred thousand US troops from around China's periphery in Asia. In his first year in office, he announced what later was called the Nixon Doctrine, a broad framework for Asia's future without massive US troop deployments. One implication seemed to be the end of the US-backed containment of China. Nixon also made several mainly symbolic gestures to the Chinese government while pursuing vigorous efforts in secret to develop communications with the Mao Zedong leadership.[8]

Meanwhile, in China, Mao succeeded in removing political rivals in the early years of the Cultural Revolution, but at tremendous cost. Many burnt urban areas testified to widespread violence and arson among competing groups. The party and government administration were severely disrupted. Experienced administrators were often purged, persecuted, or pushed aside by proponents of radical Maoist ideals or political opportunists. Expertise in economics, development, and other fields essential to nation building came to be seen as a liability in the politically charged atmosphere of repeated mass campaigns. Political indoctrination and adherence to Mao Zedong Thought overshadowed education and training in practical tasks.[9]

Military forces called into Chinese cities in order to restore order duly removed millions of disruptive Red Guards and began to lead the process of reconstituting a party and government infrastructure on the basis of military-led rule. Not surprisingly in this context, Defense Minister Lin Biao and his People's Liberation Army (PLA) associates rose to new prominence in the Chinese hierarchy. Military representation in various party and government bodies was high. Not all military leaders were as supportive of the radical policies and practices of the Cultural Revolution as Lin Biao and his associates in the high command. Some experienced civilian and military cadre had survived in office. But they appeared in the minority in a leadership featuring factional chieftains like the Gang of Four, involving Mao's wife and three other extremist party Politburo members, and such luminaries as Mao's speechwriter and sometime confidant Chen Boda and security forces and intelligence operative Kang Sheng.[10]

Under these circumstances, China was not prepared for a national security shock. Chinese troops were engaged in domestic peacekeeping and governance. They also for many years followed Maoist dictates under the leadership of Defense Minister Lin Biao and eschewed professional military training in favor of ideological training and promoting popular welfare in China. Chinese military programs for developing nuclear weapons and ballistic missiles were excluded from the violence and disruption of the Cultural Revolution, but the PLA on the whole was poorly prepared to deal with conventional military challenges.[11]

In August 1968, the Soviet Union invaded Czechoslovakia and removed its leadership, putting in power a regime more compatible with Soviet interests. The Soviet Union also made clear that it reserved the right to take similar actions in other deviant Communist states. This view came to be known as the Brezhnev Doctrine, named after the Soviet party leader Leonid Brezhnev, who ruled from the mid-1960s until the early 1980s. Of course, Chinese leaders well knew that, from the Soviet perspective, there was no Communist state more deviant than China. Moreover, since Brezhnev's takeover, the Soviet Union had backed political opposition to China with increasing military muscle, deploying ever-larger numbers of forces along the Manchurian border and, as a result of a new Soviet defense treaty with Mongolia, along the Sino-Mongolian border. The Soviet forces, mainly mechanized divisions designed to move rapidly in offensive operations, were configured in a pattern they had used when they quickly overran Japanese forces in Manchuria and northern China in the last days of World War II.[12]

The Sino-Soviet dispute had emerged in the late 1950s as an ideological dispute with wide implications. Fairly quickly it became a major issue in bilateral relations, notably with the abrupt withdrawal of Soviet assistance from China in 1960. At that time, the dispute broadened to include stark differences on international issues and how to deal with the United States. Chinese accusations of Soviet weakness in the face of the firm US stance against Soviet missiles in Cuba during the Cuban missile crisis of 1962 saw Soviet officials respond by accusing China of accommodating colonial "outhouses" held by Great Britain and Portugal in Hong Kong and Macau, respectively. Maoist China responded by reminding the world that imperialist Russia took by far the greatest tracts of Chinese territory by virtue of the so-called unequal treaties imposed on China by imperialist powers in the nineteenth and twentieth centuries. The Sino-Soviet debate now focused on competing claims to disputed border territories against the background of new uncertainty over the legitimacy of the boundaries established by the unequal treaties. Sino-Soviet negotiations soon after Brezhnev took power, following the ouster of Nikita Khrushchev in 1964, failed to resolve border uncertainties, prompting the new Soviet leader to make the force deployments and arrangements noted above in order to deal with the Chinese disputes from a position of strength. With the declared Soviet ambitions under terms of the Brezhnev Doctrine and Moscow's military preparations, the stage was set for the border dispute to evolve into the most serious national security threat ever faced by the People's Republic of China (PRC).[13]

The combination of perceived greater threat and internal weakness caused a crisis and debate in the Chinese leadership that lasted into the early 1970s. Chinese leadership decision making in the Cultural Revolution was not at all transparent. Mao seemed to remain in overall command, but official Chinese media duly reflected competing views on how to deal with the new and apparently dangerous situation in relations with the Soviet Union.[14]

Some commentary, presumably encouraged by some Chinese leaders, favored reaching out to the United States as a means to offset the Soviet threat. In November 1968, the Chinese Foreign Ministry under Premier Zhou Enlai's direction called for renewed ambassadorial talks with the newly elected Nixon administration in a statement that was notable for the absence of the then-usual Chinese invective critical of the United States. The argument used in media commentary that proposed a reaching-out to the United States was that the United States was in the process of being defeated in Indochina and was no longer the primary threat to China. It, too, faced challenges from the expanding USSR, and China could take advantage of the differences between the competing superpowers in order to secure its position in the face of the newly emerging Soviet danger.[15]

Other commentary, presumably backed by other Chinese leaders, strongly opposed an opening to the United States. These commentaries were associated with Lin Biao and his lieutenants along with the radically Maoist leadership faction the Gang of Four. They argued in favor of continued strong Chinese opposition to both the United States and the Soviet Union. Though weakened by the defeat in Vietnam, the United States could not be trusted in dealings with China. In particular, any sign of Chinese weakness toward either superpower likely would prompt them both to work together in seeking to pressure China and gain at its expense.[16]

The latter leaders held the upper hand in Chinese leadership councils during much of 1969. Chinese media rebuked and ridiculed the new US president as he took office. At the last moment Chinese leaders canceled the slated ambassadorial talks in February. The Chinese authorities took the offensive in the face of Soviet military pressure along the border, ambushing a Soviet patrol on a disputed island in early March and publicizing the incident to the world. Far from being intimidated, Brezhnev's Soviet forces responded later in the month by annihilating a Chinese border guard unit, setting the stage for escalating rhetoric and military clashes throughout the spring and summer of 1969. The clashes were capped in August by an all-day battle along the western sector of the border that saw the Soviets inflict hundreds of casualties on the Chinese. Soviet officials followed with warnings to Americans, and other foreigners sure to relay the warnings to the Chinese, that the Soviet Union was in the process of consulting with foreign powers to assure they would stand aside as the Soviet Union prepared all-out attack on China, including the possible use of nuclear weapons.[17]

In the face of such threats and pressure, Chinese leaders were compelled to shift strategy. Zhou Enlai was brought forward to negotiate with Soviet leaders. It was clear that while negotiating with the USSR would temporarily ease tensions and the danger of war, China would not accept Soviet demands. Beijing now viewed the USSR as China's number one strategic threat. Seeking international leverage, it took measures to improve strained Chinese relations with neighboring countries and with more distant powers. It was nonetheless evident that, while helpful, these improvements would not fundamentally alter China's strategic disadvantage in the face of Soviet intimidation and threat. Only one power, the United States, had that ability. Zhou and like-minded officials in the Chinese leadership were encouraged that the United States was weakened by the Vietnam War and that it was also beginning to withdraw sizeable numbers of troops from Asia and dismantle the US military containment against China. On this basis, Beijing could pursue relations with Washington as a means to deal with the Soviet threat. However,

Lin Biao and others continued to argue that both superpowers were enemies of China, and in the end they would cooperate to isolate and control China.[18]

The debate seemed to get caught up with the broader struggle for power in this period of the Cultural Revolution. Mao Zedong came to side with the view associated with Zhou Enlai. Repeated overtures by the Nixon administration to China ultimately succeeded in Sino-American ambassadorial talks being resumed in Warsaw in early 1970. China used the image of restored contacts with the United States in order to offset and undermine Soviet efforts to intimidate China. Chinese officials arranged for the meeting to be held in the secure area of their embassy in Warsaw. The usual venue, a palace provided by the Poles, was long suspected of being riddled with secret listening devices that would give the USSR and Warsaw Pact allies the full transcript of the US-China discussions. The Chinese diplomats also made a point of being unusually positive to Western reporters during the photo opportunity as American officials were welcomed to the Chinese embassy at the start of the official talks. As Chinese officials presumably hoped, Soviet commentary on the secret talks and improved atmosphere in US-China relations viewed the developments as complicating Soviet border negotiations with China and nuclear armament limitation talks with the United States. Soviet commentators even charged that Beijing, fearful of Soviet intentions, was seeking to come to terms with the United States in order to play one nuclear power against the other.[19]

The Nixon administration's expansion of the Vietnam War by invading Cambodia in spring 1970 caused China to cancel the talks and slowed forward movement. Mao highlighted a mass demonstration in Beijing on May 20, 1970, where he welcomed the Cambodian leader Norodom Sihanouk, who had been deposed by the pro-US Cambodian generals who worked with US-led invading forces. The Chinese chairman, in his last major public statement denouncing the United States, called on the people of the world to rise up against US imperialism and their "running dogs." Outwardly, it appeared that Mao was siding with the Chinese advocates of a harder line against the United States. However, clandestine US-China communication continued, as did the withdrawal of US forces from Vietnam and other parts of Asia, so that by October 1970 Mao was prepared to tell visiting US journalist Edgar Snow that Nixon could visit China.[20]

The shift in Mao's stance was accompanied by other moves that appeared to undermine the standing of Lin Biao and his radical allies in the Chinese leadership. A key radical leader, Chen Boda, dropped from public view in late 1970 in what later was shown to be intensified factional maneuvering leading up to the alleged coup plans by Lin and his allies.[21]

What role was played by differences over the opening to the United States in the life-or-death struggle in the Chinese leadership remains hidden by pervasive secrecy in Chinese leadership decision making. Emblematic of the significance of the opening to the United States in Chinese politics at the time was the unusual greeting of US National Security Adviser Henry Kissinger upon his arrival in Beijing on his secret mission in July 1971 to open US-China relations. The first Chinese official to greet Kissinger on arrival was not a protocol officer from the foreign ministry or some other appropriate official; it was Marshall Ye Jianying. Ye was one of the most senior Chinese military leaders. He survived the Cultural Revolution, advised Mao to use connections with the United States in the face of the Soviet threat, later played a key role in the arrest of the Gang of Four following Mao's death in 1976, and became president of China. His approach was close to that of Zhou Enlai and at odds with that of Lin Biao.[22]

The announcement of Kissinger's successful secret trip appeared to represent a serious defeat for Lin Biao and his allies in their debate with opponents on how to deal with the Soviet Union and the United States. The setback came amid rising pressures and adverse developments affecting the military leader. The stakes apparently were very high. Two months later, Lin and his wife, son, and close aides died as a result of an air crash in Mongolia as they were allegedly trying to escape China following a failed coup attempt against Mao and his opponents. The military high command in the PLA that had risen to power under Lin's tenure as defense minister were arrested, removed from power, and not seen again until they eventually were brought out for public trial along with the Gang of Four and other discredited radical leaders in the years after Mao's death.[23]

Though nothing like the intense factional struggles of Maoist China, US leadership and popular opposition to an opening to China were feared by President Nixon and his top aides. In particular, it was clear to the American leaders that they would have to sacrifice US official relations with Taiwan in order to meet the conditions Chinese leaders set for establishing relations with the United States. How the Chiang Kai-shek government in Taiwan would react to this new adverse turn of fate was uncertain. The so-called China lobby, both supportive of Chiang and the Chinese Nationalists and strongly anti-Communist, had been a feature of American domestic politics for more than twenty years. Chiang and the lobby had particular influence among conservatives in the president's Republican Party. Nixon had close and personal ties with the lobby.[24]

President Nixon, National Security Adviser Kissinger, and the small group of top aides involved in the opening to China dealt with potential domestic opposition through secrecy and what arguably could be seen as deception. Their motives focused on the advantages for the United States in a new relationship with China with regard to handling the difficult process of reaching an acceptable peace agreement to end US involvement in the Vietnam War and in dealing with the Soviet Union in arms limitation and other negotiations from a position of greater strength. A new order in Asian and world affairs featuring positive US-China relations seemed much less costly and more compatible for US interests than the previous US confrontation with and containment of China. President Nixon and his administration also seemed acutely aware that the political opportunity of an American opening to China could fall into the hands of a Democratic Party opponent, and they were determined to preclude such an outcome.[25]

For a time, it was difficult for scholars to construct the full picture of the Nixon administration approach to China because much of the record initially remained secret, and public pronouncements, memoirs, and other documents from administration leaders sometimes seemed very much at odds with what was actually the administration's policy and practice. It was clear that US leaders now centered their strategies and approaches in East Asia on improving relations with China and that US relations with Taiwan would decline, though the scope and extent of the decline were left ambiguous. Relations with Japan and other East Asian allies and friends also appeared secondary and were sometimes viewed as declining assets or liabilities. Also clear was evidence that the United States sought, through the new relationship with China, a means to secure US interests following the failure of US military intervention in Vietnam and the rising danger posed by the expanding power of the Soviet Union in the Asian region and elsewhere. And the ambitions of the Nixon administration to use the dramatic opening to China to garner personal prestige at home and abroad and strong domestic political support in the run-up to the 1972 US presidential race seemed evident.[26]

The American people, their representatives in Congress, the media, and others with an interest were notably left in the dark for many years regarding the full extent of the US compromises on Taiwan carried out in the early contacts between Kissinger and Nixon and Chinese leaders. The Nationalist Chinese government was in a similar situation. The record reconstructed by scholarship shows that Kissinger met Chinese conditions involving a full break in US official relations with Taiwan and other interaction with Taiwan during his initial meetings with Zhou Enlai in 1971 and that Nixon backed these steps in his initial meetings with Chinese leaders the following year. These compromises were kept from public view and also kept from many US officials responsible for the conduct of US policy toward China and Taiwan amid statements and actions by the administration indicating continued support for Taiwan and ambiguity about what the future course of US policy might be.[27]

On the basis of the compromises by Kissinger and Nixon, scholarship judges that the Chinese leadership could reasonably have concluded Taiwan would soon be theirs, as the United States would remove itself from involvement in the issue. Unfortunately, Nixon and his associates had only begun to build support in the United States and internationally for this dramatic change in policy. It was unclear whether majorities in the Congress, the media, public opinion, and the major political parties would accept it. Nixon and his aides avoided building this support as they focused on developing relations with China in secret on a foundation of compromises and accommodations poorly understood in the United States and abroad. They made a strong case that such secrecy was needed in order to avoid complications in the process of normalization. That argument would be followed by later US administrations with mixed success and some serious negative consequences for long-term US-China relations. Notably, Chinese expectations that Taiwan would soon be theirs and that the United States would remove itself from involvement in Taiwan were sorely and repeatedly tested by US actions demonstrating continued support for Taiwan, backed by American leaders often unaware of or opposed to the Nixon-Kissinger secret compromises on Taiwan.[28]

The July 1971 announcement of Nixon's trip to China came as a surprise to most Americans, who supported the initiative; Americans watched with interest the president's February 1972 visit to China. Supporting Kissinger's secret pledges in the July 1971 meetings in Beijing, Nixon privately indicated to Chinese leaders that he would break US ties with Taiwan and establish diplomatic relations with China in his second term. In the Shanghai Communiqué signed at the end of President Nixon's historic visit to China, both sides registered opposition to "hegemony" (a code word for Soviet expansion), laid out differences on a variety of Asian and other issues, and set forth the US intention to pull back militarily from Taiwan and to support a "peaceful settlement of the Taiwan question by the Chinese themselves." Subsequently, both sides agreed to establish US-China Liaison Offices staffed with senior diplomats in Beijing and Washington in 1973, despite the fact that the United States still maintained official relations with the Chinese Nationalist government in Taipei.[29]

Normalization of Relations

Progress toward establishing formal US-China relations, the so-called normalization of relations, was delayed in the mid-1970s on account of circumstances mainly involving the United States. A politically motivated break-in at the Watergate office complex in Washington, DC, and cover-up of the crime involved President Nixon in criminal activity. As congressional investigation led toward impeachment, Nixon resigned in August 1974. His promise to normalize relations with China in his second term ended with his resignation. President Gerald Ford privately reaffirmed Nixon's pledge to shift diplomatic recognition from Taiwan to China, but then he backtracked in the face of US domestic opposition and international circumstances.[30]

Chinese leaders for their part were preoccupied with Mao's declining health and subsequent death in September 1976 and the most important leadership succession struggle in the history of the People's Republic of China. The leadership turmoil in China at the time had seen Zhou Enlai die in January 1976. His purported successor, recently rehabilitated veteran leader Deng Xiaoping, gave the eulogy at the memorial service for Zhou and then disappeared from public view, purged from the leadership for a second time. The radical Gang of Four seemed to exert more influence for a time, but the demonstration of support for Zhou and his relatively moderate policies, in the form of thousands of Beijing people placing flowers and wreaths in his memory at the monument for revolutionary martyrs in the capital in April 1976, appeared to indicate that the days of radicalism were numbered. The death of senior military leader Zhu De in July 1976 preceded Mao's by two months, setting the stage for the struggle for succession following Mao's death in September.[31]

That China had far to go in creating a foreign policy that dealt with the United States and other countries in the world in conventional and normal ways was underlined by the tragedy of an earthquake in July 1976 that demolished the industrial city of Tangshan, 105 miles southeast of Beijing, and severely damaged nearby areas including the capital and the major port and industrial city of Tianjin. It later was disclosed that hundreds of thousands of Chinese died in the quake and that the needs for relief were enormous. Nevertheless, in a remarkable and extremely damaging demonstration of Maoist "self-reliance," the radical leadership in Beijing at the time refused to acknowledge these needs or to allow foreign countries and groups to assist in efforts to save lives and reduce misery.[32]

A coalition of senior leaders managed to stop the Gang of Four from gaining power after Mao's death. The coalition included veteran cadre who had survived the Cultural Revolution and administrators who had risen to prominence during the turmoil but also endeavored to avoid the harm caused by excessively radical policies. The four radical leaders were arrested. After a few years, they were put on public trial in 1980, once the Communist Party leadership had sufficiently reunited and come to overall judgment about what was correct and incorrect behavior during the Cultural Revolution. Reaching such judgment was particularly time-consuming and difficult since Chairman Mao Zedong, still seen as the revered leader of China, was personally responsible for support of the radicals and so much of the turmoil they and others carried out during the Cultural Revolution.

Following the arrest of the Gang of Four, leadership changes in China slowly evolved toward a reversal of the disruptive policies of the past and restoration to power of senior cadre committed to pragmatic reform in the interest of Chinese development and sustaining Communist rule in China. Deng Xiaoping was once again brought back to power. By the time of the third plenary session of the Eleventh Central Committee in December 1978, Deng was able to consolidate a leading position within the party, government, and military and to launch the economic and policy reforms that provided the foundation for China's recent approach to the United States and international affairs. Deng and his colleagues constantly were compelled to maneuver amid competing interests and preferences within the Chinese leadership and the broader polity in order to come up with changes they felt would advance China's wealth and shore up the legitimacy of the Chinese Communist Party, which had been severely damaged by the excesses and poor performance of the past.[33]

Not only were Chinese leaders preoccupied internally, but their priorities internationally in the latter 1970s were less focused on consummating normalization with the United States and more focused on dealing with Soviet intimidation and threat. The United States was weakened internally by Nixon's resignation, and the Ford government was hobbled by the president's pardon of Nixon. Ford was in a poor position to continue strong support for the struggling South Vietnamese government and the neighboring Cambodian government aligned with the United States. Strong Soviet assistance to Vietnamese Communist forces bolstered their efforts to take control of the south. The Cambodian regime collapsed, and Chinese-backed Khmer Rouge insurgents entered Phnom Penh in March 1975. The new regime immediately began carrying out their radical and brutal policies that would see the evacuation of the capital and the massive repression and deaths of more than one million Cambodians. North Vietnamese forces launched an all-out assault in South Vietnam. The Saigon regime disintegrated, the Americans and what Vietnamese associates they could bring with them fled in ignominious defeat, and the Communist forces barged through the gates of the presidential palace and occupied Saigon in late April.[34]

Chinese officials showed considerable alarm at the turn of events around China's periphery. Stronger efforts by the Soviet Union to use military power and relations with allies around China, like Vietnam and India, to contain and pressure the PRC mimicked the US-led containment effort against China earlier in the Cold War. Under these circumstances, Chinese leaders focused on shoring up US resolve and the resolve of other governments and forces seen as important in what China depicted as a united front against expanding Soviet power and influence in Asian and world affairs. The Chinese leaders appeared prepared to wait for the United States to meet Chinese conditions on breaking all US official ties with Taiwan, including the US-Taiwan defense treaty, before moving ahead with full normalization of PRC relations with the United States.[35]

Desiring to complete the normalization of US-China relations begun by President Nixon, President Jimmy Carter felt compelled to wait until after his success in spring 1978 in gaining Senate passage of a controversial treaty transferring control of the Panama Canal to Panama. A visit by Secretary of State Cyrus Vance to China in 1977 showed that Chinese leaders were not prepared for significant compromise on Taiwan. President Carter was aware that a complete ending of US official relations with Taiwan would alienate many in the US Senate, and he needed the support of these senators for the two-thirds Senate vote of ratification on the Panama Canal treaty. Once the Senate approved the Panama treaty in spring 1978, Carter moved forward expeditiously with normalization with China.[36]

National Security Adviser Zbigniew Brzezinski was in the lead in seeking rapid progress in normalizing US-China relations in 1978 and in subsequent steps to advance US-China relations as a means to counter Soviet power and expansion. Soviet and Soviet-backed forces had made gains and were making inroads that seemed at odds with US interests in different parts of Africa, the Middle East, Central America, and Southwest and Southeast Asia. Chinese officials were in the lead among international advocates in warning the United States to avoid the dangers of "appeasement" and to stand firm and work with China against the expanding Soviet power. Carter followed Brzezinski's advice over that of Secretary of State Cyrus Vance, who gave a higher priority to working constructively with the USSR, notably in order to reach US-Soviet arms control agreements.[37]

The process of US administration decision making followed the practices of the Nixon period. Like their Nixon-administration counterparts, the Carter administration leaders were concerned with the reactions of US supporters of Taiwan and others opposed to American normalization with China. To out-maneuver anticipated opposition and complications, Carter, Brzezinski, and their senior aides worked hard to preserve the secrecy of the negotiations with China. Though the broad direction of US policy was understood to be moving toward normalization with China, the process of the talks with Beijing and the content of US concessions were held back. The Carter administration agreement to normalize diplomatic relations with China would follow through in a public way on many of the secret agreements the US leaders had already made with China over Taiwan. Though some in the Carter administration were concerned with preserving important US ties with Taiwan after normalization, Brzezinski showed little interest, and Carter seemed contemptuous of congressional backers of Taiwan. Key Carter officials didn't expect Taiwan to survive the change in relations.[38]

The United States–China Communiqué announced in December 1978 established official US relations with the People's Republic of China under conditions whereby the United States recognized the PRC as the government of China, acknowledged that Taiwan was part of China, ended official US relations with the Republic of China (ROC) government on Taiwan, and terminated the US defense treaty with the ROC on Taiwan. Official US statements underscored US interest that Taiwan's future be settled peacefully and that the United States would continue sales of defensive arms to Taipei.[39]

US and especially Chinese leaders used the signs of improved US-China relations in the communiqué and during Chinese leader Deng Xiaoping's widely publicized visit to the United States in January 1979 to highlight Sino-American cooperation against "hegemony," notably a Soviet-backed Vietnamese military assault against Cambodia beginning in late December 1978. Returning from the United States, Deng launched a large-scale Chinese military offensive into Vietnam's northern region. Chinese forces withdrew after a few weeks but maintained strong artillery attacks and other military pressure against Vietnamese border positions until the Vietnamese eventually agreed to withdraw from Cambodia ten years later. Carter administration officials voiced some reservations about Deng's confrontational tactics against Soviet and Vietnamese expansionism, but Sino-American cooperation against the USSR and its allies increased.[40]

In pursuing normalization of relations with China, President Carter and National Security Adviser Brzezinski followed the pattern of secret diplomacy used successfully by President Nixon and National Security Adviser Kissinger in early interaction with China. Their approach allowed for very little consultation with Congress, key US allies, or the Taiwan government regarding the conditions and timing of the 1978 normalization agreement. In contrast to general US congressional, media, and popular support for the surprise Nixon opening to China, President Carter and his aides clearly were less successful in winning US domestic support for their initiatives. Many in Congress were satisfied with the stasis that developed in US-PRC-ROC relations in the mid-1970s and unconvinced that the United States had a strategic or other need to pay the price of breaking a US defense treaty and other official ties with a loyal government in Taiwan for the sake of formalizing already existing relations with the PRC. Bipartisan majorities in Congress resisted the president's initiatives and passed laws, notably the Taiwan Relations Act, that tied the hands of the administration on Taiwan and other issues.[41]

The Taiwan Relations Act was passed by Congress in March 1979 and signed by President Carter on April 10, 1979. The initial draft of the legislation was proposed by the Carter administration to govern US relations with Taiwan once official US ties were ended in 1979. Congress rewrote the legislation, adding or strengthening provisions on US arms sales, economic relations, human rights, congressional oversight, and opposition to threats and use of force. Treating Taiwan as a separate entity that would continue to receive US military and other support, the law appeared to contradict the US stance in the US-PRC communiqué of 1978 establishing official US-PRC relations. Subsequently, Chinese and Taiwan officials and their supporters in the United States competed to incline US policy toward the commitments in the US-PRC communiqué or the commitments in the Taiwan Relations Act. US policy usually supported both, though it sometimes seemed more supportive of one set of commitments than the other.[42]

Running against President Carter in 1980, California governor Ronald Reagan criticized Carter's handling of Taiwan. Asserting for a time that he would restore official relations with Taipei, Reagan later backed away from this stance but still claimed he would base his policy on the Taiwan Relations Act. The Chinese government put heavy pressure on the Reagan administration, threatening serious deterioration in relations over various issues but especially continuing US arms sales to Taiwan.[43]

Viewing close China-US relations as a key element in US strategy against the Soviet Union, Secretary of State Alexander Haig led those in the Reagan administration who favored maintaining close China-US relations and opposed US arms sales to Taiwan that might provoke China. For a year and a half, Haig and his supporters were successful in leading US efforts to accommodate PRC concerns over Taiwan, especially regarding US arms sales to the ROC, in the interest of fostering closer US-China cooperation against the Soviet Union. The United States ultimately signed with China the August 17, 1982, communiqué. In the communiqué, the United States agreed to gradually diminish arms sales, and China agreed it would seek peaceful reunification of Taiwan with the mainland. Subsequent developments showed that the vague agreement was subject to varying interpretations. President Reagan registered private reservations about the agreement, and his administration also took steps to reassure Taiwan's leader of continued US support.[44]

Looking back at the first decade of opening and developing US-China contacts leading to the normalization of relations, prevailing assessments follow a pattern that seems consistent with the perspective of realism in IR theory. They show a strong tendency on the part of US leaders to focus on relations with China as the key element in a new US approach to East Asian and world affairs. The war in Vietnam, the growing challenge of an expanding Soviet Union, the seeming decline in US power and influence in East Asian and world affairs, and major US internal disruptions and weaknesses seemed to support the emphasis on a new US approach to China with important benefits for US foreign policy and other interests. US leadership attention focused on doing what was needed to advance the new China relationship and gave secondary attention to long-standing US allies and other close relationships in

East Asia or manipulated them in ways that would accord with the China-first emphasis in US policy. Emblematic of this trend, Nixon's surprise announcement in July 1971 that he would visit China was so shocking and disturbing to the long-standing and more conservative China policy of the government of Prime Minister Eisaku Sato of Japan that it brought down the Japanese government. Available scholarship shows that Nixon deliberately withheld information of the American shift so he could "stick it to Japan" and show US frustration with Japan's trade and economic policies working against US interests.[45]

The US emphasis on China came with significant costs for the United States and US interests, though scholarship tends to depict the benefits of the US approach as justifying the costs. Notably, US leaders came to overestimate the power, influence, and utility of China in assisting US efforts to withdraw from Vietnam and to shore up international opposition to Soviet expansion. By so doing, they gave advantage to China in negotiations over contentious US-China issues regarding Taiwan and other disputes. Seeking sometimes unattainable advantages from improved relations with China, US leaders sacrificed relations with an ally, Taiwan, and treated relations with Japan and other Asian allies and associates in ways that subordinated those relations to US interests in improving relations with China. They also sacrificed attention to those US values and interests in Asian and world affairs that were inconsistent with a pragmatic pursuit of better ties with China.

The elitist approach of US leaders followed a pattern of secret diplomacy and deal making that undermined the US administration's credibility with the Congress and significant segments of the US media and public opinion. It also undermined the constitutionally mandated shared powers the executive and legislative branches hold in the conduct of US foreign policy. This experience established an atmosphere of suspicion and cynicism in American domestic politics over China policy and set the stage for often bitter and debilitating fights in US domestic politics over China policy in ensuing years that on balance are seen not to serve the overall national interests of the United States.[46]

The Pan-Asian Approach of George Shultz and Chinese Accommodation

Amid continued strong Chinese pressure tactics on a wide range of US-China disputes, US policy shifted with Haig's resignation in 1982 and the appointment of George Shultz as secretary of state. Reagan administration officers who were at odds with Haig's emphasis on the need for a solicitous US approach to China came to the fore. They were led by Paul Wolfowitz, who was chosen by Shultz as assistant secretary of state for East Asian affairs; Richard Armitage, the senior Defense Department officer managing relations with China and East Asia; and Gaston Sigur, the senior National Security Council staff aide on Asian affairs and later assistant secretary of state for East Asian affairs. While officers who had backed Haig's pro-China slant were transferred from authority over China policy, the new US leadership contingent with responsibility for East Asian affairs shifted US policy toward a less solicitous and accommodating stance toward China while giving much higher priority to US relations with Japan as well as other US allies and friends in East Asia. There was less emphasis on China's strategic importance to the United States in American competition with the Soviet Union, and there was less concern among US policy makers about China possibly downgrading relations over Taiwan and other disputes.[47]

The scholarship on the US opening to China that began in the Nixon administration, reviewed above, focuses on powerful strategic and domestic imperatives that drove the United States and China to cooperate in a pragmatic search for advantage for their respective national and leadership interests. It underlines the primacy of China in American foreign policy in Asia while relations with Japan and other East Asian allies and friends remained secondary and were sometimes viewed as declining assets or liabilities.[48]

Some scholars, often using a cost-benefit analysis seen in the realist school of thought, discern an important shift in US strategy toward China and in East Asia more broadly beginning in 1982.[49] The reevaluation of US policy toward China under Secretary of State Shultz is seen to bring to power officials who opposed the high priority on China in US strategy toward East Asia and the world and who gave much greater importance to US relations with Japan and other US allies in securing US interests amid prevailing conditions. The reevaluation on the whole is depicted as working to the advantage of the United States. It notably is seen to have added dimensions related to a changing balance of forces affecting Chinese security and other interests in Asian and world affairs, which prompted heretofore demanding Chinese leaders to reduce pressures on the United States for concessions on Taiwan and other disputed issues. The changes in Chinese policy helped open the way for several years of comparatively smooth US-China relations after a period of considerable discord in the late 1970s and early 1980s.

Other scholars also employ cost-benefit assessments, which are seen in the realist school of thought to explain the improvement in US-China relations at the time through analyses focused on the dynamics of US-China relations.[50] They discern US compromises and accommodations in negotiations and relations with China that assuaged Chinese demands and met Chinese interests over Taiwan and other issues. They tend to avoid analysis of how any shift in emphasis in US policy away from a focus on China and toward a greater emphasis on Japan and the East Asian region might have altered Chinese calculations and the overall dynamic in US interaction with China.

The analysis in the assessment detailed below supports the former view. It shows that the Chinese leaders grudgingly adjusted to the new US stance, viewing their interests best served by less pressure and more positive initiatives to the Reagan administration, seen especially in their warm welcome for the US president on his visit to China in 1984. Cooperative Chinese relations with the United States were critically important to the Chinese leadership in maintaining Chinese security in the face of continuing pressure from the Soviet Union and in sustaining the flow of aid, investment, and trade essential to the economic development and modernization underway in China—the linchpin of the Chinese Communist leadership's plans for sustaining its rule in China. Meanwhile, the Reagan leadership learned not to confront important Chinese interests over issues like Taiwan in overt and egregious ways, seeking to continue US military and other support for Taiwan in ways less likely to provoke strong Chinese reaction. Thus, the accommodations that characterized US-China relations in Reagan's second term in office were mutual, but they involved significant Chinese adjustments and changes influenced by the new posture toward China undertaken by Secretary of State Shultz and his colleagues.

In this author's assessment, the scholarship that portrays the improvement in US-China relations at that time as largely based on the dynamics of US-China relations seems too narrowly focused. In this scholarship, the United States is seen to make compromises in ways that accommodate Chinese interests and thus allow for smoother US-China relations. By limiting the focus to the dynamics of US-China ties, this scholarship seems to miss the importance of the shift in US emphasis during the tenure of George Shultz. Overall, that shift seems to have significantly enhanced US power and leverage over China in negotiations over Taiwan and other disputes and compelled China to make concessions on its part in order to ensure a positive relationship with the United States advantageous to Chinese interests. This changed dynamic, with the United States in a more commanding position vis-à-vis China, also was much more acceptable to congressional members, media, and others in US politics who had been alienated by the secrecy and perceived excessive US deference to China in the previous decade. It made executive-congressional relations over China policy much smoother than in the previous six years.

China's Shifting Strategic Calculus and the Importance of the United States

The significance of the shifts in American policy toward China and Asia undertaken during the tenure of Secretary Shultz and under the direction of such influential US officials as Wolfowitz, Armitage, and Sigur are shown below to be important for China's broader international calculations, influencing its approach toward the United States. Chinese foreign policy was strongly influenced by Chinese assessments in line with realist IR theory of the relative power and influence of the Soviet Union and the United States and the effects these had on key Chinese interests of security and development. Throughout much of the 1970s, China had been more vocal than the United States in warning of the dangers of expansion by the Soviet Union, seen as the greatest threat to China's security and integrity. Chinese officials and commentary depicted Soviet efforts to contain China in Asia through its military buildup and advanced nuclear ballistic missile deployments along the Sino-Soviet border, its deployments of mobile mechanized divisions in Mongolia, its stepped-up naval activity in the western Pacific along the China coast, its military presence in Vietnam, including active use of formerly US naval and air base facilities, and its ever-closer military relationship with India and growing involvement with and eventual invasion of Afghanistan. These Soviet actions were seen as part of a wider expansion of Soviet power and influence that China judged as needing to be countered by a united international front including China and led by the United States.[51]

For much of the 1970s, particularly after the resignation of President Nixon, Chinese officials and commentary saw the United States vacillate between a tough line toward the USSR and an approach seeking détente and accommodation with Moscow. Concern over US resolve toward Moscow saw China criticize Secretary of State Henry Kissinger for being too soft toward Moscow during the Ford administration, favoring instead the harder line advocated by Defense Secretary James Schlesinger. Carter administration officials like UN envoy Andrew Young, who took a moderate view toward Soviet-backed Cuban troop deployments and other Soviet expansion in Africa, were roundly criticized in Chinese media. More cautious official commentary registered reservations about Secretary of State Cyrus Vance's approach in seeking arms limitation talks with Moscow, while Chinese officials and commentary registered approval of National Security Adviser Brzezinski's tough anti-Soviet stance.[52]

Over time, and especially after the Soviet invasion of Afghanistan in late 1979, Chinese leaders began to recalculate the balance of forces affecting their interests and their respective approaches to the Soviet Union and the United States. The previous perceived danger that the United States would "appease" the Soviet Union and thereby allow Moscow to direct its pressure against China now appeared remote. Carter's last year in office and Reagan's initial stance toward the USSR saw a large increase in US defense spending and military preparations. Closely allied with the United States, European powers and Japan also were building forces and taking firm positions against the USSR. Meanwhile, increased complications and weaknesses affecting the power of the Soviet Union included problems of leadership succession, economic sustainability, and tensions in Poland and elsewhere in the Warsaw Pact. Faced with such adverse circumstances prior to his death in 1982, Brezhnev reached out with positive initiatives toward China, attempting to improve relations.[53]

Against this background, Chinese officials saw an ability to exert a freer hand in foreign affairs and to position China in a stance less aligned with the United States. The priority to stay close to the United States in order to encourage resolute US positions against Soviet expansion was no longer as important as in the recent past. Also, there were new opportunities to negotiate with Soviet leaders calling for talks. Beijing moved by 1981 to a posture more independent of the United States and less hostile toward the USSR. China's new "independent foreign policy" also featured a revival of Chinese relations with developing countries and in the international Communist movement, which had been neglected in favor of emphasis on the anti-Soviet front in the 1970s.[54]

However, the shift in Chinese policy away from the United States and somewhat closer to the Soviet Union did not work very well. Chinese leaders continued to speak of their new independent foreign policy approach, but they seemed to change their international calculations based on perceptions of shifts in the international balance of power affecting China. By 1983, Chinese leaders showed increasing concern about the stability of the nation's surroundings in Asia at a time of unrelenting buildup of Soviet military and political pressure along China's periphery and of serious and possibly prolonged decline in relations with the United States. They decided that the foreign policy tactics of the previous two years, designed to distance China from the policies of the United States and to moderate and improve Chinese relations with the Soviet Union, were less likely to safeguard the important Chinese security and development concerns affected by the stability of the Asian environment.[55]

The Chinese leaders appeared to recognize in particular that Beijing would have to stop its pullback from the United States for fear of jeopardizing this link, so important for maintaining its security and development interests in the face of persistent Soviet pressure in Asia. Thus, in 1983, Beijing began to retreat from some of the tactical changes made the previous two years under the rubric of an independent approach to foreign affairs. The result was a substantial reduction in Chinese pressure on the United States over Taiwan and other issues; increased Chinese interest and flexibility in dealing with the Reagan administration and other Western countries across a broad range of economic, political, and security issues; and heightened Sino-Soviet antipathy. Beijing still attempted to nurture whenever possible the increased influence it had garnered by means of its independent posture among developing countries and the international Communist movement, but it increasingly sided with the West against the USSR in order to secure basic strategic and economic interests.[56]

A key element in China's decision to change tactics toward the United States was an altered view of the likely course of Sino-American-Soviet relations over the next several years. When China began its more independent approach to foreign affairs and its concurrent harder line toward the United States in 1981–82, it had hoped to elicit a more forthcoming US attitude toward issues sensitive to Chinese interests, notably Taiwan. Beijing probably judged that there could be serious risks of alienating the United States, which had provided an implicit but vital counterweight serving Chinese security interests against the USSR for more than a decade and was assisting more recent Chinese economic development concerns. But the Chinese seemed to have assessed that their room to maneuver had been increased for the following reasons:

- The United States had reasserted a balance in East-West relations likely to lead to a continued major check on possible Soviet expansion. Chinese worries about US "appeasement" of the USSR seemed a thing of the past.
- The Soviet ability to pressure China had appeared to be at least temporarily blocked by US power, the determination of various US allies to thwart Soviet expansion, and Soviet domestic and international problems. China added to Soviet difficulties by cooperating with the United States in clandestine operations supporting fighters resisting the Soviet occupation of Afghanistan.
- At least some important US leaders, notably Secretary of State Alexander Haig and his subordinates in the State Department, continued to consider preserving and developing good US relations with China as a critically important element in US efforts to confront and contain Soviet expansion.[57]

By mid-1983, China saw these calculations upset. In particular, the United States under Secretary of State Shultz adopted a new posture that was seen to publicly downgrade China's strategic importance. The adjustment in the US position occurred after the resignation of Haig, perhaps the strongest advocate in the Reagan administration of sustaining good relations with China as an important strategic means to counter the USSR. Secretary Shultz and such subordinates as Paul Wolfowitz were less identified with this approach. Shultz held a series of meetings with government and nongovernmental Asian specialists in Washington in early 1983 to review US Asian policy in general and policy toward China in particular. The results of the reassessment—implicitly but clearly downgrading China's importance to the United States—were reflected in speeches by Shultz and Wolfowitz later in the year.[58]

US planners now appeared to judge that efforts to improve relations with China were less important than in the recent past for the following reasons:

- China seemed less likely to cooperate further with the United States (e.g., through military sales or security cooperation against the Soviet Union at a time when the PRC had publicly distanced itself from the United States and had reopened talks on normalization with the USSR).

- At the same time, China's continued preoccupation with pragmatic economic modernization and internal development made it appear unlikely that the PRC would revert to a highly disruptive position in East Asia that would adversely affect US interests in the stability of the region.

- China's demands on Taiwan and a wide variety of other bilateral disputes, and the accompanying threats to downgrade US-China relations if its demands were not met, seemed open-ended and excessive.

- US ability to deal militarily and politically with the USSR from a position of greater strength had improved, particularly as a result of the large-scale Reagan administration military budget increases and perceived serious internal and international difficulties of the USSR.

- US allies, for the first time in years, were working more closely with Washington in dealing with the Soviet military threat. This was notably true in Asia, where Prime Minister Yasuhiro Nakasone took positions and initiatives underlining common Japanese-US concerns against the Soviet danger, setting the foundation for the close "Ron-Yasu" relationship between the US and Japanese leaders.

- Japan and US allies and friends in Southeast Asia—unlike China—appeared to be more important to the United States in protecting against what was seen as the primary US strategic concern in the region—safeguarding air and sea access to East Asia, the Indian Ocean, and the Persian Gulf from Soviet attack. China appeared less important in dealing with this perceived Soviet danger.[59]

Western press reports quoting authoritative sources in Washington alerted China to the implications of this shift in the US approach for PRC interests. In effect, the shift seemed to mean that Chinese ability to exploit US interest in strategic relations with China against the Soviet Union was reduced, as was US interest in avoiding disruptions caused by China and other negative consequences that flowed from a downgrading of China's relations with the United States. Chinese ability to use these facets in order to compel the United States to meet Chinese demands on Taiwan and other questions seemed less than in the recent past. Underlining these trends for China was the continued unwillingness of the United States throughout this period to accommodate high-level PRC pressure over Taiwan, the asylum case of Chinese tennis player Hu Na, the Chinese representation issue in the Asian Development Bank, and other questions. The Reagan administration publicly averred that US policy would remain constant whether or not Beijing decided to retaliate or threatened to downgrade relations by withdrawing its ambassador from Washington or some other action.[60]

Moreover, Chinese commentary and discussions with Chinese officials suggested that Beijing perceived its leverage in the United States to have diminished at the time. Chinese media duly noted the strong revival in the US economy in 1983 and the positive political implications this had for President Reagan's reelection campaign. China also had to be aware, through contacts with leading Democrats, notably House of Representatives Speaker Tip O'Neill, who visited China that same year, that Beijing could expect little change in US policy toward Taiwan under a Democratic administration. As 1983 wore on, the Chinese saw what for them was an alarming rise in the influence of US advocates of self-determination for Taiwan among liberal Democrats. In particular, Senator Claiborne Pell took the lead in gaining passage of a controversial resolution in the Senate Foreign Relations Committee that endorsed, among other things, the principle of self-determination for Taiwan—anathema to Beijing.[61]

Meanwhile, although Sino-Soviet trade, cultural, and technical contacts were increasing, Beijing saw few signs of Soviet willingness to compromise on basic political and security issues during vice-ministerial talks on normalizing Sino-Soviet relations that began in October 1982. And the Soviet military buildup in Asia—including the deployment of highly accurate SS-20 intermediate-range ballistic missiles—continued.[62]

In short, if Beijing continued its demands and harder line against the United States of the previous two years, pressed the United States on various issues, and risked downgrading relations, it faced the prospect of a period of prolonged decline in Sino-American relations—possibly lasting until the end of Reagan's second presidential term. This decline brought the risk of cutting off the implicit but vitally important Chinese strategic understanding with the United States in the face of a prolonged danger to China posed by the USSR.

The Chinese also recognized that a substantial decline in Chinese relations with the United States would have undercut their already limited leverage with Moscow; it probably would have reduced Soviet interest in accommodating China in order to preclude closer US-China security ties or collaboration against the USSR. It also would have run the risk of upsetting China's ability to gain greater access not only to US markets and financial and technical expertise but also to those of other important capitalist countries. Now that the Chinese economy was successfully emerging from some retrenchments and adjustments undertaken in 1981–82, the Western economic connection seemed more important to PRC planners. Yet many US allies and friends, especially Japan, were more reluctant to undertake heavy economic involvement in China at a time of uncertain US-China political relations. The United States also exerted strong influence in international financial institutions that were expected to be the source of several billions of dollars of much-needed aid for China in the 1980s.

China also had to calculate as well that a serious decline in US-China relations would likely result in a concurrent increase in US-Taiwan relations. As a result, Beijing's chances of using Taiwan's isolation from the United States to prompt Taipei to move toward reunification in accord with PRC interests would be seriously set back.

The deliberations of Chinese policy makers regarding maneuvers between the United States and the Soviet Union during this period remain shrouded in secrecy. Given the upswing in Chinese public as well as private pressure against the United States during the early years of the Reagan administration over Taiwan arms sales and many other areas of dispute, any backing away from a firm line toward the United States on Taiwan and other sensitive issues almost certainly represented a difficult compromise for those leaders who had pushed this approach in 1981–82.

Unlike in the case of the United States, there was no concurrent major change in China's foreign affairs leadership, which ultimately depended on the attentive direction of strong-man ruler Deng Xiaoping. Deng appeared to have a freer hand to shift policy in foreign affairs than in the complicated mix of domestic politics at the time. Thus, for example, he was able to decide to shelve the sensitive territorial dispute of the Diaoyu/Senkaku Islands during negotiations with Japan over a peace treaty in 1978, and he allowed the agreement on normalization of relations with the United States to go forward that year despite the US intention to continue arms sales to Taiwan. Deng endorsed the most sensitive clandestine Chinese arms sale on record—the transfer of more than thirty intermediate-range nuclear-capable ballistic missiles to Saudi Arabia in the early 1980s, at a time when China also was transferring nuclear weapons technology and assistance that allowed Pakistan to develop and test a credible nuclear deterrent in the 1990s. Against this background, Deng seemed to have the domestic political standing to carry out the adjustment and moderation in China's approach to the United States without serious negative implications. No matter what might have taken place behind the scenes in Chinese decision making with regard to policy toward the United States and the Soviet Union at the time, Chinese officials did in fact pull back from pressing American leaders. The routine harangues on Taiwan and other differences that greeted senior Reagan administration visitors on the initial meetings in Beijing dropped off. Chinese leaders worked harder to curry favor with President Reagan and his associates.[63]

Moderation toward the United States

Appearing anxious to moderate past demands and improve relations with the United States, the Chinese responded positively to the latest in a series of Reagan administration efforts to ease technology transfer restrictions—announced by Commerce Secretary Malcolm Baldridge during a trip to China in May 1983. The Chinese followed up by agreeing to schedule the long-delayed visit by Secretary of Defense Caspar Weinberger in September and to exchange visits by Premier Zhao Ziyang, a Chinese senior leader, and President Reagan at the turn of the year. Not to appear too anxious to improve relations with China, Reagan administration officials were successful in getting Premier Zhao Ziyang to visit Washington for a summit in January 1984 before the US president would agree to go to China later that year.

Beijing media attempted to portray these moves as Chinese responses to US concessions and as consistent with China's avowed "independent" approach in foreign affairs and its firm stance on US-China differences over Taiwan and other issues. But as time went on, it became clear just how much Beijing was prepared to moderate past public demands and threats of retaliation over Taiwan and other issues for the sake of consolidating Sino-American political, economic, and security ties:[64]

- In 1981, Beijing had publicly disavowed any interest in military purchases from the United States until the United States satisfied China's position on the sale of arms to Taiwan. It continued to note that it was dissatisfied with US arms transfers to Taiwan after the August 1982 communiqué, which continued at a pace of more than $700 million a year, but it now was willing to negotiate with the United States over Chinese purchases of US military equipment.
- Beijing muffled previous demands that the United States alter its position regarding Taiwan's continued membership in the Asian Development Bank.
- China reduced criticism of official and unofficial US contacts with Taiwan counterparts. It notably avoided criticism of US officials being present at Taipei-sponsored functions in Washington. Beijing was even willing to turn a blind eye to the almost thirty members of Congress who traveled to Taiwan in various delegations in January 1984—coincident with Zhao Ziyang's trip to Washington. It even welcomed some of the members who traveled on to the mainland after visiting Taiwan.

- Beijing allowed Northwest Airlines to open service to China in 1984, even though the airline still served Taiwan. This was in marked contrast with the authoritative and negative Chinese position adopted in 1983 in response to Pan American World Airways' decision to reenter the Taiwan market while also serving the mainland.
- China reduced complaints about the slowness of US transfers of technology to China and about the continued inability of the administration to successfully push through legislative changes that would have allowed the Chinese to receive American assistance.[65]

China's greatest compromise was to give a warm welcome to President Reagan, despite his continued avowed determination to maintain close US ties with "old friends" on Taiwan. Visits by Speaker O'Neill and others made clear to China the importance of the China visit in serving to assist the US president's reelection bid in the fall. Chinese leaders also understood that the president was unlikely to accommodate China interests over Taiwan and some other sensitive issues during the visit. Indeed, Chinese reportage made clear that there was no change in the president's position on the Taiwan issue during the visit. Thus it appears that the best the Chinese hoped for was to try to consolidate US-PRC relations in order to secure broader strategic and economic interests while possibly expecting that such a closer relationship over time would reduce the president's firm position on Taiwan and other bilateral disputes.

The Reagan administration, meanwhile, attempted to add impetus to the relationship by accommodating Chinese concerns through the avoidance of strong rhetorical support for Taiwan that in the past had so inflamed US-PRC tensions and by moving ahead on military and technology transfers to the PRC. Nevertheless, when the US-China nuclear cooperation agreement, which had been initialed during the president's visit, became stalled because of opposition from nonproliferation advocates in the United States who were concerned about reports of China's support for Pakistan's nuclear weapons program, China went along with administration explanations of their inability to reverse the adverse situation with only minor complaint.[66]

In short, by mid-1984 it appeared that, at a minimum, Beijing was determined to further strengthen military and economic ties with the United States and to soft-pedal bilateral differences that had been stressed earlier in the decade. On the question of Taiwan, Beijing retreated to a position that asked for US adherence to the joint communiqué and accelerated reductions of US arms sales to Taiwan, but Chinese leaders were not prepared to make a significant issue of what they saw as US noncompliance unless they were seriously provoked. This meant giving lower priority to Chinese complaints about President Reagan's interpretations of the communiqué at odds with China's position and lower priority to Chinese complaints over the US president's continued strong determination to support US interests in helping the defense of Taiwan. The new Chinese position also meant downplaying Chinese criticism of methods used by the United States to calculate the value of arms sales to Taiwan at high levels, thereby allowing more than a half billion dollars of US sales to the island's armed forces for years to come. It also meant that China chose not to contest vigorously the ultimately successful maneuvers used by Taiwan and US defense manufacturers that allowed the United States to support, through commercial transfers of equipment, technology, and expertise, the development of a new group of more than one hundred new jet fighters, the so-called indigenous fighter aircraft, for the Taiwan air force.[67]

Continued Sino-Soviet Differences

China's incentive to accommodate the United States was reinforced by Beijing's somber view of Sino-Soviet relations. China appeared disappointed with its inability to elicit substantial Soviet concessions—or even a slowing in the pace of Soviet military expansion in Asia—during the brief administration of Yuri Andropov (d. 1984). Beijing saw the succeeding government of Konstantin Chernenko (d. 1985) as even more rigid and uncompromising. In response, China hardened its line and highlighted public complaints against Soviet pressure and intimidation—an approach that had the added benefit of broadening common ground between China and the West, especially the strongly anti-Soviet Reagan administration.[68]

The Sino-Soviet vice-ministerial talks on normalizing relations were revived in October 1982 following their cancelation as a result of the Soviet invasion of Afghanistan in late 1979. These talks were unable to bridge a major gap between the positions of the two sides on basic security and political issues. Beijing stuck to its preconditions for improved Sino-Soviet relations involving withdrawal of Soviet forces from along the Sino-Soviet border and from Mongolia (later China added specific reference to Soviet SS-20 missiles targeted against China), an end to Soviet support for Vietnam's military occupation of Cambodia, and withdrawal of Soviet forces from Afghanistan.[69]

In part to get around this roadblock, a second forum of vice-foreign ministerial discussions began in September 1983. The discussions covered each side's views of recent developments in the Middle East, Central America, the Indian Ocean, Afghanistan, and Indochina; concerns over arms control, including the deployment of SS-20 missiles in Asia; and other questions. No agreement was noted.

Progress in both sets of talks came only in secondary areas of trade, technology transfers, and educational and cultural exchanges. Both sides attempted to give added impetus to progress in these areas coincident with the exchange of high-level Sino-American visits in early 1984. In particular, Moscow proposed and Beijing accepted a visit to China by First Deputy Prime Minister Ivan Arkhipov. The visit was timed to occur just after President Reagan's departure from China in early May 1984. It was postponed on account of rising Sino-Soviet frictions.

Chernenko's leadership went out of its way to publicize strong support for Mongolia and Vietnam against China and underlined Soviet unwillingness to make compromises with China at the expense of third countries. Beijing also saw Moscow as resorting to stronger military means in both Europe and Asia in order to assert Soviet power and determination against China and others. In February and March, the Soviet Union deployed two of its three aircraft carriers to the western Pacific; one passed near China in late February on its way to Vladivostok. And in March, the USSR used an aircraft carrier task force to support its first joint amphibious exercise with Vietnam, which was conducted fairly close to China and near the Vietnamese port city of Haiphong. This followed the reported stationing of several Soviet medium-range bombers at Cam Ranh Bay, Vietnam, in late 1983—the first time Soviet forces were reported to be stationed outside areas contiguous with the USSR.

Meanwhile, the Chinese escalated their artillery barrages and other military pressure against the Vietnamese—taking their strongest action precisely at the time of President Reagan's visit to China in late April and early May 1984. Beijing at the same time escalated charges regarding the Soviet threat to Chinese security, especially via Vietnam, and attempted to establish publicly an identity of interests with both Japanese prime minister Nakasone, during a visit to China in March, and President Reagan in April–May, on the basis of opposition to Soviet expansion in Asia. The result was the most serious downturn in Sino-Soviet relations since the Soviet invasion of Afghanistan in late 1979.

THE SUCCESS OF THE US–PAN-ASIAN APPROACH TO CHINA

In sum, the record of developments in China's approach toward and relations with the United States and the Soviet Union in 1983 and 1984 show that the pan-Asian approach adopted by Secretary of State George Shultz and the senior officials responsible for Asian affairs during this period of the Reagan administration worked effectively in support of American interests in policy toward China in several important ways. It notably played into an array of concerns and uncertainties in Chinese foreign policy calculations and interests, causing the Chinese leaders to shift to a more accommodating posture toward the United States—a posture that played down issues that in the recent past had threatened, according to Chinese officials, to force China to take steps to downgrade US-China relations. US officials made sure their Chinese counterparts understood that the United States was no longer as anxious, as evident in the first decade of Sino-American rapprochement and normalization, to seek China's favor in improving Sino-American relations as a source of leverage against Moscow. The United States was increasingly confident in its strategic position vis-à-vis the Soviet Union and had begun a process to roll back the gains the Soviets had made in the previous decade in various parts of the developing world. It was China that appeared to face greater difficulties posed by Soviet military buildup and expansion. China needed the US relationship as a counterweight to this Soviet posture, and it increasingly needed a good relationship with the United States to allow for smooth and advantageous Chinese economic interchange with the developed countries of the West and Japan and the international financial institutions they controlled.

Under the circumstances, the Chinese leaders grudgingly adjusted to the new US stance, viewing their interests best served by less pressure and more positive overtures to the Reagan administration, seen notably in their warm welcome of the US president on his visit to China in 1984. As noted above, some scholarship portrays the improvement in US-China relations at the time largely through dynamics in US-China relations. This scholarship seems to miss the importance of the shift in US emphasis during the tenure of George Shultz, which enhanced US power and leverage over China in negotiations over Taiwan and other disputes. Facing unrelenting Soviet pressure and the danger of loss of needed engagement with the United States, China was compelled to make concessions in order to ensure a positive relationship with the United States. Placing the United States in a more commanding position vis-à-vis China was much more acceptable to congressional members, media, and others in US politics that had been alienated by the secrecy and perceived excessive US deference to China in the previous decade. It set the stage for relatively smooth US domestic politics over China policy for the remainder of the Reagan administration.

STUDY QUESTIONS

1. What motivated US and Chinese leaders to seek and achieve a breakthrough in relations during the rule of Richard Nixon and Mao Zedong?
2. Why was Nixon's opening to China widely welcomed in Congress and by US public opinion, while Carter's agreement officially normalizing relations received substantially less support?

3. How did Congress influence US relations with China and Taiwan through the Taiwan Relations Act and other means?
4. Why was China unsuccessful in pressing for a ban on US arms sales to Taiwan?
5. Was the "pan-Asian" approach of Secretary of State George Shultz more in line with US interests than the "China-first" approach followed by previous US governments since Nixon?

RELEVANT VIDEOS

"Eleanor Roosevelt: China Shadow on the Summit" (filmed discussion about China's role in world affairs, 1960, one hour) available at https://www.worldcat.org/title/prospects-of-mankind-with-eleanor-roosevelt-china-shadow-on-the-summit/oclc/8647213074&referer=brief_results

"The Shadow Circus: The CIA in Tibet" (documentary film, 2000, fifty minutes) available at https://www.worldcat.org/title/the-shadow-circus-the-cia-in-tibet/oclc/8646422926&referer=brief_results

"Nixon in China" (CSPAN, forty-five minutes) available at https://www.c-span.org/video/?507382-1/nixon-china

"United States and China" (filmstrip, 1972, thirteen minutes) available at https://www.worldcat.org/title/united-states-and-china/oclc/5547355&referer=brief_results

"China Today: Swings in Foreign Policy" (filmstrip, 1984, seventeen minutes) available at https://www.worldcat.org/title/china-today-swings-in-foreign-policy/oclc/10544344&referer=brief_results

Chapter Five

Tiananmen, Taiwan, and Post–Cold War Realities, 1989–2000

COLLAPSE OF US POLICY CONSENSUS AND EMERGING DOMESTIC DEBATE ON CHINA

Unexpected mass demonstrations centered in Beijing's Tiananmen Square and other Chinese cities in spring 1989 represented the most serious challenge to China's post-Mao leadership. Deng Xiaoping was decisive in resolving Chinese leadership differences in favor of hard-liners who supported a violent crackdown on the demonstrators and broader suppression of political dissent that began with the bloody attack on Tiananmen Square on June 4, 1989. Reform-minded leaders were purged and punished.[1]

Anticipating shock over and disapproval of the Tiananmen crackdown from the United States and the West, Deng nonetheless argued that the negative reaction would have few prolonged adverse consequences for China. The Chinese leader failed to anticipate the breadth and depth of US disapproval that would profoundly influence US policy into the twenty-first century. American public opinion of China's government dropped sharply. The US media switched coverage and opinion of China, portraying the policies and practices of the Chinese rulers in a much more critical light than in the years leading up to Tiananmen. Subsequently, American and Chinese specialists continued to see US and Western media remaining focused on the negative in reporting and commentary that deals with the Chinese government. US leaders were shocked by the brutal display of power by China's authoritarian leaders. Expectations of rapid Chinese political reform dropped; they were replaced by outward hostility at first, followed by often wary pragmatism about the need for greater US engagement with the Chinese government as it rose in prominence in Asian and world affairs. The US engagement was tempered by a private suspicion of the longer-term intentions of the Chinese rulers, which remained a prominent feature of US expectations of China into the next century.[2]

The negative impact of the Tiananmen crackdown on the American approach to China was compounded by the unforeseen and dramatic collapse of Communist regimes in the Soviet bloc and other areas, leading to the demise of the Soviet Union in 1991. These developments undermined the perceived need for the United States to cooperate pragmatically with China, despite its brutal dictatorship, on account of a US strategic need for international support against the Soviet Union. The Soviet collapse also destroyed the strategic focus of American foreign policy during the Cold War. The ability of the US president to use Cold War imperatives to override pluralistic US domestic interests seeking to influence American foreign policy declined. A variety of existing and emerging American interest groups focused on China's authoritarian regime in strongly negative ways, endeavoring to push US policy toward a harder line against China. Meanwhile, Taiwan's authoritarian government at that time was moving steadily to promote democratic policies and practices, marking a sharp contrast to the harsh political regime in mainland China and greatly enhancing Taiwan's popularity and support in the United States.[3]

Taken together, these circumstances generally placed the initiative in US-China relations with US leaders and broader forces in the United States. Chinese leaders at first focused on maintaining internal stability as they maneuvered to sustain workable economic relations with the United States and other developed countries while rebuffing major US and other Western-led initiatives that infringed on Chinese internal political control or territorial and sovereignty issues involving Taiwan, Tibet, and Hong Kong. Leadership debate about how open China should be to promoting economic reform at home and how welcoming China should be to economic interchange with the West as it consolidated authoritarian rule at home appeared to be resolved following Deng Xiaoping's tour of southern China in 1992. Deng urged continued rigorous economic reform and opening to the benefits of foreign trade, investments, and technology transfer. Beginning in 1993, as the Chinese government presided over strong economic growth, and the US and other international attention that came with it, Chinese leaders reflected more confidence as they dealt with US pressures for change. However, the Chinese leaders generally eschewed direct confrontation that would endanger the critically important economic relations with the United States unless China was provoked by US, Taiwanese, or other actions.[4]

US policy in the decade after Tiananmen worked explicitly against the central interest of the Chinese leadership to sustain the rule of the Communist Party in China (CCP). Even when US government leaders emphasized a pragmatic policy of engagement with China's leaders, they often used rationales that the engagement would lead to the demise of the authoritarian CCP rule. US policy also increased support for Taiwan, for the interests of the Dalai Lama in Tibet, and for forces in Hong Kong seen as critical of Chinese government goals and threatening to the overall territorial integrity and sovereignty of China. The United States also was in the lead in criticizing a range of Chinese foreign policies; it was seen to be strengthening strategic and other pressures on China through the reinforcement of US military relations with Japan and other allies and the improvement of American military as well as political and economic relations with other nations around China's periphery. In response, Chinese leaders and broader public opinion saw US policy and intentions in a negative way.[5]

Over time, years of pragmatic Sino-American engagement policies and generally positive treatment of the United States in state-controlled Chinese media in the first decade of the twenty-first century resulted in an improvement in Chinese public opinion about the United States. Privately, Chinese leaders were reported to remain deeply wary and suspicious of the policies and intentions of the United States. Strong public Chinese antipathy toward the United States and US policy and practice toward China also showed from time to time, over sensitive issues or during times of crisis in US-China relations.[6]

Although American leaders held the initiative in relations with China during the years after the Tiananmen incident, they had a hard time creating and implementing an effective and integrated policy. Coherent US policy toward China proved elusive in the midst of contentious American domestic debate over China policy during the 1990s. That debate was not stilled until the September 11, 2001, terrorist attack on America muffled continued US concerns over China amid an overwhelming American concern to deal with the immediate, serious, and broad consequences of the global war on terrorism.[7]

In the aftermath of Tiananmen, President George H. W. Bush tried to keep China policy under his control and to move US relations with China in directions he deemed constructive. Yet he and his administration were repeatedly criticized by Congress, the media, and organized groups with differing interests in policy toward the People's Republic of China (PRC) but with an agreed emphasis on a harder US approach to China. In this atmosphere, Bush's more pragmatic approach to China became a distinct liability for the president, notably during his failed reelection campaign in 1992.[8]

President Bill Clinton entered office on an election platform critical of the "butchers of Beijing." His administration developed a clear stance linking Chinese behavior regarding human rights issues with US trade benefits to China. Majorities in Congress and many nongovernmental groups and the media favored this position. However, the policy came under increasing pressure from other groups and their allies in both Congress and the administration who were strongly concerned with US business interests in relation to China's rising market. The opposition prompted President Clinton to end the policy of linkage in May 1994.[9]

The president's decision did not end the battle for influence over China policy on the part of competing US interest groups and their supporters in the Congress and the administration. Pro-Taiwan interests mobilized in early 1995 to change US policy in order to allow the Taiwan president to travel to the United States in a private capacity. After senior US officials assured China that no visa would be granted, President Clinton decided to allow the visit. His reversal triggered a major crisis and military face-off between the United States and China over Taiwan in 1995–96. There were periodic live-fire Chinese military exercises in the Taiwan Strait, including tests of short-range Chinese ballistic missiles, over a period of nine months beginning in mid-1995 and culminating in large exercises coincident with Taiwan's first direct election of its president in March 1996. The US government did little in public reaction to the exercises at first, but by 1996 senior US leaders privately, and eventually publicly, strongly warned Chinese leaders against them. In the end, the United States sent two aircraft carrier battle groups to the Taiwan area to face off against the perceived Chinese military provocations during the Taiwan presidential elections.[10]

Seeking to restore calm and avoid repetition of dangerous crises with China, the Clinton administration accommodated Chinese interests as US policy shifted to a strong emphasis on pragmatic engagement with China, highlighted by US-China summits in Washington and Beijing in 1997 and 1998, respectively. Through often difficult negotiations, the United States and China were able to reach agreement in late 1999, leading to China's entry into the World Trade Organization (WTO). Related to this accord, the Clinton administration secured congressional passage of a law granting China the trading status of Permanent Normal Trade Relations (PNTR) in 2000. The law removed the previous annual legal requirement for the president to publicly notify Congress of his intention to seek most favored nation (MFN) status for American trade with China and for the president's notification to be subject to possible legislation of disapproval by Congress. That legal requirement provided the focus of annual and often raucous congressional debates over the pros and cons of harsher US measures against China in the years after the Tiananmen crackdown.[11]

Clinton's policy shift toward engagement with China met strong opposition in Congress and the media and among nongovernment groups pressing for a harder policy. As for China, the US bombing of the Chinese embassy in Belgrade in May 1999 saw the Chinese government react by directing mass demonstrations that destroyed or severely damaged US diplomatic properties in Beijing and other cities. Beijing leaders also openly debated their continued emphasis on engagement with the United States, eventually coming to the conclusion that shifting to a more confrontational Chinese approach against US "hegemonism" was not in the overall interests of the Chinese administration.[12]

Those seeking to use international relations (IR) theory to understand the complicated dynamics in American policy toward China in the decade after the Tiananmen suppression of 1989 are urged to avoid emphasizing just one theory. Instead, it is important to consider various schools of thought in order to contextualize various determinants and offer a comprehensive view of the complex situation.

Liberalism helps explain the massive disappointment and hostility directed at China's rulers by American elite and public opinion following the crackdown at Tiananmen. In particular, liberalism captures the previous widespread American belief that post-Mao China's movement toward freer market economic policies and greater engagement with the West would be accompanied by social and political pluralism in line with liberal expectations. Those expectations were grievously undermined by the Tiananmen crackdown, resulting in the negative backlash in US opinion. Meanwhile, while President Clinton's motives remain unclear, he justified his policy reversal in seeking compromise and closer engagement with China after the Taiwan Straits crisis on the assumption that such engagement would lead to social and political pluralism in line with liberal thinking. US companies keenly interested in the growing China market also justified their support for continuing MFN tariff status for China on the argument that sustaining MFN treatment for China would lead to growing Sino-US economic relations that in turn would result in political pluralism in China, as forecast by liberal theory.

Realism played an important role in the determination of President George H. W. Bush and his senior aides to sustain workable relations with China, as China was seen as a major power and one of increasing international importance. Unfortunately for coherence in US foreign policy, realism also influenced those calling for sanctions and punishment of China after Tiananmen. Many such advocates used the realist argument that the demise of the Soviet Union and other Communist states meant that the United States no longer needed China's favor to offset the USSR and its allies. In this view, the reality of power in world affairs saw the US superpower ascendant, with little need to accommodate gross offenses like the Tiananmen suppression.

Constructivism helps explain the massive gap between the American identity and the Chinese identity that developed after Tiananmen. The bloody crackdown against unarmed demonstrators was anathema for most Americans, more than justifying rigorous sanctions and punishments in response. The American response focused directly on the most important priority of the Chinese government: the preservation of CCP rule. To counter the pressure, the Chinese rulers appealed to a well-developed sense of Chinese identity as a people and society of tremendous achievement that, in weakness since the nineteenth century, was subjected to various unfair modes of oppression by arrogant foreign powers. Beijing worked effectively to portray

the strident American polemics and sanctions as the latest in a long series
of foreign affronts going back to the first Opium War and the beginning of
China's gross victimization at the hands of evil foreign powers.

Post–Cold War Imperatives and American Debate over China Policy

Understanding the changes in US policy toward China in the 1990s requires
going beyond the Tiananmen crackdown and other immediate issues in
US-China relations to assess the implications of the post–Cold War debate
in US foreign policy. Because security issues and opposition to Soviet
expansion no longer drove US foreign policy, economic interests, democratization abroad, and human rights were among concerns that gained greater
prominence in American foreign policy. Various US advocacy groups and
institutions interested in these and other foreign policy concerns also showed
greater influence in policy making, including policy making with regard to
China. Historically, such fluidity and competition among priorities had more
often than not been the norm in American foreign policy making. As noted
in chapters 2 and 3, Woodrow Wilson and Franklin Roosevelt both set forth
comprehensive concepts of a well-integrated US foreign policy, but neither
framework lasted long. The requirements of the Cold War were much more
effective in establishing rigor and order in US foreign policy priorities. The
influence of these requirements in driving US interest in rapprochement and
normalization with China was described in chapter 4. By the 1990s, that
era was over.

In its place was a changed array of forces influencing American foreign
policy in general and policy toward China in particular. There was a shift
away from the elitism of the past and toward much greater pluralism. This
increased the opportunity for inputs by nongovernmental groups, including
lobby groups with interests in foreign policy, notably policy toward China.[13]

The elitist model of American foreign policy making that prevailed through
much of the Cold War included the following characteristics:

- Domination of the process by the executive branch, particularly by the
  White House, the State Department, and the Pentagon.
- Presidential consultation with a bipartisan leadership in Congress and
  mobilization through them of broad congressional support for the
  administration's foreign policy.
- Parallel consultations with a relatively small group of elites outside government, some of whom were specialists on the particular issue under
  consideration and others of whom had a more general interest in foreign
  policy as a whole.

- Mobilization of public support through major newspapers and television programs, other media outlets, and civic organizations.[14]

This process transformed in much more pluralistic directions and took on quite different characteristics following the 1980s:

- A much greater range of agencies within the executive branch became involved in foreign policy, with the rise of economic agencies (Commerce, Treasury, and US Trade Representative) of particular importance.
- A reallocation of power within the government, moving away from dominance by the executive branch and giving more power to Congress.
- Much greater participation of nongovernmental organizations including lobbying groups, which attempted to shape foreign policy to conform to their interests.
- Much less consensus within Congress and within the broader American public over the direction of US foreign policy.

Among divergent American views about foreign policy in the post–Cold War period were three discernable schools of thought.[15] The first school was in line with realism in IR theory and stressed the relative decline in US power and its implications for US ability to protect its interests abroad. It called for the United States to work harder to preserve important interests while adjusting to limited resources and reduced influence. This school of thought—reflected in the commentary of such leaders as George H. W. Bush, Henry Kissinger, and others—argued that these circumstances required the United States to work closely with traditional allies and associates. In Asia, it saw that not to preserve long-standing good relations with Japan and other allies and friends whose security policies and political-cultural orientations complemented US interests was inconsistent with US goals. It urged caution in policy toward other regional powers—Russia, China, and India. All three countries were preoccupied with internal development issues and did not appear to want regional instability. All sought closer economic and political relations with the West and with other advancing economies. Washington would be well advised, according to this view, to work closely with these governments wherever there were common interests. In considering US assets available to influence regional trends, proponents of this view called on the United States to go slow in reducing its regional military presence.[16]

A second school of thought argued for major cutbacks in US international activity, including military involvement, and a renewed focus on solving domestic American problems. Variations of this view were seen in the writings of William Hyland, Patrick Buchanan, and other well-known commentators of the time and in the political statements of the independent candidate in the 1992 presidential election, Ross Perot. Often called an "America First" or "Neo-isolationist" school, it also was in line with realism in IR theory, though it stressed different elements than the first school of thought noted above. Rather, it contended that the United States had become over-extended in world affairs and was being taken advantage of in the current world security-economic system. It called for sweeping cuts in spending for international activities, favoring US pullback from foreign bases and major cuts in foreign assistance and foreign technical-information programs. Some in this school favored trade measures that were seen as protectionist by US trading partners.[17]

A third school of thought seemed to combine elements of liberalism with realism and a strong American identity in line with constructivism. It argued for policy that would promote more vigorously US interests in international political, military, and economic affairs and would use US influence to pressure countries that do not conform to the US-backed norms on an appropriate world order. Supporters of this stance wanted the United States to maintain military forces with worldwide capabilities, to lead strongly in world affairs, and to minimize compromise and accommodation in promoting American interests and values.

Those who supported this view perceived a global power vacuum, caused mainly by the collapse of the Soviet empire, which allowed the United States to exert greater influence.[18] In the immediate post–Cold War years, some advocates of this third view were most vocal in pressing for a strong US policy in support of democracy and human rights. They opposed economic or trading policies of other countries seen as inequitable or predatory. They pressed for a strong policy against proliferation of weapons of mass destruction. Members of this school also argued variously for sanctions against countries that practiced coercive birth control, seriously polluted the environment, harbored terrorists, or promoted the drug trade. Proponents of this view came from both the left and the right in the American political spectrum. In Congress, they included conservative Republican Newt Gingrich and liberal Democrat Nancy Pelosi, both of whom would serve as speaker of the US House of Representatives.

As far as US policy toward China was concerned during the 1990s, advocates of the third group—proponents of active US leadership and international intervention—were forceful in calling for policies opposing Chinese human rights violations, weapons proliferation, and protective trade practices. They pressed Beijing to meet US-supported international norms and called for retaliatory economic and other sanctions. By contrast, the more cautious and accommodating first group believed that the advocates of strong assertion of US values and norms were unrealistic about US power and were unwilling to make needed compromises with the Chinese government in order to (1) protect and support US interests and regional stability and (2) avoid strategic enmity.[19]

As the decade wore on, it was unclear what approach to China would prevail in US policy. Some in the George H. W. Bush and Clinton administrations advocated a moderate, less confrontational policy of "engagement" with China for fear that doing otherwise could, among other things, promote divisions in—and a possible breakup of—China, with potentially adverse consequences for US interests in Asian stability and prosperity. Impressed by subsequent growth in Chinese economic and national strength later in the decade, many US officials, business interests, and others sought opportunities in closer economic and other relations with China. They also promoted engagement in order to guide China's power into channels of international activity compatible with American interests.

A tougher approach was supported by US officials and advocates outside the US government who stressed that China's leaders were biding their time and conforming to many international norms in order to avoid difficulties as China built national strength. Once the Chinese government succeeded with economic and related military modernization and development, Beijing was expected to become even less inclined to sacrifice nationalistic and territorial ambitions for the sake of cooperation in engagement policies by the United States and the West. Given this reasoning, US leaders were urged to be firm with China, to rely on military power as a counterweight to rising Chinese power, to remain resolute in dealing with economic and security disputes with China, and to work closely with US allies and friends along China's periphery in dealing with actual or potential Chinese assertiveness. Senator John McCain was identified with this view.[20]

An even tougher US approach to China at the time was advocated by some leaders in the Congress along with commentators and interest group leaders who believed that China's political system needed to change before the United States could establish a constructive relationship with Beijing. China's Communist leaders were perceived as inherently incapable of participating in truly cooperative relationships with the United States. US policy should aim to change China from within while maintaining vigilance against disruptive Chinese foreign policy. Prominent congressional leaders such as Senator Jesse Helms, Representative Frank Wolf, and Representative Christopher Smith were associated with these views.[21]

Nongovernment advocacy groups interested in influencing China policy found fertile ground in the often acute debate in the 1990s over the proper American approach to China and the broader debate over the appropriate course of US foreign policy after the Cold War. The groups endeavored to muster recruits, gain financial support, and build coalitions by focusing on issues related to China policy. Their concerns focused on issues like human rights, trade disputes, weapons proliferation, and other topics. Competing coalitions of interest groups fought bitterly, especially during major crises such as the decisions of the Bush and Clinton administrations to grant MFN tariff treatment to China.[22]

In general, the organized American interest groups active in China policy following the end of the Cold War can be divided among those dealing with economic interests, specific values or causes, ethnic issues, and issues important to foreign governments and foreign economic interests. Within the economic realm, the National Association of Manufacturers, the Chamber of Commerce, and the Business Roundtable endeavored to promote such business concerns as foreign trade and investment beneficial to American companies. The Emergency Committee for American Trade worked successfully to ensure that the United States would continue nondiscriminatory trading relations with China.[23]

Often at odds with these pro-business groups were groups representing organized labor. They favored more trade restrictions, they often viewed Chinese exports to the United States as a threat to US jobs, and they also weighed in on a variety of social justice issues including human rights and labor rights and the use of prison labor to produce Chinese exports.[24]

A number of public interest or citizen groups have common concerns of a noneconomic or nonoccupational nature. Many of these organizations focus on a single issue or a small group of issues. Examples include groups concerned with independence or greater autonomy for Tibet (e.g., the International Campaign for Tibet), freedom for political prisoners in China (e.g., Amnesty International and Human Rights Watch), religious freedom and freedom from coercive birth control and abortions (e.g., the Family Research Council, very active in the 1990s), as well as those concerned with curbing Chinese practices that endanger the regional and international environment or that promote instability and possible conflict through the proliferation of weapons of mass destruction and related technology (e.g., the Wisconsin Project, prominent in the 1990s in its focus on egregious Chinese failings in the area of weapons proliferation).[25]

Ethnic groups have long been a key factor in American foreign policy. Although Chinese Americans represent around 1 percent of the US population, they have not become a unified ethnic bloc influencing US foreign policy. However, there have been instances when segments of this group have been active in the politics of US foreign policy making. Expatriate Chinese students heavily lobbied Congress and the administration during the years immediately following the 1989 Tiananmen crackdown. Their influence waned as the students became divided over their goals regarding US policy toward China. A much more cohesive ethnic group has been the more than half million Americans who trace their family background to Taiwan.

Taiwanese Americans have formed a variety of organizations that have actively encouraged US foreign policy to respect Taiwan's separate status and autonomy from the mainland. Many of these groups are strong advocates of independence for the island.[26]

Foreign governments, foreign businesses, and other elites also work actively to influence US foreign policy. Government, business, and other leaders of Taiwan have been active for many years in pressing their points of view on the US government. With the break in official Taiwan relations with the US government in 1979, they have focused more effort to lobby the Congress. Reports have linked the Taiwan government and other groups supportive of Taiwan with sometimes large campaign contributions to US political candidates. Taiwan government and nongovernment entities also have been prominent in promoting academic, think tank, media, local government, and other research and exchanges that enhance goodwill and positive feelings between Taiwan and the United States.[27]

The mainland Chinese government, business leaders, and other elites were much less active on these fronts, though their efforts to influence US foreign policy continued to grow. Media and congressional reports in the 1990s focused on charges that the Chinese government was clandestinely funneling campaign contributions to US candidates. Chinese government and business leaders found they were more attractive to and influential with US officials and elites as a result of the rapid growth of the Chinese economy. Against this background, the Chinese government was successful in promoting regular exchanges with Congress. The Chinese government also worked closely with like-minded US business leaders and officials in sustaining vibrant economic interchange with the United States.[28]

Relations during the Bush and Clinton Administrations

Developments in US-China relations after the Tiananmen crackdown in 1989 and through the 1990s witness repeated cycles of crisis heavily influenced by the newly active domestic debate in the United States over American policy toward China. The first major turning point came during the George H. W. Bush administration with US reaction to Tiananmen and the concurrent ending of the Cold War and emergence of Taiwan democratization. The second turning point came with President Clinton's advocacy in 1993 and then his withdrawal in 1994 of linkage between Chinese human rights practices and the granting of nondiscriminatory US trade status to China. A third and more serious crisis resulted from Clinton's decision in 1995 to allow the Taiwan president to visit the United States; Chinese military demonstrations in the Taiwan area ultimately prompted the deployment of two US aircraft carrier battle groups to the area in 1996. In 1999, contentious negotiations over

China's entry into the WTO, Chinese mass demonstrations following the US bombing of the Chinese embassy in Belgrade, and a crescendo of congressional opposition to and criticism of the president and his China policy represented a fourth period of crisis since 1989.[29]

What would turn out to be a twisted course of US policy in this decade at first saw President George H. W. Bush strive to preserve cooperative ties amid widespread American outrage and pressure for retribution and sanctions against the Chinese leaders. President Bush had served as the head of the US Liaison Office in China in the mid-1970s. He took the lead in his own administration (1989–93) in dealing with severe problems in US-China relations caused by the Tiananmen crackdown and the decline in US strategic interest in China as a result of the collapse of the Soviet bloc. He resorted to secret diplomacy to maintain constructive communication with senior Chinese leaders; while senior administration officials said all high-level official contact with China would be cut off as a result of the Tiananmen crackdown, President Bush sent his national security adviser and the deputy secretary of state on secret missions to Beijing in July and December 1989. When the missions became known in December 1989, the congressional and media reactions were bitterly critical of the administration's perceived duplicity.[30]

Bush eventually became frustrated with the Chinese leadership's intransigence and took a tough stance on trade and other issues, though he made special efforts to ensure that the United States continued MFN tariff status for China despite opposition by a majority of the US Congress, much of the American media, and many US interest groups newly focused on China. Reflecting more positive US views of Taiwan, the Bush administration upgraded US interchange with the ROC by sending a cabinet-level official to Taipei in 1992, the first such visit since official relations were ended in 1979. He also seemed to abandon the limits on US arms sales set in accord with the August 1982 US communiqué with China by agreeing in 1992 to a sale of 150 advanced F-16 jet fighters, worth more than $5 billion, to Taiwan. The president's motives for the sale were heavily influenced by a need to appear to be protecting US manufacturing jobs at the F-16 plant in Texas, a key state in the Bush reelection plan.[31]

Presidential candidate Clinton used sharp attacks against Chinese government behavior, notably the Tiananmen crackdown, and President Bush's moderate approach to China to win support in the 1992 election. The presidential candidate's attacks, though probably reflecting sincere anger and concern over Chinese behavior, also reflected a tendency in the US-China debate in the 1990s to use China issues, particularly criticism of China and US policy toward China, for partisan reasons. The president-elect and US politicians in following years found that criticizing China and US policy toward China provided a convenient means to pursue political ends. For candidate Clinton and his aides, using China issues to discredit the record of the Republican candidate, incumbent George H. W. Bush, proved an effective way to take votes from him. Once Clinton won the election and was in office, he showed little interest in China policy, leaving the responsibility to subordinates.[32]

In particular, Assistant Secretary of State for East Asia Affairs Winston Lord in 1993 played the lead administration role in working with congressional leaders, notably Senate Majority Leader George Mitchell, Representative Nancy Pelosi, who was a House leader on China and human rights issues, and others to establish the human rights conditions the Clinton administration would require before renewing MFN tariff status for China. The terms he worked out were widely welcomed in the United States at the time. However, Chinese government leaders were determined not to give in on several of the US demands, and they appeared to calculate that US business interests in a burgeoning Chinese economy would be sufficient to prevent the United States from taking the drastic step of cutting MFN tariff treatment for China and risking the likely retaliation of the PRC against US trade interests. US business pressures pushed Clinton to intervene in May 1994 to reverse existing policy and allow for unimpeded US renewal of MFN status for China.[33]

Pro-Taiwan interests in the United States, backed by US public relations firms in the pay of entities and organizations in Taiwan, took the opportunity of congressional elections in 1995, which gave control of the Congress to pro-Taiwan Republican leaders, to push for greater US support for Taiwan, notably for a visit by ROC president Lee Teng-hui to his alma mater, Cornell University. Under heavy domestic political pressure, President Clinton intervened again and allowed Taiwan's president to visit the United States despite the strenuous opposition of China.[34]

The resulting military confrontation with China in the Taiwan Strait involving two US aircraft carrier battle groups saw the Clinton administration eventually move to a much more coherent engagement policy toward China. The policy received consistent and high-level attention from the president and his key aides and was marked by two US-China summit meetings in 1997 and 1998. By the end of the Clinton administration, progress included US-China agreement on China's entry into the WTO and US agreement to provide PNTR status for China. However, the new approach failed to still the vigorous US domestic debate against forward movement in US relations with China on an array of strategic, economic, and political issues.[35]

As in the case of Clinton's attacks on George H. W. Bush, many of the attacks on Clinton's engagement policy with China after 1996 were not so much focused on China and China issues for their own sake as on partisan or other concerns. Most notably, as congressional Republican leaders sought to impeach President Clinton and tarnish the reputation of his administration, they endeavored to dredge up a wide range of charges with regard to illegal

Chinese fundraising; Chinese espionage; Chinese deviations from international norms regarding human rights, nuclear weapons, and ballistic missile
proliferation; and other questions in order to discredit President Clinton's
moderate engagement policy toward China and in so doing cast serious
doubt on the moral integrity and competence of the president and his aides.[36]
The Clinton policy of engagement with China also came under attack from
organized labor interests within the Democratic Party, some of which used
the attacks on the administration's China policy as a means to get the administration to pay more attention to broader labor interests within the party. In
a roughly similar fashion, social conservatives in the Republican Party used
sharp attacks against the continuation of US MFN tariff status for China (a
stance often supported by congressional Republican leaders) despite China's
coercive birth control policies; they did this in part as a means to embarrass
and pressure the Republican leaders to pay more positive attention to the various agenda issues of the social conservatives.

During the 1990s, congressional criticism of China and moderation in US
policy toward China was easy to do and generally had benefits for those making the criticism. The criticism generated positive coverage from US media
strongly critical of China, and it generated positive support and perhaps some
fundraising and electioneering support for the congressional critics by the
many interest groups in the United States that focused criticism on Chinese
policies and practices during that decade. The Chinese government, anxious
to keep the economic relationship with the United States on an even keel,
was disinclined to punish such congressional critics or take substantive action
against them. More likely were Chinese invitations to the critical congressional members for all-expenses-paid trips to China in order to persuade them
to change their views by seeing actual conditions in China. Finally, President
Clinton, like President George H. W. Bush, often was not in a position to risk
other legislative goals by punishing congressional members critical of his
China policy.

As President Clinton and his White House staff took more control over
China policy after the face-off with Chinese forces in the Taiwan Strait in
1996, they emphasized—like George H. W. Bush—a moderate policy of
engagement, seeking change in offensive Chinese government practices
through a gradual process involving closer Chinese integration with the world
economic and political order. The US-China relationship improved but also
encountered significant setbacks and resistance. The high points included
the US-China summits in 1997 and 1998, the Sino-American agreement on
China's entry into the WTO in November 1999, and passage of US legislation in 2000 granting China PNTR status. Low points included strong congressional opposition to the president's stance against Taiwan independence
in 1998; the May 1999 bombing of the Chinese embassy in Belgrade and

Chinese demonstrators trashing US diplomatic properties in China; strident congressional criticism in the so-called Cox Committee report of May 1999, charging administration officials with gross malfeasance in guarding US secrets and weaponry from Chinese spies; and partisan congressional investigations of Clinton administration political fundraising that highlighted some illegal contributions from sources connected to the Chinese regime and the alleged impact they had on the administration's more moderate approach to the PRC.[37]

China's calculus amid the varied initiatives from the United States in the decade after the Tiananmen crackdown is explained in more detail later in this chapter. It shows that Chinese leaders had long sought the summit meetings with the United States. Coming in the wake of Chinese meetings with other world leaders in the aftermath of the international isolation of China caused by the Tiananmen crackdown, the summit meetings with the US president were a clear signal to audiences at home and abroad that the Communist government of China had growing international status and that its position as the legitimate government of China now was recognized by all major world powers.[38]

The benefits for the United States in the summit meetings were more in question, though the Clinton administration justified these steps as part of its efforts to use engagement to foster Chinese accommodation with the prevailing US-supported international economic and political order. US and other critics failed to accept this rationale and honed their criticism on what they viewed as unjustified US concessions to Chinese leaders. Heading the list were perceived concessions by the US president articulating limits on American support for Taiwan in the so-called Three No's. Speaking in Shanghai in June 1998 during his visit to China, President Clinton affirmed that the United States did not support Taiwan independence; two Chinas; or one Taiwan, one China; and that the United States did not believe Taiwan should be a member of an organization where statehood is required. The Clinton administration claimed the Three No's were a reaffirmation of long-standing US policy, but the president's action was roundly criticized in the Congress and US media as a new gesture made to accommodate Beijing and undermine Taipei.[39]

Progress in US negotiations leading to eventual agreement on China's entry into the WTO was not without serious difficulties and negative consequences. The United States took the lead among the WTO's contracting parties in protracted negotiations (1986–99) to reach agreements with China on a variety of trade-related issues before Chinese accession could move forward. Chinese premier Zhu Rongji visited Washington in April 1999, hoping to reach agreement with the United States on China's entry into the WTO. An agreement was reached and disclosed by the Americans, only to be turned down by President Clinton. The setback embarrassed Zhu and raised serious questions in the Chinese leadership about the intentions of President Clinton and his administration. Recovering from the setback, Zhu was able to complete the US-China negotiations in November 1999, paving the way for China's entry into the WTO in 2001. US legislation passed granting PNTR to China in 2000. This ended the need for annual presidential requests and congressional reviews with regard to China keeping normal trade relations tariff status, previously known as most favored nation tariff status.[40]

Making such progress in US-China relations was difficult because of incidents and developments affecting US-China relations and vitriolic US debate over the Clinton administration's China policy. Heading the list was the US bombing of the Chinese embassy in Belgrade, the most important incident in US-China relations after the Tiananmen crackdown. The reaction in China included mobs stoning the US embassy in Beijing and burning US diplomatic property in Chengdu, a provincial capital. Both governments restored calm and dealt with some of the consequences of the bombing, but China and the United States never came to an agreement on what happened and whether the United States explained its actions appropriately.[41]

Taiwan's president, Lee Teng-hui, added to Taiwan Strait tension, thus worrying American policy makers when he asserted in July 1999 that Taiwan was a state separate from China and that China and Taiwan had "special state-to-state relations." Chinese leaders saw this as a step toward Taiwan independence and reacted with strong rhetoric, some military actions, and by cutting off cross-strait communication links.[42]

Complementing difficulties abroad were the many challenges at home to the Clinton administration's moderate policy of engagement toward China. The US media ran repeated stories in the second term of the Clinton administration that linked the president, Vice President Albert Gore, and other administration leaders with illegal political fundraising involving Asian donors, some of whom were said to be connected with the Chinese government. Congressional Republican Committee chairmen Senator Fred Thompson and Representative Dan Burton held hearings, conducted investigations, and produced information and reports regarding various unsubstantiated allegations of illegal contributions from Chinese backers in return for the Clinton administration turning a blind eye to Chinese illegal trading practices and Chinese espionage activities in the United States.[43]

More damaging to the administration and its engagement policy toward China was the report of the so-called Cox Committee. Formally known as the Select Committee on US National Security and Military/Commercial Concerns with the People's Republic of China, and named for its chairman, Republican congressman Christopher Cox, the committee released in May 1999 an eight-hundred-page unclassified version of a larger, classified report.

It depicted long-standing and widespread Chinese espionage efforts against US nuclear weapons facilities, allowing China to build American-designed advanced nuclear warheads for use on Chinese missiles that were made more accurate and reliable with the assistance of US companies. It portrayed the Clinton administration as grossly negligent in protecting such vital US national security secrets. The report added substantially to congressional, media, and other concerns that the United States faced a rising security threat posed by China's rapidly expanding economic and military power.[44]

CHINA POLICY DEBATE IN PERSPECTIVE: STRENGTHS, WEAKNESS, AND IMPORTANCE

Looking back at Tiananmen from the perspective of the end of the Clinton administration in 2000, it was fair to assert that the domestic American debate over China policy had emerged powerfully in the 1990s and would continue to have a primary influence in the American approach to China for the foreseeable future. The incoming George W. Bush administration in January 2001 adopted a policy toward China that was tougher and more consistent with the widespread criticism of the Clinton administration's more moderate engagement policy. Bush's approach calmed the critics for the time being. A more lasting and significant impact on the China policy critics came with the September 11, 2001, terrorist attack on America. Though not comparable to the strategic danger posed by Soviet expansion during the height of the Cold War, the new challenge of terrorism became the focus of US government, media, and interest group attention. Those in the United States who endeavored to use criticism of China and their attacks on moderation in US policy toward China had a much harder time getting the attention of officials, media, donors, and the general public. The China debate as a force that pushed US policy toward a significantly harder line against China basically was overwhelmed by perceived American requirements to focus on other issues related to the complicated US war on terrorism. As the danger of terrorism to the United States appeared to subside and the popularity of the Bush administration also declined, the domestic US debate over China began to revive again in the middle of the decade. But it remained a secondary force influencing American China policy. It was more a drag on forward movement and improvement in US relations with China than it was a significant determinant of a more negative and critical American policy toward China.[45]

Closer examination shows that the rapid and unforeseen decline in the salience of the American domestic debate about China policy during the first year of the George W. Bush administration reflects some important weaknesses of the critics and their arguments in favor of a tougher stance toward

China. In fact, a comparison of the US China policy debate in the 1990s with that of the late 1970s and early 1980s appears to illustrate weaknesses in the resolve and approach of the critics in the later period. The resolve and commitment of critics seen in late-1970s and early-1980s episodes related to both the passage of the Taiwan Relations Act and resistance to perceived excesses in US accommodation of China at the expense of US relations with Taiwan, Japan, and other interests, appear strong. They seem notably stronger than the resolve and commitment on the part of many of the various individuals and groups seeking a tougher US approach to China after the Cold War. The comparison of the two periods of criticism of prevailing US policy leads to a conclusion that even though the number of critics and their supporters in the 1990s was larger and broader than those of critics in the late 1970s and early 1980s, the commitment of the leaders and followers was comparatively thin and expedient in the post–Cold War period.[46]

COMPARING THE US DEBATES ON CHINA: LATE 1970S/EARLY 1980S VERSUS POST–COLD WAR

Domestic debate and related domestic interests have sometimes been an important determinant pushing forward the direction of US policy toward China, including Taiwan and related issues. More often, they have been an obstacle slowing the momentum of US policy. From Richard Nixon through Jimmy Carter and into early Ronald Reagan, domestic factors generally were a brake slowing the policies led by the administration to move the United States away from ties with Taiwan and closer to the PRC. For several years following the end of the Cold War, they generally were a driver pushing US policy against China and toward closer ties with Taiwan, though they reverted to the status of brake during the second term of the Clinton administration.[47]

As noted in chapter 4, the debate in the Nixon-Reagan period (1972–83) involved important tangible costs and benefits for the United States. The US strategic posture vis-à-vis the Soviet Union and the future of Taiwan headed the list of the serious issues at stake for the United States. Reflecting deep uncertainty about US power and purpose in world affairs, US policy was prepared to make major sacrifices in order to pursue respective paths in the debate, and indeed US policy ultimately sacrificed official relations with Taiwan and took the unprecedented step of ending a defense treaty with a loyal ally for the sake of the benefits to be derived from official relations with the PRC, notably with regard to assisting the United States in dealing with expanding Soviet power.[48]

The major protagonists in the US domestic debate over policy toward the PRC and Taiwan in the Nixon-Reagan (1972–83) period argued their case mainly because they were sincerely concerned about the serious implications and consequences of the direction of US policy in this triangular relationship. Partisan interests and the influence of interest groups or constituent groups also played a role, but less so than in the US China policy debate of the 1990s. The fact that a Democrat-controlled Congress took the lead, in the Taiwan Relations Act and in other legislative actions, in modifying the perceived oversights and excesses of the Democratic Carter administration, which tilted in favor of Beijing and against Taiwan in the late 1970s up to 1981, showed that partisan interests played a secondary or relatively unimportant role in the US domestic debate. Significantly, this pattern persisted even after the Democrat-controlled Congress rewrote and passed the Taiwan Relations Act in April 1979. Democratic senators and representatives remained active in resisting the Carter administration's continuing perceived "tilt" toward the PRC and away from Taiwan. Among notable critics and skeptics of the US policy at the time were such Democratic senators as Adlai Stevenson, John Glenn, Richard Stone, and George McGovern.[49]

The congressional opposition of the day did reflect an important element of institutional rivalry between the executive branch and the Congress that colored US domestic debate over foreign policy during this period. Congress appeared determined to protect its perceived prerogatives in US foreign policy, while US administration officials were equally determined to protect the prerogatives of the executive branch in foreign affairs.[50]

Although the US domestic debate became more prominent and important in influencing the course of US policy toward China and Taiwan and related issues after the Tiananmen incident and the end of the Cold War in the late 1980s and early 1990s, major features of the debate were markedly different from the debate in the 1970s and early 1980s. The differences underlined that the resolve and commitment of the critics generally was weaker in the 1990s than in the 1970s:[51]

- US policy makers in the executive branch and the Congress were confident of US power and influence in the world, especially now that the Soviet empire had collapsed—a marked contrast from the strategic uncertainty that had underlined the US policy debate in the 1970s and early 1980s.
- In the 1970s, US officials faced and made major sacrifices in pursuit of US policy toward the PRC and Taiwan. The protagonists in the US China policy debate after the Cold War had little inclination to sacrifice tangible US interests for the sake of their preferred stance in the US-PRC-Taiwan triangle or other China policy–related questions. Thus, those in Congress, the media, and elsewhere in US domestic politics who were vocal in seeking an upgrade in US treatment for Taiwan's

President Lee Tenghui—demanding he be granted a visa to visit Cornell University in 1995—largely fell silent when Beijing reacted to the visit with forceful actions in the Taiwan Strait that posed a serious danger of US-China military confrontation. The majority of congressional members who opposed the annual waiver that granted continued MFN tariff treatment to Chinese imports had no intention of seeking a serious cutoff of US-China trade. They often explained that they were merely endeavoring to send a signal, to the administration and to China over their dissatisfaction with US and Chinese policies.

- Many were active in the US domestic debate for partisan or other ulterior motives—a marked contrast from the 1970s, when the foreign policy issues themselves seemed to be the prime drivers in the US domestic debate. Clinton used the China issue to attack the record of the Bush administration, only to reverse course after a time in office, returning to the engagement policy of the previous president. The strident rhetoric coming from Republican congressional leaders critical of the Clinton administration's engagement policy in its second term seemed to have similarly partisan motives. Labor-oriented Democrats used the China issue to discredit the pro-business leanings of the leaders of the Clinton administration, while social conservatives in the Republican Party focused in on China's forced abortions and suppression of religious freedom to embarrass their party leaders and prompt them to devote more attention to the social conservatives' political agenda in US domestic politics.[52]
- Reflecting the less serious commitment by critics in the 1990s was the fact that the US China debate notably subsided whenever the United States faced a serious foreign policy challenge. Thus, the vocal congressional debate over China policy stopped abruptly following the Iraqi invasion of Kuwait in 1990, and the Congress remained quiet about China throughout the US Desert Shield and Desert Storm operations. Once the war was over and the need for Chinese acquiescence in the United Nations over the US-led war against Iraq ended in 1991, the China debate resumed immediately, with many Democrats in Congress and elsewhere seeking to use the China issue for partisan purposes in order to tear down President George H. W. Bush's then-strong standing in US opinion polls regarding his handling of foreign affairs. As noted earlier in this chapter, the September 11, 2001, attack on America also dampened the US China debate, which was then focused notably on the threat to US interests posed by a rising China. After several months, media organs like the *Washington Times* and some in Congress resumed lower-key efforts to focus on the China threat, while pro-Taiwan groups tried to use the rebalancing of Bush administration policy in directions

more favorable to China by arguing for concurrent favorable US treatment for Taiwan.[53] These moves were small and of little consequence; they seemed to underline the weakness of US critics of China or advocates of policies opposed by China in a US foreign policy environment focused on dealing with terrorism-related issues.[54]

CHINESE PRIORITIES AND CALCULATIONS: MANAGING CRISIS-PRONE RELATIONS

Whatever their strengths and weaknesses, the shifts in US policy prompted by the US debate over China policy after the Cold War posed major and repeated challenges for Chinese leaders. Once it became clear to Chinese leaders that the strategic basis of Sino-American relations had been destroyed by the end of the Cold War and the collapse of the Soviet Union and that it would take a long time for political relations to return to more moderate engagement after the trauma of the Tiananmen incident, Chinese leaders worked throughout the 1990s to reestablish "normalized" relations with the United States on terms as advantageous as possible to China. With the US-China summits of 1997 and 1998, relations arguably were normalized, but they remained far from stable. Chinese leaders continued to give high priority to managing differences with the United States while benefiting from advantageous economic and other ties with the US superpower.[55]

Throughout the post–Cold War period, Chinese officials reflected varying degrees of suspicion regarding US intentions and remained well aware of fundamental ideological, strategic, and other differences with the United States.[56] In general, Chinese officials settled on a bifurcated view of the United States. This view held that US leaders would extend the hand of "engagement" to the Chinese government when their interests would be served but that US leaders were determined to "contain" aspects of China's rising power and block aspects of China's assertion of influence in world affairs when such aspects were seen as contrary to US interests. The Chinese emphasis on cooperating with the "soft" US "hand of engagement" or defending against the "hard" US "hand of containment" varied. The general trend from 1996 to 2001, and after adjustments in US-China relations in 2001, was to give more emphasis to the positive and less emphasis to the negative on the part of both the Chinese and US administrations.[57]

Presidents George H. W. Bush and Clinton were clear about US differences with China in several key areas. Despite Chinese disapproval, the United States was determined to expend such a vast array of resources on defense that it would remain the world's dominant power, and the dominant military power along China's periphery in East Asia, for the foreseeable future. The

United States would continue to provide support, including sophisticated arms, to Taiwan, and the United States endeavored to use growing government, commercial, and other nongovernmental contacts with China, as well as other means, to foster an environment that promoted political pluralism and change in the authoritarian Chinese Communist system.

For its part, Beijing strove for a post–Cold War world order of greater multipolarity; China would be one of the poles and would have greater opportunity for advantageous maneuvering than in a superpower-dominated order. China strove for a gradual decline in US power and influence in East Asia and globally, and Beijing called for cutbacks in US military sales and other support to Taiwan in order to help create advantageous conditions for the reunification of the island with mainland China. Finally, CCP leaders were determined to maintain the primacy of their rule in the face of economic, social, and political challenges at home and abroad, including challenges supported by the United States.

A critical problem for Chinese leaders in dealing with the United States in the 1990s involved mixing their strategies and goals with those of the United States in ways advantageous to China. In general, the Chinese approach focused on trying to work constructively with US power, concentrating on areas of common ground, building interdependent economic relations, and minimizing differences wherever possible. This was difficult to achieve, especially when US policy concentrated on the stark differences between the United States and China over human rights, Taiwan, weapons proliferation, and trade issues. In some instances, Chinese officials chose to confront the United States with threats of retaliation if the United States pursued pressure tactics against China. For the most part, however, Chinese leaders bided their time, endeavoring to avoid complications that would ensue from protracted confrontation with the United States. At bottom, they believed that China's growing economy and overall international importance would steadily win over foreign powers to a cooperative stance and encourage politically important groups in the United States, especially business groups, to press for an accommodating US approach to China.

Following this general line of approach in the 1990s, Beijing managed to end the diplomatic isolation that stemmed from the Tiananmen crackdown, weakened the Clinton administration advocates of conditioning MFN tariff treatment of Chinese imports to the United States, and prompted the president to end this policy in 1994. With the Sino-American summits of 1997 and 1998, Beijing clearly established the Chinese leaders as legitimate and respected actors in world affairs.[58]

Chinese officials duly noted during the 1990s and later that they had few illusions about beneficent US policy toward China. But they repeatedly affirmed to Western specialists and others that they—whether they personally liked it or not—also saw Chinese interests best served by trying to get along with the United States. They cited the following reasons:[59]

- The United States remained the world's sole superpower. As such, it posed the only potential strategic threat to China's national security for the foreseeable future. A confrontation with such a power would severely test China's strength and undermine Chinese economic and political programs.
- As the world's leading economic power, the United States had markets, technology, and investment important for Chinese modernization. It also played an important role in international financial institutions heavily involved in China; Western financial actors and investors viewed the status of US relations with China as an important barometer determining the scope and depth of their involvement in China.
- Internationally, establishing cooperative relations with the United States facilitated smooth Chinese relations with Western and other powers that were close to Washington. Antagonistic US-China relations would mean that China would have to work much harder, and presumably offer more in the way of economic and other concessions, to win over such powers.
- The United States continued to play a key strategic role in highly sensitive areas around China's periphery, notably Korea, Japan, the South China Sea, and especially Taiwan. It controlled sea lanes vital to Chinese trade. Cooperative US-China relations allowed Beijing to continue to focus on domestic priorities with reasonable assurance that its vital interests in these sensitive areas would not be fundamentally jeopardized by antagonistic actions by the United States. Indeed, good US-China relations tended to increase Chinese influence in these areas.

On balance, the record of Chinese relations with the United States in the 1990s showed considerable achievement for China. Beijing reestablished extensive high-level contacts with the US administration and saw the end of most Tiananmen-related sanctions against China. By 1998, the Clinton administration appeared sincerely committed to pursuing a policy of generally accommodating engagement with China. Administration officials in the United States endeavored to work closely with the Chinese government to reduce differences over US world primacy, the American strategic posture in East Asia, US support for Taiwan, and Washington's support for political pluralism in China. Chinese officials took satisfaction in the fact that the improvement in relations resulted much more from shifts toward accommodation of China's rising power and influence by the US administration than from adjustments by the Chinese government in dealing with issues sensitive to the United States.

While assessments among Chinese officials differed regarding the status and outlook of US-China relations, the prevailing view in 1999 was one of caution. There remained plenty of evidence that US policy continued to have elements of containment along with the seemingly accommodating engagement. Political forces in the United States, many interest groups, and the media still lined up against Chinese interests on a range of human rights concerns, strategic issues, Taiwan, and economic questions. Many Chinese officials remained suspicious of the ultimate motives of some members of the Clinton administration as well. As a result, Beijing was privately wary as it continued to seek advantages by building cooperative relations.[60]

The Challenges of Shifting US Policies

The Clinton administration decision in 1993 to condition MFN status for China on China's progress in human rights issues posed a major problem for the Chinese leadership. It was met indirectly by the rapid growth of the Chinese economy, which attracted strong US business interest, and the interest in turn of many visitors from Congress and the administration concerned with the growth of the US economy and economic opportunity abroad. By early 1994, Chinese officials were well aware that proponents for continuing the human rights conditions on MFN treatment for China had become isolated in the administration and centered in the State Department. The private reservations held among senior officials in US departments concerned with business, notably the Treasury Department and the Commerce Department, about these conditions on China's MFN status had become clear through their earlier visits to China and through other interactions. Moreover, US business groups had moved into high gear in warning that conditions on MFN treatment could jeopardize US access to the burgeoning Chinese market.[61]

Sino-American disagreements over human rights conditions in China and MFN status rose sharply during Secretary of State Warren Christopher's March 11–14, 1994, visit to Beijing.[62] Before and during Secretary Christopher's visit, Chinese leaders appeared defiant in the face of US human rights requirements. Most notably, Chinese security forces detained prominent dissidents immediately prior to the secretary's visit and also detained some Western journalists covering interaction between Chinese dissidents and Chinese security forces. In public interchange during the secretary's visit, Chinese leaders strongly warned against US use of trade or other pressure to prompt changes in China's human rights policy.

This tough approach reflected a determination to rebuff overt US pressure seen as targeted against the priority Chinese leadership concern of sustaining CCP rule. It also reflected the fact that the secretary's trip coincided with the annual convening of the National People's Congress. That meeting was the focal point of dissident activism in Beijing, and Chinese leaders were determined to take a hard line toward those both at home and abroad who pressed for political change.

Perhaps of most importance, Chinese leaders calculated that the time was right to press the United States to alter its human rights policy, especially the linkage with MFN renewal. They saw the Clinton administration leaders divided on the issue. They saw members of the US Congress as much more supportive than in the recent past of maintaining MFN treatment for China. Congress was perhaps influenced, too, by the fact that while the United States had been debating the issue, countries that were political allies to the United States but economic competitors, like Japan, Germany, and France, had been sending high-level officials to China—underlining their willingness to help fill the vacuum should US-China economic relations falter with the withdrawal of MFN tariff treatment.[63]

Reflecting a calculus of costs and benefits along the lines of realism in IR theory, Chinese leaders adopted a tough stance during the Christopher visit. Those in the US government favoring linkage of MFN treatment and human rights conditions were further isolated, and US leaders were forced to change their policy or lose the considerable economic opportunities in the Chinese market. In the end, Chinese leaders were generally pleased with President Clinton's May 26, 1994, decision to "delink" MFN treatment to China from US consideration of Chinese human rights practices.

Subsequently, Chinese officials and commentators in official Chinese media were anxious for the United States and China to take advantage of the improved atmosphere in bilateral relations to push for more far-reaching and comprehensive progress in the US-China relationship.[64] Whatever hopes Chinese leaders held about advancing relations with the United States were dashed by President Clinton's reversal of past policy, permitting Taiwan's president, Lee Teng-hui, to make an ostensibly private visit to Cornell University in June 1995.

Beijing's tough military and polemical responses and the Clinton administration's eventual dispatch of carrier battle groups to Taiwan highlighted mixed lessons for China.[65]

On the positive side, Chinese officials claimed several achievements resulting from the PRC's forceful reaction to Lee Teng-hui's visit to the United States:

- It intimidated Taiwan, at least temporarily, preventing it from taking further assertive actions to lobby in the US Congress or elsewhere for greater international recognition. Pro-independence advocates in Taiwan also had to reassess previous claims that the PRC was bluffing in its warnings against Taiwan independence.

- It prompted second thoughts by some pro-Taiwan advocates in the Congress and elsewhere in the United States as to the wisdom of pursuing their agenda at that time. International officials seeking to follow the US lead in granting greater recognition to Taiwan had to reevaluate their positions as well.
- It resulted in heightened sensitivity by the Clinton administration regarding China. This led to official reassurances to the PRC that US policy toward Taiwan would not deviate from past practice; it also led to an invitation for the Chinese president to visit the United States, a summit meeting long sought by Chinese leaders; and it led to tightly controlled management of significant developments in US policy toward China by the president and his senior advisers, who now sought to pursue an active engagement policy with China and to avoid significant deterioration of relations.

At the same time, Beijing appeared to have overplayed its hand in pressing the United States for pledges against Taiwan official visits to the United States and in pressing Taiwan's people to abandon Lee Teng-hui in favor of a leader more committed to reunification with the mainland. Beijing also appeared to recognize that it was not productive to continue strident accusations in official Chinese media during 1995–96 that the United States was attempting to contain China, or to shun dialogue with the United States.

Given China's perceived need to sustain a working relationship with the United States for the foreseeable future, Beijing officials tried, for example through President Jiang Zemin's meeting with President Clinton in 1995, to find and develop common ground while playing down differences. Whereas Beijing had appeared prepared in mid-1995 to freeze contacts with the Clinton administration, awaiting the results of the 1996 US elections, Beijing now appeared to have judged that endeavoring to work constructively with the current US government was in China's best interests. Also, Jiang Zemin told US reporters in October 1995 that lobbying Congress would be an important priority in the year ahead, and Chinese specialists also said that the PRC would put more effort into winning greater understanding and support from other US sectors, notably the media and business.[66] For its part, the Clinton administration continued strong efforts to avoid serious difficulties with China; to emphasize a policy of engagement with the PRC; and to seek high-level contacts, summit meetings, and tangible agreement with China on sensitive issues.

The events of the next two years in US-China relations were highlighted by the summit meetings of Presidents Jiang and Clinton in Washington in 1997 and Beijing in 1998. Despite the continued debate in the United States over the Clinton administration's new commitment to a policy of engagement with

China, Chinese officials and specialists claimed to be confident that China's rising power and influence in world affairs, and its willingness to cooperate with the United States on issues of importance to both countries, made it unlikely that the US opponents of the engagement policy would have a serious, lasting impact on US-China relations.[67]

The events of 1997 and 1998 seemed to bear out the Chinese view. The US-China summit meetings capped the Beijing leaders' decade-long effort to restore their international legitimacy after the Tiananmen incident. The results redounded to the benefit of the presiding Chinese leaders, especially President Jiang Zemin. Jiang was anxious to carve out a role as a responsible and respected international leader as part of his broader effort to solidify his political base of support at home. Basically satisfied with the results of the smooth summit meetings with the US president, Beijing saw little need to take the initiative in dealing with continuing US-China differences like human rights, trade, and weapons proliferation. It was the US side that felt political pressure to achieve results in these areas.

Responding to repeated US initiatives to reach agreements at the summit meetings and elsewhere on these kinds of questions, Chinese officials took the opportunity to make demands of their own, especially regarding US policy toward Taiwan. At the same time, Beijing was willing to marginally improve human rights practices, and it curbed nuclear and cruise missile exchanges with Iran for the sake of achieving a smoother and more cooperative US-China relationship.

In sum, despite strong and often partisan debate in the United States over policy toward China, Chinese officials were well pleased with the progress they had made in normalizing relations with the United States from the low points after the Tiananmen crackdown of 1989 and the confrontation over Taiwan in 1995–96. The progress had been made largely by changes in US policy toward China and with few concessions by Beijing in key areas of importance to China. The summits of 1997 and 1998 represented the capstone of the normalization effort, in effect strongly legitimating the PRC leaders at home and abroad—a key Chinese goal after the Tiananmen incident. Once this was accomplished, Chinese leaders could turn to their daunting domestic agenda with more assurance that the key element of US-China relations was now on more stable ground.

At the same time, Chinese leaders had few illusions about US policy. They saw plenty of opportunities for continued difficulties. American behavior continued to be seen as fitting into the pattern of engagement and containment—the "two hands" of US policy seen by Chinese officials and specialists. The main trend in 1997 and 1998 was toward greater engagement, and China endeavored to encourage that. But there remained many forces in Congress, in the media, and among US interest groups that were prepared to challenge any forward movement in US-China relations. And the fact remained that although it was clearly in China's interest to cooperate with the United States under existing circumstances, the two countries continued to have fundamentally contradictory interests over the international balance of influence, the American strategic role in East Asia, US support for Taiwan, and American support for political change in China.[68]

Events in 1999, highlighted by the US bombing of the Chinese embassy in Belgrade, posed new challenges for Chinese leadership efforts to sustain workable economic and other ties with the United States while defending key Chinese interests of sovereignty, security, and nationalism. Chinese mob violence against US diplomatic properties was accompanied by a virulent leadership debate over how to deal with the United States that was not resolved for months. In the end, Chinese leaders decided their interests were best served by working with the US administration to restore calm and to continue US-China engagement that was beneficial to China.

Amid the contentious US presidential campaign of 2000, where policy toward China figured as an issue of some importance, senior Chinese officials told senior Clinton administration officials that China was intent on approaching the United States constructively, regardless of which candidate won the election. Such comment was seen by these US officials as supporting a coherent and consistent Chinese strategy toward the United States. This strategy appeared similar to that seen in 1997 and 1998 in that it accepted US leadership in world affairs and in Asian affairs and sought Chinese development in a peaceful international environment where the United States maintained primacy.[69]

However, the limitations, fragility, and apparent contradictions of this Chinese moderate approach toward the United States also were starkly evident. Whatever this strategy entailed, it did not show Chinese willingness to curb harsh commentary and the use of military force in challenging US power and influence in Asian and world affairs. Thus, Chinese officials and commentary in 2000 and until mid-2001 continued to be full of invective against the United States, opposing alleged US power politics, hegemonism, and Cold War thinking. China repeatedly criticized the United States over a variety of key foreign policy issues, such as US plans for national missile defense in the United States and theater missile defense abroad, NATO expansion, enhanced US alliance relations with Japan, and US policy and practices in dealing with Iraq, Iran, Cuba, and other countries.[70] Chinese aircraft and ships monitoring US surveillance aircraft and ships in international waters near China carried out dangerous maneuvers in apparent efforts to harass and deter the Americans from carrying out their objectives.

STUDY QUESTIONS

1. How and why did the Chinese crackdown on dissent in the Tiananmen killings and the concurrent end of the Cold War and soon following demise of the USSR destroy a previous American consensus since the Nixon administration favoring pragmatically seeking closer relations with China in common opposition to the Soviet Union while playing down Sino-American differences over ideology and values?

2. Why did Chinese leaders view the hostile US response to the crackdown, attacking the legitimacy of one-party Communist rule in China, as a fundamental threat to their top priority concern?

3. Why was a consistent and coherent US policy toward China so hard to achieve in the 1990s? What was the importance for China policy of the US president's markedly reduced control over foreign policy making as a result of the end of the Cold War and demise of the USSR?

4. Why was Clinton compelled to reverse in 1994 his government's previous policy of linking annual US renewal of most favored nation tariff treatment for China with Beijing's human rights practices?

5. Why did Clinton's reversal of previous policy in granting a visa to the Taiwan president to visit the United States in 1995 prompt protracted and provocative demonstrations of Chinese military force against Taiwan during 1995–96, a crisis not ended until Clinton deployed two US aircraft carrier battle groups to the Taiwan area to confront Chinese forces?

6. Why did Clinton subsequently stress accommodation of Chinese interests and strong positive US engagement with China, leading to US-China summits, China's entry into the World Trade Organization, and the granting to China of US permanent most favored nation trade status?

7. Did Clinton's attacks during the 1992 election campaign on George H. W. Bush's moderate policies toward China reflect newly prominent partisan motives driving US China policy? Were such partisan motives also seen in strong Republican attacks against Clinton's accommodation of Chinese interests in his second term?

8. How did Chinese leaders assess the major progress made in US concessions and other positive advances along with continued challenges in US-China relations at the end of the Clinton government?

RELEVANT VIDEOS

"Meet the Press" (Fang Lizhi discusses Chinese reforms post Tiananmen, July 1990, thirty minutes) available at https://www.worldcat.org/title/ meet-the-press-july-8-1990/oclc/8085759821&referer=brief_results

"The China Story" (American University panel on US reaction to Tiananmen crackdown, September 11, 1989, ninety minutes) available at https://www.c-span.org/ video/?10447-1/china-story

"Ten Years after Tiananmen Square" (panel discussion on impact of the crackdown and human rights issues in US China policy, CSPAN, two hours) available at https://www.c-span.org/video/?124021-1/ten-years-tiananmen-square

"Meet the Press" (featuring Sandy Berger on China's espionage and Senator Richard Lugar and others debating China policy, 1999, one hour) available at https:// www.worldcat.org/title/meet-the-press-march-14-1999-meet-the-contenders-2000/ oclc/8085740880&referer=brief_results

"60 Minutes. Jiang Zemin" (part 1 and 2 of interview with Jiang Zemin, 2000, thirteen minutes each) available at https://www.worldcat.org/title/60-minutes-jiang-zemin-part-one/oclc/8646311640&referer=brief_results and https://www.worldcat.org/title/60-minutes-jiang-zemin-part-two/ oclc/8646336440&referer=brief_results

"60 Minutes. Spy?" (Wen Ho Lee declares his innocence, 2000, thirteen minutes) available at https://www.worldcat.org/title/60-minutes-spy/ oclc/8646523440&referer=brief_results

Chapter Six

Early Twenty-First Century Relations: Pragmatism and Rising Differences

RELATIONS DURING THE GEORGE W. BUSH ADMINISTRATION

George W. Bush became president in 2001 with a reputation of toughness toward the People's Republic of China (PRC) but no clearly articulated policy. The new US administration's approach to the Chinese government was based in large measure on a fundamental uncertainty: China was rising and becoming more prominent in Asia and world affairs, but US leaders were unsure if this process would see China emerge as a friend or foe of the United States.[1] The administration dealt with this ambiguous China situation within a broader US international strategy that endeavored to maximize US national power and influence in key situations, including relations with China. This involved strengthening

- US military and economic power;
- US relations with key allies; those in Asia, Japan, South Korea, and Australia received high priority;
- US relations with other power centers; the Bush administration was successful in moving quickly, before September 11, 2001, to build closer relations with the two major flanking powers in East Asia: Russia and India.[2]

In 2001, the new US president and his leadership team displayed a notably less solicitous approach to China than the one displayed by the outgoing Bill Clinton administration. As seen in chapter 5, the Clinton administration during its second term adopted an engagement policy toward China that received the top priority among US relations with Asia. The administration was anxious to avoid serious downturns in US-China relations over Taiwan and other issues; it also repeatedly sought negotiations with Beijing to develop "deliverables"—agreements and other tangible signs of forward movement in

US-China relations. President Clinton, senior US officials, and US specialists repeatedly made clear that key objectives of growing US engagement with China were to enmesh China in webs of interdependent relationships with the United States, international organizations, world business, and others that would constrain and ultimately change Chinese policies and practices at home and abroad that were seen as offensive to or opposed to US interests.[3]

PRC bargainers used a prevailing atmosphere of strong, public Chinese criticism of US policies and warnings of Chinese actions against Taiwan in order to press for US concessions in areas of importance to them, notably regarding US relations with Taiwan. Chinese criticism of US policy had a broad scope involving Taiwan and a wide range of issues in US foreign and security policy, including missile defense; NATO expansion; US-Japan security cooperation; US human rights policy; US efforts in the United Nations to sanction Iraq; and US policy toward Cuba, Iran, the Middle East, and other areas in the developing world. As noted in chapter 5, Clinton administration concessions fueled the white-hot US domestic debate over the proper direction of the US China policy.[4]

By contrast, the Bush administration lowered China's priority for US decision makers, placing the PRC well behind Japan and other Asian allies and even Russia and India for foreign policy attention.[5] This kind of downgrading of China's importance in US policy had last been carried out in the Reagan administration with the pan-Asian approach under the supervision of Secretary of State George Shultz discussed in chapter 4. It appeared to be no accident that the main architects of the policy shift in 2001, notably Deputy Secretary of State Richard Armitage, were among key decision makers in the similar US shift in US China policy that began in 1983. Armitage and his key aides in the State Department and close associates in the National Security Council staff were in the lead in moving US policy from the strong emphasis on compromising with China and doing what was necessary in order to preserve good relations with China in the latter years of the Clinton administration.[6]

Following the crash between a Chinese jet fighter and a US reconnaissance plane over the South China Sea during the so-called EP-3 incident of April 2001, discussed below, the Bush administration did not resort to high-level envoys or other special arrangements that were used by the Clinton administration to resolve difficult US-China issues. It insisted on working through normal State Department and Defense Department channels that did not raise China's stature in US foreign policy. In an unusual step showing that the administration was speaking firmly with one voice during the incident, US officials were instructed to avoid all but the most essential contacts with Chinese officials in Washington and elsewhere.[7]

Bush administration interest in seeking negotiations with China in order to create "deliverables" and other agreements remained low. Its reaction to the EP-3 episode, markedly increased US support for Taiwan, and a new US focus on China as a potential threat, showed Beijing leaders that the Bush government, while seeking to broaden areas of cooperation where possible, was prepared to see US-China relations worsen if necessary.[8]

Chinese leaders by mid-2001 seemed to recognize that if US-China relations were to avoid further deterioration, it was up to China to take steps to improve ties. In a period of overall ascendant US influence in Asian and world affairs, Beijing saw its interests best served by a stance that muted differences and sought common ground. Chinese officials thus significantly adjusted their approach to the United States. They became more solicitous and less acrimonious in interactions with US officials. Chinese officials and media toned down public Chinese rhetoric against the United States. They gave some tentative signs of public PRC support for the US military presence in East Asia. The US side also signaled an interest in calming the concerns of friends and allies in Asia over the state of US-China relations and pursuing areas of common ground in trade and other areas with the PRC.[9]

US-China relations faced a crisis when on April 1, 2001, a Chinese jet fighter crashed with a US reconnaissance plane, an EP-3, in international waters off the China coast. The Chinese jet was destroyed and the pilot killed. The US EP-3 was seriously damaged, but the pilot managed to make an emergency landing on China's Hainan Island. The US crew was held for eleven days and the plane for much longer by Chinese authorities. Weeks of negotiations produced compromises that allowed the crew and plane to return to the United States, but neither side accepted responsibility for the incident.[10]

Many specialists predicted continued deterioration of relations, but both governments worked to resolve issues and establish a businesslike relationship that emphasized positive aspects of the relationship and played down differences. The terrorist attack on America in September 2001 diverted US attention away from China as a potential strategic threat. Chinese officials privately indicated that they sought a constructive relationship with the new US government, and in the process they publicly showed remarkable deference in the face of the Bush government's uniquely assertive stance on Taiwan as well as its strong positions on regional and national ballistic missile defense, expansion of US-Japanese defense cooperation, NATO expansion, and other sensitive security issues that had been focal points of Chinese criticism of the United States in the recent past. The Chinese leaders seemed preoccupied at home, notably focusing on a very important and somewhat irregular leadership transition and related issues of power sharing and development policy. Against this background, Chinese leaders worked hard to moderate previous harsh rhetoric and pressure tactics in order to consolidate relations with the United States.[11]

The course of US-China relations became smoother than at any time since the normalization of those relations. US preoccupation with the wars in Afghanistan and Iraq and the broader war on global terrorism meant that US strategic attention to China as a threat remained a secondary consideration for American policy makers. Chinese leaders for their part continued to deal with an incomplete leadership transition and the broad problem of trying to sustain a one-party authoritarian political regime amid a vibrant economy and rapid social change. In this context, the two powers, despite a wide range of continuing differences ranging from Taiwan and Tibet to trade issues and human rights, managed to see their interests best served by generally emphasizing the positive. In particular, they found new common ground in dealing with the crisis caused by North Korea's nuclear weapons program beginning in 2002, and the Chinese appreciated Bush administration pressure on Taiwan's leader Chen Shui-bian to avoid steps toward independence for Taiwan that could lead to conflict in the Taiwan Strait.[12]

It is easy to exaggerate the growing Sino-American convergence during the Bush administration. The antiterrorism campaign after September 11, 2001, saw an upswing in US-China cooperation, though China was somewhat tentative and reserved in supporting the US war against Afghanistan. President Bush's visits to Shanghai in October 2001 and Beijing in February 2002 underlined differences as well as common ground. The US president repeatedly affirmed his strong support for Taiwan and his firm position regarding human rights issues in China. His aides made clear China's lower priority in the administration's view of US interests as the Bush administration continued to focus higher priority on relations with Japan and other allies in Asia and the Pacific. In its first year, the Bush administration imposed sanctions on China over issues involving China's reported proliferation of weapons of mass destruction (WMD) more times than during the eight years of the Clinton administration. The Defense Department's Quadrennial Defense Review unmistakably saw China as a potential threat in Asia. American ballistic missile defense programs, opposed by China, went forward, and rising US influence in Southwest and Central Asia and prolonged military deployments there were at odds with China's interest in securing its western flank.[13] The Defense Department's annual reports on the Chinese military pulled few punches in focusing on China's military threat to Taiwan and to US forces that might come to Taiwan's aid in the event of a conflict with the PRC. The Bush administration's September 2002 National Security Strategy Report called for better relations with China but clearly warned against any power seeking to challenge US interests with military force.[14]

It was notable that China's increased restraint and moderation toward the United States came even in the face of these new departures in US policy and behavior under the Bush administration—namely, presidential pledges along with military and political support for Taiwan, strong missile defense programs, and strong support for alliance strengthening with Japan and expanded military cooperation with India. In the recent past, such US actions would have prompted strong Chinese public attacks and possibly military countermeasures.[15]

American leaders showed an increased willingness to meet Chinese leaders' symbolic needs for summitry, and the US president pleased his Chinese counterpart by repeatedly endorsing a "constructive, cooperative, and candid" relationship with China. Amid continued Chinese moderation and concessions in 2002 and reflecting greater US interest in consolidating relations and avoiding tensions with China at a time of growing US preoccupation with the war on terrorism, Iraq, and North Korea, the Bush administration broadened cooperation with China and gave US relations with China a higher priority as the year wore on. An October 2002 meeting between President Bush and President Jiang Zemin at the US president's ranch in Crawford, Texas, highlighted this trend. Concessions and gestures, mainly from the Chinese side dealing with proliferation, Iraq, the release of dissidents, US agricultural imports, Tibet, and Taiwan, facilitated the positive Crawford summit.[16] Meanwhile, senior US leaders began to refer to China and Jiang Zemin as a "friend."[17] They adhered to public positions on Taiwan that were acceptable to Beijing. They sanctioned an anti-PRC terrorist group active in China's Xinjiang region. The Defense Department was slow to resume high-level contacts with China, reflecting continued wariness in the face of China's ongoing military buildup focused on dealing with Taiwan and US forces that may seek to protect Taiwan, but formal relations at various senior levels were resumed by late 2002.[18]

Looking back, it appears that patterns of Bush administration policy and behavior toward China began to change significantly in 2003. American officials sometimes continued to speak in terms of "shaping" Chinese policies and behavior through tough deterrence along with moderate engagement. However, the thrust of US policy and behavior increasingly focused on positive engagement. China also received increasingly high priority in US policy in Asia and the world.[19]

The determinants of the US approach now appeared to center on the Bush administration's growing preoccupations with the war in Iraq, its mixed record in other areas in the war on terror and broader complications in the Middle East, and wide-ranging international and growing domestic disapproval of Bush administration policies. The North Korean nuclear program emerged as a major problem in 2003, and the US government came to rely

heavily on China to help manage the issue in ways that avoided major negative fallout for the interests of the US government. Although Asian policy
did not figure prominently in the 2004 presidential campaign, Senator John
Kerry, the Democratic candidate, used a televised presidential debate to challenge President Bush's handling of North Korea's nuclear weapons development. President Bush countered by emphasizing his reliance on China in
order to manage the issue in accord with US interests.[20]

The Bush administration's determination to avoid trouble with China at a
time of major foreign policy troubles elsewhere saw the president and senior
US leaders strongly pressure Taiwan's government to stop initiating policies
seen as provocative by China and possible causes of confrontation and war in
US-China relations.[21] The strong rhetorical emphasis on democracy promotion in the Bush administration's second term notably avoided serious pressures against China's authoritarian system.

The US government's emphasis on positive engagement with China did
not hide the many continuing US-China differences or US efforts to plan for
contingencies in case a rising China turned aggressive or otherwise disrupted
US interests. The United States endeavored to use growing interdependence,
engagement, and dialogues with China to foster webs of relationships that
would tie down or constrain possible Chinese policies and actions deemed
negative to US interests.[22]

On the whole, the Chinese government of President Hu Jintao welcomed
and supported the new directions in US China policy. The Chinese leaders
endeavored to build on the positives and play down the negatives in relations
with the United States. This approach fit well with the Chinese leadership's
broader priorities of strengthening national development and Communist
Party legitimacy that were said to require China to use carefully the "strategic opportunity" of prevailing international circumstances seen as generally
advantageous to Chinese interests. As in the case of US policy toward China,
Chinese engagement with the United States did not hide Chinese contingency
plans against suspected US encirclement, pressure, and containment and
the Chinese use of engagement and interdependence as a type of Gulliver
strategy, discussed below, to constrain and tie down possible US policies and
actions deemed negative to Chinese interests.[23]

As China expanded military power along with economic and diplomatic
relations in Asian and world affairs at a time of US preoccupation with the
war in Iraq and other foreign policy problems, debate emerged inside and
outside the US government about the implications of China's rise for US
interests. Within the Bush administration, there emerged three viewpoints
or schools of thought, though US officials frequently were eclectic, holding
views of the implications of China's rise from various perspectives.[24]

On one side were US officials who judged that China's rise in Asia was designed by the Chinese leadership to dominate Asia and in the process to undermine US leadership in the region.[25] A more moderate view of China's rise in Asia came from US officials who judged that China's focus in the region was to improve China's position in Asia mainly in order to sustain regional stability, promote China's development, reassure neighbors and prevent balancing against China, and isolate Taiwan. Officials of this school of thought judged that China's intentions were not focused on isolating and weakening the United States in Asia. Nevertheless, the Chinese policies and behavior, even though not targeted against the United States, contrasted with perceived inattentive and maladroit US policies and practices. The result was that China's rise was having an indirect but substantial negative impact on US leadership in Asia.[26]

A third school of thought was identified with US Deputy Secretary of State Robert Zoellick, who by 2005 publicly articulated a strong argument for greater US cooperation with China over Asian and other issues as China rose in regional and international prominence.[27] This viewpoint held that the United States had much to gain from working directly and cooperatively with China in order to encourage the PRC to use its rising influence in "responsible" ways in accord with broad US interests in Asian and world affairs. This viewpoint seemed to take into account the fact that the Bush administration was already working closely with China in six-party talks to deal with North Korea's nuclear weapons development and that US and Chinese collaboration or consultations continued on such sensitive topics as the war on terror, Afghanistan, Pakistan, Iran, Sudan, Burma, and even Taiwan as well as bilateral economic, security, and other issues. Thus, this school of thought gave less emphasis than the other two on competition with China and more emphasis on cooperation with China in order to preserve and enhance US leadership and interests in Asia as China rose.

Bush administration policy came to embrace the third point of view. Senior US leaders reviewed in greater depth the implications of China's rise and the strengths and weaknesses of the United States in Asia. The review showed that US standing as Asia's leading power was basically sound. American military deployments and cooperation throughout the Asia-Pacific region were robust. US economic importance in the region was growing, not declining. Overall, it was clear that no other power or coalition of powers was even remotely able or willing to undertake the costs, risks, and commitments of the United States in sustaining regional stability and development essential for the core interests of the vast majority of regional governments.[28] Thus, China's rise—while increasingly important—posed less substantial and significant challenge for US interests than many of the published commentaries and specialists' assessments might have led one to believe.

On this basis, the US administration increasingly emphasized positive engagement and a growing number of dialogues with China, encouraging China to act responsibly and building ever-growing webs of relationships and interdependence. This pattern fit well with Chinese priorities regarding national development in a period of advantageous international conditions while building interdependencies and relationships that constrained possible negative US policies or behaviors.

Domestic criticism of US policy toward China declined sharply with the election of President Bush and Republican majorities in the Congress and the American preoccupation with the war on terrorism. As explained below, Bush's initially tougher posture toward China was in line with views of the vocal critics of Clinton administration engagement policies, and the president benefited from strong Republican leadership and discipline that kept Congress in line with the president's foreign policies. American politicians and interest groups seeking prominence and support in attacking Chinese policies and practices were overwhelmed with the shift in the country's foreign policy emphasis after the terrorist attacks of September 11, 2001. Domestic criticism of the president's management of an increasingly close engagement with China began to revive in 2005 as the war on terrorism wore on and the conflict in Iraq reflected major setbacks for the Bush administration. Economic and trade issues dominated the China policy debate. At the same time, congressional, media, and interest groups revived criticism of China on a variety of other issues involving, notably, human rights, international energy competition, and foreign relations with perceived rogue regimes.[29]

Democrats led by long-standing critics of China won majority control of both houses of Congress in the November 2006 elections. Democratic Party candidates for the 2008 presidential election generally were critical of the Bush administration's free-trade policies, which saw the US annual trade deficit with China rise to more than $250 billion and coincided with the loss of good-paying manufacturing jobs in the United States. They also tended to take a tougher line than the US administration on human rights, Tibet, and other issues in US-China relations. In the face of American criticism of China and of US government moderation toward China, the Bush administration, some in Congress, and some US interest groups emphasized pursuit of constructive engagement and senior-level dialogues as means to encourage China to behave according to US-accepted norms as a "responsible stakeholder" in the prevailing international order and thereby show that the positives in US-China relations outweighed the negatives.[30]

Viewed from the perspective of international relations theories, the patterns of US administration and Chinese government approaches to one another during this period seem well explained through cost-benefit analyses associated with realism. The differences in interests and values remained, as did the very different identities of the two societies, but pragmatic leaders on both sides viewed carefully the power realities they were attempting to change to their advantage. They weighed the costs and benefits of emphasizing various differences and, on the whole, saw the benefit in pursuing paths of convergence of mutual interest.

Of course, the calculations of US policy at this time seem shortsighted to American policy makers grappling with major challenges posed by adverse Chinese power and practices in 2021. In retrospect, those in the Bush administration and Congress who were wary of China's intentions and viewed Chinese accommodations of US interests as tactical rather than strategic adjustments seem more correct than those at that time seeking China's cooperation as a responsible stakeholder in a world order led by the United States.

Priorities and Issues in US Policy toward China

As discussed in chapter 5, the shock of the 1989 Tiananmen incident and the end of the Cold War fundamentally changed the way the United States dealt with China. A variety of US groups were in the lead among US critics who applied pressure in the Congress, the media, and in other public discourse to encourage a firmer US policy designed to press the Chinese government to conform more to US-backed norms. On the whole, such criticism and the negative impact it had on developing US-China relations was seen to decline along with the overall influence of Congress in determining American foreign policy in the twenty-first century. There were several reasons for this. First, the early actions of the Bush government supported firmer policies toward China that were backed by many in Congress regarding Taiwan, Tibet, human rights, and security concerns. Second, partisan attacks on the US administration's engagement policy toward China also diminished as the Bush White House and the Congress both were controlled by a Republican Party leadership intent on showing unity and party discipline. Third, US preoccupation with combating terrorism, including wars in Afghanistan and Iraq, overshadowed US issues with China.[31]

Human Rights Issues

China's human rights abuses remained among the most visible and persistent points of contention in US-China relations in the post–Cold War period. China's human rights record presented a mixed picture, with both setbacks and minor improvements providing plenty of ammunition for US policy debate in the Congress and elsewhere.

Crackdowns against Dissidents and the Falun Gong Group

On July 22, 1999, the Chinese government, fearing the potential of this organization to undermine Communist control, outlawed Falun Gong, a spiritual movement with an impressive nationwide organization in China. This initiated wholesale suppression of the movement involving arrests, harsh jail sentences, and torture. At that time, the Chinese government for similar reasons also cracked down on democracy activists trying to register a new independent political party, the Chinese Democracy Party.[32]

Tibet and Xinjiang

Chinese officials also harshly suppressed dissents among ethnic minorities, particularly in Tibet and in the Xinjiang-Uyghur Autonomous Region, in China's far west. Chinese suppression continued as the global war on terrorism saw the Chinese government brand dissidents in Xinjiang as terrorists with some links to al Qaeda and other international terrorist organizations. Some believed that the US government made a concession to the PRC on August 26, 2002, when it announced that it was placing one small group, the East Turkestan Islamic Movement, on the US list of terrorist groups.[33] Anti-China activism and rhetoric in Congress accompanied public protests in the United States and harsh American and other Western media criticism of China's crackdown of dissent and violence in Tibet in 2008. Congressional leaders called for a boycott of the 2008 Summer Olympic Games, but President Bush announced firmly that he would attend the games.[34]

Chinese Prisons/Prison Labor

Prisons in China were widely criticized for their conditions, treatment of prisoners, and requirements that prisoners perform productive work. One US policy issue was the extent to which products made by Chinese prisoners were exported to the US market, a violation of US law. Another involved periodic reports of Chinese security forces taking organs from executed prisoners and selling them on the black market.[35]

Family Planning/Coercive Abortion

Controversies in US population planning assistance continued with regard to China's population programs. Abortion, and the degree to which coercive abortions and sterilizations occur in China's family planning programs, remained prominent issues in these debates.[36]

Religious Freedom

The Department of State's Annual Reports on International Religious Freedom and other US government documents criticized Chinese government policies on religious practices. They were featured in congressional hearings and statements.[37]

Internet and Media Restrictions

The growth of internet, cell phone use, and text messaging led to new Chinese regulations begun in 2005 prompting congressional hearings on the extent to which US internet firms collaborated with Chinese authorities.[38]

Issues in Security Relations

US-China security and military relations never fully recovered after they were suspended following the 1989 Tiananmen Square crackdown. The EP-3 incident resulted in a temporary halt regarding most military contacts.[39]

China's Military Expansion

Some officials in the George W. Bush administration, backed by officials in Congress, the media, and others, were deeply concerned with China's military buildup focused on defeating US military forces in the event of a conflict over Taiwan. Stronger US measures to deal with this situation reinforced US-China military competition and complicated bilateral military relations.[40]

WMD Proliferation

The Bush administration, backed by many in Congress, also took a tougher position against China's WMD proliferation,[41] especially regarding weapons sales, technology transfers, and nuclear energy assistance to Iran and Pakistan.

Espionage

As noted in chapter 5, alleged Chinese espionage featured prominently in the 1999 Cox Committee report, which was sharply critical of the US administration's counterespionage activities against China.[42] Subsequently, suspicions of Chinese espionage were voiced in Congress when the State Department decided to purchase computers for use in classified communications from a Chinese company. The controversy caused the department to halt the purchase.[43] Developments later in the decade featured arrests and convictions of individuals illegally funneling advanced US technologies to China.

Economic Issues

Trade Deficit

Issues involving trade with China factored heavily into US policy debates. The US trade deficit with China surged from a $17.8 billion deficit in 1989 to $256 billion in 2008.[44]

Intellectual Property

According to calculations from US industry sources in 2006, intellectual property piracy cost US firms $2.5 billion in lost sales a year. Backed by Congress, US administration officials repeatedly pressed Chinese officials to better implement intellectual property regulations.[45]

Currency Valuation

In recent years until 2005, the PRC pegged its currency, the renminbi (RMB), to the US dollar at a rate of about 8.3 RMB to the dollar—a valuation that many critics in Congress and elsewhere in the United States concluded kept the PRC's currency undervalued, making PRC exports artificially cheap and making it harder for US producers to compete. On July 1, 2005, the PRC changed this valuation method, but the resulting slow appreciation in the RMB was not sufficient to assuage US congressional concerns.[46]

Chinese Purchase of US Government Securities

A related concern was Chinese purchases of US Treasury bills and other US government securities as a means of recycling China's massive trade surplus with the United States while maintaining the relatively low value of Chinese currency relative to the US dollar. Some congressional and other US critics warned of US overdependence on this type of investment by China.[47]

Bid for Unocal

The bid of a Chinese state-controlled oil company to acquire the US oil firm Unocal in 2005 set off an uproar in Congress and the US media that prompted the Chinese firm to withdraw the bid.[48]

China's International Rise

A set of issues emerged in the middle of the Bush administration focused on the implications of China's economic growth and increasing international engagement and influence for US interests in various parts of the world.

China notably used unconditional economic exchanges and assistance to woo governments and leaders seen as rogues or outliers by the United States and other developed countries. Chinese practices undercut Western pressures on these officials and governments to improve governance in accord with Western norms. China's increased influence also extended to many key allies and associates of the United States and to regions like Latin America, where the United States exerted predominant influence.[49]

Sovereignty Issues: Taiwan and Tibet

Taiwan

Taiwan remained the most sensitive and complex issue in US-China relations. Beijing continued a robust military buildup focused on a Taiwan contingency involving the United States. In 2001, the George W. Bush administration offered the largest package of US arms to Taiwan in ten years and allowed President Chen Shui-bian to tour more freely and to meet with congressional representatives during stopovers in the United States. President Bush publicly pledged to come to Taiwan's aid with US military power if Taiwan were attacked by mainland China. The steps were welcomed in Congress, though they reinforced Beijing's military buildup.[50] As the Taiwan government of President Chen Shui-bian in 2003 advanced pro-independence proposals, the US president and his aides took steps to curb those potentially destabilizing actions. There were only minor objections from the normally pro-Taiwan Congress.[51] Beginning in 2008, the calming of cross-strait tensions that resulted from Taiwan president Ma Ying-jeou's policies of reassurance toward China was welcomed in the administration and the Congress.[52]

Tibet

The Tibet issue flared in US-China relations in 2007 when Congress awarded the Congressional Gold Medal to the Dalai Lama in a public ceremony.[53] President Bush met the Dalai Lama during his visit to Washington, and Bush took part in the congressional award ceremony.[54] Congressional leaders spoke out firmly against the Chinese crackdown on dissent and violence in Tibet in 2008.

PRIORITIES AND ISSUES IN CHINA'S US POLICY

In the post-Mao period, Chinese Communist Party (CCP) leaders focused on economic reform and development as the basis of their continued survival as the rulers of China.[55] Support for economic liberalization and openness waxed and waned, but the overall trend emphasized greater market orientation and foreign economic interchange as critical in promoting economic advancement and, by extension, supporting the continued CCP monopoly of political power. For a time, the leaders were less clear in their attitudes toward political liberalization and change, but since the crackdown at Tiananmen in 1989, there was a general consensus among the party elite to control dissent and other political challenges.[56]

In foreign affairs, post-Mao leaders retreated from the sometimes strident calls to change the international system, and they worked pragmatically to establish relationships with important countries, especially the United States and Japan but also China's neighbors in Southeast Asia and elsewhere, who would assist China's development and enhance Beijing's overall goal of developing national wealth and power. The collapse of Soviet Communism at the end of the Cold War posed a major challenge to Chinese leaders and reduced Western interest in China as a counterweight to the USSR. But the advance of China's economy soon attracted Western leaders once again, while the demise of the USSR gave China a freer hand to pursue its interests, less encumbered by the long-term Soviet strategic threat.[57]

Against this backdrop and following the death of strong-man leader Deng Xiaoping in 1997, Chinese authorities led by the president and party chief, Jiang Zemin, were anxious to minimize problems with the United States and other countries in order to avoid complications in their efforts to appear successful in completing three major tasks for the year, involving (1) the July 1997 transition of Hong Kong to Chinese rule, (2) the reconfiguration of Chinese leadership and policy at the Fifteenth CCP Congress in September 1997, and (3) the Sino-American summit of October 1997.[58]

Generally pleased with the results of these three endeavors, Chinese leaders began implementing new policy priorities. At the top of the list was an ambitious multiyear effort to transform tens of thousands of China's money-losing state-owned enterprises into more efficient businesses by reforming them (e.g., selling them to private concerns, forming large conglomerates, or undertaking other actions). Beijing also embarked on major programs to promote economic and administrative efficiency and protect China's potentially vulnerable financial systems from any negative fallout from the 1997–98 Asian economic crisis and subsequent uncertainties.[59]

Making collective leadership work was an ongoing challenge for China's top leaders. President Jiang Zemin did not have the power exerted by Mao Zedong and Deng Xiaoping. When it came time for Jiang and his senior colleagues to retire, the leadership transition saw Jiang slow to hand over control of military power to the new leader, Hu Jintao. Hu was weaker than Jiang. He moved carefully in consolidating his leadership position. The results of the Seventeenth Congress of the CCP in October 2007 appeared to underline a continuing cautious approach to political change and international and domestic circumstances, one that was designed to reinforce Communist Party rule in China.[60]

There was little sign of disagreement among senior leaders over recent broad policy emphasis on economic reform, though sectors affected by reform often resisted strenuously. China's entrance into the World Trade Organization in 2001 increased the need for greater economic efficiency and reform. The reforms also exacerbated social and economic uncertainties, which reinforced the government's determination to maintain a firm grip on political power and levers of social control. The repression of political dissidents and related activities begun in 1998 continued into the foreseeable future.[61]

The Hu Jintao leadership gave more attention to the many negative consequences of China's rapid economic growth and social change, including glaring inequities between urban and rural sectors and coastal and interior areas; pervasive corruption by self-serving government, party, and military officials; environmental degradation; misuse of scarce land, water, and energy resources; and the lack of adequate education, health care, and social welfare for hundreds of millions of Chinese citizens.[62]

Against this background, foreign affairs generally remained an area of less urgent policy priority. Broad international trends—notably at that time, improved relations with the United States—supported the efforts by the Chinese authorities to pursue policies intended to minimize disruptions and to assist their domestic reform endeavors. The government remained wary of the real or potential challenges posed by a possible economic crisis, by Taiwan, by efforts by Japan and the United States to increase their international influence in ways seen as contrary to Beijing's interests, by India's great power aspirations and nuclear capability, by North Korea's nuclear weapons development, and by other issues. The PRC voiced special concern over the implications for China's interests of actual and reported US plans to develop and deploy theater ballistic missile defense systems in East Asia and a national missile defense for the United States. Chinese officials also voiced concern over the downturn in US-China relations at the outset of the George W. Bush administration but appeared determined to cooperate with the US-led antiterrorism campaign begun in September 2001.[63]

Overall, China's many disagreements with the United States at this time can be grouped into four general categories of disputes, which complicated US-China relations for years. China's moderation toward the United States since 2001 reduced the salience of some of these issues, but they remained important and were reflected in Chinese policies and actions. The risk-averse Hu Jintao leadership appeared to have little incentive to accommodate the United States on these sensitive questions.

As noted in chapter 1, the four categories are (1) opposition to US support for Taiwan and involvement with other sensitive sovereignty issues, including Tibet, Xinjiang, Hong Kong, and disputed islands and maritime rights along China's rim; (2) resistance to US efforts to change China's political system; (3) opposition to the United States playing the dominant role along China's periphery in Asia; and (4) resistance to many aspects of US leadership in world affairs. Some specific issues in the latter two categories included US policy in Iraq, Iran, and the broader Middle East; aspects of the US-backed security presence in the Asia-Pacific; US and allied ballistic missile defenses; US pressure on such governments as Burma, North Korea, Sudan, Zimbabwe, Cuba, and Venezuela; US pressure tactics in the United Nations and other international forums; and the US position on global climate change.[64]

Nevertheless, the Hu Jintao government prioritized reassuring neighboring countries and other concerned powers—notably the United States—that rising Chinese economic, military, and political power and influence should not be viewed as a threat but should be seen as an opportunity for greater world development and harmony. In the process, Chinese diplomacy gave ever-greater emphasis to engagement and conformity with the norms of regional and other multilateral organizations as a means to reassure those concerned over possible negative implications of China's increased power and influence.[65] Often working at odds with the above reassurances and accommodations were Chinese nationalism and Chinese security priorities. They placed a premium on building powerful Chinese military forces, strong popular patriotism, and firmness in dealing with challenges to Chinese sovereignty and security regarding Taiwan, Tibet, Xinjiang, and contested claims in the East and South China Seas.[66]

Bush's Legacy: Positive Stasis in US-China Relations

Though now sometimes seen as the result of shortsighted and flawed US foreign policy calculations, the positive stasis in US-China relations that emerged in the latter years of the George W. Bush administration met the near-term priorities of the US and Chinese governments. Converging US and Chinese engagement policies tried to broaden common ground; they dealt with differences through policies fostering ever-closer interchange that included respective strategies designed to constrain each other's possible disruptive or negative moves. The converging engagement policies involved constructive and cooperative engagement on the one hand and contingency planning or hedging on the other.[67]

Chinese and US contingency planning and hedging against one another sometimes involved actions like the respective Chinese and US military buildups focused on Taiwan. Meanwhile, each government used engagement to build interdependencies and webs of relationships that had the effect of constraining the other power from taking actions that opposed its interests. While the analogy is not precise, the policies of engagement pursued by the United States and China toward one another featured respective "Gulliver strategies" that were designed to tie down aggressive, assertive, or other negative policy tendencies of the other power through webs of interdependence in bilateral and multilateral relationships. Thus the positive stasis in US-China relations was based on an increasing convergence of these respective engagement policies and Gulliver strategies.[68]

Sustaining the positive stasis in US-China relations was also based on the fact that neither the Chinese leadership nor the US administration sought trouble with the other. Both were preoccupied with other issues. Heading the list of preoccupations for both governments was dealing with the massive negative consequences of the international economic crisis and deep recession begun in 2008. Other preoccupations of the outgoing Bush administration included Iraq, Afghanistan, Pakistan, Iran, broader Middle East issues, North Korea, and other foreign policy problems that came on top of serious adverse economic developments. Hu Jintao was preoccupied with failed attempts to achieve a strong leadership position as he struggled to meet expectations to enhance China's growth and international prominence.[69]

The US and Chinese governments worked hard to use multiple formal dialogues, high-level meetings and communications, and official rhetoric emphasizing the positive in the relationship in order to offset and manage negative implications from the many differences and issues that continued to complicate US-China relations. Neither leadership saw benefit in publicly emphasizing the major differences over key policy issues regarding economic, military, and political questions.[70]

Both governments registered close collaboration over North Korea's nuclear weapons program. They worked in parallel to manage the fallout from Taiwan's president Chen Shui-bian's repeated efforts to strengthen Taiwan's sovereignty and standing as a country separate from China. Much more limited collaboration between China and the United States influenced such international hot spots as Sudan, Iran, and Myanmar/Burma, with leaders on both sides speaking more about Sino-American cooperation than Sino-American differences over these sensitive international questions.[71] Unfortunately for those hoping for significantly greater cooperation between the United States and China, dramatic increases in cooperation seemed absent because of the major conflicting interests and disputes over a wide range of issues noted above. Cautious US and Chinese leaders seeking to avoid trouble with one another had a hard time overcoming these obstacles. Some disputes were at times hard to control, resulting in surprising upsurges in US-China tensions, such as strident criticism in Congress and the media on Beijing's crackdown on dissent in Tibet prior to the start of the 2008 Olympic Games.[72]

PRAGMATISM FALTERS DURING THE
BARACK OBAMA ADMINISTRATION

As a presidential candidate in 2008, Barack Obama was unusual in recent US presidential politics in not making a significant issue of his predecessor's China policy. Like President Bush, the new president showed a measured and deliberative course with China involving pursuing constructive contacts, preserving and protecting American interests, and dealing with challenges posed by rising Chinese influence and power.[73]

A major theme in President Obama's initial foreign policy was to seek the cooperation of other world powers, notably China, to deal with salient international concerns such as the global economic crisis and recession, climate change, nuclear weapons proliferation, and terrorism. He and his team made vigorous efforts to build common ground with China on these and related issues. China's leaders offered limited cooperation, disappointing the Obama government.[74]

More worrisome, Chinese actions and statements in 2009 and 2010 directly challenged the policies and practices of the United States:

- Chinese government patrol boats confronted US surveillance ships in the South China Sea.
- China challenged US and South Korean military exercises against North Korea in the Yellow Sea.
- Chinese treatment of US arms sales to Taiwan and President Obama's meeting with the Dalai Lama in 2010 was harsher than in the recent past.
- Chinese officials threatened to stop investing in US government securities and to move away from using the US dollar in international transactions.
- The Chinese government responded very harshly to American government interventions in 2010 urging collective efforts to manage rising tensions in the South China Sea and affirming the US-Japan security treaty during Sino-Japanese disputes over East China Sea islands.[75]

The Obama government reacted calmly and firmly to what Secretary of State Hillary Clinton called these "tests" of a new assertiveness by China. At that time, the US government also found that prominent Chinese assertiveness and truculence with the United States and neighboring Asian countries over maritime, security, and other issues seriously damaged China's efforts to portray a benign image in Asia. Asian governments became more active in working closely with the United States and in encouraging an active US presence in the Asia-Pacific. Their interest in closer ties with the United States meshed well with the Obama government's broad effort under the rubric of the US rebalance to Asia in order to "reengage" with the countries of the Asia-Pacific, ranging from India to the Pacific Islands. The overall effect was a temporary rise in the position of the United States, with China on the defensive.[76]

Explanations varied concerning the beginnings of what would turn out to be a protracted phase—up to the present—of greater competition in US-China relations overriding previous cooperation. Chinese commentators tended to see the starting point in the rising challenges China faced as the Obama government's rebalance policy was announced in late 2011. Many Chinese commentators saw the policy as encircling and designed to contain and constrain China's rising influence in Asia.[77] For their part, Obama government officials and many other Americans tended to see the new competition posed by greater Chinese assertiveness and challenges to the United States as coming from altered Chinese views of power realities between the two countries and in Asian and world affairs. On the one hand, the US-initiated international financial breakdown and massive recession added to perceived American weaknesses seen in declining American strength, notably because of the draining wars in Iraq and Afghanistan. On the other hand, China emerged from the economic crisis with strong growth, flush with cash and more confident in its state-directed growth model as opposed to the now deeply discredited American free market approach. Under these circumstances, Chinese elite and popular opinion looked with increasing disapproval on the cautious and reactive approach of the Hu Jintao government (2002–2012). In foreign affairs, accommodating the United States and regional powers over long-standing Chinese interests involving Chinese security, sovereignty, and other sensitive issues seemed overly passive and misguided. Though Hu's approach was in line with Deng Xiaoping's instruction that China should keep a low profile in foreign affairs and focus on domestic development, opinion in China now favored a more robust and prominent Chinese international approach. The result over the following years was an evolution of greater boldness, activism, and considerable use of coercion, generally short of using military force, in employing Chinese economic, political, and military power to meet the broad goals in what incoming leader Xi Jinping in 2012 called the "China Dream." The goals involved China unified with disputed territories under its control and with a stature unsurpassed in Asia as a leading world power.[78]

The explanations of rising challenges and tensions in US-China relations during the Obama government tended to use the lens of realism in international relations theory. The United States was seen in decline while China was rising. For Chinese commentators who saw containment in the Obama administration's rebalance policy, the US actions were motivated by America trying to sustain its leading position in the face of rising Chinese power and influence. For American observers, the catalyst for the rising tensions and challenges in the relationship came from more powerful China now putting aside past restraint and flexing its new muscles in pursuit of long-standing ambitions involving key differences with the United States.[79]

Constructivism played a role in some assessments of the rising tensions and acrimony in US-China relations in recent years, especially as China continued to develop a strong sense of identity based on the nationalism of an aggrieved power with an exceptional sense of self-righteousness seeking to remedy past injustices. And the United States had its constructed identity of exceptional righteousness as well, making compromise between the two nations over sensitive issues more difficult. Liberalism figured in the recent developments by showing the failure perceived in the United States of economic interchange and close diplomatic and nongovernment engagement favored by liberals as sources of stability and cooperation in relations to actually lead to mutual accommodation and greater collaboration as the main trend in the relationship. Indeed, developments in recent years showed that Americans saw economic interchange with China as working against their interests, an increasingly adverse situation that required strong remedial measures by the US government. The liberal view that closer American engagement in reaching mutually acceptable agreements with China would lead to closer relations seemed belied by the 2016 US presidential campaign rhetoric of Obama administration secretary of state Hillary Clinton, leading Republican candidate Donald Trump, and many other candidates. They argued that America had to be constantly vigilant in watching Chinese implementation of economic and other agreements, as Beijing was not to be trusted and had a record of manipulating and gaming accords to its advantage, at the expense of the United States.[80]

The administration of President Barack Obama had considerable success in implementing the various security, economic, diplomatic, and political elements of what was initially called the pivot to Asia and was soon relabeled the US rebalance policy in Asia. The policy approaches seen in the rebalance policy were considered by Obama government officials from the outset of the administration and were initiated in a series of speeches and announcements in late 2011 and early 2012. The record showed that the main initiatives of the rebalance policy were followed and duly implemented by the Obama government. Incoming president Donald Trump in 2017 ended the rebalance policy amid policy controversy and uncertainty, with potentially negative consequences for US standing in Asia.[81]

The Obama rebalance policy was also criticized in the United States and elsewhere in Asia. It was seen as too weak to deal with the challenges posed by China. And growing American opposition eventually blocked approval of the Trans-Pacific Partnership (TPP), the economic centerpiece of the rebalance policy. As noted above, China's Communist Party leader and president Xi Jinping (2012–) departed from past pragmatic Chinese cooperation with the United States in carrying out often bold and disruptive policies that notably came at the expense of China's neighbors and US interests in the Asia-Pacific region. How to deal with rising China figured prominently in the American rebalance policy from the start. The Obama government adjusted policy to take account of Chinese concerns and to more effectively manage growing Chinese challenges. Critics said that the rebalance framework needed strengthening in order to protect American interests in the face of Chinese and other challenges. Republican presidential candidate Donald Trump promised harsh measures to counter unfair Chinese economic practices, and he strongly opposed the TPP. He had little to say about the security and political aspects of US policy toward China, while his avowed policy toward Asian allies, demanding Japan and South Korea dramatically increase host nation support for US troops in the country or those troops would be withdrawn, undercut the emphasis on strengthened US-allied cooperation in the rebalance policy.[82]

The evolving and varied elements in the rebalance policy were in line with the interests of most Asia-Pacific governments, though China objected, sometimes strongly. From the outset, the initiatives reinforced long-standing US priorities in Northeast Asia involving China, Japan, and Korea, while they increased the American priority placed on the broad expanse of the Asia-Pacific ranging from India to Japan to New Zealand and the Pacific Islands. The United States adjusted the emphasis in the policy. At first (2011–2012) it focused on strategic initiatives, which were particularly controversial in China. It shifted in late 2012 to greater emphasis on economic and diplomatic initiatives, though security dimensions continued to develop. As China's challenges to US policy grew, the Obama government toughened its public posture toward China and deepened regional involvement to counter adverse Chinese behavior. The initiatives were often extensions of long-standing trends in US policy and practice; they built on and called greater attention to the positive advancements of American interests in the region by the George W. Bush and earlier administrations.[83]

Security aspects of the rebalance included the Obama government's avowed high-priority attention to the Asian-Pacific region following US military pullbacks from Iraq and Afghanistan. The Asia-Pacific's economic and strategic importance was said to warrant heightened US policy attention even as America withdrew from Southwest Asia and appeared reluctant to intervene militarily in other world conflicts. The Obama government also pledged to sustain close alliance relationships and maintain force levels and military capabilities in the Asian-Pacific region despite substantial cutbacks in overall US defense spending. If needed, funding for the Asia-Pacific security presence was said to come at the expense of other US military priorities. Meanwhile, US officials promoted more widely dispersed US forces and basing/deployment arrangements, which indicated the rising importance of Southeast Asia, the Indian Ocean, and the western Pacific in tandem with strong continuing support of long-standing American priorities, notably those in Northeast Asia. The advances involved developing deployment arrangements or supporting and supply arrangements in Australia, the Philippines, Singapore, and India, among others. The dispersal of US forces and a developing US air-sea battle concept were viewed as means to counter growing "area denial" efforts in the Asia-Pacific region, mainly by China.[84]

Economic aspects of the rebalance involved strong emphasis on the US pursuit of free trade and other open economic interchange. President Obama and his economic officers stressed that American jobs depended on freer access to Asia-Pacific markets. Against the backdrop of stalled World Trade Organization talks on international liberalization, the United States devoted extraordinary attention to the multilateral Trans-Pacific Partnership arrangement involving twelve Asian and Pacific countries in order to promote freer market access for American goods and services. The high standards of the TPP regarding such issues as safeguarding intellectual property rights and limiting state intervention in economic policies were seen to pose a challenge to China. Indeed, a successful TPP was deemed likely to prompt China to join, thereby bringing about a change in Chinese neomercantilist policies and practices that grossly disadvantaged American sales to China and competition with China in international markets.[85]

Political and diplomatic aspects of the rebalance were manifest in significantly enhanced and more flexible US activism and engagement both bilaterally and multilaterally in pursuing American interests in regional security and stability; free and open economic exchange; and political relations and values involving the rule of law, human rights, and accountable governance. The Obama government markedly advanced US relations with the Association of Southeast Asian Nations (ASEAN) and with the various regional groups convened by ASEAN. US engagement showed sensitivity to the interests of so-called third parties, notably China's neighbors, when pursuing bilateral US relations with China. The US rebalance demonstrated how the United States adapted to and worked constructively with various regional multilateral groupings, endeavoring overall to build a regional order supported by the rule of law, good governance, and other accepted norms.[86]

While the rebalance enhanced US competition with China, as well as American challenges to China's area denial security strategy and its neomercantilist economic policies and practices, it also strongly emphasized enhanced American engagement with China. Thus, the greater US engagement with Asia seen in the rebalance included greater US engagement with China. Examples of such enhanced engagement were the remarkable in-depth discussions seen in the informal summit between the Chinese and US presidents in California in June 2013 and in their later summit meetings. The greater Sino-American engagement was designed to reassure not only China but also China's neighbors that US efforts to compete for influence and to dissuade China from adopting assertive and disruptive policies toward its neighbors were done in ways that did not result in major friction or confrontation with China, which was at odds with the interests of almost all of China's neighbors. In effect, the rebalance involved a delicate "balancing act" of American resolve and reassurance toward China that seemed to work reasonably well until China's coercive expansionist efforts in disputed areas of the East and South China Seas, along with other adverse behavior, prompted a toughening in the Obama government's posture toward China.[87]

The prominence and initial success of the rebalance almost certainly influenced the Chinese leadership's most significant changes in Chinese foreign relations since the death of Deng Xiaoping. Deng had stressed that China should bide its time in foreign affairs and focus on domestic modernization. However, after the 2008 economic crisis and subsequent recession, China's comprehensive national power was rising remarkably as the United States and its allies faced protracted problems at home and abroad. Against this background, Beijing shifted to an assertive foreign policy exacerbating long-standing Chinese differences with the United States and others that was more in line with the China-centered nationalism prevalent in Chinese elite and public opinion. The shift came about with the transition from the comparatively weak and risk-adverse collective leadership of Hu Jintao to the strong-man rule carried out by Xi Jinping, who took over leadership of the Communist Party in 2012.[88]

A temporary pause in rising US-Chinese tensions came with the lead-up to the January 18–20, 2011, visit of President Hu Jintao to Washington. The harsh Chinese rhetoric criticizing American policies and practices subsided; the Chinese put aside their objections to high-level military exchanges, and Secretary of Defense Robert Gates reestablished businesslike ties at the top levels of the Chinese military during a visit to Beijing in early January 2011; China used its influence to get North Korea to stop its provocations against South Korea and to seek negotiations over nuclear weapons issues; China avoided undercutting international sanctions to press Iran to give up its nuclear weapons program; China allowed the value of its currency to appreciate in line with US interests; and Chinese officials were more cooperative over climate change issues at an international meeting in Cancun than they were a year earlier.[89] For his part, President Obama made clear during 2011 and 2012 that he would pursue closer engagement with China as part of his administration's overall new emphasis on American rebalance with the Asia-Pacific. Obama administration leaders from the president on down articulated the outlines of a new emphasis on American reengagement with the Asia-Pacific that promised more competition with China for influence in the region while averring strong US interest in greater engagement with China.[90]

Both sides endeavored to manage growing competition and rivalry with continued close engagement and pragmatism. The more than ninety official dialogues dealing with all aspects of the multifaceted relationship remained active.[91] The on-again, off-again pattern of exchanges between the military leaders of both countries—the weakest link in the array of dialogues between the two countries—was on again with improved exchanges in 2012–2015. President Obama and President Xi avowed commitment to manage differences effectively during summit meetings in 2013 and 2014 and looked positively toward their meeting slated for September 2015.

The so-called Taiwan issue—historically the leading cause of friction between the United States and China—remained on a recent trajectory of easing tensions. Taiwan's election in 2012 and the victory of incumbent president Ma validated the continued moderate approach to cross-strait relations, foreshadowing closer engagement along lines welcomed by both Beijing and Washington.[92] Local Taiwan elections in November 2014 nonetheless saw a resurgence of the opposition Democratic Progressive Party (DPP) and a decline of the ruling Nationalist (Kuomintang) Party. The DPP was viewed very suspiciously by Beijing. Once they won the January 2016 Taiwan presidential and legislative elections, cross-strait relations became tenser.[93]

Meanwhile, despite growing Sino-US distrust, there were also episodes demonstrating notable cooperation and seeming trust building between the two powers. One instance was the Sino-American handling of the case of Chen Guangcheng. The prominent Chinese civil rights activist escaped house arrest in April 2012 and fled from his home province to Beijing, where he eventually took refuge in the US embassy. After several days of talks between US officials working with Chen on one side and Chinese officials on the other, a deal was reached to safeguard Chen and his family and to provide Chen with medical treatment. Chen subsequently changed his mind and appealed for American support to go to the United States with his family. Intensive renewed US-Chinese talks concurrent with the annual Security and Economic Dialogue between top American and Chinese department leaders then underway in Beijing resulted in a second deal where Chen and his family were allowed to leave for the United States on May 19, 2012. Earlier that year, the US government showed remarkable restraint beneficial to China as it imposed strict silence on what occurred in the daylong visit of a senior deputy of the ambitious Chongqing municipality leader Bo Xilai who fled to the US consulate in Chengdu in February. The deputy was reportedly seeking refuge and safety from municipality forces; while in the consulate, an official escort to Beijing was arranged to take him to the capital, where he provided information leading to the downfall and jailing of Bo Xilai, then challenging Xi Jinping for the top leadership position. Concurrently, the American government remained silent about the extraordinary episode.[94]

Meanwhile, the Obama government after mid-2012 played down the emphasis seen in 2011 and early 2012 on American security and military moves that added directly to the growing security dilemma with China. National Security Adviser Tom Donilon went to extraordinary lengths to emphasize the nonmilitary aspects of the rebalance and to play down US competition with China prior to President Obama's trip to the region in November 2012. Concurrently, the secretary of defense and the secretary of state similarly emphasized the broad and multifaceted reasons for strong and sustained American engagement with Asia and played down competition with China.[95]

Unfortunately, the pragmatic engagement of President Obama with the Chinese leaders ran up against long-standing differences between the two countries. As discussed earlier, most relevant for China were opposition to US support for Taiwan and involvement with other sensitive sovereignty issues, including Tibet and disputed islands and maritime rights along China's rim; suspicion of perceived US efforts to change China's political system; resistance to the United States playing the dominant role along China's periphery in Asia; and criticism of many aspects of US leadership in world affairs. US differences with China involved clusters of often-contentious economic, security, political, sovereignty, foreign policy, and other issues. Most became more important for the United States as China grew to be seen as a "peer competitor" with the United States.

Xi Jinping Challenges America

After taking the leading Communist Party and government positions in late 2012 and early 2013, President Xi repeatedly placed other foreign and domestic priorities above his avowed but increasingly hollow claims to seek a positive relationship with the United States. Xi's preferred framework for US-China relations, which called for a "new type of great-power relationship" that would respect China's "core interests," was viewed warily by the United States. The framework marked the most recent in the list of proposals noted earlier that failed to create a structure to bridge differences and create lasting cooperation in the post–Cold War period.[96]

As Xi Jinping began the process of changing Chinese policies with major negative implications for the United States, the caution and low profile of Hu Jintao's leadership were viewed with disfavor. The string of Chinese actions and initiatives were truly impressive in seven different areas.

First, the government orchestrated the largest mass demonstration against a foreign target ever seen in Chinese history (against US ally Japan over disputed islands) in September 2012. It followed with diplomatic, military, and economic pressure against Japan not seen since World War II. Second, China used coercive and intimidating means to extend control of disputed territory at neighbors' expense, notably in rapidly building island military outposts in the disputed South China Sea. Third, ever-expanding advanced Chinese military capabilities were aimed at American forces in the Asia-Pacific region. Fourth, Chinese cooperation with Russia grew steadily closer as each power endeavored to undermine US influence in their respective spheres of influence. Fifth, unfair Chinese restrictions on access to China's market, demands that foreign enterprises share sensitive manufacturing and production data, industrial espionage and cybertheft for economic gain, gross infringements on foreign intellectual property rights, and reluctance to contribute to regional and global common goods all advanced as China's economy grew. Sixth, China used its large foreign exchange reserves, massive excess construction capacity, and strong trading advantages to develop international banks and to support often grandiose Chinese plans for Asian and global infrastructure construction, investments, loans, and trade areas that excluded the United States and countered American initiatives and support for existing international economic institutions. Finally, Xi Jinping tightened political control domestically in ways grossly offensive to American representatives seeking political liberalization and better human rights conditions in China.[97]

President Obama proved to be less than effective in dealing with the various challenges posed by Xi Jinping's actions. His administration gave top priority to supporting an overall positive US approach to engagement with China. Differences were usually dealt with in private consultations. Even if they seemed important, they were kept within carefully crafted channels and were not allowed to spill over and impact other elements of the relationship. Thus, the Obama government followed a deliberative and transparent approach to China policy that was predictable and eschewed "linkage," the seeking of US leverage to get China to stop behavior offensive to the United States by linking the offensive Chinese behavior to another policy area where the United States would threaten actions adverse to important Chinese interests. It was easy for China to determine how the US president was likely to act in the face of Chinese challenges; unpredictable uses of power against China seemed unlikely, allowing China to continue its advances at American expense.[98]

The administration tended to focus on the success of US-China coopera-tion on such global issues as climate change, where recent shifts in Chinese domestic energy efficiency and pollution policies made Chinese priori-ties more in line with those of the Obama government and thus facilitated US-China agreement. Meanwhile, various American government depart-ment representatives had a wide range of cooperative interactions with their Chinese counterparts. They understood that, contrary to the practice of the Obama government, the Chinese government was prone to link—specifi-cally, to punish the American or any other offending foreign government with adverse action in a policy area important to that government in retaliation against actions by the American or other foreign government that China deemed offensive. Rather than risk China cutting off their department's posi-tive interchange, these US officials tended to favor the Obama government's approach of giving top priority to the positive overall relationship and manag-ing differences within narrow channels and usually with private talks.[99]

Critics of the Obama government's approach argued that its reticence failed to dissuade China to stop offensive behavior undermining important American interests. They averred that Beijing could easily read the US gov-ernment's caution and take incremental steps forward and at odds with US interests without much worry about negative consequences. They identified particularly with the 2016 US election campaign rhetoric and the admoni-tions of Hillary Clinton in her avowed determination to halt the incremental Chinese advances made by Beijing as it "gamed" the United States on eco-nomic, security, and political issues important to the United States.[100]

The Obama government's reticence despite deepening frustration with China's advances at American expense showed during summit meetings in Washington in September 2015 and March 2016. The international nuclear security summit in Washington from March 31 to April 1, 2016, featured positive interaction between President Obama and President Xi. Both lead-ers pledged increased international nuclear security, and both promised to sign the Paris Agreement on climate change on April 22, the first day the United Nations accord would be open for government signatures. The agree-ments were central elements of the outgoing US president's historical legacy. Consistent with past practice, other issues, including growing differences over the South China Sea, were handled largely behind closed doors during one of only two one-on-one meetings President Obama held with a foreign counterpart during the summit.[101]

The cooperative atmosphere in US-China relations had deteriorated in the previous two years, and forecasted tensions over key differences seemed accepted in Washington as unavoidable consequences of America's need to protect important interests from negative Chinese practices. However, President Obama also seemed to clarify the priority of South China Sea disagreements with China; his administration's actions showed that the president judged that this most prominent area of bilateral differences had not reached a level where it would be allowed to spill over and negatively affect other sensitive areas in the relationship, like Taiwan, or jeopardize the cooperation with China that the United States sought.[102]

President Obama rarely criticized China during his first six years in office. However, he became outspoken from 2014 on about Chinese behavior. President Xi ignored the complaints, which were dismissed by lower-level officials. Sidestepping Obama's complaints, President Xi repeatedly emphasized a purported positive "new model of major country relations" with the United States; American critics increasingly saw Xi playing a double game at America's expense.[103]

After a strained US-China summit in Washington in September 2015, Obama had less to say about China. Rather, he and his administration took stronger actions, exemplified by the following:

- Much stronger pressure than seen in the past to compel China to rein in rampant cybertheft of American property.
- Much stronger pressure than seen in the past to compel China to agree to international sanctions against North Korea.
- China's continued militarization of disputed South China Sea islands followed President Xi's seemingly duplicitous promise, made during the September summit, not to do so. In tandem came much more active US military deployments in the disputed South China Sea, along with blunt warnings by US military leaders of China's ambitions.
- More prominent cooperation with allies Japan, the Philippines, and Australia, along with India and concerned Southeast Asian powers that strengthened regional states and complicated Chinese bullying.
- US action in March 2016 halted access to American information technology that impacted China's leading state-directed electronics firm ZTE. The company reportedly had earlier agreed, under US pressure, to halt unauthorized transfers to Iran of US-sourced technology, but it then clandestinely resumed them.
- The US rebuked negative Chinese human rights practices in an unprecedented statement to the UN Human Rights Council in March 2016 that was endorsed by Japan, Australia, and nine European countries.[104]

However, the impact of the actions was less than appeared at first. The public pressure regarding cybertheft and Chinese support for sanctions against North Korea subsided once bilateral talks on cybertheft began and China went along with tougher UN sanctions against North Korea. Cutting off ZTE was reversed after a few days of secret consultations. Much later, during the early Trump administration, came the news that the United States had negotiated a punishment with ZTE that required payment of a fine of more than \$1 billion.[105] The rebuke in the Human Rights Council turned out to be a one-time public occurrence. Meanwhile, the so-called Taiwan issue in Sino-American relations became more sensitive following the landslide election in January 2016 of DPP candidate Tsai Ing-wen and a powerful majority of DPP legislators. Avoiding actions that might "rock the boat," the Obama government eschewed controversy and emphasized constructive cross-strait dialogue.[106]

In sum, the Obama government's greater resolve against China's challenges seemed to end up focusing on one issue area: the South China Sea disputes and related American maneuvering with Japan, Australia, India, and some Southeast Asian nations in response to China's destabilizing and coercive measures. Defense Secretary Ashton Carter and Pacific Commander Admiral Harry Harris repeatedly spoke of China's "aggressive" actions and what Harris called Chinese "hegemony in East Asia." They and other defense officials pointed to US military plans "to check" China's advances through deployments, regional collaboration, and assistance to Chinese neighbors. American officials also expected a Chinese defeat in a ruling later in the year (noted below) at the arbitral tribunal at the Permanent Court of Arbitration in The Hague, which undermined the broad and vague Chinese claims used to justify expansion in the South China Sea.[107]

As seemed likely at the time, the opportunistic and incremental Chinese expansion in the South China Sea continued. From China's perspective, the benefits of Xi's challenges continued to appear to outweigh the costs. Notably, President Xi was viewed in China as a powerful international leader, while President Obama appeared weak. China's probing expansion and intimidation efforts in the East China Sea ran up against firm and effective Japanese efforts supported strongly by the United States, and they were complicated for Beijing by China's inability to deal effectively with provocations from North Korea. The opportunities for expansion in the South China Sea were greater, given the weaknesses of governments there. And adverse judgment in July 12 in the case at The Hague was effectively dismissed by Beijing, with the United States offering few public objections to China's flaunting its egregious opposition to the legally binding ruling.[108]

What these developments showed was that the Obama government's efforts to counter China in the South China Sea were significant. However, it was obvious to Beijing and anyone else paying attention that they were carefully measured to avoid serious disruption in the broader and multifaceted US-China relationship. The American government signaled that such measured resolve was likely to continue to the end of the Obama government, and it did. The Obama administration favored transparency and predictability in

Sino-American relations. Unpredictability was generally not favored, notably by US officials responsible for managing US-China relations, in part because of all the work involved in managing uncertainty. Unfortunately, smooth policy management seen as fostered by the predictability and transparency of Obama policy allowed the opportunistic expansionism of China to continue without danger of serious adverse consequences for Chinese interests.[109]

Against this background, US dissatisfaction with Chinese behavior at American expense grew. Republican leaders in Congress and the Republican Party platform in the 2016 election were harsh in condemning various Chinese practices and calling for stronger administration actions to counter China's challenges. The subsequent years of ever-greater Chinese challenges to US interests have tarnished the Obama government's record in managing relations with China. The Obama officials were in the lead among those accused by the Trump administration and many in Congress as being "asleep at the switch" as the China danger to America emerged as a powerful global force without significant US government countermeasures.[110]

Many China-related issues were prominent in the 2016 presidential campaign, although overall they came behind other foreign policy concerns like Islamic extremism and Russia. Going into the campaign, debates over US policy in the Asia-Pacific focused heavily on perceived US weaknesses in the face of growing challenges from China. As the US election campaign progressed, this broad concern with China remained active, but it was overshadowed by strong debate on two sets of issues—international trade and the proposed Trans-Pacific Partnership accord—and candidate Trump's controversial proposals on burden sharing among allies, nuclear weapons proliferation, and North Korea. Criticism of the TPP received broad bipartisan support and posed increasingly serious obstacles to US government approval of the pact. Trump's controversial proposals were unpopular and were opposed by senior Republicans in Congress along with many others. Mr. Trump avoided bringing them up in the immediate aftermath of the US election.[111]

STUDY QUESTIONS

1. Why and how did the early George W. Bush administration reject the solicitous and accommodating US approach toward China in Clinton's second term and revert to a more distant and firmer treatment of China in a framework reminiscent of the US pan-Asian approach of the 1980s?
2. When China moderated its policy toward the United States in response, did this lead to the remarkable new direction in Chinese foreign policy stressing reassurance of the United States and other concerned powers that China's rise would be nonthreatening and peaceful?

3. How did US preoccupation with the war on terrorism, including large-scale military commitments in Afghanistan and Iraq, along with rising tensions over North Korea's nuclear weapons development and Taiwan's provocative pro-independence initiatives, influence US government efforts to seek much closer cooperation with China?

4. Why did US domestic criticism of China subside following the September 11, 2001, terrorist attack on America?

5. How did the above developments result in a positive stasis in US-China relations where both sides emphasized positive elements of pragmatic cooperation and dealt with differences in scores of private dialogues between the two governments?

6. Why did the pragmatic cooperation falter during the Obama administration?

7. Were US observers correct in seeing China at the outset pressing Obama harder than Bush on a variety of long-standing differences over Taiwan, Tibet, and US military presence along China's rim? Did they accurately detect Chinese assessment that the 2008 economic crisis showed major US failure, weakness, and decline, and growing Chinese prowess, warranting a more assertive Chinese foreign approach toward the United States over a variety of differences?

8. How did Obama's rebalance policy strengthen US standing in Asia, indirectly challenging China? Did Chinese observers overreact in seeing the new policy as a new containment policy targeting China? Were such calculations behind Xi Jinping's broad-ranging more assertive policies involving key issues for the United States?

9. Why was the Obama government slow and ineffective in countering the Xi government's more assertive policies involving key issues of importance for the United States?

RELEVANT VIDEOS

"Meet the Press" (Richard Cheney on Bush administration foreign policy and others debating China policy, April 2001, one hour) available at https://www.worldcat.org/title/meet-the-press-april-8-2001/oclc/8085747026&referer=brief_results

"The White House and US Policy toward China: The View from the Inside" (CSPAN, May 1, 2009, ninety minutes) available at https://www.c-span.org/video/?285642-1/us-china-relations

"Jeff Bader and Dennis Wilder Talk US Policy on China at the Paulson Institute" (November 2016, seventy-seven minutes) available at https://www.paulsoninstitute.org/events/jeff-bader-and-dennis-wilder-talk-u-s-policy-on-china-at-paulson-institute

"US-China Relations" (CNN panel on US-China relations and 2012 US election, 2012, twenty-two minutes) available at https://www.worldcat.org/title/on-china-china-us-relations/oclc/8646419963&referer=brief_results

"US-China Dispute over Cyber Espionage" (CNN panel on US-China dispute over cyberespionage/security prior to Obama-Xi summit, 2015, twenty-four minutes) available at https://www.worldcat.org/title/on-china-spy-vs-spy-uschina-relations/oclc/8975935112&referer=brief_results

Chapter 7

America's Negative Turn Against China

Determinants, Evolution, and Implications

The remarkable US government hardening against Chinese challenges to American interests represented an unprecedented reversal of the previous fifty years of emphasizing growing US engagement with China. It emerged erratically in the first year of the Trump administration and reached a high point of acute competition, repeated confrontation, and tension during the 2020 US presidential election campaign and an array of anti-China initiatives by the outgoing Trump government.

The new Joseph Biden government eschewed the strident rhetoric and public posturing accompanying Trump policies and sought cooperation with China on some important issues of mutual interest. But the Biden government broadly endorsed the prevailing view of China's policies and practices posing the most important threat to US international interests and the existing global order.[1]

The new tough line against China was first articulated clearly in the National Security Strategy in December 2017, almost one year after the start of the Trump administration. At that time, the strategy document's release was overshadowed by the afterglow of President Trump's lavish treatment by Chinese president Xi Jinping during the US president's visit to Beijing in November. In a departure from his normal practice of ignoring the efforts of foreign hosts, President Trump was effusive in his public remarks of appreciation throughout the Chinese visit.[2]

The American government's targeting of China gained momentum and soon featured a wide range of hard-edged countermeasures against multifaceted challenges seen coming from Chinese government policies and actions.

It reached a high point during the heat of the 2020 presidential election campaign as the most important foreign policy issue in the campaign. This fever pitch was sustained to the end of the Trump government. The incoming Biden administration's more deliberative policy making gave a lower priority to foreign affairs but sustained and sometimes advanced the countermeasures targeting China.

Continuity in the new US policy direction came from Congress. From their outset and up to the present, countermeasures against China were strongly supported and often initiated by bipartisan majorities in Congress. These congressional majorities generally agreed with Trump administration officials that the Chinese government posed a fundamental danger to American well-being and international interests; China undermined American influence in a headlong quest to attain Asian dominance and global leadership employing coercive security measures, predatory and mercantilist economic practices, and nefarious influence operations.[3]

Democrats and Republicans in the 115th Congress (2017–2018) and the 116th Congress (2019–2020) worked closely with the Trump administration in targeting Chinese practices. Past experience in previous decades usually saw the Congress serving as a brake, impeding US administration initiatives in dealing with China. The extraordinary administration and bipartisan congressional cooperation broke that pattern. Despite acute partisanship in Washington, opposing China's various challenges to US interests came to represent one of the few areas where both sides of the congressional aisle and the controversial administration agreed. This pattern continued bipartisan congressional support for a hard line against China's challenges amid ongoing partisan wrangling on most other issues during the Biden administration.[4]

TRUMP ADMINISTRATION DEVELOPMENTS

During his campaign for election in 2016, Donald Trump repeatedly affirmed that the main problem the United States had with China was that the United States wasn't using its power to influence China. The source of US power over China, according to Trump, was US economic strength. Overall, Trump was not hostile to or confrontational with China, having said, "We desire to live peacefully and in friendship with Russia and China. We have serious differences with these two nations . . . but we are not bound to be adversaries." Trump tended to avoid discussing China as a national security threat. He averred that issues with China could be dealt with through negotiations, using American strengths as leverage.[5]

Officials and specialists in Beijing at this time saw negatives with both the Democratic candidate, Hillary Clinton, and the Republican choice, Donald

Trump. Like many Americans, they were frustrated with the downward trend in US-China relations and judged that the trend would worsen at least to some degree if Clinton were elected. Some in Beijing nonetheless voiced confidence that mutual interests and highly integrated US-China government relationships would guard against relations going seriously off track. Chinese derision of Trump earlier in 2016 shifted to seeking advantage, given the candidate's disruption of US alliances along China's rim and emphasis on seeking common ground with China through negotiations. Overall, a prevailing view was that China could "shape" President Trump to behave in line with its interests, as Donald Trump was seen as less ideological and more pragmatic than Hillary Clinton.[6]

President-elect Trump upended these sanguine Chinese views when he accepted a congratulatory phone call from Taiwan's president in December 2016. The call was reportedly facilitated by long-standing Republican Party leaders, reflecting the party's 2016 platform, which was remarkably supportive of Taiwan as well as harsh toward China. When China complained, Mr. Trump condemned Beijing's unfair economic policies and its building of military outposts in the disputed South China Sea, and he went on to question why the United States needed to support a position of one China and avoid improved contacts with Taiwan. President Trump eventually was persuaded to endorse—at least in general terms—the American view of the one-China policy. His informal summit meeting with President Xi Jinping in Florida in early April 2017 went well. The two leaders met again on the sidelines of the G-20 summit in July and held repeated phone conversations over North Korea and other issues in the lead-up to the US president's visit to Beijing in November. Despite serious differences between the two countries, both leaders seemed to value their personal rapport. As noted, President Xi organized a remarkable visit for President Trump in China, prompting President Trump's personal gratitude and appreciation.[7]

Erratic US "Whole-of-Government" Pushback Against China, 2017–18

After the Florida summit, the Trump government kept strong political pressure on China to use its leverage to halt North Korea's nuclear weapons development. Planned arms sales to Taiwan, freedom-of-navigation exercises in the South China Sea, and other US initiatives that might have complicated America's search for leverage with China in order to stop North Korea's nuclear weapons development were temporarily put on hold. The two sides also reached agreement on a one-hundred-day action plan to further bilateral economic cooperation prior to the first US-China comprehensive economic dialogue set for July.[8]

As President Trump registered dissatisfaction with China's efforts on North Korea in June, the Taiwan arms sales and freedom-of-navigation exercises went forward. And the July economic dialogue reached no agreement on actionable new steps to reduce the US trade deficit with China and ended in obvious failure. News leaks of senior administration meetings showed the president rejecting compromises with China that were supported by senior administration economic officials in lieu of unilateral punitive tariffs against adverse Chinese trade practices. The administration avoided harsh economic measures in the lead-up to the president's trip to China in November, but they emerged in 2018.[9]

The Trump government's National Security Strategy of December 2017 and its National Defense Strategy of January 2018 employed harsh words about China not seen in official administration documents since before the Nixon administration. They viewed Beijing as a predatory rival and the top danger to American national security. Added to China's military power and assertive actions in the Asia-Pacific was the danger China posed to the United States as it carried out its plan to be the leading country in various high-technology industries seen as essential for sustaining US international leadership and national security.[10]

In communications with Congress, administration leaders repeatedly highlighted the latter danger, which represented a newly prominent and important issue in 2018 added to long-standing American grievances against China. US trade representative Robert Lighthizer issued a dire warning against the many covert and overt ways China unfairly took advantage of the United States. He said such practices represented "an existential threat" to the United States. Meanwhile, FBI director Christopher Wray highlighted for Congress another newly prominent issue, Chinese overt and covert influence operations, including espionage in the United States. He warned repeatedly that America needed a "whole-of-society" effort to counter Beijing's perceived nefarious intentions.[11]

Congressional members of both parties saw the wisdom in the administration's warnings and began to take action, making 2018 the most assertive period of congressional work on China since the tumultuous decade after the Tiananmen crackdown. However, the broader impact on American politics was diluted for several reasons. First, President Trump did not use and appeared ambivalent about the anti-China language seen in the administration strategy documents. Thus, he repeatedly expressed friendship and respect for President Xi, whose support he continued to seek in dealing with North Korea. Against this background, Mr. Trump disapproved forward US movement with Taiwan as he attempted negotiations with North Korea's Kim Jung Un at a summit in Singapore in June 2018. Second, senior administration officials remained seriously divided on economic issues with China. White

House economic adviser Gary Cohn's resignation in March 2018 weakened the moderates. Initial punitive tariffs ensued. Third, public opinion generally was unaware of the China danger—it stuck to its long-standing view of not liking the Chinese government but also seeking to avoid trouble with China.[12] Fourth, the media remained largely unaware of the major shift. They tended to focus on President Trump's antics and his seeking of trade protectionism for his political supporters.[13]

The specific steps Congress used in hardening policy toward China involved the following:

- Extensive hearings on the challenges Chinese policies and practices pose for American interests.[14]
- A variety of individual bills on specific issues, some of which were incorporated into such important legislation seen as requiring congressional approval as the annual National Defense Authorization bill.[15]
- Letters to the administration signed by bipartisan congressional leaders warning of Chinese actions and urging firm responses.[16]

A bipartisan group of twenty-seven of the most senior senators, headed by Senate majority whip John Cornyn and Minority Leader Charles Schumer, sent a letter in May to the top American economic negotiators with China, urging a firm line against recent Chinese technology theft and ambitions. Another letter to senior Trump administration officials by a group of twelve senators, including prominent liberal Elizabeth Warren, urged defense against Chinese influence operations in democracies around the world. In August, a letter signed by sixteen senators including long-standing conservative critics of China and some leading liberals stressed opposition to Chinese international lending practices.[17]

Members sometimes grumbled about the adverse impact of the Trump government's punitive tariffs on their constituents, and they sometimes opposed imposing tariffs on allies at the same time tariffs were being imposed on China. Overall, there was much less opposition to the tariffs against China.[18] Congress disapproved of President Trump's decision in May 2018 to ease the harsh sanctions against the prominent Chinese high-technology firm ZTE in response to a personal plea from the Chinese president. In the end, however, Congress proved unwilling to stand against the president's compromise on sanctions on ZTE.[19]

Bills strengthening US support for Taiwan urged the American Defense Department and the US government more broadly to come up with strategies to bolster US-Taiwan military ties, assist Taiwan in countering escalating efforts by Beijing to isolate Taiwan, and promote higher-level contacts between the US and Taiwan governments. A stand-alone bill advocating more and higher-level US official visits to Taiwan, known as the Taiwan Travel Act, passed the Congress with unanimous approval and was signed by President Trump in March 2018. Taiwan generally enjoyed broad support in Congress, but achieving a unanimous vote on an issue strongly opposed by China indicated how negative a turn Congress was taking in regard to the Chinese government and its concerns.[20]

The Trump government took a variety of relatively small steps to show greater support for Taiwan despite Beijing's opposition. But after his reversal following the phone call with the Taiwan president in December 2016, President Trump reportedly remained wary of more dramatic steps on Taiwan policy that might jeopardize China's cooperation on higher-priority issues, notably North Korea. Trump reportedly was upset that a deputy assistant secretary of state in March 2018 gave a public speech in Taipei attended by the Taiwan president where he hailed ever-strengthening US-Taiwan relations. And the president reportedly reviewed the guest list of US officials attending the inauguration of the new unofficial American embassy in Taipei to ensure that no higher-level official that might be offensive to China would be attending. The Taipei office inauguration coincided with President Trump's June 12 summit with the North Korean leader in Singapore, reinforcing his unwillingness to jeopardize Chinese support at that critical time.[21]

The National Defense Authorization Act FY-2019, the most important foreign policy legislation in 2018, underlined hardening toward China.[22] Harsh language accused Beijing of using military modernization, influence operations, espionage, and predatory economic policy to undermine the United States and its interests abroad. In response, the law directed a whole-of-government US strategy targeting Chinese challenges; required the Defense Department to submit a five-year plan to bolster US, allied, and partner strength in the Indo-Pacific region; extended the authority and broadened the scope of the Maritime Security Initiative covering Southeast Asia to include the Indo-Pacific region; required a US strategy to strengthen military ties with India; prohibited China's participation in Rim of the Pacific naval exercises; required a public report on China's military and coercive activities in the South China Sea; broadened the scope of the annual report to Congress on Chinese military and security developments to now include "malign activities," including information and influence operations, as well as predatory economic and lending practices; and limited Defense Department funds for Chinese-language programs at universities that host Confucius Institutes.

The act's provisions on Taiwan reaffirmed various aspects of long-standing American commitments to Taiwan. They sought in particular to enhance US arms sales and higher-level US defense and related personnel exchanges, training, and exercises with Taiwan. The act required a comprehensive Defense Department assessment within one year of Taiwan's military forces and reserve forces, including recommendations for US actions to assist Taiwan and a plan on how the United States would implement the recommendations.

The act contained a separate set of provisions to modernize, strengthen, and broaden the scope of the interagency Committee on Foreign Investment in the United States to more effectively guard against the risk to US national security seen posed by Chinese and other predatory foreign investment. It also included key reforms in US export controls that would better protect emerging technology and intellectual property from Beijing and other potential adversaries.

Chinese officials responsible for US-China relations were aware that President Trump's approach to foreign affairs was the opposite of President Obama's as far as the former president's well-known features of deliberation, transparency, predictably, avoiding linkage, and restrained use of power were concerned. Nonetheless, they remained confident into early 2018 that whatever differences President Trump had with China could be dealt with readily through negotiations and making what the US president called "deals" that perhaps would involve some economic or other comparatively minor concessions from China. Thus, they were not well prepared for President Trump's decisive use of punitive tariffs against China beginning in 2018.[23]

An administration announcement in June promised steep tariffs on $50 billion of Chinese higher-technology imports seen to have benefited from China's abuse of American and international intellectual property rights. An announcement in July said that planned punitive tariffs of 10 percent would be imposed on $200 billion of Chinese imports. An August 1 announcement increased the rate of those proposed tariffs to 25 percent at the end of the year. As those tariffs were implemented in September, the United States threatened tariffs on an additional $267 billion of Chinese imports if Beijing retaliated, which it promptly did with Chinese punitive tariffs covering most of China's imports of American products.[24]

Throughout the fall, administration officials continued to turn up the rhetorical heat on China. In September, Trump, in the world spotlight at the UN General Assembly, condemned China for influence operations seeking to undermine the Republican Party in US midterm elections. Terry Branstad, former Iowa governor, current US ambassador to China, and "friend" of Xi Jinping (Xi favors Iowa), published a harsh editorial condemning China's influence operations in Iowa. National Security Council senior China official Matthew Pottinger at Chinese embassy National Day celebrations issued a blunt warning of impending US competition. National Security Adviser John Bolton and Secretary of State Michael Pompeo doubled down in criticism of China in prominent media interviews.

Vice President Michael Pence inaugurated a new public phase of the Trump government's toughening against China in a speech in October 2018 explaining to the American people, the media, and international audiences the wide extent of the US policy shift and its purported durability. Citing the administration's National Security Strategy, he detailed key elements in the current wide-ranging Trump administration response to China's many challenges.[25]

Other tough measures against China not seen in past US practice came from various US agencies. Sanctions were imposed on a Chinese company and officials for purchasing weapons from Russia in violation of US sanctions against Russia. Then came the publicized arrest in Belgium during an FBI-engineered sting operation and deportation to the United States of a Chinese security official involved in espionage to steal US military technology. Warning strongly against Beijing's intentions in Latin America, the administration in September condemned China's continued expansion of diplomatic relations at the expense of Taiwan in the region as adverse to US interests and regional stability. It repeatedly attacked China's self-serving and predatory ambitions seen in Xi Jinping's ever-growing Belt and Road Initiative (BRI), now involving Chinese infrastructure building, loans, investments, and port acquisitions throughout most of the world. The United States opposed continued World Bank assistance of about $2 billion in loans annually to China despite its prominent economic status, and it objected to any International Monetary Fund bailout for Pakistan that would compensate China for its large-scale "predatory lending" to the country under the rubric of China's BRI. The Trump government was reported in October to seek withdrawal from the Intermediate-Range Nuclear Forces treaty controlling intermediate ballistic missiles so that the United States could develop and deploy such missiles to counter the ballistic missile advantage in the Asia-Pacific held by China, not a signatory of the Intermediate-Range Nuclear Forces treaty.

Entering November, the Justice Department rolled out what was called a "New Initiative" to combat Chinese economic espionage. Standing in for absent President Trump, Vice President Pence repeatedly criticized Chinese economic and military practices, underscoring the administration's hard line for the international audiences in remarks at annual multilateral summit meetings in Asia. Reflecting toughening toward China, the US Navy announced its third deployment in 2018 of warships sailing through the Taiwan Strait. With the opening to China in the 1970s, the United States halted warships patrolling the Taiwan Strait. Reportedly some warship transits occasionally took place since then, but they were rare and were not publicized, presumably in deference to China's sensitivities.[26]

The overall result was a negative atmosphere for the Trump-Xi summit at the G-20 meeting in Argentina on December 1. The summit resulted in a temporary halt to escalating US punitive trade tariffs against China, pending agreement involving extensive US demands by March 2019. Indeed, on the same day of the summit came the arrest of the chief financial officer and daughter of the president of China's leading telecommunications firm, Huawei, by Canadian authorities in Vancouver for extradition to the United States. The US charges involved Huawei's involvement in subverting US sanctions against Iran. Beijing reacted strongly, arresting and detaining Canadians in China, but it avoided actions against the United States. More negatives followed with National Security Adviser John Bolton's strong attack on China's policies in Africa in a speech on December 13 and with President Trump's signing on December 31 of the Asia Assurance Initiative Act, which provided $1.5 billion in funding for carrying out US programs in Asia and US support for Taiwan and other regional partners along the lines of provisions in the National Defense Authorization Act of August, noted above.[27]

Cross Currents in America's China Debate, 2019–March 2020

Following their meeting in Argentina resulting in a halt to new trade tariffs, both President Xi and President Trump emphasized the positive in their phone conversation of December 29, with Trump averring that "big progress" was being made in preparation for official talks on economic differences slated for January. The US negotiation team was headed by US trade representative Robert Lighthizer and his subordinates known for their tough approach to China. Congress finished the year with other legislation likely to be revived in the 116th Congress taking aim at Beijing's massive crackdown on dissent among Uighur Muslims in northwestern China and continued repression in Tibet, and it proposed penalties against Chinese high-technology firms that violate US international sanctions.[28]

As trade negotiations dragged on into 2019, administration spokespersons were publicly more restrained in criticizing China. Nevertheless, the whole-of-government pushback against Chinese practices went forward. The Justice Department publicized for media use and popular information a wide array of convictions of Chinese agents or those working for Chinese authorities engaged in egregious episodes of espionage, intellectual property theft, and influence operations. Department officials featured these episodes in briefings conducted in various locations designed to inform media and the people outside Washington, DC, of the extent and impact of these Chinese challenges. Department officials also visited various universities, warning of clandestine Chinese espionage using Chinese students to seek advanced technology and influence operations through Confucius Institutes.[29]

For its part, Congress sustained an anti-China drumbeat with legislation, hearings, letters, and other public bipartisan demonstrations to reassure Asia of US support in the face of China, to criticize China-Russia cooperation, to condemn acute suppression in China's Xinjiang, and to spotlight dangers posed by Confucius Institutes. In May 2019, Senator Mark Warner, the vice chair of the Senate Intelligence Committee, broadened the scope of his unusual efforts, with Republican committee member Senator Marco Rubio, to arrange briefings by the senior leaders of the US intelligence community to alert high-technology companies and other members of Congress about the danger to the United States posed by Chinese challenges. The focus of the meetings was on Beijing's headlong push to achieve leadership and dominance in high-technology manufacturing of critical importance to the United States. A centrist Democrat previously very engaged in positive inter- action with China, Warner spoke in public on the issues at a meeting at the Brookings Institution on May 9 reflecting on his broad experience in high technology and on the Intelligence Committee to warn of the very negative implications for America of China's aspirations. For his part, Senator Rubio, long a sharp critic of Chinese practices, took aim at the US business leaders who he averred repeatedly put their companies' profits in working closely with the Chinese regime in a higher position than carrying out policies that would enhance the welfare and capacity of American workers and indigenous US manufacturing capacity.[30]

By this time, mainstream American media were no longer so distracted by President Trump's antics, and they focused on the Chinese challenges to the United States. Repeated news stories about China's perceived ambitions to overtake America's lead in high-technology industries, placing US military technology leadership in jeopardy, headed the list of issues having a negative impact on American public opinion. A widely respected annual Gallup poll in early February 2019 found a sharp deterioration in American views of China. Twenty-one percent of Americans now considered China the country's great- est enemy, compared to 11 percent at the same time in 2018. The level of American popular disapproval of the Chinese government grew by 20 percent from the previous year.[31]

The strength of American popular opposition to Chinese challenges showed in analyses demonstrating a coming together of groups of disgruntled Americans now more focused on the China danger. Those groups were seen as key elements of President Trump's so-called political base. Trump's unexpected victory brought together the following: people afraid of being displaced by alien immigrants and perceived pernicious foreign influence; workers concerned about being sold out to China and angry about the com- plicity of US elites in the betrayal; Christians frustrated with obstacles to pro- claiming the Gospel, with China as the largest malefactor; and manufacturers worried about having their technology stolen and market access blocked. All four groups now gave the China danger an overall higher importance in

American public opinion. Their respective China concerns received forceful articulation by ideologues like Steve Bannon, were echoed in the recent rhetoric of Mike Pence, were pursued in the policies advocated by such close advisers as Peter Navarro and Stephen Miller, and were encouraged by advice from hawkish Washington think tanks and nationalistic commentators on Fox News. Against this background, it was no accident that *Politico* reported that China was "the global menace" featured above any other international danger at the annual Conservative Political Action Conference that President Trump addressed at length in March 2019.[32]

The growing tensions between the US and Chinese governments resulted in the atrophy of the scores of official dialogues used in the past to manage tensions and build positive interchange in Chinese-American relations. The establishment and widespread use of consultative mechanisms, often known as dialogues, was a means to allow for private discussion of US-China differences in ways that did not negatively impact the overall relationship. China favored these dialogues to deal with sensitive issues that if publicized could cause more friction than sought by Beijing, embarrassment over compromises or unpopular commitments made by China, or criticism among Chinese elite and public opinion. American leaders also often favored keeping secret the dialogue discussions with China, notably when the current policy was being criticized by Congress, the media, and public opinion.[33]

President Trump agreed with President Xi at their first meeting at the Mar-a-Lago resort in April 2017 to establish four high-level mechanisms for senior leaders to discuss issues. They were known as the diplomatic and security dialogue, the comprehensive economic dialogue, the social and people-to-people dialogue, and the law enforcement and cybersecurity dialogue. Other important dialogues took place between the two militaries. While the various dialogues met, they did not achieve much. And rather than shielding differences from public view, US government leaders beginning in 2018 were much more public than past American administrations in registering US concerns over major differences with China, through words and actions that often embarrassed and upset Chinese government counterparts.[34]

A similar atrophy impacted the wide variety of cooperative US-China programs fostered by many US government departments and agencies with Chinese counterparts. As noted in chapter 6, in the recent past, American officials tended to avoid confronting Beijing over various disputes in order to preserve and advance such positive programs of engagement with China. Now, the tables had turned with senior US leaders giving top priority to countering China's adverse practices with much diminished concern for negative fallout for any remaining positive interchanges with Beijing.[35]

In sum, the American side used blunt rhetoric and wide-ranging government powers to counter Beijing's policies and practices deemed detrimental to the United States. China remained on the defensive, seeking to protect its rights and interests but avoiding initiatives that might worsen the situation. Indeed, to the surprise of experienced observers expecting Beijing to lash out in the face of often insulting and egregious pressures by the Trump government and the Congress, China's reaction was far more cautious—and even conciliatory at times. Avoiding confrontation, Beijing focused on limiting risks while it pursued some opportunities for gains in the turmoil created by American policy and practice. Xi Jinping took personal responsibility to carefully manage US demands. Xi and his colleagues also reassured the international community that China would be a source of stability and prosperity. They took some measures to stabilize China's immediate Asian periphery to limit its exposure to confrontation with Washington, looked for opportunities to expand its presence and influence, and advanced relations with Russia and others seeking to oppose and weaken US power.[36]

In seeming contrast with the above negative trends in US relations with China were remarks by President Trump and some administration leaders hailing the progress achieved in the "phase one" trade deal announced in January 2020. Other evidence that the US government might be moderating its approach to China included these seven pieces of evidence.[37] First, President Trump remained ambivalent and was usually more positive toward China than any other senior administration official. He rarely used the language of his tough National Security Strategy focused on China as the primary US national security danger. Seemingly underlining this reality were the contested claims by former National Security Adviser John Bolton in a book publicly available in June 2020 that the president during the summit meetings with Xi Jinping in December 2018 starting the US-China trade negotiations pleaded with Xi for China to buy more American products in order to help the US president get reelected.[38] Second, administration leaders tended to be less vocally critical of China concurrent with ups and downs in yearlong US-China trade negotiations. The phase one deal was a cause of public celebration for them. Third, the administration kept postponing the imposition of proposed export controls regarding advanced US computer chips going to Huawei, despite the US government's strong rhetoric against the firm. Fourth, Congress was very critical of China's policies on such sensitive issues as Hong Kong and Xinjiang, but its legislative impact on US policy toward China was scattered and notably less significant than in 2018. Fifth, while public opinion in 2020 registered increased disapproval for China than seen in the ratings in 2019, there was little evidence that the US public shared the urgency to counter China's behavior seen in the administration's strategies strongly backed by bipartisan congressional leaders. Sixth, more than one hundred China and foreign policy experts signed a letter disagreeing with administration policy, calling for greater moderation toward China.

Last but not least, Democratic candidates for president gave little priority to China and were much more moderate than the debate in Washington. Joseph Biden averred that the United States was notably more powerful than China and could handle challenges coming from Beijing; latecomer Michael Bloomberg remained quiet on China—presumably to avoid controversy over his extensive business dealings with Xi Jinping and other Chinese leaders. Before declaring his candidacy, Mr. Bloomberg defended Xi Jinping's harsh crackdown on Muslim Uighurs in China. When asked by a reporter, Senator Bernie Sanders said that he did not consider China as an existential threat to the United States. He, like Elizabeth Warren, saw the problem with China in economic terms and caused by US big business, not China. Warren also focused on big business, not China. Mayor Pete Buttigieg did see China's economic rise and quest for high-technology leadership as a real danger, yet his remedy was not to confront China, and he advised that cooperation with China was needed on climate change and other issues. Senator Amy Klobuchar saw utility in well-managed US-allied pressures on China, but of one hundred tasks she said she would undertake in her first hundred days as president only one related to China—steel dumping.[39]

Public opinion at this time suggested that the episodic disapproval of Chinese government practices by the Democratic Party candidates was appropriate. Jake Sullivan, who had served as Vice President Biden's national security adviser and who became President Biden's national security adviser in 2021, claimed in June 2019 that the "inside the beltway" discourse about the acute danger posed by China was countered by polls showing Americans judged that China should not be our enemy, and the United States should trade with, invest in, and work amicably with China.[40] Polling data later in 2019 supported Sullivan's view of American public ambivalence on China.[41]

Nevertheless, despite these cross currents of relative moderation, sustained hardening seemed to continue to characterize the official American posture toward China. The Justice Department and its most famous component, the FBI, in February 2020 publicly revived their high-profile initiative begun in late 2018, highlighting egregious Chinese intellectual property theft and the danger of mercantilist Chinese support for Huawei and related companies leading to high-technology dominance and US subservience.[42] Secretary of State Mike Pompeo continued a steady drum beat of charges against various Chinese targets. Pompeo also gave unprecedented support for Taiwan against China. Bipartisan congressional support for the above measures continued strong.[43] US media were now much more aware of and sometimes echoed the sense of urgency about China seen in remarks of administration and congressional officials than was the case in 2018.[44] A large volume of detailed studies by conservative, centrist, and liberal think tanks in the United States, Europe, and Australia and other countries neighboring China and in-depth journalistic accounts from a similar wide range of reporters exposed China's heretofore often disguised and hidden use of unconventional levers of power with an overall aim to undermine America. Taken together, these studies reinforced prevailing judgments in Washington that China was not to be trusted as it pursued its systematic efforts to change the world order in ways that benefited China and weakened the United States.[45] And key elements of President Trump's political base supported tough measures against China. The president appealed to this audience as he repeatedly labeled the coronavirus impacting America and much of the rest of the world as "the Chinese virus" and rebutted criticism that such labeling was unfair and racist.[46]

Defense Department leaders were clearly supportive of the hard line on China. Regarding Indo-Pacific issues, the Defense Department's Indo-Pacific Strategy Report, released in June 2019, illuminated how the acquisition and deployment of advanced capabilities, new operational concepts, and initiatives to strengthen security partnerships (highlighting Taiwan, New Zealand, and Mongolia) would contribute to the preservation of a "free and open" region and dissuade Chinese adventurism. In November, the State Department issued a paper entitled "A Free and Open Indo-Pacific," which documented a wide range of diplomatic, economic, and security programs. Collectively, the documents along with administration leaders' speeches and congressional legislation made clear the scope and resolve of the US government in countering China in the Indo-Pacific.[47]

Indo-Pacific allies and partners with advanced technologies, notably Japan and Australia, were part of US-led efforts at this time to create a growing united front of like-minded governments targeting Chinese practices against their common interests. The United States and its allies and partners, including those in the Indo-Pacific, reportedly were sharing intelligence and other information to counter adverse Chinese practices. They tightened export controls and investment approvals, condemned Chinese economic espionage, and strengthened surveillance of Chinese influence operations and espionage. An American campaign to stop allies and partners from using communications equipment from the prominent Chinese firm Huawei and other Chinese providers gradually persuaded a number of Indo-Pacific and other countries. US efforts to mobilize government and private-sector investment in the Indo-Pacific to compete with China enjoyed strong support from Australia and Japan in particular.[48]

Greater military activism and cooperation countered Chinese regional advances. With increased funding from Congress, the US military now routinely sent US naval ships through the Taiwan Strait on publicized transits; sent B-52 bombers and other warplanes to patrol around Taiwan, including along the Taiwan Strait; and conducted more frequent freedom of navigation operations in the South China Sea by warships and B-52 bombers challenging the massive Chinese territorial claim. US Indo-Pacific allies Great Britain, France, and Canada also sent warships through the Taiwan Strait, while American military operations in the South China Sea were supported or complemented by military operations of allies Australia, France, Great Britain, Japan, and South Korea and also by India.[49]

2020: US Elections, COVID-19 Pandemic, Hardening Against China

The array of US speeches and actions targeting Chinese economic, political, and military challenges against US interests reached a crescendo in the months prior to and after the November 2020 presidential election.[50] American resolve to counter Chinese practices was strongly reinforced by the impact of domestic developments determining US policy toward China, notably the coronavirus pandemic. The first wave of the coronavirus pandemic hitting the United States with devastating consequences, involving over one hundred thousand dead by June 2020 and the deepest dive in economic growth and employment in almost a century, destroyed Trump's campaign emphasis on economic growth and upended both Republican and Democratic campaigns. China tried to avoid responsibility for being the source of the virus and failing to take prompt action, allowing its spread abroad with devastating consequences, and it officially supported unsubstantiated charges that the virus was clandestinely planted in Wuhan, China, by the US military. President Trump, Secretary Pompeo, and other officials vehemently counterattacked.[51] Amid the acrimonious charges and countercharges, American public opinion turned sharply against the Chinese government. Xi Jinping was viewed with no confidence by over 70 percent of Americans. China was seen as a threat by nine in ten Americans. Republicans and Democrats differed in calling for tougher US measures in response to Chinese responsibility for the crisis, but all registered broad antipathy for the Chinese government and its leadership.[52]

By April, the Trump administration and associated political action committees set an agenda for the campaign that featured President Trump standing up firmly to Chinese challenges and depicting Vice President Biden as a holdover from the failed China policies of the past. Along these lines, the president in May 2020 tweeted a picture of all the living former presidents posing with Barack Obama in the White House in January 2009 with the caption "You can thank these men for allowing Communist China to grow to the dominant dictatorship superpower that it is!"[53]

Though the president had a phone conversation with Xi Jinping on March 27 that both sides depicted as easing tensions, he avoided such measures as he pursued a tougher posture toward China. In May, he threatened to "cut off the whole relationship" and advised in regard to negotiations with Xi Jinping that "right now I don't want to speak to him." The president led the administration's charge against the World Health Organization, labeled a "puppet" of China, for faulty warnings about the pandemic that disguised early Chinese mismanagement of the outbreak. He cut off US funding and later formally withdrew from the World Health Organization. He was ambivalent about the phase one trade deal with China, advising that "I feel differently about that than I did three months ago."[54]

Concurrently, the administration moved forward with added restrictions impeding advanced chip exports to Huawei. It blocked visas for Chinese students affiliated with Chinese military institutes who were involved with US university research on advanced science and technology. The government was considering restrictions on Chinese firms listing in US stock markets and the possible use of the US dollar as a tool in competition with Beijing. Administration officials announced success curbing the tendency of US companies to "offshore" manufacturing to China and other locales and sought further decoupling of the US and Chinese economies. President Trump blocked substantial US government pension fund investments in China.[55]

As it gave tit for tat in countering US criticism and punitive actions, the Chinese government was seen as taking advantage of international preoccupation with the pandemic to confront neighbors and to carry out repression in Hong Kong.[56] The Trump administration countered with major shows of naval and airpower in the South China Sea married with strong advances in American diplomatic support for Vietnam, the Philippines, and other claimants against what the US government emphasized as China's illegal territorial claims. There followed a remarkable series of affronts against China involving coordinated speeches by administration leaders depicting the escalating competition with China in stark Cold War terms. Sanctions against top-level Chinese leaders and many companies involved in the crackdown on Xinjiang were imposed. The United States revoked Hong Kong special status in US government regulations, furthered efforts to cut Huawei's access to high-level computer chips, further restricted visas for Chinese journalists, and canceled visas for three thousand Chinese graduate students with ties to the Chinese military. It abruptly ordered the closing of the Chinese consulate in Houston. With the president no longer interested in contact with China and Republicans seeking to use harshness toward Beijing against the Democrats in the election, the whole-of-government effort reached new heights, with future actions including the possible refusal of visas for Chinese Communist Party members, sanctions on banks in Hong Kong, and blocking Chinese firms from US stock exchanges.[57]

President Trump halted communication with President Xi. He and Republican Party strategists made hostility to China a focal point of the election campaign. Heretofore more moderate Democrats, including Joseph Biden, adopted much tougher public postures on China. Public opinion and mainstream media were more negative on China than at any time since the darkest days of the Cold War. The administration unleashed what one White House official characterized as an explosion of initiatives against China as the major systemic danger to the United States in the current period. They were fully backed by bipartisan legislation in Congress designed to defend the United States against a Chinese onslaught.[58]

The military and diplomatic dimensions of the Indo-Pacific strategy targeting China advanced. Secretary Pompeo and US envoys broke precedent in siding with other claimants rebuffing China's South China Sea claims. Freedom of navigation operations were more frequent in the South China Sea. For the first time, US warships were deployed to deter China from its use of superior security forces to threaten and intimidate ongoing oil and gas exploration operations carried out by other South China Sea claimants in their United Nations Convention on the Law of the Sea–recognized economic zones. The Defense Department supported these with unprecedented military operations, notably back-to-back aircraft carrier battle group exercises conducted by three different US carriers involving rigorous combat operations in regional waters with forces from Australia, Japan, and India during mid-2020.[59] Though the State Department avoided taking sides following the major Sino-Indian border clash in June, Secretary Pompeo separately tweeted "deepest condolences" for the Indian soldiers killed in the clash while voicing nothing about China.[60] Higher-profile US support for Taiwan's defense and diplomatic benefit advanced with high-level military and cabinet-level US visits.

As President Trump and his supporting campaign apparatus targeted Vice President Biden as weak on China,[61] Mr. Biden returned in kind. As some commentators in the United States, China, and elsewhere warned of a new Cold War, Americans broadly agreed with the hawkish policy toward China. On July 30, *Foreign Policy* concluded on the basis of recent polling published by the Pew Research Center that "American public attitudes toward China have hardened for good, which indicates that the Trump administration's aggressive approach could become the new norm burying 50 years of engagement."[62]

POSTELECTION TRANSITION AND THE BIDEN ADMINISTRATION

In the final months of 2020 and into January 2021, the Trump administration sustained an intense pace of measures to promote economic decoupling, curtail Chinese influence operations in the United States, penalize Chinese officials for undermining Hong Kong's autonomy and human rights abuses in

Xinjiang, and strengthening ties with Taiwan. For its part, the 117th Congress in its concluding weeks in 2020 faced an unprecedented number of bills (over three hundred) critical of China.[63]

Trump put aside the pretense of friendship with Chinese leader Xi Jinping and sustained a remarkable (for him) consistency in criticizing China, lasting until the end of his term and continuing as Trump emerged as the leading force in Republican Party politics going forward. Trump signed legislation and swiftly implemented sanctions targeting Chinese officials regarding repression in Hong Kong and Xinjiang. The administration further strengthened US ties with Taiwan, additional limits were imposed on visas for Chinese journalists, and dozens of Chinese companies were added to the Department of Commerce's Entity List restricting US high-technology trade with them. As it became clear that Trump would lose the election, administration leaders sought to limit the ability of the Biden administration to moderate restrictions on China and made a series of speeches to increase American public support for sustained hardening against China's challenges.[64]

As relations deteriorated markedly during the 2020 pandemic, Beijing changed its view from support of President Trump and awaited the election outcome. The major immediate costs to China of the administration and congressional countermeasures against Chinese challenges since 2017 included enduring offensive rhetorical assaults on China's policies by the US president, his lieutenants, and Congress; the impact of US punitive tariffs and export and investment controls; and much closer US strategic relationships targeting China with Australia, Japan, and India. Perhaps the biggest affront was the remarkable Trump administration multifaceted advancement of US security, diplomatic, and economic cooperation with Taiwan despite repeated stern warnings from China.[65]

Seemingly offsetting these costs was the fact that the US measures did not result in a halt of the foreign Chinese behavior challenging the United States. Those practices continued despite the US countermeasures. They involved increasing Chinese military advances focused on deterring and if needed destroying American forces; closer collaboration with Putin's Russia against US interests; continuing China's three-decade-long efforts using state-directed development polices to plunder foreign intellectual property rights and undermine international competitors, fundamentally weakening the free trade economic system; using the gains from China's state-directed economic practices to support ambitions to lead future high-technology industries, displacing the United States; seeking various narrow Chinese interests through building and exploiting economic dependencies via the BRI and other means; fostering corrupt and/or authoritarian governments against the West; coercing neighbors unwilling to defer to China's ever-increasing demands; employing widespread influence operations abroad using clandestine means;

disregarding international law and accepted diplomatic practices; and heightened domestic repression and massive human rights violations.[66]

Biden's statements during and after the 2020 election campaign suggested that he would place greater emphasis on alliances to pressure China to change its objectionable policies, attach more importance to human rights, and cooperate with China on climate change. At that time, it was deemed unlikely that the Biden administration would pursue a strategy aimed at containing China's rise.[67] Biden's priorities were seen to focus on fighting the pandemic and rejuvenating the US economy. In an interview with *60 Minutes*, Biden said that Russia posed the greatest threat to the United States. He notably eschewed calling China a threat or a rival, instead describing China as the United States' "biggest competitor."[68]

At year's end Beijing appeared to have low expectations for a reset of US-China relations after the Trump presidency ended. Chinese experts said the prevailing view in China was that the bilateral relationship had changed fundamentally for the worse. Nevertheless, they indicted that China hoped to put a floor under the relationship, reduce tensions, and find areas of cooperation.[69]

At the end of 2020, official PRC documents depicted the world as entering a period of turbulent change and forecast many challenges in the road ahead. They saw the United States in decline and the balance of power trending in China's favor. The Chinese economy rebounded from the pandemic faster than that of any other major country. International forecasts said China would overtake the United States as the world's largest economy by 2028, five years earlier than previously predicted. Chinese speeches and writings suggested that the pandemic accelerated China's emergence as a great power while hastening US decline. Reflecting this changing international power balance, a common refrain in authoritative Chinese Communist Party commentary asserted that "the profound adjustment of the international balance of power, especially that 'the East is rising, the West is declining' is the main direction for the development of the major changes."[70]

At the same time, Beijing had not reached a major inflection point in its foreign practices. In mid-2020, China's most senior intelligence analyst reaffirmed the United States had superpower status and capacity that rising China and other powers did not, arguing "the United States, like Britain after World War I, still has enough power to prevent other countries from replacing it." The United States, while in decline, was still the "one" superpower.[71] Against this background, the reasons to avoid confrontation with the United States remained: Beijing was still economically dependent on the United States, it had substantial internal preoccupations that would be worsened in protracted confrontation with the United States, and it remained insecure in key areas along its strategic rim where the United States exerted great influence.

Beijing's tough recent approaches toward India and Australia reinforced those governments to work more closely with the United States and Japan in counter-Chinese expansion.[72]

Going forward, Beijing offered no compromise on Chinese challenges for the Biden administration. It was open to dialogue and cooperation on common ground, seeing that the ball was in the hands of the Biden government. A successful Biden government effort to build a united front of regional and global allies and partners to press against negative Chinese practices would be a setback for China. But such an alignment likely would take time to build, and Beijing seemed prepared to employ tactical compromises and maneuvers to weaken a nascent front against China. In the meantime, Beijing saw little sign that the Biden government sought on its own to take significant actions to worsen relations with China.[73]

As events developed, the Biden administration sustained and sometimes advanced existing US government strictures involving trade, human rights, and other disputes with China. It demonstrated the priority of allies and partners as US leaders delayed high-level interchange with Chinese leaders until after high-level US consultations with those like-minded governments. And the Biden government delayed any significant change in US China policy until after extensive reviews of policy toward China during 2021. With an eye on China using vaccine donations to win friends abroad, the first summit meeting with the Quad leaders (Australia, India, Japan, and the United States) came in March with a major agreement of top importance to Asia to provide up to one billion doses of COVID-19 vaccine to the Association of Southeast Asian Nations, the Indo-Pacific, and beyond by the end of 2022. The developed countries of the G-7 meetings in May and June gave top priority to their issues with China. And China figured prominently in high-level US discussions with NATO, the European Union, Japan, South Korea, and Australia as the US leaders repeatedly asserted their intention to deal with China's challenges from "a position of strength."[74]

Senior US administration officials led by Secretary of State Antony Blinken and National Security Adviser Jake Sullivan worked with allies and partners in directly countering Chinese demonstrations of force targeting Taiwan and claimants in the disputed South China Sea. Such US reassurance saw the Philippines carry out their most prominent rebuke of Chinese pressure tactics in many years, while President Biden sent his close friend and top-level political adviser former senator Christopher Dodd to lead a bipartisan delegation showing support for Taiwan's president.[75]

Perhaps of most importance was President's Biden's personal assessment of the stakes involved in US competition with China. In his press statements, a speech to Congress, and various interviews, President Biden moved well beyond his common refrain during the election campaign that the United

States remained very powerful and had little to worry about from rising China, and he moved beyond earlier ambiguity as to the priority of the Chinese threat to the United States. He advised that the main inflection point facing America is the fourth industrial revolution with China confident that its authoritarian system will overtake the American one because of what Beijing views as the less efficient US democratic decision-making process. He argued "we can't let them win."[76]

Reflecting the sustained bipartisan congressional efforts to strengthen America in defense against various Chinese challenges and running in parallel with the president's recent sense of urgency about China was an enormous congressional enterprise led by Senate Majority Leader Chuck Schumer to pass multifaceted bipartisan legislation in 2021 to improve US high-technology industries and advance other measures to counter China. As Schumer advised, "We can either have a world where the Chinese Communist Party determines the rule of the road [in high-technology development] or we can make sure the United States gets there first."[77]

The administration and congressional efforts targeting China enjoyed continued strong bipartisan support in Washington, foreshadowing continued US hardening against Chinese practices for the foreseeable future. There was significant opposition, but it appeared scattered and marginalized for now amid dramatic US government pursuit of acute rivalry with China. The opposition varied and did not coalesce well. Some argued that a one-sided tough approach toward China led to counterproductive economic results as a result of the punitive tariffs implemented by the Trump administration and continued by the Biden government. US businesses with a big stake in China suffered negative consequences as a result of these measures.[78] National security experts judged that strong US support for Taiwan ran a major risk of US-China war, with possibly catastrophic results for all involved.[79] Zero-sum competition with China meant the United States would alienate those millions of Chinese who engaged positively with America over the past forty years, reducing the opportunity for a workable modus vivendi with globally prominent China.[80]

STUDY QUESTIONS

1. What were the major determinants of the sharp negative turn in US policy against China during the Trump administration?
2. Was the strong bipartisan support of Democratic and Republican majorities in Congress for the hardening of US policy toward China an important force driving the policy?

3. Did President Trump's erratic adherence to his administration's hard-line strategy to deal with Chinese challenges significantly weaken the effectiveness of the strategy?

4. Why were American public opinion, mainstream media, and Democratic presidential candidates, including Joseph Biden, ambivalent about a tougher US policy toward China until the COVID-19 pandemic struck America with a vengeance beginning in March 2020?

5. What explains Chinese leaders' uncompromising but cautious responses to the array of US countermeasures targeting Chinese policies and practices deemed threatening to US interests?

6. Why did Biden, as candidate, president-elect, and president, and his administration's foreign policy leaders come to see the wisdom of continuing and in some cases increasing the intensity and scope of Trump administration countermeasures against Chinese government behavior seen as being against US interests?

7. Given uncompromising Chinese leaders and overwhelming bipartisan congressional support for an unprecedented wave of legislation countering China in 2021, what are the prospects for US-China tensions rising to the point of military conflict? Alternatively, is there a meaningful possibility that tensions may fall as a result of unanticipated compromise by one side or the other?

RELEVANT VIDEOS

"The New China Rules" (CSIS, 2020, one hour) available at https://www.youtube.com/watch?v=IdbAcBcB714

"Communist China and the Free World's Future" (Michael Pompeo speech, July 23, 2020, twenty-five minutes) available at https://www.youtube.com/watch?v=7azj-t0gtPM

"Joe Biden Explains His Approach for US-China Relationship" (CNN interview, December 4, 2020, eight minutes) available at https://www.youtube.com/watch?v=jywSzmFa_Ig

"China Reality Check Series: Chinese Public Opinion and the Durability of Chinese Communist Party Rule" (panel discussion, CSIS, October 26, 2016, ninety-six minutes) available at https://www.csis.org/events/china-reality-check-series-chinese-public-opinion-and-durability-chinese-communist-party-rule

"How Aggressive Is China?" (panel discussion, George Washington University, March 17, 2016, ninety-six minutes) available at https://www.youtube.com/watch?v=5JZIuMgVHvI

"How Did China Succeed?" (Joseph E. Stiglitz, Norwegian Business School, September 14, 2018, fifty-four minutes) available at https://www.youtube.com/watch?v=Iaw4n9IZDdc

"What Happens When China Becomes Number One?" (Institute of Politics, Harvard University, April 9, 2015, seventy-three minutes) available at https://www.youtube.com/watch?v=bVkLqC3p0Og

Chapter Eight

Security Issues in Contemporary US-China Relations

In the course of US normalization with China since the late 1960s, security issues moved from being the main source of converging interests between the United States and China to the main source of divergence and mutual distrust between the two countries. Throughout the entire period, security issues have never been uniformly positive or negative for the relationship; their implications usually have been mixed. However, the broad pattern shows important convergence of Sino-American security interests against the Soviet Union in the period from the late 1960s through the early 1980s. This convergence can be explained using the lens of realism in international relations (IR) theory, with both the United States and China putting aside important differences in pragmatically seeking advantage in mutual collaboration against a common adversary. US-China security ties were cut drastically after the 1989 Tiananmen crackdown. This US step can be explained in part by liberalism in IR theory, with the United States asserting strong opposition to China's affront to American liberal norms involving human rights and democracy. Constructivism in IR theory helps explain what happened next. In response to US assertion of its liberal values, the Chinese government put much greater emphasis on strongly conditioning Chinese opinion to support a Communist Party–led China. Each side reinforced an identity of its state and society with divergent values and norms, complicating compromise and collaboration and reinforcing recently intense strategic rivalry.[1]

During the twenty-first century, the United States and China restored businesslike security ties and developed common ground on several international security questions. These positive elements were offset by differences on a range of security issues. The differences arose against a background of changing Asian and international power relations caused in part by China's rising power and prominence in international affairs and particularly by China's strong military modernization focused on Asian issues of key concern to the United States. A more recent US concern centered on the seemingly dire implications for the United States if China were to succeed in its headlong drive to dominate the high-technology industries of the future. This outcome would displace the US leadership in these important industries, and because high-technology industries are essential to modern militaries, it would place US military power in a weaker secondary position to China.[2]

China's growing military role in Asia and overall military capacity were supported by expanding Chinese nuclear and unconventional attack capabilities and espionage directed at the United States. The pattern in the past decade has seen China employing its increasing power and acting more boldly and assertively to change the regional and international status quo, supported by what it sees as a declining United States. Against the background of strong national identities with many antagonistic values and norms that can be understood by constructivism, the maneuvering of the two powers in the post–Cold War period can be assessed using realism, with both sides seeking advantage amid changing power realities in Asia and the world.[3]

CONVERGENCE AGAINST THE SOVIET THREAT

As discussed in chapter 4, the United States and China aligned together after decades of intense Cold War conflict and confrontation because of common security interests in the face of an expanding threat posed by the Soviet Union. Maoist China was racked by factional leadership disputes and committed to radical domestic and foreign policies and practices, but the Chinese leadership saw the need and wisdom of working closely with the United States in the face of the pressure China was receiving from the USSR. The Nixon administration and later US governments were prepared to put aside or play down a long list of American differences with China over foreign policy, economics, and values in order for American foreign policy to prioritize the development of a new opening to China for the benefit of US interests in Asian and world affairs—interests that were challenged in particular by expanding Soviet power.[4]

Both governments judged they had a lot at stake in how they worked together and in parallel to deal with security dangers posed by the Soviet Union. China was particularly vocal in complaining repeatedly in the 1970s and early 1980s that the United States was not firm enough in dealing with Soviet expansion or that the United States was too interested in bilateral agreements with Moscow that would benefit the United States but have adverse consequences for China. It took years for Chinese leaders to overcome a previous assumption that the United States would be more likely to cooperate with the Soviet Union against Chinese interests than to cooperate with China against the USSR. American leaders were concerned during this period with the possibility of a Sino-Soviet rapprochement and the negative impact this would have on US foreign policy and security. They worked hard to keep China on the US side in an international arena seen as heavily influenced by trilateral US-USSR-China relations.[5]

The Shanghai communiqué of 1972 and other official statements of both China and the United States during the 1970s and early 1980s made clear the large number of security as well as economic, political, and other issues that continued to divide the two countries. Despite secret US concessions to China over Taiwan at the start of the Sino-American normalization process, the slow pace of US withdrawal from official relations with Taiwan and the continued US commitments to the island government remained at the center of a set of key differences between the United States and China that were of fundamental importance to China. The United States was disappointed with China's position regarding the US war in Vietnam. Chinese leaders seemed from the American perspective to straddle the fence in opening closer relations with the United States while continuing support for the Vietnamese Communists fighting Americans in Indochina.[6]

The two powers were at odds over the Korean Peninsula, where they were on opposite sides, China supporting Kim Il-song's North Korea and the United States sustaining a strong alliance with and large military presence in South Korea. The close US alliance with Japan and China's avowed fear of revived Japanese "militarism" were important sources of differences between the United States and China, though China and Japan quickly normalized their relations in 1972, and China seemed more concerned in this period in shoring up Japanese resolve to join with the United States and China in struggling against the danger posed by the expanding Soviet Union. Elsewhere in international politics, China's influence was comparatively small, as Beijing was slowly rebuilding its international relationships tattered by the binge of self-righteous radicalism during the Cultural Revolution. Chinese leaders generally followed a path that focused opposition against the Soviet Union but also demonstrated strong differences with the United States. Chinese officials publicly opposed the two superpowers: the Soviet Union and the United States. The Chinese priority was building a strong international united front against expanding Soviet "hegemonism," but China continued to register strong differences with US policies in the Middle East, Africa, Latin America, and other parts of the developing world as well as US positions in international organizations and American views on international economic and political issues.[7]

Balancing American security interests with China and the Soviet Union was a repeated challenge for US policy makers. The prevailing US tendency to "play the China card," to lean closer to China in seeking US advantage against the Soviet Union, remained controversial in American politics and government decision making. Secretary of State Cyrus Vance and critics in and out of government saw US interests better served by seeking negotiations and improved relations with the USSR through arms control and other agreements. China's actual utility in assisting the United States in dealing with the expanding Soviet power also seemed limited. What exactly China would do in assisting the United States in a security confrontation with the Soviet Union was subject to debate.[8] In addition, China's sometimes strident positions and provocative actions against the USSR or its allies raised the danger of military conflict that alarmed some US officials. For example, China's military invasion of Soviet-backed Vietnam in 1979 prompted numerous statements of disagreement from prominent Americans.[9]

How US support for China in the face of the common danger posed by the Soviet Union would impact other important US security issues remained controversial. The United States was reluctant to build close military ties with China; US arms sales to the Chinese government were not an option until the early 1980s. Not only were such sales and the closer US alignment with China seen as limiting US options in relations with the Soviet Union, but US arms sales to China also had implications for long-standing US allies and associates in Asia who remained wary of Chinese intentions and expanding military capabilities. Nonetheless, the Jimmy Carter administration and the early Ronald Reagan administration continued efforts to solidify US security and other relations with China on an anti-Soviet basis. The full extent of American security cooperation with China against the Soviet Union did not become clear until years later. It involved extensive Sino-American clandestine operations directed against Soviet forces occupying Afghanistan following the Soviet invasion of December 1979 and agreements allowing US intelligence agents to monitor Soviet ballistic missile tests from sites in China.[10]

TIANANMEN AND POST–COLD WAR DIVERGENCE

US sanctions against China in reaction to the Tiananmen crackdown focused heavily on the US-China military relationship. The George H. W. Bush administration suspended military-to-military contacts and arms sales to China. US legislation in February 1990 enacted into law sanctions imposed on US arms sales and other military cooperation. In April, China canceled what had been the most significant US arms transfer to China, the so-called Peace Pearl program to upgrade avionics of Chinese fighter planes.[11]

The Bill Clinton administration began to revive military-to-military meetings with China. However, relations were marred by the Sino-American military face-off in the Taiwan Strait as a result of China's provocative military exercises there in 1995–96; the trashing of US diplomatic properties in China following the US bombing of the Chinese embassy in Belgrade in 1999; and, during the first months of the George W. Bush administration, the crash of the EP-3 US surveillance aircraft with a Chinese fighter jet in 2001.[12] During this period, Congress stuck to a harder line toward China than the administration did. It passed into law strict limits on the types of military exchanges the United States could carry out with China, and it required reports on the purpose and scope of such exchanges. It also required classified and unclassified annual reports on the purpose and scope of China's military buildup and its implications for American interests.[13]

The US reaction to the Tiananmen crackdown and the shifts in US policy toward China and Taiwan as a result of the decline and demise of the Soviet Union and the emergence of newly democratic Taiwan raised fundamental security questions in China regarding the United States. Though US administrations continued with varying vigor to pursue engagement with China, US leaders repeatedly made clear their interest in American liberal values and sought to promote change in China's authoritarian political system. The top priority of the Chinese Communist Party leadership was to preserve its rule in China, and the Chinese military and broader security apparatus focused on this task accordingly. As a result, Chinese security and other leaders came to view the US government and related nongovernment organizations and groups, notably the US media, which encouraged and fostered democratic change in China, as a fundamental threat to this key Chinese national security goal.[14]

The shift in American support for Taiwan also was seen in China as fundamentally at odds with Chinese national security objectives regarding preservation of Chinese sovereign claims and security. The fact that the Clinton administration, seen by Chinese officials as sometimes irresolute on security issues, sent two aircraft carrier battle groups to face off against Chinese forces in the Taiwan area at the height of the Taiwan Strait crisis in 1996 had important lessons for Chinese national security planners. From that time forward, Chinese security planners seemed to have little doubt that a key aspect of Chinese military preparations to counter Taiwan's moves toward independence must involve building the military capability to impede, deter, and if necessary repulse US military intervention in a possible conflict between China and Taiwan. Meanwhile, the US threat to Chinese national security and sovereignty also took other concrete forms for China, as American leaders became more prominent in support for the Dalai Lama and his calls for greater Tibetan autonomy and as they supported legislation and administrative actions pressing for democratic change and greater autonomy for Hong Kong as it passed from British to Chinese rule in 1997.[15]

TWENTY-FIRST-CENTURY DEVELOPMENTS:
REASSURANCE FOLLOWED BY GROWING TENSIONS

As reviewed in chapter 6 and discussed below, China's foreign policy approach shifted in the first decade of the twenty-first century in order to take into account concerns over the possible negative reactions of the United States and other powers to China's rising international prominence and influence. More emphasis was given to reassuring China's neighbors, and new emphasis was given to reassuring the United States; all were told that China's rise would not affect their interests in adverse ways. Opposition to "hegemonism" (a code word used by China in the past to condemn the now-collapsed Soviet Union and used prominently by Chinese officials and media throughout the 1990s to condemn the United States) had been one of the two main stated goals in major Chinese foreign policy pronouncements for decades. It was dropped from major Chinese foreign policy statements, or it received only passing reference. In its place emerged a policy of reassurance with a strong focus on the United States. The process of this evolution and change in Chinese foreign policy took several years and culminated in a major foreign policy document, "China's Peaceful Development Road," released by the Chinese government in December 2005. A few years later, China's foreign policy goal was recast by party leader Hu Jintao, who stressed that China was seeking to promote a "harmonious world" as the Chinese government also strove to achieve greater harmony inside China. The net effect of the new emphasis on "harmony" reinforced Chinese efforts to reassure American and other foreign leaders concerned with the implications of China's rise.[16]

Beginning in 2003, Chinese leaders entered a new stage in China's efforts to define China's approach toward its neighboring countries and what China's approach meant for the United States and US interests in Asia and the world. Premier Wen Jiabao addressed the topic of China's peaceful rise in a speech in New York on December 9, 2003. The exact purpose and scope of the new emphasis on China's "peaceful rise" became clearer over time.[17]

According to senior Chinese Communist Party strategists and other officials, Chinese motives rested on a leadership review of the negative experiences of China's past confrontations with the United States, Asian neighbors, and other powers and the negative experiences of earlier rising powers, such as Germany and Japan in the twentieth century. They concluded that China could not reach its goals of economic modernization and development through confrontation and conflict. As a result, they incorporated and advanced the moderate features of China's recent approach to Asia and the world into their broader definition of China's peaceful foreign policy approach.[18]

A central feature of the new Chinese approach was a very clear and carefully balanced recognition of the power and influence of the United States. In the 1990s, the Chinese leadership often worked against and confronted US power and influence in world affairs. China resisted the US superpower–led world order, seeking a multipolar world of several powers where China would enjoy more influence and room for maneuver. By contrast, in the next decade, Chinese leaders reevaluated this approach and adopted a more pragmatic attitude to the continued unipolar world led by the United States.[19]

Greater pragmatism and a strong desire to offset views in the United States that saw rising China as a competitor and a threat prompted Chinese leaders and officials to narrow sharply their view of areas of difference with the United States. They avowed that most differences with the United States now centered on the Taiwan issue and US continued support for Taiwan. The wide range of other Chinese complaints about US hegemonism in the post–Cold War period was said to be reduced. This seemed to conform to actual Chinese practice, though at times there were strong rhetorical attacks in the Chinese media against US policies and practices not related to Taiwan.[20]

In this improved atmosphere, Chinese leaders sought to build closer ties with America. They wished to integrate China more closely in the Asian and world system, which they saw as likely to continue to be dominated by US power for many years to come. They pursued closer partnership with the US leaders and wanted to avoid taking steps that would cause the US leaders to see China as a danger or threat that would warrant a concerted US resistance to Chinese development and ambitions. At the same time, they were not abandoning their past differences with US hegemonism. They still disapproved of perceived US domination and unilateralism seen in US practices in Iraq, US missile defense programs, US strengthening alliance relations with Japan, NATO expansion, and other areas that were staples in the repertoire of Chinese criticism of US practices in the 1990s. But Chinese officials were not prepared to raise such issues as significant problems in US-China relations unless they impinged directly on core Chinese interests. As a result, most important Chinese criticism of US policy focused on issues related to disputes over Taiwan.[21]

According to Chinese officials and specialists, Chinese leaders pursued the peaceful approach because they needed the appropriate environment to deal with massive internal difficulties and to avoid creating foreign opposition as China developed greater economic and other power and influence. Chinese leaders were said to judge that China faced a period of "strategic opportunity" to pursue its important and complicated nation-building tasks without major distractions, and they wanted to ensure that complications and distractions did not emerge in China's relations with the United States. The duration of this strategic opportunity was said to include the first two decades of the twenty-first century.[22]

An early indication of the weakness in Chinese reassurances to neighbors and the United States that China would invariably rise peacefully and harmoniously was seen in concurrent statements on China's national security strategy. There was a significant disconnect between China's national development policy and China's national security policy.[23] The pronouncements about China's peaceful rise and harmonious development made little or no reference to military conflict, the role of the rapidly modernizing People's Liberation Army (PLA), and other key national security questions. The broad outlines of Chinese national security policy were laid out in official Chinese documents and briefings.[24] They revealed Chinese leadership's strong concern about China's security in the prevailing regional and international order. This concern drove decades of double-digit percentage increases in China's defense budgets; it also placed China as Asia's undisputed leading military power and an increasingly serious concern to American security planners as they sought to preserve stability and US leadership in Asia.[25]

China's military growth increasingly complicated China's relations with the United States and some Asian neighbors, notably Taiwan and Japan. Leaders from the United States and some Asian countries were not persuaded by Chinese leadership pledges to pursue the road of peace and development. They saw Chinese national security policies and programs as real or potential threats to their security interests.[26]

Chinese national security pronouncements duly acknowledged that with the end of the Cold War, the danger of global war—a staple in Chinese warning statements in the 1970s and 1980s—ended. However, twenty-first-century Chinese national security statements rarely highlighted the fact that Chinese defense policy was being formulated in an environment less threatening to China than at any time in the last two hundred years.[27] Rather, they made clear that the United States remained at the center of the national security concerns of Chinese leaders.[28] Authoritative PLA briefings in 2008 presented growing US military power as the most serious complication for China's international interests; China's main security concern in the Asian region; and the key military force behind Chinese security concerns over Taiwan, Japan, and other neighbors.[29]

Chinese statements and the PLA buildup opposite Taiwan underlined that Taiwan for many years up to the present was the most likely area of US-China military conflict. The United States and its close ally Japan were portrayed as the principal sources of potential regional instability in Asia. Japan was explicitly criticized for various increased military activities and for its alleged interference in Taiwan.[30]

PLA and other Chinese officials registered strong determination to protect Chinese territory and territorial claims, including areas having strategic resources such as oil and gas. As discussed in more detail in chapters 9 and 10, Chinese-Japanese and other territorial conflicts involving energy resources in the East and South China Seas grew in scope and intensity in recent years, and they intruded ever more directly on these PLA priorities. Chinese concerns increased over US and allied forces controlling sea lines of communication, which were essential for growing Chinese shipping and increasing oil flows to China.[31]

The Obama government with some success continued the efforts of the George W. Bush administration to strengthen exchanges and dialogues between US and Chinese military leaders, which were the weakest set of links among the array of formal interchange between the two governments. As discussed in chapter 6, the Obama government also became concerned about China's perceived assertiveness and its repeated public threats and use of coercion and intimidation regarding territorial claims involving neighboring countries and US interests in unimpeded transit through Chinese-claimed air and sea spaces. Encouraged by China's neighbors, the US government embarked on a new military strategy, announced in January 2012 as part of the US administration's "rebalance" policy in Asia, which emphasized American security, economic, and diplomatic reengagement with the Asia-Pacific region.[32]

Though initial US military advances remained modest, US leaders pledged robust US military interchange with allies and associates throughout China's eastern and southern periphery, from the Korean Peninsula through Southeast Asia, Australia, New Zealand, and the Pacific Islands, and into the Indian Ocean and its central power, India. They said that with the US military withdrawal from Iraq and planned withdrawal from Afghanistan, the United States would reposition military assets and expand defense ties with many of China's neighbors, and the proportion of US warships in the Asia-Pacific region would rise from 50 percent to 60 percent of the US war fleet.[33] China's criticism of US initiatives made clear to specialists at home and abroad a forecast of greater strategic competition for influence between the United States and China—competition that would deepen the security dilemma at the heart of the pervasive distrust between the leaders of both countries. Indeed, as discussed in chapter 6, the bold and assertive initiatives of the Xi Jinping government, which began in 2012–13,

- departed from China's previous reassurance efforts under President Hu Jintao (2002–12);

- used wide-ranging coercive means short of direct military force to advance Chinese control in the East and South China Seas at the expense of neighbors and key American interests;
- advanced China's military buildup targeted mainly at the United States in the Asia-Pacific region;
- increased military, economic, and political pressure on Taiwan's government;
- rebuffed efforts for stronger pressure on North Korea's nuclear weapons development while sharply pressuring South Korea's enhanced US-supported missile defense efforts;
- cooperated ever more closely with Russia, as both powers increasingly supported one another as they pursued, through coercive and other means disruptive of the prevailing order, their revisionist ambitions in respective spheres of influence, taking advantage of opportunities coming from weaknesses in the United States, Europe, the Middle East, and Asia;
- used foreign exchange reserves and massive excess industrial capacity to launch various self-serving international economic-development programs and institutions to undermine US leadership and/or exclude the United States;
- continued cybertheft of economic assets, intellectual property rights, and grossly asymmetrical market access, investment, and currency practices; also intensified internal repression and tightened political control—all with serious adverse consequences for US interests.[34]

As noted in chapter 6, beginning in 2014, usually reserved President Obama complained often. President Xi tended to publicly ignore the complaints; he emphasized a purported "new great power relationship" with the United States to American critics who were skeptical of his intentions.[35]

As discussed in chapter 7, although President Trump vacillated between friendship and criticism in dealing with President Xi, the Trump government's National Security Strategy of December 2017 and its National Defense Strategy of January 2018 employed harsh words about China not seen in official administration documents since before the Nixon administration. They signaled the start of a fundamental shift in US government policy now viewing Beijing as a predatory rival and the top danger to American national security. Added to China's military power and assertive actions in the Asia-Pacific was the danger China posed to the United States as Beijing carried out its plan to be the leading country in various high-technology industries seen as essential for sustaining US international leadership and national security.[36]

MILITARY MODERNIZATION IN THE TWENTY-FIRST CENTURY: IMPLICATIONS FOR THE UNITED STATES

From the perspective of American defense planners and strategists, the Chinese military buildup since the 1990s has focused in considerable part on strengthening a capability to impede and deny US forces access to the Taiwan area in the event of a China-Taiwan military conflict or confrontation. The scope of this "anti-access" effort seemingly has broadened: Chinese military capabilities have grown to include the South China Sea and East China Sea, where Chinese security forces have endeavored to expand control and influence at the expense of other claimants and in the process have challenged and confronted US naval vessels and military aircraft and undermined US regional influence. Related challenges have appeared in Chinese efforts to counter US dominance in space and to use cyberattacks and other unconventional means to erode US military capabilities.[37]

As noted in earlier chapters, the United States has a fundamental interest in sustaining naval and other access to the Asia-Pacific region. And since the Japanese attack on Pearl Harbor, it has undertaken the obligations of leadership in sustaining a favorable balance of power in the region in order to protect that access and other American interests. The conflicts of the Cold War allowed for equilibrium to emerge in East Asia and the western Pacific where—in general terms and with some notable exceptions—the United States sustained dominance along the maritime rim of East Asia and the western Pacific, while continental Asia came to be dominated by China. Almost twenty years ago, this stasis was labeled the "Geography of Peace" by IR specialist Robert Ross.[38]

As of 2021, the situation has changed substantially. China has long chafed under superpower pressure along its periphery. Its military modernization gives top priority to upgrading power projection by air and naval forces along its maritime borders. While the United States seemed satisfied with the stasis Ross discussed at the end of the 1990s, American concern with Chinese anti-access efforts now grows in tandem with the increasing Chinese military capabilities to carry out the broadening scope of their anti-access goals and other expansive objectives.[39]

Key security issues involving Taiwan and other nearby contested territories, Chinese one-party rule, sovereignty, and resistance to superpower presence along China's periphery provide the foundation for Chinese security differences with the United States and help explain the suspicion and wariness that characterizes contemporary Sino-American relations. Of course, as explained in chapter 6, prevailing discourse between the US and Chinese governments previously tried to emphasize the positive for a variety of mainly pragmatic reasons important to the respective interests of the two governments. Security differences tended to be dealt with in dialogues concerning US-China military contacts and security issues in Asian and world affairs.[40]

The two governments in the recent past also developed considerable common ground on important security issues. China used to be seen by the United States as an outlier regarding issues of proliferation of weapons of mass destruction and related delivery systems. Into the 1990s, China passed nuclear weapons technology and missile systems to Pakistan and engaged in suspicious nuclear technology cooperation and missile development and sales with Iran and other nations deemed hostile to the United States. Under pressure from the United States and reflecting recalibration of Chinese foreign policy and national security priorities, China moved to a position much more consistent with American interests on weapons of mass destruction proliferation.[41] The United States and China at times demonstrated cooperation and common ground along with significant differences in dealing with North Korea's nuclear weapons and ballistic missile programs and the danger they posed for stability on the Korean Peninsula and elsewhere.[42] China also worked cooperatively and in parallel with the United States in dealing with international terrorism since the terrorist attack on America in September 2001, in managing tensions between nuclear-armed Pakistan and India in South Asia, and in managing crises precipitated by pro-independence initiatives by Taiwanese president Chen Shui-bian (2000–2008). China endeavored to moderate and then support Western-backed efforts in the UN Security Council to curb Iran's suspected nuclear weapons development program. It also was among the most active participants in sending security forces abroad as UN peacekeepers and, more recently, in contributing to the UN peacekeeping budget.[43]

Growing Military Capacity and Objectives

Overall, Chinese defense acquisition and advancement showed broad ambitions for Chinese military power. While they appeared focused on dealing with US forces in the event of a Taiwan contingency, these forces supported China's remarkably successful use of the coast guard, maritime militia, diplomatic and economic coercion, and massive dredging and construction of military installations on disputed South China Sea islets and reefs, resulting in de facto Chinese control of much of the area. Chinese military capacities ranged widely and could be used by Chinese leaders as deemed appropriate in a variety of circumstances.[44]

Salient Chinese defense acquisitions and modernization efforts included the following:

- Research and development in space and other surveillance systems to provide wide-area intelligence and reconnaissance and the development of antisatellite systems to counter the surveillance and related efforts of potential adversaries. Growing Chinese capacity in using sensors to enhance acoustical awareness in nearby seas potentially degraded the ability of US submarines to deploy in these waters.
- Cruise missile acquisitions and programs that improved the range, speed, and accuracy of Chinese land-, air-, and sea-launched weapons, including submarine-launched missiles that traveled much faster than the speed of sound and targeted sea and land surface forces. Longer-range land-based antiship cruise missiles and air-launched antiship missiles further challenged the ability of US naval forces to deploy within striking distance of Chinese targets.
- Ballistic missile programs that involved missiles with multiple warheads and that improved the range, survivability (through mobile systems in particular), reliability, accuracy, and response times of tactical, regional, and intercontinental-range weapons to augment or replace current systems.
- Development of ballistic missiles capable of targeting US or other naval combatants.
- Construction and acquisition of advanced conventional-powered submarines with subsurface-launched cruise missiles and guided torpedoes, and nuclear-powered attack and ballistic missile submarines to augment or replace older vessels in service.
- Development and acquisition of more capable naval surface ships armed with advanced antiship, antisubmarine, and air defense weapons.
- China attaining the position as the most active developer of hypersonic variants of the above-noted conventionally and nuclear-armed cruise and ballistic missiles. The speed and low-altitude trajectory of such weapons precluded effective defense in most present circumstances.
- Air force advances, including hundreds of modern multirole fighters, advanced air-to-air missiles, airborne early-warning and control system aircraft, aerial refueling capabilities, and unmanned aerial vehicles.
- Air defense systems involving modern surface-to-air missiles covering all of Taiwan and much of the maritime rim of coastal China and air defense fighters. Longer-range Chinese antiaircraft missiles posed a potential threat to such key elements of US maritime defense as Airborne Warning and Control System and tanker aircraft.
- Improved power projection for ground forces, including more sea and airlift capabilities, special operations forces, and amphibious warfare capabilities.

- Research and development of defense information systems and improved command, control, communications, and computer systems.
- Development of cyberwarfare capabilities.
- Increased tempo and complexity of exercises in order to make the PLA capable in joint interservice operations involving power projections, including amphibious operations.[45]

The Chinese advances meant that no single Asian power could match China's military power on continental Asia. With the possible exception of Japan, no Asian country was capable of challenging China's naval power and airpower in maritime eastern Asia. Should Beijing choose to deploy naval and air forces to patrol the sea lines of communication in the Indian Ocean, only India would conceivably be capable of countering China's power.[46]

Looking to the future, it is possible to bound the scope of China's military buildup. Available evidence shows that it was focused on nearby Asia. The major possible exceptions included the long-range nuclear weapons systems that targeted outside Asia and Chinese cyberwarfare and space warfare capabilities. China used its long-range nuclear weapons, now being increased significantly in number, to deter the United States and other potential adversaries by demonstrating a retaliatory, second-strike capability against them.[47]

The objectives of the Chinese military buildup seemed focused first on Taiwan, preventing its move toward independence and ensuring that China's sovereignty will be protected and restored. More generally, Chinese forces can be deployed to defeat possible threats or attacks on China, especially China's economically important eastern coastline. Apart from conflict over Taiwan, they were designed to deal with a range of so-called local war possibilities. These could involve territorial disputes with Japan, Southeast Asian countries, or India or instability requiring military intervention in Korea. Meanwhile, the Chinese military played a direct role in Chinese foreign policy; it sought to spread Chinese international influence, build military relationships with neighboring countries and others, and support a regional and international environment that will foster China's rise in power and influence. This role involved continued active diplomacy by Chinese military officials, increasing numbers of military exercises with Asian and other countries, Chinese arms sales to and training of foreign military forces, and more active participation by Chinese national security officials in regional and other multilateral security organizations and agreements.[48]

The Chinese military remained on course to continue a transformation from its past strategic outlook, that of a large continental power requiring large land forces for defense against threats to borders. The end of the threat from the Soviet Union and the improvement of China's relations with India, Vietnam, and others eased this concern. China moved away from a continental orientation requiring large land forces to a combined continental/ maritime orientation requiring smaller, more mobile, and more sophisticated forces capable of protecting China's inland and coastal periphery. Unlike the doctrine of protracted land war against an invading enemy prevalent until the latter years of the Cold War, Chinese doctrine continued its more recent emphasis on the need to demonstrate an ability to attack first in order to deter potential adversaries and to carry out first strikes in order to gain the initiative in the battlefield and secure Chinese objectives.[49]

To fulfill these objectives, Chinese forces needed and further developed the ability to respond rapidly, to take and maintain the initiative in the battlefield, to prevent escalation, and to resolve the conflict quickly and on favorable terms. Chinese military options included preemptive attacks and the use of conventional and nuclear forces to deter and coerce adversaries. Chinese forces expanded power-projection capabilities, giving Chinese forces a solid ability to deny critical land and sea access (e.g., the Taiwan Strait) to adversaries and providing options for force projection farther from Chinese borders.[50]

To achieve Beijing's national security objectives, Chinese conventional ground forces evolved, consistent with recent emphasis, toward smaller, more flexible, highly trained, and well-equipped rapid reaction forces with more versatile and well-developed assault, airborne, and amphibious power-projection capabilities. Special operations forces played an important role in these efforts. Navy forces built on recent steps forward, with more advanced surface combatants and submarines having better air defense and better antisubmarine and antiship capabilities. Their improved weaponry of cruise missiles and torpedoes, an improved naval air force, and greater replenishment-at-sea capabilities broadened the scope of their activities and posed greater challenges to potential adversaries. Air forces grew with more versatile and modern fighters; longer-range interceptor/strike aircraft; improved early-warning and air defense; and longer-range transport, lift, and midair refueling capabilities.[51]

The Chinese military in recent years was in the process of implementing a multiyear military reform effort, the most comprehensive in its history, said by some reports to be completed at the end of five years of effort in 2020. The past emphasis on ground forces was further reduced, with enhanced support for naval and air power. These military forces were reorganized with an eye toward being used increasingly in an integrated way consistent with an emphasis on joint operations that involved more sophisticated command, control, communications, computers, intelligence, and strategic reconnaissance (C4ISR); early warning; and battlefield management systems. Improved airborne and satellite-based systems aided detection, tracking, targeting, and strike capabilities and enhanced operational coordination of the various forces.[52]

Chinese strategic planners built on the advantages that Chinese strategic missile systems provided. Estimates vary, but it appeared that China possessed over 1,500 short-, medium-, and intermediate-range, solid-fuel, mobile ballistic missiles (with a range under four thousand miles) and short-range cruise missiles with increased accuracy and some with both nuclear and conventional capabilities. As it expanded its nuclear rocket forces, China also modernized and introduced a number of longer-range nuclear missiles capable of hitting the continental United States, and it was developing a viable submarine-launched nuclear missile that would broaden Chinese nuclear weapons options. Chinese nuclear missiles had smaller and more powerful warheads with multiple reentry vehicle capabilities.[53] The development of hypersonic variants of these weapons would compound already formidable defense problems for the United States and other possible opponents. The emphasis on modern surveillance, early warning, and battle management systems with advanced C4ISR assets seen in Chinese planning regarding conventional forces also applied to nuclear forces.[54]

These advances added to China's existing military abilities. They posed concerns for the United States, Taiwan, Japan, and many other Chinese neighbors; they presented an overall strategic reality of increasing Chinese military power that influenced the strategic outlook of most of China's neighbors. Those abilities included the following:[55]

- The ability to conduct intensive, short-duration air and naval attacks on Taiwan as well as prolonged air, naval, and possibly ground attacks. China's ability to prevail against Taiwan was seen as increasing steadily, especially given episodes of lax defense preparedness and political division in Taiwan. Massive US military intervention was viewed as capable of defeating a Chinese invasion, but Chinese area denial capabilities could substantially impede and slow the US intervention.
- Power-projection abilities to dislodge smaller regional powers from nearby disputed land and maritime territories and the ability to conduct air and sea denial operations for two hundred miles along China's coasts.
- Strong abilities to protect Chinese territory from invasion, to conduct ground-based power projection along land borders against smaller regional powers, and to strike civilian and military targets with a large and growing inventory of ballistic missiles and medium-range bombers armed with cruise missiles.
- A limited ability to project force against the territory of militarily capable neighboring states, notably Russia, India, and Japan.

• Continued ability to deter nuclear and other attacks from the United States and Russia by means of growing, modernized, and survivable Chinese nuclear missile forces capable of striking at these powers.

As China's military capabilities continued to grow more rapidly than those of any of its neighbors and the United States, China solidified its position as Asia's leading military power. As China's global involvement and international interests grew, its military modernization program became more focused on investments and infrastructure to support a range of missions beyond China's periphery. These missions involved power projection, sea-lane security, counterpiracy, peacekeeping, humanitarian assistance/disaster relief, and noncombatant evacuation operations. Overall, the situation clearly posed serious implications and complications in China's foreign policy. The situation made it much harder for Chinese officials to persuade skeptical neighbors, the United States, and other concerned governments that China's rising power and influence would be peaceful and of benefit to all.[56]

Finally, the challenges prompted by China's military advances were increasing because of the acute competition between the United States and China seeking leadership in the high-technology industries of the future economy, which is discussed in chapter 9. In both countries a sense of urgency prevailed in efforts to counter the other. In the United States, a strong shared administration-congressional concern centered on Chinese efforts to undermine American leadership in the high-technology industries of the future, seeking to overtake the United States and secure a dominant leadership position for China in controlling and directing these fields. Each country's defense leaders and organizations were keenly focused on using the high-technology advances for military purposes. Chinese and American military leaders recognized that the diffusion of dual-use high technologies such as artificial intelligence, big-data analytics, robotics, and other advances were often invented and produced in the commercial sector. And they were aware of the rapidity of the emergence and breakthrough of such new technologies. The result in China was a state-directed effort emphasizing military-civil fusion to absorb advanced technology from the commercial sector, and state-directed efforts to purchase companies abroad capable of advancing high-technology defense production. Continued active Chinese industrial espionage and cybertheft added to American antagonism in the intense competition with China.[57]

The outlook for intense Chinese defense challenges and competition with the United States and its allies and partners seems strong. The Xi Jinping government seeks to avoid military conflict with the United States or its allies and partners in pursuing its objectives through various tactics that leave military conflict as a last resort. These tactics are displayed in China's pursuit of its territorial and maritime claims in the East and South China Seas and along the disputed Sino-Indian border. China's continued militarization by placing antiship missiles and long-range surface-to-air missiles on outposts in the South China Sea combined with the use of coast guard forces and economic coercion to force smaller countries to bend to its demands. The Chinese defense white paper of 2019 rebuffed the Trump administration strategies targeting China. Xi Jinping's posture in the trade war with the United States did little to change the various serious frictions with the United States over intellectual property rights, industrial espionage, state-directed industrial policies, and other matters critical in the acute US-China competition to lead in the technologies driving future industries and national defense systems. China's developing ballistic missiles were capable of attacking bases as far away as Guam, striking US aircraft carriers, and penetrating US defenses to hit a range of American cities. China's advances in hypersonic variants of such weapons, its increases in nuclear weapons, its advances in sensors and other means to counter US submarines, and its advances in space and cyber-warfare all attested to the widespread rivalry and growing tension with the United States.[58]

Adding to the concern prompted by major advances in Chinese military capabilities and China's purported resolve to use these forces if necessary was the view held by many officials in neighboring governments about what their countries had experienced in past dealings with the People's Republic of China. Though the Chinese government worked hard to distort the historical record in its favor, and most Chinese seemed to believe the historical "party line" that China was never aggressive toward its neighbors, the history of the use of force in Chinese foreign policy remained well known among regional officials. The record provided little assurance that China's avowed peaceful development in the twenty-first century would be sustained. The PRC government resorted to the use of force in international affairs more than most governments in the modern period. The reasons were varied and included Chinese determination to deter perceived superpower aggression, defend Chinese territory and territorial claims, recover lost territory, and enhance China's regional and global stature. Studies of Chinese leaders' strategic thinking led to the conclusion that modern Chinese leaders, like those in the past, were more inclined than not to see the use of military force as an effective instrument of statecraft.[59]

Although facing superpower adversaries with much greater military might, Mao Zedong frequently initiated the use of military force to keep the more powerful adversary off balance and to keep the initiative in Chinese hands. Deng Xiaoping was much more focused than Mao on conventional Chinese nation building; he sought to foster a peaceful environment around China's periphery in order to pursue Chinese economic modernization. However, in 1979, Deng also undertook strong military action against Soviet-backed

Vietnam, and he continued for several years to confront Soviet power throughout China's periphery despite China's military weakness relative to the Soviet superpower. In the post–Cold War period, Chinese officials judged that the Taiwan president's visit to the United States in 1995 so challenged Chinese interests that it warranted nine months of military tensions in the Taiwan Strait. These tensions included live-fire military exercises, ballistic missile tests near Taiwan ports, and a private warning from a senior Chinese military leader of China's determination to use nuclear weapons to deter US intervention in a Taiwan confrontation.[60]

China's growing stake in the international status quo and its dependence on smooth international economic interchange were seen to argue against Chinese leaders resorting to military force to achieve international objectives. At the same time, the rapid development of Chinese military capabilities to project power and the change in Chinese doctrine to emphasize striking first to achieve Chinese objectives and advancing maritime control were seen as increasing the likelihood that China would use force to achieve the ambitions and objectives of the Chinese government. Against this background, it was not surprising that an active debate continued over Chinese national security intentions and whether they override the Chinese government's concurrent public emphasis on promoting peace and development in Chinese foreign affairs.[61]

As part of the debate, policy makers in the United States and allied countries were asked to balance their concern over Chinese military advances with an assessment of the many shortcomings seen in China's military modernization. The argument maintained that if deterrence failed in the Taiwan Strait, in the East or South China Seas, or elsewhere, US policy makers and strategic planners would need to understand and exploit the gaps in and limitations of China's military modernization to ensure that the United States and its allies were able to prevent China from using force to achieve its policy objectives. Those limitations involved the following factors:

1. Regarding leadership and quality of personnel, highlighted limitations included an outdated command structure in transition to a more effective structure, serious gaps in quality of personnel, lagging standards of professionalism, and continued corruption despite a major recent crackdown on such practices.[62]
2. Regarding weaknesses in combat capabilities, noted areas needing substantial improvement include logistical weaknesses, insufficient strategic airlift capabilities, limited numbers of special mission aircraft, and deficiencies in fleet air defense and antisubmarine warfare.
3. There remained the shortcoming of a notable lack of significant combat experience for Chinese forces and their commanders.

4. Mixed progress in carrying out joint military operations despite strenuous efforts.

5. A military structure disrupted by and still in a stage of absorbing and implementing the large-scale reforms initiated by Xi Jinping.[63]

Other Security Issues

Weapons of Mass Destruction: Development, Proliferation, and Nonproliferation

The development and deployment of nuclear weapons and ballistic missiles capable of carrying those weapons were critically important to China's national defense. They also continued to play an important role in Chinese foreign policy as a source of international power and influence.[64]

For many years, Chinese authorities followed sometimes avowed and sometimes secret policies involving the transfer of nuclear weapons, ballistic missiles, and related equipment and technology to selected countries for economic, foreign policy, and defense reasons. In the post–Cold War period, the Chinese government changed policies in these areas in important ways. While the pace and scope of Chinese nuclear weapons and ballistic missile development continued steadily to improve and expand Chinese capabilities in these areas, the Chinese government stopped its egregious proliferation policies of the past, supported and joined many leading international arms control regimes, and endeavored to change China's past international image as an outlier to that of a responsible member of the international arms control community.[65]

The recent record showed Beijing continuing to develop and increase the number of its nuclear forces capable of targeting the United States, Russia, and regional powers, while its stronger short-range and cruise missile development increased its ability to intimidate Taiwan and other neighbors and to warn their US backers. Chinese activities related to the proliferation of weapons of mass destruction narrowed and slowed markedly in the post–Cold War period as the PRC joined and adhered to varying degrees to a number of international proliferation regimes. Some Chinese proliferation activities continued to pose challenges for US and others' interests, and they sometimes met with criticism and economic sanctions from the United States.[66]

Since the end of the Cold War, the overall scope of Chinese proliferation activities declined significantly. The geographic distribution of Chinese proliferation-relevant exports narrowed from almost a dozen countries to three: Iran, Pakistan, and North Korea. The character of China's exports similarly narrowed in recent years from a broad range of nuclear materials and equipment (much of it unsafeguarded) and complete missile systems to exports of dual-use nuclear, missile, and chemical technologies. In addition, during much of the 1980s and 1990s, China's nuclear and missile assistance directly contributed to the nuclear and missile programs in other countries; in recent years, such assistance was indirect at best. The frequency of such exports also declined. Chinese leaders were loath to restrict China's own national defense programs; they appeared to weigh carefully the pros and cons of restrictions on Chinese weapons and weapons technology transfers abroad, leading to some ambiguities and loopholes in their commitments that were criticized by the United States and others.[67]

Among some perceived gaps in Chinese adherence to international arms control efforts, China is not yet a member of the Missile Technology Control Regime (MTCR) or the Australia Group. In June 2004, China expressed willingness to join the MTCR. China did not join the ninety-three countries signing the International Code of Conduct against Ballistic Missile Proliferation in The Hague on November 25, 2002. China did not join the Proliferation Security Initiative announced by President George W. Bush on May 31, 2003. China cooperated with UN-backed efforts against North Korea's missile and nuclear tests in 2006, 2009, 2013, and 2017, though it remained reluctant to impose sanctions or other pressure on Pyongyang. China also cooperated to varying degrees with US-backed efforts to sanction Iran for its reported development of nuclear weapons capabilities. China agreed with the Barack Obama government and other members of the UN Security Council in support of the Joint Comprehensive Plan of Action, signed in 2015, which seeks to curb Iran's suspected development of nuclear weapons. It criticized the Trump administration's withdrawal from the plan.[68]

The 1987 Intermediate Nuclear Forces Agreement between the United States and the Soviet Union prohibited cruise and ballistic missiles with range capabilities between 500 and 5,500 kilometers. Citing Russian development of such weapons, the Trump administration withdrew from the agreement in 2019. US officials reportedly sought to use the withdrawal to allow US development of such weapons to counter China, which was not a party to the agreement. China developed a large array of ballistic and cruise missiles of these ranges, giving Beijing a large strategic advantage against American forces in the Asia-Pacific region. China sharply criticized US withdrawal from the agreement and made clear that Beijing would not limit its arms development in US-proposed trilateral US-Russia-China arms agreements.[69]

CHINA'S APPROACH TO
INTERNATIONAL TERRORISM

Other features of Chinese national security policy that significantly impacted China's foreign policy and relations with the United States included Chinese policies and practices related to international terrorism. Chinese leaders broadly supported the US-led war on terrorism that began after September 11, 2001. Chinese leaders opposed the US-led military intervention against Iraq, but they were careful that China's opposition, as voiced in the UN Security Council and other venues, was less salient than that voiced by fellow UN Security Council permanent members. Letting France and Russia take the lead, China avoided serious problems in Chinese efforts to sustain positive ties with the George W. Bush administration.[70]

Presumably related to the withdrawal of US-led forces from Afghanistan were notable Chinese security involvement and activities with Tajikistan and Afghanistan's Wakhan Corridor. Increased Chinese security presence in both areas was seen to maintain domestic security in Tajikistan and prevent Afghan instability spreading to Tajikistan and China's restive Xinjiang region. The deployment of the People's Armed Police based in Tajikistan, as well as joint operations with Tajik and Afghan forces, remained focused on securing the Afghan border with Tajikistan and China. It remained to be seen what other measures China would undertake to secure borders in the weeks following the crisis caused by the rapid takeover in Afghanistan by the Taliban forces and concurrent rushed withdrawal of remaining US and allied forces in August 2021.[71]

As acute international antiterrorist efforts waned after a decade of US-led war against terrorism following the September 2001 attack on America, Chinese leaders focused on internal security in the restive Xinjiang Autonomous Region of the People's Republic of China and its large Muslim ethnic Uighur population. Violent actions by antiregime Uighurs occurred periodically in the region and elsewhere in China. They were linked to the East Turkestan Islamic Movement (ETMI) and related groups opposed to Chinese rule and favoring independence for Xinjiang. ETMI was classified by the US government as a terrorist group. An increase in such domestic antiregime attacks in 2012–2014 was followed by the unprecedented Chinese government "Strike Hard" campaign.[72] In the following years, China's crackdown in Xinjiang escalated to include internment camps, forced labor, and daily indoctrination programs for over a million Uighur and other Muslims in Xinjiang. Beijing also made extensive use of technological advancements to monitor Xinjiang residents. Besides surveillance cameras equipped with facial recognition, the government also collected information such as biometric data, data usage, and location. This sweeping approach was used to combat what China considered to be a serious terrorism threat. The longer-term objective encouraged cultural assimilation and internal migration to areas where Turkic minorities predominated, resulting in marginalizing dissent and cultural opposition to regime norms.[73]

The internment camps and other harsh Chinese measures were sharply criticized in the media and by politicians in the United States and other Western countries; significant sanctions were imposed on leading officials in the region and on foreign purchases of goods produced by Xinjiang people under duress. Beijing's strong relationships with predominantly Islamic countries resulted in little official criticism from these governments. Beijing continued to work constructively with an array of countries, such as Saudi Arabia, whose policies fostered the spread of Salafi ideas that China opposed at home, as well as other countries, like Iran, which the United States considered a sponsor of terrorism. Many governments concerned with terrorism or anxious to monitor domestic dissent were attracted to Chinese surveillance methods, equipment, and technical expertise for use in their countries. China's ever-increasing role in the United Nations and other international bodies acted as a brake on international condemnation and raised the chance of Beijing's approach to terrorism becoming a more widely accepted world practice. A variety of international terrorist groups targeted China as a result of the crackdown in Xinjiang, raising the possibility of terrorist danger for the ever-increasing large numbers of Chinese working and traveling abroad, notably in Pakistan, Nigeria, and other countries with significant terrorism problems.[74]

STUDY QUESTIONS

1. How did US-Chinese security relations change from being the most important determinant of US-China cooperation against the Soviet Union during the last two decades of the Cold War to becoming the most dangerous area of acute US-China rivalry in recent years?

2. Were US policy makers correct in cutting ties with Taiwan, downplaying relations with Asian allies and partners, and putting aside differences in values and norms in order to advance close security cooperation with China against the USSR?

3. What is the nature of the security dilemma posed by the respective military buildups, underway for three decades, of US and Chinese forces facing one another along China's rim? Do the buildups represent a so-called Thucydides Trap, foreshadowing superpower war?

4. Were US policy makers during the post–Cold War period up to the Trump administration more influenced by China's emphasis on reassuring the United States that China's rise would be peaceful or by concurrent Chinese defense reports and actual military deployments targeting US forces in the Asia-Pacific region?

5. What advances in Chinese weapons systems, military organization, and defense spending change the balance of power in Asia, challenging US leadership? How important are Chinese gray zone operations using robust coast guard and maritime militia to suppress neighboring countries and undermine the ability of interested outside powers, notably the United States, to counter China's gains at the expense of others, notably in the disputed South China Sea?

6. Is it correct for US policy makers to view China's rise as a leader of high-technology industries of the future as fundamentally important for America in order to maintain a military superior to China's?

7. What are recommended US countermeasures against Chinese challenges involving air and naval defenses in China's area denial efforts along its rim; high-technology industries; military power projection; and space, cyberwarfare, and hypersonic weapons?

8. Is China now prepared to put aside past constraint in order to confront and risk military conflict with the United States? Over Taiwan? Some other issue?

RELEVANT VIDEOS

"What Is China's Grand Strategy?" (Heritage Foundation forum, May 23, 2019, one hour) available at https://www.youtube.com/watch?v=qx-7Q3HEbDM

"Global China Webinar: Assessing China's Growing Regional Influence and Strategy" (Brookings Institution forum, July 29, 2020, ninety-seven minutes) available at https://www.brookings.edu/events/global-china-webinar-assessing-chinas-growing-regional-influence-and-strategy/

"The Hundred-Year Marathon: China's Secret Strategy to Replace America as the Global Superpower" (Michael Pillsbury lecture, Hudson Institute, February 3, 2015, ninety-two minutes) available at https://www.youtube.com/watch?v=u-QRVYVg50g

"Active Defense: China's Military Strategy Since 1949" (M. Taylor Fravel lecture, National Committee on U.S.-China Relations, September 10, 2019) available at https://www.ncuscr.org/event/active-defense-china-military-strategy/video

"Jamestown's Ninth Annual China Defense and Security Conference" (Jamestown Foundation conference proceedings, September 10, 2019) available at https://jamestown.org/event/jamestowns-ninth-annual-china-defense-and-security-conference/

"China Initiative Conference" (CSIS conference proceedings, February 6, 2020) available at https://www.csis.org/events/china-initiative-conference

"China's Military Power Projection and U.S. National Interests" (day-long hearing of US-China Economic and Security Review Commission, February 20, 2020, four hours) available at https://www.uscc.gov/hearings/chinas-military-power-projection-and-us-national-interests

Chapter Nine

Economic and Environmental Issues in Contemporary US-China Relations

Today, China's greatest global importance is as the world's second-largest economy. China's modernization and economic advance spread and deepened throughout the vast country and into all corners of the globe. China's economy experienced a 10 percent average annual growth rate for thirty years; it declined to 6 to 7 percent recently. China has become the largest manufacturer, trader, creditor, and holder of foreign exchange ($3 trillion), and it is the second-largest economy and recipient of foreign investment. It is forecast to become the world's largest economy, surpassing the United States, late in this decade.[1]

China accounts for 30 percent of the world's manufacturing output versus 16 percent for the United States. In recent years, it has contributed one-third of the growth in the global economy. China has become an important exporter as well as importer of technology. It accounts for over 40 percent of world e-commerce. In 2025, China is projected to have a larger science, technology, engineering, and math workforce than the United States and all other thirty-four Organisation for Economic Co-operation and Development countries put together. China's ambitious Belt and Road Initiative, begun in 2013, for several years featured more financing for infrastructure development abroad than the US-backed World Bank and related international financial institutions.[2]

China's economic modernization has had a staggering impact on the lives of Chinese people. It is the foundation of the legitimacy of the ruling Chinese Communist Party, the source of China's growing military power, and the main reason for China's international prominence in the twenty-first century. The implications of Chinese economic development also have had negative features at home and abroad, notably regarding wide-ranging trade and economic disputes and issues in environmental protection.[3]

The economic development supports active diplomacy in multilateral and bilateral relations. It provides large and growing leverage that Chinese leaders use often in conventional ways by winning favor and showing disapproval to countries through giving or taking away advantageous trade, investment, financing, and access to China's state-restricted market. And it provides leverage that Chinese leaders use often in unconventional ways, such as widespread covert bribery and other corrupt practices; elite capture (e.g., providing high-paid employment for standing or recently retired foreign leaders) and related influence operations; and penetration and control of media, communications, surveillance systems, and other key infrastructure for purposes of political manipulation and espionage as well as economic benefit. As noted, China's economic progress also provides the basis for the fastest-growing military modernization of any country in the post–Cold War period. Taken together, China's growing economic and military capacity changes the balance-of-power calculus of China's neighbors and other concerned countries, notably the United States.[4]

As the world's leading economy, source of foreign investment and technology, and leading importer of Chinese products, the United States has had an important influence on, and in turn has been influenced in important ways by, China's economic advance and integration into existing international economic structures and agreements. The burgeoning Sino-American economic relationship had a positive effect on relations between the two countries in the post–Cold War period. It replaced the strategic cooperation between the United States and China against the Soviet Union that had provided the key foundation of US-China cooperation in the 1970s and 1980s. The two world economies became increasingly interdependent. They were so important for each country's development that in the twenty-first century, signs of serious economic dispute or confrontation between the great economic powers had profound impacts on world markets detrimental to the well-being of each country.[5]

On the whole, China's rapid growth and rise to great-power status as a leading world economy showed the process in recent years as highly beneficial to China's interests. The Chinese government generally avoided major initiatives that had the potential to disrupt existing economic relationships seen as largely beneficial for its interests.[6]

As discussed in chapters 6 and 7, complaints and initiatives to change existing economic relations came largely from the US side of the Sino-American relationship, providing leading reasons for the remarkable hardening in US relations with China carried out since the start of the Donald Trump administration. The US complaints reflected a broad range of US interests and constituencies disadvantaged by widely perceived unfair negative aspects of the massive US-China economic relationship. They were supported by bipartisan majorities in Congress, American public opinion, and media commentary, and they received growing support from other developed countries subjected to egregiously unfair Chinese economic practices.[7]

Increasingly, US experts and government leaders and those of many US allies and partners with important stakes in the existing free market world economic system came to see as incorrect their past expectation, consistent with the liberal school of international relations (IR) theory, that growing trade and economic interchange would prompt China to conform more to international economic practices in line with the existing US-led economic order. What they found, as explained in a prominent report by the Asia Society in February 2017, was that Chinese practices reinforced, from a decade earlier, state-directed "zero-sum, mercantilist trade and investment policies that are highly . . . damaging to US commercial and economic interests."[8]

This darker view of Chinese economic behavior was more in line with the realist school of IR theory. Using that lens, China was increasingly seen in the United States and elsewhere in the world, especially among developed countries, as deliberately eschewing economic reforms that would open China more to investment and trade advantageous for the United States and other developed countries. The Chinese government practiced a form of state-controlled capitalism that used its control of bank lending and important state-owned enterprises (SOEs) and its influence over China's dynamic private sector to carry out industrial policies designed to advance a wide range of protected segments of the Chinese economy; and in this way, China, through illegal as well as legal means, eventually acquired advanced technology from abroad in a high-priority effort to create national industries that would prevail in the protected China market and then be launched with heavy state subsidies to wipe out international competitors and dominate international markets at the expense of the United States and other developed nations.[9]

As seen in the discussion in chapter 11 on China's various challenges to the existing system of global governance, Beijing's economic policies and practices came to be viewed as a critically important part of fundamental challenges to the existing order that not only impacted the particular interests of various developed countries but also undermined and overshadowed the existing world order with one dominated by an authoritarian party-state focused on advancing Chinese wealth and power at the expense of others. The latter included a wide range of countries with a strong interest in sustainable economic development and nonpredatory lending, noncorrupt business practices, government accountability, national interdependence, rule of law, human rights, and popular political empowerment.[10]

RECENT ECONOMIC AND TRADE ISSUES

The so-called US-China trade war started in 2018 with the Trump administration's punitive tariffs in reaction to unfair trade practices, massive theft
of intellectual property, and other Chinese economic challenges. The tariffs
grew to cover most US imports from China. Beijing reciprocated with tariffs on US imports and other measures that negatively impacted American
business with China. Negotiations to ease trade tensions begun in late 2018
moved in fits and starts, leading to a phase one deal in January 2020 that
remained to be implemented under very uncertain circumstances notably
caused by the COVID-19 pandemic and downward spiral of US-China relations over that and other issues.[11]

The United States accompanied the tariffs with tighter controls on Chinese
purchases of US high technology and the companies that make high technology. The government imposed major restrictions on US purchases of
equipment and services from China's leading high-technology and communications company Huawei and other such high-technology firms. It led efforts
with allies and partners to restrict Chinese purchases of high technology and
to restrict the access of Huawei and other such high-technology companies
to the markets of allies and partners. A major justification was that Huawei
(and other such companies) would comply with Chinese government man-
dates to secretly share with them sensitive information on foreign countries
held by Huawei as a result of its role in the communications infrastructure
of those states. Another justification was the substantial leverage the Chinese
government gained and often used to compel recipient governments' compliance with Chinese policy preferences or risk their difficult-to-maintain and
hard-to-replace sophisticated Chinese infrastructure.[12]

Additional US government steps to counter China included export controls
that could further hamper Chinese companies' access to high technology from
the United States and the many other countries that used US high technology.
Efforts to curb widespread Chinese spying and theft to acquire US high technology illegally saw an upsurge in counterespionage efforts targeting China
and restrictions on visas for Chinese specialists working in high-technology
fields in the United States. In a high-profile case, the United States had
Canada arrest the chief financial officer of Huawei, the daughter of the company's founder and leader, in Vancouver for extradition to the United States
on charges of illegally subverting sanctions on Iran.[13]

The trade war was only part of the dramatic hardening in American policy
toward China during the Trump administration. The US whole-of-government
countermeasures to varied Chinese challenges featured a variety of US government efforts targeting adverse Chinese practices over many issues that had

long bedeviled the relationship. The US efforts often centered on fair trade and investment practices, theft of intellectual property, predatory industrial policies, unsustainable foreign lending, and currency manipulation.[14]

New issues emerged to give a much greater sense of urgency to American efforts to counter often long-standing Chinese challenges. One was the awareness that China used a variety of covert and unconventional means along with traditional propaganda and lobbying to influence American elite and popular opinion in directions favoring China and weakening US resolve in countering China. The FBI director was outspoken on the need for a whole-of-society American effort to counter what was seen as nefarious Chinese efforts to beguile American opinion while stealing US industrial and security secrets in seeking to undermine US power and influence perceived as standing in the way of Chinese dominance in Asia and world leadership. The charges were fully supported in Congress, where conservatives and liberals came together in hearings, letters to the responsible administration leaders, and legislation in calling for a whole-of-government US pushback against China.[15]

An even more important driver in creating a sense of urgency in American efforts to counter China was the shared administration-congressional concern with Chinese efforts to undermine American leadership in the high-technology industries of the future, seeking to overtake the United States and secure a dominant leadership position for China in controlling and directing these fields. The consequences of such dominance were viewed as dire. They not only included America becoming second to and dependent on China economically but American military power, reliant on high technology, becoming second to China and thereby less able to counter China's expansive ambitions for leadership and control in Asia and the world.[16]

As noted chapter 7, the high-technology fields that received strong attention in the American debate about China included artificial intelligence, 5G communications networks, the Internet of Things, nano- and biotechnology, aviation and space, and electric vehicles. Specialist literature and media investigations assessing whether China or the United States was winning in the race for leadership in such fields often had a hard time supporting judgments on which side was ahead and why. Part of the problem was that important advances in these fields were not yet invented. What did become clear was acute US-China competition to build the next generation of industrial and military power, which was at the heart of the recent US-China rivalry. The so-called fourth industrial revolution saw advanced states headed by the United States and China attempting to exploit emerging high-technology breakthroughs for industrial purposes to promote economic growth and competitiveness.[17]

US and Chinese defense leaders and organizations were also keenly focused on using high-technology advances for military purposes. Chinese

and American military leaders were aware that dual-use high technologies such as artificial intelligence, big-data analytics, robotics, and other
advances were often invented and produced in the commercial sector. And
they were aware of the rapidity of the emergence and breakthrough of such
new technologies. The result in China was a state-directed effort emphasizing
a military-civil fusion to absorb advanced technology from the commercial
sector and state-directed efforts to purchase companies abroad capable of
advancing high-technology defense production.[18]

One key element of this high-technology competition between the United
States and China involved technology that was already invented and developed. It concerned digital network competition. As the ever-growing world
need for improved high-speed internet communications advanced, China was
often depicted as well ahead of the United States in developing and deploying the next generation of wireless communication, the fifth generation or
5G. China's robust domestic construction of 5G infrastructure was married
to plans for the so-called digital Silk Road abroad, encompassing a Chinese
effort to export telecommunications equipment and infrastructure, fiber-optic
submarine cables, mobile networks, cloud computing systems, electronic
commerce, and so-called smart cities. China's strong state-supported and
state-directed effort at home and abroad seemed to put US efforts led by
competing private companies dealing with issues posed by national and local
governments at a disadvantage. China attaining the "first mover" advantage
in developing and employing 5G systems also meant that international rules
determining how the world regulated the internet would be more heavily
influenced by China. Since Chinese party control of key Chinese industries
and economic enterprises grew under Xi Jinping, and China's national intelligence law was judged to require Chinese companies to cooperate with
Chinese government requests for information, the expansion of China's
digital communications equipment and infrastructure meant that Chinese
digital infrastructure deployed abroad could be used by Chinese authorities
for purposes of intelligence, influence operations, and other means advantageous to the state.[19]

American concern over China's 5G development was at the heart of the
Trump administration's restrictions targeting Huawei, China's leading company developing and deploying 5G and related technology and infrastructure
abroad. The US government worked with considerable success to persuade
intelligence officials among US allies of the dangers to security posed by
communications equipment provided by Huawei or other Chinese companies.
The American effort for a time was less successful in persuading government
decision makers in several allied states, but sometimes China's strident and
lurid warnings against countries joining the US-led boycott backfired as the
governments viewed with growing concern the harsh demands coming from

Beijing. Meanwhile, the US efforts were viewed by some allies and partners as coming late, as Huawei was already involved in their respective communications systems, and purging the Chinese firm would be costly and wasteful. Also, Huawei and related firms provided equipment that Western-aligned competitors, without the strong state support Chinese companies enjoyed, might be unable to provide in an expeditious way. And the Trump government was less than uniform in its opposition to Huawei, notably avoiding blanket restrictions in order to allow rural American communities to proceed with plans to use Huawei telecommunications equipment.[20]

Tempering keen American angst over China's advances in 5G development and deployment were some US specialists who judged that the "first mover" advantage might be exaggerated. Huawei's products were attractive because they were less expensive due to heavy financial support by the Chinese government, but they were viewed as being highly insecure. What was deemed more important by these specialists was that the United States creates secure 5G networks from the start. They advised coordinated and funded US government efforts focused on reliable 5G, along with close cooperation with American allies and partners.[21]

On entering office, the Biden administration said it would need time to review the numerous trade and investment restrictions actions taken against China by the Trump administration; predictions said the review could take much of 2021. Nonetheless, administration leaders from President Biden on down showed consistent resolve to compete with China for the leading position in the technologies of the twenty-first century. In the Interim National Security Strategic Guidance released on March 3, the Biden White House pledged to sustain America's innovation edge and pledged in response to China's adverse practices that the United States will confront unfair and illegal trade practices, cybertheft, and coercive economic practices that hurt American workers and undercut US advanced and emerging technologies. The new administration maintained the Trump administration's commitment to exposing Chinese corporate influence in the United States when the Federal Communications Commission identified five Chinese companies as a threat to national security on March 12. The Commerce Department then served subpoenas to multiple Chinese companies that provide information and communications technology and services in the United States. The Securities and Exchange Commission issued its final interim amendments to the Holding Foreign Companies Accountable Act (signed into law under the Trump administration), which mandated that companies disclose their associations with the Chinese Communist Party. In April, seven Chinese supercomputing companies were placed under strong export controls by the Department of Commerce because they were "involved with building supercomputers used by China's military actors, its destabilizing military modernization efforts, and/or weapons of mass destruction programs."[22]

As noted in chapter 7, President Biden in his April 28 address to a Joint Session of Congress sounded the alarm in calling on the United States to compete successfully with China. He said, "China and other countries are closing in fast. We have to develop and dominate the products and technologies of the future, the advanced batteries, biotechnology, computer chips."[23]

Meanwhile, Biden government officials sustained the Trump administration's punitive tariffs, even though they had been repeatedly attacked as counterproductive by Biden and other Democratic presidential candidates during the 2020 election campaign. And the Democratic candidates' campaign rhetoric ridiculing the phase one trade deal of January 2020 was put aside as Biden officials promised to hold China accountable for meeting its obligations under the agreement.[24]

Official Chinese commentary registered disappointment and some criticism of the Biden government's approach on these issues. There was no sign of any significant Chinese compromise, though on various occasions Beijing expressed its desire for a mutually beneficial trade and economic relationship with the United States. Beijing's "dual circulation policy" featured in China's Fourteenth Five-Year Economic Plan (2021–2025) demonstrated in essence that China sought to preserve as much as possible Chinese access to US and other advanced high technology and markets, to increase the world's dependence on the Chinese market, and to reduce Chinese dependence on foreign markets.[25]

US Trade Deficit with China

In addition to the important issues discussed above, related salient issues in US-China economic relations included the US trade deficit with China, which remained very important in American politics and policy dealing with China. The deficit was a sore point for US policy makers for many years. The deficit leveled off and declined during the major global economic crisis in 2008–2009 but then rose again, reaching record levels of $273 billion in 2010, $296 billion in 2011, and $315 billion in 2012. The merchandise trade deficit with China was $367 billion in 2015 and $347 billion in 2016. It was the largest of any country or group of countries.[26] US-China trade felt the impact of the US-Chinese tariffs and concurrent negative implications of the global pandemic and economic decline. Nonetheless, in 2020, China was the largest US goods trading partner (with total trade at $659.5 billion), the third-largest US export market (at $120.3 billion), and the largest source of US imports (at $539.2 billion). The official US trade deficit in goods with

China was \$311 billion. US goods imports from China fell by \$103.8 billion between 2018 and 2020.[27]

Offsetting to a small degree the negative implications of the merchandise trade deficit was a surplus in US service trade with China. In 2016, China was the United States' fourth-largest service trading partner at \$69.6 billion, the third-largest services export market at \$53.5 billion, and the eleventh-largest source of services imports at \$16.1 billion. That year the United States ran a \$37.3 billion services trade surplus with China, which was the largest services surplus of any US trading partner.[28] In contrast, bilateral services trade fell by 35 percent between January and September 2020 over that same period in 2018.[29]

The enormous US trade deficit with China was accompanied by long-standing complaints voiced by the US government policy makers in the administration and the Congress as well as media, public opinion surveys, and interest groups that focused on the massive trade gap as a key indicator that China's economic and trade policies were unfair and disadvantageous for the United States. Chinese officials publicly and privately resented US attempts to "politicize" the trade deficit, which Chinese trade figures showed as significantly less than shown by US trade figures, largely because of the way China counts its exports to Hong Kong that were actually going to the United States. They tended to see the American complaints as "protectionist" efforts by special interests in the United States that were disadvantaged by international economic trends associated with economic globalization. They found little fault in Chinese policies or practices and viewed American criticisms of China as unjustified.[30]

An important dimension of the recent increase in US imports of Chinese manufactured goods was the movement in production facilities from other Asian countries to China. Various manufactured products that used to be made in Japan, Taiwan, Hong Kong, South Korea, and Southeast Asian nations and then exported to the United States were now being made in China (in many cases by foreign firms in China using components and materials imported from foreign countries) and exported to the United States. Such processing trade often did not provide much overall value for the ultimate exporter, China.[31]

Investment Issues

Active foreign direct investment (FDI) in China continued in recent years, and growing Chinese investment abroad surpassed China's FDI in 2016.[32] China's trade, which continued to play a major role in China's rapid economic growth, featured strong dependence on foreign investment coming into China and trade relations managed by Chinese officials in ways that provided China with a large trade surplus each year. Foreign-invested enterprises (FIEs) were responsible for a significant portion of China's foreign trade; FIEs accounted for 42 percent of Chinese exports and 44 percent of Chinese imports in 2018. There were reportedly 445,244 FIEs registered in China in 2010, employing 55.2 million workers, or 15.9 percent of the urban workforce.[33]

The large role of FIEs and their often extensive supply-chain networks meant that a large portion of Chinese trade was so-called processing trade, where firms in China obtained raw materials and intermediate inputs from abroad, processed them locally, and exported value-added goods. Estimates of the extent of such processing trade vary. Among higher estimates, experts from Peking University reported in 2012 that processing trade constituted about half of China's total trade. According to China's Commerce Department in 2019, the total value generated by the exports of China's processing trade in 2018 was $797 billion and accounted for 32 percent of China's total exports that year.

Meanwhile, China's investments in US assets can be broken down into two categories: holdings of US securities (e.g., US Treasury securities, US government agency securities, corporate securities, and stocks) and FDI. China's holdings of US public and private securities were significant and constituted the largest category by far of Chinese investment in the United States. These securities included US Treasury securities, US government agency (such as Freddie Mac and Fannie Mae) securities, corporate securities, and equities (such as stocks). China's investment in public and private US securities totaled $1.84 trillion as of June 2015, making China the second-largest holder after Japan. US Treasury securities, which helped the federal government finance its budget deficits, were the largest category of US securities held by China. China's holdings of US Treasury securities increased from $118 billion in 2002 to $1.24 trillion in 2014 but fell to $1.06 trillion in 2016, making China the second-largest foreign holder of US Treasury securities after Japan.[34] Meanwhile, US holdings of Chinese securities were comparatively small. The US government estimated the value of such holdings (mainly equities such as stocks) at $107 billion in 2015. This was comparable to US holdings in Brazil and represented a very small percentage of total US holdings of foreign securities.[35] The Rhodium Group estimated that, as of December 2020, US investors held $100 billion of Chinese debt and $1.1 trillion in Chinese equities while Chinese investors held $1.4 trillion in US debt and $720 billion in US equities.[36]

Regarding bilateral FDI, China's FDI in the United States remained small until the past decade, when it rapidly expanded. In part because much Chinese investment in the United States comes via tax havens, estimates of the size of Chinese investment in the United States varied. The US government said the amount was $5.8 billion in cumulative investment through 2010. In 2015,

China ranked as the twelfth-largest investor in the United States, with investment that year amounting to $5 billion and the stock of cumulative investment valued at $14.8 billion. Private estimates of Chinese investment were higher. US FDI in China declined during the recession in 2009 but grew by $9.6 billion in 2010 for a cumulative figure of $60.4 billion. In 2015, the respective figures were $7.3 billion and $74.6 billion. While the overall value of US investment in China was relatively low, amounting to about 10 percent of US investment in the Asia-Pacific region, the investment was very important for certain US companies seeking investment and sales in China. China had the world's largest mobile phone network and hundreds of millions of mobile phone users, it was the largest market for commercial aircraft outside the United States, it had the largest number of internet users in the world, and more recently China became the world's largest market for new cars. US firms invested substantially in China as they endeavored to expand to meet the needs of these Chinese markets.[37] Foreign direct investment flows in both directions slowed with the US-China trade war.

Regarding Chinese holdings of US securities, US government leaders and other Americans encouraged Chinese investment in such US securities as a means for the United States to meet its investment needs and to fund the large US federal budget deficit. On the other hand, US policy makers at times in the past raised concerns that the Chinese investment could give China increased leverage over the United States on major economic or other issues.[38]

Chinese practices in holding US securities in recent years seemed to support the arguments of those who judged that China's holdings of US debt did not provide much practical leverage over the United States. They argued that, given China's economic dependency on a stable and growing US economy, and its substantial holdings of US securities, any attempt to try to sell a large share of those holdings would likely damage both the US and Chinese economies. Such a move could also cause the US dollar to sharply depreciate against global currencies, which could reduce the value of China's remaining holdings of US dollar assets.[39]

Regarding Chinese and US restrictions on foreign investment, as Chinese investment in the United States rose, the American debate on the perceived pros and cons of such investment intensified. On one side were US specialists and advocates who judged that greater Chinese FDI in the United States would create new jobs for US workers and have an overall beneficial economic impact on US interests. On the other side were American specialists and critics who assessed that Chinese investment was geared toward unfair, state-directed industrial policies designed to improve the competitive position of Chinese firms through mergers and acquisition of US technology. They saw Chinese firms as directly or indirectly controlled by Chinese officials bent on acquiring US economic assets in a drive to outperform the United

States in higher-valued industries and services. There also was a growing concern of China using investment to gain access to secret US national security technology.[40]

Meanwhile, American concerns rose over growing restrictions on American and other foreign investments in China. The restrictions especially involved the many highly protected sectors of the Chinese economy that were being developed by the state as "national champions," which were seen as designed to dominate the Chinese and international markets at the expense of America's leading firms in advanced production and technology. Such practice reinforced the view that China's growing acquisitions of high-technology American and other foreign firms were part of an overall industrial strategy that came at the expense of the United States. Against this background, FDI flows in both directions declined. In 2018, Congress enacted laws (P.L. 115–232) to boost US efforts against perceived predatory Chinese investment in US high-technology industries. Some in Congress remained concerned, however, that gaps in US authorities over greenfield and venture capital investments persisted. Among other actions, the Trump administration established the Committee for the Assessment of Foreign Participation in the US Telecommunications Services Sector, and it blocked China Mobile and China Telecom in the US market.[41]

Chinese "State Capitalism" and Its Implications for the United States

The practices of the state-directed Chinese economy included extensive networks of trade and investment barriers, financial support, and indigenous innovation policies that sought to promote and protect domestic sectors and firms deemed by the government to be critical to the country's future economic growth. Such practices of Chinese "state capitalism" involved government-directed cybertheft of US trade, technology, and other economic secrets; selective implementing of World Trade Organization (WTO) obligations; government-led financial policies that promoted high savings and allowed surpluses favoring state-guided industries; and a history of managing exchange rate policy to the advantage of China and the disadvantage of the United States, among others.[42]

US government agencies and many others argued that the Chinese government's intervention in various sectors through industrial policies had increased in recent years. The central and local Chinese governments promoted industries deemed crucial to the country's future economic development by using various means that critics judged to be grossly out of line with international norms, such as subsidies, tax breaks, preferential loans, trade barriers, foreign investment restrictions, discriminatory regulations and standards, export restrictions, technology transfer requirements imposed on foreign firms, public procurement rules that gave preferences to domestic firms, and weak enforcement of intellectual property rights (IPR).[43]

China's state sector centered on SOEs, which accounted for more than 40 percent of China's nonagricultural gross domestic product (GDP). A wide range of industries where Beijing decided that the state should dominate included autos, aviation, banking, coal, construction, environmental technology, information technology, insurance, media, oil and gas, power, railways, shipping, steel and other metals, telecommunications, and tobacco. The state-controlled banks provided generous funding for SOEs in various sectors selected by the government.[44]

"Indigenous Innovation": Made in China 2025

A major focus of the government's attention since 2008 was to transform China from a global center for low-technology manufacturing into a major center for innovation by the end of this decade and a global innovation leader by 2050. Concurrently, Beijing sought to reduce sharply the country's dependence on foreign technology, notably that sold by advanced US firms that led in these fields. This stress on so-called indigenous innovation meant that China curbed foreign sales in the China market while Beijing acquired advanced technology through coercing American and other foreign high-technology firms seeking access to the China market to share their advanced technology with favored Chinese companies. Beijing also sought such advanced technology through cyber and human industrial espionage and the acquisition of generally smaller high-technology foreign firms to gain access to their advanced techniques for the benefit of the protected Chinese enterprise while allowing no such acquisition of Chinese firms by foreign companies.[45]

China's use of industrial policies, subsidies, and regulatory authorities (e.g., antitrust, procurement, and standards) to advance economic, technological, and military development goals were of growing concern to US policy makers. Policies such as Made in China 2025 aimed to create competitive advantages for China in strategic industries, in part by first obtaining technology and expertise from US firms to gain core competencies. These policies appeared to incentivize technology transfer, licensing, and joint venture requirements; state-directed technology and intellectual property (IP) theft; and government-funded acquisitions of US companies. Also of concern was potentially widespread Chinese economic, academic, and cyber-enabled espionage—including reports of cyberattacks on US universities and companies engaged in COVID-19 vaccine research—and China's military-civil fusion program, which sought to leverage Made in China 2025 advancements for military applications.[46]

Related is the emphasis on these matters in China's Fourteenth Five-Year Plan (FYP) for 2021–2025. In the plan, Chinese leaders emphasized technology independence and indigenous innovation—long-standing themes in China's industrial policies—while prioritizing China's ability to circumvent recent US and other restrictions and countermoves in order to continue to access foreign technology and global markets. Innovation was viewed as the core driver of China's development, a direction set in 2006 with China's Medium- and Long-Term Plan for Science and Technology and the Thirteenth FYP. The plans called for developing indigenous capabilities, decreasing dependence on foreign technology, and advancing emerging technologies. This process of "indigenous" innovation involved the introduction, absorption, and adaptation of foreign technology that was rebranded as indigenous Chinese capabilities. The party's emphasis on developing domestic innovation capabilities underpinned aspects of China's industrial policies of concern to US policy makers, such as forced technology transfer, industrial subsidies, state-financed acquisitions of foreign firms in strategic sectors, cyberintrusions, and IP theft.[47]

Meanwhile, the Chinese city Shenzhen was piloting Fourteenth FYP innovation priorities that included a focus on foreign partnerships and overseas centers for basic research. China's talent plan incentives included visas and permits to facilitate frequent cross-border travel, work, and permanent residence of foreign experts in China. Reforms sought to commercialize research, transfer government patent rights to innovators, and revitalize national labs. China sought to securitize IP and develop digital IP rights to foster the trade of IP. In the process, China targeted foreign collaboration in basic research, open technology, and overseas research centers in order to exploit areas that at least ostensibly were outside current application of export controls and remained open for US cooperation. These ties allowed China to develop capabilities in priority areas, such as semiconductor design. Many countries' export controls focused on applied (but not basic) research and technology transfer across national borders. China's new semiconductor policies encouraged foreign academic and industry collaboration and Chinese corporate R&D centers overseas. In June 2020, Chinese firms Huawei and San'an Optoelectronics announced a $1.2 billion R&D center in the United Kingdom to develop semiconductor chips. Many top Chinese technology firms— including Alibaba, Baidu, and Tencent—had US R&D centers.[48]

Technology Transfer Issues

As noted above, related to the broader US concerns with China's "indigenous innovation" came concern about coerced technology transfer. When China entered the WTO in 2001, it agreed that foreign firms would not be pressured by government entities to transfer technology to a Chinese partner as part of the cost of doing business in China. However, many US firms argued that this was a common Chinese practice, although this was difficult to quantify because US business representatives often appeared to try to avoid negative publicity regarding the difficulties they encountered doing business in China out of concern over retaliation by the Chinese government. In addition, Chinese officials reportedly pressured foreign firms through oral communications to transfer technology (e.g., as a condition to invest in China), but they avoided putting such requirements in writing to evade being accused of violating WTO rules. In 2011, then US Treasury secretary Timothy Geithner charged that "we're seeing China continue to be very, very aggressive in a strategy they started several decades ago, which goes like this: you want to sell to our country, we want you to come produce here. If you want to come to produce here, you need to transfer your technology to us." Thirty-three percent of the respondents to a 2012 Am-Cham China survey reported that technology transfer requirements were negatively affecting their businesses.[49]

Information Communications Technology and Semiconductors

For the past ten years, many US and other foreign business groups registered increasing concerns over a continuing stream of Chinese laws and regulations on information and communications technology products and services that had the effect of limiting foreign companies' access to this important Chinese market. Several Chinese proposals said that critical information infrastructure should be "secure and controllable," an ambiguous term that was not precisely defined by Chinese authorities. Other proposals laid out policies to promote indigenous information and communications technology industries or required foreign firms to hand over proprietary information. Overall, such requirements had a significant impact on US firms, which exported $12 billion of these kinds of services to China in 2015. Summarizing US concerns, the Commerce Department said the Chinese requirements caused long-term damage to American efforts to participate in China's information and communications market valued at $465 billion in 2015.[50]

In its most recent five-year economic plan, China is developing strategic technologies and digital infrastructure (including a cryptocurrency) and aims to advance its digital infrastructure and domestic rules globally. China recently committed $1.4 trillion over five years for digital infrastructure,

including 5G, smart cities, and Internet of Things applications for manufacturing. US business expressed concerns that (1) these sectors are already
restricted, and (2) procurement in areas such as cloud computing could favor
Chinese firms and require technology disclosure and data localization.[51]

Against this background and other abusive Chinese industrial policies that
sought global civilian and military leadership in emerging technologies, the
Trump administration sought to tighten oversight over technology transfer to
China. It also increased scrutiny of academic ties, strengthened investment
review authorities, tightened export controls, and banned US investment in
firms tied to China's military. It also banned Huawei, China Mobile, and
China Telecom from the US market and encouraged other countries to follow
suit. These policies remained under review in the Biden administration, which
avowed strong countermeasures to adverse Chinese industrial policies.[52]

The Trump administration also issued an executive order allowing a ban
on information communications technology (ICT) transactions that posed
undue risks. Concerned about sanctions violations, IP theft, and espionage, it
tightened technology exports to China's ICT firm Huawei and its affiliates by
adding them to the Commerce Department's Bureau of Industry and Security
(BIS) Entity List, requiring a license for the sale or transfer of US technology,
but issued waivers. BIS amended rules to curtail Huawei's ability to contract
semiconductor chips from overseas facilities that use US technology, such as
Taiwan Semiconductor Manufacturing Company (TSMC). The US government restricted the use of funds to buy Huawei equipment and advocated to
dissuade other governments from using Huawei products in 5G networks.
Meanwhile, the US government negotiated with TSMC to build a $12 billion
5nm chip foundry in Arizona. Congress included provisions in the National
Defense Authorization Act for FY2021 to boost US capabilities. Legislative
proposals and debates about possible new controls on US ICT equipment,
tools, and IP that enable China's advancement persisted.[53]

Intellectual Property Rights and Industry Standards

For three decades, the United States, along with Japan and other developed
countries, pressed China to abide by internationally accepted IPR guidelines.
Episodic progress was repeatedly upset by new developments of Chinese
infringements that disadvantaged US firms and angered senior US officials.
As discussed in chapter 7, China's use of cyberattacks to steal American commercial technology and other know-how prompted usually reticent President
Obama and his advisers to sharply criticize China and to publicly sanction a
few of those responsible. The US administration pressed hard for China to
engage in senior-level talks and seek agreements on how to curb the offensive
Chinese practice.

Steps to protect IPR go back to 1991, when the United States threatened to impose $1.5 billion in trade sanctions against China if it failed to strengthen its IPR laws. Although China later implemented a number of new IPR laws, it often failed to enforce them, which led the United States to threaten China once again with trade sanctions. The two sides reached a trade agreement in 1995, which pledged China to take immediate steps to stem IPR piracy by cracking down on large-scale producers and distributors of pirated materials and prohibiting the export of pirated products, to establish mechanisms to ensure long-term enforcement of IPR laws, and to provide greater market access to US IPR-related products.[54]

Under the terms of China's WTO accession in 2001, China agreed to immediately bring its IPR laws into compliance with the WTO agreement on Trade-Related Aspects of Intellectual Property Rights. Chinese officials repeatedly highlighted advances in improved IPR protection in China, and the Office of the United States Trade Representative (USTR) stated on a number of occasions that China made great strides in improving its IPR protection regime.[55] However, the USTR continued to indicate that much work needed to be done to improve China's IPR protection regime. According to a US International Trade Commission report in 2011, US intellectual property–intensive firms that conducted business in China in 2009 lost $48.2 billion in sales, royalties, and license fees because of IPR violations in China. The Congressional Research Service estimated in 2009 that counterfeits accounted for 15 to 20 percent of all products made in China and accounted for 8 percent of China's GDP. China's enforcement agencies and judicial system often lacked the resources or the will needed to vigorously enforce IPR laws; convicted IPR offenders generally faced minor penalties. In addition, while market access for US and other foreign IPR-related products improved, high tariffs, quotas, and other barriers continued to hamper US exports; such trade barriers were believed by US analysts to be partly responsible for illegal IPR-related smuggling and counterfeiting in China. In addition, China accounted for a significant share of imported counterfeit products seized by US Customs and Border Protection officers ($110 million, or 62 percent of total goods seized, in FY2011 and $1.1 billion, or 88 percent of total goods seized, in 2015).[56] Meanwhile, the USTR called into question the safety of products imported from China by stating that Chinese counterfeit products, such as pharmaceuticals, electronics, batteries, auto parts, industrial equipment, and toys, "pose a direct threat to the health and safety of consumers in the United States, China, and elsewhere."[57]

In government testimony in 2010, a representative of the US Chamber of Commerce offered a graphic indictment in charging that Chinese IPR policies were part of a coherent and government-directed, or at least government-motivated, strategy to lessen China's perceived reliance on foreign innovations and IP. He charged,

> China is actively working to create a legal environment that enables it to intervene in the markets for IP, help its own companies "reinnovate" competing IPR as a substitute to American and other foreign technologies and potentially misappropriate US and other foreign IP as components of its industrial policies and internal market regulations. . . . The common themes throughout these policies are: (1) undermine and displace foreign IP; (2) leverage China's large domestic market to develop national champions and promote its own IP, displacing foreign competitors in China; and (3) building on China's domestic successes by displacing competitors in world markets.[58]

Standards and IPR Enforcement

China's Fourteenth Five-Year Plan (2021–2025) called for standards development and IPR enforcement to advance industrial policies. The latter represents a new turn in Chinese IPR enforcement as China enters world markets with advanced Chinese technologies. Under the plan guidelines, China continued to advance sectors and projects prioritized by Made in China 2025—including aerospace, artificial intelligence, biotechnology, information technology, semiconductors, quantum computing, robotics, advanced machinery and rail, deep sea technologies, and new materials. Under the most recent plan, China was expected to introduce new projects and areas of emphasis as well as policies to advance its next stage of development in these areas, including commercialization, standardization, financing, and export promotion. Beijing was forecast to use standards development and antitrust and IPR enforcement to advance its industrial policies. These tools were used during China's Twelfth and Thirteenth FYPs to require foreign technology and IP licensing, joint ventures, and divestitures to Chinese state firms. In 2018, China consolidated market competition, IP, and standards authorities in a powerful new regulator—the State Administration for Market Regulation (SAMR)—that was charged to play a key role in implementing the Fourteenth FYP. Since then, China's Academy of Engineering and SAMR have been developing China Standards 2035, a plan to set standards to advance Chinese industrial goals and create interoperable civilian and military standards, raising questions about the dual-use nature of Chinese overseas infrastructure. China's standards setting was seen to focus on new technologies where China is likely to have greater influence in the absence of existing rules.[59]

Cybersecurity Issues

Leaders of the US intelligence community and their congressional overseers warned for several years that China's use of human agents for industrial, economic, and national security espionage was complemented by a massive Chinese use of cyberespionage targeting information, held by American companies, which would be useful in advancing China's goal of innovation and leadership in key economic areas. This issue eventually prompted substantial US action. On May 19, 2014, the US Department of Justice issued a thirty-one-count indictment against five members of the Chinese People's Liberation Army for cyberespionage for commercial advantage against five US firms and a labor union. This marked the first time the federal government initiated such action against state actors. It was later disclosed that in March 2014 a Chinese government hacking effort stole 22.5 million security clearance records from the Office of Personnel Management.[60] On April 1, 2015, President Obama issued an executive order authorizing certain sanctions reportedly targeting Chinese cyberthieves. Shortly before Chinese president Xi's state visit to the United States in September 2015, press reports indicated that the Obama administration was considering the imposition of sanctions against Chinese entities over cybertheft, possibly doing so even before the arrival of President Xi in Washington later that month. China sent a high-level delegation to Washington, DC. It held four days of talks with US officials over cyber issues. The result of the talks allowed President Xi and President Obama to announce at their summit that they had reached an agreement on cybersecurity. The agreement stated that neither country's government would conduct or knowingly support cyber-enabled theft of IP, trade secrets, and related information, with the intent of providing competitive advantages to companies or commercial sectors. They set up a high-level dialogue mechanism to address cybercrime. The first meeting was held in December 2015 in Washington, DC; the second was held in Beijing in June 2016. Both resulted in signs of progress in a complicated and usually secret area of international relations.[61] Subsequent periodic reports of Chinese government cyberintrusions to influence US domestic politics were overshadowed by egregious Russian efforts, but cybersecurity issues with China reached new prominence when the Biden administration faced the challenge of a major breach of Microsoft Corporation email systems used by key military contractors and others by what Microsoft said was a state-sponsored Chinese group.[62]

World Trade Organization Implementation Issues

An important benchmark in Chinese leaders' embrace of economic globalization and interdependence was the decision to join the WTO under terms requiring major concessions from China to its international trading partners. On September 13, 2001, China concluded a WTO bilateral trade agreement with Mexico, the last of the original thirty-seven WTO members to have requested such an accord. On September 17, 2001, the WTO Working Party handling China's WTO application announced that it had resolved all outstanding issues regarding China's WTO accession. China's WTO membership was formally approved at the WTO Ministerial Conference in Doha, Qatar, on November 10, 2001. On November 11, 2001, China notified the WTO that it had formally ratified the WTO agreements, which enabled China to enter the WTO on December 11, 2001.[63]

Under the WTO accession agreement, China set forth various concessions and actions to accommodate the interests of its major trading partners. It agreed to do the following:

- Reduce the average tariff for industrial goods to 8.9 percent and for agricultural goods to 15 percent; most tariff cuts were to come by 2004.
- Limit subsidies for agricultural production to 8.5 percent of the value of farm output and end export subsidies for agricultural exports.
- By 2004, grant full trade and distribution rights to foreign enterprises (with some exceptions).
- Provide nondiscriminatory treatment to all WTO members; foreign firms in China were to be treated no less favorably than Chinese firms for trade purposes; price controls would not be used to provide protection to Chinese firms.
- Implement the WTO's standards on IPR seen in the organization's Trade-Related Aspects of Intellectual Property Rights agreement.
- Accept a twelve-year safeguard mechanism, available to other WTO members in cases where a surge in Chinese exports caused or threatened to cause market disruption to domestic producers.
- Fully open the Chinese banking system to foreign financial institutions by 2006; joint ventures in insurance and telecommunications would be permitted, with various degrees of foreign ownership allowed.[64]

The subsequent record of implementation of the Chinese agreement with the WTO was a source of considerable criticism from the United States and some others among China's major trading partners. These criticisms, in turn, prompted Chinese government complaints. As a result of burgeoning Chinese exports of a variety of manufactured products, the United States, the European Union, and others imposed restrictions on Chinese imports of these products, which met with vocal complaints from the Chinese government. Surges in Chinese exports involving agricultural products were a frequent source of complaint from some of China's Asian trading partners, who tried to restrict the imports in ways that antagonized the Chinese authorities.[65]

The US government took the lead among WTO members in reaching the agreements leading to China's joining the organization. It viewed the US market as by far China's largest export market and had a growing concern over the unprecedented US trade deficit with China. As a result, it maintained a leading role in measuring Chinese compliance with WTO commitments, and its complaints met with dissatisfaction and criticism from the Chinese government.[66]

The USTR issued annual reports assessing China's WTO compliance, as did prominent US nongovernmental organizations such as the US-China Business Council. These reports tended to give China mixed evaluations. On the one hand, China was seen as making significant progress in meeting such commitments as formal tariff reductions; on the other hand, the reports raised a host of concerns involving quotas, standards, lack of transparency, and protection of IPR, all of which were seen to impact negatively on US trade interests. As time went on, the US government reports highlighted evidence of trends toward a more restrictive trade regime. The USTR's 2015 report on China's WTO compliance summarized US concerns over China's trade regime as follows: "Many of the problems that arise in the US-China trade and investment relationship can be traced to the Chinese government's interventionist policies and practices and the large role of state-owned enterprises and other national champions in China's economy, which continue to generate significant trade distortions that inevitably give rise to trade frictions."[67]

The specific priority areas of US concern identified in the report dealt with IPR, Chinese industrial policies disadvantaging US firms, restriction on services provided by US companies in the China market, restrictions on US agricultural products sold to China, inadequate transparency in the production and announcement of Chinese laws and regulations, and restrictions working against US firms in licenses and related matters.

The United States utilized the WTO dispute settlement mechanism on a number of occasions to address China's alleged noncompliance with its WTO commitments. It brought twenty-one dispute settlement cases against China (or more than half of the total number of cases against China brought by all WTO members through January 2017). The United States generally prevailed in these cases; several were resolved before going to a WTO panel. China in turn brought more dispute settlement cases against the United States than any other WTO member: ten (or two-thirds of all cases against the United States). Several Chinese complaints were against US antidumping and countervailing duty measures. In December 2016, China initiated a dispute resolution case against the United States for its continued treatment of China as a nonmarket economy for the purpose of calculating and imposing antidumping measures.[68]

American concerns about Chinese industrial policies that limited market access for non-Chinese goods and services and promoted Chinese industries that compete with US and other firms in international markets were brought up repeatedly by senior US officials in various dialogues with China, and while some issues were addressed by Chinese officials, they were not resolved and their negative impact grew with the growth of the Chinese economy and US-China economic interchange.[69]

It was against this background that in March 2018, the Trump administration's US Trade Representative, acting under Section 301 of the Trade Act of 1974 (19 U.S.C. §2411), concluded that Chinese violations of WTO commitments and other assurances saw China engaged in forced technology transfer, cyber-enabled theft of US intellectual property and trade secrets, discriminatory and nonmarket licensing practices, and state-funded strategic acquisitions of US assets. As noted in chapter 7, USTR Robert Lighthizer concluded that such practices represented an "existential threat" to the United States, thereby justifying the start of the US government's punitive tariffs and other measures to counter predatory Chinese practices.[70]

China's Currency Policy

Criticism in the United States over China's currency policy emerged against the background of the massive and growing US trade deficit with China and complaints from US manufacturing firms and workers over competitive challenges posed by Chinese imports that benefit from the Chinese currency's value relative to the US dollar. Unlike most advanced economies, China did not maintain a market-based floating exchange rate. Between 1994 and 2005, China pegged its currency, the renminbi (RMB) or yuan, to the US dollar at about 8.28 yuan to the dollar. In July 2005, China began what it called a "managed float," based on a basket of major foreign currencies, including the US dollar. In order to maintain a target rate of exchange with the dollar and other currencies, the Chinese government maintained restrictions and controls over capital transactions and made large-scale purchases of US dollars and dollar assets. At that time and continuing in following years, many US policy makers, business leaders, union representatives, and academic specialists charged that China's currency policy made the RMB significantly undervalued relative to the US dollar. Estimates of undervalue ranged from 15 to 40 percent. The American critics maintained that China's currency policy made Chinese exports to the United States cheaper and US exports to China more expensive than they would have been if exchange rates were determined by market forces. They complained that this policy particularly hurt several US manufacturing sectors (such as textiles and apparel, furniture, plastics, machine tools, and steel), which were forced to compete against low-cost imports from China. The Chinese currency policy was seen by the American critics to add to the size and growth of the US trade deficit with China. Responsive to these complaints, representatives in Congress introduced numerous bills in recent years designed to pressure China to either significantly appreciate its currency or let it float freely in international markets. As the 2012 Republican presidential candidate, Mitt Romney pledged to take strong action against Chinese currency "manipulation."[71]

Experts continued to differ strongly on the RMB's valuation against the dollar and other currencies. The IMF had criticized the low value of the yuan in the past, but it said in May 2015 that the currency was no longer undervalued. The US Department of the Treasury said in April 2015 that the RMB remained "significantly undervalued," but it concluded that the RMB remained "under its appropriate mid-term valuation."[72]

During the 2016 presidential election campaign, Donald Trump was outspoken in criticizing Chinese manipulation of the value of RMB for the sake of trading advantage over the United States. The first Treasury report on exchange rates under the Trump administration, issued on April 14, 2017, did not conclude that China (or any country) had manipulated its currency. President Trump told the *Wall Street Journal* in April 2017 that he had changed his mind and no longer viewed China as such a currency manipulator.[73] In 2019, for the first time in twenty-five years, the US government labeled China a currency manipulator under the 1988 Trade Act but lifted the designation in January 2020, citing currency provisions in the "phase one" trade deal.[74]

Opposition to China's Belt and Road Initiative

US opposition continued strongly against Xi Jinping's signature Belt and Road Initiative (BRI) involving Chinese-financed and-implemented commitments to often large-scale infrastructure projects in over one hundred countries, including many poorly endowed or badly governed states seen as weak credit risks. The BRI aimed to develop China-centered and-controlled global infrastructure, transportation, trade, and production networks. It promoted China's information and communications technology supply chains, including hardware and optical cable and satellite networks, and it expanded the use of China's credit information system and currency. China used these advances to foster Chinese leadership in setting world economic standards in line with Beijing's China Standards 2035 strategy. During the recent pandemic, Beijing focused on providing protective equipment, vaccines, and medical missions to various BRI partners as part of a "Health Care Silk Road," and it promoted global collaboration in health, research, and standards setting.[75]

Responding to the BRI, Congress with Trump administration support passed the Better Utilization of Investments Leading to Development (BUILD) Act of 2018 (P.L. 115–254) and reauthorized the Export-Import Bank of the United States. Trump administration efforts to enhance US ability to finance competitive projects overseas included the Infrastructure Technology Assistance Network, the Transaction Advisory Fund, and the Blue Dot Network with Japan and Australia.[76]

The US opposition to BRI was commonly understood in China and elsewhere as a competition between the United States and China for economic advantage and accompanying international influence, but the drivers of US opposition were more broad-ranging and serious.[77]

Notably, US policy saw China using the BRI to gain the support of the United Nations and other international legitimacy, thereby strengthening China's mercantilist and heavily state-directed economic model undermining the existing free market economic system. The BRI promoted Huawei and other paramount beneficiaries of China's unfair mercantilist practices, building connections that allowed deep Chinese penetration and control of the economies and decision making of weaker states. More than any other power, China built through the BRI and used recipient countries' dependencies on China for maintenance of modern infrastructure, financing, investment, technology, and trade to compel compliance with ever-expanding Chinese requirements. Some of these requirements involved granting access to ports of use by more widely dispersed Chinese military forces. Meanwhile, BRI contracts repeatedly fostered egregious corruption and unaccountable governance, and they enabled expansion of authoritarian rule at the expense of national interest and popular sovereignty. BRI also contracted opportunistically, taking advantage of poorer countries that had benefited from recent interventions and supporting actions by the IMF and the OECD countries in the Paris Club to restore fiscal integrity, only to become burdened by unsustainable debt to China and thereby seek once again the support and intervention of the IMF and the Paris Club countries.[78]

Challenges Facing China's Economic Leadership, Including Energy and Environment

The impact of the trade war and related acute rivalry with the United States headed the list of serious economic problems for the Chinese government in the period ahead. The phase one agreement did not deal with many fundamental economic differences. It was quickly overtaken by events with the Trump government hurtling toward the November 2020 election finish line with a platform focused on sharp criticism of Chinese handling of the coronavirus and a host of other US complaints. Economic performance was important for President Trump and his election campaign in 2020, but it was probably even more important for the legitimacy of the Chinese one-party state than it was for the democratically elected US president. Meanwhile, the COVID-19 pandemic placed both world-leading economies in an economic downturn of major proportions.

Among the immediate consequences of the trade war and broader US-China economic competition in 2018 and 2019 were the following:

- An across-the-board negative impact on China's economy, reducing the growth of Chinese exports to close to zero and depressing exports to the United States in absolute terms.
- Investors at home and abroad slowed investment in China's trade-intensive sectors.
- The trade networks producing manufactured products for export, with China at the center, were shifting away from reliance on China and toward other locales for export to the United States.
- China was stressing more self-reliance and less dependence on the US market, but there was no immediate market available to purchase the output of the existing production chains focused on the United States and its heretofore lucrative market.[79]

Meanwhile, as discussed above, US-led efforts blocked Chinese purchase of and access to high-technology companies in developed countries. They complicated Chinese companies' access to high-technology equipment and curbed Chinese advances in the control of telecommunications in developed countries. US criticisms added to the serious complications facing China's Belt and Road Initiative as heretofore hidden or denied Chinese ambitions for local penetration; influence operations; and control of communications, media, and discourse; and military expansion increased broad international wariness of Beijing's intentions.

The above problems came as the growth rate of the Chinese economy continued to gradually decline, as did the workforce. The list of ongoing domestic challenges for the Chinese economy reviewed below involved protracted issues with no easy solution, encumbering Chinese international advances in the years ahead.[80] All the above difficulties were compounded by the impact the coronavirus had on China and its longer-lasting impact on the various countries China relied on for inputs and to purchase Chinese exports.

- *Industrial policy and state-owned enterprises.* China failed to implement the 2013 reforms for a more efficient, more market-oriented economy. It doubled down on industrial policies employing state-owned enterprises and targeted ostensibly private firms to lead state-directed industrial policies at home and abroad. Accounting for about one-third of Chinese industrial production and employing a large part of China's urban workers, SOEs put a heavy strain on China's economy in terms of inefficiency and the need for heavy financial backing by state banks.[81]

- *State-dominated banking sector, excess credit, and growing debt.* China's banking system remained largely dominated by state-owned or state-controlled banks. Banking in China faced several major difficulties because of its financial support of SOEs and its failure to operate more on market-based principles. Results included excessive and wasteful production of unneeded goods and rising debt levels. Relatedly, China's combined household, corporate, and government debt levels rose rapidly over the past decade. Much of the rise in that debt came from the corporate sector, supported by the state banking system. In dollar terms, China's corporate debt rose from $3 trillion in 2006 to $17.8 trillion in 2016 (up $14.8 trillion) and greatly exceeded US corporate debt levels. Such credit growth risked undermining future growth by sharply boosting debt levels, causing overcapacity in many industries, contributing to bubbles (such as in real estate), and reducing productivity by providing preferential treatment to SOEs and other government-supported entities.[82]

- *Rule of law.* The absence of the rule of law in China led to widespread government corruption, financial speculation, and misallocation of investment funds. The Xi Jinping government conducted an unprecedented anticorruption campaign to curb such abuses. The government also reemphasized Communist Party discipline throughout the economic system of China. Nevertheless, it remained commonly held that government "connections," not market forces, were the main determinant of successful firms in China, leading to greater expense and waste in production and other economic enterprises.[83]

- *Growing pollution.* Despite extensive publicity surrounding Xi Jinping as a leader in the fight against climate change and international efforts to create a cleaner environment, the fact remained that the level of pollution in China continued to pose extraordinary problems for Chinese development. The Chinese government often disregarded its own environmental laws in order to promote rapid economic growth. Authoritative foreign reports said that China contributed about 60 percent of the growth in global carbon dioxide (CO_2) emissions from 2000 to 2016 and that its emissions would surpass the combined CO_2 levels of the United States and EU by 2025. The health costs of China's air pollution in 2015 were said to be $1.4 trillion; as a percentage of GDP, the costs of water pollution and soil degradation were an additional 2.1 percent and 1.1 percent, respectively. Remedial measures were underway, but the problems were enormous. Meanwhile, China became a major global producer and user of clean and renewable energy technology.[84]

- *Aging population.* The number of people aged over sixty was growing fast and reached 240 million in 2020 and was expected to reach 360 million by 2030. The population share of people aged over sixty was 20 percent in 2020 and was forecast to be 27 percent by 2030. With a low birth rate as a result of the long-standing "one child per family" policy and other factors, the working population was declining as the elderly population rose. The Chinese government and the families of the elderly faced challenges trying to meet the costs to the country of expanded spending on health care and elderly services.[85]

Against this background, Chinese leaders in major meetings in late 2020 and early 2021 signaled policies to counter what they described as new global constraints on China. They sought to leverage the global economy to advance Beijing's goals in ways that would challenge or reshape global rules and counter US interests and policies. President Xi's emphasis on a "dual circulation" policy meant leveraging the dual forces of domestic and global demand or, in other words, developing domestic capacity while pursuing openings in global markets. In 2009, the government used this approach to subsidize increased production in thirteen industries while global industry contracted. This generated excess capacity that China then exported to the detriment of other producers in world markets. President Xi also advanced a strong state role in the economy and advocated for Chinese leadership in global standards setting. A digital campaign called for $1.4 trillion over five years in 5G, smart cities, and other technology infrastructure and a push to adopt this approach globally. Chinese leaders called for strengthening party control of the private sector to "build a backbone of private economic actors that are reliable and useful at critical moments." Chinese leaders played up self-reliance and indigenous innovation while seeking to sustain access to foreign markets and technology. An emphasis on basic research called for foreign collaboration. A new policy for semiconductors called for overseas research and production centers. The government was advancing a cryptocurrency to influence global finance and e-commerce and diversify from US dollar financing. China issued an export control law and rules to review foreign investment on national security grounds, potentially to counter US policy actions.[86]

Substantial foreign economic challenges facing China in addition to the troubles initiated by the United States include energy security and various environmental and climate change issues treated below.

Uncertain Energy Security

In the past two decades, the need to be on guard to deal with economic vulnerability was very apparent in Chinese leaders' approach to China's fast-growing need for imported raw materials, especially oil. China became the world's largest importer of oil, and it consumed a large share of other international raw materials, including iron ore, copper, aluminum, nickel, and timber. Chinese leaders at times adopted an overtly mercantilist approach to gaining access to oil and gas resources overseas. They showed serious reservations about the international market in these critically important commodities. This led Chinese purchasers of international oil to strive vigorously to diversify sources. In the recent past, China's top suppliers were Saudi Arabia and Iran, but China bought even more oil from a diverse range of suppliers that included Sudan, Russia, and Angola. More recently, Russia at times became China's top crude oil supplier, surpassing Saudi Arabia. Meanwhile, government-backed Chinese enterprises sought control of foreign oil fields that were available for purchase and paid a premium for the rights to develop those fields.[87]

China's growing dependence on imported oil and gas, especially Middle East oil, also meant that China depended even more on US forces to secure the sea lines of communication between the Persian Gulf and the Chinese coast. Chinese strategists worried that the US Navy might close these channels and try to "strangle" China in the event of conflict over Taiwan or other issues. Despite predictions by some Western commentators and in Chinese government pronouncements about the expanding reach of China's emerging "blue-water" navy, Chinese strategists had few realistic options to counter US power so far from Chinese shores, at least over the next five years. Their longer-term plans were seen to involve a series of ports and other access points useful in securing very exposed lines of shipping from the Persian Gulf to China. The first Chinese military base abroad was begun in Djibouti in 2017. Reports forecast future bases in Pakistan, Cambodia, and elsewhere, while Chinese island building and militarization of outposts in the South China Sea strengthened Chinese control in those shipping lanes.[88] As noted above and discussed in chapter 11, China's Belt and Road Initiative saw Chinese leaders leverage dependence of weaker countries along sensitive transportation routes on Chinese financing; debt relief, investment, and trade; port construction and management; and construction and maintenance of transportation, communication, and surveillance systems. Beijing used such dependence to allow access to facilities in these countries for use by Chinese military forces or to reserve that option for future use depending on circumstances.

Environmental and Climate Change Issues

China for many years remained on the defensive regarding its environmental practices and the consequences of China's rapid growth on the Chinese and world environment. Throughout the 1990s and into the next decade, Chinese leaders worked hard, on the one hand, to avoid China being considered an international laggard on environmental practices while, on the other, to avoid environmental obstacles to the rapid development of China's economy. On the positive side, Chinese leaders since the early 1990s took serious steps to deal with worsening environmental conditions in China. Premier Li Peng was particularly instrumental in putting ecology on the political map. Laws were passed on air, water, solid waste, and noise pollution. Enforcement mechanisms were bolstered, and funds for cleanup, inspection, education, and enforcement increased repeatedly in the 1990s.[89] Despite good intentions at the top, Beijing had serious problems, especially compliance and follow-through with funding and implementation of promised programs. Enforcement authority remained weak and fragmented, and penalties were anemic. Local officials tended to judge proposed projects by the number of jobs they created and the revenue they generated rather than by the environmental damage or good they did.[90]

With close to 10 percent annual growth and extensive foreign investment in China focused on manufacturing, China faced enormous environmental problems at the start of the twenty-first century. Demand for electric power grew rapidly and was met predominantly by coal-fired plants. Automobiles clogged roads in major cities. Air pollution went from bad to worse. Efforts to develop hydropower using dams on China's rivers were controversial, as the projects displaced large numbers of people and had major environmental impacts on people in China and in other countries downstream from the new dams. Serious depletion of water resources in northern China was exacerbated by water pollution, pervasive throughout China.[91]

The Chinese leadership at the time gave more emphasis than its predecessors to the need for sustainable development in China. However, the results more often than not were mixed.[92] As they had done in the past, Chinese officials responsible for environmental protection agreed in 2006 that an investment of 1.5 percent of GDP was required to effectively curb pollution and that an investment of 3 percent of GDP was needed to substantially improve the environment. The Chinese government appeared more serious than in the past about reducing the wasteful use of energy in Chinese production, and significant progress was made in this area during the Eleventh Five-Year Plan (2005–2010) and continued into the next decade. China also continued its stronger emphasis on increasing the importance of renewable energy, notably hydroelectric power, and made major gains in becoming a world leader in manufacturing and using solar panels and wind turbines.

The nation still lacked a powerful national body that was able to coordinate, monitor, and enforce environmental legislation. The devolution of decision-making authority to local levels often placed environmental stewardship in the hands of officials who were more concerned with economic growth than with the environment. Meanwhile, the capital and will needed to promote the massive spending necessary to reverse several decades of environmental damage remained enormous.

The international consequences of China's environmental problems were varied and usually negative. Dust storms from eroding land in northern China polluted the atmosphere in Korea and Japan, leading to popular and sometimes official complaints and concerns. Air pollution from China affected locales to the east as far away as the Pacific coast of the United States. Chinese dams on the Mekong River and other Asia rivers originating in Tibet had negative impacts on the livelihood of people in neighboring countries, complicating official relations. Extensive international publicity regarding China's poor environmental record made international opinion less patient with Chinese government explanations that China, as a developing country, should not be held to strict environmental standards. As a result, China's image in world affairs declined.[93]

China avoided the negative international spotlight when the United States refused to agree to the Kyoto Protocol to reduce pollution and other emissions. The US position became the focal point of international criticism, with little attention devoted to China's refusal to agree to binding commitments on greenhouse gas emissions.[94] In response to growing domestic and international pressures for stronger Chinese actions to curb environmental damage, the Chinese government in 2007 and 2008 established senior-level working groups to deal with international pressure that China conform more to growing world efforts to curb the negative effects of climate change. Chinese diplomats and senior officials were at the forefront in bilateral and multilateral meetings in calling attention to China's concerns over climate change. They emphasized that China and other developing countries should not see their growth thwarted by environmental restrictions and that developed countries should bear the initial responsibility for concrete actions to deal with the growing issue. At home, Chinese officials took new measures to curb investment in energy-intensive industries and to improve the poor standard of energy efficiency in Chinese manufacturing.[95]

China was seen in the West as partly responsible for the collapse of the international climate change meeting in Copenhagen in December 2009. Chinese leaders defended their position that Chinese economic development should not be encumbered by binding commitments to reduce greenhouse gases. The energy intensity of Chinese production continued to decline according to goals set by the Chinese government plans, though China's position as the world's largest emitter of greenhouse gases solidified, with ever-larger Chinese emissions. The massive global economic crisis beginning in 2008 distracted attention from broad-gauge international solutions to climate change, reducing the negative spotlight on China's role and responsibility.[96]

China worked cooperatively with the Obama administration and other developed countries seeking international accords that would curb the growth of greenhouse gas emissions; Beijing sought to avoid major complications for Chinese economic development. China's stress on greater success in achieving energy efficiency in recent years and its future plans along these lines were nonetheless unlikely to offset projections that China's CO_2 emissions in 2035 would be double the amount seen in 2011.[97] Over time, China's stronger interest in domestic energy efficiency and curbing pollution in the country resulted in energy use policies more in line with international climate change ambitions. Notably, Beijing now saw its overall interests better served by putting aside China's past opposition to undertaking domestic economic changes to meet standards proposed at the Copenhagen Climate Change Conference in 2009, and it supported the requirements of the Paris Climate Change agreement in 2016. With the Trump government decision to withdraw from the Paris agreement, Xi Jinping and Chinese publicists positioned Beijing as the world leader in climate change efforts.[98]

China in 2021 was the top emitter of greenhouse gases, burned more than half of the coal used globally, and was faulted for reemphasizing coal industries at home and exporting coal-fired electricity generation plants abroad under the BRI rubric. Nevertheless, Beijing was also the leading market for solar panels, wind turbines, and electric vehicles, and it manufactured two-thirds of solar cells installed worldwide. China was making significant progress in shifting energy use to renewables and in increasing energy efficiency. China's diplomatic stature in discussions on climate change was especially high, as the Trump administration opposed international climate change agreements. China began to develop the world's largest carbon trading scheme, meant to cover 25 percent of global CO_2 emissions. China continued to take the side of developing countries in calling on developed countries to do more in line with their greater responsibilities under international climate change agreements. China continued to insist that it was a developing country.[99]

The incoming US administration of President Joseph Biden in 2021 initiated an unprecedented range of domestic and foreign efforts to counter climate change. China's cooperation in these efforts was deemed very important, and the new US government strove diligently to make progress on climate change issues with China even while pursuing strong rivalry in countering many serious challenges for US interests posed by adverse Chinese policies and practices. The Chinese president participated constructively in President Biden's climate change summit in April. At that time, the US president's special envoy for climate change, former senator and secretary of state John Kerry, held talks with leading officials in China promising future cooperation between the two countries on climate issues.[100]

STUDY QUESTIONS

1. Is China's economic rise the most important element in China's competition with the United States for regional and global leadership?
2. Are leading US policy makers correct in arguing that China's headlong pursuit of wealth and power, employing many unfair and disruptively self-serving practices and features of the Chinese economic model, represents an existential threat to the US economy and to other economies of developed and developing countries with a stake in the prevailing international economic system?
3. Are US countermeasures warranted in targeting Chinese mercantilist trade and investment practices, notably developing real or potential world champion industries in the highly protected Chinese market and seeking dominance there before they are launched with enormous subsidies to wipe out international competitors in the global market?
4. How are the profits from such state capitalist practices combined with widespread cyber and human industrial espionage and coerced or covert technology transfer to foster China's avowed goal to lead the high-technology industries of the future? Are US policy makers correct in judging that such efforts will displace the US leading position in these high-technology industries, placing the United States in a secondary and subservient position to China? And will the efforts also make the US military, highly dependent on high-technology industries, second and subservient to China?
5. Why does the United States oppose China's Belt and Road Initiative?
   - Are the reasons more than competition with China for global markets and influence?
   - What is the importance of other reasons involving sustainable lending, transparent deal making, and popular accountability?
   - Is it true that the BRI record shows widespread corruption in nontransparent deals supporting authoritarian leaders unaccountable to their publics?
   - Does the record show China using for various foreign policy advantages the leverage provided by economic dependences of BRI

recipient countries for financing, investment, trade, and maintenance of difficult-to-replace, sophisticated infrastructure?
- ◦ Do dependencies on Chinese information communication technology and so-called smart cities technologies have the added benefit of allowing Chinese covert surveillance of BRI recipients' government and other sensitive communications?
- ◦ And are the dependencies salient in countries having strategic locations sought for Chinese existing or future military operations?
6. Were Trump government countermeasures against Chinese economic challenges warranted and effective? Why has the Biden government continued and added to these countermeasures?
7. What are the prospects for US-China cooperation over environmental issues and climate change amid strong Sino-American rivalry?

RELEVANT VIDEOS

"China: Power and Prosperity" (PBS documentary, November 22, 2019, 144 minutes) available at https://www.youtube.com/watch?v=JovtmKFxi3c

"How Did China Succeed?" (Joseph E. Stiglitz, Norwegian Business School, September 14, 2018, one hour) available at https://www.youtube.com/watch?v=Iaw4n9IZDdc

"What Is China's Grand Strategy?" (Heritage Foundation forum, May 23, 2019, one hour) available at https://www.youtube.com/watch?v=qx-7Q3HEbDM

"Global China Webinar: Assessing China's Growing Regional Influence and Strategy" (Brookings Institution forum, July 29, 2020, ninety-seven minutes) available at https://www.brookings.edu/events/global-china-webinar-assessing-chinas-growing-regional-influence-and-strategy/

"China Century of Humiliation?" (documentary, Mitch Anderson, July 16, 2017, seventy-seven minutes) available at https://www.youtube.com/watch?v=boPkMCJSYSs

"The Chinese View of Strategic Competition with the United States" (hearing, US-China Economic and Security Review Commission, June 24, 2020, five hours) available at https://www.uscc.gov/hearings/chinese-view-strategic-competition-united-states

"US-China Trade Relations" (CSPAN testimony of Robert Lighthizer, February 27, 2019, three hours) available at https://www.c-span.org/video/?458285-1/us-china-trade-relations

"US-China Trade War: Questions and Answers with the *Economist*" (November 2019, thirty-eight minutes) available at https://www.youtube.com/watch?v=ABQd0ckeLQk

"Is China's Belt Road a Path to Power?" (TRT, April 2, 2018, twenty-six minutes) available at https://www.youtube.com/watch?v=aO5Oyx9s4rA

Chapter Ten

Taiwan and East Asian Maritime Disputes in Contemporary US-China Relations

There is much to support the judgment of experts on both sides of the Taiwan Strait and in the United States that the so-called Taiwan issue in US-China relations is sui generis, encompassing a unique set of sensitive elements that stand on their own as they influence the US-China relationship in negative and positive ways. Thus, past editions of this volume duly treated Taiwan as the subject of a separate chapter. Nevertheless, as reviewed in chapter 7, the serious challenges to US interests posed by President Xi Jinping's assertive and expansionist behavior in the disputed East China Sea to the north of Taiwan and the South China Sea to the south of Taiwan represented a leading cause of hardening US attitudes toward China by the US administration, Congress, the media, and various elite and public opinion outlets. That hardening did not spill over to change the Barack Obama administration's tightly managed relations with Taiwan that carefully avoided serious controversy with China.[1]

Nevertheless, even though President Donald Trump remained personally ambivalent about Taiwan's importance for US interests, his administration, with strong support from bipartisan majorities in Congress and much of US media, carried out despite China's objections a series of often unprecedented and largely incremental advances in US military, diplomatic, and economic relations with Taiwan that were endorsed and continued by the Biden administration. The Taiwan issue no longer received the special handling under the rubric of the strictly enforced US one-China policy seen in the Obama and most earlier US governments. It became caught up in the broader American pushback against adverse challenges posed by Chinese expansionism along the Asian rim as well as a host of other Chinese measures seen collectively posing the most serious danger facing the United States in the twenty-first century. In response to the US changes and developments in Taiwan, tensions rose with strong Chinese military, economic, and diplomatic pressures targeting the US-backed Taiwan government involving impressive shows of military force by Chinese air and naval forces intruding into Taiwan air and sea space and US forces deployed in nearby waters including transiting the Taiwan Strait. Taiwan reemerged as a critical flashpoint of possible superpower conflict, prompting debate on whether or not the United States should go further in efforts to deter possible Chinese military attack on Taiwan by amending or ending the existing framework of the US one-China policy to include an explicit statement committing the United States to support Taiwan if it is attacked by China.[2]

This chapter assesses Taiwan issues and their impact on US-China relations, with a special focus on the recent reemergence of acute US-China rivalry and tension in the Taiwan Strait in the context of recent unprecedented tension over territorial disputes in the East China Sea and the South China Sea that surround Taiwan. The issues examined in this chapter regarding Taiwan and the maritime disputes probably are best understood using a realist lens in international politics: seeing China and the United States engaged in an often zero-sum competition for influence and control. Of course, realism could result in negotiations leading to compromises that would markedly improve relations, say, for example, if the US government in economic negotiations with China saw such progress for US interests that it was prepared in turn to substantially reduce US support for Taiwan. Advocates of liberalism in international relations theory might see such an outcome as reflective of the importance of economic engagement and as thus reflective of the salience of their perspective in recent US-China relations. Meanwhile, the constructivist perspective seems more likely than not to perceive that the strong nationalistic identities being built in China, Taiwan, and other nearby states as factors that make significant compromise over territorial and related disputes more difficult, which adds to the prevailing trend of competition and distrust.

TAIWAN ISSUES AND CONTEMPORARY US-CHINA RELATIONS

As explained in chapter 4, the process of normalization of US-China relations saw Henry Kissinger and Richard Nixon privately pledge to meet firm Chinese demands about ending US official relations with Taiwan in return for the perceived strategic and other benefits the United States would gain from the breakthrough in official relations with China. To avoid controversy in American domestic politics and in US interaction with Taiwan and other concerned powers, these commitments remained hidden from the American public, the Congress, most officials in the Nixon government, Taiwan, and other foreign governments. The US-China normalization process stalled on account of Nixon's forced resignation over the Watergate scandal. Unaware of the Kissinger-Nixon secret commitments, American public opinion and mainstream views in Congress supported continuing US ties with Taiwan while moving ahead with China.[3]

The Jimmy Carter administration endeavored to complete the normalization of diplomatic relations and eventually met most Chinese demands on ending US official ties with Taiwan. China seemed basically satisfied, though Carter's insistence on continuing some US arms sales to Taiwan after breaking official relations remained an outstanding dispute. The backlash in the United States severely complicated the Carter understanding with China. Bipartisan congressional leaders rewrote the administration's proposed bill governing future unofficial relations with Taiwan, passing the Taiwan Relations Act, which underlined continued strong US interest in protecting Taiwan from Chinese pressure and sustaining close economic, arms sales, and other ties with Taiwan.[4]

Ronald Reagan highlighted his record of support for Taiwan in defeating Carter in the 1980 presidential election. Strong Chinese pressure against the seeming reversal of US policy resulted in a compromise over US arms sales to Taiwan in a Sino-American communiqué in 1982. Whatever Chinese expectations continued about the United States withdrawing from Taiwan diminished further with concurrent US efforts to support Taiwan in international organizations; to transfer to Taiwan the equipment, technology, and expertise to produce its own jet fighters; and to increase high-level US officials' meetings with Taiwan counterparts. American officials from Reagan on down saw US interests well served by preserving a balance in American relations with Taiwan and China where Taiwan would be sufficiently supported by the United States through military and other means that it would not feel compelled to come to terms with China on reunification or other issues seen as adverse to Taiwan's interests. Reagan's successor, George H. W. Bush, continued this approach, notably by sending the first US cabinet member to visit Taiwan and by selling more than $5 billion of advanced jet fighters to Taiwan in a deal that was widely seen to have undermined the understandings reached in the 1982 communiqué with China.[5]

As discussed in chapter 5, Sino-American interaction over the issues associated with Taiwan became much more complicated as democracy and a strong movement toward self-determination emerged in Taiwan in the post–Cold War period. The American antipathy to China's government following the Tiananmen crackdown added to the shift in American attitudes against China and in favor of Taiwan. American attraction to growing democracy in Taiwan overshadowed US attention to the profound implications for China of moves by Taiwan's democratic leaders toward greater separation from China. The moves were popular among many Taiwanese people and their supporters in the United States but were fundamentally at odds with China's concerns over sovereignty and nationalism.[6]

The clash of Sino-American interests reached a high point with the military crisis in the Taiwan Strait in 1995–96, caused by Chinese military reaction to President Bill Clinton's unexpected reversal of US policy in granting Taiwan's president Lee Teng-hui a visa in order to visit the United States and give a speech at his alma mater, Cornell University. Following the face-off of US and Chinese forces in the Taiwan area in 1996, China's strong political pressure against Taiwan and its US supporters continued along with concerted Chinese efforts to build up military forces in the Taiwan area designed to coerce Taiwan, prevent its movement toward permanent separation from China, and deter US military efforts to intervene. American policy reflected a complicated mix of efforts to preserve a balance of power favorable to the United States and Taiwan and thereby deter China's coercive pressures, on the one hand, while trying to dampen pro-independence initiatives in Taiwan and thereby reassure China regarding US commitment to a one-China policy, on the other.[7]

The period from the Lee Teng-hui visit to the United States in 1995 until the end of the administration of President Chen Shui-bian in 2008 featured repeated episodes of escalating tensions in US-China relations regarding Taiwan. They usually were prompted by the actions of Taiwan's government, often in reaction to escalating coercive pressure from China, to move in directions seen by China as supporting Taiwan's independence. As indicated in chapters 5 and 6, the Clinton and George W. Bush administrations had a hard time in efforts to deter the two sides from provocative actions, to calm tensions when one side or the other took steps that worsened cross-strait relations, and thereby to sustain the broad American interest in preserving peace and stability in the Taiwan area.[8]

The election of Ma Ying-jeou as president of Taiwan in 2008 significantly reduced cross-strait tensions and the salience of the Taiwan issue in Sino-American relations. Ma reversed the policies and practices of his immediate predecessors that were seen by China as moving Taiwan toward independence from China. He put aside the zero-sum competition that had generally prevailed in Taiwan-China relations for sixty years. He opened Taiwan to much greater interchange with China that made the Taiwan economy more dependent than ever on close and cooperative relations with China. China reciprocated with policies and practices designed to foster closer ties and build closer identity between Taiwan and the mainland. US policy makers in the Bush and Obama administrations warmly welcomed the moderation of cross-strait tensions.[9]

The domestic foundations of Ma's positive engagement with China remained unsteady. Vocal oppositionists continued attacking as they grew in political prominence. Domestic opinion in Taiwan turned against closer ties with China, and mass demonstrations opposed agreements seen as making Taiwan more dependent on China. Ma's overall approval rating plummeted, and his Nationalist (or Kuomintang, KMT) Party lost the presidential and legislative elections in 2016 by such wide margins that it was questionable how soon it would revive as a leading force in Taiwan politics. The incoming Tsai Ing-wen administration promised to sustain the status quo in cross-strait relations as it refused Chinese demands and pressures to accommodate Chinese interests. Beijing gradually increased negative military, diplomatic, and economic pressures with an eye to weakening Taiwan and thereby eroding domestic support for the Tsai government.[10] Though the KMT revived and scored impressive victories in island-wide local elections in 2018, and Tsai's approval rating remained low in early 2019, voters in Taiwan reacted strongly against the People's Republic of China (PRC) pressures. And months of mass demonstrations against PRC rule in Hong Kong beginning in mid-2019 increased Taiwan voter antipathy to China, leading to Tsai's strong reelection in January 2020 and setting the stage for continued impasse and rising tensions with Beijing.[11]

American Support for Taiwan under Ma Ying-jeou[12]

In response to the dramatic shift in Taiwan's approach to China under President Ma Ying-jeou, the US government played down past emphasis on Taiwan's role in cooperation with the United States in sustaining a favorable military balance in the Taiwan Strait. Rather, it sought to support Ma's new approach of reassurance as an important means of sustaining stability and peace. Despite the shifts toward greater criticism and competition regarding various issues in US-China policy in the years following Ma's ascendance, the Obama government policy toward Taiwan was more durable and consistent. The Obama government sold a large amount of weapons to Taiwan but avoided provoking Chinese ire with the sale of advanced fighter aircraft or submarines requested by Taiwan. China viewed with suspicion the Obama government's rebalance in Asia policy highlighted since 2011. The Obama government was careful to keep Taiwan outside the scope of the rebalance in its initial explanations of the new policy, and later official US references affirming Taiwan's role avoided specifics or actions that risked raising China's ire over the very sensitive Taiwan issue in US-China relations.[13]

American policy makers concerned with Taiwan repeatedly highlighted the very good state of bilateral relations and the calm that prevailed in cross-strait ties, a welcome comparison to the headaches for US policy posed by active nearby hot spots in the East and South China Seas and North Korea. Signs of low US tolerance for Taiwan actions that could disrupt cross-strait ties included US officials warning against the Democratic Progressive Party (DPP) candidate, Tsai Ing-wen, regarding her China policy following US official meetings with the candidate prior to the Taiwan election in 2012. This episode marked a rare American official intervention into a friendly democracy's electoral process.[14]

Specialists and media highlighted declines in US support for Taiwan under the Obama government. The administration strongly disagreed, but it followed policies in the rebalance in dealing with sales of sensitive weapons and in reacting to the approach of the DPP presidential candidate, noted above, that underlined declining support for policy initiatives that would support Taiwan but risk upsetting China and come at a possibly significant cost for US relations with China. By contrast, George W. Bush started his administration with a strong rebalancing against perceived Chinese assertiveness in Asia by placing Taiwan at the center of his approach, warning that he would do "whatever it takes" to help Taiwan defend itself against Chinese attack.[15]

Congress at times was the source of strong support for Taiwan and pressure on the administration to do more for Taiwan. But the weak congressional signs of support of Taiwan in the first term of the Obama government were overshadowed by declining interest and opposition to Taiwan's wishes. Few members visited the island, and those who did sometimes came away with views adverse to Taiwan's interests. After visiting Taiwan in August 2010, Senator Arlen Specter came out against irritating China by selling Taiwan the F-16 aircraft sought by President Ma.[16] Likewise, in a public hearing in June 2010, Senate Intelligence Committee chairwoman Dianne Feinstein cast US arms sales to Taiwan as a liability for US foreign policy and pressed Secretary of Defense Robert Gates for options to resolve the impasse between the United States and China over the issue.[17]

The decline in congressional support was also influenced by the fracturing and decline of the Taiwan lobby in Washington. Reflecting the often intense competition in Taiwan politics between the Nationalist or Kuomintang Party and the Democratic Progressive Party in recent decades, DPP representatives in Washington and like-minded US interest groups, such as the Formosan Association for Public Affairs on one side and KMT representatives in Washington and supporting interest groups on the other side, repeatedly clashed while lobbying congressional members. Ma Ying-jeou's appointment of the head of the KMT's Washington office, a veteran of these partisan squabbles with the DPP, as his choice to lead the Taiwan government's office in Washington saw the partisan divisions persist. An overall result was confusion on Capitol Hill and a decline in Taiwan's influence there.[18]

Since 2012 and 2013, rising American tensions with China over disputes in the East and South China Seas were accompanied by an increase in congressional, nongovernmental specialist, and media attention to Taiwan's role in proposed American plans for dealing with Chinese assertiveness. For its part, the Obama government remained generally mum on Taiwan's role in this regard. While US government representatives eventually came to say that Taiwan was part of the rebalance, they avoided disclosing how this would assist in dealing with Chinese assertiveness. One reason for the Obama government restraint was presumably that such discussion would heighten attention to the Taiwan issue in US-China differences in Asia, causing more serious friction in US-China relations than the Obama government judged warranted under the circumstances. The Obama government, congressional representatives, and specialists were in agreement in complimenting the actions of the Ma Ying-jeou government—a major stakeholder in the contested East China Sea and South China Sea claims—for generally adhering to peaceful means in dealing with differences and in reaching pragmatic understandings with Japan and the Philippines over fishing rights in disputed territories. They also appreciated Taiwan's criticism of China's abrupt declaration of an air defense identification zone over the disputed East China Sea islands in late 2013.[19]

Pushing against Obama government restraint regarding Taiwan and China was an array of congressional representatives, specialists, and commentators arguing in favor of greater US attention to Taiwan in this period of tension with China. The push against Obama government restraint was intensified by the now common discourse in congressional deliberations and media commentary that the Obama government was too timid in the face of challenges in such sensitive international areas as Ukraine, Syria, Iraq, Afghanistan, and elsewhere.[20] The critics also saw the stakes in competition with China as long term and serious; they argued for stronger American actions that would show negative costs for China's interests if it pursued its coercive means of incremental expansion of control—so-called salami slicing—in nearby disputed territories. They were prepared to risk some of the negative consequences for the United States that would flow from serious disruption of the existing relationship with China.[21]

Against this background, Taiwan was involved in some proposed American actions to counter China as the United States moved from the positive engagement side of the policy spectrum to an approach that balanced against and endeavored to deter Chinese expansionism. Strategists and specialists argued that to effectively deter expanding China required credible American strategies to deal with confrontation with China. Taiwan was often at the center of such proposed strategies and was seen by some as "the cork in the bottle" if the United States needed to shore up radars, defenses, and other anti-China military preparations along the first island chain running from Japan through Taiwan to the Philippines.[22]

Taiwan was also involved in options raised in congressional deliberations and specialist commentaries on what the United States could do in order to raise the cost for China of its continued salami slicing in the nearby seas. According to this view, by raising the costs to China with these Taiwan-related options (as well as other options), the United States could show Beijing that its interests would be better served with a less aggressive approach in the East and South China Seas.[23] The Ma Ying-jeou government reacted very warily to these suggestions, while the Obama government ignored them. They included using the sale of advanced jet fighters to Taiwan as a way to upset the Chinese security calculus along its periphery in ways costly to China, with the implicit understanding that more such disruptions of Chinese plans would come unless it ceased its assertiveness and expansion in the East and South China Seas.

Meanwhile, another US option regarding Taiwan built on the Obama government's strong criticism of China's use of coercion and intimidation of neighbors in disputes in the East and South China Seas. The new US government rhetoric raised the question of why the United States was not showing the same concern with long-standing Chinese military coercion and intimidation of Taiwan. Strong American statements against such intimidation, if backed by substantive support, would seriously complicate China's plans for what Beijing saw as the resolution of the Taiwan issue—a major cost to the Chinese government.[24]

The increased attention to Taiwan related to the hardening US policy toward China was reinforced by other factors increasing the American focus on Taiwan. Thanks in part to stronger efforts by the Taiwan office in Washington and to the particular interest in Taiwan by committee chairs and ranking members in the House and Senate, the number of members of Congress visiting Taiwan and the stature of these members increased.[25] In 2012, a general election year when overseas congressional travel usually declines, there were fifteen representatives who visited Taiwan. In 2013, there were four senators and eighteen representatives who visited Taiwan. In January–August 2014, one senator and fourteen representatives visited Taiwan. Chairman Ron Wyden (D-OR) of the Senate Committee on Finance visited in August, and Chairman Buck McKeon (R-CA) of the House Armed Services Committee led a congressional delegation that same month. Congress continued to pass legislation and urge the US administration in various ways to encourage Taiwan's democratization, to meet Taiwan's self-defense needs, and to assist with Taiwan's bid to participate in regional economic integration and international organizations such as the World Health Assembly and the International Civil Aviation Organization.[26]

TAIWAN AND THE HARDENING OF
CONTEMPORARY US-CHINA RELATIONS

President Xi Jinping's government remained resolute in pursing pressure tactics to compel the Tsai Ing-wen government to compromise and accept the 1992 consensus and to move toward the one country, two systems formula Beijing used in the reunification of Hong Kong and Macao with the PRC. The consensus was a compromise Beijing reached with the KMT allowing for a vague recognition of the one-China principle required by Beijing before formal agreements and cross-strait interchange would be allowed. It provided the foundation for the extensive trade, travel, communications, and other cross-strait accords reached during the Ma Ying-jeou government. Now the opposition party to Tsai's ruling DPP, the KMT, and much of the Taiwan business community supported the 1992 consensus. The PRC's proposed one country, two systems formula was more uniformly unpopular in Taiwan. Tsai and her party long held a negative view of both measures, believing they would undermine Taiwan's sovereignty and pave the way for absorption of Taiwan under Beijing's control, following the trajectory of Hong Kong and Macao as they lost control and were integrated with China beginning in the 1990s.[27]

Among various coercive measures to isolate and intimidate Taiwan, Xi Jinping's government established diplomatic relations with seven countries that previously recognized Taiwan; pressured host countries to force Taiwan's unofficial representative offices to change their names; forced US and other foreign firms to change how they publicly dealt with Taiwan to conform with Chinese-approved guidelines; blocked Taiwan's participation as an observer at international meetings; stepped up deployments and provocative military operations of the PRC military near Taiwan; reduced the number of mainland Chinese tourists visiting Taiwan; demanded that other countries return Taiwan citizens accused of crimes to the PRC rather than to Taiwan; and, for the first time, tried a Taiwan activist on charges of attempted subversion of the PRC state.[28]

Perhaps of more significance, Taiwan was put on the front lines of threats from China's "sharp power," or malign authoritarian influence that tried to take advantage of the island's open democratic system to build support for China. Taiwan's Mainland Affairs Council said in July 2019 that the Chinese Communist Party was stepping up its united front work and efforts to infiltrate Taiwan, following Chinese president Xi Jinping's firm speech on reunification with Taiwan on January 1. Beijing's recent influence operations in Taiwan involved an aggressive political propaganda campaign in Taiwan through its penetration into Taiwan's information and political environments.

In this information war, Chinese agents sought to influence Taiwanese political actors and society through distortion of information on social media and
other platforms—all to ultimately benefit Chinese interests and objectives.[29]

Beijing long relied on the KMT and other like-minded political parties
of the so-called pan-blue group to counter the policies and preferences of
the DPP and the so-called pan-green parties opposed to China's ambitions.
Chinese officials were pleased with the strong KMT victory in the 2018
island-wide local elections that promised the removal of the DPP president
and the DPP-controlled legislature in the January 2020 elections. During the
2018 and 2020 Taiwan election campaigns, Beijing intensified its efforts to
add to its pan-blue influence by bypassing the central government in Taiwan
and the ruling DPP. Instead, it relied increasingly on co-opted candidates,
political parties, and various proxies in Taiwan to undermine democratic
institutions, sow confusion within the public, and engineer electoral outcomes
in its favor. In the view of some experts, this new approach was seen as an
admission that previous strategies had failed and an acknowledgement that,
as long as it stands, Taiwan's commitment to an identity as a democratic
country unwilling to succumb to China's demands will prevent outcomes
desired by Beijing.[30]

Now facing the adverse results of the DPP victories in the January 2020
presidential and legislative elections and four more years of DPP presidential
and legislative rule, Beijing continued to apply the pressures of the recent
past. The appeal of the KMT for China seemed reduced as the new KMT
leadership appeared less than firm in their support of the 1992 consensus.
The coronavirus that emerged first in China underlined for many in Taiwan
concrete reasons to remain separate from PRC control. Public opinion in
Taiwan strongly opposed Beijing's use of its influence in the World Health
Organization to prevent Taiwan participation in World Health Organization
deliberation about the coronavirus, which was heavily impacting Taiwan as
well as the PRC.[31]

Trump Administration Support for Taiwan

Perhaps of more importance in Beijing's deliberations over strategy toward
Taiwan was the remarkable strengthening of US support for Taiwan and the
Tsai Ing-wen government. A major bright spot amid mediocre accomplish-
ments of Trump administration foreign policy was unprecedented improvement in US relations with Taiwan despite the risk of objection from China, a
change in US policy warmly welcomed by Taiwan's leaders.[32]

Many incremental and some more substantial advances in US military,
diplomatic, and economic support for Taiwan reached high points in 2019 and
2020. They offset President Trump's personal ambiguity about dealing with

Taiwan. The president reportedly told National Security Adviser John Bolton that he cared little for Taiwan against the background of US interests regarding China. Historically, Mr. Trump had demonstrated little known commitment to or concern regarding Taiwan. Candidate Trump did not feature Taiwan in his 2016 election campaign. He accepted President Tsai's 2016 phone call, but he came to side strongly with Xi Jinping against Taiwan. He reportedly disapproved of a high-profile visit to Taiwan by a State Department official in 2017 and sought to avoid friction over Taiwan in the lead-up to his June 2018 summit with Kim Jong Un.[33]

On balance, however, the overall impact of US policy measures in support of Taiwan during the Trump administration represented a significant US counter to increased Chinese military, diplomatic, and economic pressures on Taiwan in the lead-up to and the aftermath of Taiwan's January 2020 elections. The United States sought to reassure Taiwan and preserve the status quo that Beijing was attempting to change with intimidation and coercion. The US steps raised tensions regarding Taiwan to high levels not seen since the Taiwan Straits crisis of 1995–96, prompting significant debate among US specialists as the incoming Biden government continued strong engagement with Taiwan in a period of acute rivalry with China.[34]

Recent US Advances Despite China's Objections

Military

Military advances involved joint consultations, planning, exercises, exchanges of intelligence, and other matters out of public view. Public advances involved the sale of over $11 billion in arms to Taiwan, including sixty-six F-16 jet fighters approved in 2019. Also, US warships were passing regularly through the Taiwan Strait. As noted earlier, when establishing ties with Beijing, the US publicly halted warship patrols in the Taiwan Strait. Some US warships secretly passed through the strait in later years. The Trump government began publicizing US warships passing through the strait (nine went through from mid-2018 to mid-2019). Meanwhile, the Defense Department's Indo-Pacific Strategy in June 2019, for the first time in an authoritative executive branch document in several decades, declared that Taiwan was a "country."[35]

Diplomatic

The Department of State no longer acted as a gatekeeper more concerned with avoiding offending Beijing and thus restricting relations between Taiwan and other departments and Congress. Showing often unprecedented support for Taiwan, widely publicized visits by deputy assistant secretaries, carried out rarely in the past, were now common. Such high-profile meetings in Taiwan in 2019 dealt with Southeast Asia, China's advances in the Pacific Islands, and cooperation in the Indo-Pacific. Another unprecedented move saw the recall in September 2018 of US ambassadors from three Latin American countries after their governments switched diplomatic relations from Taiwan to Beijing. In 2020 and in the closing days of the administration in 2021, Secretary of State Pompeo was in the lead in measures of support for Taiwan. There was a proposed visit of the US representative to the United Nations to Taiwan, which, if it had been carried out, would have been the second Trump cabinet-level official to visit the island; Pompeo also oversaw the State Department's removal of the formal restrictions that had limited US officials' interchange with Taiwan for over forty years.

Relatedly, National Security Adviser John Bolton held a publicized meeting with his Taiwan counterpart in May 2019. Past practice kept such meetings secret and at the level of deputy national security advisers. Another unprecedented move saw Tsai Ing-wen's running mate, vice president elect Lai Ching-te, visit the National Security Council while in Washington to attend the National Prayer Breakfast in February 2020. Since 2019, US ambassadors in the Pacific Island states were publicly helping Taiwan to sustain its official diplomatic relations among those small nations. Secretary Pompeo in October 2019 issued a statement urging Tuvalu to maintain diplomatic relations with Taiwan. Vice President Pence in September 2019 registered disapproval of the Solomon Islands breaking ties with Taiwan.

The American Institute in Taiwan, responsible to the State Department, offered unprecedented pledges of US support for Taiwan. The director said in June 2019 that Taiwan can "count on" US support for a "shared future" between the two, adding that "Taiwan will always have a home in the community of democracies."[36]

Economic

Economic support came notably in June 2019 when visiting director of the US Overseas Private Investment Corporation promised assistance in helping Taiwan retain its diplomatic partners. Meanwhile, the scope and activism of the US-Taiwan Global Cooperation and Training Framework grew markedly, involving and impacting more foreign governments.[37]

There were four driving forces supporting the advances of US relations with Taiwan during this period. First was Beijing's growing military, diplomatic, and economic pressure on Taiwan, which endeavored to change the status quo in cross-strait relations. The US pushback acted to counter Chinese pressures and sustain the status quo. Second, Taiwan's location and role in the Indo-Pacific region and its important high-technology industries centered on the production of sophisticated computer chips were deemed very important for US plans to counter adverse Chinese advances. Third, Taiwan's political democracy, free market economy, and support for other such international norms were valued by US leaders who saw China's rising challenge to these norms as a major threat to US interests. Fourth, US relations with Taiwan imposed costs on Beijing.[38]

There remained several factors that served to brake the forward movement of US support for Taiwan that Beijing opposed, but their importance was diminished in several cases. First, US government concern that advances with Taiwan would upset US relations with China was lessened now that the already acute US rivalry with China had intensified. Second, US government concern that US tensions with China over Taiwan would upset US allies and partners in the Asia-Pacific was also overtaken by the US-China rivalry. Third, US government suspicion that Taiwan leaders would use greater US support to move provocatively toward independence continued to be low during Tsai Ing-wen's presidency. The fourth factor braking forward US movement with Taiwan did not diminish. Beijing's rising military, political, and economic power remained the most important brake on advancing US support that might prompt strong PRC reactions.[39]

Biden Administration and the Future of the US One-China Policy

Top leaders of the Joseph Biden administration continued the Trump government's remarkable advances of US relations with Taiwan despite China's objections. High-level US government rebukes and military countermeasures, including repeated warship passages in the Taiwan Strait, targeted Chinese air and naval shows of force attempting to intimidate Taiwan. An extraordinary visit to Taiwan in April by a delegation of top policy makers in the Barack Obama and George W. Bush administrations led by Biden's close friend and trusted trouble shooter, former senator Christopher Dodd, featured high-profile consultations with President Tsai Ing-wen and other Taiwan leaders. The US-led G-7 and Secretary of State Antony Blinken both called for Taiwan's inclusion in the World Health Assembly despite China's opposition. Administration and congressional spending plans involving tens of billions of dollars of outlays to compete with China in computer technology, 5G communications, and high-technology industries featured keen awareness of Taiwan's central role in the production of advanced microchips critical to US success over China.[40]

Such Biden administration actions reflected a continuing sharp turn away from the pattern followed by most US administrations since the normalization of US-China relations of strictly implementing the US one-China policy in ways that would avoid serious upset of Beijing. As noted above, such strict implementation was carried out by senior officials of the Obama administration, including now President Biden as well as his secretary of state and national security adviser. Taiwan elites had been very concerned that the Biden administration would revert to the Obama administration's strict interpretation of the US one-China policy; they were encouraged by the new US government's early policies and practices. The Biden administration's continuation of the Trump advances in relations with Taiwan also underscored remarkable change in the determinants of the US one-China policy, adding to questions as to the utility of continuing this framework brought on by the rising tensions in US-China relations over the Taiwan issue.[41]

Why and how have determinants of the US one-China policy changed? The main reason remained Beijing's growing determination to expand its wealth and power at others' expense as its economic and military capacities advance Chinese influence and control in Asia and the world. China's drive continued to be broadly seen by bipartisan majorities in Congress and elsewhere in Washington as posing a series of serious challenges to America. If not met effectively, these would lead to substantial erosion of US power and influence relative to China. This risks Chinese dominance in Asia and in high-technology industries and an international order detrimental not only to narrow US national interests but also to regional and global free economic interchange, national independence, popular sovereignty, and personal freedom.[42]

In the case of Taiwan, this drive continues to involve multifaceted military, diplomatic, and economic pressures to change the status quo in China's favor. US policy now works vigorously to push back and sustain the status quo. Taiwan's key location and role in the Indo-Pacific region and its strong position amid keen US-China competition over the high-technology industries of the future remain important elements valued by US policy makers seeking to compete with and counter adverse Chinese advances. Taiwan's political democracy, free market economy, and support for international norms America seeks to advance are valued by Biden administration and congressional leaders opposed to expanding authoritarian rule. US relations with Taiwan also provide leverage for US policy makers seeking to influence PRC behavior.[43]

The brakes that heretofore curbed US advances in relations with Taiwan that risked antagonizing Beijing continue to decline in importance in current US policy making focused on countering China's adverse challenges. In particular, worry that US advances with Taiwan would upset the overall US relationship with China has been overtaken by events involving acute US rivalry with China, as has the related US worry that tensions with China over Taiwan would upset US allies and partners in Asia-Pacific. Meanwhile, the steady and determined Tsai Ing-wen leadership continues to counter past US concerns that advances in US support for Taiwan would prompt Taiwan leaders to move toward independence and thereby provoke Beijing.[44]

Outlook: Tensions with China and the US One-China Policy

Going forward, Beijing's ever-rising military power and related political and economic influence remained as the most important brake on advancing American support that might prompt strong PRC reactions adverse to US interests. The tense situation in the Taiwan Strait was seen as dangerous. Analysts predicted increasing danger as rising Chinese military capacities appeared to outpace American military strength, changing the overall balance of power to the advantage of China.[45]

Nevertheless, countervailing factors seemed important. Heading the list was China's clearly demonstrated reluctance to confront America in ways that would lead to military conflict. The reasons included the adverse impact of such conflict on China's many internal priorities, its still strong economic dependence on the United States, and its vulnerabilities along the rim of Asia and in control of important sea lines of communication.[46]

Obviously, deterring China from attacking Taiwan would be more difficult as the balance of forces in the Taiwan Strait continues to change in Beijing's favor. That US forces could no longer guarantee a quick victory over Chinese attack was important, but the United States and its allies in the Cold War were able to deter successfully major asymmetries in military capacity in Europe vis-à-vis the massive Soviet Union forces there and presumably could do so in the case of Taiwan today.[47]

A more immediately relevant countervailing factor was Beijing's effort to slow or reverse the overall hardening of American resolve to resist Chinese challenges. China sought to avoid a cutoff of economic, high-technology, and other interchange with the United States that was needed and advantageous for China's development. The United States focusing the spotlight on China's aggression against Taiwan could further energize calls for American resistance, seriously curbing the many advantages China gets from economic, technology, and other US interchange. Such focus would reduce the influence of US business and other interests in sustaining involvement with China advantageous for their companies and organizations but increasingly seen as adverse to overall US national security.[48]

As for the US one-China policy, an advisable path forward seems to be to avoid a possible major disruption caused by a US declaration formally changing policy toward Taiwan and China, such as a widely suggested US official statement declaring that the United States would militarily support Taiwan if it were attacked by China. Such a statement was suggested by leading specialists to end what is seen as dangerous "strategic ambiguity" about the US commitment to defend Taiwan. According to proponents, without the declaration, Beijing would be more inclined to use force against Taiwan.[49]

Rather, this writer's long experience with cross-strait tensions supported a recommendation in favor of continuing the recent steady and incremental steps that solidify Taiwan's relationship with the United States using a broad and flexible interpretation of the US one-China policy in a likely prolonged period of intense US-China rivalry in the years ahead. In this context, formally asserting US readiness to protect Taiwan from PRC attack in a way that would appear to undermine the one-China policy seemed unadvisable. Though advocated by some in the interest of avoiding US ambiguity on this matter given the end of the US defense alliance with Taiwan over forty years ago, it seemed provocative and unnecessary amid acute US determination to counter Chinese adverse ambitions across the board.[50]

EAST ASIAN MARITIME DISPUTES AND CONTEMPORARY US-CHINA RELATIONS

As reviewed in chapter 6, early Chinese tests of the Obama administration's resolve on sensitive issues in US-China relations reached a more assertive stage around the time of the Obama government's launching of its rebalance to Asia policy in 2011 and the ascendance to power of President Xi Jinping, strong-man ruler and Communist Party leader, in 2012. Although President Hu Jintao's last visit to the United States in January 2011 stressed commitments to peace and development,[51] 2012 saw unprecedented demonstrations of Chinese power short of using military force in defense of Chinese claims to disputed territories in the South China Sea and the East China Sea. The Chinese demonstrations of coercive power went well beyond established international norms and resulted in extralegal measures and in some cases in widespread violence and property destruction. They placed China's neighbors and concerned powers, notably the United States, on guard. The implications for regional order clearly took a negative turn in 2012.[52]

Against this background, it appeared difficult for US policy makers to determine and carry out a clear strategy on how the United States should deal with the subsequent mix of China's determination to advance its disputed claims at the expense of neighbors and of the US position as security guarantor of the Asia-Pacific, with China's continued summitry and close engagement with the United States to move forward on important areas of common ground, manage differences, and avoid military conflict. As noted earlier, the Obama government was pleased overall with its record in dealing with China, including over the disputes in the maritime regions adjoining China's mainland. Senior officials in the Trump administration supported by bipartisan majorities in Congress viewed negatively the Obama government's restricted US responses to Chinese affronts, resulting in substantial setbacks and lost influence as China advanced to become an overriding national security danger to the Asian order and global governance. They undertook much tougher American approaches to counter Chinese challenges.[53] The incoming Biden administration, including President Biden and senior leaders with deep experience in dealing with China during the Obama administration, showed clear resolve to sustain a tough stance on Chinese expansion around Asia's rim.[54]

As discussed in chapter 6, the Obama government rebalance policy strengthened the US military, economic, and diplomatic position in Asia while also strengthening the capacities of Asian countries to preserve and advance their development free from coercion and in accord with existing international norms.[55] The Obama government's reengagement in Asia ran up against rising Chinese assertiveness and coercive and intimidating actions to protect and advance Chinese sovereignty and security interests in disputed territories along China's rim. The Chinese actions were influenced and strongly supported by patriotic elite and public opinion that viewed the US activism as a justification for China to take more coercive actions to protect and advance its interests. In effect, the US and Chinese initiatives represented the most important challenge or test of the durability of cooperative Sino-American engagement during 2012, and the testing would continue until the end of Obama's term.

The pattern of assertiveness showed remarkable features in defending Chinese disputed claims in the South China Sea and the East China Sea in 2012.[56] The first round of Chinese assertiveness over territorial issues in 2012 involved the South China Sea. Chinese disagreement with the Philippines in April over Philippine officers' attempt to arrest Chinese fishermen in disputed Scarborough Shoal, which led to a face-off between Philippines and Chinese security forces and a US-mediated agreement calling for mutual withdrawal, which in the end China did not do,[57] left Beijing in control of the shoal ever since. There followed impressive and extraordinary demonstrations of Chinese security, economic, administrative, and diplomatic power to have their way in the South China Sea. Highlights included the following:

- China employed its large and growing force of maritime and fishing security ships; targeted economic sanctions out of line with international norms and World Trade Organization rules; and repeated diplomatic warnings to intimidate and coerce Philippine officials, security forces, and fishermen to respect China's claims to disputed Scarborough Shoal.
- China created a new, multifaceted administrative structure backed by a new military garrison that covered wide swaths of disputed areas in the South China Sea. The coverage was in line with China's broad historical

claims, depicted in Chinese maps with a nine-dashed line and encompassing most of the South China Sea.

- The large claims laid out in Chinese maps also provided justification for a state-controlled Chinese oil company to offer nine new blocks in the South China Sea for foreign oil companies' development that were far from China but very close to Vietnam.
- China advanced cooperative relations with the 2012 Association of Southeast Asian Nations (ASEAN) chair, Cambodia, thereby ensuring that with Cambodia's cooperation, South China Sea disputes did not receive prominent treatment in ASEAN documents and meetings from that time forward.

Chinese officials meanwhile continued public emphasis on peaceful development and cooperation during meetings with Southeast Asian representatives and those of other concerned powers, including the United States.

In sum, China set forth an implicit choice for the Philippines, Vietnam, other Southeast Asian disputants of China's South China Sea claims, ASEAN, and other governments and organizations with an interest in the South China Sea, notably the United States. On the one hand, based on recent practice, pursuit of policies and actions at odds with Chinese claims in the South China Sea would meet with more of the demonstrations of Chinese power seen above. On the other hand, concurrent Chinese leaders' statements and official commentary indicated that others' moderation and/or acquiescence regarding Chinese claims would result in mutually beneficial development.[58]

The Philippines, Vietnam, and other disputants of Chinese claims did not seem to be in an advantageous position in the face of Chinese power and intimidation. ASEAN remained divided on how to deal with China. The United States and other concerned powers remained ambivalent about the territorial claims, and the United States remained vague about the applicability of its alliance to the Philippines to the South China Sea areas disputed by Beijing.[59]

The second round of Chinese assertiveness on sensitive sovereignty and security issues came with a dispute, more widely publicized at the time, with Japan over the Senkaku (Diaoyu) Islands.[60] Even more so than in the recent case in the South China Sea, China's response to a perceived affront by Japan involved a variety of extralegal measures sharply contrary to international norms. The Japanese government had endeavored to avoid a crisis prompted by Japanese politicians hostile to China who sought to buy three of the contested islands and develop them in ways sure to antagonize China. Instead, the Japanese government intervened and purchased the islands. The purchase triggered an extraordinary Chinese reaction. It included trade sanctions and failure to provide security for Japanese people and property in

China. As large anti-Japanese demonstrations, fostered by well-orchestrated publicity efforts of Chinese authorities, emerged in more than one hundred Chinese cities, the security forces tended to stand aside as agitated Chinese demonstrators destroyed Japanese properties and manhandled Japanese citizens. The displays of violence were eventually mildly criticized by Chinese official media commentary, but the publicity organs of China were full of support of Chinese people's "righteous indignation" against Japan as the widespread violence spread throughout the country. Meanwhile, the Chinese authorities deployed maritime security forces and official aircraft and took legal steps that showed Japan and other concerned powers that the status quo of Japan's control of the islands had changed amid continued challenge from China employing security forces and other means short of direct use of military force.[61]

Chinese popular and elite opinion reacted positively to the Chinese actions in the South China Sea and the East China Sea. Chinese media continued to strongly criticize alleged US efforts to support American allies and partners against China and to exploit Chinese differences with neighboring countries in order to advance American influence in the Asia-Pacific region. Meanwhile, in apparent recognition of the weak US response to the Chinese affronts, some Chinese officials advised that the Obama administration leaders seemed less willing in 2012 to confront China on such assertive actions regarding territorial disputes, in contrast to what they saw as a more prominent and assertive US stance against Chinese interests regarding the territorial disputes in 2010.[62]

Overall, Chinese commentary and elite and public opinion argued that China was successful in its muscular reactions to US allies the Philippines and Japan despite the widely touted US reengagement with the Asia-Pacific. It triumphed with effective use of often extralegal coercive measures to advance China's territorial claims and show firm resolve against perceived challenges.[63]

Subsequent developments in the East China Sea disputes saw the election of Liberal Democratic Party leader Shinzo Abe as Japan's prime minister, defeating the discredited Democratic Party in elections in late 2012. Abe was firm in the face of Chinese pressure. Japan's experienced coast guard forces—backed by Japan's modern and well-trained naval and air forces— were up to the new challenges posed by the patrolling Chinese coast guard fleet. The Obama government welcomed Abe's ascendance. America shifted from a mediating role to a tougher stance critical of China's coercive behavior.[64] The US position overlapped closely with Abe's defensive but firm stance toward China. China stridently attacked Abe as he also sought support against Chinese pressures by strengthening defense at home and seeking support in visits to all members of ASEAN as well as India, Australia, and others. For

his part, President Obama, visiting Japan in April 2014, embraced close collaboration with Japan in Asia and underlined America's defense commitment
to all areas under Japanese administrative control, including the Senkaku
(Diaoyu) Islands. Prime Minister Abe's visit to the United States in April
2015 advanced defense cooperation and international coordination between
the two allies. President Obama, heretofore reluctant to speak out publicly
against Chinese actions, began to criticize China for "flexing its muscles" to
intimidate neighbors and gain control of disputed territory.[65]

In sum, while China continued repeated coast guard and naval and air intru-
sions, it had no success in trying to intimidate Japan, backed firmly by the
United States. A highlight of Chinese assertiveness was Beijing's November
2013 announcement that it would establish an air defense identification zone
(ADIZ) over the East China Sea to include the disputed Senkaku (Diaoyu)
Islands. Outside of China, the ADIZ was widely interpreted as a challenge
to Japanese administration of the Senkaku (Diaoyu) Islands. Washington
weighed in strongly against China's actions.[66] The United States and Japan
coordinated closely and at a high level in their individual and collective
responses to the new situation.

Stymied in the East China Sea, Beijing found it easier to advance against
weaker Southeast Asian states and a less resolute America. Domestic nationalism and demands for a less deferential and more activist foreign policy
drove Chinese policy. The Xi government's widely publicized policies met
with domestic approval as they advanced Chinese South China Sea claims.
Rapidly expanding Chinese military and paramilitary capabilities along with
impressive oil rigs, fishing fleets, dredging machines, and construction abilities allowed and probably prompted China's leaders to expand in areas that
were long claimed by China. Xi's China married its tough policy on South
China disputes with visionary publicity of China's proposed Silk Road Belt
and Maritime Silk Road (later called China's Belt and Road Initiative) and
related proposals, including the still-forming Asian Infrastructure Investment
Bank and related economic initiatives. In effect, China set forth a choice for
the Philippines, Vietnam, other Southeast Asian disputants of China's South
China Sea claims, ASEAN, and other governments and organizations with an
interest in the South China Sea, notably the United States. Pursuit of policies
and actions at odds with Chinese claims in the South China Sea would meet
with more of the demonstrations of Chinese power seen in China's takeover
of Scarborough Shoal from the Philippines in 2012, its deployment of an oil
rig and an imposing armada of defending ships near islands very sensitive to
Vietnam in 2014, and its subsequent massive land reclamation for force projection in the far reaches of the South China Sea. At the same time, Southeast
Asian and other neighbors' moderation and/or acquiescence regarding

Chinese South China Sea claims would result in mutually beneficial development flowing from Chinese economic largess.[67]

The regional reaction to the Sino-Vietnamese confrontation in 2014 appeared to show unwillingness by most Southeast Asian countries to take a stand against China. While the United States avoided major controversy with China over the deployment of its oil rig in Vietnamese claimed waters in 2014, by 2015, US criticism of Chinese dredging to create outposts for power projection in the far reaches of the South China became common.[68]

Xi Jinping's government entered its third year registering significant success in advancing control in the disputed South China Sea. China's bold tactics involving massive dredging and rapid construction, shows of force involving large military exercises, deployments of China's impressive coast guard fleet, and movement of massed fishing vessels and large oil rigs warned weaker neighbors of China's power and determination to have its way. US Pacific Commander Admiral Harry Harris said in July 2015 that the dredging over the past eighteen months rapidly created three thousand acres of Chinese island territory, which was widely seen as being for military use and maritime control.

In early 2016, Chinese–Southeast Asian relations were dominated by China's unremitting expanding control in disputed territory in the South China Sea in the face of complaints, maneuvers, and challenges by a range of regional governments and concerned powers headed by the United States. At the top of the list of American-led challenges to Chinese expansion were military shows of force, expanded military presence, and freedom-of-navigation operations accompanied by strong rhetoric from American defense leaders warning of Chinese ambitions. China rebuked the American actions and pressed ahead with military deployments, construction of defense facilities, and island expansion. Beijing remained determined to gain greater control in the disputed sea despite earlier indications of moderation, notably President Xi Jinping's pledge not to militarize disputed territory made during his September 2015 summit in Washington. Reflecting the Obama government's careful management of South China Sea tensions with China, the rising tension did not spill over and impede the constructive outcome of the US-China summit on March 31, 2016. This served to reinforce various indications showing Southeast Asian governments and other concerned powers that Washington sought to avoid confrontation, as did Beijing, though China was prepared to risk tensions with the United States caused by its expansion in the South China Sea.[69]

Against that background, when China reacted with harsh rhetoric and intimidating threats to the July 2016 decision of an international tribunal in The Hague ruling against China's South China Sea claims in a case brought by former Philippines president Benigno Aquino, the onslaught worked to

China's advantage. The United States was in the lead among regional powers in calling for restraint and moderation, and no other regional country was willing to get out in front of Washington. In contrast to the high tempo of large-scale US and US-led naval exercises and other military maneuvers in the South China Sea prior to the decision, there were no US military actions signaling pressure on China in the weeks following the July 12 decision. Japan and Australia, important American allies in the Asia-Pacific and concerned with China's territorial expansion, joined the United States in restricting reactions mainly to official statements of approval of the tribunal's decision. The Philippines, a US ally and the initiator of the case, had come under a new government on June 30 and was much more interested in seeking common ground with China.[70]

In 2017, Chinese officials showed growing confidence and satisfaction that the cooling tensions in the South China Sea demonstrated increasing regional deference to Beijing's interests, while China's economic importance to Southeast Asia loomed large. For the time being at least, the way seemed open to a steady Chinese consolidation and control of holdings and rights in the South China Sea, a Chinese-supported code of conduct in the South China Sea, Chinese diplomatic initiatives to promote closer ties and reduce regional suspicion of Chinese intentions, and an array of economic blandishments in line with Beijing's ambitious Silk Road programs.[71]

Trump Administration Counters China; Biden Government Shows Resolve

As part of the Trump administration's National Security Strategy and National Defense Strategy came reinforcement of the Obama government's firm backing of Japan in the face of Chinese continued challenges to Japanese control of the disputed Senkaku (Diaoyu) Islands and much stronger support for Taiwan and much stronger measures against Chinese challenges to US interests in the disputed South China Sea. The focus at first involved stepped-up US naval and air power shows of force along the maritime periphery of China, including numerous bilateral and multilateral exercises involving Japan, Australia, and India, thereby solidifying defense cooperation of the newly emerging four-power "Quad" seen as targeted on countering Chinese challenges. There now were publicized US warships transiting the Taiwan Straits many times each year and shows of force countering Chinese warship deployments around Taiwan and in the South China Sea. Senior leaders repeatedly called out China for "bullying" its neighbors and for seeking regional dominance in a Chinese-led order where neighbors would be required to defer to Beijing's requirements.

Much more frequent US freedom-of-navigation exercises were carried out by US warships passing close to Chinese fortified islands in the South China Sea in ways that directly challenged Beijing's territorial claims deemed illegal by the United Nations Convention on the Laws of the Sea (UNCLOS) tribunal in 2016. As those efforts continued, there followed successful efforts to get allies Japan, Australia, Great Britain, France, and South Korea, as well as such important regional partners as India, to join in deployments in the disputed waters. Unlike in the Obama years, the US government now explicitly said that the US defense treaty with the Philippines would apply in the event of conflict between Chinese and Philippine forces in the disputed South China Sea; it began a practice to send warships to shadow Chinese security forces attempting to intimidate ships of South China Sea claimants carrying out surveys for oil and gas exploitation in their UNCLOS-recognized exclusive economic zone that Beijing disputes on the basis of its nine-dash line claim. In contrast to long-standing US noncommitment regarding the disputed South China Sea claims, the US government now led allies and partners in supporting the stance of South China Sea claimants that China's nine-dash line claim is illegal. Meanwhile, the United States also joined with allies Japan and Australia in promoting investment mechanisms and related economic support that would compete with Beijing's Belt and Road Initiative, notably in Southeast Asia.[72]

Seeming to respond to overt angst in Taiwan and more hidden anxiety in Japan and Southeast Asia that the Biden government might return to the less resolute US posture of the Obama administration in the face of Chinese expansionism at neighbors' expense along Asia's maritime rim,[73] the incoming Biden administration lost no time in making clear its attentive resolve to counter any adverse Chinese challenges. In addition to the steps taken to reassure Taiwan against the China threats discussed above, the Biden administration from the president on down solidified opposition to China's ambitions in discussions with Prime Minister Suga Yoshihide, who served as Prime Minister Abe's cabinet secretary for eight years before taking over as prime minister following Abe's resignation because of health reasons in 2020. Suga was honored at the White House as the first foreign leader to meet with President Biden in a summit resulting in strong statements of mutual support, including over Taiwan, the application of the US defense treaty to the disputed Senkaku (Diaoyu) Islands, and other matters sensitive to China.[74]

Perhaps more remarkable was the Biden government's firm counters to Chinese ambitions in the South China Sea and Southeast Asia. Southeast Asian views of the United States as a positive force in the region declined during the Donald Trump administration. The Southeast Asian views remained questionable at the outset of the Joseph Biden presidency.[75] Some months on, however, two developments helped to offset such negative perceptions.[76]

The first summit of Biden and his Quad counterparts in March affirmed that the group would deliver up to one billion COVID-19 vaccine doses to ASEAN, the Indo-Pacific, and beyond by the end of 2022. Though obviously subject to changing circumstances like India's acute need for vaccines, the Quad initiative—and other groups working on deliverables such as climate change and critical and emerging technologies—helped to offset the negative depiction by China and some in Southeast Asia of the United States as being disruptive in Southeast Asia and the Quad as ineffective and ephemeral.

More strikingly, the Biden government also seemed on target in reaffirming the long-standing alliance with the Philippines. Beginning in March 2021, top Biden national security officials worked effectively with their Philippines counterparts—and in conjunction with supporting US and Philippines military exercises—to counter China's coercive attempt to occupy the Philippines-claimed Whitsun Reef. Highlighting China's strong-arm tactics, which starkly belied Beijing's self-proclaimed image as a regional "stabilizer," Philippines-US criticism saw senior Philippines leaders attack China's practices in the South China Sea in harsh language unprecedented in the years of President Rodrigo Duterte. Known for his negative views of the United States and positive views of China, Duterte did not join the barrage of criticism. Yet he did not attempt to stop it, until he issued an order in mid-May for his cabinet to avoid public comments on China and the South China Sea.

Over two hundred ships, purportedly from the People's Armed Forces Maritime Militia (PAFMM), occupied the disputed territory in early March. The reef is within the Philippines' exclusive economic zone and is also claimed by Vietnam. As noted earlier, China's expansive South China Sea entitlement was deemed illegal by a United Nations Law of the Sea Tribunal in 2016. The Chinese ship presence was first reported by the Philippines government on March 20. The foreign ministry protested, the defense minister condemned the presence, and Philippines navy and coast guard forces were dispatched to the area. Even Duterte reportedly asserted the Philippines' position in a meeting with the Chinese ambassador on March 25.

Chinese diplomats said the territory belonged to China and that the Chinese vessels were fishing boats seeking shelter, not maritime militia. A growing body of evidence suggested otherwise. Research by Andrew Erickson and Ryan Martinson showed conclusively that a number of PAFMM vessels were deployed at Whitsun Reef. And research by Zachary Haver showed Chinese authorities supply all fishing vessels in the South China Sea with surveillance equipment as the "first line in defending China's maritime rights and interests."

The US embassy promptly backed the Philippines' criticisms. In late March, US National Security Adviser Jake Sullivan followed up with a phone conversation with his Philippines counterpart, emphasizing US support and the applicability of the US-Philippines Mutual Defense Treaty to the area. Japan, Australia, Great Britain, Canada, and the European Union also sided with the Philippines.

In early April, forty-four Chinese vessels were at the reef. The Philippine defense minister warned strongly that Chinese militia vessels sought to occupy other disputed areas. In unusually sharp language by officials in President Duterte's presidential office, his legal counsel and the presidential spokesperson added to the criticism, and the foreign ministry initiated daily protests.

Steadfast US support reached a high point with Secretary of State Antony Blinken's April 8 phone conversation with Philippines foreign minister Teodoro Locsin. Both men expressed their "shared concerns" with China's actions. Like Sullivan, Blinken affirmed the applicability of the US-Philippines Mutual Defense Treaty to the South China Sea. Two days later Secretary of Defense Lloyd Austin had a similarly supportive phone conversation with his Philippines counterpart.

Foreign reports in mid-April said only "a handful" of Chinese vessels remained at Whitsun Reef, which seemingly ended the standoff then. President Duterte's first public remarks on the controversy came in a briefing on April 19, arguing against the Philippines' confrontation with China.

Nevertheless, the Duterte government's public opposition to China's affronts followed on an unprecedented scale. On April 24, Philippines coast guard and related security forces began conducting prolonged widely publicized exercises in the disputed waters, prompting a Chinese complaint. The Philippines' defense and foreign ministers strongly rejected China's opposition. Mr. Locsin, the country's chief diplomat, used rather undiplomatic and coarse language in demanding that China withdraw its ships. The firm Philippine government resolve presumably was reinforced by the annual US-Philippines Balikatan exercises held for two weeks in mid-April. Exercise Balikatan was the latest in a series of repeated US naval shows of force, with a US carrier strike group carrying out exercises in the disputed waters.

China's next moves in the controversy remained unclear amid Duterte's continued ambivalence. The mercurial president continued to see China as "a good friend" while periodically affirming strong resolve to protect Manila's territorial claims. The Biden government working closely with senior Philippines leaders appearing at cross purposes with Duterte added to the ambiguity. This uncertainty seemed likely to characterize Philippines-China-US relations in the last year of Duterte's term. For now, however, the Biden administration showed a steady hand in effective moves seeking to win friends and influence developments in competition with China. The prospects of continued active Sino-American rivalry in Southeast Asia and over the South China Sea remained strong. How successful the United States would be in reversing a recent overall decline in US influence relative to rising China in Southeast Asia remained to be determined.

STUDY QUESTIONS

1. Why is the so-called Taiwan issue so often viewed as the most important problem in US-China relations? Though Taiwan's importance to China seems easy to understand, why is Taiwan so important for the United States? What is the role of Congress in US support for Taiwan?
2. Why did subsequent US leaders fail to meet Chinese expectations resulting from Nixon's private assurances that the United States would pull away from supporting Taiwan, seemingly opening the way for reunification with China?
3. How did democracy emerging in Taiwan beginning in the 1990s seriously complicate Chinese and US policies regarding Taiwan?
4. What drove the Trump administration's remarkable increase in support for Taiwan in contrast with strict restrictions in earlier US governments against advances in relations with Taiwan that risked serious upset in US relations with China?
5. Is the rise in US-China tension over Taiwan in the recent period of acute US-China rivalry likely to lead to war?
6. What explains Chinese leaders in the early twenty-first century departing from reassuring neighbors and the United States that China's rise was not a threat and becoming more assertive in advancing claims and control in disputed territory in the East and South China Seas?
7. Why did China employ pressure tactics short of using direct military force to advance control in the disputed seas?
8. Why were the results mixed—a stalemate with Japan in the East China Sea and remarkable gains in control against South China Sea claimants?
9. Did the Obama administration's mixed responses to the Chinese advances featuring strong support for Japan but more ambivalence about South China Sea disputes play a role in Beijing's mixed results? And why did the Trump administration initiative show much stronger opposition to Chinese advances at neighbors' expense in the South China Sea?
10. Will the Biden administration continue recent practice showing sustained resolve against Chinese challenges regarding Taiwan and disputes in the South and East China Seas?

RELEVANT VIDEOS

"Council Special Report: The United States China and Taiwan" (Council on Foreign Relations, March 15, 2021, one hour) available at https://www.youtube.com/watch?v=2Rc6yFv_J3I

"US Taiwan Policy in 2021 and Beyond" (Brookings Institution, November 12, 2020, one hour) available at https://www.youtube.com/watch?v=DqW7t23pjpQ

"The United States and China in Southeast Asia: Is Confrontation Inevitable?" (Georgetown University, May 27, 2021, ninety minutes) available at https://www.youtube.com/watch?v=JPmBCoHbKEE

"China, Japan, Taiwan and the Diaoyu/Senkaku-Islands Dispute" (blog post, 2019, fifteen minutes) available at https://www.youtube.com/watch?v=XyXWqRDqUhk

"Media Narratives and the Diaoyu/Senkaku Islands Dispute" (University of Southern California, December 22, 2014, 56 minutes) available at https://www.youtube.com/watch?v=bRXN6zZZnSM

Chapter Eleven

Issues of Human Rights and Governance in Contemporary US-China Relations

Issues of human rights and governance in US-China relations reflect a wide range of values dealing with economic, social, political, cultural, and other interests and concerns of groups and individuals. Differences over human rights issues have long characterized Sino-American relations. The differences have their roots in the respective backgrounds of the American and Chinese societies, governments, and peoples. Those backgrounds foster values that are often at odds.[1]

Governance in this chapter refers to structures and processes of ruling authorities that are designed to ensure accountability, transparency, responsiveness, rule of law, stability, equity and inclusiveness, empowerment, and broad-based participation. The strong US-Chinese differences on these matters also reflect different values based on different backgrounds and experiences of American and Chinese societies, governments, and peoples. Governance differences were obvious to all as China was ruled by a Communist Party–led governing system exerting strong control over state power and society, and the United States was ruled by a liberal democratic system exerting much less control and encouraging frequent changes in leaders of different political parties with contending policy platforms through regularly scheduled popular elections. Those differences were salient as elements of a strong ideological struggle between the communist systems including China's and the democratic systems fostered by the United States during the Cold War. They tended to get much less attention as closer US-Chinese engagement developed beginning in the 1970s. They rose in prominence for a few years following the Tiananmen crackdown of 1989, and they became major issues in the past decade, influenced by China's rising international power and prominence. Contemporary Chinese leaders were determined to use their new power and influence to counter what were viewed as widespread American efforts after the Cold War to spread democratic values and undermine authoritarian rule in China and other authoritarian countries. Through a wide range of overt state-craft as well as hidden, disguised, or denied levers of power, Beijing came to be seen in the United States and among US allies and partners as determined to undermine and weaken the power and influence of their system of gover-nance, favoring authoritarian rule.[2]

Such differences may be understood through the constructivist school of thought in the field of international relations, which sees national identity as an important determinant of international affairs. As discussed in chapter 1 and noted elsewhere, the governments and societies of China and the United States reflect a self-centered exceptionalism that comes from their very well developed national identities. The US identity has evolved over more than two centuries, while China's has developed over millennia. Adding to this mix, the Communist Party (CCP)–ruled government of China, seeking to pre-serve its rule, works very hard to reinforce an identity based on China's past. Overall, these circumstances make it difficult for either power to compromise with the other on issues of values and norms that impact their respective deeply rooted identities.

Meanwhile, the school of thought of liberalism in the field of interna-tional relations can deepen understanding of a fundamental ingredient in the American incentive to engage positively with China despite wide differences, especially over values and norms. That is, America's engagement with China, especially after the Cold War, was premised on a commonly held assumption by liberals that economic change and integration of China with developed countries having free market economies and pluralistic political systems would eventually lead to social and then political change toward pluralism and democracy in China. As noted earlier and discussed below, a major reason for a growing sense among Americans in recent years that US engagement with China has failed is the fact that many Americans previously optimistic that engagement with China would lead to change in China's political system and other norms and values in line with American norms and values have become more pessimistic about the possibility of this kind of change.

A common pattern following the opening of Sino-American relations in the early 1970s was the Chinese and American governments endeavoring to man-age differences over human rights and the two sides' respective authoritarian and democratic governments in ways that did not block progress in other important areas of Sino-American relations. At times when one side or the other focused high priority on human rights issues, as did the United States following the Tiananmen crackdown of 1989, US-China relations tended to stall or retrogress. As US and Chinese leaders more often devoted only secondary consideration to human rights and related differences, the obstacles posed by these issues for Sino-American relations were also less significant.[3]

The importance of human rights and governance differences between the United States and China also was influenced by changes in policies and practices, especially on the part of China. In a broad sense, the United States sought to prompt the Chinese authorities to adopt policies and practices in line with the international values and norms prevalent in modern developed countries of the West. The review of economic issues in chapter 9 and the examination of security issues in chapter 8 show how Chinese leaders have at times seen their interests better served by conforming more to international norms in these areas. Economically, China's government embraced many of the norms of the globalized international economy and adapted comprehensively to economic market demands. A significant benchmark in this process was China's decision to join the World Trade Organization (WTO) with an agreement demanding extensive changes in Chinese economic policies and practices. Evidence of shortcomings of the process included rising complaints by Americans and others regarding China's failure to live up to WTO commitments. China's conformity to world norms in the security area was slower but substantial, especially in areas involving such sensitive issues as the proliferation of weapons of mass destruction. Meanwhile, as will be discussed below, as China grew in international power and prominence, it endeavored to create new international norms in economic and security matters more in line with its interests and often at odds with US-backed norms.[4]

China's leadership also endeavored at various times to appear more in line with international norms regarding issues affecting political power and processes in China. Chinese officials engaged in a broad range of discussions, dialogues, and agreements with various countries and international organizations designed to advance political rights in line with world norms supported by the United States. China signed international covenants dealing with economic, social, and political rights. Chinese leaders routinely pledged cooperation with other countries in promoting human rights. They fostered reforms emphasizing the rule of law, greater transparency, and accountability, and they promoted democracy and democratic decision making in handling various human rights concerns in China. At times, the progress of Chinese reform in these areas encouraged some Chinese and foreign specialists to anticipate continued change leading to the transformation of China's authoritarian one-party political system.[5] However, other specialists in China and abroad saw the Chinese leadership as following policies of adaptation and adjustment in the area of political reform and related human rights.[6] The reforms in these areas were seen as undermining neither Chinese leadership control of political power in China nor what was viewed as the overriding concern of Chinese leaders to sustain and strengthen one-party rule in China through authoritarian as well as more liberal means.

CHANGING IMPORTANCE OF HUMAN RIGHTS ISSUES, 1969–2021

It's hard to imagine two societies and governments with more different sets of values than the United States and Maoist China. The progress made in US-China reconciliation during the initial efforts of normalization begun by President Richard Nixon and Chairman Mao Zedong is a testament to the pragmatism of their respective leaderships. Other interests—notably each country's need for support in the face of rising Soviet power and other complications—overrode differences regarding political and other values that divided the United States and China.[7]

President Jimmy Carter rose to power on a platform pledging to devote more concern to American political values in the conduct of US foreign policy. He pledged to put aside the realpolitik calculations seen as prevalent in the policies of the Nixon and Gerald Ford administrations. This shift in policy resulted in divergence and confrontation between the United States and some authoritarian governments, but it had little effect on US relations with China. In the case of China, President Carter and his key aides pursued the pragmatic search for strategic leverage begun by Nixon; they did not allow differences over human rights and values to impede advances in relations, leading to the normalization of diplomatic relations in 1979.[8]

During the 1970s, there were signs of domestic debate and disagreement in both the United States and China over issues involving how the two countries differed with regard to values and human rights and the tendencies of the respective governments to give little overt attention to these differences in the pursuit of other interests. Leadership debate in China at the end of the Maoist period included disagreements over the alleged corrupting effect American and broader Western values would have on the prevailing authoritarian political order and social and economic structure of China. Removal of the radical Chinese leadership faction known as the Gang of Four following Mao's death in 1976 reduced the debate. Deng Xiaoping's return to power in 1978 coincided with a remarkable demonstration of freer speech in the posting of various proposals for reform, individual freedom, and democracy in Beijing's so-called Democracy Wall. After one year of publicizing proposals for sometimes radical reform, including some calling for the end of Communist rule in China, the Chinese leadership closed this channel of free speech and arrested and imprisoned some prominent reform advocates.[9]

American public and elite opinion supported Nixon's opening to China and gave comparatively little attention to human rights issues in relations with China. A minority of media commentators, specialists, members of Congress, and other influential Americans called attention to President Carter's apparent double standard in pushing human rights issues in relations with various authoritarian governments but not doing so in his administration's approach to China. The Democracy Wall caught the attention of the American and other foreign media and their audiences. As China opened to greater foreign contact and Chinese intellectuals were able to write about some of the searing experiences of Maoist rule, reporters, academic specialists, and other American and foreign commentators showed greater awareness of the enormous abuses of human rights in China and the wide gap between the United States and China over political and other values.[10]

The disclosures of human rights abuses in Maoist China and the closing of the Democracy Wall and arrests and imprisonment of prominent dissidents had little effect on the forward momentum in US-China relations. Deng Xiaoping's reform programs were widely seen in the United States and elsewhere in the West to be advancing the material well-being of Chinese people while curbing many of the capricious uses of authoritarian administrative power that had prevailed during the Maoist period. Broadly gauged human rights conditions in China were seen to be improving with post-Mao economic and political reforms and opening to greater international interchange. Some American officials, advocacy groups, and media commentators focused on the negative implications of China's continued Communist rule for imprisoned or otherwise suppressed political dissidents and for religious and ethnic groups, notably Tibetan followers of the Dalai Lama. US supporters of democracy and self-determination for Taiwan also joined Americans pressing for continued US support for Taiwan's status separate from the control of China's Communist government. In contrast, President Ronald Reagan seemed to capture the generally more optimistic American view about trends in China during his remarks at the time of his official visit to China in 1984. Reagan approved of emerging capitalist economic development in China and tended to soft-pedal criticism of China's authoritarian political system, referring to "so-called Communist China," a sharp contrast with his trademark criticism of the "evil empire" seen as prevalent in the Communist-ruled Soviet Union.[11]

The economic and political reforms in China in the 1980s saw continued Chinese debate over the implications of closer Chinese interchange with the United States and the West. American and broader Western values of individual freedom were widely seen in elite and public opinion in China as a threat to the Communist system in China. Conservatives railed against the danger of the so-called spiritual pollution from US political values and culture that would undermine and weaken Chinese resiliency and power in the face of international forces, including the United States, that were often seen as unfriendly to China. The conservatives included key leaders in the old guard in the CCP hierarchy and many other senior leaders said to be retired but who actually exerted great influence in Chinese decision making. The conservatives continued to influence the reformists leading the Chinese Communist government, forcing them to curb initiatives at home and abroad that might undercut the traditional power and prerogatives of Communist rule in China.[12]

The conservative leaders played a key role in support of the decision to suppress the demonstrators in Tiananmen Square in Beijing and in other Chinese cities in June 1989. Communist Party leaders advocating more moderate treatment of the demonstrators and continued political reform were removed from power. Over time, a Chinese leadership consensus emerged in favor of continued economic reform and outreach to the world for the benefit of Chinese modernization and development, on the one hand, and strong efforts, on the other hand, to sustain authoritarian political rule in China and to resist pressures and other influences coming from US and Western governments and other advocates of political and other change that could lead to the end of CCP rule in China. With the demise of the Soviet Union, the main "threat" to China was seen to come from the United States and its allies. The US and other Western governments and a broad array of nongovernmental forces in these countries were seen to be pressing and undermining Communist Party rule and endeavoring to weaken and constrain its influence in Asian and world affairs.[13]

A resumption of more moderate policies of engagement with China by the United States and other governments later in the 1990s helped reassure Chinese authorities of the intentions of those governments, and it diminished Chinese concern with the immediate threat of US and other pressure regarding human rights and American values. But the Communist authorities remained on guard against US values; they were diligent and generally effective in suppressing political dissidents and perceived deviant religious organizations, ethnic groups, and other nongovernmental organizations (NGOs) and individuals. The latter organizations and individuals sometimes received support from individuals and groups, including some government-sponsored organizations, in the United States or other countries favoring change in China's authoritarian political system in line with American and broader Western values.[14]

The Chinese crackdown on the Tiananmen demonstrators and the emerging consensus in the Chinese leadership on the need for a continued hard line against political dissent and unauthorized religious and ethnic movements placed human rights issues in the forefront of American differences with

China. For a period after the Tiananmen crackdown, human rights advocates seemed to have the initiative in setting US policy toward China. The George H. W. Bush administration was on the defensive, endeavoring to preserve key elements of the US partnership with China despite the ending of the Cold War and the perceived diminished importance of China as a counterweight to the now sharply declining Soviet Union. Congressional leaders for a few months gave top priority to the often idiosyncratic and inconsistent views of Chinese students in the United States advocating reform in China and punishment for the Chinese authorities suppressing the demonstrators at Tiananmen.[15]

For more than a decade, the annual congressional consideration of the president's decision to renew most favored nation trade status for China provided an opportunity for American human rights advocates to publicize their criticisms of China and to seek government as well as media and broader public support for their efforts. Human rights advocates were soon joined by other Americans with interests regarding economic and security relations involving China and advocates for stronger US support for Taiwan, Tibet, and political rights in Hong Kong. As noted in chapter 5, the criticism of Chinese policies and practices in Congress was pervasive, though congressional commitment to a harder line against China often seemed thin. Partisan motives, apart from concern with human rights and other differences with China, frequently appeared to motivate critics of Chinese policies involved in the annual debates over whether to renew most favored nation trade treatment for China. When crises emerged in other areas affecting Sino-American interests, as they did during the war over Iraq's invasion of Kuwait in 1990 and the Taiwan Straits crisis of 1995–96, the congressional criticism of China's human rights policies and practices subsided as American officials pursued pragmatic interaction with the Chinese government. The Bill Clinton administration succeeded in ending the annual congressional deliberations over China by reaching agreement with China on entry into the WTO and getting Congress to pass related legislation granting China permanent normal trade relations with the United States.[16]

Developments in the early years of the twenty-first century reinforced American tendencies to deal pragmatically with China and to play down differences. The terrorist attack on America in 2001 and the global economic crisis beginning in 2008–9 prompted US leaders to minimize differences over human rights and related values in pursuit of closer cooperation with China for the sake of other American interests. However, these issues continued to be raised by US leaders in discussions with China. President George W. Bush continued to voice concern with human rights issues, especially freedom of religion, in China. He met several times with the Dalai Lama and also met with prominent political dissidents from China.[17]

President Barack Obama seemed to capture the balance in the US government's concerns with human rights issues at that time when he spoke to the annual Sino-American leadership dialogue meeting in Washington in July 2009. He advised his Chinese colleagues that the American government did not seek to force China to conform to its view of human rights, but it would nonetheless continue to press China and others to conform to the values of human rights so important to the United States. He said, "Support for human rights and human dignity is ingrained in America. Our nation is made up of immigrants from every part of the world. We have protected our unity and struggled to perfect our union by extending basic rights to all our people. And those rights include the freedom to speak your mind, to worship your God, and to choose your leaders. They are not things that we seek to impose—this is who we are. It guides our openness to one another and the world."[18]

Chinese leaders for their part highlighted the great progress made in advancing economic, social, and other considerations affecting the lives of the vast majority of Chinese people during the post-Mao period. Public opinion in China tended to be supportive of prevailing conditions in the country. Chinese officials also underlined China's increasing cooperation with foreign governments and international organizations to promote human rights abroad. They nonetheless drew a line against US and other foreign government and nongovernment efforts to interfere in Chinese internal affairs in ways that would undermine the sovereignty of China and the integrity of its Communist institutions. They also strongly opposed US and Western-backed efforts supporting popular empowerment against foreign authoritarian rulers in various so-called color revolutions (peaceful democratic movements involving mass demonstrations supported by Western governments and nongovernment groups that toppled post-Communist authoritarian administrations in such former Soviet states as Georgia, Ukraine, and Kyrgyzstan)[19] and the uprisings seen in the Middle East in the so-called Arab Spring. They resisted foreign efforts to spotlight Chinese deviations from international norms in international organizations or world media.[20]

At times, these diverging Sino-American approaches came together in ways that complicated US-China relations. For example, an unanticipated uprising in Tibet in March 2008 saw a strenuous Chinese crackdown against dissent in Tibet. The developments received widespread negative media treatment in the United States and other Western countries. They coincided with an international Olympic torch relay that the Chinese government had organized leading up to the Summer Olympic Games in China in 2008. The Olympic torch relay traveled through several Western countries, including the United States, and was greeted by hostile demonstrators supporting Tibetan rights and condemning Chinese policies. Some Western leaders vacillated on whether to participate in the opening ceremony of the Summer Olympics. Chinese

official and public resentment against the Western demonstrations, supportive media coverage, and political leaders sympathetic to the Dalai Lama and
Tibetan rights were strong. President Bush said firmly that he would attend
the Olympic Games in China, easing the tension in Sino-American relations
over the episode, but the Tibet issue remained highly sensitive in Chinese
interaction with some Western European countries, and it then became a focal
point of Chinese pressure on the incoming Obama administration. President
Obama delayed a meeting with the Dalai Lama so as not to complicate his
first visit to China in November 2009. He met with the Tibetan leader in
February 2010, prompting much tougher Chinese criticism than seen in earlier US presidential meetings with the Dalai Lama. That Chinese pressure was
viewed by Americans as one of several signs of growing Chinese assertiveness over differences with the United States.[21]

Broadly speaking, human rights remained a secondary concern in American
policy toward China during the Obama administration. Incoming president
Donald Trump promised a "pragmatic" approach to human rights issues in
China and elsewhere, treating them with lower priority than economic and
security interests of the United States. President Trump personally avoided
criticism of China on human rights and related issues, but other administration leaders, notably Secretary of State Michael Pompeo, focused on human
rights issues in what was portrayed in US leadership pronouncements especially in 2019 and 2020 as a profound international struggle between the
Chinese Communist Party and its authoritarian rule encompassing a wide
range of human rights abuses versus the human rights and governance practices favored by the United States and many of its allies and partners.[22]

For his part, China's more assertive and internationally active leader, Xi
Jinping, strongly affected American concerns about human rights in China.
His government tightened political controls over the media, academic institutions, and cultural activities; arrested dissidents and lawyers defending dissidents; and curbed NGOs supported by the United States and others in the
West that were promoting change seen as challenging to CCP rule. The Xi
government's push for the CCP's greater authoritarianism and firmer control
of public discourse, social interchange, and key elements of the Chinese
economy added to the perception widely held among specialists, media, various interest groups, and members of Congress that the decades of American
and Western engagement in China were moving in the wrong direction, leading to failure. There was little sign of the above-noted anticipated result of
closer engagement with China of a hoped-for, gradual political liberalization
in China going along with China's greater involvement in world affairs. The
actual result was increasingly seen as a much stronger Chinese government
more capable of societal and economic management and control that effectively squelched signs of dissent or other liberalization and used its growing

international power and influence to advance authoritarian rule and undermine and weaken US-backed international governance.[23]

CONTEMPORARY HUMAN RIGHTS PRACTICES AND ISSUES

Early in the twenty-first century, the Chinese government and party leader
Hu Jintao (2002–12) continued efforts to deal with public grievances and
domestic and foreign calls for redress and reform while suppressing activists
who attempted to organize mass protests or create organizations at odds with
CCP rule. The results were some improvements in human rights along with
continued serious abuses. On the one hand, China's developing legal system
still featured corruption and political interference, but it also provided activists in China with tools with which to promote human rights. Although generally supportive of the status quo, the urban middle class showed increased
willingness to engage in narrowly targeted protests against local government
policies. Their activism added to more widespread social unrest among wage
laborers and rural residents demonstrating against local government policies
and practices and other conditions. Despite a massive effort by the Chinese
authorities to control and censor information available to the public, the
internet and other communications technologies made it more difficult for
the government to clamp down on information as fully as before. On the
other hand, the human rights abuses by Chinese authorities included unlawful
killings by security forces, torture, unlawful detention, the excessive use of
state security laws to imprison political dissidents, coercive family planning
policies and practices, state control of information, and religious and ethnic
persecution. Tibetans, ethnic Uighur Muslims, and Falun Gong adherents
were singled out for especially harsh treatment.[24]

The US government duly acknowledged Chinese advances and shortcomings, notably in a series of congressionally supported official reports including the State Department's annual report on human rights conditions in world
countries. US government efforts to promote human rights in China included
formal criticism of the Chinese government's policies and practices, official
bilateral dialogues, public diplomacy, congressionally sponsored legislation,
hearings, visits, and research. The US government also provided funding for
rule of law, civil society development, participatory government, labor rights,
preserving Tibetan culture, internet access, and other related programs in
China. The US government attention to human rights conditions in China was
backed by more wide-ranging media coverage of human rights conditions in
China and issues in US-China relations and by reports and other publicity
from prominent nongovernment groups and individuals in the United States

with a strong interest in promoting advancement of human rights conditions in China.[25]

American activism and pressure on China regarding human rights issues were tempered by an ongoing debate on whether human rights conditions in China were improving or not. On the negative side were US media, congressional, and other commentators who highlighted evidence of increasing Chinese legal restrictions on freedoms and cases of political and religious persecution. The annual State Department reports on human rights conditions in China were said by some to register no major or overall improvements. On the positive side were those who emphasized the expansion of economic and social freedoms in people's lives.[26]

Further complicating the debate were the efforts of the Chinese government to become more populist, accountable, and law-based, while rejecting Western democracy and more far-reaching political reforms. Party leader and President Hu Jintao and other senior officials showed sympathy with segments of the population who were left behind in the Chinese economic advance. The central leadership also acknowledged human rights as a concern of the state, continued to develop legal institutions, and implemented limited institutional restraints on the exercise of state power. These steps forward came amid continuing administrative practices that retained a large degree of arbitrary power for the ruling authorities.[27]

Indeed, the American debate about human rights conditions in China mirrored a debate among Chinese authorities on where to strike the balance between efforts to improve governance and reduce sources of social and political instability through anticorruption campaigns and the implementation of political reforms and efforts to check mass pressures for greater change. Some Chinese leaders expressed fears that China's small but growing civil society, combined with foreign government and nongovernment assistance for advocacy groups in China, could bring about a "color revolution" in China. With this kind of fear in mind and with continuing determination to sustain and support CCP rule in China, the Chinese authorities enacted legislation aimed at preventing human rights abuses but without protecting the activities of human rights activists who were subject to apparently arbitrary arrest and detention; it tolerated protests against official policies but arrested protest leaders and organizers; public discourse on a wide variety of topics became routine, but politically sensitive issues remained off-limits.[28]

Getting the right balance of flexibility and coercion seemed especially important as increasing economic and social changes fostered tensions along with growing rights consciousness and social activism. Many efforts by citizens to express grievances and demand redress, having been met by government inaction or opposition, erupted into large-scale public protests.[29]

The mixed picture of positives and negatives in Chinese human rights policies and behavior was well illustrated in the annual State Department reports on conditions in China, which tended to focus on infractions and other negative developments, and assessments by Chinese and foreign specialists highlighting various positive Chinese reforms and advances. Thus, the State Department reports in this period noted episodes of unlawful or politically motivated killings, including people who died in detention because of torture. Torture seemed to be used commonly against Falun Gong adherents, Tibetans, Uighur Muslims, and other prisoners of conscience as well as criminal suspects. The "reeducation through labor" system, in which individuals were held in administrative detention for antisocial activity, without formal charges or trial, for a period up to four years, remained a central feature of social and political control in China. Unlawful detention and house arrest remained widespread, particularly against human rights activists, lawyers, and journalists sympathetic to their cause and leaders of unofficial Christian churches. Thousands of persons were viewed by the State Department as political prisoners, serving jail time for "endangering state security" or the former political crime of "counterrevolution." China's "one-child policy" continued with fewer reports of occurrences that were more common in earlier decades of coercive abortions, forced sterilization, and other unlawful government actions against individuals.[30]

This list of infractions and violations of human rights from the perspective of the American government was balanced by positive developments assisting greater freedom and helping ensure human rights. NGOs were often encouraged by the authorities to remain active in order to improve governance and to allow people to give vent to their frustrations in ways that did not directly oppose one-party rule. Some representatives from these organizations and others outside the CCP-controlled system became more involved in advising with regard to government policies and behavior on a variety of topics. Media freedom was expanded in order to target corruption and other abuses of power. Freedom of worship within the range of government-approved religious organizations and churches remained strong; freedom of movement was enhanced by government policies that tried to accommodate the more than 10 percent of Chinese citizens who left their rural homesteads to pursue opportunities in the wealthier urban areas.[31]

The purpose and scope of NGOs grew substantially in this period. At this time early in the twenty-first century, there were more than three hundred thousand registered NGOs in China and more than one million in total, including more than two hundred international organizations. Environmental groups were at the forefront of NGO development in China. Other areas of NGO activity included poverty alleviation, rural development, public health, education, and legal aid. The Chinese government from time to time tightened restrictions on NGOs and voiced opposition to foreign support for groups pushing reforms not favored by the Chinese authorities, but the overall scope and activism of the NGOs continued to grow.[32]

Another area of positive development was the human rights legislation and reforms enacted by the Chinese government. In 2006, the government enacted prohibitions of specific acts of torture and requirements that interrogations of suspects of major crimes be recorded. Use of the death penalty, still egregiously high by international standards, declined markedly under instituted review by the Supreme People's Court. A new labor contract law went into effect in 2008, prompting increases in dispute arbitration cases and lawsuits over wages and benefits. Farmers were provided with new measures in 2008 that allowed them more easily to lease, transfer, and sell rights to property allocated to them by the state. Government measures took effect in 2008 to require government institutions, especially local government administrations seen as more prone to corruption than other government bodies, to reveal financial accounts related to land seizures in rural areas. Responding to international criticism that organs were being removed from executed prisoners in order to profit from organ transplants, the government enacted new regulations stipulating that the donation of organs for transplant must be free and voluntary.[33]

The advent of party and government leader Xi Jinping (2012–) saw much greater emphasis on Communist Party control and the dangers posed by liberalizing forces inside China that were supported from abroad. There was particularly strong concern over the activities of NGOs potentially challenging authoritarian rule. There also was a resurgence of official state-sponsored Chinese propaganda focused on the United States and other so-called hostile foreign forces as threats to China's stability and well-being. Domestically, the overall message fostered public suspicion of the United States and of individuals and NGOs in China with ties to the United States, Japan, or others associated with Western values. Meanwhile, China's impressive, well-financed, and broad-ranging public diplomacy and propaganda efforts abroad featured media distortions, censorship, and defamation of democratic values. When combined with stepped-up Chinese pressure tactics and control efforts targeted against individuals and organizations abroad that were seen as adverse by the CCP regime, the result was a more serious challenge to American-supported values and norms.[34]

When Xi Jinping became general secretary of the CCP in 2012, he began carrying out a crackdown on dissent and activism that surprised many observers for its scope and severity; it included the detentions and arrests of hundreds of government critics, human rights lawyers, well-known bloggers, investigative journalists, outspoken academics, civil society leaders, and ethnic minorities. Indictments for state security crimes, which often are political in nature, rose in 2013 to 1,384 cases, the highest level since the Tibetan unrest of 2008. The government imposed growing restrictions on Chinese microblogging and mobile text services, which had become important sources of news for many Chinese people and platforms for public opinion. The Chinese government passed or considered new laws that strengthened the role of the state security apparatus in overseeing a wide range of social activities, including those of foreign NGOs; placed additional restrictions on defense lawyers; and authorized greater governmental controls over the internet.[35]

Summarizing adverse conditions in 2016, the State Department disclosed in its annual human rights report that severe repression and coercion was targeted against organizations and individuals involved in civil and political rights advocacy, and such severe repression also was targeted against organizations and individuals involved with public interest and ethnic minority issues. Past hopes that free elections would spread from use in the very lowest levels of governance were thwarted. Citizens did not have the right to choose their government. Authorities prevented independent candidates from running in elections, even on such low levels as selecting delegates to local people's congresses. Citizens had limited forms of redress against official abuse. Other serious human rights abuses included arbitrary or unlawful deprivation of life; executions without due process; illegal detentions at unofficial holding facilities known as "black jails"; torture and coerced confessions of prisoners; and detention and harassment of journalists, lawyers, writers, bloggers, dissidents, petitioners, and others whose actions the authorities deemed unacceptable. There was also a lack of due process in judicial proceedings; political control of courts and judges; closed trials; the use of administrative detention; failure to protect refugees and asylum seekers; extrajudicial disappearances of citizens; restrictions on NGOs; and discrimination against women, minorities, and persons with disabilities. The government imposed a coercive birth-limitation policy that, despite lifting one-child-per-family restrictions, denied women the right to decide the number of their children and in some cases resulted in forced abortions (sometimes at advanced stages of pregnancy). On the work front, severe labor restrictions continued.[36]

Since 2017, the PRC government has enacted laws and policies that enhance the legal authority of the state to counter potential ideological, social, political, and security challenges, including the Law on Overseas Nongovernmental Organizations, the Cybersecurity Law, and the National Intelligence Law. In 2018, Xi backed a constitutional amendment removing the previous limit of two five-year terms for the presidency, clearing the way for him potentially to stay in power indefinitely. PRC methods of social and political control were evolving to include sophisticated technologies. The government was developing a "social credit system" that aggregated data on individuals' credit scores, consumer behavior, internet use, and criminal records and scored citizens' "trustworthiness." China deployed tens of millions of surveillance cameras as well as facial, voice, iris, and gait recognition equipment to reduce crime generally as well as to track the movements of politically sensitive groups. These and other salient human rights issues are treated below.

Recent Human Rights Issues

A wide range of human rights issues continued to prompt critical attention from American officials in the Congress and the executive branch of government as well as American media, human rights groups, and other groups and individuals with an interest. Some issues—like the status of student demonstrators and others arrested during the Tiananmen crackdown and those suffering as a result of widespread abuses in China's family planning regime—subsided with the passage of time and changed circumstances. Others, like the human rights conditions in Tibet and among Uighur Muslims in China's restive Xinjiang region, became more salient as a result of violence in both Tibet and Xinjiang in recent years. Meanwhile, China's increasingly strong and assertive efforts abroad to manipulate opinion and squelch dissent and opposition to the Communist government and its policies and practices became a new set of recently prominent human rights concerns.[37]

Uighurs

Since an outbreak of Uighur demonstrations and unrest in the Xinjiang Uyghur Autonomous Region (XUAR) in 2009, and sporadic clashes involving Uighurs and Xinjiang security personnel that spiked between 2013 and 2015, PRC leaders have sought to "stabilize" the region through large-scale arrests and more intensive security and assimilation measures aimed at combating what China repeatedly refers to as the "three evils: terrorism, separatism and religious extremism."[38] In particular, the government undertook forceful attempts to transform the thought and customs of Uighurs, a Turkic ethnic group who practice a moderate form of Sunni Islam, and assimilate them into Han Chinese culture; the efforts were widely seen abroad as designed to result in the destruction of Uighur culture and identity. According to some estimates, between 2017 and 2020, XUAR authorities arbitrarily detained roughly 1.5 million Turkic Muslims, mostly Uighurs, in "reeducation" centers. Detainees were compelled to renounce many of their Islamic beliefs and customs as a condition for their possible release. By 2020, many detainees were said to have been formally convicted of crimes and placed in higher-security facilities. The government relocated other former detainees and their families to residential compounds with restricted access.

Since 2019, thousands of Uighurs, including many former detainees, were employed in textile and other labor-intensive industries in Xinjiang and other provinces under circumstances that some observers argued indicated the use of forced labor. Uighurs who refused to accept such employment risked detention. Factory employment also often involved heavy surveillance and political indoctrination during and after work.[39]

Referring to the situation in Xinjiang, Secretary of State Mike Pompeo in July 2019 said, "China is home to one of the worst human rights crises of our time; it is truly the stain of the century."[40] The Trump administration was reported to be considering sanctions under the Global Magnitsky Human Rights Accountability Act against officials in Xinjiang. In January 2021, the Trump government issued a determination that China had committed crimes against humanity and genocide "against the predominantly Muslim Uyghurs and other ethnic and religious minority groups" in China's Xinjiang region.[41] Earlier US actions on Xinjiang included adding PRC firms to the Department of Commerce's Entity List, restricting their trading opportunities with the United States; imposing sanctions on certain PRC officials and organizations; and blocking imports from China tied to forced labor. Presidential candidate Joseph Biden and others vying for the Democratic Party nomination during the 2020 election campaign often criticized Chinese policy in Xinjiang. Secretary of State Antony Blinken said he concurred with the Trump administration "genocide" determination. He also emphasized the need to prevent the import of goods made with forced labor and the export of technologies used for repression. The Biden administration in March imposed sanctions under the Global Magnitsky Human Rights Accountability Act against officials in Xinjiang. Stepped-up enforcement by the Biden administration and other Western governments of prohibitions of imports of products involving forced labor prompted several Western firms to cut supplies coming from Xinjiang or from factories employing contract workers from Xinjiang.[42]

Religious and Ethnic Minority Policies

In line with the crackdown on Muslim Uighurs in Xinjiang, Xi Jinping in 2016 launched a policy of "Sinicization" requiring religious practitioners and ethnic minorities to "assimilate" or conform to Han Chinese culture, China's overall socialist system, and the policies of the Chinese Communist Party. Han Chinese, the majority ethnic group in China, make up about 91 percent of the country's population. New regulations on religious practice further restricted travel to foreign countries for religious reasons and contacts with foreign religious organizations and tightened bans on religious practice among party members and religious education of children. All religious venues now were required to teach traditional Chinese culture and "core socialist values." Meanwhile, the government intensified pressure on Christian churches that were not officially registered to apply for government approval or risk closure. Authorities also removed crosses from roughly four thousand church buildings in recent years, ostensibly for not complying with regulations.[43]

Tibetans

Apart from the suppression of Uighurs in Xinjiang, human rights issues in Tibetan areas in China include the curtailment of rights and freedoms to a greater degree than elsewhere in the country. They involve arbitrary detention and imprisonment of Tibetans and ideological reeducation of Tibetan Buddhist monks and nuns. Authorities accelerated forced assimilation in Tibetan areas, including by "forcibly resettling and urbanizing nomads and farmers, and weakening Tibetan-language education in public schools and religious education in monasteries," according to the US Department of State.[44] The PRC government insisted that Chinese laws, and not Tibetan Buddhist religious traditions, would govern the process by which lineages of Tibetan lamas are reincarnated and that the state had the right to choose the successor to the Tibetan spiritual leader, the eighty-six-year-old (at time of writing) fourteenth Dalai Lama, who lives in exile in India.[45]

Hong Kong

A former British colony, Hong Kong reverted to PRC sovereignty in 1997 under the provisions of a 1984 treaty in which China promised the city a "high degree of autonomy" and stated that Hong Kong's social and economic systems would remain unchanged for at least fifty years. After a series of mass demonstrations during 2019–20 against proposed restrictions on Hong Kong people's rights, in June 2020, China imposed a sweeping national security law on Hong Kong that many saw as breaking promises of autonomy. On July 14, 2020, President Trump issued an executive order stating that the Hong Kong Special Administrative Region (HKSAR) "is no longer sufficiently autonomous to justify differential treatment in relation to the People's Republic of China" and suspending such differential treatment.[46] The special treatment was important for Hong Kong's economic relationship with the United States. The order also authorized the secretaries of State and the Treasury to impose visa and economic sanctions on HKSAR and PRC officials determined to be responsible for the erosion of the HKSAR's autonomy, the undermining of democracy in Hong Kong, or the loss of the rights of Hong Kong residents. Subsequently, twenty PRC officials and eight HKSAR officials were sanctioned by the US government. The HKSAR government described the sanctions as "blatant interference in the internal affairs of the

PRC, violating international law and basic norms governing international relations."[47] The PRC government imposed visa and other sanctions on US officials.[48]

Criticizing the Chinese policies and practices on Hong Kong was a staple in election campaign remarks of candidate Biden and other Democrats. After Hong Kong in February 2021 charged prodemocracy politicians and activists with subversion under the 2020 national security law, Secretary of State Blinken in March affirmed the new US administration would adhere to the tough Trump administration measures on Hong Kong.[49]

Restrictions on Free Speech

From 2013 to 2021, China dropped four places, to 177 out of 180 countries, on Reporters Without Borders' World Press Freedom Index. And Freedom House judged that China had the worst conditions in the world for internet freedom for six consecutive years. The PRC government oversaw one of the most extensive and sophisticated internet censorship systems in the world, including expansive censorship and blocking many of the world's most used foreign websites. State authorities and private companies also monitored and regulated social media use in order to prevent sensitive topics and information from being discussed and disseminated. The Chinese party-state's control of information had dire consequences in dealing with the COVID-19 outbreak centered in Wuhan, China, in December 2019–March 2020. There was a crackdown on disclosures of information that if known and acted on by Chinese authorities would have led to actions preventing the disastrous worldwide contagion.[50]

Use of Surveillance Technology

PRC methods of social and political control evolved to include the widespread use of sophisticated surveillance and big-data technologies. Increasingly, Chinese companies were exporting data and surveillance technologies around the world. In April 2019, the Australian Strategic Policy Institute, an Australian-based nonpartisan think tank, showed Chinese firms involved in installing 5G networks in thirty-four countries and deploying so-called safe cities surveillance technologies in forty-six countries. In October 2018, Freedom House reported thirty-eight countries in which Chinese companies had installed internet and mobile networking equipment, eighteen countries that had deployed intelligent monitoring systems and facial recognition developed by Chinese companies, and thirty-six countries in which media elites and government officials had traveled to China for trainings on new media or information management.[51]

Arbitrary Arrest

According to human rights groups, there were two dozen high-profile cases of arbitrary arrest of political dissidents and rights defenders and activists in 2019–20. One such group, the Dui Hua Foundation, compiled information on over 7,500 political and religious prisoners in China as of September 2020 (not including Uighurs detained in reeducation facilities in Xinjiang).[52]

Persecution of Political Dissent at Home and Abroad

China's state security law was used liberally and often arbitrarily against political dissidents. In May 2013, the CCP issued a classified directive (Document No. 9) identifying seven negative topics largely aimed at the media and liberal academics. According to the document, topics to be avoided in public discussion included universal values, constitutional democracy, freedom of the press, civil society, civil rights, an independent judiciary, and criticism of the CCP. Universities were warned against using textbooks that spread "Western values" and making remarks that "defame the rule of the Communist Party."[53]

One of the focal points of Chinese authorities cracking down on dissent involved a number of extraterritorial disappearances. One case involved journalist Li Xin, who fled to India in 2015 after allegedly leaking documents detailing the CCP's propaganda policies, went missing on a train in Thailand in January, and later reappeared in China in custody of security officials. He told his wife by telephone that he had returned voluntarily, but Thai immigration officials told the media they had no exit record for Li. Five men working in Hong Kong's publishing industry disappeared between October and December 2015. In addition to being Hong Kong residents, two had foreign citizenship, which was ignored by the Chinese government in its repression efforts. Gui Minhai was a Swedish citizen and was taken while he was in Thailand; Lee Bo was a British citizen taken from Hong Kong. Media coverage of the cases noted that the men worked for a publishing house and bookstore in Hong Kong that was known for selling books critical of the CCP and its leaders. In a televised "confession" released by Chinese authorities, Gui Minhai said he had "voluntarily returned" to China to "bear the responsibility" for a traffic accident that supposedly occurred more than a decade before. Another bookseller, Hong Kong resident Lam Wing Kee, was detained at the border crossing into Shenzhen in October 2015 and released after five months. Upon his return to Hong Kong, Lam immediately recanted his televised confession, saying it was scripted and recorded under extreme pressure. He also said he was forced to sign away his legal rights when he was taken to Ningbo by men who claimed they were from a "central special unit." With the exception of Swedish citizen Gui Minhai, the other detained booksellers were released during the year but remained under surveillance, travel restrictions, and the threat of punishment after returning to Hong Kong. Gui's location—presumably under incommunicado detention in the mainland—remained unknown for years. In 2020, he received a ten-year prison sentence.[54] During these years, the Swedish government insisted on their right to meet with their citizen. A human rights group in Sweden recognized Gui for a human rights award, a move favored by the Swedish government, leading to a major controversy involving the Chinese embassy and foreign ministry.[55] Meanwhile, the US FBI repeatedly warned against Chinese government agents working illegally in the United States to harass and pressure Chinese residents in the United States to return to China to face charges. The FBI arrested five such accused Chinese agents in October 2020.[56]

Falun Gong

Falun Gong is a movement that combines spiritual beliefs with an exercise and meditation regimen derived from traditional Chinese practices known as qigong. The movement remained out of the public spotlight while it gained millions of adherents across China in the 1990s. On April 25, 1999, thousands of adherents gathered in Beijing to protest the government's growing restrictions on their activities. The demonstration seemed to take the Chinese leadership by surprise. The ability of the movement to mobilize such an impressive show of support at the seat of Chinese administrative power was viewed as a threat—one that reflected infiltration of Falun Gong supporters throughout the police and security forces and other sensitive apparatus of the Chinese government.[57]

Party leader Jiang Zemin led a major crackdown against the movement that continued for years. The harsh measures against suspected adherents who refused to recant their beliefs and cooperate with the authorities led to widespread reports of torture; estimates of adherents who died in state custody ranged from several hundred to a few thousand. The Chinese government acknowledged that deaths while in custody occurred but denied that they were caused by mistreatment. As the Chinese suppression succeeded in wiping out the movement in China, its salience as a human rights issue in US-China relations declined.[58]

China's International Challenges to Human Rights

With its expanding international profile and greater assertiveness under President Xi Jinping, Chinese government and Chinese Communist Party organs have been expanding the reach of their censorship and control activities beyond purely domestic affairs into the United States and other countries.

Examples include the abductions and detainments of foreign nationals and Hong Kong residents, which were discussed above. Chinese consular and embassy officials warned US and other foreign think tanks, churches, media outlets, NGOs, and universities against giving public platforms to people they deemed politically unacceptable. Chinese officials also pressured or boycotted international cultural events ranging from book fairs to beauty pageants in order to censor certain topics or expel certain participants for political reasons. Beijing agents targeted relatives of Chinese living abroad who expressed views that challenged party orthodoxy, not only by denying them visas to visit ailing and dying parents but also by threatening the human rights of relatives within China. Meanwhile, as also noted above, there was China's massive public diplomacy/propaganda efforts that featured media distortions, censorship, and defamation of democratic values.[59]

ISSUES OF GOVERNANCE IN CONTEMPORARY US-CHINA RELATIONS

Though the United States registered varying degrees of concern over human rights and related governance issues inside China since the establishment of US official relations with China in the 1970s, Americans came late in appreciating the challenge to broader international governance posed by rising Chinese power and influence. Even in the past decade, expert assessments of China's performance in international governance often focused on measuring the degree of Chinese conformity to the norms and practices of the post–Cold War international order heavily influenced by the United States.[60]

In contrast, over the past four years came a variety of progressive, moderate, and conservative think tank reports and in-depth academic studies, often supported by government reports and investigative journalism, that documented a wide variety of cases of Chinese practices throughout the world that demonstrated heretofore often underappreciated challenges to the United States and its allies and partners with an interest in the existing liberal order.[61] They were written by specialists in the United States, Europe, Australia, and other countries around China's periphery that were on the receiving end of the Chinese challenges. They showed Chinese party, government, and military agents working in often disguised and hidden ways that could be and were denied by the Chinese authorities to undermine existing governance policies and practices seen in the way of China fulfilling its broadening international ambitions. These efforts were demonstrated to have ever-greater support from the Chinese government, allowing for in-depth action across the globe. Overall, the evidence showed that China was not yet ready to call for the overhaul of the international order, but its actions in support of ambitions to change the world order had reached a point where China was actively presenting the China model for international emulation.[62]

Summarized here are some of the salient features of China's push for greater foreign influence involving challenges to this order.

Exploitative Economic Practices

The most impactful Chinese practices advancing influence and undermining the prevailing international order came within the scope of China's three-decades-long effort using state-directed development polices, which plunder foreign intellectual property rights and undermine international competitors. Beijing did so with hidden and overt state-directed economic coercion, egregious government subsidies, import protection, and export promotion using highly protected and state-supported products to drive out foreign competition in key industries. The profits went into efforts to achieve dominance in major world industries and build military power to secure China's primacy in Asia and world leadership. They allowed companies like Huawei to attempt to dominate international communications enterprises.[63] The profits also supported the massive state-directed Chinese efforts to lead high-technology industries that will define economic and eventually military leadership in world affairs. Beijing disguised these practices with avowed support for globalization. China's Belt and Road Initiative (BRI) also sought and gained avid support from the UN secretary general and other world leaders, thereby legitimating Chinese predatory economic practices.[64]

Building and Exploiting Economic Dependence

As the world's leading trader and creditor, China disregarded WTO norms and its avowed support for globalization in order to weaponize economic dependence to compel states to defer to Chinese demands on political, sovereignty, security, and other issues.[65] Many countries relied heavily on exports to and/or imports from China, and many states depended on the inflow of Chinese tourists and students to their countries. Coercion was applied or threatened by the Chinese government directly or through party channels mobilizing boycotts, demonstrations, and other pressures in China against foreign targets. The many foreign countries subjected to these kinds of threats in recent years included Argentina, Australia, Canada, France, Germany, Great Britain, Japan, New Zealand, Norway, the Philippines, South Korea, Sweden, Taiwan, and the United States.

As a creditor, China undermined World Bank, International Monetary Fund, and Organisation for Economic Co-operation and Development lending guidelines. A graphic example was the so-called debt trap for a number of states brought about by excessive and unsustainable borrowing from Chinese state banks.[66] Often large amounts of debt were accumulated by shortsighted, selfish, and corrupt foreign leaders; their successors found that easing the debt burden was impossible without China's close cooperation as the costs of canceling overly ambitious Chinese-financed infrastructure projects often precluded this action. Such debt dependency had strategic implications as China compelled these states to accommodate Chinese demands for equity (e.g., land, ports, and airfields) for repayment and/or Chinese requests for access to military facilities or other favors.[67]

Fostering Corrupt and/or Authoritarian Governments Aligned with China Against the West

China's Belt and Road Initiative and other programs relied on bilateral non-transparent deals involving extensive Chinese financing. They were attractive to many foreign corrupt and/or authoritarian leaders adverse to existing international lending norms. The agreements enabled profitable Chinese infrastructure development and deepened Chinese influence while serving the power and personal wants of the authoritarian and/or corrupt foreign leaders.[68] This symbiosis of Chinese-foreign government interests represented a strong asset in China's growing international influence as the world was full of such regimes.

Added to this bond was Chinese provision of communications and surveillance systems that assisted the foreign leaders to track and suppress opponents. Related was robust Chinese interchange with media outlets in various states. Those outlets pursued news coverage that was positive concerning the government leadership and China. Meanwhile, Chinese communications and surveillance systems along with Chinese-provided hydroelectric dams, railroads, and port operations caused recipient countries to rely ever more on Chinese firms for maintenance, and they made the Chinese ties difficult and expensive to replace by another provider. Communications and surveillance systems also assisted Chinese intelligence collection and manipulation of opinion in the country.[69]

The array of foreign governments influenced in these ways was global in scope. Salient examples included Venezuela and Ecuador in Latin America; Serbia, Montenegro, and at times arguably Italy and Greece in Europe; Djibouti and Zambia in Africa; the Maldives and Sri Lanka in South Asia; and Cambodia, Laos, Malaysia, Myanmar, and the Philippines in Southeast Asia. Many authoritarian governments in the Middle East and Central Asia were seen as inclined to work closely with China along these lines.[70]

Coercing Neighbors, Leveraging Unconventional Assets

In addition to Chinese forces' clashes in 2020, without the use of firearms, with Indian forces along the disputed boundary, other unconventional coercive methods used to intimidate neighboring states involved usually unpublicized Chinese deployment of maritime militia and coast guard vessels to deter and "bully" governments challenging China's expansive claims in the South China Sea and the East China Sea. In tandem with such deployments, China privately warned disputants that countering China on these matters would lead to their decisive military defeat. Repeated shows of force by Chinese naval and air forces in the South and East China Seas and around Taiwan were used to deter these governments from countering China's demands for deference. Beijing bombers in 2019 teamed up with Russian bombers to probe and challenge the air space of South Korea and Japan, thereby serving notice of China-Russia cooperation against the claims of these US allies.[71]

Among unconventional assets used to pressure Southeast Asian neighbors, Chinese dams controlled the flow of water in the Mekong River, strongly impacting downriver countries Myanmar, Laos, Thailand, Cambodia, and Vietnam and influencing their postures toward China. Beijing's strong ties with armed separatist groups inside Myanmar provided a major source of leverage in regard to that country.[72]

Influence Operations, Elite Capture

The well-funded influence operations abroad of Chinese party and state agents and the front organizations they support achieved significant success in (1) mobilizing the Chinese diaspora in various countries, (2) achieving success in so-called elite capture—winning over foreign dignitaries to work in support of Chinese objectives, and (3) gaining influence with and control over media and journalism in a number of states.[73] They were backed by diplomats abroad prepared to resort to outrageous invective and threats in demanding deference to China's objectives supported by the influence operations. Behind the influence operations rested strong efforts to penetrate foreign high-technology centers for desired information through the Chinese government's thousand talents program and other means, including common intellectual property theft. Also active were Chinese agents recruiting foreign individuals to serve the purposes of Chinese espionage.[74]

Disregard for International Law

China's disregard for international law in pursuit of expansionism showed egregiously in its rejection of the July 2016 ruling of a United Nations Convention on the Law of the Sea tribunal finding against China's expansive

South China Sea claims. Also, China practiced illegal abduction of and prolonged detention in China of Chinese nationals resident abroad and holding foreign citizenship, ignoring provisions of international conventions. Beijing also used arrests and detentions of foreigners in China as leverage against foreign governments.[75]

Supporting Russian Disruptions; Undermining ASEAN, European Unity

Though China denied malign intent, China and Russia worked ever more cooperatively to reduce US influence in their respective spheres of influence—China in Asia and Russia in Europe and the Middle East.[76] With similar denials, China also worked steadily to weaken the unity of ASEAN and of the European Union. It appealed to some members at the expense of the unity of the group, which otherwise would impede Chinese ambitions in Southeast Asia and Europe.[77]

PRINCIPLE VERSUS PRACTICE: THE CHALLENGE OF CHINA'S JANUS-FACED STRATEGIES

Reinforcing the wide gap between the United States and China over issues of international governance and the difficulty the United States and other stakeholders faced in the existing international order in dealing with the negative implications for prevailing international governance flowing from the above Chinese practices were China's Janus-faced public postures regarding these often malign efforts targeting Western interests and norms. The following discussion juxtaposes some of Beijing's self-serving and often malign behavior targeting Western interests and norms with China's avowed positions in foreign affairs. Beijing said it followed long-standing principles that lead to moral behavior reassuring to concerned nations, arguing that China was not a revisionist power intent on disrupting the world order. The contrast between the avowed reassuring principles and the actual Chinese behavior showed duplicity that added to difficulties in discerning the impact of China's actions.[78]

China's Avowed "Noninterference in Internal Affairs" versus Chinese Influence Operations and Political Warfare

Despite China's decades-long assertion that it did not interfere in other countries' internal affairs, Chinese foreign practices interfered in often gross ways in the political, social, and related affairs of targeted countries. They included mobilization of the ethnic Chinese and Chinese students. These practices involved embassy and consulate officials and other agents to recruit, monitor, and control ethnic Chinese abroad, employing them for purposes in line with Chinese interests. A subset involved efforts to control and influence Chinese students abroad to counter perceived anti-China forces in various countries. The scope of such efforts focused on the many countries with large ethnic Chinese and Chinese student populations. The United States and Australia were notable examples. The efforts became more prominent when developments in the country concerned moved in directions opposed by the Chinese government.[79]

A second area of Chinese interference in other countries' internal affairs came with substantial financial and other assistance to key individuals and institutions that were prepared to support China's interests. This involved large campaign contributions to political parties in some democracies, employment of recently retired or active government or political leaders in paid positions in organizations backed by the Chinese government favoring Chinese interests, and recruitment of local business leaders with high salaries and benefits to work in organizations backed by China to pursue Chinese interests. Examples included Italy, Australia, New Zealand, and Tonga among many others. Also involved were the use of corrupt practices involving payments and padded contracts to win support for Chinese infrastructure and other projects in line with China's BRI and other efforts. Among the many salient examples here were Cambodia, Malaysia, the Maldives, Ecuador, Kyrgyzstan, and Montenegro. Collectively, these efforts were labeled "elite capture," allowing the Chinese government to use such influential individuals for Chinese purposes.[80]

A third area of interference involved China leveraging trade and investment dependencies to coerce countries to follow China's interests. Such practices became routine in Chinese statecraft as seen in an illuminating report from the Center for New American Security.[81] A recent episode came when Australia's support for an independent investigation of the origins of the coronavirus in China prompted Chinese cutoff of Australian beef imports. The restrictions quickly escalated, bringing relations between the two countries to a new low.[82] A very costly and ostensibly nongovernment Chinese boycott of South Korean business and tourism came in retaliation to the deployment of the US THAAD antimissile system in South Korea, which Beijing deemed against its interest. And Chinese officials warned Germany and other European countries that their large trade interests in China would be seriously impacted if they did not favor the Chinese company Huawei for their telecommunications modernization, despite strenuous opposition from the United States.[83] Meanwhile, Chinese interference increasingly targeted foreign businesses, carrying out or threatening retaliation for the statements or actions deemed offensive to China by the enterprises or their representatives, including large sports groups like the National Basketball Association.[84]

A fourth area of Chinese interference in other countries' internal affairs saw Beijing resorting to arrests and detentions of foreigners or dual citizens holding foreign passports in retaliation for actions by foreign governments or in pursuit of foreign-based dissidents. Notable examples included the arrests of Canadians in China on account of Canada's detention of the Huawei chief financial officer for extradition to the United States, reported extralegal abduction and rendition to China of dissidents from Thailand and Hong Kong noted earlier, and Chinese security agents illegally coming to the United States and other countries to carry out intimidation of anti-China dissidents.[85]

A fifth area of Chinese intrusion in other countries' internal affairs saw Chinese interference in foreign elections in, among others, Australia, New Zealand, Malaysia, and most recently the United States.[86]

Two other areas of Chinese interference involved large-scale information operations to build support in foreign media, seeking media control in some developing countries (e.g., Kenya) with poor media infrastructures and greater influence in more developed countries (e.g., Italy).[87] And it involved fostering pro-China views in educational institutions employing such elements as the Confucius Institutes and the wide-ranging training and educational opportunities provided by the Chinese government and party.[88]

Recent in-depth analyses showed the impressive and expanding scope of the Chinese overseas United Front influence operations carried out by the Chinese Communist Party, its overt International Liaison Department, and various disguised or hidden influence and espionage operations. Many of the operations were under the direction of the United Front Department of the Communist Party with others directed by the military and the espionage agencies. These efforts seemed relatively benign in countries closely aligned with China's interests, but they appeared very much focused on interfering in the internal affairs of countries that seemed opposed or resistant to Chinese interests.[89]

"China Committed to Globalization" versus Seeking State-Directed Industrial Dominance and Other Interests

"China Committed to Globalization" was the *China Daily* headline of the Chinese vice premier Han Zheng's message at the Fiftieth World Economic Forum at Davos, Switzerland, in January 2020.[90] In contrast, the reality of Chinese economic practices examined by Center for American Progress (CAP) and other think tanks showed determination to use China's economic size and importance to compel acceptance of Chinese practices that eroded existing free market norms and grossly disadvantaged the United States and many allied and other developed countries.

Examples of egregious Chinese erosion of economic norms of open and free markets in globalization involved the common practices highlighted by CAP of the Chinese government supporting Chinese industrial firms to gain access to US advanced technology through state-backed funding, espionage, required joint ventures, and/or coerced technology transfers. These steps allowed developing competing industries in China without permitting US or other foreign competition. These Chinese firms then emerged on the international market with heavily state-subsidized products that wiped out international competition and placed China in the lead of key new industries.[91]

US industry complaints about such predatory Chinese practices risked losing access to China's market. And even if advanced US industries did not follow coerced technology transfer demands from China, they still risked cybertheft and human agent espionage. Past authoritative US estimates of the loss of US wealth to Chinese cybertheft and other espionage ranged around several hundreds of billions of dollars annually.[92]

In 2015, Beijing released its "made in China 2025" plan, which called for Chinese firms to supplant their foreign competitors in China and in global markets and provided financial and regulatory support to achieve these goals. Reinforcing this effort, China presented US businesses with a host of new self-serving Chinese market regulations that disadvantaged foreign companies and a new cybersecurity law that required foreign firms to hand over proprietary source codes and other trade secrets. The United States Trade Representative in its report on China in March 2018 laid out a long list of Chinese practices at odds with international economic norms, asserting that they represented an "existential threat" to the American economy.[93]

Meanwhile, Marriott Corporation, other hotel chains, and various airlines in 2018 had to change their treatment of Taiwan to accord with China's view that Taiwan is part of China or risk losing their business in China.[94] That retribution very much out of line with economic norms of globalization became the norm in China's foreign policy became clearer when the coach of the Houston Rockets basketball team voiced support for prodemocracy demonstrators in Hong Kong in 2019. The result was immediate loss of market access to China until the team and the National Basketball Association apologized profusely and restricted any team member or those attending the games in the United States or elsewhere from showing support for the Hong Kong demonstrators.[95]

"No Matter How Far China Develops, It Will Never Seek Hegemony" versus Common Chinese Applications of Coercion and Intimidation to Achieve China's Advances at Others' Expense

The quoted remarks from a Xi Jinping speech in December 2018 were a common refrain used specially to reassure China's neighbors.[96] Beijing often added that its BRI and other economic ventures were designed to bring China and its neighbors closer together in a "community of common destiny."[97]

Unfortunately, the rhetoric and economic interchange were often accompanied by strong applications of force, short of military attack. Beijing's hard sticks were applied in unpublicized coercion in 2019 and 2020 of Vietnam, the Philippines, and Malaysia—claimants disputing China's broad claim in the South China Sea. They included chilling private warnings to the first two that contesting Chinese claims would lead to defeat in war, and harassment of ongoing oil and gas exploitation efforts of Vietnam and Malaysia. Among China's goals was to halt and expel foreign ventures from the contested sea, making China the only acceptable partner for the other claimants in pursuing development of the oil and gas resources.[98]

Acting in ways that if carried out by the United States would be viewed by China as practicing hegemony, Beijing rebuked the UN Law of the Sea tribunal's ruling in July 2016 against China's expansive claims in the South China Sea, manipulated China-dependent Cambodia and Laos in order to thwart ASEAN statements on the ruling, and strongly coerced all ASEAN countries to avoid support or even mention of the ruling. Those Southeast Asian states increasing security ties with the United States were privately and sometimes publicly warned of adverse consequences. In protracted negotiations, China sought an ASEAN-China code of conduct regarding the South China Sea that would limit the ability of Southeast Asian nations to call on the US military for support.[99] If neighboring countries hosting regional meetings were seen to allow even veiled criticism of China in the concluding statements, Chinese diplomats put aside diplomatic norms and barged into offices demanding changes in the documents, as happened in Papua New Guinea in 2018 in an episode later labeled as "tantrum diplomacy." Such improper behavior also happened with Chinese officials attending the annual Pacific Islands Forum meeting in September 2018.[100]

Chinese diplomats lobbying in Europe in favor of Huawei in 2019–20 were similarly obnoxious and bullying. In Asia and Europe, China looked to exploit opportunities in ways beyond the pale of normal international governance to drive wedges between the United States and its allies, such as seen in the strong ostensibly nongovernment retribution against South Korea over the THAAD deployment. And, despite its avowed constructive relationship with the European Union, Beijing showed the other side of a Janus-faced policy as it gave top priority in wooing the less advanced Central and Eastern European members of the EU, getting some of the latter to weaken EU efforts sought by leading EU powers to counter offensive Chinese policies.[101]

IMPLICATIONS

Taken as a whole, the above evidence supported the judgment of Council of Foreign Relations specialist Elizabeth Economy that China had reached a stage where it was challenging and endeavoring to undermine the United States as it exported its political and development model abroad.[102] The evidence also seemed to validate specialists such as Liza Tobin of the US government who warned that Xi Jinping's promotion of the community of common destiny masked a concerted effort to restructure global governance in order to enable China to integrate with the world and attain global leadership. A global network of partnerships centered on China would replace US treaty alliances; the international community would regard the Beijing authoritarian governance model as superior to Western electoral democracy; and the world would credit the Communist Party of China for developing a new path to peace, prosperity, and modernity that other countries can follow.[103]

In sum, assessing the breadth and depth of heretofore often denied, disguised, and hidden multifaceted means used by the Chinese government to expand influence abroad in ways that undermined, weakened, and challenged existing international norms favored by the United States and its allies and partners underlined challenges these governments faced in seeking to preserve the existing status quo they favored. Whether or not these Chinese efforts actually changed the overall balance of international power and global influence between the United States and China also depended on many important variables, like military and economic power, national unity, and effective leadership that remained to be seen.

STUDY QUESTIONS

1. Why were differences over ideology and values regarding human rights and related issues so important in US-Chinese relations in the 1950s and 1960s?
2. What explains both sides playing down those differences during growing engagement over the next two decades?
3. How did the Tiananmen crackdown, the end of the Cold War, and the rise of democratic rule in Taiwan make differences over ideology and

values regarding human rights and related issues much more serious for both the United States and China?

4. Why did subsequent strong efforts on both sides to pragmatically promote positive engagement while managing differences over human rights and related issues of ideology and values fail to substantially diminish these sources of US-China tension?

5. How does one explain the recently strong competition between the United States and China over ideological and values differences regarding global governance?

6. How threatening to China's authoritarian rulers are US efforts to promote human rights, popular sovereignty, and democracy abroad?

7. And how threatening to US rulers are Chinese efforts opposing such efforts and supporting authoritarian and corrupt governments that align with China against US challenges in favor of an alternate order where China's rise would be less encumbered by American challenges?

RELEVANT VIDEOS

"A Clash of Civilizations" (South China Morning Post panel, July 6, 2020, thirty minutes) available at https://www.youtube.com/watch?v=e4grWwFxhe0

"Global China: Examining China's Approach to Global Governance" (Brookings Institution, September 21, 2020, seventy-five minutes) available at https://www.youtube.com/watch?v=Gp0SL3wwKPI

"The New China Rules" (CSIS, 2020, one hour) available at https://www.youtube.com/watch?v=IdbAcBcB714

"China Reality Check Series: Chinese Public Opinion and the Durability of Chinese Communist Party Rule" (panel discussion, CSIS, October 26, 2016, ninety-six minutes) available at https://www.csis.org/events/china-reality-check-series-chinese-public-opinion-and-durability-chinese-communist-party-rule

"How Xi Jinping Is Transforming China at Home and Abroad" (PBS, September 26, 2019, twelve minutes) available at https://www.pbs.org/newshour/show/how-president-xi-jinping-is-transforming-china-at-home-and-abroad

"Imagining China in 2023—China's Domestic and Foreign Posture under Xi Jinping" (Kevin Rudd, National University of Singapore, April 9, 2014, eighty-two minutes) available at https://www.youtube.com/watch?v=3lmpGTGkkos&list=PUakbhT1zJqJ9iod01nFEYhw

"The Chinese Communist Party's Strategy for Survival" (Bruce Dickson, University of Michigan, May 19, 2016, eighty-one minutes) available at https://www.youtube.com/watch?v=90CrKOxlLqg

Chapter Twelve

Outlook

The twists and turns in US-China relations assessed in this book argue for caution in predicting the future direction of the relationship. This volume has depicted tenets of realism in international relations (IR) theory as useful in understanding these shifts from negative to positive and vice versa, especially since the Cold War. The kinds of cost-benefit analysis seen in realism seem evident in decision making in Beijing and Washington during key episodes—notably, the breakthrough under Nixon and Mao in the 1970s, Deng Xiaoping's pullback from pressing the Ronald Reagan administration in the 1980s, the mutual accommodation in line with China's avowed "peaceful rise" during the George W. Bush administration, and the Chinese government's greater international assertiveness at US expense in the past decade.[1]

Liberalism in IR theory has been employed to explain promoting cooperation through increased engagement—notably, economic interchange. Liberalism also has been used to explain the strong US disapproval of the Tiananmen crackdown of 1989 as Chinese leaders reversed nascent politically liberal trends in the period of reform. US disappointment also was registered recently in the face of the Xi Jinping government's tightening of control over Chinese civil society.[2]

Constructivism in IR theory has been used to explain the positive significance of mutual learning by participants on both sides as they discerned and acted on areas of common ground and mutual interest. At the same time, constructivism has also explained the distinct and often strongly divergent identities of China and the United States that seriously impede improving relations, especially in sensitive policy areas involving ideology, sovereignty, and security.[3]

Powerful elements of convergence and divergence have long characterized US-China relations. Since the opening of official relations seen in President Richard Nixon's summit with Mao Zedong in 1972 until the sharply negative US turn against China in the Donald Trump administration, the changing mix of areas of close cooperation with enduring differences saw relations shift

305

in positive or negative directions. In this book, the recent negative turn was explained using realism and constructivist concepts, while liberalism seemed notable in its absence.

As the new US administration of President Joseph Biden took power in 2021, the momentum in support of continued acute US rivalry with China was strong. While employing more measured and less virulent rhetoric than Trump administration leaders, President Biden and his lieutenants committed strongly to efforts at home and abroad to mobilize American power and that of allies and partners in protracted competition and struggle with China for regional and global leadership. The current US posture recalled some of the adverse practices seen in the decades of Sino-American Cold War antagonism, though Biden was open to cooperation with China on climate change, pandemic relief, and other areas of common ground. A number of US foreign policy specialists, along with business groups and other Americans with interests in China, argued that the negative US turn against China was extreme, counterproductive, and unsustainable, particularly given the close economic and other US-China interdependent relationships, and it overestimated China's dangers to the United States.[4] Their views often mirrored those of counterparts in China.[5] But such reservations were offset by the administration's multibillion-dollar programs to advance US high technology and other capacities to compete with China coming in tandem with an unprecedented legislative outpouring backed by bipartisan majorities in Congress to counter challenges from China seen as the major danger for the United States in the twenty-first century.[6]

CHINA'S CURRENT CHALLENGES TO AMERICA—HIGH-STAKES IMPLICATIONS

As discussed in consideration on international governance issues in chapter 11 and China's military advances targeting US forces in nearby Asia in chapter 8, the drivers of the negative turn in US policy remained strong as the stakes for American interests were seen as very high. Until recently, US perceptions viewed challenges posed by Chinese policies and practices as significant but not particularly dangerous or strong. For many years they were offset by the avowed reassurances of China's peaceful and constructive interaction with the United States along with China's comparative weakness in the face of comprehensive US power. Those circumstances changed remarkably in recent years. Overall the changed circumstances saw Chinese challenges targeting and weakening the prevailing US-led international order in a variety of serious ways. The overall trend risked Chinese dominance in Asia and in high-technology industries and an international order detrimental not only to narrow US national interests but also to regional and global free economic interchange, national independence, popular sovereignty, and personal freedom.[7]

Perhaps of most importance among the changed circumstances was China's current salience as the world's second-largest and still strongly growing economy. China was the world's top trader with over 120 countries, the world's largest manufacturer, and the largest holder of foreign exchange reserves. China accounted for over one-quarter of global economic growth. Chinese advances in a robust state-directed drive to achieve leadership in the high-technology industries of the future, including artificial intelligence, 5G communications networks, the Internet of Things, nano- and biotechnology, aviation and space, and electric vehicles, were captured in the government-fostered Made in China 2025 program and other comprehensive efforts seen as challenging and preparing to overtake the United States' lead in these key areas.[8]

The Chinese advances further strengthened Chinese military forces targeting American forces, fundamentally changing the balance of power along China's periphery in particular. Beijing used this altered military balance to its advantage in coercively gaining control of most of the South China Sea despite opposition from regional claimants and other concerned powers, including the United States.[9]

Chinese mendacity about its peaceful intent and nonmilitarizing South China Sea holdings added to US reevaluation of other challenges posed by China that were often denied or hidden by Chinese authorities. The challenges added substantially to the momentum behind recent US determination to counter China.

Adding to the list of China's challenges undermining US influence and leadership was China's partnership with Russia, which continued to strengthen significantly. President Vladimir Putin and President Xi Jinping, both foreseen to stay in power for the foreseeable future, supported forward momentum. The powers posed increasingly serious challenges to the US-supported order in their respective priority spheres of concern—Russia in Europe and the Middle East, and China in Asia. China backed Russia in carrying out military exercises to intimidate countries in Europe and the Middle East and in efforts to divide NATO and the European Union. Russia backed China in carrying out exercises supporting Beijing's expansionism in the South China Sea, Chinese pressure tactics to weaken US alliances with South Korea and Japan, and efforts to undercut US-led sanctions against North Korea.[10]

China's long-standing use of state-directed development polices to plunder foreign intellectual property rights and undermine international competitors had profound negative impacts on US and Western interests. Beijing employed hidden and overt state-directed economic coercion, egregious government subsidies, import protection, and export promotion using highly protected and state-supported products to weaken and often destroy foreign competition in key industries. The profits went into efforts to achieve dominance in major world industries and build military power to secure China's primacy in Asia and world leadership. As a result, companies like Huawei emerged in international markets endeavoring to dominate international communications enterprises. The profits also supported massive state-directed Chinese efforts to lead high-technology industries that will define economic and military leadership in world affairs. Also, China increasingly used economic leverage to gain international legitimacy for its predatory economic practices from the UN secretary general and other world leaders.[11]

More than any other power in recent memory, China leveraged economic dependence to compel states to defer to Chinese demands, many with negative implications for US interests and influence. The dependence involved trade, financing, investment, and tourist and student exchanges. Coercion was applied or threatened by the Chinese government directly or through party channels mobilizing boycotts, demonstrations, and other pressures in China against foreign targets. As a creditor, China undermined World Bank, International Monetary Fund, and Organisation of Economic Co-operation and Development lending guidelines. Repeatedly when these donors supported poorer countries to return to solvency, Beijing used the opportunity to strike development deals, making the state heavily dependent on China, sometimes to the point where the state needed new bailouts provided by the above-noted Western-aligned institutions. China sometimes compelled these debt-dependent states to accommodate Chinese demands for equity (e.g., land, ports, and airfields) for repayment and/or Chinese requests for access to military facilities or other favors. Meanwhile, Chinese-provided communications and surveillance systems along with Chinese-provided hydroelectric dams, railroads, and port operations caused recipient countries to rely ever more on Chinese firms for maintenance, and they made the Chinese ties difficult and expensive to replace with another provider.[12]

China's bilateral nontransparent deals involving extensive Chinese financing were attractive to many foreign corrupt and/or authoritarian leaders adverse to existing international lending norms. The agreements deepened Chinese influence while serving the power and personal wants of the authoritarian and/or corrupt foreign leaders. In addition was Chinese provision of communications and surveillance systems to assist authoritarian foreign leaders to track and suppress opponents. Robust Chinese interchange with media outlets in various states promoted news coverage that was positive concerning the government leadership and China. Communications and surveillance systems also assisted Chinese intelligence collection and manipulation of opinion in the country.[13]

Coercion of neighbors, often allies or partners of the United States, involved Chinese forces along the border with India and Chinese maritime militia and coast guard forces, backed by Chinese naval and air forces, intimidating governments that challenged China's claims in the South China Sea, the East China Sea, and Taiwan. China privately warned some South China Sea disputants that countering China on these matters would lead to their decisive military defeat. Backing the warnings were major shows of force by Chinese naval and air forces in the South and East China Sea and around Taiwan. Beijing bombers in 2019 teamed up with Russian bombers to probe and challenge the air space of US allies South Korea and Japan.[14]

Among unconventional means of leverage, Chinese dams controlling the flow of water in the Mekong River influenced downriver countries Myanmar, Laos, Thailand, Cambodia, and Vietnam. Beijing's strong ties with armed separatist groups inside Myanmar provided a major source of influence on Myanmar. Such leverage added to reasons for these governments to follow policies on issues in US-China relations that tended to avoid criticism of China.[15]

Other areas where China posed challenges to US interests included well-funded Chinese agents and front organizations achieving significant success in (1) mobilizing the Chinese diaspora, (2) winning over foreign dignitaries to work in support of Chinese objectives, and (3) influencing media and journalism in a number of states. They were backed by diplomats abroad prepared to resort to invective and threats in demanding deference to China's objectives supported by the influence operations. Related were strong efforts to penetrate foreign high-technology centers for desired information through the Chinese government's thousand talents program and intellectual property theft. Chinese agents actively recruited foreigners for espionage.[16]

Added to this mix was China's repeated disregard of international law. China rejected the July 2016 ruling of a United Nations Convention on the Law of the Sea tribunal finding against China's expansive South China Sea claims. It used illegal abduction of and prolonged detention of Chinese residents abroad and holding foreign citizenship, ignoring provisions of international conventions. Beijing repeatedly arrested and detained foreigners as leverage against their governments. Finally, China worked steadily to weaken the unity of the Association of Southeast Asian Nations and of the European Union. It appealed to some members at the expense of the unity of the group, which otherwise would impede Chinese ambitions in Southeast Asia and Europe.[17]

HOW TO GAUGE CHINA'S FOREIGN ASCENDANCE AMID ACUTE RIVALRY WITH AMERICA

An underlying question addressed in this volume involves how to assess the implications for the United States and the US-China relationship of China's international rise, and its various attendant challenges to the United States, since the end of the Cold War. As discussed in chapters 8 and 9, the ongoing debate in the United States over China's rise stressed recently the danger of Chinese dominance in high-technology industries deemed essential in determining leadership in international economic and national security. Unfortunately, this writer and apparently many others have been frustrated in seeking a clear view of whether China or the United States is winning in the newly prominent competition to lead in production of high technology that will dominate international economic and national security. The field of high-technology industry and production has many ambiguous elements and is subject to constant change, making clear assessment very difficult even for specialists.[18]

Against this background, the US intelligence community offered only general findings in an authoritative outlook for 2021 and a longer-range forecast reaching to 2040. In discussing dangers posed by China, the outlook for 2021 said China will remain the top threat to US technological competitiveness as the Chinese Communist Party (CCP) targeted key technology sectors and proprietary commercial and military technology from US and allied companies and research institutions associated with defense, energy, finance, and other sectors. Beijing used a variety of tools, from public investment to espionage and theft, to advance its technological capabilities. The intelligence community outlook also advised that China will maintain its major innovation and industrial policies because Chinese leaders see this strategy as necessary to reduce dependence on foreign technologies, enable military advances, and sustain economic growth and thus ensure the CCP's survival. And Beijing was seen as increasingly combining its growing military power with its economic, technological, and diplomatic clout to preserve the CCP, secure what it viewed as its territory and regional preeminence, and pursue international cooperation at Washington's expense.[19]

The longer-range US intelligence community forecast said technology, particularly military technologies, will continue to be central to a country's security and global influence. Cutting-edge artificial intelligence, biotechnology, and data-driven decision making will provide states with a range of advantages for military as well as economic growth, manufacturing, health care, and societal resiliency. With these technologies, there will be a first mover advantage, enabling states and nonstate actors to shape the views and decision making of populations, to gain information advantages over competitors, and to better prepare for future shocks.[20]

It was predicted up to 2040 that no single actor will be positioned to dominate across all regions and in all domains and that the growing contest between China and the United States and its close allies is likely to have the broadest and deepest impact on global dynamics, including the pace and direction of technological change. It added that Beijing is poised to continue to make military and technological advancements that will further shift the geopolitical balance in China's favor, particularly in Asia.[21]

One result of such useful but inconclusive findings is that analysts attempting to gauge the impact of China's rising power on the overall "balance of power" between the United States and China are brought back to more traditional but still valid ways of assessing in which way the overall balance of power is evolving. American strategists have long focused on the US-China balance of power in Asia as the most important area of Sino-American competition.[22] Many still do so in recent years.[23] The reasons include the following: China has long given top priority to nearby Asia in its foreign policy. The area is also of top priority in recent American foreign policy. If China is attaining leading international control, that development should show up first in nearby Asia. Without control of its surroundings, rising China's leadership elsewhere would remain vulnerable. Thus, measuring how well or poorly China's influence is spreading in the region at the expense of the United States, the long-standing leading power in the region, represents a useful way to gauge the realities of relative power between the two states, showing whether or not traditional US leadership in Asia is in jeopardy and China's rise to regional and global dominance is imminent.[24]

Chinese leaders have made strenuous efforts to advance China's power and influence in Asia that generally came at the expense of US interests. Salient recent achievements included China's control of much of the South China Sea and China's strong influence in Cambodia, Laos, and arguably Myanmar, thereby impeding the Association of Southeast Asian Nations from taking positions or steps that China opposes. Beijing's Belt and Road Initiative (BRI) consolidated Chinese influence in Central Asian countries and in important countries in South Asia and East Asia. The Chinese relationship with Russia moved well beyond its past status as an axis of convenience, becoming instead an axis of the world's leading authoritarian countries seeking largely compatible mutual interests.

Nevertheless, the following assessment using conventional metrics of international influence, involving economic, military, political, and cultural elements making up China's overall regional importance, provides some confidence in this writer's judgment that Beijing will not soon become Asia's leader and that the United States remains in a leading position in the region in several important respects.

XI JINPING'S FOREIGN POLICY VISION

Xi Jinping and supporting publicists built on gains in China's rising influence in Asian and world affairs to craft a vision called the China Dream. Though supported by Chinese elite and popular opinion, Xi's vision of a powerful and benign China moving smoothly to international leadership proved weak in the face of realities constraining China.[25] Xi Jinping's China dream of "national rejuvenation" sought a unified and powerful China as Asia's leader and a great power. As noted earlier, Xi broke with the more restrained policies of previous leaders following Deng Xiaoping's instructions in foreign affairs. Xi was bolder and no longer emphasized reassurance of the United States, Asian neighbors, and others.

To remind, Xi's new foreign policy approach involved major challenges for the United States and its interests in the prevailing international order as reviewed above. In summary, they involved the following:

- Growing military, paramilitary, economic, and other state power coerced neighbors to give way to China's broad territorial claims and other interests, thereby challenging the United States and its defense of regional stability and the status quo.
- Often hidden efforts by Chinese spies and other party, government, and military agents fostered influence and favorable elite and public opinion in a wide range of developed and developing countries. Beijing sought support for Chinese foreign policies at odds with those backed by the United States.
- The Belt and Road Initiative and other institutions that undermined US leadership or excluded the United States used China's large foreign exchange reserves and massive excess industrial capacity to launch various self-serving international economic development programs.
- China's military buildup was aimed at American forces in the Asia-Pacific region, and China built forces for use beyond China's rim while fostering debt and other dependencies among smaller, strategically located states, thus allowing for positive responses from them to host Chinese military forces overseas.
- An ever-stronger entente with Russia in pursuit, through coercive and other means, of revisionist ambitions undermining US interests in respective spheres of influence.

- Continuing gross violations of World Trade Organization norms and practices showed in cybertheft of economic assets, widespread intellectual property rights violations, unfair market access restrictions on US and other developed countries' companies, state-directed industrial policies leading to targeted acquisition of US and other high technology, large-scale overcapacity disadvantaging US and other foreign producers, and currency practices disadvantaging US and other foreign traders. Made in China 2025, a massive effort benefiting from the above economic practices, sought dominance in high-technology industries to protect China from feared US technological leadership.
- Intensified internal repression and tightened political control had serious adverse consequences for US interests and those of other developed countries.

As shown in chapter 6, President Barack Obama was slow and ineffective in responding to Xi Jinping's advances. American critics, who rose in influence after President Obama left office, saw Xi Jinping duplicitously playing a double game, pretending to seek cooperation while relentlessly undermining America.[26] At this time, US opinion was negative about the Chinese government but sought to avoid confrontation. Though China was not deemed a high priority by most candidates, a tougher US approach toward China was endorsed by both leading candidates and most others in the 2016 US presidential election campaign.[27]

International factors facilitating Xi's foreign advances in fulfilling the China Dream were an irresolute American government; a decline in the ability and willingness of US allies and partners to counter China's affronts; weaknesses in Asia, notably Southeast Asia, allowing Chinese expansion of control into the disputed South China Sea; and Russia facing strong sanctions in the West and thus becoming ever more dependent on China.[28] Against this background, Xi and Chinese officials and publicists fostered an image of China as a generous and benign power, contributing more to the United Nations and other international organizations favored by Beijing and fostering growth through the BRI and other China-favored mechanisms. They even reinterpreted Chinese history to support a historical assertion common in Beijing today that China never was aggressive in its long history and would not be so today.[29]

IMAGE MEETS REALITIES:
CONSTRAINTS ON CHINA'S RISE

Constraints on Chinese influence in regional and world affairs started at home. Chinese leaders faced an ongoing and major challenge in trying to sustain one-party rule in the world's largest society, one that was both dynamic and economically vibrant. To sustain one-party rule required massive expenditures and widespread leadership attention to internal security and control and strong continued economic growth that advanced the material benefits of the Chinese people and ensured general public support and legitimacy for the Communist government. As shown below, these domestic concerns were multifaceted, expensive to deal with, and very hard to resolve; they represented the main focus of China's large government and Communist Party apparatus.[30]

Moreover, the prime importance of economic growth and continued one-party rule required stability at home and abroad, especially in nearby Asia, where conflict and confrontation would have a serious negative impact on Chinese economic growth. Unfortunately for uniform adherence to these policy priorities, the Chinese leaders had other seemingly contradictory priorities. They involved protecting Chinese security and advancing Chinese control of sovereign claims. These other top concerns were evident in the long and costly buildup of military forces to deal with a Taiwan contingency involving the United States and more recent use of various means of state power to advance territorial control in nearby disputed seas. Of course, these priorities seemed to contradict the priority of stability in Asia for the sake of needed economic development. This made for a muddled Chinese approach to its nearby neighbors and other concerned powers, notably the United States. China's portrayal as benevolent and focused on mutual benefit was mixed with strong determination to have its way at others' expense on sensitive sovereignty disputes and related security issues.[31]

Meanwhile, looking beyond nearby Asia, there was less clarity among specialists in China and abroad as to where Chinese international ambitions for regional and global leadership fit in the current priorities of China's leaders. However, there was little doubt that domestic concerns got overall priority.[32] Significant domestic concerns involved problems in leadership legitimacy, corruption, widening income gaps and social division, widespread social turmoil and mass demonstrations,[33] a highly resource-intensive economy and related enormous environmental damage, an aging population, and an economic model at the point of diminishing returns with no clear path to effective reform.

Domestic preoccupations, reinforced by extraordinary measures to deal with the COVID-19 pandemic, meant China's continued reluctance to undertake the costs and risks of international leadership because it had so many important requirements at home. One result was that China continued to rely on the US-led world order where it benefited China while moving incrementally to displace US leadership.[34]

As far as international constraints were concerned, the so-called trade war with the United States brought home to Chinese leaders how strongly China depended on the United States economically. The United States exerted much greater influence than China on international technology and financial and trade flows that China depended on. The economic face-off with America caused major harm to Chinese economic development—the linchpin of regime legitimacy in China.[35] China also depended on the United States for secure passage of its growing imports of oil and gas from the Persian Gulf. Moreover, neither side could deal effectively with North Korea without the other. Additional areas of interdependence involved climate change, antiterrorism, nuclear nonproliferation, and cybersecurity.

The respite in the trade war provided by the so-called phase one trade agreement in January 2020 was quickly overshadowed by strident acrimony and acute rivalry prompted by the COVID-19 pandemic. Notably, China launched a world propaganda campaign that covered up responsibility for initially mishandling the virus and causing a global plague. China was portrayed as effectively curbing the virus at home and generously offering medical supplies abroad. Some prominent Americans argued for closer US government cooperation with China to deal with the crisis, but President Trump, Democratic presidential candidates, bipartisan congressional majorities, mainstream media, and public opinion all viewed China more negatively. US hardening deepened as it became clear that in the initial stages of the outbreak China cornered the world market in the medical equipment and supplies needed to fight the virus. The result was that many states, ill stocked to deal with the outbreak, including the United States, found no available supplies because of Chinese hoarding, profiteering, and targeted international donations to burnish China's world image.[36]

The broad negative US view of China also prompted forecasts that Republican political strategists would continue through the election year to blame China and thereby distract attention from the Trump administration's ineffective handling of the crisis. President Trump shifted sharply against China, alleging that Beijing was working against his reelection. One source of acrimony was the Trump administration mustering evidence to show that Chinese malfeasance in a highly sensitive research laboratory in Wuhan was the likely cause of the epidemic, calling for an international investigation into the matter, and charging that Beijing should be held liable for the massive international costs.[37]

Regarding China's ascendance in its top foreign policy priority area, nearby Asia, Beijing's record remained mediocre. An inventory of China's relationships with other leading regional powers, notably Japan and India, and important middle powers like South Korea and Australia, showed serious reversals over the past two decades. Similarly serious downturns occurred in areas keenly sensitive to Chinese interests: Taiwan, Hong Kong, and North Korea. In particular, Beijing's passivity in the face of protracted anti-China mass demonstrations in Hong Kong in 2019 and its failure in attempting to influence Taiwan's elections in 2020 projected a constrained rather than decisive Chinese leadership. These setbacks offset widely touted gains China made in the South China Sea and among some Southeast Asian and other neighboring countries. Beijing's strong intervention in 2020 forcing implementation of a national security law and coercive law enforcement measures seemed to overwhelm opposition in Hong Kong but deepened strong disapproval of the Chinese government among democratic governments and some other foreign countries.[38] This mixed record had persisted for thirty years as China tried with mediocre results to expand its influence in nearby Asia after the Cold War. Unfortunately for China, negative legacies of past Chinese violent and coercive policies and practices prompted regional wariness of contemporary Chinese intentions. Chinese foreign policy in post–Cold War Asia also showed conflicting objectives involving peaceful development of mutual interest on the one hand and steely determination to gain control of disputed territories and resources at neighbors' expense on the other. There were repeated switches, at times stressing reassurance and peaceful development and at other times stressing determination and intimidation in pursuing sensitive issues of sovereignty and security.[39]

Looking out, whether or not China's importance as a powerful military force and prime trader and investor with nearby Asia will override security, sovereignty, and other differences is hard to predict and is unlikely to be resolved anytime soon. Meanwhile, uncertainty over US resolve to sustain regional leadership remained an important determinant in China's quest for Asian primacy, though, as shown below, recent US government hardening toward China clearly complicated and constrained China's rise going forward.

Including but going well beyond nearby Asia, Chinese foreign policy concerns in the broad-ranging Belt and Road Initiative begun in 2013 saw Beijing advance and modify the strong "going out" policies of Chinese investment and financing abroad seen in the previous decade.[40] That past effort focused on attaining access to oil and other raw materials needed for China's resource-hungry economy. Recent Chinese economic reforms sought to reduce such intense resource use. The recent push for Chinese foreign investment and financing was to enable construction abroad of Chinese-supplied infrastructure provided by the enormous excess capacity of Chinese companies for such construction and supply now that major infrastructure development inside China had been curtailed under recent economic reforms. Locating some of China's heavily resource-intensive and polluting industries abroad eased China's serious pollution problems and enhanced its ability to meet commitments to international climate change agreements. Economically, the recent push also helped to connect the poorer regions of central and western China to international markets and thereby advanced their development. The BRI provided investment opportunities promising better returns for China's $3 trillion foreign exchange reserves invested in low-yield foreign securities, and the initiative broadened the international use of China's currency. Strategically, the BRI improved Chinese access to key international land and sea corridors, reduced China's vulnerability posed by actual or possible US military control of transit choke points for Chinese shipping, and advanced overall Chinese relations with important countries. Several countries became "debt dependent" on Chinese financing; many more became dependent on sophisticated Chinese-supplied and-maintained information and communications technology products, hydroelectric dams, advanced port facilities, and other infrastructure very difficult and expensive to replace.[41]

The BRI was also the centerpiece of exaggerated Chinese image building that portrayed China as a confident and generous global economic leader. The realities seen in summing up the results of China's decade-long "going out" strategy and the trends in recent Chinese economic behavior showed substantial growth in Chinese economic activism, influence, and power but also pervasive constraints and strong negative international reactions.[42]

In particular, trade significantly declined in importance as an element of Chinese influence abroad. After China joined the World Trade Organization in 2001, Beijing relied on its burgeoning trade with Asian and international markets as the primary source of Chinese international economic influence. For several years China's trade grew at double the rate of China's economic growth of around 10 percent. In contrast, while the Chinese economy continued to grow at a rate of around 7 percent in 2015 and 2016, the growth of Chinese trade collapsed—growth was zero in those two years. The value of trade began to rise again in 2017, but a return to the days of previous high annual growth seemed unlikely, and that judgment came even before the onset of the major negative impacts of the US-China trade war and the COVID-19 pandemic.[43]

There also were substantial constraints in Chinese investments and loans. "Going out" policies begun twenty years before were accompanied by massive publicity for Chinese multibillion-dollar agreements to invest in various developing countries and to promote infrastructure constructed by Chinese companies with loans from Chinese banks. The recent BRI and related initiatives were also accompanied by such positive publicity. In contrast, foreign expert assessments were more sober. China's actual investment in developing countries remained limited. Its more important position as the leading world provider of financing for infrastructure resulted in only a few instances, often very controversial, where China represented the dominant international economic power (e.g., Venezuela, Cambodia, Djibouti). More commonly, Beijing was seen as a growing source of influence but still as only "one among several" foreign sources of economic influence and support.[44]

Serious shortcomings emerged in China's role as a provider of infrastructure financing to developing countries. The past record of China announcing massive deals and delivering much less continued. The reasons hinged on the difficulty in carrying out large projects in poorly governed countries that were bad credit risks. Other factors included changes in governments and much greater opposition to Chinese practices by the United States and some other developed countries. The US government as well as think tanks and the media in the United States and other developed countries were in the lead recently in exposing how the Chinese government used loans and economic dependency to infiltrate and influence decision making in vulnerable developing countries to benefit Chinese expansion abroad. Special attention was devoted to China seeking ports in the Indo-Pacific region for its forces, the expansion of Chinese telecommunications to dominant positions in these countries, and backing for Chinese expansion in the South China Sea and its egregious crackdown against dissent in the Xinjiang region of China.[45]

The US Position in Asia

Until the past decade, a comparison of Chinese policies and practices with those of the United States in the Asia-Pacific region and the rest of the world underlined how far China had to go to supersede American leadership. However, after many years of US accommodation of China's rise through constructive engagement and the downplaying of differences came the erratic and unpredictable foreign policy behavior of US president Donald Trump, adding to regional and international uncertainty about American leadership. Extraordinary domestic distractions, notably the congressional impeachment of the president in 2019, the pandemic of 2020, and the violent attack on the Capitol on account of disputes over the 2020 election process and results compounded the difficulties of leaders throughout the world in predicting American resolve to stay the course in Asian and world affairs. The rushed US and allied military withdrawal in the face of the Taliban's surprisingly rapid takeover of Afghanistan in August 2021 reinforced regional doubt about

US leadership. Going forward, would the United States persist in its past leadership role in competition with China in the Asia-Pacific region? Other possibilities ranged from retrenchment to conflict. In particular, retrenchment meant that existing constraints on China in Asia would weaken substantially and China would have a freer hand in advancing toward regional dominance.[46]

Nevertheless, realities of US power and practice demonstrated enduring strengths. And the Trump years saw a sharp US policy shift away from past drift in order to confront rising China, now widely viewed as America's number-one opponent. The new American toughness was led by the administration and bipartisan congressional leaders. It was reinforced by an ever-growing outpouring of government and nongovernment assessments disclosing in detail China's heretofore often hidden measures to expand at American expense while publicly avowing cooperation. Beijing was now widely viewed as duplicitous, making meaningful agreements and accommodation more difficult going forward. Media and public opinion became significantly more negative, and sharp criticism of China came from the leading Democratic presidential candidates.[47]

China's leaders did not anticipate the recent American shift and the array of troubles it posed for China's economy, international influence, security, and sovereignty. Facing an aroused America, Xi Jinping's strategy in pursuit of the China Dream came under revision. There was a notable increase in emphasis on economic self-reliance, especially in the development of high-technology industries that heretofore depended on US-provided technology and equipment. This effort was accompanied by stronger multifaceted initiatives to work around US restrictions on high-technology interchange with China in order to gain the needed access to US high technology through indirect, illegal, and other means that avoided US government restrictions. Senior Chinese leaders and diplomats were much more active in efforts to counter US-backed efforts to win support in its rivalry with China from states threatened by China along Asia's rim and by countries in Europe now reconsidering their ties with China amid American warnings of the dangers Beijing's advances pose for the West. Beijing had no easy remedy for the counterproductive impact of its ratcheting up military, economic, and diplomatic pressure on Taiwan, resulting in deepening Taiwan's ever-closer relationship with the United States. And a similar counterproductive process followed Chinese pressures on Japan, Australia, and India, resulting in substantial progress in the US-led Quad alignment targeting China.[48]

Adding to challenging developments for China's interests in Asia, the Biden administration entered office with a much more attentive and accommodating stance toward US allies and partners in the Indo-Pacific. The US consultative approach was broadly welcomed and enhanced the new US government's efforts in pursuing a top foreign policy priority to build alignments among allies and partners to counter multifaceted challenges coming from the US government's designated main danger, China, as part of its hard work to solidify regional efforts focused on challenges posed by China. Asia was the new US government's top foreign policy arena, and China was targeted as the main international danger.[49]

The Biden initiatives came on a foundation of basic determinants of US strength and influence in the Asia-Pacific region involving five factors, starting with security.[50] In most of Asia, governments were viable and made the decisions that determined their direction in foreign affairs. Popular, elite, media, and other opinions might influence government officials in their policy toward the United States and other countries, but in the end officials made decisions on the basis of their own calculus. In general, officials saw their governments' legitimacy and success resting on nation building and economic development, which required a stable and secure international environment. Unfortunately, Asia was not particularly stable, and most regional governments were privately wary of, and tended not to trust, each other. As a result, they looked to the United States to provide the security they needed to pursue goals of development and nation building in an appropriate environment. They recognized that the US security role was very expensive and involved great risk, including large-scale casualties if necessary, for the sake of preserving Asian security. They also recognized that neither rising China, nor any other Asian power or coalition of powers, was able or willing to undertake even a small part of these risks, costs, and responsibilities.

Second, the nation-building priority of most Asian governments depended greatly on export-oriented growth. Much of Chinese and Asian trade depended heavily on exports to developed countries, notably the United States. America ran a massive annual trade deficit with China amid much larger annual trade deficits with Asia regularly surpassing US$500 billion. Asian government officials recognized that China, which consistently ran an overall trade surplus, and other trading partners in Asia were unwilling and unable to bear even a fraction of the cost of such large trade deficits, which nonetheless were very important for Asian governments.

Third, despite the negative popular view in Asia of the George W. Bush administration's policies in Iraq and the broader war on terror, the administration was generally effective in its interactions with Asia's powers—notably China, Japan, and India. The Obama administration built on these strengths. The Obama government's broad rebalancing with regional governments and multilateral organizations had a scope ranging from India to the Pacific Island states to Korea and Japan. Its emphasis on consultation with and inclusion of international stakeholders before coming to policy decisions on issues of importance to Asia and the Pacific was also broadly welcomed and stood in contrast with the previously perceived unilateralism of the Bush administration. Meanwhile, the US Indo-Pacific Command and other US military commands and security and intelligence organizations were at the edge of wide-ranging and growing US efforts to build and strengthen webs of military and related intelligence and security relationships throughout the region.

Fourth, the United States for decades, reaching back to past centuries, engaged the Asia-Pacific region through business, religious, educational, media, and other interchange. Such active nongovernment interaction put the United States in a unique position and reinforced overall American influence. Meanwhile, more than fifty years of generally color-blind US immigration policy, since the ending of discriminatory American restrictions on Asian immigration in 1965, resulted in the influx of millions of Asia-Pacific migrants who called America home and who interacted with their countries of origin in ways that underpinned and reflected well on the US position in the region.

Fifth, part of the reason for the success of US efforts to build webs of security-related and other relationships with Asia-Pacific countries had to do with active contingency planning by many Asia-Pacific governments. As power relations changed in the region, notably on account of China's rise, regional governments generally sought to work positively and pragmatically with rising China on the one hand, but they sought the reassurance of close security, intelligence, and other ties with the United States on the other hand in case rising China shifted to greater assertiveness or dominance.

Against a background of repeated episodes of Chinese demands, coercion, and intimidation, the Asia-Pacific governments' interest in closer ties with the United States often meshed well with the US administration's engagement with regional governments and multilateral organizations. The US concern with maintaining stability while fostering economic growth overlapped constructively with the priorities of the majority of regional governments as they pursued their respective nation-building agendas.

Under President Trump, the positive role of the Indo-Pacific Command, legal immigration, and nongovernment American engagement in Asia noted above continued. On the other hand, the president's rhetoric and actions denigrating alliances and demanding much more host nation support from Japan and South Korea raised lasting questions about US support for alliances, even though the president's positions were offset to some degree with high-level US reassurance and the actions of US national security policy makers. America's role as economic partner was in doubt with the scrapping of the Trans-Pacific Partnership and the disruptive trade war with China, but the US market continued to absorb massive flows of regional imports. US and Asian media rightfully highlighted President Trump's disruptive relations with the region as he ended the rebalance and the US commitment to the Trans-Pacific

Partnership, causing a decline in confidence in the United States. Employing unpredictable unilateral actions, he cast doubt on past US commitment to positive regional relations. He also junked related policy transparency, carefully measured responses, and avoidance of dramatic action, linkage, or spillover among competing interests. Those features of US foreign policy had been stressed by the Obama and earlier administrations and were welcomed by Asia-Pacific allies and partners. Trump's presidency showed episodic engagement featuring special attention to North Korea and China.[51]

The Biden administration, full of veterans of the Obama administration, promised a much more consistent, consultative, and respectful American government approach toward allies and partners in Asia. The administration also registered determination to continue Trump administration initiatives to counter challenges coming from China. The mix of the two trends was overall viewed in the region as better than Trump's policies, though the outlook was clouded not only by the uncertainties about US-China rivalry but by immediate problems posed by the enduring pandemic and the protracted crisis leading to a failed-state situation in Myanmar.[52]

Overall, China remained encumbered in nearby regions of Asia, but US influence in the region was in decline. If the US decline continued, China would advance, foreshadowing a major power shift in Asia. Much depended on the effectiveness of American leadership going forward.

Before coming to a conclusion on the evolving US-China balance of power and influence in Asia, the above examination following past practice and assessing mainly conventional Chinese behavior and levers of power and influence in foreign affairs needs to add an assessment of newly prominent, unconventional aspects of Chinese actions and levers of influence. Those aspects and levers have heretofore been disguised, hidden, denied, or otherwise neglected or unappreciated by foreign specialists assessing Chinese foreign relations. As noted above and discussed in chapters 9 and 11, they involved coercive use of maritime and other security forces; predatory economic policies; widespread coercive use of economic leverage often fostered by enticements leading to economic dependencies on China; fostering closer alignments with Russia and other authoritarian states countering the heretofore prevailing liberal international order; influence operations including elite capture, use of the Chinese diaspora, coopting high-technology researchers, media and information technology communications control, and espionage; and disregard for international law and diplomatic practices.

Many of these tools clearly advanced Chinese power and influence, but these advances seemed more than offset by many negative outcomes for Chinese interests. The most negative outcomes for Chinese interests were the reactions of the United States and some of its allies and partners. In particular, many of the hidden, denied, or otherwise neglected and unappreciated elements of Chinese foreign policy practice showed American and other policy makers that engagement with China, an ostensibly positive policy toward building constructive relations, was repeatedly being manipulated and exploited by the Chinese party-state in often nefarious ways to undermine the power and influence of the United States and other countries in world affairs. And adding to the duplicity and mendacity seen coming from senior Chinese officials on these matters were platitudes of China's benign intent under such rubrics as seeking a "new type of great-power relationship" with the United States and a "community of common destiny" abroad.[53]

Chinese leaders for their part remained uncompromising as Beijing prepared for a period of protracted competition with the United States. They endeavored to avoid military conflict and preserve advantageous economic, technological, and other relationships. They continued working from a position of increasing strength and influence on remedying long-standing grievances against US policies and practices involving Taiwan, US security presence in Asia, and many elements of US foreign policy.[54]

They saw the US government working consistently to undermine China's one-party system of governance. The failures of US governance in creating the 2008 global economic crisis and in dealing ineffectively with the COVID-19 pandemic, resulting in more than six hundred thousand US deaths (at time of writing), reinforced Chinese elite and popular views in the superiority of China's one-party authoritarian rule. The spectacle of mass demonstrations against racial injustice, repeated mass shootings killing hundreds of innocent bystanders, and the chaotic aftermath of the 2020 presidential election culminating in a mass demonstration targeting the US Capitol endorsed by the president reinforced antipathy for US governance in favor of China's authoritarian system. Chinese leaders regularly highlighted the massive negative consequences coming from violent US international interventions in recent years. They denounced the United States on these grounds for its failure as US troops left Afghanistan in August 2021. They saw mendacity and duplicity in US rhetorical support for a one-China policy while working to shore up Taiwan's position separate from China.[55]

Though unexpected events like the death of a leader, the outbreak of military conflict, or a turn to moderation by either the United States or China could change the recent negative trajectory in US-Chinese relations, the overall circumstances forecast continued tense competition with possible more serious trouble ahead. The superpower struggle will put a premium on unproven conflict management skills on both sides. The "contest for supremacy" predicted by Aaron Friedberg in Asia ten years ago has now become much broader, impacting the domestic and foreign policies and practices of both countries.[56]

What lessons academic specialists in the United States, China, and elsewhere will discern from this very consequential negative turn in US relations with China remains ill-defined and seemingly very broad. As noted in chapter 1, one element this writer intends to pursue is a comparative examination of the role of the executive branch versus the role of the US Congress in the making and execution of US policy toward China since the opening of relations in the early 1970s. The record is varied, but it commonly shows repeated efforts by the executive branch to advance US relations with China, even at the expense of American interests and values given lower priority by the executive branch. And it commonly shows repeated counterefforts in the Congress that overall slowed and thwarted the forward movement at the expense of US interests and values that were of higher priority to congressional policy makers. The proposed examination will focus on the question of which branch of government, the executive or the Congress, was a better steward of American interests in dealing with China. As suggested in brief comments and assessments in chapters 4–7, this writer believes that Congress, with all its many shortcomings, was a better steward of American interests than the executive branch.

STUDY QUESTIONS

1. Why has the Biden administration continued strong US rivalry with China begun by the Trump administration?
2. What is at stake for the United States in countering various serious challenges seen coming from China's behavior?
3. Why is US-China rivalry unlikely to diminish easily under prevailing circumstances?
4. Are perceived rising Chinese influence and declining US influence in world affairs likely to continue?
5. Why are US-Chinese competition for leadership in high-technology industries and the two powers' respective positions in the balance of power in Asia seen as important gauges showing which power is achieving regional and global leadership?
6. What explains major uncertainties about the trajectories and outcomes of the above competitions?

RELEVANT VIDEOS

"Global China: Assessing China's Growing Role in the World" (Brookings Institution, speech by Mark Warner, May 10, 2019, one hour) available at https://www.youtube.com/watch?v=u1z5Y3f7aBM

"Imagining China in 2023—China's Domestic and Foreign Posture under Xi Jinping" (Kevin Rudd, National University of Singapore, April 9, 2014, eighty-two minutes) available at https://www.youtube.com/watch?v=3lmpGTGkkos&list=PUakbhT1zJqJ9iod01nFEYhw

"Transition 2021 Series, Confronting China" (Council on Foreign Relations, February 9, 2021, one hour) available at https://www.youtube.com/watch?v=0DL7tc_Qgel

"Jia Qingguo on Future US-China Relations" (Channel News Asia, January 29, 2020, twenty-four minutes) available at https://www.channelnewsasia.com/news/video-on-demand/in-conversation-fy1920/jia-qingguo-former-dean-school-of-international-studies-peking-12316960

Notes

CHAPTER ONE

1. Ryan Hass, *Stronger: Adapting America's China Policy in an Age of Competitive Interdependence* (Washington, DC: Brookings Institution, 2021); Evan Medeiros, "The Changing Fundamentals of US-China Relations," *The Washington Quarterly* 42, no. 3 (Fall 2019): 93–119; Wu Xinbo, "The China Challenge," *The Washington Quarterly* 43, no. 3 (Fall 2020): 99–114; Wang Dong and Travis Tanner, eds., *Avoiding the "Thucydides Trap": US-China Relations in Strategic Domains* (New York: Routledge, 2020); Timothy Heath, Derek Grossman, and Asha Clark, *China's Quest for Global Dominance* (Washington, DC: RAND Corporation, 2021); Evan Medeiros, "Major Power Rivalry in East Asia," Council on Foreign Relations Discussion Paper (April 2021). For earlier assessments of this topic see Wang Jisi, "Trends in the Development of U.S.-China Relations and Deep-Seated Reasons," *Danddai Yatai* (Beijing), June 20, 2009, 4–20; Yan Xuetong, "The Instability of China-U.S. Relations," *Chinese Journal of International Politics* 3, no. 3 (2010): 1–30; Aaron Friedberg, *A Contest for Supremacy: China, America, and the Struggle for Mastery in Asia* (New York: W. W. Norton, 2011); Michael Swaine, *America's Challenge: Engaging a Rising China in the Twenty-First Century* (Washington, DC: Carnegie Endowment for International Peace, 2011); Jeffrey Bader, *Obama and China's Rise* (Washington, DC: Brookings Institution, 2012); David Shambaugh, ed., *Tangled Titans: The United States and China* (Lanham, MD: Rowman & Littlefield, 2012).

2. Robert Sutter, *Chinese Foreign Relations: Power and Policy of an Emerging Global Force*, 5th ed. (Lanham, MD: Rowman & Littlefield, 2021), 2.

3. Robert Sutter and Satu Limaye, *A Hardening of US-China Competition: Asia Policy in American's 2020 Elections and Regional Responses* (Honolulu, HI: East-West Center, 2020), 6–7.

4. White House, *National Security Strategy of the United States*, December 2017, https://www.whitehouse.gov/wp-content/uploads/2017/12/NSS-Final-12-18-2017-0905.pdf; US Department of Defense, *Summary of the National Defense Strategy of the United States*, January 2018, https://www.defense.gov/Portals/1/Documents/pubs/2018-National-Defense-Strategy-Summary.pdf; Anthony Capaccio, "US Faces 'Unprecedented Threat' on China Tech Takeover," *Bloomberg*, June 22, 2018, https://www.bloomberg.com/news/articles/2018-06-22/china-s-thousand-talents-called-key-in-seizing-u-s-expertise.

5. Capaccio, "US Faces 'Unprecedented Threat'"; "Bipartisan Groups of Senators Urge Administration to Safeguard Critical Military and Dual-Use Technology from China," United States Senate Release, May 22, 2018, https://www.cornyn.senate.gov/content/news/bipartisan-group-senators-urge-administration-safeguard-critical-military-and-dual-use; transcript of speech of Senator Mark Warner at Brookings Institution, Washington, DC, May 9, 2019, https://www.brookings.edu/wp-content/uploads/2019/05/fp_20190509_global_china_transcript.pdf.

6. Christopher Johnson, "Xi Jinping Unveils His Foreign Policy Vision," *Thoughts from the Chairman* (Washington, DC: Center for Strategic and International Studies, December 2014); Yun Sun, "China's Peaceful Rise: Peace through Strength?," *PacNet* 25 (Honolulu, HI: Pacific Forum CSIS, March 31, 2014); Yong Deng, "China: The Post-Responsible Power," *Washington Quarterly* 37, no. 4 (Winter 2015): 117–32; Center for a New American Security, *More Willing and Able: Charting China's International Security Activism* (Washington, DC: Center for a New American Security, 2015); Christopher Johnson, *Decoding China's Emerging "Great Power" Strategy in Asia* (Washington, DC: Center for Strategic and International Studies, June 2014); Ashley Tellis, *Balancing without Containment* (Carnegie Endowment for International Peace Report, January 22, 2014); David Michael Lampton, "A Tipping Point in U.S.-China Relations Is upon Us," May 11, 2015, https://www.uscnpm.com/model_item.html?action=view&table=article&id=15789); Harry Harding, "Has U.S. China Policy Failed?," *The Washington Quarterly* 38, no. 3 (2015): 95–122; Robert Blackwill and Ashley Tellis, *Revising U.S. Grand Strategy toward China* (Council on Foreign Relations, *Council Special Report*, April 2015).

7. Zheng Bijian, "China's 'Peaceful Rise' to Great-Power Status," *Foreign Affairs* 84, no. 5 (September–October 2005): 18–24; Wang Jisi, "China's Search for Stability with America," *Foreign Affairs* 84, no. 5 (September–October 2005): 39–48; Avery Goldstein, *Rising to the Challenge: China's Grand Strategy and International Security* (Stanford, CA: Stanford University Press, 2005); Bates Gill, *Rising Star: China's New Security Diplomacy* (Washington, DC: Brookings Institution, 2007).

8. Aaron Friedberg, *The Contest for Supremacy* (New York: Norton, 2011); Denny Roy, *Return of the Dragon: Rising China and Regional Security* (New York: Columbia University Press, 2013); Ashley Tellis, *Balancing without Containment* (Washington, DC: Carnegie Endowment for International Peace Report, January 22, 2014); Michael Pillsbury, *The Hundred Year Marathon* (New York: Holt, 2015).

9. Peter Martin, "Biden's Asian Czar Says Era of Engagement with China Is Over," *Bloomberg*, May 26, 2021, https://www.bloomberg.com/news/articles/2021-05-26/biden-s-asia-czar-says-era-of-engagement-with-xi-s-china-is-over.

10. Bader, *Obama and China's Rise*; Kenneth Lieberthal, "The China-U.S. Relationship Goes Global," *Current History* 108, no. 719 (September 2009): 243–46; "China-U.S. Dialogue Successful—Vice Premier," *China Daily*, July 29, 2009, 1; Hillary Clinton and Timothy Geithner, "A New Strategic and Economic Dialogue with China," *Wall Street Journal*, July 27, 2009, https://www.wsj.com/articles/SB100 01424052970204886304574308753825396372.

11. Bonnie Glaser, "The Diplomatic Relationship: Substance and Process," in *Tangled Titans: The United States and China*, ed. David Shambaugh (Lanham, MD: Rowman & Littlefield, 2013), 151–80.

12. Prominent Americans identified with this view include Zbigniew Brzezinski and C. Fred Bergsten. For critical response, see Elizabeth Economy and Adam Segal, "The G-2 Mirage," *Foreign Affairs* 88, no. 3 (May–June 2009): 56–72.

13. Jeffrey Bader, "U.S.-China Challenges: Time for China to Step Up," Brookings Institute, January 12, 2017, https://www.brookings.edu/research/u-s-china-challenges-time-for-china-to-step-up.

14. Robert Sutter and Satu Limaye, *America's 2016 Election Debate on Asia Policy and Asian Reactions* (Honolulu, HI: East-West Center, 2016). That report used campaign statements and other materials made available in "2016 Presidential Candidates on Asia," Asia Matters for America, http://www.asiamattersforamerica.org/asia/2016-presidential-candidates-on-asia.

15. Bader, "U.S.-China Challenges"; Harding, "Has U.S. China Policy Failed?"; Blackwill and Tellis, *Council Special Report: Revising U.S. Grand Strategy toward China*; Orville Schell and Susan Shirk, chairs, *U.S. Policy toward China: Recommendations for a New Administration*, Task Force Report (New York: Asia Society, 2017).

16. Interviews with Chinese officials and specialists, Beijing 2016, reviewed in Sutter and Limaye, *America's 2016 Election Debate*, 21–28.

17. Bonnie Glaser and Alexandra Viers, "China Prepares for Rocky Relations in 2017," *Comparative Connections* 18, no. 3 (January 2017): 21–22.

18. Shi Jiangtao, "Tempest Trump: China and U.S. Urged to Make Plans for 'Major Storm' in Bilateral Relationship," *South China Morning Post*, January 30, 2017.

19. The above developments are reviewed in Bonnie Glaser and Alexandra Viers, "Trump and Xi Break the Ice at Mar-a-Lago," *Comparative Connections* 19, no. 1 (May 2017): 21–32.

20. Heath, Grossman, and Clark, *China's Quest for Global Dominance*; Sutter, *Chinese Foreign Relations*, 301–3, 312–14.

21. On Chinese perspectives, see Nina Hachigian, ed., *Debating China* (New York: Oxford University Press, 2014). See also contrasting US views of various differences in China-US relations in Michael Swaine, *Creating a Stable Asia: An Agenda for a U.S.-China Balance of Power* (Washington, DC: Carnegie Endowment for International Peace, 2016); Bader, "U.S.-China Challenges"; Harding, "Has U.S. China Policy Failed?"; Blackwill and Tellis, *Council Special Report*; Schell and Shirk, *U.S. Policy toward China*; Shambaugh, *Tangled Titans*; Friedberg, *A Contest for Supremacy*; and Swaine, *America's Challenge*. Earlier contrasting perspectives are seen in David M. Lampton, *The Three Faces of Chinese Power* (Berkeley: University

of California Press, 2008); Gill, *Rising Star*; and Susan Shirk, *China: Fragile Superpower* (New York: Oxford, 2007).

22. Kurt Campbell and Ely Ratner, "How American Foreign Policy Got China Wrong," *Foreign Affairs* (March–April 2018), https://www.foreignaffairs.com/articles/china/2018-02-13/china-reckoning); Schell and Shirk, *US Policy toward China*; Larry Diamond and Orville Schell, *Chinese Influence and American Interests* (Stanford, CA: Hoover Institution, 2018); Orville Schell and Susan Shirk, *Course Correction: Toward and Effective and Sustainable China Policy* (Asia Society and University of California San Diego Task Force Report, February 2019); Aaron Friedberg, "Competing with China," *Survival* 60, no. 3 (June 2018): 7–64; Aaron Friedberg, "A New US Economic Strategy towards China?," *The Washington Quarterly* 40, no. 4 (December 2017): 97–114; "Special Report: China and America," *The Economist*, May 18, 2019, 3–16; Yuan Peng, "The New Coronavirus Epidemic Situation and Centennial Changes," June 2020, https://sinocism.com/p/flooding-cicir-head-on-the-pandemic; Evan Medeiros, "China Reacts: Assessing Beijing's Response to Trump's New China Strategy," *The China Leadership Monitor*, March 1, 2019; Medeiros, "The Changing Fundamentals of US-China Relations"; Wu, "The China Challenge."

23. Aaron Friedberg, "The Future of U.S.-China Relations: Is Conflict Inevitable?," *International Security* 30, no. 2 (Fall 2005): 7–45.</notes>

CHAPTER TWO

1. John K. Fairbank, *Trade and Diplomacy on the China Coast: The Opening of the Treaty Ports, 1842–1854* (Cambridge, MA: Harvard University Press, 1953); Li Changjiu and Shi Lujia, *Zhongmei guanxi liangbainian* [Two hundred years of Sino-American relations] (Peking: Xinhua Publishing House, 1984).

2. Warren Cohen, *America's Response to China: A History of Sino-American Relations* (New York: Columbia University Press, 2010), 8–28; Michael Hunt, *The Making of a Special Relationship: The United States and China to 1914* (New York: Columbia University Press, 1983).

3. Daniel Bays, ed., *Christianity in China* (Stanford, CA: Stanford University Press, 1996).

4. Michael Hunt, *Frontier Defense and the Open Door: Manchuria in Chinese-American Relations, 1895–1911* (New Haven, CT: Yale University Press, 1973); Michael Schaller, *The United States and China: Into the Twenty-First Century* (New York: Oxford University Press, 2015), 26–48.

5. Akira Iriye, *After Imperialism: The Search for a New Order in the Far East, 1921–1931* (Cambridge, MA: Harvard University Press, 1965); Dorothy Borg, *The United States and the Far Eastern Crisis of 1933–1938* (Cambridge, MA: Harvard University Press, 1964).

6. John K. Fairbank, *The United States and China* (Cambridge, MA: Harvard University Press, 1983); Cohen, *America's Response to China*; Schaller, *The*

United States and China; Gordon H. Chang, *Fateful Ties: A History of America's Preoccupation with China* (Cambridge, MA: Harvard University Press, 2015).

7. Ernest R. May and John K. Fairbank, eds., *America's China Trade in Historical Perspective: The Chinese and American Performance* (Cambridge, MA: Harvard University Press, 1986).

8. John Fairbank and Suzanne W. Barnett, eds., *Christianity in China* (Cambridge, MA: Harvard University Press, 1985).

9. Walter LaFeber, *The New Empire: An Interpretation of American Expansion, 1860–1898* (Ithaca, NY: Cornell University Press, 1963).

10. Cohen, *America's Response to China*, 29–88.

11. John Fairbank, Edwin Reischauer, and Albert Craig, *East Asia: Tradition and Transformation* (Boston: Houghton Mifflin, 1973), 593–95, 766.

12. Ronald Takaki, *Strangers from a Different Shore: A History of Asian America* (Boston: Little, Brown, 1998).

13. Hunt, *Making of a Special Relationship*; Li and Shi, *Zhongmei guanxi liangbainian* [Two hundred years of Sino-American relations].

14. Cohen, *America's Response to China*, 8–59.

15. Paul Cohen, *China and Christianity: The Missionary Movement and the Growth of Chinese Antiforeignism, 1860–1870* (Cambridge, MA: Harvard University Press, 1963).

16. Delber McKee, *Chinese Exclusion versus the Open Door Policy, 1900–1906* (Detroit, MI: Wayne State University Press, 1977).

17. Li Tien-yi, *Woodrow Wilson's China Policy, 1913–1917* (New York: Twayne, 1952).

18. Dorothy Borg, *American Policy and the Chinese Revolution, 1925–1928* (New York: Macmillan, 1947); Borg, *The United States and the Far Eastern Crisis*; Akira Iriye and Warren I. Cohen, eds., *American, Chinese, and Japanese Perspectives on Wartime Asia, 1939–1949* (Wilmington, DE: Scholarly Resources, 1990).

19. Jonathan Goldstein, *Philadelphia and the China Trade* (University Park: Pennsylvania State University Press, 1978).

20. Cohen, *America's Response to China*, 4.

21. Peter Ward Fay, *Opium War, 1840–1842* (Chapel Hill: University of North Carolina Press, 1997).

22. Fairbank, *Trade and Diplomacy on the China Coast*.

23. Edward Gulick, *Peter Parker and the Opening of China* (Cambridge, MA: Harvard University Press, 1973).

24. Eugene Boardman, *Christian Influence upon the Ideology of the Taiping Rebellion 1850–1864* (Madison: University of Wisconsin Press, 1952).

25. David Anderson, *Imperialism and Idealism: American Diplomats in China, 1861–1898* (Bloomington: University of Indiana Press, 1985); Cohen, *America's Response to China*, 23–24.

26. Fairbank, Reischauer, and Craig, *East Asia: Tradition and Transformation*, 558–96.

27. Immanuel C. Y. Hsu, *The Rise of Modern China* (New York: Oxford University Press, 2000), 297–99.

28. Schaller, *The United States and China*, 18–24.

29. Fairbank, Reischauer, and Craig, *East Asia: Tradition*, 570–75.

30. Anderson, *Imperialism and Idealism*, 154–70.

31. Tyler Dennett, *Americans in Eastern Asia: A Critical Study of the Policy of the United States with Reference to China, Japan, and Korea in the 19th Century* (New York: Macmillan, 1922), 485–504; Hunt, *Making of a Special Relationship*; Cohen, *America's Response to China*, 32–34.

32. Robert Sutter, *Historical Dictionary of United States–China Relations* (Lanham, MD: Scarecrow Press, 2006), 108.

33. Marilyn Young, *The Rhetoric of Empire: American China Policy, 1895–1901* (Cambridge, MA: Harvard University Press, 1968).

34. Cohen, *America's Response to China*, 29–88; Schaller, *The United States and China*, 26–48.

35. John Fairbank, Edwin Reischauer, and Albert Craig, *East Asia: The Modern Transformation* (Boston: Houghton Mifflin, 1965), 476–77.

36. Joseph Esherick, *The Origins of the Boxer Uprising* (Berkeley: University of California Press, 1987).

37. Cohen, *America's Response to China*, 42–55.

38. Hunt, *Frontier Defense and the Open Door*; Cohen, *America's Response to China*, 56–58.

39. Sutter, *Historical Dictionary*, 25–26.

40. Cohen, *America's Response to China*, 52–57, 65.

41. Sutter, *Historical Dictionary*, 25–26.

42. Edward Rhodes, *China's Republican Revolution: The Case of Kwangtung, 1895–1913* (Cambridge, MA: Harvard University Press, 1975), 176–81.

43. Hunt, *Frontier Defense and the Open Door*.

44. Sutter, *Historical Dictionary*, 192.

45. Cohen, *America's Response to China*, 68–70.

46. Hunt, *Frontier Defense and the Open Door*.

47. Li, *Woodrow Wilson's China Policy*; Fairbank, Reischauer, and Craig, *East Asia: The Modern*, 571, 645, 665.

48. Iriye, *After Imperialism*; Fairbank, Reischauer, and Craig, *East Asia: The Modern*, 674–76.

49. James Sheridan, *China in Disintegration: The Republican Era in Chinese History, 1912–1949* (New York: The Free Press, 1975).

50. Fairbank, Reischauer, and Craig, *East Asia: The Modern*, 685.

51. Benjamin Schwartz, *Chinese Communism and the Rise of Mao* (Cambridge, MA: Harvard University Press, 1958).

52. Cohen, *America's Response to China*, 107–9; Fairbank, Reischauer, and Craig, *East Asia: The Modern*, 688–91.

53. Schaller, *The United States and China*, 42–43.

54. Borg, *The United States and the Far Eastern Crisis*; Cohen, *America's Response to China*, 126–27.

55. Schaller, *The United States and China*, 51.

56. Sutter, *Historical Dictionary*, 78–79.

57. Fairbank, Reischauer, and Craig, *East Asia: The Modern*, 608–12.

58. Schaller, *The United States and China*, 54, 63.

59. Cohen, *America's Response to China*, 137–38.

60. Patricia Neils, *China Images in the Life and Times of Henry Luce* (Lanham, MD: Rowman & Littlefield, 1990); Graham Peck, *Two Kinds of Time* (Boston: Houghton Mifflin, 1967).

61. James C. Thomson Jr., *While China Faced West: American Reformers in Nationalist China, 1928–1937* (Cambridge, MA: Harvard University Press, 1968).

62. Fairbank, Reischauer, and Craig, *East Asia: The Modern*, 701–6.

CHAPTER THREE

1. Michael Schaller, *The U.S. Crusade in China, 1938–1945* (New York: Columbia University Press, 1979); Herbert Feis, *The China Tangle: The American Effort in China from Pearl Harbor to the Marshall Mission* (Princeton, NJ: Princeton University Press, 1953); Barbara Tuchman, *Stilwell and the American Experience in China, 1911–1945* (New York: Macmillan, 1971); Tsou Tang, *America's Failure in China, 1941–1950* (Chicago: University of Chicago Press, 1963); Jay Taylor, *The Generalissimo: Chiang Kai-shek and the Struggle for Modern China* (Cambridge, MA: Harvard University Press, 2009); Wang Taiping, ed., *Xin Zhongguo waijiao wushinian* [Fifty years of diplomacy of the new China] (Beijing: Beijing Chubanshe, 1999).

2. Feis, *The China Tangle*.

3. Russell Buhite, *Patrick J. Hurley and American Foreign Policy* (Ithaca, NY: Cornell University Press, 1973).

4. Dorothy Borg and Waldo Heinrichs, eds., *Uncertain Years: Chinese-American Relations, 1947–1950* (New York: Columbia University Press, 1980).

5. Taylor, *The Generalissimo*; Schaller, *The U.S. Crusade in China*.

6. Buhite, *Patrick J. Hurley and American Foreign Policy*; John Beal, *Marshall in China* (Garden City, NY: Doubleday, 1970).

7. Warren Cohen, "The Development of Chinese Communist Policy toward the United States, 1922–1938," *Orbis* 2 (1967): 219–37.

8. James Reardon-Anderson, *Yenan and the Great Powers: The Origins of Chinese Communist Foreign Policy, 1944–1946* (New York: Columbia University Press, 1980).

9. Odd Arne Westad, *Brothers in Arms: The Rise and Fall of the Sino-Soviet Alliance, 1945–1963* (Stanford, CA: Stanford University Press, 1998).

10. Borg and Heinrichs, *Uncertain Years*; Zi Zhongyun, *Meiguo duihua zhengce de yuanqi he fazhan, 1945–1950* [The origins and development of American policy toward China, 1945–1950] (Chongqing: Chongqing, 1987).

11. Tsou, *America's Failure in China*.

12. Charles Romanus and Riley Sunderland, *Time Runs Out on CBI* (Washington, DC: Department of the Army, 1959).

13. Charles Romanus and Riley Sunderland, *Stilwell's Command Problems* (Washington, DC: Department of the Army, 1956).

14. Tuchman, *Stilwell and the American Experience in China*.

15. Michael Schaller, *The United States and China: Into the Twenty-First Century* (New York: Oxford University Press, 2002), 59–61.

16. Ibid., 72; Warren Cohen, *America's Response to China: A History of Sino-American Relations* (New York: Columbia University Press, 2010), 138.

17. Tuchman, *Stilwell and the American Experience in China.*

18. Kenneth Shewmaker, *Americans and the Chinese Communists, 1927–1945: A Persuading Encounter* (Ithaca, NY: Cornell University Press, 1971).

19. Robert Sutter, *China Watch: Toward Sino-American Reconciliation* (Baltimore: Johns Hopkins University Press, 1978), 12–14.

20. Sutter, *China Watch*, 14–18.

21. Immanuel C. Y. Hsu, *The Rise of Modern China* (New York: Oxford University Press, 2000), 603–4.

22. Sutter, *China Watch*, 18–23.

23. Hsu, *The Rise of Modern China*, 604–5.

24. Buhite, *Patrick J. Hurley and American Foreign Policy.*

25. Schaller, *The United States and China*, 94–96.

26. Cohen, *America's Response to China*, 159–62.

27. Robert Sutter, *Historical Dictionary of United States–China Relations* (Lanham, MD: Scarecrow Press, 2006), 57–58.

28. Schaller, *The United States and China*, 99–102.

29. Cohen, *America's Response to China*, 192.

30. John Fairbank, Edwin Reischauer, and Albert Craig, *East Asia: The Modern Transformation* (Boston: Houghton Mifflin, 1965), 858–59.

31. Schaller, *The United States and China*, 115.

32. Nancy Bernkopf Tucker, *Strait Talk: United States-Taiwan Relations and the Crisis with China* (Cambridge, MA: Harvard University Press, 2009), 13.

33. Schaller, *The United States and China*, 116–17; Zi, *Meiguo duihua zhengce de yuanqi he fazhan* [The origins and development of American policy toward China].

34. Yu-ming Shaw, *An American Missionary in China: John Leighton Stuart and Chinese-American Relations* (Cambridge, MA: Harvard University Press, 1992).

35. Tucker, *Strait Talk*, 13; Sutter, *China Watch*, 31–34.

36. Chen Jian, *China's Road to the Korean War* (New York: Columbia University Press, 1994); Westad, *Brothers in Arms*; Zi Zhongyun and He Di, eds., *Meitai Guanxi Sishinian* [Forty years of US-Taiwan relations] (Beijing: People's Press, 1991).

37. Allen Whiting, *The Chinese Calculus of Deterrence: India and Indochina* (Ann Arbor: University of Michigan Press, 1975); Robert S. Ross and Jiang Changbin, eds., *Re-examining the Cold War: U.S.-China Diplomacy, 1954–1973* (Cambridge, MA: Harvard University Press, 2001).

38. Chen Jian, *Mao's China and the Cold War* (Chapel Hill: University of North Carolina Press, 2001); Thomas Christensen, *Useful Adversaries: Grand Strategy, Domestic Mobilization, and Sino-American Conflicts, 1949–1958* (Princeton, NJ: Princeton University Press, 1996).

39. Richard Wich, *Sino-Soviet Crisis Politics* (Cambridge, MA: Harvard University Press, 1980).

40. Ralph Clough, *Island China* (Cambridge, MA: Harvard University Press, 1978), 5–10.

41. Tucker, *Strait Talk*, 13–26.

42. Robert Blum, *Drawing the Line: The Origins of the American Containment Policy in East Asia* (New York: W. W. Norton, 1982); William Stueck, *The Korean War: An International History* (Princeton, NJ: Princeton University Press, 1997); Chen, *China's Road to the Korean War*.

43. Schaller, *The United States and China*, 152–62.

44. Bruce Cumings, *The Origins of the Korean War* (Princeton, NJ: Princeton University Press, 1990).

45. Cohen, *America's Response to China*, 186–91.

46. Schaller, *The United States and China*, 129–35.

47. Rosemary Foot, *A Substitute for Victory: The Politics of Peacemaking and the Korean Armistice Talks* (Ithaca, NY: Cornell University Press, 1990).

48. Barry Naughton, *The Chinese Economy: Transitions and Growth* (Cambridge, MA: MIT Press, 2007), 55–83.

49. Chen, *Mao's China and the Cold War*.

50. Christensen, *Useful Adversaries*.

51. Schaller, *The United States and China*, 144–46.

52. Ross Koen, *The China Lobby in American Politics* (New York: Harper and Row, 1974).

53. Tucker, *Strait Talk*, 13–15.

54. Clough, *Island China*, 10–14.

55. Sutter, *China Watch*, 34–46.

56. Zhang Baijia and Jia Qingguo, "Steering Wheel, Shock Absorber, and Diplomatic Probe in Confrontation: Sino-American Ambassadorial Talks Seen from the Chinese Perspective," in Ross and Jiang, eds., *Re-examining the Cold War*, 173–99; Sutter, *China Watch*, 34–46.

57. Sutter, *Historical Dictionary of United States–China Relations*, 4.

58. Steven Goldstein, "Dialogue of the Deaf? The Sino-American Ambassadorial-Level Talks, 1955–1970," in Ross and Jiang, eds., *Re-examining the Cold War*, 200–237.

59. Tucker, *Strait Talk*, 14–17.

60. Chen, *Mao's China and the Cold War*.

61. Schaller, *The United States and China*, 152–56.

62. Tucker, *Strait Talk*, 17–21.

63. Cohen, *America's Response to China*, 210–13; Goldstein, "Dialogue of the Deaf?," 229–37.

64. Tony Saich, *Governance and Politics of China* (New York: Palgrave Macmillan, 2004), 44–56.

65. Hsu, *The Rise of Modern China*, 689–702.

66. Roderick MacFarquhar and Michael Schoenhals, *Mao's Last Revolution* (Cambridge, MA: Harvard University Press, 2006).

67. Sutter, *China Watch*, 65–67.

68. Peter Van Ness, *Revolution and Chinese Foreign Policy* (Berkeley: University of California Press, 1970).

69. Jisen Ma, *The Cultural Revolution in the Foreign Ministry of China* (Hong Kong: Chinese University Press, 2004).

70. Schaller, *The United States and China*, 156–62.

71. Tucker, *Strait Talk*, 21–26.

CHAPTER FOUR

1. A. Doak Barnett, *A New U.S. Policy toward China* (Washington, DC: Brookings Institution, 1971); Rosemary Foot, *The Practice of Power: U.S. Relations with China since 1949* (New York: Oxford University Press, 1997); Evelyn Goh, *Constructing the U.S. Rapprochement with China, 1961–1974* (New York: Cambridge University Press, 2005); Gong Li, *Kuayue: 1969–1979 nian Zhong-Mei guanxi de yanbian* [Across the chasm: The evolution of relations between China and the United States, 1969–1979] (Henan, China: Henan People's Press, 1992).

2. Chen Jian, *Mao's China and the Cold War* (Chapel Hill: University of North Carolina Press, 2001).

3. Foot, *The Practice of Power*; Goh, *Constructing the U.S. Rapprochement with China*.

4. Robert Ross, *Negotiating Cooperation: The United States and China, 1969–1989* (Stanford, CA: Stanford University Press, 1995); Robert Sutter, *China Watch: Toward Sino-American Reconciliation* (Baltimore: Johns Hopkins University Press, 1978), 83–102; Thomas Gottlieb, *Chinese Foreign Policy Factionalism and the Origins of the Strategic Triangle* (Santa Monica, CA: Rand, 1977); John Garver, *China's Decision for Rapprochement with the United States, 1968–1971* (Boulder, CO: Westview Press, 1982); Wang Zhongchun, "The Soviet Factor in Sino-American Normalization, 1969–1979," in *Normalization of U.S.-China Relations*, ed. William Kirby, Robert Ross, and Gong Li (Cambridge, MA: Harvard University Press, 2005) 147–174.

5. James Mann, *About Face: A History of America's Curious Relationship with China, from Nixon to Clinton* (New York: Knopf, 1999).

6. Sutter, *China Watch*, 1–62.

7. The developments in the United States during 1968 noted here and below are covered in *American History Online—Facts on File* (http://www.fofweb.com) and *CQ Almanac 1968* (Washington, DC: Congressional Quarterly News Features, 1968).

8. Mann, *About Face*, 13–25.

9. Li Jie, "China's Domestic Politics and the Normalization of Sino-U.S. Relations, 1969–1979," in Kirby, Ross, and Li, eds., *Normalization of U.S.-China Relations*, 56–89; Philip Bridgham, "Mao's Cultural Revolution: The Struggle to Seize Power," *The China Quarterly* 41 (1970): 1–25.

10. Gottlieb, *Chinese Foreign Policy Factionalism*; Roderick Mac-Farquhar and Michael Schoenhals, *Mao's Last Revolution* (Cambridge, MA: Harvard University Press, 2006).

11. Harlan Jencks, *From Muskets to Missiles: Politics and Professionalism in the Chinese Army, 1945–1981* (Boulder, CO: Westview Press, 1982).

12. Thomas Robinson, "The Sino-Soviet Border Dispute: Background, Development and the March 1969 Clashes," *American Political Science Review* 66, no. 4 (December 1972): 1175–78; Alice Lyman Miller and Richard Wich, *Becoming Asia* (Stanford, CA: Stanford University Press, 2011), 116–36, 182–93.

13. John Garver, *Foreign Relations of the People's Republic of China* (Englewood Cliffs, NJ: Prentice Hall, 1993), 304–20.

14. Gottlieb, *Chinese Foreign Policy Factionalism*.

15. Sutter, *China Watch*, 72–75; Ibid., 75–78.

16. Garver, *Foreign Relations of the People's Republic of China*, 306–10.

17. Sutter, *China Watch*, 78–102.

18. Michael Schaller, *The United States and China: Into the Twenty-First Century* (New York: Oxford University Press, 2002), 170.

19. Ross, *Negotiating Cooperation*, 28, 34–35.

20. Immanuel C. Y. Hsu, *The Rise of Modern China* (New York: Oxford University Press, 2000), 711–14, 822.

21. Sutter, *Historical Dictionary of United States–China Relations* (Lanham, MD: Scarecrow Press, 2006), 190–91.

22. Hsu, *The Rise of Modern China*, 710–14, 820–23.

23. Nancy Bernkopf Tucker, *Strait Talk: United States-Taiwan Relations and the Crisis with China* (Cambridge, MA: Harvard University Press, 2009), 35–40.

24. Ibid., 52, 68; Mann, *About Face*, 51–52.

25. An authoritative account of the US-China opening is in Tucker, *Strait Talk*.

26. Ibid., 52.

27. House Committee on Foreign Affairs, *Executive-Legislative Consultations over China Policy, 1978–1979* (Washington, DC: US Government Printing Office, 1980).

28. Schaller, *The United States and China*, 178–84; Tucker, *Strait Talk*, 29–68; Ross, *Negotiating Cooperation*, 17–54.

29. Warren Cohen, *America's Response to China: A History of Sino-American Relations* (New York: Columbia University Press, 2010), 220.

30. Hsu, *The Rise of Modern China*, 763–73.

31. John K. Fairbank and Merle Goldman, *China: A New History* (Cambridge, MA: Harvard University Press, 1999), 404–5.

32. Hsu, *The Rise of Modern China*, 817–23.

33. Fairbank and Goldman, *China*, 406–10; Ezra Vogel, *Deng Xiaoping and the Transformation of China* (Cambridge, MA: Harvard University Press, 2011), 91–183.

34. Nayan Chanda, *Brother Enemy: The War after the War* (New York: Harcourt Brace Jovanovich, 1986).

35. Garver, *Foreign Relations of the People's Republic of China*, 166–77, 310–11.

36. Cohen, *America's Response to China*, 221–25.

37. Mann, *About Face*, 82–92.

38. Tucker, *Strait Talk*, 101–15.

39. Harry Harding, *A Fragile Relationship: The United States and China since 1972* (Washington, DC: Brookings Institution, 1992), 80–81.

40. Ross, *Negotiating Cooperation*, 125–26; Mann, *About Face*, 98–100.

41. House Committee on Foreign Affairs, *Executive-Legislative Consultations over China Policy*.

42. Harding, *A Fragile Relationship*, 86–87.

43. Schaller, *The United States and China*, 193–96.

44. Tucker, *Strait Talk*, 129–52.

45. Schaller, *The United States and China*, 177.

46. On the costs, see Tucker, *Strait Talk*, 52, 68, 153; Ross, *Negotiating Cooperation*, 163–245; Mann, *About Face*, 125–36; Schaller, *The United States and China*, 177; House Committee on Foreign Affairs, *Executive-Legislative Consultations over China Policy*.

47. See discussion of congressional debates on China policy in chapter 5, below.

48. Tucker, *Strait Talk*, 153–60.

49. Harding, *A Fragile Relationship*; Ross, *Negotiating Cooperation*; Mann, *About Face*. Major works covering later developments are Tucker, *Strait Talk*; David M. Lampton, *Same Bed, Different Dreams: Managing U.S.-China Relations, 1989–2000* (Berkeley: University of California Press, 2001); Robert Suettinger, *Beyond Tiananmen: The Politics of U.S.-China Relations, 1989–2000* (Washington, DC: Brookings Institution, 2003); Jean Garrison, *Making China Policy: From Nixon to G. W. Bush* (Boulder, CO: Lynne Rienner, 2005). Garrison's analysis (80–85) identifies two competing groups of US decision makers regarding China policy in the early 1980s as the "China-first" group and the "pan-Asian" group. The analysis in this book builds on the Garrison analysis.

50. Ross, *Negotiating Cooperation*, 170–245; Mann, *About Face*, 119–36; Garrison, *Making China Policy*, 79–106; Tucker, *Strait Talk*, 153–60.

51. Harding, *A Fragile Relationship*, 131–45. David Shambaugh, "Patterns of Interaction in Sino-American Relations," in *Chinese Foreign Policy: Theory and Practice*, ed. Thomas Robinson and David Shambaugh (New York: Oxford University Press, 1994), 203–5.

52. Garver, *Foreign Relations of the People's Republic of China*, 310–19.

53. Robert Sutter, *Chinese Foreign Relations: Developments after Mao* (New York: Praeger, 1986), 18–96.

54. Garver, *Foreign Relations of the People's Republic of China*, 98–103, 317–19.

55. Ross, *Negotiating Cooperation*, 164–74.

56. Sutter, *Chinese Foreign Relations*, 182; Ibid., 178.

57. Garver, *Foreign Relations of the People's Republic of China*, 98–103; Ross, *Negotiating Cooperation*, 170–200.

58. Tucker, *Strait Talk*, 153–60; Mann, *About Face*, 128–33.

59. Sutter, *Chinese Foreign Relations*, 178.

60. Richard Nations, "A Tilt towards Tokyo," *Far Eastern Economic Review*, April 21, 1983, 36; Ross, *Negotiating Cooperation*, 228–33.

61. Sutter, *Chinese Foreign Relations*, 178–79.

62. Ibid.

63. On Deng's role in these foreign policy issues and overall political standing, see Vogel, *Deng Xiaoping and the Transformation of China*.

64. Ross, *Negotiating Cooperation*, 233–45; Tucker, *Strait Talk*, 160–61.

65. Sutter, *Chinese Foreign Relations*, 180–81.

66. Ross, *Negotiating Cooperation*, 233–44; Sutter, *Chinese Foreign Relations*, 181–82.

67. Tucker, *Strait Talk*, 155–60.

68. Gerald Segal, *Sino-Soviet Relations after Mao*, Adelphi Papers, no. 202 (London: International Institute for Strategic Studies, 1985).

69. The review of Sino-Soviet relations in the remainder of this section is adapted from Sutter, *Chinese Foreign Relations*, 182–86. See also Segal, *Sino-Soviet Relations after Mao*.

CHAPTER FIVE

1. Tony Saich, *Governance and Politics of China* (New York: Palgrave Macmillan, 2004), 70–74; Ezra Vogel, *Deng Xiaoping and the Transformation of China* (Cambridge, MA: Harvard University Press, 2011).

2. Jean Garrison, *Making China Policy: From Nixon to G. W. Bush* (Boulder, CO: Lynne Rienner, 2005), 210–17; Carola McGiffert, ed., *China in the American Political Imagination* (Washington, DC: CSIS Press, 2003); David M. Lampton, *Same Bed, Different Dreams: Managing U.S.-China Relations, 1989–2000* (Berkeley: University of California Press, 2001), 276–78; Kenneth Lieberthal, "Why the US Malaise over China?" YaleGlobal Online, January 19, 2006, http://yaleglobal.yale.edu/content/why-us-malaise-over-china; Kenneth Lieberthal and Wang Jisi, *Addressing U.S.-China Strategic Distrust* (Washington, DC: Brookings Institution, 2012).

3. Lampton, *Same Bed, Different Dreams*, 17–55.

4. Barry Naughton, *The Chinese Economy: Transitions and Growth* (Cambridge, MA: MIT Press, 2007), 98–100.

5. Carola McGiffert, ed., *Chinese Images of the United States* (Washington, DC: CSIS Press, 2006).

6. Kenneth Lieberthal, "China: How Domestic Forces Shape the PRC's Grand Strategy and International Impact," in *Strategic Asia 2007–2008*, ed. Ashley Tellis and Michael Wills (Seattle, WA: National Bureau of Asian Research, 2007), 63.

7. Garrison, *Making China Policy*, 182–83; Michael Swaine, *Reverse Course? The Fragile Turnabout in U.S.-China Relations*, Policy Brief 22 (Washington, DC: Carnegie Endowment, February 2003).

8. Warren Cohen, *America's Response to China: A History of Sino-American Relations* (New York: Columbia University Press, 2000), 229.

9. Michael Schaller, *The United States and China: Into the Twenty-First Century* (New York: Oxford University Press, 2015), 211–14.

10. John Garver, *Face Off: China, the United States, and Taiwan's Democratization* (Seattle: University of Washington Press, 1997).

11. Lampton, *Same Bed, Different Dreams*, 55–63.

12. Robert L. Suettinger, *Beyond Tiananmen: The Politics of U.S.-China Relations, 1989–2000* (Washington, DC: Brookings Institution, 2003), 358–409.

13. Robert Sutter, *U.S. Policy toward China: An Introduction to the Role of Interest Groups* (Lanham, MD: Rowman & Littlefield, 1998).

14. Harry Harding, *Public Engagement in American Foreign Policy* (New York: The American Assembly, Columbia University, February 23–25, 1995), 8–9.

15. Charlotte Preece and Robert Sutter, *Foreign Policy Debate in America*, CRS Report 91–833F (Washington, DC: Congressional Research Service of the Library of Congress, November 27, 1991).

16. Sutter, *U.S. Policy toward China*, 12.

17. "Ross Perot on the Issues," On the Issues, accessed September 21, 2009, http://www.issues2000.org/Ross_Perot.htm.

18. Sutter, *U.S. Policy toward China*, 13–14; Joseph Nye, *Bound to Lead* (Cambridge, MA: Harvard University Press, 1992).

19. Sutter, *U.S. Policy toward China*, 14–15; Lampton, *Same Bed, Different Dreams*, 17–63.

20. "John McCain on the Issues," On the Issues, accessed September 21, 2009, http://www.issues2000.org/John_McCain.htm.

21. Lampton, *Same Bed, Different Dreams*, 332–35, 338–39.

22. Kerry Dumbaugh, "Interest Groups: Growing Influence," in *Making China Policy: Lessons from the Bush and Clinton Administrations*, ed. Ramon Myers, Michel Oksenberg, and David Shambaugh (Lanham, MD: Rowman & Littlefield, 2001), 113–78.

23. Sutter, *U.S. Policy toward China*, 16.

24. Kent Wong, "The AFL-CIO and China," *U.S.-China Media Brief*, 2008, UCLA Asian American Studies Center, accessed September 21, 2009, http://www.aasc.ucla.edu/uschina/ee_aflciochina.shtml.

25. Dumbaugh, "Interest Groups," 150, 158–59, 161, 162, 170–71.

26. Sutter, *U.S. Policy toward China*, 16–17.

27. Nancy Bernkopf Tucker, *Strait Talk: United States-Taiwan Relations and the Crisis with China* (Cambridge, MA: Harvard University Press, 2009).

28. Suettinger, *Beyond Tiananmen*, 294, 330.

29. The four crises are identified and reviewed in Lampton, *Same Bed, Different Dreams*, 17–63. See also Suettinger, *Beyond Tiananmen*.

30. Schaller, *The United States and China*, 204–5.

31. Sutter, *U.S. Policy toward China*, 26–44.

32. James Mann, *About Face: A History of America's Curious Relationship with China, from Nixon to Clinton* (New York: Knopf, 1999), 274–78.

33. Cohen, *America's Response to China*, 229–31.

34. Schaller, *The United States and China*, 214–19.

35. Cohen, *America's Response to China*, 234–39.

36. For this and the next two paragraphs, see Robert Sutter, *Historical Dictionary of United States–China Relations* (Lanham, MD: Rowman & Littlefield, 2006), lxix–lxx.

37. Schaller, *The United States and China*, 219–27.

38. Cohen, *America's Response to China*, 235–36.

39. Tucker, *Strait Talk*, 217–18, 231–43.

40. Sutter, *Historical Dictionary of United States–China Relations*, lxxi.

41. Suettinger, *Beyond Tiananmen*, 369–77.

42. Tucker, *Strait Talk*, 239–44.

43. Lampton, *Same Bed, Different Dreams*, 95–97.

44. Garrison, *Making China Policy*, 148–52.

45. Ibid., 165–82; Robert Sutter, "The Democratic-Led 110th Congress: Implications for Asia," *Asia Policy* 3 (January 2007): 125–50.

46. The following analysis summarizes points made at greater length in Robert Sutter, "U.S. Domestic Debate over Policy toward Mainland China and Taiwan: Key Findings, Outlook, and Lessons," *American Journal of Chinese Studies* 8, no. 2 (October 2001): 133–44; and Robert Sutter, "The Bush Administration and U.S. China Policy Debate," *Issues and Studies* 38, no. 2 (June 2002): 14–22.

47. Tucker, *Strait Talk*; Myers, Oksenberg, Shambaugh, eds., *Making China Policy*; Lampton, *Same Bed, Different Dreams*; Mann, *About Face*; Sutter, *U.S. Policy toward China*; Robert Sutter, *The China Quandary* (Boulder, CO: Westview Press, 1983).

48. Tucker, *Strait Talk*, 29–52.

49. Reviewed in ibid., 116–28; Sutter, *The China Quandary*, 5, 19, 85, and 146.

50. House Committee on Foreign Affairs, *Executive-Legislative Consultations over China Policy, 1978–1979* (Washington, DC: US Government Printing Office, 1980).

51. Ramon Myers, Michel Oksenberg, and David Shambaugh, eds., *Making China Policy: Lessons from the Bush and Clinton Administrations* (Lanham, MD: Rowman & Littlefield, 2001), 79–222.

52. Robert Sutter, "U.S. Domestic Debate over Policy toward Mainland China and Taiwan," in *Making China Policy: Lessons from the Bush and Clinton Administrations*, ed. Ramon Myers, Michel Oksenberg, and David Shambaugh (Lanham, MD: Rowman & Littlefield, 2001), 37.

53. Bill Gertz and Rowan Scarborough, "Inside the Ring," *Washington Times*, March 22, 2002; Murray Hiebert and Susan Lawrence, "Crossing Red Lines," *Far Eastern Economic Review*, April 4, 2002.

54. Sutter, "The Bush Administration and U.S. China Policy Debate," 16.

55. Lampton, *Same Bed, Different Dreams*; Chu Shulong, "Quanmian jianshe xiao-kang shehui shiqi de zhongguo waijiao zhan-lue," *Shijie Jingji yu Zhengzhi* 8 (August 2003); Fu Hao and Li Tongcheng, eds., *Lusi shui shou? Zhongguo waijiaoguan zai Meiguo* [Who will win the game? Chinese diplomats in the United States] (Beijing: Hauqiao Chubanshe, 1998).

56. Song Qiang, Zhang Changchang, and Qiao Bian, *Zhongguo keyi shuo bu: Lengzhanhou shidai de zhengzhi yu qinggan jueze* [China can say no: The decision between politics and sentiment in the post–Cold War] (Beijing: Zhonghua Gongshang Lianhe Chubanshe, 1996).

57. Robert Sutter, *Chinese Policy Priorities and Their Implications for the United States* (Lanham, MD: Rowman & Littlefield, 2000), 40–41; Wang Jisi, *China's Changing Role in Asia* (Washington, DC: The Atlantic Council of the United States, January 2004), 1–5, 16–17; Qian Qichen, "Adjustment of the United States National Security Strategy and International Relations in the Early New Century," *Foreign Affairs Journal* (Beijing) 71 (March 2004): 1–7; Wang Jisi, "Xinxingshi de zhuyao tedian he Zhongguo waijiao," *Xiabdai Guoji Guanxi* (Beijing) 4 (April 2003): 1–3;

Yuan Peng, "Bumpy Road Ahead for Sustainable Sino-U.S. Ties," *China Daily*, May 8, 2007, 11; Lieberthal, "Why the US Malaise over China?"; Fu Mengzi, "Sino-U.S. Relations," *Xiandai Guoji Guanxi* (Beijing) 17 (January 2007): 32–46.

58. Suettinger, *Beyond Tiananmen*, 340–51; Schaller, *The United States and China*, 223–24.

59. Sutter, *Chinese Policy Priorities*, 41–42.

60. "Experts Appraise Sino-U.S. Relations," *Jeifang Junbao* (June 1995), 5; Wang Jisi, "Deepening Mutual Understanding and Expanding Strategic Consensus," *Renmin Ribao* (June 16, 1998), 6; "Questions and Answers at Qian Qichen's Small-Scale Briefing," *Wen Wei Pao* (Hong Kong; November 4, 1997), A6; Sutter, *Chinese Policy Priorities*, 42.

61. Lampton, *Same Bed, Different Dreams*, 39–45; Sutter, *U.S. Policy toward China*, 47–65.

62. David M. Lampton, "America's China Policy in the Age of the Finance Minister: Clinton Ends Linkage," *China Quarterly* 139 (September 1994): 597–621.

63. Sutter, *Chinese Policy Priorities*, 43–44.

64. Lampton, *Same Bed, Different Dreams*, 45.

65. Sutter, *Chinese Policy Priorities*, 52; Garver, *Face Off*. See also Su Ge, *Meiguo: Dui hua Zhengce yu Taiwan wenti* [America: China policy and the Taiwan issue] (Beijing: Shijie Zhishi Chubanshe, 1998).

66. *U.S. News and World Report*, October 23, 1995, 72.

67. Suettinger, *Beyond Tiananmen*, 264–357.

68. Sutter, *Chinese Policy Priorities*, 57–58.

69. Susan Shirk, *China: Fragile Superpower* (New York: Oxford University Press, 2007), 220.

70. Robert Sutter, *China's Rise in Asia* (Lanham, MD: Rowman & Littlefield, 2005), 12–13.

CHAPTER SIX

1. Murray Hiebert, *The Bush Presidency: Implications for Asia* (New York: Asia Society, 2001), 5–9.

2. Robert Sutter, "Grading Bush's China Policy: A−," *PacNet* 10 (March 8, 2002), https://www.csis.org/analysis/pacnet-10-grading-bushs-china-policy.

3. James Shinn, ed., *Weaving the Net: Conditional Engagement with China* (New York: Council on Foreign Relations, 1996).

4. Bonnie Glaser, "Bilateral Relations on Reasonably Sound Footing as 2000 and the Clinton Administration Come to a Close," *Comparative Connections*, January 2001, https://csis-prod.s3.amazonaws.com/s3fs-public/legacy_files/files/media/csis/pubs/0004qus_china.pdf.

5. Bonnie Glaser, "First Contact: Qian Qichen Engages in Wide-Ranging, Constructive Talks with President Bush and Senior U.S. Officials," *Comparative Connections*, April 2001, https://csis-prod.s3.amazonaws.com/s3fs-public/legacy_files/files/media/csis/pubs/0101qus_china.pdf.

6. Sutter, "Grading Bush's China Policy."

7. John Keefe, *Anatomy of the EP-3 Incident* (Alexandria, VA: Center for Naval Analysis, 2002).

8. Robert Sutter, "US-China Relations after the Sixteenth Party Congress: Prospects and Challenges," *Journal of Asian and African Studies* 38, no. 4 (2003): 447–63.

9. Nick Cummings-Bruce, "Powell Will Explain Bush's Asia Policy," *Wall Street Journal*, July 23, 2001, A11; Sutter, "US-China Relations after the Sixteenth Party Congress: Prospects and Challenges," 452–53.

10. Michael Swaine and Zhang Tuosheng, eds., *Managing Sino-American Crises* (Washington, DC: Carnegie Endowment for International Peace, 2006).

11. Sutter, "US-China Relations after the Sixteenth Party Congress: Prospects and Challenges," 451–52.

12. Thomas Christensen, "Optimistic Trends and Near-Term Challenges: Sino-American Security Relations in Early 2003," *China Leadership Monitor* 6 (Spring 2003), https://www.hoover.org/research/optimistic-trends-and-near-term-challenges-sino-american-security-relations-early-2003.

13. "Concern over U.S. Plans for War on Terror Dominate Jiang Tour," Reuters, April 7, 2002, http://www.taiwansecurity.org; Willy Wo-Lap Lam, "U.S., Taiwan Catch Jiang Off-Guard," CNN.com, March 19, 2002, http://edition.cnn.com/2002/WORLD/asiapcf/east/03/18/willy.column.

14. Bonnie Glaser, "Playing Up the Positive on the Eve of the Crawford Summit," *Comparative Connections*, October 2002, http://cc.csis.org/2002/10/playing-positive-eve-crawford-summit.

15. Sutter, "US-China Relations after the Sixteenth Party Congress: Prospects and Challenges," 453.

16. "U.S. Says China Regulations Should Free Up Soybean Exports," statement of the Office of the U.S. Trade Representative, October 18, 2002, http://ustr.gov; "Mainland Offers Taiwan Goodwill Gesture," *China Daily*, October 18, 2002, http://www.taiwansecurity.org; "China Tightens Rules on Military Exports," Reuters, October 21, 2002, http://www.taiwansecurity.org; "Ashcroft to Open China FBI Office," Reuters, October 22, 2002, http://www.taiwansecurity.org; "U.S. and China Seal Billion Dollar Deals," *BBC*, October 22, 2002, http://www.taiwansecurity.org; "U.S. and China Set New Rights Talks," *Washington Post*, October 24, 2002, http://www.taiwansecurity.org.

17. Lu Zhenya, "Jiang Zemin, Bush Agree to Maintain High-Level Strategic Dialogue," *Zhongguo Xinwen She* (Beijing), October 26, 2002.

18. Shirley Kan, *U.S.-China Military Contacts: Issues for Congress*, CRS Report RL32496 (Washington, DC: Congressional Research Service of the Library of Congress, June 19, 2012), 2–4.

19. Victor Cha, "Winning Asia: Washington's Untold Success Story," *Foreign Affairs* 86, no. 6 (November–December 2007): 98–133.

20. "Bush, Kerry Square Off in 1st Debate," *Japan Today*, October 1, 2004, http://www.japantoday.com/jp/news/313422/all (site discontinued).

21. Robert Sutter, "The Taiwan Problem in the Second George W. Bush Administration—U.S. Officials' Views and Their Implications for U.S. Policy," *Journal of Contemporary China* 15, no. 48 (August 2006): 417–42.

22. Secretary of State Condoleezza Rice, remarks at Sophia University, Tokyo, Japan, March 19, 2005, http://www.state.gov/secretary/rm/2005/43655.htm (site discontinued); Evan Medeiros, "Strategic Hedging and the Future of Asia-Pacific Stability," *Washington Quarterly* 29, no. 1 (2005–6): 15–28.

23. Rosemary Foot, "Chinese Strategies in a U.S.-Hegemonic Global Order: Accommodating and Hedging," *International Affairs* 82, no. 1 (2006): 77–94; Wang Jisi, "China's Search for Stability with America," *Foreign Affairs* 84, no. 5 (September–October 2005): 39–48; Yong Deng and Thomas Moore, "China Views Globalization: Toward a New Great-Power Politics," *Washington Quarterly* 27, no. 3 (Summer 2004): 117–36.

24. Off-the-record interviews with US officials reviewed in Robert Sutter, "Dealing with a Rising China: U.S. Strategy and Policy," in *Making New Partnership: A Rising China and Its Neighbors*, ed. Zhang Yunlin (Beijing: Social Sciences Academic Press, 2008), 370–74.

25. Among published sources, see U.S.-China Economic and Security Review Commission, *2005 Report to Congress* (Washington, DC: US Government Printing Office, 2005), 143–90.

26. Author interviews with US officials.

27. Remarks of Deputy Secretary of State Robert Zoellick, "Wither China? From Membership to Responsibility," National Committee for U.S.-China Relations, September 21, 2005, http://www.cfr.org/china/whither-china-membership-responsibility/p8916 (site discontinued).

28. Cha, "Winning Asia"; Daniel Twining, "America's Grand Design in Asia," *Washington Quarterly* 30, no. 3 (2007): 79–94; Robert Sutter, *The United States in Asia* (Lanham, MD: Rowman & Littlefield, 2008), 270–76, 281–83.

29. Kerry Dumbaugh, *China-U.S. Relations: Current Issues and Implications for U.S. Policy*, CRS Report RL33877 (Washington, DC: Congressional Research Service of the Library of Congress, May 25, 2007).

30. Dumbaugh, *China-U.S. Relations* (May 25, 2007); Robert Sutter, "The Democratic-Led 110th Congress: Implications for Asia," *Asia Policy*, no. 3 (January 2007): 125–50.

31. Kerry Dumbaugh, *China-U.S. Relations*, IB 98018 (Washington, DC: Library of Congress, July 17, 2001); Robert Sutter, "Domestic American Influences on US-China Relations," in *Tangled Titans: The United States and China*, ed. David Shambaugh (Lanham, MD: Rowman & Littlefield, 2013), 110.

32. Tony Saich, *Governance and Politics of China* (New York: Palgrave Macmillan, 2004), 83.

33. Dumbaugh, *China-U.S. Relations*, IB 98018, 5.

34. Kerry Dumbaugh, *Tibet: Problems, Prospects, and US Policy*, CRS Report RL34445 (Washington, DC: Congressional Research Service of the Library of Congress, July 30, 2009).

35. Kerry Dumbaugh, *China and the 105th Congress: Policy Issues and Legislation, 1997–1998*, CRS Report RL30220 (Washington, DC: Congressional Research Service of the Library of Congress, June 8, 1999); Thomas Lum and Hannah Fisher, *Human Rights in China*, CRS Report RL34729 (Washington, DC: Congressional Research Service of the Library of Congress, July 13, 2009), 15–16.

36. Larry Q. Nowels, *U.S. International Population Assistance: Issues for Congress*, CRS IB96026 (Washington, DC: Congressional Research Service of the Library of Congress, June 15, 2001); Lum and Fisher, *Human Rights in China*, 3.

37. "Religion in China: When Opium Can Be Benign," *Economist*, February 1, 2007, http://www.economist.com/node/8625817.

38. Erica Werner, "U.S. Lawmakers Criticize Yahoo Officials," *Washington Post*, November 6, 2007, A1.

39. Shirley Kan, *US-China Military Contacts*, CRS Report RL32496 (Washington, DC: Congressional Research Service of the Library of Congress, October 27, 2014), 1–8.

40. Richard Weitz, "Persistent Barriers to Sino-American Military Dialogue," Jamestown Foundation China Brief, September 6, 2006, https://jamestown.org/program/persistent-barriersto-sino-american-military-dialogue.

41. Kerry Dumbaugh, *China-U.S. Relations in the 109th Congress*, CRS Report RL32804 (Washington, DC: Congressional Research Service of the Library of Congress, December 31, 2006), 20.

42. Shirley Kan, *China: Suspected Acquisition of U.S. Nuclear Weapons Secrets*, CRS Report RL30143 (Washington, DC: Congressional Research Service of the Library of Congress, 2006).

43. Amy Argetsinger, "Spy Case Dismissed for Misconduct," *Washington Post*, January 7, 2005, A4; Steve Lohr, "State Department Yields on PC's from China," *New York Times*, May 23, 2006, http://www.nytimes.com/2006/05/23/washington/23lenovo.html.

44. Wayne Morrison, *China-U.S. Trade Issues*, CRS Report RL33536 (Washington, DC: Congressional Research Service of the Library of Congress, April 23, 2007).

45. Dumbaugh, *China-U.S. Relations in the 109th Congress*, 19.

46. Morrison, *China-U.S. Trade Issues*.

47. Ibid.

48. Dumbaugh, *China-U.S. Relations in the 109th Congress*, 4.

49. Ibid., 27.

50. Bonnie Glaser, "Mid-Air Collision Cripples Sino-U.S. Relations," *Comparative Connections*, April–June 2001, https://csis-prod.s3.amazonaws.com/s3fs-public/legacy_files/files/media/csis/pubs/0102qus_china.pdf.

51. Dumbaugh, *China-U.S. Relations in the 109th Congress*, 8.

52. Kerry Dumbaugh, *Taiwan-US Relations: Developments and Policy Implications*, CRS Report R40493 (Washington, DC: Congressional Research Service of the Library of Congress, April 2, 2009).

53. Dumbaugh, *China-U.S. Relations*, IB98018, 10–11.

54. Peter Grier, "Why Bush Risks China's Ire to Honor Dalai Lama," *Christian Science Monitor*, October 17, 2007, 1.

55. For sources and examples, see Robert Sutter, *Chinese Foreign Relations: Power and Policy since the Cold War*, 3rd ed. (Lanham, MD: Rowman & Littlefield, 2012), 1–2.

56. David Shambaugh, "China's 17th Party Congress: Maintaining Delicate Balances," *Brookings Northeast Asia Commentary*, November 1, 2007, https://www.brookings.edu/opinions/chinas-17th-party-congress-maintaining-delicate-balances.

57. Denny Roy, *China's Foreign Relations* (Lanham, MD: Rowman & Littlefield, 1998).

58. Robert Sutter, *Chinese Policy Priorities and Their Implications for the United States* (Lanham, MD: Rowman & Littlefield, 2000), 18. See review of this period in Barry Naughton, *The Chinese Economy: Transitions and Growth* (Cambridge, MA: MIT Press, 2007), and Saich, *Governance and Politics of China*.

59. Sutter, *Chinese Policy Priorities and Their Implications for the United States*, 18.

60. Kerry Dumbaugh, *China's 17th Party Congress, October 15–21, 2007*, Congressional Research Service Memorandum, October 23, 2007.

61. Sutter, *Chinese Policy Priorities and Their Implications for the United States*, 19.

62. Maureen Fan, "China's Party Leadership Declares New Priority: 'Harmonious Society,'" *Washington Post*, October 12, 2006, A18.

63. Sutter, *Chinese Policy Priorities and Their Implications for the United States*, 19–21.

64. See contrasting views of China's approach to the United States at this time and of various differences in China-US relations in Bates Gill, *Rising Star: China's New Security Diplomacy* (Washington, DC: Brookings Institution, 2007); Susan Shirk, *China: Fragile Superpower* (New York: Oxford University Press, 2007); David M. Lampton, *The Three Faces of Chinese Power: Might, Money, and Minds* (Berkeley: University of California Press, 2008); Michael Swaine, *America's Challenge: Engaging a Rising China in the Twenty-First Century* (Washington, DC: Carnegie Endowment, 2011); Aaron Friedberg, *A Contest for Supremacy: China, America, and the Struggle for Mastery in Asia* (New York: W. W. Norton, 2011); and Jeffrey Bader, *Obama and China's Rise* (Washington, DC: Brookings Institution, 2012).

65. These developments and determinants are reviewed in Sutter, *Chinese Foreign Relations*, 3rd ed., 2–3.

66. Ibid.

67. Evan Medeiros, "Strategic Hedging and the Future of Asia-Pacific Security," *Washington Quarterly* 29, no. 1 (2005): 173–89.

68. This dualism and respective Gulliver strategies are discussed in Robert Sutter, "China and U.S. Security and Economic Interests: Opportunities and Challenges," in *US-China-EU Relations: Managing the New World Order*, ed. Robert Ross and Oystein Tunsjo (London: Routledge, 2010), 143–163.

69. See reviews of Chinese leaders' priorities following the major party and government meetings in Robert Sutter, *Positive Equilibrium in US-China Relations: Durable or Not?* (Baltimore: University of Maryland School of Law, 2010), 33–49,

https://digitalcommons.law.umaryland.edu/cgi/viewcontent.cgi?referer=https://www.google.com/&httpsredir=1&article=1198&context=mscas.

70. Ibid.

71. Testimony on US-China relations before the House Foreign Affairs Committee of Deputy Secretary of State John Negroponte, May 1, 2007, https://2001-2009.state.gov/s/d/2007/84118.htm; Cha, "Winning Asia," 98–113.

72. Dumbaugh, *Tibet: Problems, Prospects, and US Policy*.

73. For an overview of the Obama government's approach to China, see notably Bader, *Obama and China's Rise*. See also Robert Sutter, "The Obama Administration and China: Positive but Fragile Equilibrium," *Asian Perspective* 33, no. 3 (2009): 81–106.

74. Bader, *Obama and China's Rise*; Sutter, *Positive Equilibrium in US-China Relations: Durable or Not?*

75. Bonnie Glaser and Brittany Billingsley, "Friction and Cooperation Co-exist Uneasily," *Comparative Connections* 13, no. 2 (September 2011): 27–40; Minxin Pei, "China's Bumpy Ride Ahead," *The Diplomat*, February 16, 2011; Sutter, *Positive Equilibrium in US-China Relations: Durable or Not?*

76. Bader, *Obama and China's Rise*, 69–129; "Interview of Hillary Clinton with Greg Sheridan of the *Australian*," November 8, 2010, https://2009-2017.state.gov/secretary/20092013clinton/rm/2010/11/150671.htm.

77. See assessments of prominent Chinese specialists in Nina Hachigian, ed., *Debating China: The U.S.-China Relationship in Ten Conversations* (New York: Oxford University Press, 2014), and Wu Xinbo, "Chinese Visions of the Future of U.S.-China Relations," in *Tangled Titans: The United States and China*, ed. David Shambaugh (Lanham, MD: Rowman & Littlefield, 2013), 371–88.

78. Christopher Johnson, "Xi Jinping Unveils His Foreign Policy Vision," *Thoughts from the Chairman* (Washington, DC: Center for Strategic and International Studies, December 2014); Yun Sun, "China's Peaceful Rise: Peace through Strength?," *PacNet* 25 (Honolulu, HI: Pacific Forum CSIS, March 31, 2014); Yong Deng, "China: The Post-Responsible Power," *Washington Quarterly* 37, no. 4 (Winter 2015): 117–32.

79. David Shambaugh, "Introduction," in *China and the World*, ed. David Shambaugh (New York: Oxford University Press 2020), 16.

80. Robert Sutter and Satu Limaye, *America's 2016 Election Debate on Asia Policy and Asian Reactions* (Honolulu, HI: East-West Center, 2016), 4–5, 18–28.

81. Robert Sutter, *The United States and Asia*, 2nd ed. (Lanham, MD: Rowman & Littlefield, 2020), 64.

82. Ibid., 64–65.

83. Mark E. Manyin, Stephen Daggett, Ben Dolven, Susan V. Lawrence, Michael F. Martin, Ronald O'Rourke, and Bruce Vaughn, *Pivot to the Pacific? The Obama Administration's "Rebalancing" toward Asia*, CRS Report 42448 (Washington, DC: Congressional Research Service of the Library of Congress, March 28, 2012); Philip Saunders, *The Rebalance to Asia: U.S.-China Relations and Regional Security* (Washington, DC: National Defense University, Institute for National Security Studies, 2012); Richard Ellings, testimony before the House Committee on Foreign Affairs Subcommittee on Asia and the Pacific, Washington, DC, Hearing on the

Obama Administration's Pivot to Asia, December 6, 2016, https://www.nbr.org/publication/step-or-stumble-the-obama-administrations-pivot-to-asia; Choi Kang and Lee Jayhyon, eds., "What Asia Wants from the US: Voices from the Region," Asan Report (Seoul: Asan Institute, September 2018), http://en.asaninst.org/contents/what-asia-wants-from-the-us; Robert Sutter, Michael Brown, and Timothy Adamson, *Balancing Acts: The U.S. Rebalance and Asia-Pacific Stability* (Washington, DC: George Washington University, Elliott School of International Affairs, 2013); Timothy Adamson, Michael Brown, and Robert Sutter, *Rebooting the U.S. Rebalance to Asia* (Washington, DC: George Washington University, Elliott School of International Affairs, 2014). For a book-length compendium on the rebalance, see Hugo Meijer, ed., *Origins and Evolution of the U.S. Rebalance toward Asia: Diplomatic, Military and Economic Dimensions* (London: Palgrave Macmillan, 2015). For an authoritative account of a key US official, see Kurt Campbell, *The Pivot* (New York: Hachette, 2016).

For an overview of US relations with allies and partners in Asia, see Ashley Tellis, Abraham Denmark, and Greg Chaffin, eds., *Strategic Asia 2014–15: U.S. Alliances and Partnerships at the Center of Global Power* (Seattle, WA: National Bureau of Asian Research, 2014). For an in-depth assessment foreseeing gradual American decline in Asia, see Xenia Dormandy, with Rory Kinane, *Asia-Pacific Security: A Changing Role for the United States* (London: Chatham House, Royal Institute of International Affairs, April 2014).

84. This concept dropped from use in 2015 as it was incorporated into the Defense Department's Joint Concept for Access and Maneuver in the Global Commons, https://news.usni.org/2015/01/20/pentagon-drops-air-sea-battle-name-concept-lives. Sutter, *The United States and Asia*, 65.

85. Campbell, *The Pivot*, 267–68.

86. Sutter, *The United States and Asia*, 66.

87. Sutter, Brown, and Adamson, *Balancing Acts: The U.S. Rebalance and Asia-Pacific Stability*.

88. Denny Roy, *Return of the Dragon* (New York: Columbia University Press, 2013); Yun Sun, "China's New Calculations in the South China Sea," *Asia-Pacific Bulletin*, no. 267 (June 10, 2014).

89. "Beyond the US-China Summit," Foreign Policy Research Institute, February 4, 2011.

90. Bonnie Glaser and Brittany Billingsley, "Strains Increase and Leadership Transitions," *Comparative Connections* 14, no. 3 (January 2012): 29–40; Mark Manyin, *Pivot to the Pacific?*

91. Daljit Singh, "US-China Dialogue Process: Prospects and Implications," *East Asia Forum*, November 2, 2012, http://www.eastasisforum.org.

92. Richard Bush, *Uncharted Strait* (Washington, DC: Brookings Institution, 2013), 213–50.

93. Aries Poon, Jenny Hsu, and Fanny Liu, "Taiwan Election Results Likely to Complicate Relations with China," *Wall Street Journal*, December 1, 2014, http://www.wsj.com/articles/taiwan-election-results-set-to-complicate-relations-with-china-1417366150.

94. Bonnie Glaser and Brittany Billingsley, "Xi Visit Steadies Ties; Dissident Creates Tension," *Comparative Connections* 14, no. 1 (May 2012): 29–30; Bonnie Glaser and Brittany Billingsley, "Creating a New Type of Great Power Relations," *Comparative Connections* 14, no. 2 (September 2012): 29.

95. Donilon's speech and US officials' media briefing on the president's Asia trip were released on November 15, 2012, at http://www.whitehouse.gov/the-press-office.

96. Robert Sutter, "Trump, America and the World—2017 and Beyond," H-Diplo/ISSF POLICY Series, January 19, 2019, https://networks.h-net.org/node/28443/discussions/3569933/issf-policy-series-sutter-trump%E2%80%99s-china-policy-bi-partisan.

97. Orville Schell and Susan Shirk, *US Policy toward China* (New York: Asia Society, 2017).

98. Robert Sutter, "Obama's Cautious and Calibrated Approach to an Assertive China," *YaleGlobal online*, April 23, 2016, https://www.eurasiareview.com/23042016-obamas-cautious-and-calibrated-approach-to-an-assertive-china-analysis.

99. Author consultations with US administration officials, Washington, DC, August 2016.

100. Sutter and Limaye, *America's 2016 Election Debate*, 20.

101. Sutter, "Obama's Cautious and Calibrated Approach to an Assertive China"; Jeffrey Bader, "A Framework for U.S. Policy toward China," Asia Working Group Paper 3, March 2016, Brookings, https://www.brookings.edu/wp-content/uploads/2016/07/us-china-policy-framework-bader-1.pdf; Deputy Secretary Blinken Testimony on US-China Relations: Strategic Challenges and Opportunities, Senate Foreign Relations Committee, April 27, 2016.

102. David M. Lampton, "A Tipping Point in U.S.-China Relations Is upon Us," *US-China Perception Monitor*, May 11, 2015; Harry Harding, "Has U.S. China Policy Failed?" *Washington Quarterly* 38, no. 3 (2015): 95–122.

103. Sutter, "'Obama's Cautious and Calibrated Approach to an Assertive China."

104. Ibid.

105. "China's ZTE to Pay Massive U.S. Fine over Iran, North Korea Sanctions Busting," Euronews, March 7, 2017, http://www.euronews.com/2017/03/07/china-s-zte-to-pay-massive-us-fine-over-iran-north-korea-sanctions-busting.

106. Author consultations with US administration officials, Washington, DC, August 2016.

107. Robert Sutter and Chin-Hao Huang, "Countering Adverse Tribunal Ruling," *Comparative Connections* 18, no. 2 (September 2016): 59–69.

108. Sutter, "'Obama's Cautious and Calibrated Approach to an Assertive China."

109. Ibid; author consultations with US administration officials, Washington, DC, August 2016.

110. Republican National Committee, *Republican Platform 2016*, https://prod-cdn-static.gop.com/media/documents/DRAFT_12_FINAL%5B1%5D-ben_1468872234.pdf.

111. Candidate Trump notably called for Japan and South Korea to pay more for America's defense, and if they didn't, he advocated US withdrawal. He allowed that the powers then might seek to develop nuclear weapons, which he viewed as an

unfortunate but unavoidable consequence. On North Korea, Mr. Trump called for direct talks between US and North Korean leaders. The coverage of the US election in this chapter builds on the findings in Robert Sutter and Satu Limaye, *America's 2016 Election Debate on Asia Policy and Asian Reactions* (Honolulu, HI: East-West Center, 2016).

CHAPTER SEVEN

1. Joe Biden, "My Trip Is about America Rallying the World's Democracies," *Washington Post*, June 6, 2021, A25; David Brunnstrom, Alexandra Alper, and Yew Lun Tian, "China Will 'Eat Our Lunch,' Biden Warns after Clashing with Xi on Most Fronts," Reuters, February 10, 2021.

2. Kinling Lo, "Donald Trump Tweets from Beijing about His 'Unforgettable Afternoon' with Xi Jinping," *South China Morning Post*, November 8, 2017, https://www.scmp.com/news/china/society/article/2119016/trump-tweets-beijing-about-his-unforgettable-afternoon-xi-jinping.

3. "Special Report: China and America," *The Economist*, May 16, 2019, https://www.economist.com/special-report/2019/05/16/trade-can-no-longer-anchor-americas-relationship-with-china; Robert Sutter, "Trump, America and the World—2017 and Beyond," H-Diplo/ISSF POLICY Series, January 19, 2019, https://networks.h-net.org/node/28443/discussions/3569933/issf-policy-series-sutter-trump%E2%80%99s-china-policy-bi-partisan; White House, *National Security Strategy of the United States*, December 2017, https://www.whitehouse.gov/wp-content/uploads/2017/12/NSS-Final-12-18-2017-0905.pdf; US Department of Defense, *Summary of the National Defense Strategy of the United States*, January 2018, https://www.defense.gov/Portals/1/Documents/pubs/2018-National-Defense-Strategy-Summary.pdf.

4. Tony Romm, "Senate Approves $250 Billion to Trim China's Ambitions," *Washington Post*, June 9, 2021, A18; David Sanger, Catie Edmondson, David McCabe, and Thomas Kaplan, "In Rare Show of Unity, Senate Poised to Pass a Bill to Counter China," *New York Times*, June 7, 2021, A10.

5. Maggie Haberman, "Donald Trump Says He Favors Big Tariffs on Chinese Exports," New York Times, January 7, 2016, http://www.nytimes.com/politics/first-draft/2016/01/07/donald-trump-says-he-favors-big-tariffs-on-chinese-exports; Donald Trump, "'America First' Foreign Policy Speech," Washington, DC, April 27, 2016.

6. Robert Sutter and Satu Limaye, *America's 2016 Election Debate on Asia Policy and Asian Reactions* (Honolulu: East-West Center, 2016), 21.

7. Robert Sutter, "The United States and Asia in 2017," *Asian Survey* 58, no. 1 (2018): 10–20.

8. Bonnie Glaser and Collin Norkiewicz, "North Korea and Trade Dominate the Agenda," *Comparative Connections* 19, no. 2 (September 2017): 21–34.

9. Bonnie Glaser and Kelly Flaherty, "Hurtling toward a Trade War," *Comparative Connections* 20, no. 1 (May 2018): 19–22; these various events are reviewed in Sutter, "Trump, America and the World—2017 and Beyond."

10. White House, *National Security Strategy of the United States*, December 2017, https://www.whitehouse.gov/wp-content/uploads/2017/12/NSS-Final-12-18-2017-0905.pdf; US Department of Defense, *Summary of the National Defense Strategy of the United States*, January 2018, https://www.defense.gov/Portals/1/Documents/pubs/2018-National-Defense-Strategy-Summary.pdf.

11. David Lynch, "Trump's Raise the Stakes Strategy," *Washington Post*, July 21, 2018, A14; for an overview of developments, see Robert Sutter, "Pushback: America's New China Strategy," *The Diplomat*, November 2, 2018, https://thediplomat.com/2018/11/pushback-americas-new-china-strategy.

12. Chicago Council on Global Affairs, "China Not Yet Seen as a Threat by the American Public," October 19, 2018.

13. The discussion of congressional actions in the remainder of this section is taken from Robert Sutter, "Congress and Trump Administration China Policy," *Journal of Contemporary China* 28, no. 118 (2019): 519–37, https://www.tandfonline.com/doi/full/10.1080/10670564.2018.1557944.

14. Reviewed in Sutter, "Trump, America and the World—2017 and Beyond."

15. US Congress, House Armed Services Committee, "Reform and Rebuild: The Next Steps—National Defense Authorization Act FY-2019," July 2018, https://republicans-armedservices.house.gov/sites/republicans.armedservices.house.gov/files/wysiwyg_uploaded/FY19%20NDAA%20Conference%20Summary%20.pdf.

16. "Bipartisan Group of Senators Urge Administration to Safeguard Critical Military and Dual-Use Technology from China," United States Senate Release, May 22, 2018, https://www.cornyn.senate.gov/content/news/bipartisan-group-senators-urge-administration-safeguard-critical-military-and-dual-use; "Senators Urge Trump Administration to Counter Chinese Meddling in Democracies," *Daily Beast*, June 12, 2018, http://commentators.com/senators-urge-trump-administration-to-counter-chinese-meddling-in-democracies; Siobhan Hughes and Josh Zumbrun, "Senators Signal Concerns over China's Global Investments," *Wall Street Journal*, August 5, 2018, https://www.wsj.com/articles/senators-signal-concerns-over-chinas-global-investments-1533517099.

17. Bill Gertz, "Congress to Crack Down on Chinese Influence in US," *Washington Free Beacon*, June 4, 2018, http://freebeacon.com/national-security/congress-crack-chinese-influence-u-s; "Bipartisan Group of Senators"; "Senators Urge Trump"; "Senators Signal Concerns."

18. Burgess Everett, "Republicans Gobsmacked by Trump's Tariffs," *Politico*, May 31, 2018, https://www.politico.com/story/2018/05/31/trump-tariffs-canada-mexico-republican-response-615479.

19. Shannon Tiezzi, "Brace Yourselves: The US-China Trade War Is about to Begin," *The Diplomat*, June 5, 2018, https://thediplomat.com/2018/06/brace-yourselves-the-us-china-trade-war-is-about-to-begin; Lara Seligman, "Congress Caves to Trump in Fight over China's ZTE," *Foreign Policy*, July 26, 2018.

20. Bonnie Glaser and Kelly Flaherty, "Hurtling toward a Trade War," *Comparative Connections* 20, no. 1 (2018): 23.

21. Jackson Diehl, "Taiwan Seems to Be Benefiting from Trump's Presidency," *Washington Post*, April 29, 2018, https://www.washingtonpost.com/opinions/

global-opinions/taiwan-seems-to-be-benefiting-from-trumps-presidency-so-why-is-no-one-celebrating/2018/04/29/f5d38166-4966-11e8-827e-190efaf1f1ee_story. html?utm_term=.e5c764f91b55; Zhenhua Lu, "To Avoid Beijing's Ire, Trump Won't Send High-Level Officials to Opening of De-Facto Embassy in Taiwan," *South China Morning Post*, June 5, 2018, https://www.politico.com/story/2018/06/05/trump-china-taiwan-embassy-598150.

22. *Reform and Rebuild: The Next Steps*; Vivian Salama, "Trump Signs Defense Bill to Boost Military, Target China," *Wall Street Journal*, August 13, 2018, https://www.wsj.com/articles/trump-signs-defense-bill-to-boost-military-target-china-1534196930.

23. See Sutter, "Pushback: America's New China Strategy"; see also Robert Sutter, "United States and Asia 2018," *Asian Survey* 59, no. 1 (2019): 10–20.

24. US Special Trade Representative, *Update Concerning China's Acts, Policies and Practices*, November 20, 2018, https://ustr.gov/sites/default/files/enforcement/301Investigations/301%20Report%20Update.pdf; "China Releases White Paper on Facts and Its Position on Trade Friction with US," *Xinhua*, September 24, 2018, http://www.xinhuanet.com/english/2018-09/24/c_137490176.htm.

25. The developments in these two paragraphs are reviewed in Sutter, "Trump, America and the World—2017 and Beyond." See also discussion in "Special Report: China and America."

26. For coverage of developments in late 2018, see Bonnie Glaser, "US-China Relations," *Comparative Connections* 20, no. 3 (2019): 21–30; see also Sutter, "Trump, America and the World—2017 and Beyond" and "Special Report China and America."

27. Sutter, "Trump, America and the World—2017 and Beyond."

28. Sutter, "The United States and Asia 2018."

29. Robert Sutter, "Washington's 'Whole of Government' Pushback against Chinese Challenges—Implications and Outlook," *PacNet* 26, Pacific Forum CSIS, April 23, 2019, https://www.pacforum.org/sites/default/files/20190423_PacNet_26.pdf.

30. "Special Report China and America," 5; Mark Warner, "The China Challenge and Critical Next Steps for the United States," Brookings Institution, May 15, 2019, https://www.brookings.edu/blog/order-from-chaos/2019/05/15/the-china-challenge-and-critical-next-steps-for-the-united-states/; James Hohmann, "Marco Rubio Slams CEO for Bad China Deals," *Powerpost*, May 15, 2019, https://www.washingtonpost.com/news/powerpost/paloma/daily-202/2019/05/15/daily-202-marco-rubio-slams-ceos-for-bad-china-deals-short-term-thinking-and-not-investing-in-u-s-workers/5cdaf5841ad2e544f001dd1a/?utm_term=.c2bd79e6cad2.

31. Justin McCarthy, "Americans' Favorable Views of China Take a 12 Point Hit," *Gallup News*, March 11, 2019, https://news.gallup.com/poll/247559/americans-favorable-views-china-point-hit.aspx.

32. Reviewed in Sutter, "Washington's 'Whole of Government' Pushback"; see also Ben Schreckinger, "CPAC's New Boogeyman: China," *Politico*, February 28, 2019, https://www.politico.com/story/2019/02/28/cpac-conservatives-china-1194212.

33. Bonnie Glaser, "The Diplomatic Relationship," in *Tangled Titans: United States and China*, ed. David Shambaugh (Lanham, MD: Rowman & Littlefield, 2013), 172–76.

34. Shannon Tiezzi, "Is a Thaw Coming in US-China Relations?," *The Diplomat*, November 7, 2018, https://thediplomat.com/2018/11/is-a-thaw-coming-in-us-china-relations.

35. Robert Sutter, *US-China Relations: Perilous Past, Uncertain Present* (Lanham, MD: Rowman & Littlefield, 2018), 156.

36. Evan Medeiros, "China Reacts: Assessing Beijing's Response to Trump's New China Strategy," *The China Leadership Monitor*, March 1, 2019, https://www.prcleader.org/medeiros.

37. Sources for the evidence discussed below are Robert Sutter, "Has US Government Angst over the China Danger Diminished?," East-West Center Washington, Asia-Pacific Bulletin No. 497, January 22, 2020, https://www.eastwestcenter.org/publications/has-us-government-angst-over-the-china-danger-diminished; Bonnie Glaser and Kelly Flaherty, "US-China Relations Hit New Lows amid Pandemic," *Comparative Connections* 22, no. 1 (May 2020): 28–39; "Episode 135: How Might a Democratic President Deal with China?," Carnegie-Tsinghua Center for Global Policy: China in the World (podcast transcript), June 25, 2019, https://carnegieendowment.org/files/Episode_-_How_Might_a_Democratic_President_Deal_with_China_1.pdf; Craig Kafura, "American Favor US-China Trade, Split over Tariffs," The Chicago Council on Global Affairs, September 3, 2019, https://www.thechicagocouncil.org/publication/lcc/americans-favor-us-china-trade-split-over-tariffs; Ryan Hass, "Why Has China Become Such a Big Political Issue?," Brookings Institution, November 15, 2019, https://www.brookings.edu/policy2020/votervital/why-has-china-become-such-a-big-political-issue/; Richard Fontaine, "Great-Power Competition Is Washington's Top Priority—but Not the Public's," *Foreign Affairs*, September 9, 2019, https://www.foreignaffairs.com/articles/china/2019-09-09/great-power-competition-washingtons-top-priority-not-publics; Kathrin Hille, "US 'Surgical' Attack on Huawei Will Reshape Tech Supply Chain," *Financial Times*, May 18, 2020, https://www.ft.com/content/c614afc5-86f8-42b1-9b6c-90bffbd1be8b; Democratic candidates' remarks taken from East-West Center Washington, "2020 US Presidential Candidates on the Indo-Pacific."

38. Jordan Fabian, Nick Wadhams, and *Bloomberg*, "John Bolton's New Book Claims Trump Sought Xi Jinping's Help to Win 2020 Election," *Fortune*, June 17, 2020, https://fortune.com/2020/06/17/john-bolton-book-trump-2020-xi-china/.

39. Sutter, "Has US Government Angst over the China Danger Diminished?"

40. "Episode 135: How Might a Democratic President Deal with China?"

41. Kafura, "American Favor US-China Trade, Split over Tariffs"; Hass, "Why Has China Become Such a Big Political Issue?"; Fontaine, "Great-Power Competition Is Washington's Top Priority."

42. "Attorney General William Barr Delivers the Keynote Address to the Department of Justice's China Initiative Conference," Department of Justice News, February 6, 2020, https://www.justice.gov/opa/speech/attorney-general-william-p-barr-delivers-keynote-address-department-justices-china.

43. Ren Qi, "Anti-China Stance at Munich Security Conference Criticized," *China Daily*, February 18, 2020, https://www.chinadaily.com.cn/a/202002/18/WS5e4b47b5a310128217278510.html.

44. Josh Rogin, "Covid-19 Sparks Unity on US China Policy," *Washington Post*, May 22, 2020, A23.

45. Kat Devlin, Laura Silver, and Christine Huang, "US Views of China Increasingly Negative amid Coronavirus Outbreak," Pew Research Center, April 21, 2020, https://www.pewresearch.org/global/2020/04/21/u-s-views-of-china-increasingly-negative-amid-coronavirus-outbreak/; Marc Caputo, "Anti-China Sentiment Is on the Rise," *Politico*, May 20, 2020, https://www.politico.com/news/2020/05/20/anti-china-sentiment-coronavirus-poll-269373.

46. Jonathan Martin and Maggie Haberman, "GOP Aiming to Make China the Scapegoat," *New York Times*, April 19, 2020, A1; David Lynch, "President Ties Trade Angst to China's Virus Response," *Washington Post*, May 16, 2020, A1; Emily Rauhala, Teo Armus, and Gerry Shih, "With Ultimatum, Trump Deepens Crisis with World Health Organization," *Washington Post*, May 20, 2020, A29; Morgan Phillips, "Trump on China Trade Deal," Fox News, May 19, 2020, https://www.foxnews.com/politics/trump-china-trade-deal-i-feel-differently. Daniel Lynch and Emily Rauhala, "Trump Lashes Out at China, Orders Action on Hong Kong," *Washington Post*, May 30, 2020, A1.

47. Department of Defense, *Indo-Pacific Strategy Report* (Washington, DC: Department of Defense, July 2019), https://media.defense.gov/2019/Jul/01/2002152311/-1/-1/1/DEPARTMENT-OF-DEFENSE-INDO-PACIFIC-STRATEGY-REPORT-2019.PDF; Joel Wuthnow, *Just Another Paper Tiger? Chinese Perspectives on the US Indo-Pacific Strategy*, National Defense University Report SF no. 305, June 2020; Department of State, *A Free and Open Indo-Pacific* (Washington, DC: Department of State, November 4, 2019), https://www.state.gov/wp-content/uploads/2019/11/Free-and-Open-Indo-Pacific-4Nov2019.pdf.

48. Robert Sutter, *The United States and Asia: Regional Dynamics and Twenty-First Century Relations*, 2nd ed. (Lanham, MD: Rowman & Littlefield, 2020), 112–13, 115–16.

49. Sutter, "Washington's 'Whole of Government' Pushback"; Robert Sutter and Chin Hao Huang, "China-Southeast Asia Relations," *Comparative Connections* 21, no. 3 (January 2020).

50. "Attorney General William Barr Delivers the Keynote Address to the Department of Justice's China Initiative Conference," Department of Justice News, February 6, 2020, https://www.justice.gov/opa/speech/attorney-general-william-p-barr-delivers-keynote-address-department-justices-china; Ren Qi, "Anti-China Stance at Munich Security Conference Criticized," *China Daily*, February 18, 2020, https://www.chinadaily.com.cn/a/202002/18/WS5e4b47b5a310128217278510.html; Glaser and Flaherty, "US-China Relations Hit New Lows amid Pandemic," 32–34, 39; Robert Sutter and Chin-Hao Huang, "From Low Priority to High Tensions," *Comparative Connections* 22, no. 1 (May 2020): 65–67.

51. Glaser and Flaherty, "US-China Relations Hit New Lows amid Pandemic," 28–32.

52. Caputo, "Anti-China Sentiment Is on the Rise."

53. Martin and Haberman, "GOP Aiming to Make China the Scapegoat"; William Davis, "Trump Calls Himself 'the Chosen One' to Take on China," *The Daily Caller*, August 21, 2019, https://dailycaller.com/2019/08/21/

donald-trump-chosen-one-china-israel/; May 10, 2020, Trump retweet received by author.

54. Martin and Haberman, "GOP Aiming to Make China the Scapegoat"; Lynch, "President Ties Trade Angst to China's Virus Response"; Rauhala, Armus, and Shih, "With Ultimatum, Trump Deepens Crisis with World Health Organization"; Phillips, "Trump on China Trade Deal."

55. Josh Rogin, "Trump's China Hawks Are on the Loose," *Washington Post*, June 26, 2020, A23; Lynch and Rauhala, "Trump Lashes Out at China"; Robert Lighthizer, "The Era of Offshoring US Jobs Is Over," *New York Times*, May 12, 2020, A27; Hille, "US 'Surgical' Attack on Huawei Will Reshape Tech Supply Chain."

56. Steven Lee Myers, "China's Military Provokes Its Neighbors but the Message Is for the United States," *New York Times*, June 26, 2020, https://www.nytimes.com/2020/06/26/international-home/china-military-india-taiwan.html.

57. Edward Wong and Steven Lee Myers, "Hawks Set China and US on Path to Lasting Divide," *New York Times*, July 26, 2020, A1; Meredith McGraw, "Trump Accelerates China Punishments in Time for Reelection," *Politico*, July 22, 2020, https://www.politico.com/news/2020/07/22/trump-china-punishments-reelection-377405; "Would a Biden Administration Be Softer Than Trump on China?," *The Economist*, July 29, 2020, https://www.economist.com/united-states/2020/07/30/would-a-biden-administration-be-softer-than-trump-on-china.

58. Robert Sutter and Satu Limaye, *A Hardening US-China Competition: Asia Policy in America's 2020 Elections and Asian Responses* (Honolulu, HI: East-West Center, 2020).

59. Sutter and Huang, "China-Southeast Asia Relations."

60. "US Extends Condolence to India," *The Tribune* (India), June 19, 2020, https://www.tribuneindia.com/news/world/us-extends-condolences-to-india-on-loss-of-its-soldiers-lives-in-clashes-with-chinese-troops-101316.

61. Wong and Myers, "Hawks Set China and US on Path to Lasting Divide."

62. Dan Haverty and Augusta Saraiva, "When It Comes to China, Americans Think Like Trump," *Foreign Policy*, July 30, 2020, https://foreignpolicy.com/2020/07/30/pew-research-trump-china-american-public/; Laura Silver, Kat Delvin, and Christine Huang, "Americans Fault China for Its Role in the Spread of COVID-19," Pew Research Center, July 30, 2020, https://www.pewresearch.org/global/2020/07/30/americans-fault-china-for-its-role-in-the-spread-of-covid-19/.

63. Bonnie Glaser and Hannah Price, "Joe Biden Is Elected President amid a Plummeting US-China Relationship," *Comparative Connections* 22, no. 3 (January 2021): 29–39.

64. Ibid.; Bonnie Glaser and Hannah Price, "Continuity Prevails in Biden's First 100 Days," *Comparative Connections* 23, no. 1 (May 2021): 29–37.

65. Robert Sutter, "Testimony before the US-China Economic and Security Review Commission Hearing on US-China Relations at the Chinese Communist Party Centennial, Panel I—The State of US-China Relations Heading into 2021," https://www.uscc.gov/sites/default/files/2021-01/Robert_Sutter_Testimony.pdf.

66. Robert Sutter, "China's Foreign Behavior Warrants Sustained US Countermeasures," *PacNet* 59, October 29, 2020, https://pacforum.org/publication/

pacnet-59-chinas-foreign-behavior-warrants-sustained-us-countermeasures; Ryan Hass, "How China Is Responding to Escalating Strategic Competition with the US," *China Leadership Monitor*, March 1, 2021, https://www.prcleader.org/hass.

67. Sutter and Limaye, *A Hardening US-China Competition: Asia Policy in America's 2020 Elections and Asian Responses*, 20–22, 73.

68. The interview is available at https://www.youtube.com/watch?v=kSAo_1mJg0g.

69. Sutter and Limaye, *A Hardening US-China Competition: Asia Policy in America's 2020 Elections and Asian Responses*, 22; Hass, "How China Is Responding."

70. "China Plays Up Ascendancy Over West as It Sets Economic Path," *Wall Street Journal*, March 4, 2021, https://www.wsj.com/articles/china-plays-up-ascendancy-over-west-as-it-sets-economic-path-11614854159.

71. Yuan Peng, "The New Coronavirus Epidemic Situation and Centennial Changes," in 袁鹏, "新冠疫情与百年变局," June 17, 2020, http://www.aisixiang.com/data/121742.html, translated in *Reading the China Dream*, https://www.readingthechinadream.com/yuan-peng-coronavirus-pandemic.html.

72. Sutter, Testimony.

73. Hass, "How China Is Responding"; Sutter, Testimony.

74. Ralph Cossa and Brad Glosserman, "Change in Style, Continuity in Asia Policy," *Comparative Connections* 23, no. 1 (May 2021): 1–7.

75. Sutter and Huang, "China-Southeast Asia Relations," 70–72; Nick Aspinwall, "Biden Delegation Pledges US Support for Taiwan Self-Defense," *The Diplomat*, April 17, 2021, https://thediplomat.com/2021/04/biden-delegation-pledges-us-support-for-taiwan-self-defense/.

76. US-China Policy Foundation Newsletter, "US View of China Competition," May 21, 2021, https://uscpf.org/v3/2021/05/21/us-china-competition/.

77. Romm, "Senate Approves $250 Billion to Trim China's Ambitions"; Sanger et al., "In Rare Show of Unity, Senate Poised to Pass a Bill to Counter China."

78. Simon Lester and Huan Zhu, *The US-China Trade War: Is There an End in Sight?* (CATO Institute, Winter 2020), https://www.cato.org/cato-journal/winter-2020/us-china-trade-war-there-end-sight; Yen Nee Lee, "US Businesses Are Bearing the Brunt of Trump's China Tariffs," *CNBC*, May 18, 2021.

79. Richard Bush, Bonnie Glaser, and Ryan Hass, "Don't Help China by Hyping Risk of War over Taiwan," *NPR*, April 8, 2021, https://www.npr.org/2021/04/08/984524521/opinion-dont-help-china-by-hyping-risk-of-war-over-taiwan.

80. "Open Letter: China Is Not an Enemy," National Committee on U.S. China Relations, July 2019, https://www.ncuscr.org/news/open-letter-china-is-not-the-enemy

CHAPTER EIGHT

1. Ren Xiao and Liu Ming, *Chinese Perspectives on International Relations in the Xi Jinping Era* (Seattle, WA: National Bureau of Asian Research, June 2020); Peter Gries, "Nationalism, Social Influences, and Chinese Foreign Policy," in *China and the World*, ed. David Shambaugh (New York: Oxford University Press, 2020); Aaron

Friedberg, "Competing with China," *Survival* 60, no. 3 (June 2018): 7–64; Elizabeth Economy, *The Third Revolution: Xi Jinping and The New Chinese State* (New York: Council on Foreign Relations, 2018).

2. Satoru Mori, "US Technological Competition with China: The Military, Industrial and Digital Network Dimensions," *Asia-Pacific Review* 26, no. 1 (2019): 77–120; Elsa Kania, "Technology and Innovation in China's Strategy and Global Influence," in *China's Global Influence*, ed. Scott McDonald and Michael Burgoyne (Honolulu, HI: Asia-Pacific Center for Security Studies, 2020), 229–46; Graham Allison, "Is China Beating America to AI Supremacy?," *National Interest*, December 22, 2019, https://nationalinterest.org/feature/china-beating-america-ai-supremacy-106861. A useful framework for understanding recent American debate on this issue is in Kenneth Boutin, *Economic Security and Sino-American Relations* (Northamton, MA: Edward Elgar, 2019).

3. Ryan Hass, *Stronger: Adapting America's China Policy in an Age of Competitive Interdependence* (Washington, DC: Brookings Institution, 2021); Evan Medeiros, "The Changing Fundamentals of US-China Relations," *The Washington Quarterly* 42, no. 3 (Fall 2019): 93–119; Wu Xinbo, "The China Challenge," *The Washington Quarterly* 43, no. 3 (Fall 2020): 99–114; Wang Dong and Travis Tanner, eds., *Avoiding the "Thucydides Trap": US-China Relations in Strategic Domains* (New York: Routledge, 2020); Timothy Heath, Derek Grossman, and Asha Clark, *China's Quest for Global Dominance* (Washington, DC: RAND Corporation, 2021); Evan Medeiros, "Major Power Rivalry in East Asia," Council on Foreign Relations Discussion Paper, April 2021.

4. In addition to sources noted in chapter 4, see Wang Zhongchun, "The Soviet Factor in Sino-American Normalization, 1969–1979," in *Normalization of U.S.-China Relations*, ed. William Kirby, Robert Ross, and Gong Li (Cambridge, MA: Harvard University Press, 2005), 147–174.

5. John Garver, *Foreign Relations of the People's Republic of China* (Englewood Cliffs, NJ: Prentice Hall, 1993), 166–77, 310–11.

6. James Mann, *About Face: A History of America's Curious Relationship with China, from Nixon to Clinton* (New York: Knopf, 1999), 33–35.

7. Garver, *Foreign Relations of the People's Republic of China*, 166–73; Harry Harding, *A Fragile Relationship: The United States and China since 1972* (Washington, DC: Brookings Institution, 1992), 119–22, 332–33.

8. House Committee on Foreign Affairs, Subcommittee on Asian and Pacific Affairs, *Playing the China Card: Implications for United States-Soviet Union-Chinese Relations* (Washington, DC: US Government Printing Office, 1979).

9. Robert Sutter, *The China Quandary: Domestic Determinants of U.S. China Policy, 1972–1982* (Boulder, CO: Westview Press, 1983), 99–100, 111–26.

10. Mann, *About Face*, 98–100, 109–14; Yitzhak Shichor, "The Great Wall of Steel: Military and Strategy in Xinjiang," in *Xinjiang: China's Muslim Borderland*, ed. S. Frederick Starr (Armonk, NY: M. E. Sharpe, 2004), 148–50.

11. Harding, *A Fragile Relationship*, 224–34.

12. David M. Lampton, *Same Bed, Different Dreams: Managing U.S.-China Relations, 1989–2000* (Berkeley: University of California Press, 2001), 39–63; Jean

Garrison, *Making China Policy: From Nixon to G. W. Bush* (Boulder, CO: Lynne Rienner, 2005), 165–72.

13. Shirley Kan, *U.S.-China Military Contacts: Issue for Congress*, CRS Report RL32496 (Washington, DC: Congressional Research Service of the Library of Congress, April 15, 2009), 6–11.

14. Lampton, *Same Bed, Different Dreams*, 71–110.

15. The Chinese reactions and motivations concerning these developments are reviewed in Lampton, *Same Bed, Different Dreams*, and Robert Suettinger, *Beyond Tiananmen: The Politics of U.S.-China Relations, 1989–2000* (Washington, DC: Brookings Institution, 2003).

16. Robert Sutter, *China's Rise in Asia* (Lanham, MD: Rowman & Littlefield, 2005), 265–78; People's Republic of China State Council Information Office, "China's Peaceful Development Road," *People's Daily Online*, December 22, 2005, http://english.peopledaily.com.cn/200512/22/eng20051222_230059.html; "Full Text of Chinese President Hu Jintao's Speech at Opening Session of Boao Forum," *China Daily*, April 15, 2011, www.chinadaily.com.cn/china/2011-04/15/content_12335312.htm.

17. Bonnie Glaser and Evan Medeiros, "The Ecology of Foreign Policy Decision-Making in China: The Ascension and Demise of the Theory of Peaceful Rise," *China Quarterly* 190 (June 2007): 291–310.

18. Sutter, *China's Rise in Asia*, 265–76.

19. Avery Goldstein, *Rising to the Challenge: China's Grand Strategy and International Security* (Stanford, CA: Stanford University Press, 2005).

20. Robert Sutter, *Chinese Foreign Relations: Power and Policy since the Cold War* (Lanham, MD: Rowman & Littlefield, 2008), 177.

21. Ibid., 178.

22. David M. Lampton, *The Three Faces of Chinese Power: Might, Money, and Minds* (Berkeley: University of California Press, 2008), 27.

23. People's Republic of China State Council Information Office, "China's Peaceful Development Road," *People's Daily Online*, December 22, 2005, http://english.peopledaily.com.cn/200512/22/eng20051222_230059.html; "Full Text of Chinese President Hu Jintao's Speech at Opening Session of Boao Forum," *China Daily*, April 15, 2011, www.chinadaily.com.cn/china/2011-04/15/content_12335312.htm; People's Republic of China State Council Information Office, "China's National Defense in 2004" (Beijing, December 27, 2004); People's Republic of China State Council Information Office, "China's National Defense in 2006" (Beijing, December 29, 2006); People's Republic of China State Council Information Office, "China's National Defense in 2008" (Beijing, January 2009); People's Republic of China State Council Information Office, "China's National Defense in 2010" (Beijing, March 2011).

24. Briefings, Academy of Military Science, Beijing, June 2008 and June 2011; briefings by senior representatives of the academy at a public meeting at Georgetown University, Washington, DC, October 2, 2008.

25. Paul Godwin, "China as a Major Asian Power: The Implications of Its Military Modernization (A View from the United States)," in *China, the United States, and*

Southeast Asia: Contending Perspectives on Politics, Security, and Economics, ed. Evelyn Goh and Sheldon Simon (New York: Routledge, 2008), 145–66; Ashley J. Tellis and Travis Tanner, eds., *Strategic Asia 2012–2013: China's Military Challenge* (Seattle, WA: National Bureau of Asian Research, 2012); Chu Shulong and Lin Xinzhu, "It Is Not the Objective of Chinese Military Power to Catch Up and Overtake the United States," *Beijing Huanqiu Shibao*, June 26, 2008, 11; Christopher Twomey, "The Military-Security Relationship," in *Tangled Titans: The United States and China*, ed. David Shambaugh (Lanham, MD: Rowman & Littlefield, 2012), 235–62.

26. United States Department of Defense, *Annual Report on the Military Power of the People's Republic of China, 2009* (Washington, DC: US Department of Defense, March 2009); United States Department of Defense, *Annual Report to Congress: Military and Security Developments Involving the People's Republic of China 2012*, https://www.defense.gov/Portals/1/Documents/pubs/2012_CMPR_Final.pdf.

27. People's Republic of China State Council Information Office, "China's National Defense in 2004," 2–4.

28. Andrew Scobell and Larry M. Wortzel, eds., *Shaping China's Security Environment: The Role of the PLA* (Carlisle, PA: Strategic Studies Institute, US Army War College, 2006), 2; Andrew Nathan and Andrew Scobell, *China's Search for Security* (New York: Columbia University Press, 2012).

29. Briefings, Beijing, June 2008; Georgetown University, Washington, DC, October 2, 2008.

30. Hu Xiao, "Japan and U.S. Told, Hands Off Taiwan," *China Daily*, March 7, 2005, 1; for background see Michael Yahuda, *Sino-Japanese Relations after the Cold War* (New York: Routledge, 2014).

31. "China-Southeast Asia Relations," *Comparative Connections* 9, no. 3 (October 2007): 75.

32. Robert Sutter, Michael Brown, and Timothy Adamson, *Balancing Acts: The U.S. Rebalance and Asia-Pacific Stability* (Washington, DC: George Washington University, Elliott School of International Affairs, 2013); Timothy Adamson, Michael Brown, and Robert Sutter, *Rebooting the U.S. Rebalance to Asia* (Washington, DC: George Washington University, Elliott School of International Affairs, 2014).

33. On the military aspects of the Obama government's reengagement policies, see Mark Manyin, Steven Daggett, Ben Dolvin, Susan Lawrence, Michael Martin, and Ronald O'Rourke., *Pivot to the Pacific? The Obama Administration's "Rebalancing" toward Asia*, CRS Report 42448 (Washington, DC: Congressional Research Service of the Library of Congress, March 28, 2012), and Kurt Campbell, *The Pivot* (New York: Twelve-Hachette Book Group, 2016).

34. Robert Sutter, *Chinese Foreign Relations: Power and Policy of an Emerging Global Force* (Lanham, MD: Rowman & Littlefield, 2021), 301–3.

35. Robert Sutter, "Obama's Cautious and Calibrated Approach to an Assertive China," *YaleGlobal online*, April 23, 2016, https://www.eurasiareview.com/23042016-obamas-cautious-and-calibrated-approach-to-an-assertive-china-analysis.

36. White House, *National Security Strategy of the United States*, December 2017, https://www.whitehouse.gov/wp-content/uploads/2017/12/NSS-Final-12-18-2017-0905.pdf; US Department of Defense, *Summary of the National*

Defense Strategy of the United States, January 2018, https://www.defense.gov/Portals/1/Documents/pubs/2018-National-Defense-Strategy-Summary.pdf.

37. United States Department of Defense, *Annual Report to Congress . . . 2012*; Nathan and Scobell, *China's Search for Security*; Tellis and Tanner, eds., *Strategic Asia 2012–2013*; Ian Rinehart, *The Chinese Military: Overview and Issues for Congress*, CRS Report 44196 (Washington, DC: Congressional Research Service of the Library of Congress, March 24, 2016); "Full Text: China's National Defense in the New Era," *Xinhua*, July 24, 2019, http://www.xinhuanet.com/english/2019-07/24/c_138253389.htm; Anthony Cordesman, *China's New Defense White Paper* (Washington, DC: Center for Strategic and International Studies, July 24, 2019), https://csis-prod.s3.amazonaws.com/s3fs-public/publication/190724_China_2019_Defense.pdf; Department of Defense, "Annual Report to Congress: Military and Security Developments Involving the People's Republic of China 2020," https://media.defense.gov/2020/Sep/01/2002488689/-1/-1/1/2020-DOD-CHINA-MILITARY-POWER-REPORT-FINAL.PDF; *China's Naval Modernization*, Congressional Research Service Report RL33153, March 7, 2021; Caitlin Campbell, *China's Military, The People's Liberation Army*, Congressional Research Service Report R46808, June 4, 2021.

38. Robert S. Ross, "The Geography of Peace: East Asia in the Twenty-First Century," *International Security* 23, no. 4 (Spring 1999): 81–118.

39. Aaron Friedberg, *A Contest for Supremacy: China, America, and the Struggle for Mastery in Asia* (New York: W. W. Norton, 2011); Elsa Kania and Peter Wood, "Major Themes in China's 2019 Defense White Paper," *Jamestown Foundation China Brief* 19, no. 14 (July 31, 2019), https://jamestown.org/program/major-themes-in-chinas-2019-national-defense-white-paper; US Defense Intelligence Agency, *China Military Power* (Washington, DC: US Defense Intelligence Agency, 2019), https://www.dia.mil/Portals/27/Documents/News/Military%20Power%20Publications/China_Military_Power_FINAL_5MB_20190103.pdf.

40. Kan, *U.S.-China Military Contacts*.

41. Evan Medeiros, *Reluctant Restraint: The Evolution of China's Nonproliferation Policies and Practices, 1980–2004* (Stanford, CA: Stanford University Press, 2007).

42. Bonnie S. Glaser, "China's Policy in the Wake of the Second DPRK Nuclear Test," Asia Foundation, accessed July 19, 2017, https://asiafoundation.org/resources/pdfs/GlaserChinaSecurity2.pdf; Jeffrey Bader, *Obama and China's Rise* (Washington, DC: Brookings Institution, 2012), 26–39, 83–93.

43. Evan Medeiros, *China's International Behavior*, 96–101; Bader, *Obama and China's Rise*, 140–50; "China to Become Second-Largest Contributor to UN Peacekeeping Budget," *China Watch*, June 6, 2016, http://www.telegraph.co.uk/sponsored/china-watch/politics/12210677/china-contributions-un-peacekeeping-budget.html.

44. Dan Blumenthal, "Fear and Loathing in Asia," *Journal of International Security Affairs* (Spring 2006): 81–88; US Department of Defense, *Military and Security Developments Involving the People's Republic of China, 2010*; US Defense Intelligence Agency, *China Military Power.*

45. Godwin, "China as a Major Asian Power"; US Department of Defense, *Military and Security Developments Involving the People's Republic of China, 2010*; Andrew Erickson and David Yang, "On the Verge of a Game-Changer," *Proceedings* 135, no. 5 (May 2009): 26–32; US Defense Intelligence Agency, *China Military Power*; Ashley Tellis, "Overview," in *Strategic Asia 2019: China's Expanding Strategic Ambitions*, ed. Ashley Tellis, Allison Szalwinski, and Michael Wills (Seattle, WA: National Bureau of Asian Research, 2019), 34–40; US Department of Defense, *Military and Security Developments Involving the People's Republic of China, 2020* (Washington, DC: Office of the Secretary of Defense, 2020).

46. Ashley J. Tellis and Travis Tanner, eds., *Strategic Asia 2012–13: China's Military Challenge* (Seattle, WA: National Bureau of Asian Research, 2012); Tellis, "Overview," in *Strategic Asia 2019: China's Expanding Strategic Ambitions*.

47. Michael Swaine, "China's Regional Military Posture," in *Power Shift: China and Asia's New Dynamics*, ed. David Shambaugh (Berkeley: University of California Press, 2005), 266; David Michael Lampton, *The Three Faces of Chinese Power: Might, Money, and Minds* (Berkeley: University of California Press, 2008), 40–42; Eric Heginbotham et al., *China's Evolving Nuclear Deterrent* (Santa Monica, CA: RAND Corporation, 2017); US Defense Intelligence Agency, *China Military Power*, 36–39; Campbell, *China's Military, The People's Liberation Army*, 36–37.

48. David Shambaugh, "China's Military Modernization: Making Steady and Surprising Progress," in *Strategic Asia 2005–06: Military Modernization in an Era of Uncertainty*, ed. Ashley Tellis and Michael Wills (Seattle, WA: National Bureau of Asian Research, 2005), 67–104; Ashley Tellis, "China's Military Modernization and Asian Security," in *Strategic Asia 2012–13: China's Military Challenge*, ed. Ashley J. Tellis and Travis Tanner (Seattle, WA: National Bureau of Asian Research, 2012), 3–26; Tellis, "Overview"; US Defense Intelligence Agency, *China Military Power*, 107–8.

49. US Defense Intelligence Agency, *China Military Power*, 12–13, 23–30.

50. The discussion here and in the following several paragraphs was adapted from an analytical frameworks used in Swaine, "China's Regional Military Posture," 268–72. The discussion was updated with reference to annual Department of Defense reports to Congress on the Chinese military and a variety of other authoritative reports. See US Department of Defense, *Military and Security Developments Involving the People's Republic of China, 2019* (Washington, DC: Office of the Secretary of Defense, 2019); US Defense Intelligence Agency, *China Military Power*; Tellis, "Overview"; Kania and Wood, "Major Themes in China's 2019 Defense White Paper"; Cordesman, *China's New Defense White Paper*.

51. Campbell, *China's Military, The People's Liberation Army*, 26–33.

52. The section benefited from the comprehensive treatment of recent PLA developments and reforms in Phillip Saunders, Arthur Ding, Andrew Scobell, Andrew N. D. Yang, and Joel Wuthnow, eds., *Chairman Xi Remakes the PLA* (Washington, DC: National Defense University Press, 2019); see also US Defense Intelligence Agency, *China Military Power*; US Department of Defense, *Military and Security Developments Involving the People's Republic of China, 2019*; Tellis, "Overview."

53. Campbell, *China's Military, The People's Liberation Army*, 35–38.

54. Ibid., 38–39.

55. These abilities are addressed in among others Campbell, *China's Military, The People's Liberation Army*; US Defense Intelligence Agency, *China Military Power*; Tellis, "Overview"; *China's Naval Modernization*, Congressional Research Service Report RL33153; see also Eric Heginbotham et al., *The U.S.-China Military Scorecard: Forces, Geography, and the Evolving Balance of Power, 1996–2017* (Santa Monica, CA: RAND Corporation, 2018).

56. Joel Wuthnow, Arthur Ding, Phillip Saunders, Andrew Scobell, and Andrew N. D. Yang, eds., *The PLA Beyond Borders* (Washington, DC: National Defense University Press, 2021).

57. Campbell, *China's Military, The People's Liberation Army*, 47–51; Satoru Mori, "US Technological Competition with China: The Military, Industrial and Digital Network Dimensions," *Asia-Pacific Review* 26, no. 1 (2019): 77–120; Graham Allison, "Is China Beating America to AI Supremacy?," *National Interest*, December 22, 2019, https://nationalinterest.org/feature/china-beating-america-ai-supremacy-106861; Julian Baird Gewitz, "China's Long March to Technology Supremacy," *Foreign Affairs*, August 27, 2019, https://www.foreignaffairs.com/articles/china/2019-08-27/chinas-long-march-technological-supremacy; Elsa Kania, "Technology and Innovation in China's Strategy and Global Influence," in *China's Global Influence*, ed. Scott McDonald and Michael Burgoyne (Honolulu, HI: Asia-Pacific Center for Security Studies, 2020), 229–46.

58. Campbell, *China's Military, The People's Liberation Army*; Tellis, "Overview"; *China's Naval Modernization*, Congressional Research Service Report.

59. John Garver, *Foreign Relations of the People's Republic of China* (Englewood Cliffs, NJ: Prentice Hall, 1993), 249–64; Thomas Christensen, "Windows and War: Trend Analysis and Beijing's Use of Force," in *New Directions in the Study of China's Foreign Policy*, ed. Alastair Iain Johnston and Robert S. Ross (Stanford, CA: Stanford University Press, 2006), 50–85; Robert Sutter, *Foreign Relations of the PRC* (Lanham, MD: Rowman & Littlefield, 2013), 10–14.

60. Robert Suettinger, *Beyond Tiananmen: The Politics of U.S.-China Relations, 1989–2000* (Washington, DC: Brookings Institution, 2003), 200–63.

61. Phillip Saunders, "China's Global Military-Security Interactions," in *China and the World*, ed. David Shambaugh (New York: Oxford University Press, 2020), 188–93.

62. Saunders et al., *Chairman Xi Remakes the PLA*, 1–44.

63. Michael Chase, Jeffrey Engstrom, Tai Ming Cheung, Kristen Gunness, Scott Harold, Susan Puska, and Samuel Berkowitz, *China's Incomplete Military Transformation* (Santa Monica, CA: RAND Corporation, 2015); Saunders et al., *Chairman Xi Remakes the PLA*, 203–519; Campbell, *China's Military, The People's Liberation Army*, 45–46.

64. Michael Swaine, "Chinese Views of Weapons of Mass Destruction," in US National Intelligence Council, *China and Weapons of Mass Destruction: Implications for the United States*, Conference Report (Washington, DC: US National Intelligence Council, November 5, 1999), 165–82; Bates Gill, "China and Nuclear Arms Control," *SIPRI Insights* 4 (April 2010); M. Taylor Fravel and Evan Medeiros, "China's

Search for Assured Retaliation," *International Security* 35, no. 2 (Fall 2010): 48–87; Heginbotham et al., *China's Evolving Nuclear Deterrent.*

65. Evan Medeiros, *Reluctant Restraint: The Evolution of China's Nonproliferation Policies and Practices, 1980–2004* (Stanford, CA: Stanford University Press, 2007).

66. For background, see Shirley Kan, *China and Proliferation of Weapons of Mass Destruction and Missiles: Policy Issues*, Congressional Research Service Report RL31555 (Washington, DC: Library of Congress, January 5, 2015). See also Saunders et al., *Chairman Xi Remakes the PLA*, 393–518. For Chinese views, see the periodic defense white papers referenced previously.

67. Evan Medeiros, "The Changing Character of China's WMD Proliferation Activities," in US National Intelligence Council, *China and Weapons of Mass Destruction*, 135–38; Kan, *China and Proliferation.*

68. Kan, *China and Proliferation*, 2–3, 7–18, 18–49; Kinling Lo, "China Backs Iran Nuclear Deal as US Walks Away," *South China Morning Post*, May 9, 2018, https://www.scmp.com/news/china/diplomacy-defence/article/2145406/china-backs-iran-nuclear-deal-united-states-walks-away.

69. Pranay Vaddi, *Leaving the INF Treaty Won't Help Trump Counter China* (Washington, DC: Carnegie Endowment for International Peace, January 31, 2019), https://carnegieendowment.org/2019/01/31/leaving-inf-treaty-won-t-help-trump-counter-china-pub-78262; https://www.newsweek.com/china-arms-deal-us-russia-1431025.

70. Sutter, *Chinese Foreign Relations*, 250.

71. Nadege Rolland, ed., *Securing the Belt and Road Initiative*, NBR Special Report No. 80 (Seattle, WA: National Bureau of Asian Research, September 2019), 72, https://www.nbr.org/wp-content/uploads/pdfs/publications/sr80_securing_the_belt_and_road_sep2019.pdf.

72. Murray Scott Tanner, *China's Response to Terrorism* (Washington, DC: Center for Naval Analysis, June 2016), https://www.cna.org/CNA_files/PDF/IRM-2016-U-013542-Final.pdf.

73. *China Primer: Uighurs*, Congressional Research Service Report IF10281, June 7, 2021.

74. Daniel Byman and Israa Saber, *Is China Ready for Global Terrorism?* (Washington, DC: Brookings Institution, September 2019), https://www.brookings.edu/wp-content/uploads/2019/09/FP_20190930_china_counterterrorism_byman_saber-1.pdf: Sutter, *Chinese Foreign Relations*, 120.

CHAPTER NINE

1. Wayne Morrison, *China's Economic Rise*, Congressional Research Service Report RL33534 (Washington, DC: Library of Congress, June 25, 2019); *China's Economy: Current Trends and Issues*, Congressional Research Service Report IF11667 (Washington, DC: Library of Congress, January 12, 2021); *China's 14th Five-Year Plan: A First Look*, Congressional Research Service Report (Washington, DC: Library of Congress, January 5, 2021); Larry Elliott,

"China to Overtake the US as World's Biggest Economy," *The Guardian*, December 25, 2020, https://www.theguardian.com/world/2020/dec/26/china-to-overtake-us-as-worlds-biggest-economy-by-2028-report-predicts.

2. Ambassador Chas Freeman Jr., "Playing at War Games with China," remarks to the Washington Institute of Foreign Affairs, February 11, 2021, https://chasfreeman.net/playing-war-games-with-china/; *China's Belt and Road: Implications for the United States* (New York: Council on Foreign Relations, 2021).

3. Barry Naughton, "China's Global Economic Interactions," in *China and the World*, ed. David Shambaugh (New York: Oxford University Press, 2020), 113–36; Nicholas Lardy, *The State Strikes Back: The End of Economic Reform in China* (Washington, DC: Peterson Institute for International Economics, 2018); Arthur Kroeber, *China's Economy* (New York: Oxford University Press, 2016); Barry Naughton, *The Chinese Economy: Transitions and Growth* (Cambridge, MA: MIT Press, 2018); David M. Lampton, *The Three Faces of Chinese Power: Might, Money, and Minds* (Berkeley: University of California Press, 2008), 78–116; David Shambaugh, *China Goes Global* (New York: Oxford University Press, 2013), 156–206; C. Fred Bergsten, Charles Freeman, Nicholas Lardy, and Derek Mitchell, *China's Rise: Challenges and Opportunities* (Washington, DC: Peterson Institute for International Economics, 2008), 105–37; Nicholas Lardy, *Sustaining China's Economic Growth after the Global Financial Crisis* (Washington, DC: Peterson Institute for International Economics, 2012); Wayne Morrison, *China's Economic Conditions*, CRS Report RL33534 (Washington, DC: Congressional Research Service of the Library of Congress, December 4, 2012); Wang Jisi, "Trends on the Development of U.S.-China Relations and Deep-Seated Reasons," lecture delivered at the Chinese Academy of Social Science, Asia Pacific Institute, *Dangdai Yatai* (Beijing), June 20, 2009, 4–20.

4. On China's covert use of economic leverage in foreign affairs, see Daniel Russel and Blake Berger, *Navigating the Belt and Road Initiative* (New York: Asia Society Policy Institute, June 2019); Melanie Hart and Blaine Johnson, *Mapping China's Global Governance Ambitions* (Washington, DC: Center for American Progress, February 2019); Melanie Hart and Kelly Magsamen, *Limit, Leverage and Compete: A New Strategy on China* (Washington, DC: Center for American Progress, April 2019); Matt Schrader, *Friends and Enemies: A Framework for Understanding Chinese Political Influence in Democratic Countries* (Washington, DC: German Marshall Fund, April 22, 2020); David Shullman, ed., *Chinese Malign Influence and the Corrosion of Democracy* (Washington, DC: International Republican Institute, 2019); Daniel Kliman, Rush Doshi, Kristine Lee, and Zack Cooper, *Grading China's Belt and Road* (Washington, DC: Center for New American Security, April 2019); Ashley Tellis, Alisson Szalwinski, and Michael Wills, eds., *Strategic Asia 2020: US-China Competition for Global Influence* (Seattle, WA: National Bureau of Asian Research, 2020); Nadege Rolland, *China's Vision for a New World Order* (Seattle, WA: National Bureau for Asian Research, January 2020); Scott McDonald and Michael Burgoyne, eds., *China's Global Influence* (Honolulu, HI: Asia-Pacific Center for Security Studies, 2020); Thomas Mahnken, Ross Babbage, and Toshi Yoshihara, *Countering Comprehensive Coercion* (Washington, DC: Center for Strategic and Budgetary

Assessments, 2018); Ross Babbage, *Winning without Fighting: Chinese and Russian Political Warfare Campaigns* (Washington, DC: Center for Strategic and Budgetary Assessments, 2018).

5. Bergsten et al., *China's Rise*, 9–32; C. Fred Bergsten, Bates Gill, Nicholas Lardy, and Derek Mitchell, *China: A Balance Sheet* (New York: Public Affairs, 2006), 73–117; Wayne Morrison, *China-U.S. Trade Issues*, CRS Report RL33536 (Washington, DC: Congressional Research Service of the Library of Congress, May 21, 2012); Jeffrey Bader, *Obama and China's Rise* (Washington, DC: Brookings Institution, 2012), 111–27.

6. Kenneth Lieberthal, "How Domestic Forces Shape the PRC's Grand Strategy and International Impact," in *Strategic Asia 2007–2008*, ed. Ashley Tellis and Michael Wills (Seattle: National Bureau of Asian Research, 2007), 29–68; Lampton, *The Three Faces of Chinese Power*, 207–51; Lardy, *Sustaining China's Economic Growth*; Kroeber, *China's Economy*, 233–62.

7. Demetri Sevastopulo and Michael Peel, "US and EU to Revive Joint Effort to Handle More Assertive China," *Financial Times*, March 23, 2021, https://www.ft.com/content/89049954-96e8-410e-aecf-b75a7e4123a3.

8. Orville Schell and Susan Shirk, *US Policy toward China* (New York: Asia Society, 2017), 60.

9. Hart and Magsamen, *Limit, Leverage and Compete: A New Strategy on China*.

10. Robert Sutter, "China's Foreign Behavior Warrants Sustained US Countermeasures," *PacNet* 59, Pacific Forum CSIS, October 29, 2020.

11. Bonnie Glaser, "US-China Relations," *Comparative Connections* 22, no. 1 (January–April 2020).

12. Satoru Mori, "US Technological Competition with China: The Military, Industrial and Digital Network Dimensions," *Asia-Pacific Review* 26, no. 1 (2019): 77–120; *US-China Trade Relations*, Congressional Research Service Report, February 9, 2021, 2.

13. The developments in this and later paragraphs are assessed in Robert Sutter, "Trump, America and the World—2017 and Beyond," H-Diplo/ISSF POLICY Series, January 19, 2019, https://networks.h-net.org/node/28443/discussions/3569933/issf-policy-series-sutter-trump%E2%80%99s-china-policy-bi-partisan.

14. *US-China Relations*, Congressional Research Service Report, February 3, 2021, 1–2.

15. "Special Report: China and America," *The Economist*, May 16, 2019, https://www.economist.com/special-report/2019/05/16/trade-can-no-longer-anchor-americas-relationship-with-china.

16. This paragraph and following paragraphs are based on Mori, "US Technological Competition with China"; Elsa Kania, "Technology and Innovation in China's Strategy and Global Influence," in McDonald and Burgoyne, *China's Global Influence*, 229–46; Graham Allison, "Is China Beating America to AI Supremacy?," *National Interest*, December 22, 2019, https://nationalinterest.org/feature/china-beating-america-ai-supremacy-106861. A useful framework for understanding recent American debate on this issue is in Kenneth Boutin, *Economic Security and Sino-American Relations* (Northamton, MA: Edward Elgar, 2019); see updates in Tony

Romm, "Senate Approves $250 Billion to Trim China's Ambitions," *Washington Post*, June 9, 2021, A18; David Sanger, Catie Edmondson, David McCabe, and Thomas Kaplan, "In Rare Show of Unity, Senate Poised to Pass a Bill to Counter China," *New York Times*, June 7, 2021, A10; *US-China Relations*, February 3, 2021, 1–2.

17. US-China Policy Foundation Newsletter, "US View of China Competition," May 21, 2021, https://uscpf.org/v3/2021/05/21/us-china-competition/.

18. Caitlin Campbell, *China's Military*, Congressional Research Service Report R46808, June 4, 2021, 48–50.

19. Rush Doshi, Emily de la Bruyere, Nathan Pucarsic, and John Ferguson, *China as a "Cyber Great Power"* (Washington, DC: Brookings Institution, April 2021).

20. See, among others, Elsa Kania, "The China Challenge in 5G," in *Securing Our 5G Future* (Washington, DC: Center for New American Security, November 2019), 7–11.

21. Kania, *Securing Our 5G Future*, 11–23; David Sacks, "China's Huawei Is Winning the 5G Race," Council on Foreign Relations (blog post), March 29, 2021, https://www.cfr.org/blog/china-huawei-5g.

22. Bonnie Glaser and Hannah Price, "Continuity Prevails in Biden's First 100 Days," *Comparative Connections* 23, no. 1 (May 2021): 32.

23. Ibid.

24. "US and China Trade Officials Hold 'Candid' First Talks of Biden Era," *BBC News*, May 27, 2021, https://www.bbc.com/news/business-57264346.

25. *China's Fourteenth Five-Year Plan*, 1–2.

26. Morrison, *China-U.S. Trade Issues* (May 21, 2012), 2; Howard Schneider, "U.S. Trade Deficit Drops for 2012," *Washington Post*, February 8, 2013, https://www.washingtonpost.com/business/economy/us-trade-deficit-drops-for-2012/2013/02/08/36dd01f0-7235-11e2-8b8d-e0b59a1b8e2a_story.html?utm_term=.e35e7f89dabe; Morrison, *China-U.S. Trade Issues* (April 24, 2017), 10.

27. *US-China Trade Relations*, Congressional Research Service Report, February 9, 2021, 1.

28. Morrison, *China-U.S. Trade Issues* (April 24, 2017), 9–10.

29. *US-China Trade Relations*, 1.

30. "China Criticizes US Trade Protectionism Measures," *Xinhua*, April 17, 2012, http://www.globaltimes.cn/content/705258.shtml; Evelyn Cheng, "Chinese Foreign Minister Calls for the US to Remove Tariffs and Sanctions," *CNBC*, February 21, 2021, https://www.cnbc.com/2021/02/22/chinas-foreign-minister-calls-for-us-to-remove-tariffs-sanctions.html.

31. Morrison, *China-U.S. Trade Issues* (December 29, 2016), 3–8, 11–14.

32. "China's Outward Investment Tops $161 Billion in 2016," *Reuters*, December 26, 2016, http://www.reuters.com/article/us-china-economy-investment-idUSKBN14F07R.

33. Wayne Morrison, *China's Economic Rise*, Congressional Research Service Report RL33534 (Washington, DC: Library of Congress, September 15, 2017), 13.

34. Morrison, *China-U.S. Trade Issues* (April 24, 2017), 19.

35. Morrison, *China-U.S. Trade Issues* (May 21, 2012), 15; Morrison, *China-U.S. Trade Issues* (December 29, 2016), 18; Department of the Treasury, *U.S. Portfolio*

Holdings of Foreign Securities as of December 31, 2015, October 2016, http://ticdata.treasury.gov/Publish/shca2015_report.pdf.

36. *US Capital Markets and China*, Congressional Research Service Report IF11803 (April 5, 2021), 1.

37. Morrison, *China-U.S. Trade Issues* (June 3, 2009), 9; Morrison, *China-U.S. Trade Issues* (May 21, 2012), 17–20; Morrison, *China-U.S. Trade Issues* (December 29, 2016), 20.

38. Susan Lawrence and David MacDonald, *U.S.-China Relations*, Congressional Research Service Report R41108, August 2, 2012, 30.

39. Morrison, *China-U.S. Trade Issues* (November 29, 2012), 17.

40. Morrison, *China-U.S. Trade Issues* (May 21, 2012), 20–23; *US-China Trade Relations*, February 9, 2021, 2.

41. Schell and Shirk, *US Policy toward China*, 60–61; *US-China Trade Relations*, February 9, 2021, 2.

42. Discussed in Morrison, *China-U.S. Trade Issues* (April 24, 2017), 27–31.

43. See review of complaints in Schell and Shirk, *US Policy toward China*, 60–64.

44. Morrison, *China-U.S. Trade Issues* (December 29, 2016), 27–29.

45. Schell and Shirk, *US Policy toward China*, 61.

46. *"Made in China 2025" Industrial Policies*, Congressional Research Service Report IF10964, August 11, 2020, 1.

47. *China's Fourteenth Five-Year Plan*, 1–2.

48. *China's Fourteenth Five-Year Plan*, 1.

49. This paragraph is taken from Morrison, *China-U.S. Trade Issues* (December 29, 2016), 40–41.

50. Morrison, *China-U.S. Trade Issues* (April 24, 2017), 35.

51. *China's Fourteenth Five-Year Plan*, 1.

52. *US-China Trade Relations*, February 9, 2021, 2.

53. *US Export Control Reforms and China*, Congressional Research Service Report IF11627, January 15, 2021, 1; *Semiconductors: US Industry, Global Competition, and Federal Policy*, Congressional Research Service Report R46581, October 26, 2020, 1.

54. Robert Sutter, *Chinese Policy Priorities and Their Implications for the United States* (Lanham, MD: Rowman & Littlefield, 2000), 11, 46, 53.

55. Robert Sutter, *Chinese Foreign Relations: Power and Policy since the Cold War* (Lanham, MD: Rowman & Littlefield, 2008), 99.

56. Morrison, *China-U.S. Trade Issues* (May 16, 2006), 13–14; Morrison, *China-U.S. Trade Issues* (June 3, 2009), 20; Morrison, *China-U.S. Trade Issues* (May 21, 2012), 29–30; Morrison, *China-U.S. Trade Issues* (April 24, 2017), 37–46.

57. U.S. Special Trade Representative, "Priority Watch List," annual report, April 25, 2008, http://www.ustr.gov/sites/default/files/asset_upload_file558_14870.pdf.

58. *Hearing on China: Intellectual Property Infringement, Indigenous Innovation Policies, and Framework for Measuring Effects on the U.S. Economy* (testimony of Jeremie Waterman, senior director, Greater China, US Chamber of Commerce, before the US International Trade Commission, June 15, 2010).

59. *China's Fourteenth Five-Year Plan*, 2.

60. Mike Levine and Jack Date, "22 Million Affected by OPM Hack," *ABC News*, July 9, 2015, https://abcnews.go.com/US/exclusive-25-million-affected-opm-hack-sources/story?id=32332731.

61. Morrison, *China-U.S. Trade Issues* (April 24, 2017), 42–46.

62. Frank Bajak, Eric Tucker, and Matt O'Brien, "Chinese Hackers Blamed for Massive Microsoft Server Hack," *The Diplomat*, March 10, 2021, https://thediplomat.com/2021/03/chinese-hackers-blamed-for-massive-microsoft-server-hack/.

63. Sutter, *Chinese Foreign Relations*, 97.

64. Deepak Bhattasali, Shantong Li, and Will Martin, eds., *China and the WTO* (Washington, DC: World Bank, 2004).

65. David Barboza, "Trade Surplus Tripled in '05, China Says," *New York Times*, January 12, 2006, http://www.nytimes.com/2006/01/12/business/worldbusiness/trade-surplus-tripled-in-05-china-says.html; Morrison, *China-U.S. Trade Issues* (May 21, 2012), 35–39.

66. Sutter, *Chinese Foreign Relations*, 76.

67. Cited in Morrison, *China-U.S. Trade Issues* (December 29, 2016), 46.

68. Morrison, *China-U.S. Trade Issues* (April 24, 2017), 48; Lawrence and MacDonald, *U.S.-China Relations*, 30–31.

69. William Pentland, "China Pulls Back Indigenous Innovation Policies," *Forbes*, July 3, 2011, https://www.forbes.com/sites/williampentland/2011/07/03/china-pulls-back-indigenous-innovation-policies/#d61709d425c6; Morrison, *China-U.S. Trade Issues* (May 21, 2012), 26–28.

70. David Lynch, "Trump's Raise the Stakes Strategy," *Washington Post*, July 21, 2018, A14.

71. Morrison, *China-U.S. Trade Issues* (December 29, 2016), 50–52; Donald Keyser, "President Obama's Re-election: Outlook for U.S.-China Relations in the Second Term," *China Policy Institute: Analysis* (blog), November 12, 2012, http://blogs.nottingham.ac.uk/chinapolicyinstitute/2012/11/07.

72. Morrison, *China-U.S. Trade Issues* (December 29, 2016), 50–52.

73. "President Trump's WSJ Interview: Highlights," *Wall Street Journal*, April 12, 2017, http://www.wsj.com/podcasts/president-trump-wsj-interview-highlights/632F7842-135C-407A-AB30-6F6D7409F38B.html.

74. "US Says China No Longer a Currency Manipulator," *New York Times*, January 13, 2020, https://www.nytimes.com/2020/01/13/us/politics/treasury-china-currency-manipulator-trade.html.

75. For an up-to-date comprehensive treatment of this large and evolving topic, see *China's Belt and Road: Implications for the United States* (New York: Council on Foreign Relations, 2021).

76. *China's Belt and Road Initiative: Economic Issues*, Congressional Research Service Report IF11735, January 22, 2021.

77. For more detailed discussion, see Robert Sutter, "Why America Opposes the Belt and Road Initiative (BRI)," *PacNet* 38, July 2, 2020.

78. Ibid.

79. Victor Shih, "US-China Relations in 2019," testimony before the US-China Economic and Security Review Commission, September 4, 2019, https://www.uscc.gov/sites/default/files/Panel%20I%20Shih_Written%20Testimony.pdf.

80. See treatment of these difficulties in Morrison, *China's Economic Rise*, 25–34.

81. Morrison, *China's Economic Rise*, 25–26; "China Steels Its Resolve, but 'Zombies' Abound," *Wall Street Journal*, July 29, 2016, http://blogs.wsj.com/chinarealtime/2016/07/29/csteel0729/.

82. Morrison, *China's Economic Rise*, 26–29; Ing. Jan Bejkovsky, "State Capitalism in China: The Case of the Banking Sector," August 2016, http://globalbizresearch.org/IAR16_Vietnam_Conference_2016_Aug/docs/doc/PDF/VS611.pdf.

83. Morrison, *China's Economic Rise*, 31–32; Transparency International, "Corruption Perceptions Index 2016," January 2017, https://www.transparency.org/news/feature/corruption_perceptions_index_2016.

84. Morrison, *China's Economic Rise*, 29–31; OECD, "The Rising Cost of Ambient Air Pollution Thus Far in the 21st Century, Results from the BRIICS and the OECD Countries," July 2017, 22, http://www.oecd-ilibrary.org/docserver/download/d1b2b844-en.pdf?expires=1517681542&id=id&accname=guest&checksum=9B43144FCF78931DCE50EBEC9B8F84E8.

85. Morrison, *China's Economic Rise*, 32–33; Weizhen Tan, "China's Aging Population Will Be 'a Big Shock' to the Global Supply Chain," *CNBC*, May 12, 2021, https://www.cnbc.com/2021/05/13/chinas-aging-population-could-be-a-big-shock-to-global-supply-chain.html.

86. *China's Fourteenth Five-Year Plan*, 1.

87. Vanand Meliksetian, "China's Energy Dependences to Grow Despite Major Oil Discoveries," OilPrice.com, December 25, 2020, https://oilprice.com/Energy/Energy-General/Chinas-Energy-Dependence-To-Grow-Despite-Major-Oil-Discoveries.html; Joanna Lewis and Laura Edwards, "Assessing China's Energy and Climate Goals," Center for American Progress, May 6, 2021, https://www.americanprogress.org/issues/security/reports/2021/05/06/499096/assessing-chinas-energy-climate-goals/.

88. Aaron Friedberg, "'Going Out': China's Pursuit of Natural Resources and Implications for the PRC's Grand Strategy," *NBR Analysis* 17, no. 3 (September 2006): 1–35; David Brewster, *China's New Network of Indian Ocean Bases*, Lowy Institute, January 30, 2018, https://www.lowyinstitute.org/the-interpreter/chinas-new-network-indian-ocean-bases.

89. Robert Sutter, *Chinese Policy Priorities and Their Implications for the United States* (Lanham, MD: Rowman & Littlefield, 2000), 188.

90. Elizabeth Economy, "China's Environmental Challenge," *Current History* 105, no. 692 (September 2005): 278–79; Sutter, *Chinese Policy Priorities and Their Implications for the United States*, 189.

91. Elizabeth Economy, "China: A Rise That's Not So 'Win-Win,'" *International Herald Tribune*, November 15, 2005.

92. Te Kan, "Past Successes and New Goal," *China Daily*, December 26, 2005–January 1, 2006, supplement, 9.

93. Joanna Lewis, "The State of U.S.-China Relations on Climate Change," *China Environmental Series* 11 (2010–2011): 7–39.

94. Hua Jianmin, "Strengthen Cooperation for Clean Development," Chinese Foreign Ministry statement, January 12, 2006, http://www.fmprc.gov.cn/eng.

95. Kenneth Lieberthal and David Sandalow, *Overcoming Obstacles to U.S.-China Cooperation on Climate Change*, John L. Thornton China Center Monograph Series 1 (Washington, DC: Brookings Institution, January 2009).

96. Lewis, "The State of U.S.-China Relations on Climate Change."

97. Joel Kirkland, "Global Emissions Predicted to Grow through 2035," *Scientific American*, May 26, 2010, http://www.scientificamerican.com/article/global-emissions-predicted-to-grow.

98. Carolyn Beeler, "Is China Really Stepping Up as the World's New Climate Leader," *PRI*, November 9, 2017, https://www.usatoday.com/story/news/world/2017/11/09/china-really-stepping-up-worlds-new-climate-leader/847270001.

99. Elizabeth Economy, "Why China Is No Climate Leader," *Politico*, June 12, 2017, https://www.politico.com/magazine/story/2017/06/12/why-china-is-no-climate-leader-215249; *US-China Relations*, Congressional Research Service Report R45898 (Washington, DC), August 29, 2019 (see pp. 39–40 on climate change issues).

100. Lewis and Edwards, "Assessing China's Energy and Climate Goals"; Elizabeth Economy, "China's Climate Strategy," *China Leadership Monitor*, June 1, 2021, https://www.prcleader.org/economy.

CHAPTER TEN

1. *China/Taiwan: Evolution of the "One China" Policy—Key Statements from Washington, Beijing, and Taipei*, Congressional Research Service Report RL30341, January 5, 2015; Robert Sutter and Satu Limaye, *A Hardening US-China Competition: Asia Policy in America's 2020 Elections and Asian Responses* (Honolulu, HI: East-West Center, 2020), 45–48, 71–73.

2. Richard Haass and David Sacks, "American Support for Taiwan Must Be Unambiguous," *Foreign Affairs*, September 2, 2020, https://www.foreignaffairs.com/articles/united-states/american-support-taiwan-must-be-unambiguous; Richard Bush, Bonnie Glaser, and Ryan Hass, "Don't Help China by Hyping Risk of War Over Taiwan," *NPR*, April 8, 2021, https://www.npr.org/2021/04/08/984524521/opinion-dont-help-china-by-hyping-risk-of-war-over-taiwan.

3. Nancy Bernkopf Tucker, *Strait Talk: United States-Taiwan Relations and the Crisis with China* (Cambridge, MA: Harvard University Press, 2009), 11–89.

4. Steven Goldstein, *China and Taiwan* (Cambridge, UK: Polity Press, 2015), 43–60.

5. Tucker, *Strait Talk*, 129–94.

6. Tucker, *Strait Talk*, 171–94; Goldstein, *China and Taiwan*, 70–98.

7. Cal Clark, "The Taiwan Relations Act and the US Balancing Role in Cross-Strait Relations," *American Journal of Chinese Studies* 17, no. 1 (April 2010): 3–18.

8. Tucker, *Strait Talk*, 231–73; Goldstein, *China and Taiwan*, 99–118.

9. Goldstein, *China and Taiwan*, 119–90; Shirley Kan, *U.S.-Taiwan Relationship: Overview of Policy Issues*, CRS Report R41592 (Washington, DC: Congressional Research Service of the Library of Congress, December 11, 2014).

10. Alan Romberg, "Tsai Ing-wen Takes Office: A New Era in Cross-Strait Relations," *China Leadership Monitor* no. 50 (Summer 2016), http://www.hoover.org/research/tsai-ing-wen-takes-office-new-era-cross-strait-relations.

11. *Taiwan: Political and Security Issues*, Congressional Research Service Report IF10275, January 4, 2021, 1

12. Taken from Robert Sutter, "More American Attention to Taiwan amid Heightened Competition with China," *American Journal of Chinese Studies* 22, no. 1 (April 2015): 1–16.

13. Sutter, "More American Attention to Taiwan," 6.

14. Shirley Kan and Wayne Morrison, *U.S.-Taiwan Relationship*, Congressional Research Service Report R41592, December 11, 2014, 14.

15. "Upsetting China," *The Economist*, April 27, 2001, http://www.economist.com/node/594078.

16. William Lowther, "U.S. Senator Not Convinced on F-16 Bid," *Taipei Times*, September 23, 2010.

17. "Senator Questions Arms Sales to Taiwan," Reuters, June 16, 2010.

18. Kerry Dumbaugh, "Underlying Strains in Taiwan-U.S. Political Relations," Congressional Research Service Report RL33684 (Washington, DC: Library of Congress, April 20, 2007); Robert Sutter, "Taiwan's Future: Narrowing Straits," *NBR Analysis*, May 2001, 19–22.

19. Daniel Russel, "Evaluating U.S. Policy on Taiwan on the 35th Anniversary of the Taiwan Relations Act," testimony before the Senate Committee on Foreign Affairs Subcommittee on East Asian and Pacific Affairs, April 3, 2014; Joseph Yeh, "Taiwan Lauded for Response to Beijing ADIZ Move: AIT," *China Post*, December 14, 2013.

20. Josh Hicks, "Obama Foreign Policy Sparks Bi-partisan Criticism," *Washington Post*, August 31, 2014; "Inviting an Asian Crimea," *Wall Street Journal*, April 6, 2014; William Lowther, "US Senator Rubio Seeks Answers on the 'Six Assurances,'" *Taipei Times*, April 5, 2014, 1; William Lowther, "US Academic Warns over Pace, Extent of Cross Strait Moves," *Taipei Times*, June 20, 2014, 3.

21. Sutter, "More American Attention to Taiwan."

22. Dean Cheng, "Taiwan's Maritime Security," *Heritage Foundation Backgrounder*, March 19, 2014, http://www.heritage.org/research/reports/2014/03/taiwans-maritime-security-a-critical-american-interest; William Lowther, "US Study Urges 'Offshore Control' Strategy for China," *Taipei Times*, January 12, 2014, 3; Wendell Minnick, "US Might Tap into Taiwan Early Warning Radar," *Defense News*, May 8, 2014.

23. The options noted below are discussed in Robert Sutter, "Dealing with America's China Problem in Asia—Target China's Vulnerabilities," *PacNet* 58 (Honolulu, HI: Pacific Forum CSIS, July 21, 2014).

24. Ibid.

25. The author thanks the Taiwan Economic and Cultural Representative Office in Washington, DC, for their assistance in filling out the full scope of these interchanges.

26. Kan and Morrison, *U.S.-Taiwan Relationship*.

27. *Taiwan: Political and Security Issues*; Richard Bush, "From Persuasion to Coercion: Beijing's Approach to Taiwan and Taiwan's Response,"

Brookings Institution, November 2019, https://www.brookings.edu/research/from-persuasion-to-coercion-beijings-approach-to-taiwan-and-taiwans-response.

28. Syaru Shirley Lin, "How Taiwan's High Income Trap Shapes Its Options in US-China Competition," in *Strategic Asia 2020: US-China Competition for Global Influence*, ed. Ashley Tellis, Alison Szalwinski, and Michael Wills (Seattle, WA: National Bureau of Asian Research, 2020), 133–62; Bush, "From Persuasion to Coercion: Beijing's Approach to Taiwan and Taiwan's Response"; Michael Chase, "A Rising China's Challenges to Taiwan," in *Strategic Asia 2019: China's Expanding Strategic Ambitions*, ed. Ashley Tellis, Alison Szalwinski, and Michael Wills (Seattle, WA: National Bureau of Asian Research, 2019), 111–42; Lauren Dickey, "Taiwan Policymaking in Xi Jinping's 'New Era,'" *China Brief*, November 10, 2017, https://jamestown.org/program/taiwan-policymaking-xi-jinpings-new-era.

29. Rush Doshi, "China Steps Up Its Information War Against Taiwan," *Foreign Affairs*, January 9, 2020, https://www.foreignaffairs.com/articles/china/2020-01-09/china-steps-its-information-war-taiwan.

30. Ibid.

31. David Brown and Kyle Churchman, "Coronavirus Embitters Cross-Strait Relations," *Comparative Connections* 22, no. 1 (May 2020): 73–82.

32. The paragraphs below are taken from Robert Sutter, "The US and Taiwan Embrace Despite China's Objections," *PacNet* 58, November 12, 2019, https://pacforum.org/publication/pacnet-58-the-us-and-taiwan-embrace-despite-chinas-objections-but-will-it-last; see also, Sutter and Limaye, *A Hardening US-China Competition*, 45–48, 71–73.

33. Sutter, "The US and Taiwan Embrace Despite China's Objections."

34. Haass and Sacks, "American Support for Taiwan Must Be Unambiguous"; Bush, Glaser, and Hass, "Don't Help China by Hyping Risk of War Over Taiwan."

35. Sutter, "The US and Taiwan Embrace," 1.

36. Ibid.

37. Ibid., 2.

38. Ibid.

39. Ibid.

40. David Keegan and Kyle Churchman, "Taiwan Prospers, China Ratchets Up Coercion, and US Support Remains 'Rock Solid,'" *Comparative Connections* 23, no. 1 (May 2021): 77–84.

41. Sutter and Limaye, *A Hardening US-China Competition*, 45–48, 71–73; Robert Sutter, "Biden, China and US High Technology Competition," *Taiwan Insight*, December 4, 2020, https://taiwaninsight.org/2020/12/04/biden-taiwan-and-us-china-high-technology-competition/; Robert Sutter, "Biden & Taiwan: Advancing a Flexible US One China Policy," *Taiwan Insight*, May 28, 2021, https://taiwaninsight.org/2021/05/28/biden-taiwan-advancing-a-flexible-us-one-china-policy/.

42. Robert Sutter, "China's Foreign Behavior Warrants Sustained US Countermeasures," *PacNet* 59, October 29, 2020.

43. Sutter, "Biden & Taiwan: Advancing a Flexible US One China Policy."

44. Ibid.

45. Charles Glaser, "Washington Is Avoiding the Tough Questions on Taiwan and China," *Foreign Affairs*, April 28, 2021, https://www.foreignaffairs.com/articles/asia/2021-04-28/washington-avoiding-tough-questions-taiwan-and-china.

46. Sutter, "Biden & Taiwan: Advancing a Flexible US One China Policy."

47. Chip Gregson, Russell Hsiao, and Stephen Young, "How the Biden Administration Can Support Taiwan," *The Diplomat*, April 30, 2021, https://thediplomat.com/2021/04/how-the-biden-administration-can-support-taiwan/.

48. Sutter, "Biden & Taiwan: Advancing a Flexible US One China Policy."

49. Haass and Sacks, "American Support for Taiwan Must Be Unambiguous."

50. Sutter, "Biden & Taiwan: Advancing a Flexible US One China Policy."

51. Bader, *Obama and China's Rise*, 69–92.

52. Ronald O'Rourke, *Maritime Territorial and Exclusive Economic Zone (EEZ) Disputes Involving China: Issues for Congress*, CRS Report 42784 (Washington, DC: Congressional Research Service of the Library of Congress, December 10, 2012).

53. There appeared to be serious disagreement within the Obama government: military leaders like Defence Secretary Ashton Carter and Pacific Commander Admiral Harry Harris adopted much tougher public postures than the Obama White House staff regarding Chinese provocations in the East China Sea and the South China Sea. There were repeated media reports that Harris was muzzled by the president's aides. David Larter, "4-Star Admiral Wants to Confront China; White House Says 'Not So Fast,'" *Navy Times*, April 6, 2016 (republished September 26, 2016), https://www.navytimes.com/articles/4-star-admiral-wants-to-confront-china-the-white-house-says-not-so-fast.

54. Sheila Smith and Charles McClean, "Suga and Biden Off to a Good Start," *Comparative Connections* 23, no. 1 (May 2021): 21–27; Robert Sutter and Chin Hao Huang, "Beijing's Advances Complicated by Myanmar Coup and US Resolve," *Comparative Connections* 23, no. 1 (May 2021): 67–72.

55. Robert Ross, "The Problem with the Pivot," *Foreign Affairs* (November–December 2012): 70-82; Shawn Brimley and Ely Ratner, "Smart Shift," *Foreign Affairs* (January–February 2013): 177–81. The full scope of the rebalance policy is addressed in Kurt Campbell, *The Pivot* (New York: Twelve-Hachette Book Group, 2016); see also Mark Manyin, Stephen Daggett, Ben Dolvin, Susan Lawrence, Michael Martin, and Ronald O"Rourke, *Pivot to the Pacific? The Obama Administration's "Rebalancing" toward Asia*, CRS Report 42448 (Washington, DC: Congressional Research Service of the Library of Congress, March 28, 2012); and Robert Sutter, *The United States and Asia: Regional Dynamics and Twenty-First Century Relations* (Lanham, MD: Rowman & Littlefield, 2020), 62–67.

56. The following discussion comes from Robert Sutter and Chin-Hao Huang, "China Muscles Opponents on South China Sea," *Comparative Connections* 14, no. 2 (September 2012): 61–69; Robert Sutter and Chin-Hao Huang, "China Gains and Advances in South China Sea," *Comparative Connections* 14, no. 3 (January 2013): 69–76; and James Przystup, "China-Japan Relations," *Comparative Connections* 14, no. 3 (January 2013): 109–24.

57. Asia Maritime Transparency Initiative, *Counter Coercion Series: Scarborough Shoals Standoff*, May 22, 2017, https://amti.csis.org/counter-co-scarborough-standoff/.

58. Sutter and Huang, "China Gains and Advances in South China Sea."

59. Ibid.; *Counter Coercion Series: Scarborough Shoals Standoff.*

60. Przystup, "China-Japan Relations."

61. Robert Sutter, *Chinese Foreign Relations: Power and Policy of an Emerging Global Force* (Lanham, MD: Rowman & Littlefield, 2021), 180–82.

62. Su Xiaohui, "Obama Will Be 'Smarter' in Rebalancing towards Asia and Engaging China," *China-US Focus*, November 8, 2012.

63. Bonnie Glaser, *Beijing as an Emerging Power in the South China Sea* (Washington, DC: CSIS, 2012).

64. Mark Valencia, "Asian Threats, Provocations Giving Rise to Whiffs of War," *Japan Times*, June 9, 2014, http://www.japantimes.co.jp/opinion/2014/06/09/commentary/world-commentary/asian-threats-provocations-giving-rise-whiffs-war/#.U6VP6JRdXxA.

65. White House Office of the Press Secretary, *Fact Sheet: U.S.-Japan Global and Regional Cooperation*, April 25, 2014; Matt Spetalnick and Nathan Layne, "Obama Accuses China of Flexing Muscles in Disputes with Neighbors," Reuters, April 28, 2015, http://www.reuters.com/article/2015/04/29/us-usa-japan-idUSKBN0NJ09520150429.

66. Emma Chanlette-Avery, coord., *Japan-US Relations*, CRS Report RL33436 (Washington, DC: Congressional Research Service of the Library of Congress, April 23, 2015), 2.

67. Sutter and Huang, "China Muscles Opponents on South China Sea"; and Sutter and Huang, "China Gains and Advances in South China Sea."

68. Michael Green and Ernest Bower, *Carter Defends South China Sea and Shangri-La* (Washington, DC: Center for Strategic and International Studies, May 29, 2015); "Facing U.S. Led Resistance in the South China Sea," *Comparative Connections* 17, no. 2 (September 2015): 65–73.

69. The above developments are reviewed in Dean Cheng, "South China Sea after the Tribunal Ruling—Where Do We Go from Here?," *National Interest* (blog), July 16, 2016, http://nationalinterest.org/blog/the-buzz/south-china-sea-after-the-tribunal-ruling-where-do-we-go17011; "Countering Adverse Tribunal Ruling," *Comparative Connections* 18, no. 2 (September 2016): 59–67; "Beijing Presses Its Advantages," *Comparative Connections* 18, no. 3 (January 2017): 43–48.

70. "Countering Adverse Tribunal Ruling," 59–67; "Beijing Presses Its Advantages," 43–48.

71. "China Consolidates Control and Advances Influence," *Comparative Connections* 19, no. 1 (May 2017): 51–58; Steven Stashwick, "US Freedom of Navigation Challenges in South China Sea on Hold," *Diplomat*, May 8, 2017, http://thediplomat.com/2017/05/us-freedom-of-navigation-challenges-in-south-china-sea-on-hold.

72. For Trump and Biden policy regarding disputes in East and South China Seas, see Ronald O'Rourke, *US-China Strategic Competition in South and East China Seas*, Congressional Research Service Report R42784, March 18, 2021. For background on US policy toward Japan-East China Sea disputes, see Sutter, *The United States and Asia*, 189–90; on US policy toward South China Sea disputes, see Sutter, *Chinese Foreign Relations*, 207–8. For recent US policy on Taiwan, see Sutter, "The

US and Taiwan Embrace Despite China's Objections," and Sutter, "Biden & Taiwan: Advancing a Flexible US One China Policy."

73. Sutter and Limaye, *A Hardening US-China Competition*, 31–35, 39–45, 45–48.

74. Smith and McClean, "Suga and Biden Off to a Good Start."

75. Sutter and Limaye, *A Hardening US-China Competition*, 39–45.

76. The following discussion for the remainder of this chapter comes from Robert Sutter, "Philippines-US Cooperation on Whitsun Reef: A 'Win' for the Biden Team in Southeast Asia?," *Fulcrum*, May 21, 2021, https://fulcrum.sg/philippine-us-cooperation-on-whitsun-reef-a-win-for-the-biden-team-in-southeast-asia/. For background, see Sutter and Huang, "Beijing's Advances Complicated by Myanmar Coup and US Resolve."

CHAPTER ELEVEN

1. For historical treatment of these differences, see John K. Fairbank, *The United States and China* (Cambridge, MA: Harvard University Press, 1983).

2. Robert Sutter, *Chinese Foreign Relations: Power and Policy of an Emerging Global Forces*, 5th ed. (Lanham, MD: Rowman & Littlefield, 2021), 71–95; Timothy Heath, Derek Grossman, and Asha Clark, *China's Quest for Global Dominance* (Washington, DC: RAND Corporation, 2021).

3. See the discussion of human rights issues in Harry Harding, *A Fragile Relationship: The United States and China since 1972* (Washington, DC: Brookings Institution, 1992); James Mann, *About Face: A History of America's Curious Relationship with China, from Nixon to Clinton* (New York: Knopf, 1999); David M. Lampton, *Same Bed, Different Dreams: Managing U.S.-China Relations, 1989–2000* (Berkeley: University of California Press, 2001); and Ming Wan, *Human Rights in Chinese Foreign Relations: Defining and Defending National Interests* (Philadelphia: University of Pennsylvania Press, 2001). See also People's Republic of China State Council Information Office, *National Human Rights Action Plan of China (2009–2010)*, April 13, 2009, http://www.china.org.cn/archive/2009-04/13/content_17595407.htm.

4. "Don't Call It the New Chinese Global Order (Yet)," *Foreign Policy*, March 7, 2017, http://foreignpolicy.com/2017/03/07/dont-call-it-the-chinese-global-order-yet-xi-jinping-donald-trump-values; Melanie Hart and Blaine Johnson, *Mapping China's Global Governance Ambitions* (Washington, DC: Center for American Progress, February 2019); Heath, Grossman, and Clark, *China's Quest for Global Dominance*.

5. Yu Keping, "Ideological Change and Incremental Democracy in Reform-Era China," in *China's Changing Political Landscape: Prospects for Democracy*, ed. Cheng Li (Washington, DC: Brookings Institution, 2008), 44–60.

6. Jacques deLisle, "Legalization without Democratization in China under Hu Jintao," in *China's Changing Political Landscape*, ed. Cheng Li (Washington, DC: Brookings Institution, 2008), 185–211.

7. Gong Li, "The Difficult Path to Diplomatic Relations: China's U.S. Policy, 1972–1978," in *Normalization of U.S.-China Relations: An International History*,

ed. William Kirby, Robert Ross, and Gong Li (Cambridge, MA: Harvard University Press, 2005), 116–146.

8. Harding, *A Fragile Relationship*, 198–99; Warren Cohen, *America's Response to China: A History of Sino-American Relations* (New York: Columbia University Press, 2000), 213.

9. Cohen, *America's Response to China*, 212–13.

10. Harding, *A Fragile Relationship*, 198–206; Mann, *About Face*, 100–9.

11. Michael Schaller, *The United States and China into the Twenty-First Century* (New York: Oxford University Press, 2002), 197.

12. John K. Fairbank and Merle Goldman, *China: A New History* (Cambridge, MA: Harvard University Press, 1999), 419–26.

13. Lampton, *Same Bed, Different Dreams*, 130–53.

14. Song Qiang, Zhang Changchang, and Qiao Bian, *Zhongguo keyi shuo bu: Lengzhanhou shidai de zhengzhi yu qinggan jueze* [China can say no: The decision between politics and sentiment in the post–Cold War] (Beijing: Zhonghua Gongshang Lianhe Chubanshe, 1996).

15. Mann, *About Face*, 200–1.

16. Lampton, *Same Bed, Different Dreams*, 15–63.

17. Sheryl Gay Stolberg, "Bush Meets 5 Dissidents from China before Games," *New York Times*, July 30, 2008, http://www.nytimes.com/2008/07/30/sports/olympics/30prexy.html?mcubz=1.

18. "Remarks by the President at the U.S./China Strategic and Economic Dialogue," The White House, Office of the Press Secretary, July 27, 2009, https://obamawhitehouse.archives.gov/the-press-office/remarks-president-uschina-strategic-and-economic-dialogue.

19. Gideon Rachman, "China's Strange Fear of Colour Revolution," *Financial Times*, February 9, 2015, https://www.ft.com/content/9b5a2ed2-af96-11e4-b42e-00144feab7de.

20. C. Fred Bergsten, Bates Gill, Nicholas Lardy, and Derek Mitchell, *China: The Balance Sheet* (New York: Public Affairs, 2006), 62–72; "China Hits Back on U.S. Human Rights," CNN, May 25, 2012, http://www.cnn.com/2012/05/25/world/asia/china-us-human-rights/index.html.

21. Kerry Dumbaugh, *Tibet: Problems, Prospects, and U.S. Policy*, CRS Report RL34445 (Washington, DC: Congressional Research Service of the Library of Congress, July 30, 2008); Jeffrey Bader, *Obama and China's Rise* (Washington, DC: Brookings Institution, 2012), 48–52, 72–75.

22. Thomas Lum and Michael Weber, *Human Rights in China and US Policy: Issues for the 117th Congress*, Congressional Research Service Report R46750, March 31, 2021, 21–22.

23. Orville Schell and Susan Shirk, chairs, *U.S. Policy toward China: Recommendations for a New Administration*, Task Force Report (New York: Asia Society, 2017), 53; Hart and Johnson, *Mapping China's Global Governance Ambitions*; Heath, Grossman, and Clark, *China's Quest for Global Dominance*.

24. Bergsten et al., *China*, 62–72; Cheng Li, "Will China's 'Lost Generation' Find a Path to Democracy?," in *China's Changing Political Landscape: Prospects for*

Democracy, ed. Cheng Li (Washington, DC: Brookings Institution, 2008), 98–120; Joseph Few Smith, "Staying in Power: What Does the Chinese Communist Party Have to Do?," in *China's Changing Political Landscape: Prospects for Democracy*, ed. Cheng Li (Washington, DC: Brookings Institution, 2008), 212–28; US Department of State, Bureau of Democracy, Human Rights and Labor, *Country Reports on Human Rights Practices for 2011: China* (includes Tibet, Hong Kong, and Macau), https://www.state.gov/j/drl/rls/hrrpt/2011/eap/186268.htm; US Department of State, Bureau of Democracy, Human Rights and Labor, *Country Reports on Human Rights Practices for 2016: China* (includes Tibet, Hong Kong, and Macau), https://www.state.gov/documents/organization/265540.pdf.

25. US Department of State, *Country Reports on Human Rights Practices for 2011*; Congressional-Executive Commission on China, *Annual Report 2012*, October 10, 2012, https://www.cecc.gov/publications/annual-reports/2012-annual-report; US Commission on International Religious Freedom, *Annual Report of the U.S. Commission on International Human Rights*, March 2012, http://www.uscirf.gov/sites/default/files/resources/Annual%20Report%20of%20USCIRF%202012(2).pdf; Amnesty International, *Annual Report 2012—China, 2012*, accessed March 5, 2013, https://www.amnestyusa.org/files/air12-report-english.pdf; Human Rights Watch, *World Report 2013–China*, accessed March 5, 2013, https://www.hrw.org/world-report/2013/country-chapters/china-and-tibet.

26. Thomas Lum and Hannah Fischer, *Human Rights in China: Trends and Policy Implications*, CRS Report RL34729 (Washington, DC: Congressional Research Service of the Library of Congress, July 17, 2009), 1; Susan Lawrence and David MacDonald, *U.S.-China Relations: Policy Issues*, CRS Report R41108 (Washington, DC: Congressional Research Service of the Library of Congress, August 2, 2012), 35–42.

27. Andrew Nathan, "China at the Tipping Point?," *Journal of Democracy* 24, no. 1 (January 2013): 20–25; People's Republic of China State Council Information Office, *National Human Rights Action Plan of China (2012–2015)*, June 14, 2012, http://news.xinhuanet.com/english/china/2016-06/14/c_135435326.htm.

28. Bergsten, *China*, 62–64; Lawrence and MacDonald, *U.S.-China Relations*, 35–42; Lum and Fischer, *Human Rights in China*, 2. As seen from source notes below, reports from the Department of State and the Congressional Research Service of the Library of Congress provide comprehensive and balanced coverage of human rights issues in China of use to researchers and specialists.

29. "Recent High-Profile Mass Protests in China," *BBC News*, July 3, 2012, http://www.bbc.co.uk/news/world-asia-china-18684903.

30. Thomas Lum and Hannah Fischer, *Human Rights in China: Trends and Policy Implications*, CRS Report RL34729 (Washington, DC: Congressional Research Service of the Library of Congress, October 31, 2008), 3–4; US Department of State, *Country Reports on Human Rights Practices for 2011*.

31. Yu Keping, *Democracy Is a Good Thing* (Washington, DC: Brookings Institution, 2008); C. Fred Bergsten, Charles Freeman, Nicholas Lardy, and Derek Mitchell, *China's Rise: Challenges and Opportunities* (Washington, DC: Peterson

Institute for International Economics, 2008), 38; Nathan et al., "China at the Tipping Point?"

32. Paul Mooney, "How to Deal with NGOs—Part 1, China," YaleGlobal Online, August 1, 2006, http://yaleglobal.yale.edu/content/how-deal-ngos-part-i-china; Raymond Li, "Li Keqiang Wants Tax Breaks for NGOs Specializing in AIDS/HIV Work," *South China Morning Post*, November 29, 2012, http://www.scmp.com/news/china/article/1093457/li-keqiang-wants-tax-breaks-ngos-specialising-aidshiv-work.

33. Lum and Fischer, *Human Rights in China*, 5–7.

34. Schell and Shirk, *U.S. Policy toward China*, 53–55; US Department of State, *Country Reports on Human Rights Practices for 2016* (see "Executive Summary").

35. Thomas Lum, *Human Rights in China and U.S. Policy*, CRS Report R43964 (Washington, DC: Congressional Research Service of the Library of Congress, September 17, 2015); see "Summary" pages.

36. US Department of State, *Country Reports on Human Rights Practices for 2016* (see "Executive Summary").

37. Lum and Weber, *Human Rights in China and US Policy*; US Department of State, *2020 Country Reports on Human Rights Practices*; Human Rights Watch, *China: Events of 2020* (2021), https://www.hrw.org/world-report/2021/country-chapters/china-and-tibet#; Amnesty International, *China 2020* (2021), https://www.amnesty.org/en/countries/asia-and-the-pacific/china/report-china/.

38. Enshen Li, "Fighting the 'Three Evils,'" *Emory International Law Review* 33, no. 3 (2019), https://scholarlycommons.law.emory.edu/eilr/vol33/iss3/1.

39. *China Primer: Uyghurs*, Congressional Research Service Report IF10281, June 1, 2021.

40. Amy Gunia, "Pompeo Calls China's Treatment of Uyghurs the 'Stain of the Century,'" *Time*, July 18, 2019.

41. Ibid.

42. Bonnie Glaser and Hannah Price, "Continuity Prevails in Biden's First 100 Days," *Comparative Connections* 23 (May 1, 2021): 35–36.

43. Lum and Weber, *Human Rights in China and US Policy*, 5, 10.

44. *Human Rights in China*, Congressional Research Service Report IF11240, January 13, 2021, 2.

45. Ibid.

46. *Hong Kong: Key Issues in 2021*, Congressional Research Service Report IF11711, December 23, 2020, 1

47. Ibid.

48. *Hong Kong: Key Issues in 2021*, 2.

49. "US Reaffirms Trump-Era Ruling that Hong Kong Lacks Autonomy," *Aljazeera*, March 31, 2021, https://www.aljazeera.com/news/2021/3/31/blinken-reaffirms-trump-era-ruling-on-hong-kong-autonomy.

50. *Human Rights in China*, 1.

51. Lum and Weber, *Human Rights in China and US Policy*, 5–6.

52. *Human Rights in China*, 1.

53. Lum, *Human Rights in China and U.S. Policy*, 6; Linda Yeung, "Campus Crackdown on 'Western Values,'" University World News, February 6, 2015, http://www.universityworldnews.com/article.php?story=2015020710141145.

54. "Hong Kong Bookseller Gui Minhai Jailed for 10 Years in China," *The Guardian*, February 25, 2020, https://www.theguardian.com/world/2020/feb/25/gui-minhai-detained-hong-kong-bookseller-jailed-for-10-years-in-china.

55. US Department of State, *Country Reports on Human Rights Practices for 2016*, 5–6; "Swedish Rights Groups Honours Detained Bookseller Gui Minho," AFP via HKFP, April 22, 2017, https://www.hongkongfp.com/2017/04/22/swedish-rights-group-honours-detained-bookseller-gui-minhai.

56. Masood Farivar, "FBI Arrests Five People in China's 'Operation Fox Hunt,'" *VOA*, October 28, 2020, https://www.voanews.com/usa/fbi-arrests-five-people-chinas-operation-fox-hunt.

57. Maria Hsia Chang, *Falun Gong: The End of Days* (New Haven, CT: Yale University Press, 2004).

58. Thomas Lum, *China and Falun Gong*, CRS Report 33437 (Washington, DC: Congressional Research Service of the Library of Congress, May 25, 2006).

59. Schell and Shirk, *U.S. Policy toward China*, 54–55.

60. Sutter, *Chinese Foreign Relations*, 77–78.

61. Notable reports supporting this judgment and providing more clarity on the breadth and depth of Chinese challenges to the United States are listed here. Individual reports and/or other evidence are cited in dealing with specific examples of Chinese challenges below. Daniel R. Russel and Blake Berger, *Navigating the Belt and Road Initiative* (New York: Asia Society Policy Institute, June 2019); Melanie Hart and Blaine Johnson, *Mapping China's Global Governance Ambitions* (Washington, DC: Center for American Progress, February 2019); Melanie Hart and Kelly Magsamen, *Limit, Leverage and Compete: A New Strategy on China* (Washington, DC: Center for American Progress, April 2019); Matt Schrader, *Friends and Enemies: A Framework for Understanding Chinese Political Influence in Democratic Countries* (Washington, DC: German Marshall Fund, April 22, 2020); David Shullman, ed., *Chinese Malign Influence and the Corrosion of Democracy* (Washington, DC: International Republican Institute, 2019); Daniel Kliman, Rush Doshi, Kristine Lee, and Zack Cooper, *Grading China's Belt and Road* (Washington, DC: Center for New American Security, April 2019); Ashley Tellis, Alison Szalwinski, and Michael Wills, eds., *Strategic Asia, 2020: US-China Competition for Global Influence* (Seattle, WA: National Bureau of Asian Research, 2020); Nadege Rolland, *China's Vision for a New World Order* (Seattle, WA: National Bureau for Asian Research, January 2020); Larry Diamond and Orville Schell, coordinators, *Chinese Influence and American Interests* (Stanford, CA: Hoover Institution Press, 2018); Scott McDonald and Michael Burgoyne, eds., *China's Global Influence* (Honolulu, HI: Asia-Pacific Center for Security Studies, 2020); Thomas Mahnken, Ross Babbage, and Toshi Yoshihara, *Countering Comprehensive Coercion* (Washington, DC: Center for Strategic and Budgetary Assessments, 2018); Ross Babbage, *Winning Without Fighting: Chinese and Russian Political Warfare Campaigns and How the West Can Prevail* (Washington, DC: Center for Strategic and Budgetary Assessments, 2018);

Matt Geraci, "An Update on American Perspectives on the Belt and Road Initiative," *ICAS Issue Primers*, January 23, 2020; Nadege Roland, ed., *Securing the Belt and Road Initiative* (Seattle, WA: National Bureau of Asian Research, September 3, 2019); Andrew Foxall and John Hemmings, *The Art of Deceit* (London: The Henry Jackson Society, 2019); Samantha Hoffman, *Engineering Global Consent* (Canberra: APSI Policy Brief, 2019); Peter Harrell, Elizabeth Rosenberg, and Edoardo Saravalle, *China's Use of Coercive Economic Measures* (Washington, DC: Center of New American Security, June 11, 2018).

62. Elizabeth Economy, *The Third Revolution: Xi Jinping and the New Chinese State* (New York: Council on Foreign Relations, 2018); Heath, Grossman, and Clark, *China's Quest for Global Dominance.*

63. As Huawei takes over a country's telecommunications, it can collect information from users of its systems. Although billed as a private company, civilian entities in the PRC like Huawei and ZTE are legally required to provide information to the party government. US Department of Justice, "Attorney General William P. Barr Delivers the Keynote Address at the Department of Justice's China Initiative Conference," Washington, DC, February 6, 2020, https://www.justice.gov/opa/speech/attorney-general-william-p-barr-delivers-keynote-address-department-justices-china.

64. Hart and Magsamen, *Limit, Leverage and Compete*, 3–5; United Nations Secretary General, "Secretary-General's Remarks at the Opening Ceremony of the Belt and Road Forum for International Cooperation," April 26, 2019, https://www.un.org/sg/en/content/sg/statement/2019-04-26/secretary-generals-remarks-the-opening-ceremony-of-the-belt-and-road-forum-for-international-cooperation.

65. Harrell, Rosenberg, and Saravalle, *China's Use of Coercive Economic Measures*, 2–3.

66. Kliman et al., *Grading China's Belt and Road* (see challenge #3 "unsustainable financial burdens" covered throughout the report); Russel and Berger, *Navigating the Belt and Road Initiative*, 11–14.

67. Shullman, *Chinese Malign Influence*, 13–14; Krzysztof Iwanek, "No, Pakistan's Gwadar Port Is Not a Chinese Naval Base (Just Yet)," *The Diplomat*, November 19, 2019, https://thediplomat.com/2019/11/no-pakistans-gwadar-port-is-not-a-chinese-naval-base-just-yet.

68. Russel and Berger, *Navigating the Belt and Road Initiative*, 16–17; Kliman et al., *Grading China's Belt and Road* (see challenge #7 "significant potential for corruption" covered throughout the report).

69. Shullman, *Chinese Malign Influence*, 13–14, 18–19, 22–23, 27–28, 32–33, 36–37, 40–41, 44, 47, 52–53, 56–57; Hart and Johnson, *Mapping China's Global Governance Ambitions*, 16–17; Kliman et al., *Grading China's Belt and Road* (see challenge #1 "erosion of national sovereignty" covered throughout the report); Russel and Berger, *Navigating the Belt and Road Initiative*, 11–12; Hoffman, *Engineering Global Consent*, Executive Summary.

70. For an up-to-date comprehensive treatment of recent Chinese foreign relations, see Sutter, *Chinese Foreign Relations: Power and Policy*, 5th ed.

71. "Chronology of China-Southeast Asia Relations," *Comparative Connections* 22, no. 1 (May 2020): 65–68; David Brown and Kyle Churchman, "Coronavirus

Embitters Cross-Strait Relations," *Comparative Connections* 22, no. 1 (May 2020): 76; "First Russian-Chinese Air Patrol in Asia-Pacific Draws Shots," Reuters, July 22, 2019, https://www.reuters.com/article/us-southkorea-russia-aircraft/first-russian-chinese-air-patrol-in-asia-pacific-draws-shots-from-south-korea-idUSKCN1UI072.

72. "Chronology of China-Southeast Asia Relations," 68–69.

73. Diamond and Schell, *Chinese Influence and American Interests*, 145–86, 148, 152, 158–59, 161–63, 170–72; Mahnken, Babbage, and Yoshihara, *Countering Comprehensive Coercion*, 25–52; Babbage, *Winning Without Fighting*, 17–72, 32–33, 52; Foxall and Hemmings, *The Art of Deceit*, 14–17.

74. "How Sweden Copes with Chinese Bullying," *The Economist*, February 20, 2020, https://www.economist.com/europe/2020/02/20/how-sweden-copes-with-chinese-bullying; Jeffrey Mervis, "When Europeans Do Science in China," *Science*, September 11, 2019, https://www.sciencemag.org/news/2019/09/when-europeans-do-science-china; Alan Crawford and Peter Martin, "How Belgium Became Europe's Den of Spies and Gateway for China," *Bloomberg*, November 28, 2019, https://www.bloomberg.com/news/articles/2019-11-28/how-belgium-became-europe-s-den-of-spies-and-a-gateway-for-china.

75. "Beijing Rejects Tribunal Ruling in South China Sea Case," *The Guardian*, July 12, 2016, https://www.theguardian.com/world/2016/jul/12/philippines-wins-south-china-sea-case-against-china; "How Sweden Copes with Chinese Bullying"; Mike Blanchfield, "The Chill Is Real," *CTV News*, February 7, 2020, https://www.ctvnews.ca/politics/the-chill-is-real-ambassador-on-canada-china-relationship-1.4799020; Hart and Johnson, *Mapping China's Global Governance Ambitions*, 12–13 (paragraphs 12 and 13).

76. Robert Sutter, *China-Russia Relations: Strategic Implications and US Policy Options* (Seattle, WA: National Bureau of Asian Research, NBR Special Report No. 73, September 2018), 3–8.

77. Robert Sutter and Chin-hao Huang, "Beijing Leads Regional Agenda, Rejects US Challenges," *Comparative Connections* 21, no. 3 (January 2020): 60–64; Laura Zhou, "Chinese President Xi Jinping to Take Over as Host of 17+1 Summit," *South China Morning Post*, January 2, 2020, https://www.scmp.com/news/china/diplomacy/article/3044359/chinese-president-xi-jinping-take-over-host-171-summit.

78. Sutter, *Chinese Foreign Relations*, 82–88.

79. Babbage, *Winning Without Fighting*, 30–31, 38–42, 50–52, 59–60; Diamond and Schell, *Chinese Influence and American Interests*, 29–38, 147–48, 151–52, 157–58, 162, 170–71, 177–78, 180–81.

80. Babbage, *Winning Without Fighting*, 32, 39–43, 52; Foxall and Hemmings, *The Art of Deceit*, 14–17; Shullman, *Chinese Malign Influence*, 12–15, 17–18, 21–22, 26–28, 32–33, 36–37, 48, 51–52, 55–56, 59–61; Hart and Johnson, *Mapping China's Global Governance Ambitions*, 17–18, 21–22; Kliman et al., *Grading China's Belt and Road*, 6–7, 10, 13, 15, 16, 18; Russel and Berger, *Navigating the Belt and Road Initiative*, 11–14, 16–17.

81. Harrell, Rosenberg, and Saravalle, *China's Use of Coercive Economic Measures*, 11–33. See also, Elizabeth Rosenberg, Peter Harrell, and Ashley Feng, *A*

New Arsenal for Competition (Washington, DC: Center for New American Security, April 2020), 22–39.

82. "China Cuts Australian Beef Imports as Coronavirus Tensions Escalate," *Los Angeles Times*, May 12, 2020, https://www.latimes.com/world-nation/story/2020-05-12/china-cuts-australian-beef-imports-coronavirus-tension; "China-Southeast Asian Relations," *Comparative Connections* 23, no. 1 (May 2021): 72–73.

83. Harrell, Rosenberg, and Saravalle, *China's Use of Coercive Economic Measures*, 7–8, 10; Erik Brattberg and Philippe Le Corre, *The EU and China in 2020: More Competition Ahead* (Washington, DC: Carnegie Endowment, February 19, 2020), see section "Potential Chinese Backlash on 5G Decisions"; "Chinese Donation Diplomacy Raises Tensions," *New York Times*, April 14, 2020, https://www.nytimes.com/2020/04/14/us/politics/coronavirus-china-trump-donation.html.

84. Rosie Perper, "China and the NBA Are Coming to Blows over a Pro-Hong Kong Tweet," *Business Insider*, October 22, 2019, https://www.businessinsider.com/nba-china-feud-timeline-daryl-morey-tweet-hong-kong-protests-2019-10; Benjamin Haas, "Marriott Apologizes to China over Tibet and Taiwan Error," *The Guardian*, January 12, 2018, https://www.theguardian.com/world/2018/jan/12/marriott-apologises-to-china-over-tibet-and-taiwan-error.

85. "How Sweden Copes with Chinese Bullying"; "US to Order Drastic Reduction in Chinese Diplomats amid Surge of Spy Cases," *Washington Times*, July 28, 2020, https://www.washingtontimes.com/news/2020/jul/28/us-china-standoff-trump-administration-order-reduc/.

86. Fumi Matsumoto and Kensaku Ihara, "Fear of China's Election Meddling Triggers Reforms across Pacific," *Nikkei Asian Review*, December 7, 2019, https://asia.nikkei.com/Politics/International-relations/Fear-of-China-s-election-meddling-triggers-reforms-across-Pacific; "Joe Biden Warns of Chinese Interference in Presidential Election," *The Telegraph*, July 18, 2020, https://www.telegraph.co.uk/news/2020/07/18/joe-biden-warns-chinese-interference-presidential-election/.

87. Hart and Johnson, *Mapping China's Global Governance Ambitions*, 16–17; Foxall and Hemmings, *The Art of Deceit*, 17–18.

88. Peter Mattis, *China's Digital Authoritarianism: Surveillance, Influence and Political Control* (Washington, DC: Testimony before the House Permanent Select Committee on Intelligence, May 16, 2019); Shullman, *Chinese Malign Influence*, 14, 18–19, 22–23, 27–28, 36–37, 40, 44, 48, 52–53.

89. Alexander Bowe, *China's Overseas United Front Work* (Washington, DC: US-China Economic and Security Review Commission, August 18, 2018).

90. "China Committed to Globalization," *China Daily*, January 23, 2020, http://www.chinadaily.com.cn/a/202001/23/WS5e2901eca310128217272f52.html.

91. Hart and Magsamen, *Limit, Leverage and Compete*, 17–19.

92. *US-China Trade Issues*, Congressional Research Service Report IF10030 (Washington, DC: Library of Congress, June 23, 2019), 2.

93. Wayne M. Morrison, *China's Economic Rise*, Congressional Research Service Report RL33534 (Washington, DC: Library of Congress, June 25, 2019), 36–37; Wayne M. Morrison, *US-China Trade Issues*, Congressional Research Service Report RL33536 (Washington, DC: Library of Congress, June 30, 2018), 1–2; David Lynch,

"Trump's Raise the Stakes Strategy Raises Anxiety," *Washington Post*, July 21, 2018, A14.

94. Haas, "Marriott Apologizes to China."

95. Perper, "China and the NBA Are Coming to Blows."

96. Yanan Wang, "Xi Says China 'Will Never Seek Hegemony,'" *Associated Press*, December 18, 2018, https://www.theglobeandmail.com/business/international-business/asia-pacific-business/article-chinas-xi-pledges-unswerving-reforms-but-on-own-terms/.

97. Jacob Mardell, "The Community of Common Destiny in Xi Jinping's New Era," *The Diplomat*, October 25, 2017, https://thediplomat.com/2017/10/the-community-of-common-destiny-in-xi-jinpings-new-era/.

98. "Chronology of China-Southeast Asia Relations," 61–62.

99. Ibid., 65–68.

100. Ibid., 55. For a detailed Chinese assessment of the South China Sea and China's objection to the US role there, see Wu Shicun, *The US Military Presence in the Asia Pacific 2020* (Haikou, China: National Institute for South China Sea Studies, June 2020), 1–15, 56–59, 66–74.

101. Harrell, Rosenberg, and Saravalle, *China's Use of Coercive Economic Measures*, 7–8, 10; Brattberg and Le Corre, *The EU and China* (see section "Potential Chinese Backlash on 5G Decisions"); Zhou, "Chinese President Xi Jinping to Take Over as Host."

102. Economy, "Yes, Virginia, China Is Exporting Its Model."

103. Tobin, "Xi's Vision for Transforming Global Governance," 54–56.

CHAPTER TWELVE

1. Warren Cohen, *America's Response to China* (New York: Columbia University Press, 2010), and Michael Schaller, *The United States and China: Into the Twenty-First Century*, 4th ed. (New York: Oxford University Press, 2015), commonly employ a realist perspective in explaining the often turbulent course of US-China relations.

2. David Shambaugh, ed., *Tangled Titans* (Lanham, MD: Rowman & Littlefield, 2012), a widely used volume, takes an eclectic approach, with different authors seeing the utility of liberalism as well as realism and constructivism in understanding developments in US-China relations.

3. Employing a line of assessment that could be viewed as constructivist, a highly regarded historical account, Gordon H. Chang, *Fateful Ties: A History of America's Preoccupation with China* (Cambridge, MA: Harvard University Press, 2015), focuses on the positive attraction of China to the United States.

4. Michael Swaine, "China Doesn't Pose an Existential Threat for America," Quincy Institute for Responsible Statecraft, April 22, 2021, https://quincyinst.org/2021/04/22/china-doesnt-pose-an-existential-threat-for-america/; Ryan Hass, "China Is Not Ten Feet Tall," *Foreign Affairs*, March 3, 2021, https://www.foreignaffairs.com/articles/china/2021-03-03/china-not-ten-feet-tall; Ryan Hass, "Playing the China Card," *NOEMA*, May 20, 2021, https://www.noemamag.com/playing-the-china-card/;

"Decoupling with China Not Economically Viable for Americans," Press Release of US-China Business Council, January 14, 2021, https://www.uschina.org/media/press/decoupling-china-not-economically-viable-americans.

5. Wu Xinbo, "The China Challenge," *The Washington Quarterly* 43, no. 3 (Fall 2020): 99–114; Jia Qingguo, "Malign or Benign? China-US Strategic Competition under Biden," East Asia Forum, March 28, 2021, https://www.eastasiaforum.org/2021/03/28/malign-or-benign-china-us-strategic-competition-under-biden/.

6. Joe Biden, "My Trip Is About America Rallying the World's Democracies," *Washington Post*, June 6, 2021, A25; David Brunnstrom, Alexandra Alper, and Yew Lun Tian, "China Will 'Eat Our Lunch,' Biden Warns after Clashing with Xi on Most Fronts," Reuters, February 10, 2021; "US View of China Competition," US-China Policy Foundation Newsletter, May 21, 2021, https://uscpf.org/v3/2021/05/21/us-china-competition/; "China Discussed in Defense Budget Hearing," US-China Policy Foundation Newsletter, June 18, 2021, https://uscpf.org/v3/news/; Tony Romm, "Senate Approves \$250 Billion to Trim China's Ambitions," *Washington Post*, June 9, 2021, A18; David Sanger, Catie Edmondson, David McCabe, and Thomas Kaplan, "In Rare Show of Unity, Senate Poised to Pass a Bill to Counter China," *New York Times*, June 7, 2021, A10.

7. Robert Sutter, "China's Foreign Behavior Warrants Sustained US Countermeasures," *PacNet* 59, October 29, 2020, https://pacforum.org/publication/pacnet-59-chinas-foreign-behavior-warrants-sustained-us-countermeasures; Ryan Hass, "How China Is Responding to Escalating Strategic Competition with the US," *China Leadership Monitor*, March 1, 2021, https://www.prcleader.org/hass.

8. David Lynch, "Trump's Raise the Stakes Strategy," *Washington Post*, July 21, 2018, A14; *China's Economy: Current Trends and Issues*, Congressional Research Service Report IF11667, January 12, 2021; *China's 14th Five-Year Plan*, Congressional Research Service Report IF11684, January 5, 2021.

9. Matt Pottinger, "Testimony before US Senate Armed Services Committee," June 8, 2021, https://www.hoover.org/sites/default/files/written_testimony_to_sasc1.pdf.

10. Jeff Seldin, "US Intelligence Warns China, Russia Determined to Erode Washington's Influence," *VOA*, April 13, 2021, https://www.voanews.com/usa/us-intelligence-warns-china-russia-determined-erode-washingtons-influence; "An Emerging China-Russia Axis?," Hearing of US-China Economic and Security Review Commission, March 21, 2019, https://www.uscc.gov/hearings/emerging-china-russia-axis-implications-united-states-era-strategic-competition.

11. Melanie Hart and Blaine Johnson, *Mapping China's Global Governance Ambitions* (Washington, DC: Center for American Progress, February 2019).

12. *China's Belt and Road: Implications for the United States*, Council on Foreign Relations Independent Task Force Report No. 79 (2021), 17–19, 50.

13. *China's Belt and Road*, 17–19, 43, 50, 67–70; Robert Sutter, *Chinese Foreign Relations: Power and Policy of an Emerging Global Force* (Lanham, MD: Rowman & Littlefield, 2021), 46, 58–59, 209, 238, 288.

14. Sutter, *Chinese Foreign Relations: Power and Policy of an Emerging Global Force*, 139, 204–9.

15. Sutter, "China's Foreign Behavior Warrants Sustained US Countermeasures," 2.

16. Sutter, *Chinese Foreign Relations: Power and Policy of an Emerging Global Force*, 314.

17. Sutter, "China's Foreign Behavior Warrants Sustained US Countermeasures," 3.

18. John Deutch, "Is Innovation China's New Great Leap Forward?," *Issues in Science and Technology* (Summer 2018): 37–47.

19. *Annual Threat Assessment of the US Intelligence Community*, Office of the Director of National Intelligence, April 9, 2021, 6–9.

20. *Global Trends 2040*, US National Intelligence Council, March 2021, 94–95.

21. Ibid.

22. Aaron Friedberg, *Beyond Air-Sea Battle: The Debate over US Military Strategy in Asia*, Adelphi Paper 444 (London: International Institute for Strategic Studies, 2014).

23. Denny Roy, "US Strategy toward China: Three Key Questions for Policy-Makers," *PacNet* 30 (Honolulu, HI: Pacific Forum CSIS, May 28, 2019), https://www.pacforum.org/sites/default/files/20190528_PacNet_30.pdf.

24. For differing views on China and the United States in Asia, see Dennis Blair, "A Strong Foundation but Weak Blueprint for National Security," in *Strategic Asia 2015–16: Foundations of National Power in the Asia-Pacific*, ed. Michael Wills, Ashley J. Tellis, and Alison Szalwinski (Seattle, WA: National Bureau of Asian Research, 2016), 224–58; "Roundtable: Contending Visions of the Regional Order in East Asia," *Asia Policy* 13, no. 2 (April 2018); Ashley Tellis, Alison Szalwinski, and Michael Wills, eds., *Strategic Asia 2019: China's Expanding Strategic Ambitions* (Seattle, WA: National Bureau of Asian Research, 2019); Ashley J. Tellis, Alison Szalwinski, and Michael Wills, *Strategic Asia 2020: US-China Competition for Global Influence* (Seattle, WA: National Bureau of Asian Research, 2020); Christopher Layne, "The US-Chinese Power Shift and the End of the Pax Americana," International Affairs 94, no. 1 (January 2018): 89–111; Ashley J. Tellis, "Waylaid by Contradictions: Evaluating Trump's IndoPacific Strategy," *The Washington Quarterly* 43, no. 4 (2020): 123–54; Ren Xiao and Liu Ming, *Chinese Perspectives on International Relations in the Xi Jinping Era* (Seattle, WA: National Bureau of Asian Research, June 2020); Wang Dong and Weizhan Meng, "China Debating the Regional Order," *The Pacific Review* 33 (2020): 497–519; *Regional Responses to US-China Competition in the Indo-Pacific* (Washington, DC: RAND Corporation, 2020); Yuan Peng: "The New Coronavirus Epidemic Situation and Centennial Changes in 袁鹏, "新冠疫情与百年变局," June 17, 2020, http://www.aisixiang.com/data/121742.html, translated in *Reading the China Dream*, https://www.readingthechinadream.com/yuan-peng-coronavirus-pandemic.html; Chen Zhimin and Xueying Zhang, "Chinese Conceptions of the World Order in the Turbulent Trump Era," *The Pacific Review* 33 (2020): 438–68; Timothy Heath, Derek Grossman, and Asha Clark, *China's Quest for Global Dominance* (Washington, DC: RAND Corporation, 2021); Evan Medeiros, *Major Power Rivalry in East Asia* (Washington, DC: Council on Foreign Relations, April 2021).

25. Over the past twenty years, this writer has assessed the strengths and weaknesses of China's rise in Asian and world affairs in various publications. Those detailed assessments duly considered differing perspectives on China's strengths and

weaknesses and those of the United States and other concerned powers. For those interested in the evolution of these assessments and various sources used, see Robert Sutter, *The United States and Asia* (Lanham, MD: Rowman & Littlefield, 2020), 327–34; Robert Sutter, *Foreign Relations of the PRC* (Lanham, MD: Rowman & Littlefield, 2019), 297–301; Sutter, *Chinese Foreign Relations: Power and Policy of an Emerging Global Force*, 301–14; and the earlier editions of this book. The assessment in this chapter builds on those previous assessments.

26. Robert Sutter, "Obama's Cautious and Calibrated Approach to an Assertive China," *YaleGlobal Online*, April 19, 2016, http://yaleglobal.yale.edu/content/obamas-cautious-and-calibrated-approach-assertive-china.

27. Robert Sutter and Satu Limaye, *America's 2016 Election Debate on Asia Policy and Asian Reactions* (Honolulu, HI: East-West Center, 2016).

28. Robert Sutter, *Russia-China Relations: Assessing Common Ground and Strategic Fault Lines* (Seattle, WA: National Bureau of Asian Research, July 2017), http://nbr.org/publications/element.aspx?id=950.

29. Sutter, *Chinese Foreign Relations: Power and Policy of an Emerging Global Force*, 301–3.

30. See, among others, Elizabeth Economy, *The Third Revolution: Xi Jinping and the New Chinese State* (New York: Council on Foreign Relations, 2018); Sebastian Heilmann, ed., *China's Political System* (Lanham, MD: Rowman & Littlefield, 2017); David Shambaugh, *China's Future* (Cambridge, UK: Polity Press, 2016); Bruce Dickson, *The Dictator's Dilemma: The Chinese Communist Party's Strategy for Survival* (New York: Oxford University Press, 2016); Arthur Kroeber, *China's Economy: What Everyone Needs to Know* (New York: Oxford University Press, 2016); Elizabeth Perry, "Growing Pains: Challenges for a Rising China," *Daedalus* 143, no. 2 (Spring 2014): 5–13; Martin King Whyte, "China's Dormant and Active Volcanoes," *China Journal* (January 2016): 9–37; Deborah Davis, "Demographic Challenges for a Rising China," *Daedalus* 143, no. 2 (Spring 2014): 26–38; Cheng Li, "The End of the CCP's Resilient Authoritarianism? A Tripartite Assessment of Shifting Power in China," *China Quarterly* 211 (September 2012): 595–623; Minxin Pei, *China's Crony Capitalism: The Dynamics of Regime Decay* (Cambridge, MA: Harvard University Press, 2016); Daniel Lynch, *China's Futures: PRC Elites Debate Economics, Politics, and Foreign Policy* (Stanford, CA: Stanford University Press, 2015); William Callahan, *China: The Pessioptimist Nation* (Oxford, UK: Oxford University Press, 2010).

31. See, for example, China's recent conflicted approach to the Philippines in "China-Southeast Asia," *Comparative Connections* 23, no. 1 (May 2021): 68–72.

32. See David Shambaugh, *China's Future* (Cambridge, UK: Polity Press, 2016).

33. Ben Blanchard and John Ruwitch, "China Hikes Defense Budget, to Spend More in Internal Security," Reuters, March 5, 2013, http://www.reuters.com/article/2013/03/05/us-china-parliament-defence-idUSBRE92403620130305.

34. Sutter, *Chinese Foreign Relations: Power and Policy of an Emerging Global Force*, 304.

35. Victor Shih, "US-China Relations in 2019: A Year in Review," testimony before the US-China Economic and Security Review Commission, September 4, 2019, https://www.uscc.gov/Hearings/us-china-relations-2019-year-review.

36. *COVID-19: China Medical Supply Chains and Broader Trade Issues*, Congressional Research Service Report R46304 (Washington, DC: Library of Congress, April 6, 2020).

37. Josh Rogin, "The Coronavirus Is Turning Americans in Both Parties Against China," *Washington Post*, April 8, 2020, https://www.washingtonpost.com/opinions/2020/04/08/coronavirus-crisis-is-turning-americans-both-parties-against-china; Paul Heer, "Why the Coronavirus Is a Hinge for the Future of US-China Relations," *National Interest*, April 7, 2020, https://nationalinterest.org/feature/why-coronavirus-hinge-future-us-china-relations-141792?page=0%2C1; Henry Olsen, "Get Ready for an Election All about China," *Washington Post*, May 5, 2020, A23; *COVID-19 and China: A Chronology of Events*, Congressional Research Service Report R46354 (Washington, DC: Library of Congress, May 13, 2020).

38. Vivian Wong and Alexandra Stevenson, "In Hong Kong, Arrests and Fear Mark First Day of New Security Law," *New York Times*, July 1, 2020, https://www.nytimes.com/2020/07/01/world/asia/hong-kong-security-law-china.html.

39. Sutter, *Chinese Foreign Relations: Power and Policy of an Emerging Global Force*, 200–9.

40. For background and sources, see discussion in chapter 3 and chapters 9–12 covering regional relations. Notable summations include David Shinn, "China Just Another Great Power in Africa," East Asia Forum, May 17, 2018, https://www.eastasiaforum.org/2018/05/17/china s-just-another-great-power-in-africa, and Margaret Myers, "The Reasons for China's Cooling Interest in Latin America," *Americas Quarterly*, April 23, 2019, https://www.americasquarterly.org/content/how-beijing-sees-it.

41. Robert Sutter, "Why America Opposes the Belt and Road Initiative (BRI)?," *PacNet* 38, July 2, 2020.

42. *China's Belt and Road*.

43. Sutter, *Chinese Foreign Relations: Power and Policy of an Emerging Global Force*, 49–50; Shih, "US-China Relations."

44. Shinn, "China Just Another Great Power in Africa"; Myers, "The Reasons for China's Cooling Interest in Latin America."

45. Ashley Tellis, Alison Szalwinski, and Michael Wills, eds., *Strategic Asia 2020: U.S.-China Competition for Global Influence* (Seattle, WA: National Bureau of Asian Research, 2020); Sutter, *Chinese Foreign Relations: Power and Policy of an Emerging Global Force*, 307.

46. Robert Sutter and Satu Limaye, *A Hardening US-China Competition: Asia Policy in America's 2020 Elections and Asian Responses* (Honolulu, HI: East-West Center, 2020), 24–74.

47. Robert Sutter, "Has US Government Angst over the China Danger Diminished?," *Asia-Pacific Bulletin*, January 22, 2020, https://www.eastwestcenter.org/publications/has-us-government-angst-over-the-china-danger-diminished; Rogin, "The Coronavirus Is Turning Americans in Both Parties Against China"; Paul Heer,

"Stop the Coronavirus Blame Game," *National Interest*, May 15, 2020, https://www. realclearworld.com/2020/05/15/stop_the_coronavirus_blame_game_491681.html.

48. "Regional Overview," *Comparative Connections* 31, no. 1 (May 2021): 1–6.

49. Peter Martin, "Biden's Asian Czar Says Era of Engagement with China Is Over," *Bloomberg*, May 26, 2021, https://www.bloomberg.com/news/articles/2021-05-26/ biden-s-asia-czar-says-era-of-engagement-with-xi-s-china-is-over.

50. The discussion of the five factors below is taken from Sutter, *Chinese Foreign Relations: Power and Policy of an Emerging Global Force*, 308–11; for earlier assessments of these factors see Sutter, *The United States and Asia* (Lanham, MD: Rowman & Littlefield, 2020), 327–34; Robert Sutter, *Foreign Relations of the PRC* (Lanham, MD: Rowman & Littlefield, 2019), 297–301.

51. Sutter and Limaye, *A Hardening US-China Competition*, 24–74.

52. "Regional Overview," *Comparative Connections* 31, no. 1 (May 2021): 1–7.

53. Sutter, *Chinese Foreign Relations: Power and Policy of an Emerging Global Force*, 312–14.

54. US China Economic and Security Review Commission, "US-China Relations at the Chinese Communist Party's Centennial," Hearing, January 28, 2021 (statements by Carolyn Bartholomew and Roy Kamphausen; testimony by Robert Sutter and Zach Cooper), https://www.uscc.gov/hearings/ us-china-relations-chinese-communist-partys-centennial.

55. Hass, "How China Is Responding to Escalating Strategic Competition with the US"; Yuan Peng, "The New Coronavirus Epidemic Situation and Centennial Changes"; Kacie Miura and Jessica Chen Weiss, "Chinese Leaders Say Biden Offers 'a New Window of Hope.' Their Experts Are More Skeptical," *Washington Post*, January 21, 2021, https://www.washingtonpost.com/politics/2021/01/21/chinas-leaders-say-that-biden-offers-new-window-hope-their-experts-are-more-skeptical/.

56. Aaron Friedberg, *A Contest for Supremacy: China, America and the Struggle for Mastery in Asia* (New York: W. W. Norton, 2011).

Selected Bibliography

Accinelli, Robert. *Crisis and Commitment: United States Policy toward Taiwan, 1950–1955*. Chapel Hill: University of North Carolina Press, 1996.

Allison, Graham. *Can China and American Escape the Thucydides Trap?* Boston: Houghton Mifflin Harcourt, 2017.

Bachrack, Stanley D. *The Committee of One Million: "China Lobby" Politics, 1953–1971*. New York: Columbia University Press, 1976.

Bader, Jeffrey. *Obama and China's Rise*. Washington, DC: Brookings Institution, 2012.

Barnett, A. Doak. *China and the Major Powers in East Asia*. Washington, DC: Brookings Institution, 1977.

———. *U.S.-China Relations: Time for a New Beginning—Again*. Washington, DC: Johns Hopkins University, School for Advanced International Studies, 1994.

Bays, Daniel H., ed. *Christianity in China*. Stanford, CA: Stanford University Press, 1996.

Beal, John R. *Marshall in China*. Garden City, NY: Doubleday, 1970.

Bernstein, Richard, and Ross H. Munro. *Coming Conflict with China*. New York: Knopf, 1998.

Borg, Dorothy. *American Policy and the Chinese Revolution, 1925–1928*. New York: Macmillan, 1947.

———. *The United States and the Far Eastern Crisis of 1933–1938*. Cambridge, MA: Harvard University Press, 1964.

Borg, Dorothy, and Waldo Heinrichs, eds. *Uncertain Years: Chinese-American Relations, 1947–1950*. New York: Columbia University Press, 1980.

Brazinsky, Gregg. *Winning the Third World: Sino-American Rivalry during the Cold War*. Chapel Hill: University of North Carolina Press, 2017.

Buhite, Russell D. *Patrick J. Hurley and American Foreign Policy*. Ithaca, NY: Cornell University Press, 1973.

Bush, Richard. *At Cross Purposes: U.S.-Taiwan Relations since 1942*. Armonk, NY: M. E. Sharpe, 2004.

————. *Hong Kong in the Shadow of China*. Washington, DC: Brookings Institution, 2016.

————. *Uncharted Strait*. Washington, DC: Brookings Institution, 2013.

————. *Untying the Knot*. Washington, DC: Brookings Institution, 2005.

Chang, Gordon. *Fateful Ties: A History of America's Preoccupation with China*. Cambridge, MA: Harvard University Press, 2015.

————. *Friends and Enemies: The United States, China, and the Soviet Union, 1948–1972*. Stanford, CA: Stanford University Press, 1990.

Chen, Dean. *US-China Rivalry and Taiwan's Mainland Policy*. Cham, UK: Palgrave, 2017.

Chen, Jian. *Mao's China and the Cold War*. Chapel Hill: University of North Carolina Press, 2001.

Christensen, Thomas. *The China Challenge: Shaping the Choices of a Rising Power*. New York: W. W. Norton, 2016.

————. *Useful Adversaries: Grand Strategy, Domestic Mobilization, and Sino-American Conflicts, 1949–1958*. Princeton, NJ: Princeton University Press, 1996.

Cohen, Paul. *China and Christianity: The Missionary Movement and the Growth of Chinese Anti-foreignism 1860-1870*. Cambridge, MA: Harvard University Press, 1963.

Cohen, Warren I. *America's Response to China: A History of Sino-American Relations*. New York: Columbia University Press, 2010.

Dennett, Tyler. *Americans in Eastern Asia: A Critical Study of the Policy of the United States with Reference to China, Japan, and Korea in the 19th Century*. New York: Macmillan, 1922.

Diamond, Larry, and Orville Schell, coordinators. *Chinese Influence and American Interests: Promoting Constructive Vigilance*. Stanford, CA: Hoover Institution Press, 2018.

Dong Mei, ed. *Zhong-Mei guanxi ziliao xuanbian* [Selected materials on Sino-American relations]. Beijing: Shishi Chubanshe, 1982.

Downs, Jacques M. "American Merchants and the China Opium Trade, 1800–1840." *Business History Review* 42, no. 4 (1968): 418–442.

Dulles, Foster Rhea. *American Policy toward Communist China, 1949–1969*. New York: Thomas Y. Crowell, 1972.

Economy, Elizabeth. *The Third Revolution: Xi Jinping and the New Chinese State*. New York: Council on Foreign Relations, 2018.

Engel, Jeffrey, ed. *The China Diary of George H W Bush: The Making of a Global President*. Princeton, NJ: Princeton University Press, 2008.

Evans, Paul. *John Fairbank and the American Understanding of Modern China*. New York: Blackwill, 1988.

Fairbank, John K. *The United States and China*. Cambridge, MA: Harvard University Press, 1983.

Fairbank, John K., and Suzanne W. Barnett, eds. *Christianity in China*. Cambridge, MA: Harvard University Press, 1985.

Foot, Rosemary. *The Practice of Power: U.S. Relations with China since 1949*. New York: Oxford University Press, 1997.

Foxall, Andrew, and John Hemmings. *The Art of Deceit: How China and Russia Use Sharp Power to Subvert the West*. London: Henry Jackson Society, 2019.

Fravel, M. Taylor. *Active Defense: China's Military Strategy since 1949*. Princeton, NJ: Princeton University Press, 2019.

Friedberg, Aaron. *A Contest for Supremacy: China, America, and the Struggle for Mastery in Asia*. New York: W. W. Norton, 2011.

———. *Beyond Air-Sea Battle: The Debate over US Military Strategy in Asia*. London: IISS/Routledge, 2014.

Fu Hao, and Li Tongcheng, eds. *Lusi shui shou? Zhongguo waijiaoguan zai Meiguo* [Who will win the game? Chinese diplomats in the United States]. Beijing: Hauqiao Chubanshe, 1998.

Garrison, Jean. *Making China Policy: From Nixon to G. W. Bush*. Boulder, CO: Lynne Rienner, 2005.

Garver, John W. *China's Decision for Rapprochement with the United States, 1968–1971*. Boulder, CO: Westview Press, 1982.

———. *Face Off: China, the United States, and Taiwan's Democratization*. Seattle: University of Washington Press, 1997.

———. *The Sino-American Alliance: Nationalist China and American Cold War Strategy in Asia*. Armonk, NY: M. E. Sharpe, 1997.

Goh, Evelyn. *Constructing the U.S. Rapprochement with China, 1961–1974*. New York: Cambridge University Press, 2005.

———. *The Struggle for Order: Hegemony, Hierarchy and Transition in Post–Cold War East Asia*. Oxford: Oxford University Press, 2013.

Goldstein, Lyle. *Meeting China Halfway*. Washington, DC: Georgetown University Press, 2015.

Goldstein, Steven. *China and Taiwan*. Cambridge: Polity Press, 2015.

Gong Li. *Deng Xiaoping yu Meiguo* [Deng Xiaoping and America]. Beijing: Zhonggong dangshi chubanshe, 2004.

———. *Kuayue: 1969–1979 nian Zhong Mei guanxi de yanbian* [Across the chasm: The evolution of China-US relations, 1969–1979]. Henan, China: Henan People's Press, 1992.

Gong Li, William Kirby, and Robert Ross, eds. *Zong jiedong zouxiang jianjiao: Zhong Mei guanxi zhengchanghua jincheng zai tantuo* [From thaw to normalization: A reexamination of the normalization of US-China relations]. Beijing: Zhongyang Wenxian Chubanshe, 2004.

Griswold, A. Whitney. *The Far Eastern Policy of the United States*. New York: Harcourt Brace, 1938.

Hachigian, Nina, ed. *Debating China: The U.S.-China Relationship in Ten Conversations*. New York: Oxford University Press, 2014.

Haddah, John Rogers. *The Romance of China: Excursions to China in US Culture, 1776–1876*. New York: Columbia University Press, 2008.

Han Nianlong, and Xue Mouhong, eds. *Dangdai Zhongguo waijiao* [Contemporary Chinese diplomacy]. Beijing: Zhongguo Shehui Kexue Chubanshe, 1990.

Harding, Harry. *A Fragile Relationship: The United States and China since 1972.* Washington, DC: Brookings Institution, 1992.

Harding, Harry, and Yuan Ming, eds. *Sino-American Relations, 1945–1955.* Wilmington, DE: Scholarly Resources, 1989.

Hass, Ryan. *Stronger: Adapting America's China Policy in an Age of Competitive Interdependence.* Washington, DC: Brookings Institution, 2021.

Heath, Timothy, Derek Grossman, and Asha Clark. *China's Quest for Global Dominance.* Santa Monica, CA: RAND Corporation, 2021.

Heginbotham, Eric, et al. *China's Evolving Nuclear Deterrent: Major Drivers and Issues for the United States.* Santa Monica, CA: RAND Corporation, 2017.

Heginbotham, Eric, et al. *The U.S.-China Military Scorecard: Forces, Geography, and the Evolving Balance of Power, 1996–2017.* Santa Monica, CA: RAND Corporation, 2018.

Herzstein, Robert Erwin. *Henry R. Luce, Time, and the American Crusade in Asia.* New York: Cambridge University Press, 2005.

House Committee on Foreign Affairs. *Executive-Legislative Consultations over China Policy, 1978–1979.* Washington, DC: US Government Printing Office, 1980.

Hu Sheng, ed. *Zhongguo gongchandang de qishi nian* [Seventy years of the Chinese Communist Party]. Beijing: Zhonggong Dangshi Chubanshe, 1991.

Huang Hua. *Qinli yi Jianwen; Huang Hua huiyi lu* [Witnessing and experiencing at first hand: The memoirs of Huang Hua]. Beijing: Shijie Zhishi Chubanshe, 2007.

Hunt, Michael H. *The Making of a Special Relationship: The United States and China to 1914.* New York: Columbia University Press, 1983.

Iriye, Akira. *Across the Pacific: An Inner History of American–East Asian Relations.* New York: Harcourt, Brace and World, 1967.

Iriye, Akira, and Warren I. Cohen, eds. *American, Chinese, and Japanese Perspectives on Wartime Asia, 1939–1949.* Wilmington, DE: Scholarly Resources, 1990.

Isaacs, Harold R. *Scratches on Our Minds: American Images of China and India.* New York: John Day, 1958.

Jacoby, Neil H. *U.S. Aid to Taiwan.* New York: Praeger, 1966.

Jespersen, T. Christopher. *American Images of China, 1931–1949.* Stanford, CA: Stanford University Press, 1996.

Jia Qingguo. *Wei Shixian de Hejie: Zhongmei Guanxi de Gehe yu Weiji* [The unmaterialized rapprochement: Estrangement and crisis in Sino-American talks in retrospect]. Beijing: Shijie Zhishi Chubanshe, 1985.

Jiang Changbin, and Robert S. Ross, eds. *1955–1971 Nian de Zhong Mei Guanxi—Huanhe Zhigian: Lengzhan Chongtu yu Keshi de Cai Tantao* [US-China relations 1955–1971—before détente: An examination of Cold War conflict and restraint]. Beijing: Shijie Zhishi Chubanshe, 1998.

———. *Cong Duizhi zouxiang Huanhe: Lengzhan Shiqi Zhong Mei Guanxi zai Tantao* [From confrontation toward détente: A reexamination of US-China relations during the Cold War]. Beijing: Shijie Zhishi Chubanshe, 2000.

Jing Li. *China's America: The Chinese View of the United States, 1900–2000.* New York: State University of New York Press, 2011.

Johnston, Alastair Iain. "Is China a Status Quo Power," *International Security* 27, no. 4 (2003): 5–56.

Kirby, William, Robert Ross, and Gong Li, eds. *Normalization of U.S.-China Relations*. Cambridge, MA: Harvard University Press, 2005.

Kissinger, Henry. *On China*. New York: Penguin, 2011.

Koen, Ross Y. *The China Lobby in American Politics*. New York: Harper and Row, 1974.

Lampton, David M. *Same Bed, Different Dreams: Managing U.S.-China Relations, 1989–2000*. Berkeley: University of California Press, 2001.

Lardy, Nicholas. *The State Strikes Back*. Washington, DC: Petersen Institute, 2019.

Latourette, Kenneth S. *The History of Early Relations between the United States and China, 1784–1844*. New Haven, CT: Yale University Press, 1917.

Lee, David Tawei. *The Making of the Taiwan Relations Act: Twenty Years in Retrospect*. New York: Oxford University Press, 2000.

Li Changjiu, and Shi Lujia. *Zhongmei guanxi liangbainian* [Two hundred years of Sino-American relations]. Peking: Xinhua Publishing House, 1984.

Lieberthal, Kenneth, and David Sandalow. *Overcoming Obstacles to US-China Cooperation on Climate Change*. John L. Thornton China Center Monograph Series 1. Washington, DC: Brookings Institution, January 2009.

Lieberthal, Kenneth, and Wang Jisi. *Addressing U.S.-China Strategic Distrust*. Washington, DC: Brookings Institution, 2012.

Lin, Bonnie, et al. *Regional Responses to US-China Competition in the Indo-Pacific*. Santa Monica, CA: RAND Corporation, 2020.

Lin Qing. *Zhou Enlai zaixiang shengya* [The career of Prime Minister Zhou Enlai]. Hong Kong: Changcheng Wenhua Chubanshe, 1991.

Liu Xiaoyuan. *A Partnership for Disorder: China, the United States, and Their Policies for the Postwar Disposition of the Japanese Empire*. New York: Cambridge University Press, 1996.

MacMillian, Margaret. *Nixon in China*. Toronto: Viking Canada, 2006.

Madsen, Richard. *China and the American Dream: A Moral Inquiry*. Berkeley: University of California Press, 1995.

Mahnken, Thomas, Ross Babbage, and Toshi Yoshihara. *Countering Comprehensive Coercion*. Washington, DC: Center for Strategic and Budgetary Assessments, 2018.

Mann, James. *About Face: A History of America's Curious Relationship with China, from Nixon to Clinton*. New York: Knopf, 1999.

———. *The China Fantasy*. New York: Viking, 2007.

May, Ernest R. *The Truman Administration and China, 1945–1949*. New York: Lippincott, 1975.

May, Ernest R., and John K. Fairbank, eds. *America's China Trade in Historical Perspective: The Chinese and American Performance*. Cambridge, MA: Harvard University Press, 1986.

Mazarr, Michael, Timothy Heath, and Astrid Stuth Cevallos. *China and the International Order*. Santa Monica, CA: RAND Corporation, 2018.

McGiffert, Carola, ed. *Chinese Images of the United States*. Washington, DC: CSIS, 2006.

Medeiros, Evan. "Strategic Hedging and the Future of Asia-Pacific Stability." *Washington Quarterly* 29, no. 1 (2005–2006): 145–67.

Miller, Stuart Creighton. *The Unwelcome Immigrant: The American Image of the Chinese, 1785–1882*. Berkeley: University of California Press, 1969.

Myers, Ramon, ed. *A Unique Relationship: The United States and the Republic of China under the Taiwan Relations Act*. Stanford, CA: Hoover Institution, 1989.

Myers, Ramon, Michel Oksenberg, and David Shambaugh, eds. *Making China Policy*. Lanham, MD: Rowman & Littlefield, 2001.

Nathan, Andrew, and Andrew Scobell. *China's Search for Security*. New York: Columbia University Press, 2012.

Neils, Patricia. *United States Attitudes toward China: The Impact of American Missionaries*. Armonk, NY: M. E. Sharpe, 1990.

Ninkovich, Frank. *The United States and Imperialism*. Oxford: Blackwell, 2001.

Peck, Graham. *Two Kinds of Time*. Boston: Houghton Mifflin, 1967.

Pei Jianzhang. *Yanjiu Zhou Enlai: Waijiao sixiang yu shijian* [Researching Zhou Enlai: Diplomatic thought and practice]. Beijing: Shijie Zhishi Chubanshe, 1989.

———. *Zhonghua renmin gongheguo waijiao shi, 1949–1956* [A diplomatic history of the People's Republic of China, 1949–1956]. Beijing: Shijie Zhishi, 1994.

Pillsbury, Michael. *The Hundred-Year Marathon*. New York: St. Martin's Press, 2015.

Pomfret, John. *The Beautiful Country and the Middle Kingdom*. Boston: Henry Holt, 2016.

Qian Qichen. *Ten Episodes in China's Diplomacy*. New York: HarperCollins, 2005.

Qing Simei. *From Allies to Enemies: Visions of Modernity, Identity and US-China Diplomacy 1945–1960*. Cambridge, MA: Harvard University Press, 2007.

Roberts, Sean. *The War on the Uyghurs: China's Internal Campaign Against a Muslim Minority*. Princeton, NJ: Princeton University Press, 2020.

Rolland, Nadege. *China's Vision for a New World Order*. Seattle, WA: National Bureau for Asian Research, January 2020.

Romberg, Alan. *Rein In at the Brink of the Precipice*. Washington, DC: Henry Stimson Center, 2003.

Rosen, Daniel, and Thilo Hanemann. *An American Open Door: Maximizing the Benefits of Chinese Foreign Direct Investment*. New York: Asia Society, 2011.

Ross, Robert S. *Negotiating Cooperation: The United States and China, 1969–1989*. Stanford, CA: Stanford University Press, 1995.

Ross, Robert S., and Jiang Changbin, eds. *Re-examining the Cold War: U.S.-China Diplomacy, 1954–1973*. Cambridge, MA: Harvard University Press, 2001.

Roy, Denny. *Return of the Dragon: Rising China and Regional Security*. New York: Columbia University Press, 2013.

Russel, Daniel, and Blake Berger. *Navigating the Belt and Road Initiative*. New York: Asia Society Policy Institute, June 2019.

Sandalow, David. *Guide to Chinese Climate Policy 2019*. New York: Columbia University Center on Global Energy Policy, September 13, 2019.

Saunders, Phillip. "China's America Watchers: Changing Attitudes toward the United States." *China Quarterly* (March 2000): 41–65.

Schaller, Michael. *The United States and China: Into the Twenty-First Century*. New York: Oxford University Press, 2015.

———. *The U.S. Crusade in China, 1938–1945*. New York: Columbia University Press, 1979.

Schell, Orville, and Susan Shirk, chairs. *Course Correction: Toward an Effective and Sustainable China Policy*. New York: Asia Society, 2019.

———. *US Policy toward China: Recommendations for a New Administration*. New York: Asia Society, 2017.

Schrader, Matt. *Friends and Enemies: A Framework for Understanding Chinese Political Influence in Democratic Countries*. Washington, DC: German Marshall Fund, April 22, 2020.

Shambaugh, David. *Beautiful Imperialist: China Perceives America, 1972–1980*. Princeton, NJ: Princeton University Press, 1991.

———, ed. *Tangled Titans: The United States and China*. Lanham, MD: Rowman & Littlefield, 2012.

Shaw, Yu-ming. *An American Missionary in China: John Leighton Stuart and Chinese-American Relations*. Cambridge, MA: Harvard University Press, 1992.

Shewmaker, Kenneth E. *Americans and the Chinese Communists, 1927–1945: A Persuading Encounter*. Ithaca, NY: Cornell University Press, 1971.

Shinn, James, ed. *Weaving the Net: Conditional Engagement with China*. New York: Council on Foreign Relations, 1996.

Shullman, David, ed. *Chinese Malign Influence and the Corrosion of Democracy*. Washington, DC: International Republican Institute, 2019.

Snow, Edgar. *Red Star over China*. New York: Random House, 1938.

Solomon, Richard H. *The China Factor: Sino-American Relations and the Global Scene*. Englewood Cliffs, NJ: Prentice Hall, 1982.

Song Qiang, Zhang Changchang, and Qiao Bian. *Zhongguo keyi shuo bu: Lengzhanhou shidai de zhengzhi yu qinggan jueze* [China can say no: The decision between politics and sentiment in the post–Cold War]. Beijing: Zhonghua Gongshang Lianhe Chubanshe, 1996.

Storey, Ian James. *The United States and ASEAN-China Relations: All Quiet on the Southeastern Asian Front*. Carlisle, PA: Strategic Studies Institute, U.S. Army War College, 2007.

Su Ge. *Meiguo: Dui hua Zhengce yu Taiwan wenti* [America: China policy and the Taiwan issue]. Beijing: Shijie Zhishi Chubanshe, 1998.

Suettinger, Robert L. *Beyond Tiananmen: The Politics of U.S.-China Relations, 1989–2000*. Washington, DC: Brookings Institution, 2003.

Sutter, Robert G. *China's Rise: Implications for U.S. Leadership in Asia*. Washington, DC: East-West Center, 2006.

———. *U.S. Policy toward China: An Introduction to the Role of Interest Groups*. Lanham, MD: Rowman & Littlefield, 1998.

———. *The United States and Asia*. Lanham, MD: Rowman & Littlefield, 2020.

Sutter, Robert, and Satu Limaye. *A Hardening US-China Competition: Asia Policy in America's 2020 Elections and Asian Responses*. Honolulu, HI: East-West Center, 2020.

Swaine, Michael. *America's Challenge: Engaging a Rising China in the Twenty-First Century.* Washington, DC: Carnegie Endowment for International Peace, 2011.

———. "China's Regional Military Posture." In *Power Shift: China and Asia's New Dynamics*, edited by David Shambaugh, 266–88. Berkeley: University of California Press, 2005.

———. *Creating a Stable Asia: An Agenda for a U.S.-China Balance of Power.* Washington, DC: Carnegie Endowment for International Peace, 2016.

Swaine, Michael, and Zhang Tuosheng, eds. *Managing Sino-American Crises.* Washington, DC: Carnegie Endowment for International Peace, 2006.

Tan, Andrew T. H., ed. *Handbook of US-China Relations.* Cheltenham, UK: Edward Elgar, 2016.

Tang Tsou. *America's Failure in China, 1941–1950.* Chicago: University of Chicago Press, 1963.

Tao Wenzhao. *Zhong Mei guanxi shi* [The history of Sino-US relations]. Shanghai: Renmin Chubanshe, 2004.

Taylor, Jay. *The Generalissimo: Chiang Kai-shek and the Struggle for Modern China.* Cambridge, MA: Harvard University Press, 2009.

Tellis, Ashley. *Balancing without Containment.* Washington, DC: Carnegie Endowment for International Peace Report, January 22, 2014.

Tellis, Ashley, Alisson Szalwinski, and Michael Wills, eds. *Strategic Asia, 2020: US-China Competition for Global Influence.* Seattle, WA: National Bureau of Asian Research, 2020.

Thomson, James C. Jr. *While China Faced West: American Reformers in Nationalist China, 1928–1937.* Cambridge, MA: Harvard University Press, 1968.

Tian Zengpei, ed. *Gaige kaifang yilai de Zhongguo waijiao* [Chinese diplomacy since reform and opening]. Beijing: Shijie Zhishi Chubanshe, 1993.

Tuchman, Barbara. *Stilwell and the American Experience in China, 1911–1945.* New York: Macmillan, 1971.

Tucker, Nancy Bernkopf. *China Confidential: American Diplomats and Sino-American Relations, 1945–1996.* New York: Columbia University Press, 2001.

———, ed. *Dangerous Strait: The U.S.-Taiwan-China Crisis.* New York: Columbia University Press, 2005.

———. *Strait Talk: United States-Taiwan Relations and the Crisis with China.* Cambridge, MA: Harvard University Press, 2009.

Varg, Paul A. *Missionaries, Chinese and Diplomats: The American Protestant Missionary Movement in China, 1890–1952.* Princeton, NJ: Princeton University Press, 1958.

———. *The Making of a Myth: The United States and China, 1897–1912.* East Lansing: Michigan State University Press, 1968.

Wachman, Alan M. *Why Taiwan?* Stanford, CA: Stanford University Press, 2007.

Wang Bingnan. *Zhongmei huitan jiunian huigu* [Nine years of Sino-American ambassadorial talks]. Beijing: Shijie Zhishi, 1985.

Wang Dong. *The United States and China: A History from the Eighteenth Century to the Present.* Lanham, MD: Rowman & Littlefield, 2013.

Wang Dong, and Travis Tanner, eds., *Avoiding the "Thucydides Trap": US-China Relations in Strategic Domains*. New York: Routledge, 2020.

Wang Taiping, ed. *Xin Zhongguo waijiao wushinian* [Fifty years of diplomacy of the new China]. Beijing: Beijing Chubanshe, 1999.

White, Hugh. *The China Choice*. Collingwood, Australia: Black Inc., 2012.

Xia Yafeng. *Negotiating with the Enemy: U.S.-China Talks during the Cold War, 1949–1972*. Bloomington: Indiana University Press, 2006.

Xiang Liling. *Zhongmei quanxi shi quanbian* [A comprehensive history of US-China relations]. Shanghai: Huadongshifandaxue, 2002.

Xie Xide, and Ni Shixiong. *Quzhe de licheng: Zhong Mei jianji ershi nian* [From normalization to renormalization: Twenty years of Sino-US relations]. Shanghai: Fudan Daxue Chubanshe, 1999.

Xiong Zhiyong, *Banian Zhengmei quanxi* [100 years of US-China relations]. Beijing: Shijie Zhishi Chubanshe, 2006.

Xue Mouhong, and Pei Jianhang, eds. *Danggai Zhongguo waijiao* [The diplomacy of contemporary China]. Beijing: Zhongguo Shehui Kexue Chubanshe, 1987.

Yan Xuetong. "The Instability of China-U.S. Relations." *Chinese Journal of International Politics* 3, no. 3 (2010): 1–30.

———. *Zhongguo guojia liyi fenxi* [The analysis of China's national interest]. Tianjin, China: Tianjin Renmin Chubanshe, 1996.

Yan Xuetong, Wang Zaibang, Li Zhongcheng, and Hou Roushi. *Zhongguo jueqi: Guoji huanjing pinggu* [International environment for China's rise]. Tianjin, China: Renmin Chubanshe, 1998.

Young, Kenneth T. *Negotiating with the Chinese Communists: The United States Experience, 1953–1967*. New York: McGraw-Hill, 1968.

Young, Marilyn B. *The Rhetoric of Empire: American China Policy, 1895–1901*. Cambridge, MA: Harvard University Press, 1968.

Zhang Shu Guang. *Deterrence and Strategic Culture: Chinese-American Conflicts, 1949–1959*. Ithaca, NY: Cornell University Press, 1992.

Zhang Yunling, ed. *Hezou haishi duikang: Lengzhanhou de Zhongguo, Meiguo he Riben* [Cooperation or confrontation: China, the United States, and Japan after the Cold War]. Beijing: Zhongguo Shehui Kexue Chubanshe, 1997.

Zi Zhongyun. *Meiguo duihua zhengce de yuanqi he fazhan, 1945–1950* [The origins and development of American policy toward China, 1945–1950]. Chongqing, China: Chongqing, 1987.

Zi Zhongyun, and He Di, eds. *Meitai Guanxi Sishinian* [Forty years of US-Taiwan relations]. Beijing: People's Press, 1991.

Zou Jing-wen. *Li Denghui Zhizheng Gaobai Shilu* [Record of revelations on Lee Teng-hui's administration]. Taipei: INK, 2001.

Index

Abe, Shinzo, 263–64
abortion, coercive, 138, 284
abuses, of human rights by Chinese,
    282–83, 286
accession agreement, WTO, 230
accommodations, Chinese, 83–85
Acheson, Dean, 52
ADIZ. *See* air defense
    identification zone
Afghanistan: Soviet invasion of, 94; US
    withdrawal from, 206, 318–19
Afghanistan war, 132
Africa, 86, 169; Zhou Enlai visit to, 63
Afro-Asian Conference (1955), 59
aging population, 237
agreements, US-China, 102
agricultural products, exports of, 230–31
air attacks, US, 46–47
air defense identification zone
    (ADIZ), 264
air force, Taiwan, 94
air pollution, 240
ambassadorial talks, Sino-American, 74
American–Chinese Nationalist
    alignment, 48
American Civil War, 23
American Military Observer Mission
    Group, 48, 69
Americans, violence against, 33

Amnesty International, 108
Andropov, Yuri, 94
anti-American boycott, 19–20, 29
anti-imperialism, 33
antimissionary riots, 19
anti-terrorism, 132, 133
antiwar sentiment, US, 69
Aquino, Benigno, 265
arbitrary arrests, 291
Arkhipov, Ivan, 95
Armitage, Richard, 83–84, 130
arms sales, US: to China, 188; to
    Taiwan, 92, 94, 110, 120
arrests: arbitrary, 291; of foreigners
    in China, 297, 299; of political
    dissidents, 277
ascendance, of China, 310–12, 314–18
ASEAN. *See* Association of Southeast
    Asian Nations
Asia Assurance Initiative Act, 169
Asian economic crisis, 142
Asian-Pacific immigrants, 321
Asia Society report, on China
    policy, 213
assertiveness, by China, 146–47
assimilation, forced, 288, 289
Association of Southeast Asian Nations
    (ASEAN), 150, 262–63, 297
attack, Tiananmen Square, 99–100

attacks, on missionaries, 27, 29
Australia, 178, 180, 298
Australian Strategic Policy Institute, 290
authoritarianism, 2, 3, 99, 295–97
autonomy: Hong Kong and, 177–78, 289–90; Taiwan and, 109; for Tibet, 108, 189

Bannon, Steve, 171
Belt and Road Initiative (BRI), 168, 211, 264, 316–18; economic practices and, 294; opposition to, 233–34
benefits, of US-China relations, 121
benefits and costs, 11
Better Utilization of Investments Leading to Development (BUILD) Act (2018), 234
Biden, Joseph, 1, 3, 161, 177–81, 306; on climate change, 241–42; competition with China and, 180–81, 218; on Hong Kong, 290; initiatives from, 320; one-China policy and, 257–59; resolves with China and, 266–70
BIS. *See* Bureau of Industry and Security
"black jails," 286
Bloomberg, Michael, 173
Bolton, John, 256
bombing, of the Chinese embassy (1999), 102, 112–13, 126
Boxer Protocol, 28
Boxer Uprising, 27–29
Bo Xilai, 153
boycotts: anti-American, 19; of Hong Kong, 33; international events by Chinese, 293
Branstad, Terry, 167
Brezhnev, Leonid, 71
Brezhnev Doctrine, 71
BRI. *See* Belt and Road Initiative
Bryan, William Jennings, 31–32
Brzezinski, Zbigniew, 80
Buddhism, 289

budget deficits, US, 8
BUILD Act. *See* Better Utilization of Investments Leading to Development Act
bullying, 296
Bureau of Industry and Security (BIS), 226
Burlingame, Anson, 17–18, 23
Bush, George H. W., 10, 101, 103, 279; China policy and, 109–15, 119; support for Taiwan, 247–48, 250; US foreign policy and, 107
Bush, George W., 3, 129–37, 320; China military expansion and, 139; foreign policy toward China of, 115–16; legacy of, 144–46; Taiwan and, 141
Buttigieg, Pete, 173

Cambodia, 74
Canton, 21
capitalism, state-controlled, 213
capitol attack, US (2021), 318
Carter, Jimmy, 80, 81, 116–17; Taiwan and, 247; US foreign policy and, 276–77
CCP. *See* Communist Party of China
censoring of information, by China, 282
Chang Chih-tung, 26, 28–29
Chen Boda, 71, 74
Chen Guangcheng, 152–53
Chennault, Claire, 46–47
Chen Shui-bian, 132, 141, 145, 196, 248
Chernenko, Konstantin, 94
Chiang Kai-shek, 31, 33–34, 36–37, 42–43; Korean War and, 58; during 1940s, 44–52; relationship with US, 64; Roosevelt, F., and, 45, 46; Taiwan and, 59
China: approach to terrorism, 206–7; arrests of foreigners in, 297; ascendance of, 310–12, 314–18; assertiveness by, 146–47; censoring of information by, 282; coercion of neighbors by, 296, 309; constraints on, 314–18; corrupt government in,

295–97, 298; earthquake (1976), 78; manufacturing output for, 211; one-party system, 323; Prisons/Prison Labor in, 138; rise of in 2000s, 134–35; Russia collaborating with, 178, 297; tariffs against, 167; trade and, 15–16, 21, 36, 102, 108. *See also specific topics and places*
China Aid Act (1948), 51
China Cultural Revolution (1966), 55
"China Dream," 147, 312–13, 319
China policy: Asia Society report on, 213; Bush, G. W., and, 136; Clinton, B., and, 109–15, 118; human rights issues in, 137–39; issues in security relations, 139; late-1970s to early-1980s *versus* post Cold War, 116–19; in 1999, 121–22; sovereignty issues, 141; strengths and weaknesses, 115–16; Trump hardening of, 165, 177; US debate over, 104–9, 116–19
"China's Peaceful Development Road," 190
China theater, 45
Chinese accommodations, 83–85
Chinese Americans, 16, 18–20, 24
Chinese anti-American boycott, 19
Chinese Civil War, 41–43, 44, 50–52
Chinese conservative leaders, 278
Chinese control, of technology, 286–87
Chinese currency policy, 232–33
Chinese Customs Service, 26
Chinese debt, 220–21
Chinese debt trap, 294–95, 308
Chinese diaspora, mobilization of, 309
Chinese economy, 91, 211–13; high technologies and, 307; state controlled capitalism and, 222–23
Chinese elites, 19–20
Chinese embassy bombing (1999), 102, 112–13, 126
Chinese espionage, 114–15, 139, 164, 169, 296, 300
Chinese exceptionalism, 9
Chinese expansionism, 245–46

Chinese foreign investments, 316–17
Chinese foreign policy, 2, 8, 25, 68, 95–96, 322–23; "hegemonism" and, 190; independent, 87; IR theory and, 86; in 1976, 78; as peaceful, 190–91; trade policy and, 218–19; Xi Jinping vision of, 312–13
Chinese gentry class, 24–25
Chinese history, reinterpretation of, 313
Chinese human rights abuses, 282–83, 286
Chinese immigrants, 18–19, 24, 25–26
Chinese Imperial Maritime Customs Service, 23
Chinese industrial policies, 226
Chinese influence operations, 296, 311–12
Chinese infrastructure, 168, 295, 317
Chinese interests, actions and perceptions, 19–20
Chinese international challenges, to human rights, 292–93
Chinese legislation, on human rights, 285
Chinese media, 125; government and, 295; state-controlled, 101
Chinese military forces, 8
Chinese nationalism, 2, 34, 41
Chinese "noninterference in internal affairs" *versus* influence operations and political warfare, 297–302
Chinese propaganda, 293
Chinese sovereignty, 32
Chinese-Soviet alliance, 60
Chinese state security, 286
Chinese students, 108–9, 298; espionage through, 170
Chinese technology theft, 165, 170–71
Ch'i-ying, 21
Christianity, 22, 37
Christian missionaries, 15–16
Christopher, Warren, 122–23
civil wars: American, 23; China, 41–43, 44, 50–52

climate change, 144, 151, 236, 239–42, 317; cooperation with China on, 173, 179, 306; Obama on, 146, 155
Clinton, Bill, 101–2, 107, 124; China policy and, 109–15, 118, 119, 129–30; MFN status and, 123
Clinton, Hillary, 5–6, 146, 148, 163
coerced technology transfer, 225
coercion, economic, 294
coercion of neighbors, by China, 296, 309
coercive abortion, 138, 284
Cohn, Gary, 165
Cold War, 7, 52, 53, 54–55, 100
Cold War containment strategy, 55
Committee for the Assessment of Foreign Participation in the USTelecommunications Services Sector, 222
communications systems, 216–17
communism, 33, 273; international movement of, 88; US policy and, 55; in Vietnam, 63, 64, 79
Communist-Nationalist confrontation, 47–48
Communist-Nationalist peacetalks, 49
Communist Party of China (CCP), 33–34, 41–43, 62, 142–43; Document No. 9 by, 291; interactions 1950s and 1960s, 55–64; interactions in the 1940s, 44–52; Jinping and, 285–86; Maoist period and, 54; propaganda by, 291; supercomputing companies and, 217–18; technologies and, 310; United Front influence operations, 299; US and, 100
competition. *See* US-China competition
Confucius Institutes, 169–70
conservative leaders, Chinese, 278
constraints, on China, 314–18
constructivism, 103, 106, 148, 274, 305–6
containment policy, 79–80, 119
Convention on the Law of the Sea, UN, 297–98

converging and conflicting interests, 3–7
cooperation, US-China, 135
Copenhagen Climate Change Conference (2009), 240–41
corrupt government, in China, 295–97, 298
cost-benefit assessments, 84; in realism, 305
costs and benefits, 11
counterfeit products, 227
countermeasures, US, 2
coup attempt, 75
COVID-19 pandemic, 174, 175–77; Chinese propaganda and, 315–16; free speech restrictions and, 290; trade during, 214
COVID-19 vaccine, 180, 268
Cox, Christopher, 114
Cox Committee report (1999), 113, 114–15
crackdown, Tiananmen, 10, 99–100
Crawford summit, 133
crisis-prone relations, managing of, 119–22
cryptocurrency, 237
Cuban missile crisis (1962), 72
Cultural Revolution, 61, 64, 68, 70–71, 74, 187
currency exchange rate, 232–33
currency policy, Chinese, 232–33
current challenges, US-China relations, 306–9
Currie, Lauchlin, 46
Cushing, Caleb, 17–18, 21
cyberattacks, 223–24, 226–27, 229
cyberespionage, 223, 229
cybersecurity, 229, 315
Cybersecurity Law, PRC, 286
cybertheft, 154, 156–57, 194, 201, 300
cyberwarfare, 198
Czechoslovakia, 71

Dalai Lama, 141, 189, 277, 281, 289
debt, US and Chinese, 220–21
debt trap, Chinese, 294–95, 308

decrease, in US-China relations, 90
defense budgets, Chinese, 192
defense spending, US, 86–87
defense strategies, Chinese, 201–2
deficit, US trade, 218–19
democracy, 273
Democracy Wall, 277
Democratic candidates 2020 US
  election, 173
Democratic Progressive Party (DPP),
  152, 157, 250, 254
democratization, of Taiwan, 109
demonstrations, Tiananmen
  Square, 99, 278
Denby, Charles, 25
Deng Xiaoping, 1, 78, 79, 91, 142;
  Reagan and, 305; return to power,
  276; Tiananmen attack and, 99;
  Vietnam and, 202–3
Desert Storm operations, 118
deterioration, of US-China
  relations, 131
Diaoyu/Senkaku Islands, 91
diplomacy, secret, 110
diplomatic advances, US, 255–56
discrimination, against Chinese
  Americans, 16, 18–20, 24
dissidents, political, 138; arrests of, 277;
  persecution of, 291–92
Document No. 9, CCP, 291
Dodd, Christopher, 257
Donilon, Tom, 153
DPP. *See* Democratic Progressive Party
"dual circulation policy," 218
Dui Hua Foundation, 291
Dulles, John Foster, 58
Duterte, Rodrigo, 268–69

earthquake (1976), China, 78
East Asian affairs, US, 83, 84
East Asian maritime disputes, 260–66
East China Sea, 245, 251, 264–65
East Turkestan Islamic Movement
  (ETMI), 206
e-commerce, 211

economic advances, US-Taiwan, 256–57
economic coercion, 294
economic crisis (2008), 145, 151
economic dependence, Chinese
  exploitation of, 294–95
economic reform, 100
economy, free market, 103. *See also*
  Chinese economy
educational exchanges, 37
Eisenhower, Dwight D., 56, 57–58
elections: 1992 US, 110–11; 2016 US,
  5, 6; 2020 US, 162, 173, 175–77;
  2000 US, 126
Eleventh Five-Year Plan (2005–
  2010), 239–40
elites, Chinese, 19–20
Emergency Committee for American
  Trade, 108
energy, and environment
  challenges, 234–37
energy security, 238
engagement, enhancement of
  US-China, 151–52
"engagement" policy, 107, 119, 125–26,
  129–30; Bush, G. W., and, 144; in
  late 1990s, 278
environmental challenges,
  234–37, 239–42
EP-3 incident (2001), 130–31
espionage: China recruiting foreigners
  for, 309; Chinese, 114–15, 139,
  164, 169, 296, 300; cyber, 223, 229;
  industrial, 154, 201
ethnic groups, US foreign
  policy and, 108
ethnic minorities and religious
  policies, 288–89
ETMI. *See* East Turkestan
  Islamic Movement
exceptionalism, 274; Chinese,
  9; US, 8–9
exclusion movement, 18–19
expansion, counter-Chinese, 180
expansionism, Chinese, 245–46
exploitative economic practices, 294

exports, Chinese, 108, 235–36, 320; of
   agricultural products, 230–31
extraterritorial rights, 46
extremism, religious, 287

Falun Gong, 138, 284, 292
family planning, 138
Far Eastern Agreement, 50
FDI. *See* foreign direct investment
FIEs. *See* Foreign-invested enterprises
financial institutions, international, 96
financial markets, US, 90
5G wireless communications, 216–17
"Flying Tigers," 36, 46
forced assimilation, 288, 289
forced labor, 288
forced sterilization, 284
Ford, Gerald, 77–78, 276
foreign direct investment (FDI), 219–22
Foreign-invested enterprises (FIEs), 220
Fourteenth Five-Year Plan (FYP)
   (2021–2025), 224, 228
fourth industrial revolution, 215–16
freedom, of religion, 279, 289
freedom-of-navigation
   exercises, US, 267
free enterprise, 47
free market economy, 103
free speech, restrictions on, 290
free trade, 150
free-trade policies, 136
French military, 57–58
Friedberg, Aaron, 12
FYP. *See* Fourteenth Five-Year Plan

G-2 world order, 4
G-20 summit meeting, 168–69
Gang of Four, 73, 78–79, 276
Gates, Robert, 151
Geary Act, 24
Geneva Conference (1954), 57
genocide, 288
gentry class, in China, 24–25
"Geography of Peace," 195
Gingrich, Newt, 106

globalization, 299–300
Global Magnitsky Human Rights
   Accountability Act, 288
Gore, Albert, 114
governance, 273, 275; contemporary
   issues of, 293–95; international, 306
Grant, Ulysses S., 25
Great Britain, 17
Great Depression, 16
Great Leap Forward campaign, 61, 62
Gui Minhai, 291, 292

Haig, Alexander, 82, 83
Han Chinese culture, 287, 288–89
Hankow-Canton railway, 29
Harris, Harry, 157
Hay, John, 27–28
"hegemonism," 102, 187, 191, 301
"hegemony" code word, 77, 190
high technologies, 201–2, 215, 235,
   319; Chinese economy and, 307;
   supercomputing companies, 217–18;
   US-China competition with, 216
history, reinterpretation of Chinese, 313
HKSAR. *See* Hong Kong Special
   Administrative Region
Holding Foreign Companies
   Accountable Act, 217
Hong Kong, 100, 142, 176, 177–78,
   189, 249; boycott of, 33; human
   rights issues in, 289–90; protests in,
   63, 300, 316
Hong Kong Special Administrative
   Region (HKSAR), 290
Hoover, Herbert, 34
Hornbeck, Stanley, 35
Huang Hua, 52
Huawei, 169, 174, 176, 214;
   communications systems out of, 217;
   economic practices and, 294
Hu Jintao, 134, 143–44, 151, 154
Hull, Cordell, 35
human rights, 108, 273; abuse in
   Xinjiang, 178; changing issues 1969–
   2021, 276–82; Chinese abuse of,

282–83, 286; Chinese international challenges to, 292–93; Chinese legislation on, 285; Chinese policies on, 284; contemporary practices and issues, 282–87; governance and, 275; issues in China over, 101, 111, 122; issues in Tibet, 277, 280–81, 289; issues in US foreign policy over, 137–39; recent issues, 287–93; after Tiananmen crackdown, 274–75; Uighur Muslims and, 169, 173, 206–7, 287–88; US foreign policy on, 104, 123

Human Rights Watch, 108

Hung Hsiu-ch'uan, 22

Hurley, Patrick, 49–50

ICT. *See* information communications technology

identities: Chinese, 103–4; US, 103–4, 106

immigrants: Asian-Pacific, 321; Chinese, 18–19, 24, 25–26; prejudice against, 23–24

immigration policy, US, 46

imperialism, 33

imperialism, US, 74

improvements, in US-China relations, 84–85, 89, 96

Inchon landing, 56

India, 133, 166, 196, 198, 296; Sino-Indian border clash, 177; US and, 86

indigenous innovation, 223–25

Indochina, 57–58

Indo-Pacific allies, 174

Indo-Pacific Command, US military, 321–22

Indo-Pacific strategy, 174, 177

industrial economy, China, 57

industrial espionage, 154

industrial policies, Chinese, 226

influence operations, Chinese, 296, 311–12

information communications technology (ICT), 225–26

infrastructure, Chinese, 168, 295, 317

infrastructure financing, developing countries, 318

Ing-wen, Tsai, 157, 250

innovation, indigenous, 223–25

intellectual property rights (IPR), 223, 231–32; industry standards for, 226–28

intellectual property theft, 173, 223–24

Intermediate Nuclear Forces Agreement (1987), 205

Intermediate-Range Nuclear Forces treaty, 168

International Campaign for Tibet, 108

International Code of Conduct against Ballistic Missile Proliferation, 205

international financial institutions, 96

international law, China disregard for, 296–97, 309

international relations (IR) theories, 12, 68, 86, 185; constructivism and, 274, 305–6; liberalism in, 274, 305–6; realism and, 103, 105, 106, 305–6; US foreign policy and, 105–6

internet and media regulations, 139, 216, 286

internment camps, in China, 207

investment dependencies, 298

investment issues, 219–22. *See also* foreign direct investment (FDI)

investments, Chinese foreign, 316–17

Iowa, 167

IPR. *See* intellectual property rights

IR. *See* international relations

Iraq war, 131, 133

Janus-face strategies, 297

Japan, 16, 25, 34–35, 48–49, 154; industrial interests in China, 31–32; militarism of, 187, 192–93; Nixon and, 83; Obama visiting, 264; "Ron-Yasu" relationship with US, 89; Senkaku (Diaoyu) Islands, 262–63; Sino-Japanese War (1894–95), 26–28; Twenty-One Demands and,

20, 26, 31, 32; war against China
    1937, 35, 36, 50
Jiang Zemin, 124, 125, 133, 142, 292
Johnson, Lyndon, 69–70
Joint Comprehensive Plan of Action
    (2015), 205

Kang Sheng, 71
Kellogg, Frank, 34
Kellogg-Briand Pact (1928), 34
Kennedy, John, 61
Kennedy, Robert, 70
Kerry, John, 134
Khrushchev, Nikita, 72
Kim Il-song, 187
Kim Jong Un, 255
King, Martin Luther Jr., 70
Kissinger, Henry, 75, 105
Klobuchar, Amy, 173
KMT. *See* Nationalist Party of China
Korean Peninsula, 187
Korean War, 54, 55–56
Kuomintang. *See* Nationalist party
Kuwait, invasion of, 118
Kyoto Protocol, 240

labor, forced, 288
Lam Wing Kee, 291
land collectivization, 57
Law on Overseas Nongovernmental
    Organizations, PRC, 286
League of Nations, 34
Lee Bo, 291, 292
Lee Teng-hui, 111, 114, 118,
    123–24, 248
lend-lease program, 36
liberalism, 103, 106, 274, 305–6
Lien-Chou massacre (1905), 29
Lighthizer, Robert, 164, 232
Li Hung-chang, 25–26, 28
Lin Biao, 62, 71, 75
Li Peng, 239
"little red book" (Mao Zedong), 62
Li Xin, 291
Lord, Winston, 111

Manchukuo, 34
Manchuria, 16, 28, 29–31, 34, 51
manufacturing output, China, 211
Mao Zedong, 1, 7, 43, 49, 53–54, 78;
    Cultural Revolution and, 70–71,
    74; Eisenhower administration and,
    56; Great Leap Forward campaign
    and, 61, 62; Nixon and, 276, 305–6;
    Taiwan and, 60
maritime disputes, 251–52, 267–70;
    China coercing neighbors and, 296,
    309; East Asian, 260–66
Marshall, George, 51
Ma Ying-jeou, 4, 248–49, 252; US
    support and, 249–52
May Thirtieth movement, 33
McCain, John, 107
McCarthy, Joseph, 56
McKinley, William, 27
media: Chinese, 101, 125, 295; foreign,
    299; US, 99, 170–71
MFN. *See* most favored nation
microblogging restrictions, 286
Middle East, 94–95, 133
Middle East policy, US, 7
military, Chinese, 8, 62, 63, 95,
    132, 306; defense acquisitions
    for, 196–202; doctrine for, 199;
    expansion of, 107, 134, 139, 192–93,
    199–201; intimidation of neighbors
    by, 296; limitations of, 203–4;
    maritime disputes and, 263–70;
    PLA, 71, 192–93; reform effort for,
    199–200; Taiwan conflict, 195; US
    forces targeted by, 307; Xi Jinping
    and, 193–94
military, French, 57–58
military, Soviet, 86–87, 96
military, Taiwan, 92–94
military, US, 23, 52, 119–20, 193–94;
    advances, 255; Beijing ties with,
    93–94; Chinese military targeting,
    307; cutbacks on, 105–6; Desert
    Storm operations, 118; Indo-Pacific
    allies and, 174–75; Indo-Pacific

Command, 321–22; Indo-Pacific strategy, 174, 177; Korean War and, 55–56; maritime disputes and, 263–70; Navy, 195; observer mission by, 48; support for Taiwan, 133, 189; Vietnam War, 69–70

military conflict, 1, 259

military face-off, over Taiwan (1995–96), 102

military modernization, twenty-first century, 195; capacity and objectives, 196–204; security issues, 204–5

military technologies, 310–11

military-to-military relations, 188–89

Missile Technology Control Regime (MTCR), 205

missionaries, 15–16, 17–18, 22, 37; antimissionary riots, 19; attacks on, 27, 29

mob violence, Chinese, 126

moderation, toward US, 92–94

Morgenthau, Henry, 35–36

most favored nation (MFN) status, 102, 108, 122–23

MTCR. *See* Missile Technology Control Regime

multipolarity, 120

Muslims: Turkic, 287; Uighur, 169, 173, 206–7, 287–88

Myanmar, 322

Nanking incident, 34

National Basketball Association, 299, 300

National Defense Authorization Act, 166

National Intelligence Law, PRC, 286

nationalism, Chinese, 2, 34, 41, 151

Nationalist-Communist peacetalks, 49

Nationalist Party of China (Kuomintang) (KMT), 33–35, 36–37, 41–43, 152, 249, 254; interactions 1950s and 1960s, 55–64; interactions in the 1940s, 44–52; Maoist period and, 54

National Origins Act (1924), 24

National People's Congress, 122–23

national security, China, 57, 121, 203; international terrorism and, 206–7

national security, US, 164

National Security Strategy (2007), 161

National Security Strategy Report (2002), 132

Navy, US, 195

Nazi Germany, 36

"Neo-isolationist" school, 106–7

"New Initiative," 168

NGOs. *See* nongovernmental organizations

Nine Power Treaty, 20, 27, 32

nineteenth-century encounters, 20–26

Nixon, Richard, 1, 7, 70, 75–76, 116, 277; China visit, 83; Mao Zedong and, 276, 305–6; secrecy and, 10, 76–78; Taiwan and, 246–47

Nixon Doctrine, 70

nongovernmental organizations (NGOs), 278, 281, 284–85

"noninterference in internal affairs" *versus* influence operations and political warfare, Chinese, 297–302

normalization of relations, 77–83

Northern Expedition, 33

North Korea, 55–56, 157; nuclear weapons and, 132, 133–34, 135, 145; Trump and, 322

nuclear cooperation agreement, US-China, 93

nuclear weapons, 57, 60–61, 64, 93; Chinese espionage and, 115; North Korea and, 132, 133–34, 135, 145; WMDs, 132, 139, 196, 204–6

Obama, Barack, 3, 4, 5–6, 146–53; on Chinese cyberattacks, 226–27, 299; on climate change, 146; environmental policies of, 241; on human rights, 280; Japan and, 264; maritime disputes and, 260–61; military talks with China, 193, 194; one-China policy and, 258;

policy toward China, 156, 157–58; rebalance policy, 148, 149, 261, 320; Xi Jinping and, 154–56, 313
oil embargo, US (1941), 36
oil imports, 238
Olympic Games (2008), 146
Olympics, 280–81
"one-child policy," 284, 286
one-China policy, 6, 257–60, 323
one-party system, in China, 323
Open Door Notes, 26–27
opium, 21
Opium War, 20, 21, 104
opposition to US support, for Taiwan, 144

Pacific Islands Forum, 301
PAFMM. *See* People's Armed Forces Maritime Militia
Pakistan, 196
Pakistan, China support for, 93
Panama Canal treaty, 80
pan-Asian approach, in US foreign policy, 95–96, 130
pandemic. *See* COVID-19 pandemic
Paris Climate Change agreement (2016), 241
Paris Club, 234
Parker, Peter, 22
Peace Pearl program, 188
peacetalks, Communist-Nationalist, 49
Pearl Harbor, attack on, 9, 41
Pelosi, Nancy, 106
Pence, Michael, 167–68
Peng Dehuai, 62
People's Armed Forces Maritime Militia (PAFMM), 268
People's Liberation Army (PLA), 71, 192
People's Republic of China (PRC), 7, 9, 53, 58, 123–24; Cybersecurity Law, 286; Law on Overseas Nongovernmental Organizations, 286; National Intelligence Law, 286; policy toward (1972–83), 116–17;

surveillance technologies and, 290; US interest in, 89–90
Permanent Normal Trade Relations (PNTR), 102
Perot, Ross, 106
Philippines, 265–66, 267–69
PLA. *See* People's Liberation Army
PNTR. *See* Permanent Normal Trade Relations
policies: "dual circulation policy," 218; free-trade, 136; Middle East, 7; one-China, 6, 323; rebalance, 148, 149, 261, 320; religious and ethnic minorities, 288–89; "Sinicization," 288. *See also* China policy; Chinese foreign policy; "engagement" policy; US foreign policy
political dissidents, 138; arrests of, 277; persecution of, 291–92
political goals, US, 105
political prisoners, 291
political warfare, Chinese, 297–302
pollution, air, 240
Pompeo, Mike, 173, 177, 288
population growth, 236–37
PRC. *See* People's Republic of China
predictions, of US-China relations, 179
prejudice, against immigrants, 23–24
priorities and calculations, Chinese, 119–22
prisoners, political, 291
Prisons/Prison Labor, in China, 138
propaganda, Chinese, 215, 285, 293; CCP, 291; COVID-19 pandemic and, 315–16; in Taiwan, 253–54
Protestant missionaries, 17
protests, in Hong Kong, 63, 300, 316
Putin, Vladimir, 307

al Qaeda, 138

Qing dynasty, 15, 19, 31
"Quad," four-power, 266, 268
Quotations from Chairman Mao Tse-Tung, 62

race relations, US, 70
racism, 24
railway building, 30–31
Reagan, Ronald, 82, 93, 247; Deng Xiaoping and, 305
realism, 84, 103, 105, 106, 305–6
rebalance policy, Obama, 148, 149, 261, 320
recession (2008), 145
Red Guards, 62, 63, 71
reformist ideas and influence, American, 37
refugees, 286
religious and ethnic minorities policies, 288–89
religious extremism, 287
religious freedom, 139, 279, 289
renminbi (RMB), 232–33
repression, technologies used for, 288
Republic of China (ROC), 81, 110
restrictions: for China, 176; on free speech, 290
revolutionary ideology, 53
riots, antimissionary, 19
rise, of China (2000s), 134–35
rivalry, US-China, 90, 310–12
RMB. *See* renminbi
ROC. *See* Republic of China
Romney, Mitt, 233
"Ron-Yasu" relationship, Japan and US, 89
Roosevelt, Franklin D., 35, 41, 45, 46, 49, 104
Roosevelt, Theodore, 29
Rubio, Marco, 170
rule of law, 236
Russia, 28–29, 30–31; China collaborating with, 178, 297

SAMR. *See* State Administration for Market Regulation
Sanders, Bernie, 173
Schumer, Chuck, 181
Scott Act, 24
secret diplomacy, 110

security, US, 149–50, 153
security interests, 196; Chinese, 87, 88; US, 187–88
security issues, US-China, 185
semiconductors, 225–26
Senkaku (Diaoyu) Islands, 262–64, 266
separatism, 287
September 11, 2001, terrorist attack, 101, 115, 131, 279
Seventeenth Congress, CCP (2007), 142–43
Shanghai Communiqué (1972), 77, 187
Shanghai Municipal Council, 33
Shultz, George, 83–85, 86, 95
Sihanouk, Norodom, 74
"Sinicization" policy, 288
Sino-American ambassadorial talks, 74
Sino-American trade treaty, 28
Sino-Indian border clash, 177
Sino-Japanese War (1894–95), 26–27
Sino-Soviet relations, 72, 94–95
"social credit system," 286–87
SOEs. *See* state-owned enterprises
South China Sea disputes, 157, 166, 252, 261–62, 265–70
Southeast Asia, 60–61
South Korea, 55–56
sovereignty, 8; Chinese, 32; issues of, 141, 314
Soviet embassy invasion, 63
Soviet military expansion, in Asia, 94
Soviet Union, 33, 42, 58, 62–63, 71–73; Chinese-Soviet alliance, 60; collapse of, 106; demise in 1991, 100; interactions during 1950s and 1960s, 56–57; invasion of Afghanistan, 94; invasion of China by, 68; military force by, 86, 88; nuclear weapons and, 205; trade with, 90; US-China convergence against, 186–88; US relations with, 88; Yalta conference (1945), 50–51
space warfare, 197, 198
spies, Chinese, 113
Stalin, Joseph, 27, 33

State Administration for Market Regulation (SAMR), 228
state-controlled capitalism, 213, 222–23
state-directed development polices, China, 294
state-owned enterprises (SOEs), 213, 235–37
sterilization, forced, 284
Stilwell, Joseph, 45, 46, 49
Straight, Willard, 30
strategic calculus shift, Chinese, 85–92
strategies and goals, China with US, 120
"Strike Hard" campaign, 206
students, Chinese, 108–9, 170, 298
Suga Yoshihide, 267
Sullivan, Jake, 173
summit meetings: G-20, 168–69; US-China, 113, 125, 155
supercomputing companies, 217–18
surveillance, 287; Chinese government, 295, 308–9; in South China Sea, 268–69
surveillance technologies, 290

Taft, William H., 26, 30–31
Taiping Rebellion, 22, 23
Taiwan, 10, 54, 108, 114, 123–24, 180; air force, 94; arms sold to, 92, 94, 110, 120; Chinese military conflict with, 195; Chinese opposition to US support for, 144, 181, 189, 250–52; Chinese propaganda in, 253–54; contemporary US-China relations and, 246–54, 256–57, 259–60; democratization of, 109, 252; economic advances with US and, 256–57; human rights issues and, 279; Jinping and, 253–54; military, 92–94; military conflict with China, 111, 112; military face-off (1995–96) over, 102; 1995–96 confrontation over, 125; one-China policy and, 257–59; sovereignty issues, 141; Trump policy toward, 164, 165–67; Trump supporting,
254–55; US-China agreements on, 152; US-China differences over, 4, 5, 7, 58–60, 88, 92–93; US foreign policy toward, 117–18; US relations with, 76–77, 81–82, 111, 133, 166–67, 178; US visits to, 252
Taiwanese Americans, 109
Taiwan Relations Act (1979), 10, 81–82, 116, 117
Taiwan Semiconductor Manufacturing Company (TSMC), 226
Taiwan Strait, 56, 57, 59, 111, 189, 203
Taiwan Travel Act, 166
Tajikistan, 206
Tang Shao-yi, 29–30
tariffs: against China, 167; MFN, 103, 108; by Trump, 214, 218
technologies: CCP and, 310; Chinese control of, 286–87; ICT, 225–26; indigenous innovation and, 223–25; military, 310–11; semiconductors and, 225–26; surveillance, 290; transfer issues with, 225; used for repression, 288. *See also* high technologies
technology theft, Chinese, 165, 170–71
technology transfer restrictions, 92, 93
telecommunications, 222, 318
Terranova, Francesco, 21
territorial disputes, Chinese, 198
terrorism, 115, 118–19, 138, 287; anti-, 132, 133; China approach to, 206–7; war on, 136, 206
terrorist attack, September 11, 2001, 101, 115, 131, 279
"three evils," 287
Three No's, 113
three pillars of power, 62
Tiananmen crackdown, 10, 99–100, 103, 108, 125; human rights after, 274–75; US-China divergence after, 188–89
Tibet, 138, 141, 169; autonomy for, 108, 189; human rights issues and, 277, 280–81, 289

torture, 284
TPP. *See* Trans-Pacific Partnership
trade, 111, 226–27; China and, 15–16, 21, 36, 102, 108; during COVID-19 pandemic, 214; free, 150; free-trade policies, 136; investment issues and, 219–22; issues on, 214–18; MFN status and, 103, 108, 122; "phase one" deal, 172; with Soviet Union, 90; US annual trade deficit, 320. *See also* World Trade Organization
Trade Act of 1974, US, 232
trade deficit, US with China, 218–19
trade war, US-China, 5, 214–15, 235, 317
Trans-Pacific Partnership (TPP), 149, 150, 321–22
transparency, 158
Treaty of Nanjing, 21
Treaty of Wang-hsia, 21
treaty system, 23
Truman, Harry, 50, 51–52
Trump, Donald, 1, 2, 5–6, 148, 162, 315–16; anti-China policy, 161, 178, 194; anti-China sentiment, 174, 175–76, 177; China countering by, 266–70; on currency exchange, 233; on human rights issues, 281, 288; Indo-Pacific Command, 321–22; maritime disputes and, 260–61; North Korea and, 322; policy with Taiwan, 164, 165–67; Taiwan supported by, 254–55; tariffs by, 214, 218; trade policies by, 232; unpredictability of, 318; Xi Jinping and, 163, 164–65, 169, 171–72, 175–76
TSMC. *See* Taiwan Semiconductor Manufacturing Company
Turkic Muslims, 287
Twenty-One Demands (1915), 20, 26, 31, 32

Uighur Muslims, 169, 173, 206–7, 287–88
UN. *See* United Nations

UNCLOS. *See* United Nations Convention on the Laws of the Sea
United Front influence operations, CCP, 299
United Nations (UN), 56, 64, 207
United Nations Convention on the Laws of the Sea (UNCLOS), 267
United States (US): budget deficits, 8; capitol attack (2021), 318; debate over China policy, late-1970s to early-1980s *versus* post Cold War in, 116–19; economy of, 162, 212; exceptionalism in, 8–9; India and, 86; interests, actions and perceptions, 17–19; media on China in, 170–71; Middle East policy of, 7; National Security Strategy, 2; oil embargo (1941), 36; political goals of, 105; position in Asia, 318–24; Taiwan relations with, 76–77, 81–82, 111, 133, 166–67, 178. *See also specific topics*
United States Trade Representative (USTR), 227, 231
UN peacekeepers, 196
US. *See* United States
US annual trade deficit, 320
US-backed security presence, in Asia-Pacific, 7–8
US-China agreements, 102
US-China competition, 150–51, 152, 180–81, 308, 323–24; ascendance of China and, 310–12; high technologies, 216, 218
US-China cooperation, 135
US-China diverging interests and values, 7–11, 68–69
US-China nuclear cooperation agreement, 93
US-China rivalry, 90, 310–12
US-China security issues, 185
US-China strategic and economic dialogue, 4, 69
US-China trade war, 5, 214–15, 235, 317

US foreign policy, 11; challenges of shifting, 122–26; debate over China policy and, 104–9; "engagement" with China, 107; ethnic groups and, 108; human rights issues in, 137–39; IR theory and, 105; negative opinion of, 101; Obama and, 146–47; pan-Asian approach in, 130; post-Cold War, 104–5; security relations issues, 139; Taiwan and, 117
US-pan-Asian approach, 95–96
US policy, China, 8–9, 141–44; communism and, 55; Taiwan and, 102
USTR. *See* United States Trade Representative

vaccine, COVID-19, 180, 268
Versailles Peace Treaty, 32
"victim mentality," of China, 9
Vietnam, 60, 63, 64, 68, 202–3; Chinese invasion of, 81, 188; communism in, 79
Vietnam War, 69–70, 74
violence, against Americans, 33

Wallace, Henry, 48–49
Ward, Frederick Townsend, 23
Ward, John, 22–23
warfare: cyber-, 198; political 297–302, 198; space, 197, 198
Warner, Mark, 170
Warren, Elizabeth, 165, 173
wars, 2; Afghanistan war, 132; American Civil War, 23; Chinese Civil War, 41–43, 44, 50–52; Iraq war, 131, 133; Korean War, 54, 55–56; Opium War, 20, 21, 104; possibility of US-China, 181; Sino-Japanese War (1894–95), 26–27; on terrorism, 136; trade war, 5, 214–15, 235, 317; World War I, 16, 20; World War II, 44
Washington Conference (1921–22), 32–33

weapons, nuclear, 57, 60–61, 64
weapons of mass destruction (WMD), 132, 139, 196, 204–6
Wen Jiabao, 190
Whitsun Reef, 268, 269
Wilson, Woodrow, 20, 31, 104
WMD. *See* weapons of mass destruction
Wolfowitz, Paul, 83–84
world affairs, China and, 129–30
World Health Organization, 176
World Press Freedom Index, 290
World Trade Organization (WTO), 102, 110, 113–14, 143, 222, 225; China joining, 317; implementations issues with, 229–32
World War I, 16, 20
World War II, 44; US-China relations during, 41–42, 45
Wray, Christopher, 164
WTO. *See* World Trade Organization

xenophobia, 64
Xi Jinping, 1–2, 3, 4–6, 151, 301; BRI, 168; CCP and, 285–86; challenges America, 153–58; "China Dream" and, 147, 312–13, 319; foreign policy vision by, 312–13; human rights issues and, 281, 282, 292–93; maritime disputes and, 265; movements 2012–2013, 193–94; Obama and, 154–56, 313; Putin and, 307; Taiwan and, 253–54; Trump and, 163, 164–65, 169, 171–72, 175–76
Xinjiang, 138, 177–78, 206–7, 287–88
Xinjiang Uyghur Autonomous Region (XUAR), 287

Yalta conference (1945), 50
Ye Jianying, 75
Yuan Shih-kai, 30

Zhao Ziyang, 92
Zhou Enlai, 47–48, 59, 63, 73, 78
Zhu Rongji, 113, 114

Zoellick, Robert, 135

ZTE, 156–57, 165

CPSIA information can be obtained
at www.ICGtesting.com
Printed in the USA
BVHW030014010322
628762BV00010B/1

9 781538 157169